The Doctrine of Res Judicata

SPENCER BOWER AND TURNER

The Doctrine of Res Judicata

The Original Text by

GEORGE SPENCER BOWER

Sometime one of His Majesty's Counsel and a
Master of the Bench of the Inner Temple

The Second Edition by

THE RIGHT HONOURABLE

SIR ALEXANDER KINGCOME TURNER,

M.A., LL.B. (N.Z.), HON. LL.D. (AUCKLAND)

A Judge of the Court of Appeal of New Zealand

"οὐκ ἄν ποτε
κατάστασις γένοιτ' ἂν οὐδενὸς νόμου,
εἰ τοὺς δίκῃ νικῶντας ἐξωθήσομεν
καὶ τοὺς ὄπισθεν εἰς τὸ πρόσθεν ἄξομεν."

Sophocles, *Ajax*, 1246–49

LONDON

BUTTERWORTHS

1969

ENGLAND: BUTTERWORTH & CO. (PUBLISHERS) LTD.
LONDON: 88 KINGSWAY, W.C.2

AUSTRALIA: BUTTERWORTH & CO. (AUSTRALIA) LTD.
SYDNEY: 20 LOFTUS STREET
MELBOURNE: 343 LITTLE COLLINS STREET
BRISBANE: 240 QUEEN STREET

CANADA: BUTTERWORTH & CO. (CANADA) LTD.
TORONTO: 14 CURITY AVENUE, 16

NEW ZEALAND: BUTTERWORTH & CO. (NEW ZEALAND) LTD.
WELLINGTON: 40/51 BALLANCE STREET
AUCKLAND: 35 HIGH STREET

SOUTH AFRICA: BUTTERWORTH & CO. (SOUTH AFRICA) LTD.
DURBAN: 33/35 BEACH GROVE

Standard Book Number: 406 38210 7

Printed in Great Britain by
William Clowes and Sons Limited, London and Beccles

SPENCER BOWER AND TURNER

The Doctrine of Res Judicata

The Original Text by

GEORGE SPENCER BOWER

Sometime one of His Majesty's Counsel and a Master of the Bench of the Inner Temple

The Second Edition by

THE RIGHT HONOURABLE

SIR ALEXANDER KINGCOME TURNER,

M.A., LL.B. (N.Z.), HON. LL.D. (AUCKLAND)

A Judge of the Court of Appeal of New Zealand

"οὐκ ἄν ποτε
κατάστασις γένοιτ' ἂν οὐδενὸς νόμου,
εἰ τοὺς δίκῃ νικῶντας ἐξωθήσομεν
καὶ τοὺς ὄπισθεν εἰς τὸ πρόσθεν ἄξομεν."

Sophocles, *Ajax*, 1246–49

LONDON

BUTTERWORTHS

1969

ENGLAND: BUTTERWORTH & CO. (PUBLISHERS) LTD.
LONDON: 88 KINGSWAY, W.C.2

AUSTRALIA: BUTTERWORTH & CO. (AUSTRALIA) LTD.
SYDNEY: 20 LOFTUS STREET
MELBOURNE: 343 LITTLE COLLINS STREET
BRISBANE: 240 QUEEN STREET

CANADA: BUTTERWORTH & CO. (CANADA) LTD.
TORONTO: 14 CURITY AVENUE, 16

NEW ZEALAND: BUTTERWORTH & CO. (NEW ZEALAND) LTD.
WELLINGTON: 40/51 BALLANCE STREET
AUCKLAND: 35 HIGH STREET

SOUTH AFRICA: BUTTERWORTH & CO. (SOUTH AFRICA) LTD.
DURBAN: 33/35 BEACH GROVE

Standard Book Number: 406 38210 7

Printed in Great Britain by
William Clowes and Sons Limited, London and Beccles

The Director of Public Prosecutions,[1] the source of inspiration of Chapter XI, was decided in 1964; and in Divorce *Travers* v. *Holley*[2] dates only from 1953, while *Indyka* v. *Indyka*[3] was decided in the Lords only in the present decade. Beside the topics which I have mentioned, to which this second edition has devoted four separate new chapters, there are other subjects upon which the text has had to be almost completely reconstituted, although they are still dealt with in the same part of the book as in the first edition. Instances of these may be found in judgments by default,[4] foreign judgments,[5] and issue estoppel,[6] and the interrelation of these topics *inter se*, and in the place of public policy as an answer to the plea of *res judicata*.[7] The basic philosophy of the plea of *res judicata* has also seemed to me to need some original treatment in this volume;[8] for it does not seem by any means as certain now as when Mr Spencer Bower wrote that the public good does always require litigation to be brought abruptly to an end, so far at least as to prohibit reinvestigation of *all* matters which have been resolved, perhaps a little hastily, between the same parties in earlier litigation.

I hope that I have been forthright enough, in editing Mr Spencer Bower's almost hallowed text, to say clearly where I have disagreed with his original writings, and why. In the places where there is any substantial difference between our opinions, the reader should be able to see without difficulty whether he is reading the text of the original author, respectfully approved by the present editor, or whether he is reading the present editor, in difference on the point from Mr Spencer Bower's original text.

As with the *Estoppel by Representation* I have added, where I have thought them of assistance, the principal Australian and New Zealand cases. In the discussion of issue estoppel, especially, the Australian cases should be found helpful, if indeed they do not prove to be positively the best authorities. I have again omitted the Canadian cases, not having sufficient reading in them or in Canadian law to feel confident in making any judicious or comprehensive selection.

I must again point out, as in the case of *Estoppel by Representation*, that I have been under the disadvantage, in carrying out my self-imposed task, that no one has collected, during the forty-five years which have gone by since the original publication, any note of the slips and errors which must

---

1 [1964] A.C. 1254, H.L.
2 [1953] P. 246, C.A.
3 [1967] 2 All E.R. 689, H.L.
4 Chapter II, paras. 46 *et seq*.
5 Chapter IV, paras. 157 *et seq*.
6 Chapter VI, *passim*.
7 The topic is dealt with in Chapter XIV.
8 The discussion of this subject, developed later in the text, is introduced in Chapter I, para 11.

Preface to the Second Edition

Mr Spencer Bower felt no need for any elaborate *apologia* justifying the publication of his *Res Judicata*. His preface to it occupied six lines of print. He signed it in 1924; he died while the work was still becoming established. Nearly half a century has now elapsed during which its authority has steadily increased; but no one has ventured to re-edit the text. For the same reasons, then, as led me to set about rewriting his *Estoppel by Representation* I have been moved to take in hand this book, which without some friend willing to render it such a service might soon have fallen first into disuse, and then even into oblivion.

As with the *Estoppel by Representation*, I found that it was of no use to attempt a second edition simply by adding notes of the authorities decided since the original date of publication, with such consequent amendments to the original script as these might involve. Large tracts of the text needed rewriting, some of it of a drastic kind, and several topics almost unnoticed by the original author had in the last forty-five years acquired importance sufficient to require exposition at length in any book purporting to cover the subject. Instances are to be found in the cases dealing with highway accidents, those dealing with taxation and revenue matters, the plea of *autrefois acquit*, and the matrimonial cases. Each of these subjects has in this edition a complete chapter to itself, for which, since I wrote the whole of it, I must take the entire responsibility. These four chapters are concerned in great part with special developments of the law which were unforeseen, at least in detail, by Mr Spencer Bower. The application of the plea of *res judicata* to highway accidents as a development of the law of issue estoppel was not given any special notice in the first edition; and all the group of cases of which *Marginson* v. *Blackburn Borough Council*[1] was the first, which are dealt with *seriatim* in Chapter IX, have been decided since the original author's death. So with the taxation cases, in which the period 1925–61 gave us the law as it now stands.[2] *Connelly* v.

---

[1] [1939] 2 K.B. 426.

[2] *Broken Hill Pty. Co., Ltd.* v. *Broken Hill Municipal Council*, [1926] A.C. 94, P.C.; *Hoystead* v. *Commissioner of Taxation*, [1926] A.C. 155; *C.I.R.* v. *Sneath*, [1932] 2 K.B. 362; *Society of Medical Officers of Health* v. *Hope* [1960] A.C. 551, H.L.; *Caffoor* v. *Commissioner of Income Tax*, [1961] A.C. 584, P.C.

have been noticed from time to time in the first edition. All I can say in this regard is that I have endeavoured to consider the text of the first edition sentence by sentence, and I hope that the number of errors which have escaped me is not great.

My affection for the original text has led me to retain, with a nostalgic sense of the pleasure with which I first read them, a number of passages in which are preserved the characteristic idioms of the first author, even in some cases where my own enthusiasm would not have led me quite so far. To have abandoned these would have been to lose some of the flavour and inspiration of the original work.[1]

In conclusion I express my grateful thanks, for the assistance they have given me in the preparation and publication of this edition, to Miss Olivia Spencer Bower of Christchurch, New Zealand, for the gift of a copy of the original text (now almost unpurchasable) inscribed by its author; to Mrs. W. Everitt, my Judge's Associate, for her untiring secretarial work in transcribing the MS; to my wife for bearing with me in the course of its writing, and for translating from the Greek for my edification the passage from Sophocles which Mr Spencer Bower placed upon its title page; and to the proprietors of *The Times* for permission to reproduce the material for the Memoir, which relies in large measure on the Obituary Notice of September 5th, 1928.

The law has been stated, I hope, as at September 30th, 1968.

A. K. TURNER

Wellington,
NEW ZEALAND
December 1968

[1] Instances may be found in Chapter II, paras. 66 *et seq.*, in para. 395, and in Appendix B.

Preface to the First Edition

The design, scope, and arrangement of this treatise are clearly indicated in the following: (1) the Introduction, (2) Part I, Ch. I, Sect. 4, (3) Part II, Ch. I, Sect. 4, and (4) the Table of Contents.

The programme thus disclosed will, I hope, render unnecessary any other prefatory announcement or observations.

G. SPENCER BOWER

2 Hare Court, Temple

March, 1924

Memoir

George Spencer Bower was born on October 12th, 1854, the son of George Bower of St. Neots. He died on September 4th, 1928, aged 73 years. He was a scholar of Winchester and New College, retaining all his life an intense Wykehamical patriotism. His record at Oxford was a distinguished one, including first classes in both the Classical Schools, the Gaisford Greek Prose and the Chancellor's English Essay; and classical literature never ceased to be the interest nearest to his heart.

He was called to the Bar by the Inner Temple in 1880, and acquired an extensive and miscellaneous junior practice. Like many of his profession he enjoyed the society of actors, being a friend of some of the most notable theatrical personalities of the day, including Sir Henry Irving and Sir Charles Wyndham, whose daughter he married in 1885. He took silk in 1903, and, although his practice within the Bar was never very extensive, it included such famous cases as that which ended with the "Osborne Judgment" of the House of Lords in 1909. Spencer Bower was one of the two leading counsel for the successful appellant, Osborne. He was made a Bencher of his Inn in 1912, an honour that he greatly appreciated and of which he took full advantage. He thoroughly enjoyed the social life of the Benchers, among whom he was the acknowledged arbiter on points of classical scholarship.

His name is remembered by lawyers—and will long continue so to be remembered—for the series of textbooks which he published in the 1920's, all on some aspect of the law as to representations of fact. These books, besides remaining classic authorities on the subjects with which they deal, have a special charm in the great wealth of literary illustration (largely drawn from his beloved classical authors) with which Spencer Bower delighted to illustrate his work. It was said of him that a quotation from Horace might set him off on a veritable flood-tide of reminiscences of great advocates and judges; a point of law reported from the Courts might give him occasion to quote a hundred lines of Shakespeare, Homer, or Sophocles (he could actually recite the whole of the *Oedipus Tyrannus*). It was as a scholar of the old type, knowing the ancient authors through and through by constant daily intercourse, that he himself said that he would best like to be remembered; and those who read this book may add this thought to the regard in which they continue to hold him, half a century after his death, still as a contemporary expositor of the living law.

Contents

Table of Cases

B

C

D

E

F

G

L

M

N

S

U

V

Table of Statutes

References to "Stats." are to Halsbury's Statutes of England (2nd Edn.) showing the volume and page at which the annotated text of the Act will be found. Figures in heavy type indicate where the Act is set out in part or in full.

AUSTRALIA

NEW ZEALAND

Introduction

Introductory

1 In English jurisprudence a *res judicata*, that is to say a final judicial decision pronounced by a judicial tribunal having competent jurisdiction over the cause or matter in litigation, and over the parties thereto, disposes once and for all of the matters decided, so that they cannot afterwards be raised for re-litigation between the same parties or their privies. The effect of such a decision is two-fold.

Parties estopped from averring to the contrary

2 In the first place, the judicial decision estops or precludes any party to the litigation from disputing, against any other party thereto, in any later litigation, the correctness of the earlier decision in law and fact.[1] The same issue cannot be raised again between them, and this principle extends to all matters of law and fact which the judgment, decree, or order necessarily established as the legal foundation or justification of the conclusion reached by the Court.[2]

Transit in rem judicatam

3 In the second place, by virtue of the decision the right or cause of action set up in the suit is extinguished, merging in the judgment which is pronounced. *Transit in rem judicatam.* The result is that no further claim may be made upon the same cause of action in any subsequent proceedings between the same parties or their privies.[3]

4 Every judicial decision such as is described in paragraph 1 above operates, in a word, both as an estoppel and as a merger. It is conclusive in both capacities because on the one hand, as Coke would put it, it is of such "uncontrollable credit and verity" that no party may presume to

---

[1] See para. 9, *post*, for a more detailed statement of the rule.

[2] Per DIXON J. in *Blair* v. *Curran* (1939), 62 C.L.R. 464 (H. Ct. of Aus.) at p. 531. This dictum crystallises the essence of the doctrine of issue estoppel.

[3] "The very right or cause of action claimed or put in suit has in the first proceedings passed into judgment, so that it merged and has no longer an independent existence"—per DIXON J. in *Blair* v. *Curran* (1939), 62 C.L.R. 464 (H. Ct. of Aus.) at p. 532.

impeach it,[1] and, on the other, it is of such an exalted nature that it extinguishes the original cause of action, and consequently bars the successful party from afterwards attempting to resuscitate what has been so extinguished, and stir the dust which has received such honourable sepulture; or, in modern phraseology, because in both cases alike it is against public policy, and oppressive to the individual, to re-agitate disputes which have been litigated once for all to a finish.

5 It is of the utmost importance, in every case in which considerations of *res judicata* arise, to distinguish clearly between the two consequences of a judicial decision to which we have already adverted. Much confusion of thought has been engendered by the failure of text-writers, counsel,[2] and judges,[3] to keep clearly in mind which of the two consequences of *res judicata* arise, or are invoked, in particular matters before the Court. It is hoped that in the present work the terminology to be adopted in this edition may assist towards the clarity of thought always essential to a study of this subject.

Terminology

6 The terms "*res judicata*" and "estoppel by record" have at times been indiscriminately used to signify either, or both, of the two doctrines which we have mentioned. It is proposed in this edition to use the term *res judicata* as a phrase of general application applicable to both the doctrines. The first of the two consequences of a *res judicata*, by virtue of which a party to litigation is precluded thereafter, as against the other or

---

1 2 Coke on Litt. 260A.

2 In the judgment of SOMERVELL L.J. in *Greenhalgh* v. *Mallard*, [1947] 2 All E.R. 255 a considerable passage is occupied (at p. 258) in dealing with an argument in which the two doctrines had obviously been hopelessly confused, Counsel having put forward *Brunsden* v. *Humphrey*, *infra*, (in which the question of merger, not of issue estoppel, was the sole matter for argument) in support of a plea of what amounted to issue estoppel. So, too, in *Carl-Zeiss-Stiftung* v. *Rayner and Keeler, Ltd.* (*No.* 2), [1966] 2 All E.R. 536, H.L. Lord HODSON refers at p. 561 to "another argument put forward by the appellant, which I do not find it possible to accept", the argument being obviously based on a confusion between the two quite separate consequences which follow upon a judgment.

3 See, for instance, *Ord* v. *Ord*, [1923] 2 K.B. 432, a case of issue estoppel pure and simple, where at p. 443 LUSH J. reinforced his judgment by a reference to *Brunsden* v. *Humphrey* (1884), 14 Q.B.D. 141, C.A., a case in which merger was essentially the question in dispute. Another typical example is the judgment of LEWIS J. at first instance in *Marginson* v. *Blackburn Borough Council*, [1938] 2 All E.R. 539; this was reversed on appeal in [1939] 1 All E.R. 273; [1939] 2 K.B. 426. Cf. *in New Zealand* the judgments of OSTLER J. in *Priest* v. *Mouat*, [1937] N.Z.L.R. 431 and of SMITH J. in *National Insurance Co. of New Zealand Ltd.* v. *Geddes*, [1936] N.Z.L.R. 1004, and the criticism of these in *Wilson* v. *Matheson*, [1955] N.Z.L.R. 927, at p. 930, adopted by SHORLAND J. in *Clyne* v. *Yardley*, [1959] N.Z.L.R. 617, at p. 628. Even in the Lords, Lord GUEST is to be found in *Carl-Zeiss-Stiftung* v. *Rayner and Keeler, Ltd.*, (*No.* 2), [1966] 2 All E.R. 536, H.L. at p. 567 speaking in the same sentence of merger and of issue estoppel as if the two were instances of the operation of the same doctrine. *Cf.*, however, the less receptive attitude of Lord HODSON to this part of appellant's argument at p. 561.

others, from denying in subsequent litigation the correctness of a decision on a matter of law or fact given in the earlier litigation between them, will in this treatise be called "estoppel *per rem judicatam*". The second consequence—*viz.* the merger of the original cause of action in the judgment concluding the litigation—will be referred to hereafter in this work as "merger in judgment".

The term "estoppel by record", though it has been widely accepted as applicable to one or both of the consequences of a *res judicata* which have been referred to above,[1] must be acknowledged, on any careful examination of the doctrines supporting those consequences in their present form, to be both misleading and inconvenient. If the first of these two consequences—estoppel *per rem judicatam*—be the topic to be considered, it is at once to be observed that it is the *res judicata*, not the record, which creates the estoppel. As will be seen hereafter, it is immaterial whether the judicial decision is pronounced by a tribunal which is required by law, or authorised by custom, to keep written memorials of its decisions, or by a tribunal which is not so required or authorised.[2] As regards this result of a *res judicata*, then, though it is correctly described as an estoppel, its description as "estoppel by matter of record" or (more shortly) "estoppel by record" is a misnomer. The term, as applied by Coke and the other Elizabethan jurists, did undoubtedly reflect the views in their day obtaining as to the characteristics and limits of this class of estoppel. At a time when it was considered a sacrilege to question the inviolable "credit and verity" of a judicial *record*, rather than an injustice and scandal to impeach and re-agitate a judicial *decision*, the phrase was natural and appropriate enough. But, now that the latter aspect of the doctrine has superseded the former, the retention of the expression "estoppel by record" has become little more than an archaic survival.[3]

[1] The term is used generically by *Halsbury's Laws* (3rd Edn. Vol. 15); *cf. Everest and Strode* 3rd Edn. (1923), *Phipson on Evidence* 10th Edn. 845–846.

[2] See (e.g.) per Lord GUEST in *Carl-Zeiss-Stiftung* v. *Rayner and Keeler, Ltd.*, (*No.* 2), [1966] 2 All E.R. 536, H.L. at p. 564: "As it is now quite immaterial whether the judicial decision was pronounced by a tribunal which is required to keep a written record of its decisions, this nomenclature has disappeared, and it may be convenient to describe *res judicata* in its true and original form as 'cause of action estoppel'."

[3] "Estoppel by matter of record" is the first of the three classes of estoppel mentioned in 2 Coke on Littl. 352a. Coke there describes "matter of record" as including "letters patent, fine, recovery, pleading, taking of continuance, confession, imparlance, warrant of attorney, admittances", without mentioning judgments at all,—a curious omission,—but, in an earlier part of the same treatise (2 Coke on Littl. 260a), after defining "recordum" as a memorial or remembrance in rolls of parchment of the "proceedings and acts"—which would include judgments—"of courts of record", he proceeds to state, as a fundamental rule of evidence, that "the rolls being the records or memoranda of the judges of the courts of record, import in them such uncontrollable credit and verity as they admit no averment, plea, or proof to the contrary"—which is as much as to say, though the word itself is not used, that there is an estoppel against contradicting or impeaching the records of judicial "proceedings and acts". Now, if this rule

As regards the other of the consequences of *res judicata*—merger in judgment—the term "estoppel by record", though it is used in this connection by some high authorities, must be regarded as even more inept and open to objection, since this consequence of a *res judicata* is seen, when examined, not to be attributable to estoppel at all.

The use of the terms "estoppel by matter of record" or "estoppel by record" is accordingly sedulously avoided in this work, as is also that of their horrible companion "estoppel quasi of record".[1]

Treatment of the subject

7 The two doctrines which we have now been at pains to separate one from the other will be dealt with in completely different parts of this treatise, of which Part I will deal with the principles governing estoppel *per rem judicatam*. Under this general heading the subjects of cause of action estoppel and of issue estoppel[2] must logically be dealt with. After an exposition in the earlier chapters of this Part of the principles underlying the doctrine of estoppel *per rem judicatam*, a number of applications of

---

had been expressed so as to embrace all judicial decisions, and no more, it would, in substance, correspond to the rule of estoppel *per rem judicatam*; but it is not so expressed, for, in the first place, it is limited to the record of the decision, not the decision itself; secondly, the records referred to include, in addition to those of judgments, many of which are deemed in modern times to create either no estoppel at all, or only an estoppel by representation; whilst, lastly, it is only the decisions of courts of record which are stated to be subjects of estoppel. It is accordingly submitted, for reasons which will be elaborated in Chapter I, *post*, that the term "estoppel by record" ought now to be discarded altogether, in the interests of scientific nomenclature.

Dealing with the term "estoppel by record", and contrasting with it the more modern use of "issue estoppel", FULLAGAR J. wrote (of "issue estoppel") in *Jackson* v. *Goldsmith* (1950), 81 C.L.R. 446 (H. Ct. of Aus.) at p. 466: "It has the great advantage of being quite unambiguous. The term 'estoppel by record' is an alternative to 'issue estoppel', and it is a term which has been in use for a very long time. But while it is not open to any *prima facie* objection, it has become *ancipitis usus*, being used sometimes as equivalent to issue estoppel, sometimes as equivalent to *res judicata*, and sometimes as describing a supposed common principle from which both the rule as to *res judicata* and the rule as to issue estoppel are derived." In this work "estoppel *per rem judicatam*" is used to include all cases of estoppel precluding the contradiction of matters previously determined between the parties. These include (a) cases where it is sought to challenge the decision itself, and this is precluded by estoppel ("cause of action estoppel"), and (b) cases where, though the decision in the previous proceedings is not challenged, some issue forming an essential constituent of it is. The principle which precludes the latter type of challenge is in this work called "issue estoppel".

[1] 15 *Halsbury's Laws*, 3rd Edn., pp. 168–169, 212 *et seq*; *cf*. the notes to *The Duchess of Kingston's Case* in 2 Smith's Leading Cases 13th Edn. 689.

[2] For the place of these terms in the systematic classification of estoppels *per rem judicatam*, see the judgment of DIPLOCK L.J. in *Thoday* v. *Thoday*, [1964] P. 181, at p. 197. He appears to have been the first to use the term "cause of action estoppel". "Issue estoppel" is a term perhaps first suggested in Australia by HIGGINS J. in *Hoysted* v. *Federal Taxation Commissioner* (1921), 29 C.L.R. 537 (H. Ct. of Aus.) at p. 561. It was taken up by DIXON J. in *Blair* v. *Curran* (1939), 62 C.L.R. 464 (H. Ct. of Aus.) at p. 531 and by FULLAGAR J. in *Jackson* v. *Goldsmith* (1950), 81 C.L.R. 446 (H. Ct. of Aus.) at p. 466. It has been adopted in English courts by DIPLOCK L.J. in *Thoday* v. *Thoday*, [1964] P. 181, at p. 198 and by Lord DENNING, M.R. in *Fidelitas Shipping Co., Ltd.* v. *V/O Exportchleb*, [1965] 2 All E.R. 4, at p. 8.

these principles will be examined, and it will be seen in successive chapters how these principles are applied to such special subjects as running-down cases, taxation and rating cases, and matrimonial proceedings. The plea of *autrefois acquit* (the plea by which this doctrine is applied to criminal matters) is dealt with in a separate chapter in this section of Part I, and this Part concludes with a chapter dealing with affirmative answers to a plea of estoppel.

Part II will deal with merger in judgment—the doctrine whereby recovery of judgment by one party operates as a bar to further proceedings by him in respect of the same cause of action. After an exposition of the principles underlying this doctrine, the plea of *autrefois convict* in criminal matters will receive consideration in a separate chapter.

Each Part will conclude with a chapter dealing with the rules as to pleading and procedure applicable to that part of the subject. Four Appendices are added to the text; in the first two of these will be found short excursus dealing with (a), the inherent jurisdiction of the Court enabling the dismissal of proceedings in cases where *res judicata* cannot be strictly established, and (b), the doctrine of *Res Judicata* in Roman Law, while the last two are devoted to the legislative repeal of the rule in *Hollington* v. *F. Hewthorn & Co., Ltd.*[1]

[1] [1943] K.B. 587.

PART I

Estoppel Per Rem Judicatam

CHAPTER

Preliminary

8 In this introductory chapter it is proposed to deal successively with, first, the principle sustaining estoppel *per rem judicatam*, secondly, the theory on which the doctrine is based, thirdly, the terminology of this part of the subject, and lastly, the constituent elements of *res judicata* in its operation as estoppel.

Statement of the principle of estoppel per rem judicatam

9 The rule of estoppel by *res judicata*, which, like that of estoppel by representation, is a rule of evidence,[1] may thus be stated: where a final judicial decision has been pronounced by either an English, or (with certain exceptions) a foreign,[2] judicial tribunal of competent jurisdiction over the parties to, and the subject-matter of, the litigation, any party or privy to such litigation, as against any other party or privy thereto, and, in the case of a decision *in rem*, any person whatsoever, as against any other person, is estopped in any subsequent litigation from disputing or questioning such decision on the merits,[3] whether it be used as the foundation of an action,[4] or relied upon as a bar to any claim, indictment or complaint,[5] or to any affirmative defence, case, or allegation, if, but not unless, the party

---

[1] *Humphries* v. *Humphries*, [1910] 2 K.B. 531, C.A. per FARWELL J. delivering the judgment of the court, at p. 536; *Marginson* v. *Blackburn Borough Council*, [1939] 2 K.B. 426, per SLESSER L.J. at p. 437. ("the broader rule of evidence which prohibits the reassertion of a cause of action"); *Morrison, Rose & Partners* v. *Hillman*, [1961] 2 Q.B. 266, per PEARSON L.J. at p. 277 ("To my mind the correct line of approach to this question is to regard the previous decision as conclusive evidence").

[2] See Chapter II, para. 69, *post*, as to foreign *res judicatae*.

[3] This passage of the text, reprinted from the first edition, was expressly approved by Lord GUEST in *Carl-Zeiss-Stiftung* v. *Rayner and Keeler, Ltd.*, (*No.* 2), [1966] 2 All E.R. 536, H.L. at p. 564.

[4] See para. 18, *infra*, as to the principle, in cases where an action is brought on the *res judicata*, being precisely the same as in cases where the decision is set up as a bar, though not usually denominated "estoppel" in the former type of case. As to the cases in which an action will not lie at all on a judgment, see Chapter II, paras. 77 *et seq.*, *post*.

[5] The plea of *autrefois acquit*, which is in its nature a plea of estoppel *per rem judicatam* in criminal cases, is dealt with in Chapter XI.

interested raises the point of estoppel at the proper time and in the proper manner.[1]

This rule is sometimes expressed in the concise Latin maxim *res judicata pro veritate accipitur*.[2]

Theories on which the doctrine is based

10 There are two theories (which, however, on analysis, may perhaps be regarded as merely two aspects or sides of one and the same theory) whereon the doctrine of estoppel *per rem judicatam* is commonly justified;[3] *viz.* first, the general interest of the community in the termination of disputes, and in the finality and conclusiveness of judicial decisions; and, secondly, the right of the individual to be protected from vexatious multiplication of suits and prosecutions at the instance of an opponent whose superior wealth, resources and power may, unless curbed by the estoppel, weigh down judicially declared right and innocence.[4] The former is

---

[1] See Chapter XIV, *post*.

[2] By (for instance) Lord MACDERMOTT, delivering the report of the Judicial Committee, in *Sambasivam* v. *Public Prosecutor, Federation of Malaya*, [1950] A.C. 458, P.C. at p. 479.

[3] One may disregard here certain archaic and metaphysical theories, originating mainly with Coke, such as that of the inviolable sanctity of "the record", as such (2 Coke on Littl. 260a), which is of "so high and conclusive a nature as to admit of no contradiction thereof" (2 Coke on Littl. 352a), or the fanciful view, quite in the Baconian spirit, that, as nature abhors a vacuum, so "the common law . . . abhors infiniteness" (*Ferrer* v. *Arden* (1599), 6 Co. Rep. 7a), and *infinitum in jure reprobatur* (*Randal* v. *Higgens* (1605), 6 Co. Rep. 44b), or the still more curious and scholastic suggestion that it would be a monstrous inversion of the natural order of things that, men being mortal, litigation should be immortal (*ne lites immortales essent dum litigantes mortales sunt*) cited by the Court of Common Pleas at p. 239 of *Ellis* v. *M'Henry* (1871), L.R. 6 C.P. 228), or, lastly, the idea that, on the principle of *cuilibet in sua arte perito est credendum*, a sort of intercurial comity ought to prevail, in obedience to which the judgment of a court of exclusive jurisdiction ought not to be questioned by any other court, though deemed by the latter erroneous (*Bunting* v. *Lepingwell* (1585), 4 Co. Rep. 29a).

[4] In 2 Coke on Littl. 260a, the doctrine is made to rest upon public convenience only: "for otherwise (as our old authors say, and that truly) there should never be an end of controversies, which should be inconvenient". *Cf.* BRETT M.R., at p. 518 of *Re May* (1885), 28 Ch.D. 516, C.A.: "it is one of the most fundamental doctrines of all courts, that there must be an end to all litigation". This was also the view of the Roman jurists: see App. B., *post*. On the other hand, both of the theories referred to in the text are expressly relied upon in *Ferrer* v. *Arden* (1599), 6 Co. Rep. 7a, where *expedit reipublicae ut sit finis litium* is first given summarily as the foundation of the rule (p. 7a), and, later (at p. 9a) there follows an expansion of the formula in these terms: "*interest reipublicae ut sit finis litium*; otherwise great oppression might be done under colour and pretence of law; for if there should not be an end of suits, then a rich and malicious man would infinitely vex him that had right by suits and actions; and in the end (because he cannot come to an end) compel him (to redeem his charge and vexation) to relinquish his right". The court then enlarges on the scandal of an infinity of verdicts, recoveries, and judgments in one and the same cause, with possibly "contrariety" between some of them, and the protraction of litigation thence resulting, and concludes with the quaint expression cited in the last note—"all this tends to the dishonour of the common law, which abhors infiniteness". *Cf.* CASSELS J. in *Johnson* v. *Cartledge and Matthews*, [1939] 3 All E.R. 654, at p. 657: "it seems lamentable that it should be possible for so many Courts to be engaged at different times in different places considering the unfortunate results of the negligent driving of a motor car". Lord BLACKBURN, at p. 530 of *Lockyer* v. *Ferryman* (1877), 2 App. Cas. 519, H.L., preached the two theories as separate and distinct from one another, and as the two recognised foundations of the doctrine: "The object of the rule of *res judicata* is always put upon two grounds—the one *public policy*, that it is in the

public policy, and is succinctly expressed in the maxim, *interest (or expedit) reipublicae ut sit finis litium:* the latter is private justice, and is reflected in the maxims, *nemo debet bis vexari pro una et eadem causa*, and, in connection with criminal litigation, to which the theory is equally applicable,[1] *nemo debet bis vexari pro uno et eodem delicto*. "The utility and equity of estoppel by *res judicata*, from either of the above points of view", (said Mr Spencer Bower in the first edition of this work) "is so obvious that, with scarcely any exception,[2] both professional and popular criticism has refrained from fastening on this class of estoppel the odium which, with equal injustice, but far more superficial plausibility, has in times past gathered round the doctrine of estoppel by representation".[3] This opinion was fully supported by the decisions at the time when it was written, and indeed it has been said even in recent years in the House of Lords that:

> "the doctrine of estoppel (*per rem judicatam*) is one founded on considerations of justice and good sense. If an issue has been distinctly raised and decided in an action, in which the parties are represented, it is unjust and unreasonable to permit the same issue to be litigated afresh between the same parties or persons claiming under them".[4]

---

interest of the State that there should be an end of litigation, and the other, the *hardship on the individual* that he should be vexed twice for the same cause". This dictum is recalled with approval by HOLROYD PEARCE L.J. in *Morrison, Rose and Partners* v. *Hillman*, [1961] 2 Q.B. 266, at p. 276, and again by Lord REID in his judgment in the Lords in *Carl-Zeiss-Stiftung* v. *Rayner and Keeler, Ltd.*, (*No.* 2), [1966] 2 All E.R. 536, H.L. at p. 549. Reference may also be made to the judgment of Lord GUEST at p. 564 in the same case. See further *Green* v. *Weatherill*, [1929] 2 Ch. 213, at p. 221, "The plea of *res judicata* is not a technical doctrine, but a fundamental doctrine based on the view that there must be an end to litigation" (MAUGHAM J.). (It is to be noted, however, that this was a merger case.) *Cf.* the cases cited in note 2, *infra*.

[1] For a full exposition of the doctrine of *autrefois acquit* and of the application of the doctrine of issue estoppel to criminal cases, see Chapter XI, *post*.

[2] There appear to be few, if indeed any, instances of express judicial characterisation of estoppel *per rem judicatam* as "odious", though in one case, a very sound and accurate judge permitted himself the rather loose expression that "in one sense" (he did not say what sense, and it is not easy to conceive any) it may be said to exclude the truth (HOLMES L.J., at p. 584 of *Irish Land Commission* v. *Ryan*, [1900] 2 I.R. 565: "it would be contrary to public policy to allow the same parties to re-agitate the same matter in subsequent proceedings. Estoppel by matter of record rests on this principle, and though it may be said in one sense to exclude the truth, it is essentially just and righteous"). In *Cox* v. *Dublin City Distillery Co., Ltd.* (*No.* 3), [1917] 1 I.R. 203, Sir IGNATIUS O'BRIEN L.C. (Ir.), said, at p. 230, that "the principle" of estoppel "has often been made the subject of disapproval from the time of Coke to that of L.J. FITZGIBBON. For myself, I fail to see why this should be so, because it appears to me a convenient means, and sometimes the only means, of defending a position which may be just and fair as between man and man." In *Hayward* v. *Hayward*, [1961] 1 All E.R. 236; [1961] P. 152 PHILLIMORE J. permitted himself some critical observations as to the possible effects of the application of estoppels in the divorce jurisdiction; but it must be remembered that divorce is a very special field, and, moreover, in that case he was provided with a legitimate answer to the plea of estoppel—*viz.* the illegality of the marriage which was to be set up by the plea.

[3] See the authors' *Law of Estoppel by Representation* 2nd Edn. (1965) paras. 14 *et seq*.

[4] *New Brunswick Rail. Co.* v. *British and French Trust Corporation, Ltd.*, [1939] A.C. 1, H.L. per Lord MAUGHAM L.C. at pp. 19–20. *Cf.* LAWTON J.'s pleasant reconciliation of justice and equity with the "curious and excellent kinde of learning" of the doctrine of estoppel in *Randolph* v. *Tuck*, [1962] 1 Q.B. 175, at p. 184.

Criticisms of the doctrine

11 But notwithstanding the opinions, above expressed, of Mr Spencer Bower in the first edition of this book in 1924, and of Lord MAUGHAM L.C. in the House of Lords in 1939,[1] doubts have been expressed more and more frequently in more recent years as to how far the application of the doctrine can be pushed before it breaks down as a matter of practical common sense. As yet legal philosophy has been spared the shock of any vigorous attack from a high quarter upon the doctrine as a whole; but some cracks have appeared in a structure which half a century ago was considered impregnable. As is often the case when a legal doctrine comes under fire, matters of detail, particular aspects, rather than the doctrine as a whole, have first become the subject of criticism. In the case of estoppel *per rem judicatam*, the questions which have been raised have not been concerned with the doctrine as generally enunciated, but with particular applications of it. It has been questioned, for instance, whether judgments by default ought always to have the same authority, binding the parties by estoppel *per rem judicatam*, as judgments in which the issues have been decided after contest;[2] and, again, whether judgments in foreign courts should not be more carefully examined, before being held to be binding by estoppel, than domestic judgments.[3] After much exploratory litigation it has ultimately been found impracticable to bind revenue and rating

---

[1] *New Brunswick Rail. Co.* v. *British and French Trust Corporation*, [1939] A.C. 1, H.L. per Lord MAUGHAM L.C. at pp. 19–20.

[2] *New Brunswick Rail. Co.* v. *British and French Trust Corporation*, [1939] A.C. 1, H.L. per Lord WRIGHT at p. 37 and Lord ROMER at p. 41; *Kok Hoong* v. *Leong Cheong Kweng Mines, Ltd.*, [1964] A.C. 993, J.C. per Lord RADCLIFFE at p. 1010. ("... while from one point of view a default judgment can be looked upon as only another form of a judgment by consent (see *Re South American and Mexican Co., Ex parte Bank of England*, [1895] 1 Ch. 37, at p. 45 and, as such, capable of giving rise to all the consequences of a judgment obtained in a contested action or with the consent or acquiescence of the parties, from another a judgment by default speaks for nothing but the fact that a defendant for unascertained reasons, negligence, ignorance or indifference, has suffered judgment to go against him in the particular suit in question. There is obvious and, indeed, grave danger in permitting such a judgment to preclude the parties from ever reopening before the court on another occasion, perhaps of different significance, whatever issues can be discerned as having been involved in the judgment so obtained by default."). See, too, *Carl-Zeiss-Stiftung* v. *Rayner and Keeler, Ltd.*, (*No. 2*), [1966] 2 All E.R. 536, H.L. per Lord REID at p. 554, dealing with a judgment by default in a foreign court, the effect of which is referred to in note 3, *infra*. And see, generally, under the heading "Judgments by Default" paragraphs 46 *et seq. post.*

[3] *Carl-Zeiss-Stiftung* v. *Rayner and Keeler, Ltd.*, (*No. 2*), [1966] 2 All E.R. 536, H.L. per Lord REID at p. 554. Dealing with estoppels which were contended for on the foundation of a foreign default judgment, Lord REID said: "The difficulty which I see about issue estoppel is a practical one. Suppose the first case is one of trifling importance, but it involves for one party proof of facts which would be expensive and troublesome; and that party can see the possibility that the same point may arise if his opponent later raises a much more important claim. What is he to do? The second case may never be brought. Must he go to great trouble and expense to forestall a possible plea of issue estoppel if the second case is brought? This does not arise in cause of action estoppel: if the cause of action is important, he will incur the expense; if it is not, he will take the chance of winning on some other point. It seems to me that there is room for a good deal more thought before we settle the limits of issue estoppel ..."

authorities from year to year by estoppel *per rem judicatam*, and so a gloss has been placed upon the doctrine, resulting in each year's assessment being considered as a different question from the assessment of the year before;[1] in running-down cases it has been seriously doubted whether a decision as between A and B (for instance) as to their respective contributions, in respect of the injuries suffered by one passenger in the car of one of them ought always to estop them when their contributions to another passenger's damages are under consideration;[2] and in divorce the courts have firmly declined to allow "the Court to be estopped" from making full and fresh inquiry into allegations of matrimonial misconduct, even though the same point has been the subject of a previous decision between the same parties.[3] All these separate instances taken together must be taken to indicate some substantial degree of resistance on the part of the courts against extending the application of the doctrine any further; and indeed may demonstrate a definite tendency towards positively restricting its future operation, in the face of the increasing complexity of many of the problems of modern litigation.

12 The theoretical foundation of estoppel *per rem judicatam* is as stated in para. 10, *supra*, not only where the *res judicata* is set up as a bar to a cause of action, claim, or affirmative case which contradicts the former decision, but also where an action is brought on the *res judicata*, for the purpose of preventing the opposite party from disputing such former decision on the merits. Though the word "estoppel" is hardly ever used in the latter class of case, the rule of evidence applied is in substance precisely the same, and its object and effect is the same, *viz.* to preclude any party to the *res judicata* from ever afterwards, as against any other party thereto, impeaching its correctness.[4]

13 The applicability of the rule both to civil and to criminal proceedings, both to decisions of courts of record and to those of other judicial tribunals, and both to English and to foreign *res judicatae*, is justified by, and rests upon, the same theoretical basis of public policy and private justice.

The doctrine is the product of the adversary system of litigation

14 The doctrine of estoppel *per rem judicatam* is the product of the adversary system of litigation practised in English Courts. Its essence is that *as between opposed parties* an issue, once litigated, should be regarded as

---

[1] For a discussion of the development of the exception to the general principle, applicable to taxation and rating cases, see Chapter X, *post*.

[2] For a separate discussion of the doctrine as applied to running-down cases see Chapter IX, *post*.

[3] The doctrine as applied in matrimonial proceedings is discussed in Chapter XII, *post*.

[4] See para. 17, *infra*.

for ever decided. In a different system of jurisprudence where the court exercised an inquisitorial function, it might be thought unjust or inexpedient that it should be impeded in its search for truth by the principle *res judicata inter partes pro veritate accipitur*. But this is not the system under which English courts administer justice, except possibly for the divorce jurisdiction, in which it has become clear that considerations of estoppel *inter partes* will not be allowed to stifle full inquiry into the facts founding allegations of matrimonial offences. DIPLOCK L.J. has commented interestingly on the philosophical background of the matter as follows:

> "Estoppel merely means that, under the rules of the adversary system of procedure upon which the common law of England is based, a party is not allowed, in certain circumstances, to prove in litigation particular facts or matters which, if proved, would assist him to succeed as plaintiff or defendant in an action. If the court is required to exercise an inquisitorial function and may inquire into facts which the parties do not choose to prove, or would under the rules of the adversary system be prevented from proving, this is a function to which the common law concept of estoppel is alien. It may well be a rational rule to apply in the exercise of such an inquisitorial function to say that if a court having jurisdiction to do so has once inquired into the truth of a particular allegation of fact and reached a decision thereon, another court of co-ordinate jurisdiction in the exercise of its own discretion should not re-embark upon the same inquiry, but should accept the decision of the first court. But this is a different concept from estoppel as hitherto known in English law. It will be interesting to watch its development in future cases, but fortunately it is not, in my view, necessary to develop it in the present appeal. For, whatever this new concept may involve, it would appear from those cases in which it has been adumbrated that it only becomes relevant in cases where, under the old common law concept of estoppel, a party to matrimonial proceedings would be prevented from proving facts or matters which the court, in the exercise of its inquisitorial functions, might regard as relevant to its decision in those proceedings."[1]

The doctrine that the decision of the Court is binding thereafter on those only who were parties to the suit is subject to an exception in the case of judgments *in rem*, which will receive consideration in a later chapter.[2]

Correctness of the decision not a relevant consideration

15 It is not essential, or even relevant, to prove that the decision relied upon to found an estoppel is itself correct, or well founded in law or fact; if it is pronounced as a final judicial decision, by a tribunal having jurisdiction, as to the same question, and between the same parties, it will be conclusively deemed correct, as between these parties, unless and until upset on appeal. This proposition rests on the well-known fact that a

---

1 *Thoday* v. *Thoday*, [1964] P. 181, C.A. at p. 197.

2 See Chapter VIII, *post*.

competent tribunal has jurisdiction to give a wrong judgment. It has jurisdiction to decide wrongly, as well as rightly,[1] and if it makes a mistake that mistake is conclusive between the parties unless and until corrected by an appeal duly constituted.[2]

Res judicata *and judicial precedent contrasted*

16 There is an essential difference between the doctrine of estoppel *per rem judicatam* and the doctrine of judicial precedent. By virtue of the former a final decision of a concrete issue between parties, by any court having jurisdiction to determine that issue, will for ever thereafter preclude either party from raising the same issue against the other party to the decision, whether before the same court, or before any court exercising a higher or lower jurisdiction.[3] The doctrine of judicial precedent, on the other hand, is not concerned with concrete issues as between parties. Its effect is to declare the law, not the facts, and to declare it so as to be binding upon all persons, whether parties to the proceedings or not, in all courts of inferior, and in some cases of the same, jurisdiction; but not so as to be binding on courts of higher jurisdiction, in which the *ratio decidendi* of the former decision becomes re-arguable. The doctrine of precedent does not depend upon the maxims *interest reipublicae sit finis litium* or *res judicata pro veritate accipitur*, but depends simply upon the desirability of certainty and uniformity in the law. The difference between the doctrines of *res judicata* and judicial precedent is interestingly illustrated in the twin cases of *Re Waring, Westminster Bank, Ltd.* v. *Awdry*[4] decided in 1942 and 1948 respectively. In the first of these, on an originating summons issued by trustees, FARWELL J. held that section 25 of the Finance Act 1941 was not applicable to a certain annuity fund set up by the trust; on appeal, the Court of Appeal reversed this decision, and held the provisions of the section applicable to the fund.[5] At this stage the effect of the decision of the Court of Appeal was two-fold; it decided as a matter of *res judicata* for ever, as between the parties to the appeal, that section 25 applied to the particular fund. It also declared to all the world that courts up to and including the Court of Appeal would thereafter interpret the law as laid

---

1 See for instance per Lord HOLT C.J. in *Philips* v. *Bury* (1694), Skin. 447—"his sentence must have some effect to make a vacancy, be it never so wrong" (p. 485).

2 Per ISAACS J. in *Meyers* v. *Casey* (1913), 17 C.L.R. 90 (H. Ct. of Aus.) at pp. 114–115.

3 See, for instance, *Marginson* v. *Blackburn Borough Council*, [1939] 2 K.B. 426, C.A. at p. 438—"This seems to us to be a clear discussion on the same issue, between the same persons litigating in the present case, and establishes conclusively, *albeit in the county court*, in a claim by the defendants against the present plaintiff, that both were equally to blame."

4 FARWELL J.'s decision on the first application in the *Waring* litigation is reported in [1942] Ch. 309. The decision was reversed in the Court of Appeal—[1942] Ch. 426. The second application is reported in [1948] Ch. 221.

5 *In Re Waring, Westminster Bank, Ltd.* v. *Awdry*, [1942] 2 All E.R. 250; [1942] 1 Ch. 426, C.A.

down in that case, in disputes as between any parties whomsoever. In 1946 *Berkeley* v. *Berkeley*[1] came before the House of Lords; the decision of the House in that case (in which none of the parties in *Re Waring* was concerned) was to the opposite effect. The result of *Berkeley* v. *Berkeley* was that the law was thereby stated, as a matter of judicial precedent, to all the world to the opposite effect from what had previously been stated in *Re Waring*. But although such was the effect of *Berkeley* v. *Berkeley* as a matter of judicial precedent, it had no effect at all, as regards the persons concerned in the Waring Trust, as *res judicata*. Although the law was, as to all the rest of the world, now as decided in *Berkeley* v. *Berkeley*, the parties to the 1942 decision in *Re Waring* continued to be bound by the result of that case. In 1948 the trustees in the Waring estate made a further application to the court,[2] seeking directions as between themselves and another beneficiary who had not been joined in the first proceedings. The result—it is submitted in accordance with principle—was that, following the application of the principle of *res judicata*, all those who had been parties to the first proceedings in 1942 remained bound *inter partes* by the decision, from which there had been no appeal; but, as between the trustees and beneficiaries who had not been parties to the 1942 proceedings, the application of the doctrine of judicial precedent brought about a different position—*viz*. that laid down in *Berkeley* v. *Berkeley*.[3]

Use of the term "estoppe" land its equivalents, where the res judicata *is relied upon as a bar*

17 Where a judicial decision is pleaded or relied upon as a bar to any claim, counter-claim, affirmative defence, or allegation which purports to impeach the correctness of such decision, the *res judicata* clearly operates as an "estoppel" in the strictest sense of the word, as has been recognised at various stages in the history of the doctrine by such eminent authorities, to take a few examples out of the many, as BULLER J.,[4] Lord ELLENBOROUGH C.J.,[5] Lord TENTERDEN, then ABBOTT C.J.,[6] Lord SELBORNE

---

1 *Countess of Berkeley* v. *Berkeley*, [1946] 2 All E.R. 154; [1946] A.C. 555, H.L.

2 *In Re Waring, Westminster Bank, Ltd.* v. *Burton-Butler*, [1948] 1 All E.R. 257; [1948] Ch. 221 (JENKINS J.).

3 *In New Zealand* the difference between the two doctrines was referred to by Sir HAROLD BARROWCLOUGH C.J. in *Gisborne Sheepfarmers' Mercantile Co., Ltd.* v. *Inland Revenue Commissioner*, [1962] N.Z.L.R. 810, S.C. at p. 814.

4 At p. 377 of *Duffield* v. *Scott* (1789), 3 Term Rep. 374.

5 At pp. 353, 358 of *Outram* v. *Morewood* (1803), 3 East 346. In the same year, Lord ELLENBOROUGH C.J. is reported, at p. 59 of *Strutt* v. *Bovingdon* (1803), 5 Esp. 56 as having directed a jury that "the record of the first cause should not be deemed a legal estoppel, so as to conclude the rights of the parties by its production, but it was binding so far that he should consider himself bound to tell the jury to consider it as conclusive of the rights of the parties". (Then why should it "not be deemed a legal estoppel"?)

6 At p. 155 of *Hannaford* v. *Hunn* (1825), 2 C. & P. 148.

L.C.,[1], Lord PARKER, then PARKER J.,[2] and, to come to more recent times, Lord MAUGHAM L.C., Lord RUSSELL OF KILLOWEN, and Lord WRIGHT,[3] whether the *res judicata* be a judgment, or a judicial decision which is not technically so denominated, such as the sentence of a court martial,[4] or an award.[5] In Australia, the decision of the committee of a racing club disqualifying a race horse owner has been held *res judicata* between the parties thereto.[6] Accordingly, the use of the word "estoppel" in connection with the class of case under discussion has now become quite common,[7] though in earlier times it was more sparingly and hestitatingly employed. There is no magic, however, in this or any other particular name, and in nearly all the cases in which the word "estoppel" is absent from the judgment,[8] it will be found that exact variants or equivalents such as "conclusive" or "cannot be questioned",[9] "preclude", "bar",[10] "obstacle",[11] and the like have been used in its place, and that, under this substituted nomenclature, the principle, that every *res judicata* bars or precludes a party from setting up a case the object or effect of which is to dispute the correctness of that *res judicata*, is as efficiently stated as if the actual expression "estoppel" were a thousand times repeated.[12]

---

[1] At p. 304 of *R.* v. *Hutchings* (1881), 6 Q.B.D. 300, C.A.—"estoppel *per rem judicatam*".

[2] At p. 583 of *Re Surfleet's Estate, Rawlings* v. *Smith* (1911), 105 L.T. 582 ("estoppel by *res judicata*").

[3] In *New Brunswick Rail. Co.* v. *British and French Trust Corporation*, [1938] 4 All E.R. 747; [1939] A.C. 1.

[4] *Hannaford* v. *Hunn* (1825), 2 C. & P. 148. See Chapter II, *post*, for other illustrations of decisions which are not judgments.

[5] In *Commings* v. *Heard* (1869), L.R. 4 Q.B. 669 an award was described in the argument for the defendant as having the effect of an "estoppel quasi of record", adopting the phraseology of *Smith's Leading Cases*. In the judgments the court hesitated to apply the term "estoppel", preferring phrases (which are really equivalent) such as "concluded", "precluded", "prohibited", "bar", etc. etc. (*per* LUSH J. at pp. 672, 673 and 674): but on p. 231 of *Duke of Buccleuch* v. *Metropolitan Board of Works* (1870), L.R. 5 Exch. 221, BLACKBURN J. spoke of an award as an estoppel in unqualified terms. *Cf. Hopkins* v. *Hopkins*, [1914] P. 282, where a withdrawal of a charge was described as an "estoppel" by BARGRAVE DEANE J. at p. 286. A more modern instance of the use of the term "estoppel" where the decision was one of an umpire on an arbitration is *Fidelitas Shipping Co., Ltd.* v. *V/O Exportchleb*, [1965] 2 All E.R. 4; [1966] 1 Q.B. 630.

[6] *Meyers* v. *Casey* (1913), 17 C.L.R. 90 (H. Ct. of Aus.) per ISAACS J. at p. 114 ("the objections . . . are, by reasons of the Committee's decision, *res judicatae* as much as if, instead of the Committee, it had been the Supreme Court unappealed from that had so held".

[7] For modern instances see for instance *Marginson* v. *Blackburn Borough Council*, [1939] 1 All E.R. 273; [1939] 2 K.B. 426, C.A.; *Morrison, Rose & Partners* v. *Hillman*, [1961] 2 All E.R. 891; [1961] 2 Q.B. 266, C.A.

[8] In some cases, though absent from the judgment, it was used in the argument—*e.g.* in *A.-G.* v. *King* (1817), 5 Price 195 and *The Challenge and Duc D'Aumale*, [1904] P. 41.

[9] As in *London County Council* v. *Galsworthy*, [1917] 1 K.B. 85, D.C.

[10] As in *Commings* v. *Heard* (1869), L.R. 4 Q.B. 669 where also the terms "concluded", "precluded", and "prohibited" appear in the judgment of LUSH J. at pp. 673, 674.

[11] "Obstacle to the recovery" is the phrase used by Lord DENMAN, C.J., delivering the judgment of the Queen's Bench at p. 521 of *Palmer* v. *Temple* (1839), 9 Ad. & El. 508.

[12] "Conclusive evidence" is treated as a synonym of "estoppel" by KNIGHT BRUCE V.C. at p. 171 of *Holland* v. *Clark* (1842), 1 Y. & C. Ch. Cas. 151; *cf.* the judgment of PEARSON L.J. in

Terminology employed where the res judicata is the foundation of an action

18 Where an action, or counterclaim, is founded on a judgment or other judicial decision, assuming it to lie at all, as is the case with all foreign, but only some English, *res judicatae*, the judicial decision is precisely to the same extent, and precisely for the same reasons, and under precisely the same conditions, conclusive and binding upon the parties and their privies, so as to preclude any of them from impeaching its correctness, as it is when set up as a bar or obstacle to a claim or case which involves such an impeachment. There is, therefore, no logical justification for applying the term "estoppel" to the one class of case, and withholding it from the other, since in substance and principle both are equally the subject of the doctrine. But there has been a reluctance to use the term in such proceedings, and in both pleadings and judgments there has appeared a preference—not to be explained upon logical grounds—for such phraseology as that the decision is not "examinable" or "impeachable" on the merits, or is "not to be inquired into", or that the defendant is not "suffered", or "permitted", or "allowed", to contradict it.

The necessary constituents of estoppel per rem judicatam

19 Any party who is desirous of setting up *res judicata* by way of estoppel, whether he is relying on such *res judicata* as a bar to his opponent's claim, or as the foundation of his own, and who has taken the preliminary steps required in order to qualify him for that purpose, must establish all the constituent elements of an estoppel of this description, as already indicated in the general proposition enunciated at the commencement of this chapter.[1] That is to say, the burden is on him of establishing (except as to any of them which may be expressly or impliedly admitted) each and every of the following:

(i) that the alleged judicial decision was what in law is deemed such;
(ii) that the particular judicial decision relied upon was in fact pronounced, as alleged;

Morrison, Rose & Partners v. *Hillman*, [1961] 2 Q.B. 266, at p. 277—"to my mind the easiest line of approach to this question is to regard the previous decision as conclusive evidence". "Estoppel or bar" is the expression used by JAMES L.J. at p. 751 of *Massam* v. *Thorley's Cattle Food Co.* (1880), 14 Ch.D. 748, C.A., he evidently regarding the two terms as convertible. In *Stokes* v. *Stokes*, [1911] P. 195 the doctrine in question is spoken of by EVANS P., delivering the judgment of himself and BARGRAVE DEANE J. at p. 198, as "the doctrine of *res judicata*, or of estoppel".

[1] SLESSER L.J. thus put the essentials in *Marginson* v. *Blackburn Borough Council*, [1939] 2 K.B. 426, C.A. at p. 438: "This seems to us a clear decision on the same issue between the same persons litigating in the present case, and establishes conclusively, albeit in the county court, in a claim by the defendants against the present plaintiff that both were equally to blame. We think, therefore, on this head, that the appeal succeeds . . . and that the plaintiff is estopped from bringing his first cause of action".

(iii) that the judicial tribunal pronouncing the decision had competent jurisdiction in that behalf;
(iv) that the judicial decision was final;
(v) that the judicial decision was, or involved, a determination of the same question as that sought to be controverted in the litigation in which the estoppel is raised;
(vi) that the parties to the judicial decision, or their privies, were the same persons as the parties to the proceeding in which the estoppel is raised, or their privies, or that the decision was conclusive *in rem*.

20 The above six *probanda* form the subjects of the next seven chapters of this Part,[1] the treatment of the sixth of them being divided between Chapters VII and VIII. Then follow four chapters dealing with particular applications of the principles which have up to this point been enunciated.[2] Part I then concludes with a chapter on affirmative answers which are in law deemed sufficient to defeat a *prima facie* case of estoppel *per rem judicatam*; and by a final chapter[3] on the procedure which must be followed by a party entitled to raise a plea of estoppel.[4]

---

[1] Chapter II, *post*, first examines the question of what constitutes a judicial decision, which (since such a decision must have been pronounced by a judicial tribunal) involves a discussion of two questions, *viz*: what constitutes a judicial tribunal, and what is in law deemed a decision; it then deals with English criminal *res judicatae*, and foreign *res judicatae*, both of which, with certain qualifications, are shown to come within the doctrine of *res judicata*; and, finally, it discusses and distinguishes the classes of judicial decision on which an action will lie, and those on which it will not: Chapter III, *post*, deals with the mode of proving that the particular judicial decision relied upon as the foundation of the estoppel was in fact pronounced: Chapter IV, *post*, is occupied with an investigation of what is required to establish that the judicial tribunal had a competent jurisdiction over the subject of the litigation, and the parties: Chapter V, *post*, is devoted to the question of the finality of the decision, and what is involved in that expresssion: Chapter VI, *post*, treats of the identity of the subject-matter of the *res judicata* with that of the proceedings in which the estoppel is raised. The subject of issue estoppel is dealt with at length at this point of the text. Chapter VII, *post*, deals with the topic of parties in actions *in personam*; proceedings *in rem* are considered in Chapter VIII.

[2] These are: Chapter IX (Running-down Cases); Chapter X (Taxation and Rating Cases); Chapter XI (The Plea of *Autrefois Acquit*); and Chapter XII (Matrimonial Proceedings).

[3] Chapter XIII.

[4] Chapter XIV.

CHAPTER II

What in Law Constitutes a Res Judicata

Introduction

21 A *res judicata* is a judicial decision, pronounced by a judicial tribunal. It is of no avail to prove that the alleged *res judicata* was a decision, or even that it was a judicial one, in the sense that it was pronounced according to judicial principles, unless it be also established that it emanated from a judicial tribunal in the exercise of its judicial functions; nor, on the other hand, is it sufficient to shew that it was pronounced by a judicial tribunal, unless it be also shewn that it was a decision, and a judicial one, as distinguished from a termination of the proceedings otherwise than by a judicial decision. It is vital, therefore, to the present inquiry to fix at the outset the proper definition, first, of "judicial tribunal", and then, of "judicial decision".

What is a judicial tribunal?

22 In determining the characteristics and *differentiae* of a "judicial tribunal", the first essential is to get rid, once and for all, of the antiquated view, entertained by Sir Edward Coke,[1] which is the source of the misleading, but still surviving, expression, "estoppel by record",[2] that only a court of record[3] can be a judicial tribunal for the purpose of the doctrine of estoppel *per rem judicatam*. It is now well established that it is quite immaterial whether the tribunal which pronounced the decision relied upon

[1] See 2 Coke on Litt. 260a.

[2] See Introduction, para. 6, *ante*.

[3] Defined by Coke, *ubi sup.*, as "a court of justice which hath power to hold plea according to the course of the common law of real or mixed actions, or of actions *quare vi et armis*, or of personal actions, whereof the debt or damage amounts to forty shillings or above", and which is "created by parliament, letters patent, or prescription", as distinguished from "inferior", or "any other courts which proceed not *secundum legem et consuetudinem Angliae*". This is a very odd definition, or description, since it entirely omits all reference to a record of any sort. One

as a ground of estoppel is a court of record, or not,[1] or whether it is what has been denominated by custom, or statute, a superior court, or not,[2] or even whether it is known by the name of a court at all.[3] Nor does it signify whether the tribunal, if English, be one of civil, or of criminal, jurisdiction;[4] nor (with certain exceptions) whether it be English or foreign.[5] It is enough if the alleged "judicial tribunal" can properly be described as a person, or body of persons, exercising judicial functions by common law, statute, patent, charter, custom, or otherwise in accordance with the law of England, or, in the case of a foreign tribunal, the law of the particular foreign state, whether he, or they, be invested with permanent jurisdiction to determine all causes of a certain class as and when submitted, or be clothed by the State, or the disputants, with merely temporary authority to adjudicate on a particular dispute, or group of disputes.[6] Thus, taking,

---

would have thought that, to justify the name, the definition would be—"a court required or empowered by statute, common law, or prescription, to record, and to preserve records, of its acts and proceedings". HOLT C.J., at p. 467 of *Groenvelt* v. *Burwell* (1699), 1 Ld. Raym. 454, seems to have thought that the distinguishing feature of a court of record was a "power to fine and imprison", which again ignores the word "record" altogether.

[1] See *Williams* v. *Jones* (1845), 13 M. & W. 628 (per POLLOCK C.B., at p. 633, PARKE B., at p. 633, and ALDERSON B., at p. 634); *Re May* (1885), 28 Ch.D. 516, C.A. (per BRETT M.R., at p. 518): "the counsel for the petitioner has argued first of all that this is not *res judicata*, because there was no record, and the doctrine of *res judicata* only applies where there is a record. To my mind that argument cannot be sustained. The doctrine of *res judicata* is *not a technical doctrine applicable only to records.* It is a very substantial doctrine, and it is one of the most fundamental doctrines of *all courts*, that there must be an end to all litigation, and that the parties have no right of their own accord, having tried a question between them, and obtained *a decision of a court*, to start that litigation over again on precisely the same question".

[2] See the references in the last note to passages from the judgments in *Williams* v. *Jones*, *sup.* In modern times this has become so completely accepted as not to need authority to support it; but if express modern authority is desired an instance may be found in *Marginson* v. *Blackburn Borough Council*, [1939] 2 K.B. 426, C.A. where it is said in the judgment of the Court of Appeal at p. 438 "This seems to us to be a clear decision on the same issue between the same persons litigating in the present case, *and establishes conclusively*, *albeit in the county court*, in a claim by the defendants . . ."

[3] At p. 485 of *Philips* v. *Bury* (1694), Skin. 447, a case which raised the question whether a sentence of deprivation passed by the Visitor of a college was, or was not, conclusive and unimpeachable on the merits, HOLT C.J., whose dissentient judgment in the K.B., was affirmed and adopted in the H.L., said: "you will say that this man *hath no Court*: will you conclude a man by the sentence of one that hath no Court? *It is not, I say, at all material whether he hath a Court, or no*; *all the matter is, whether he hath a jurisdiction*: if he hath a jurisdiction, and conusance of the matter and the person, and he gives sentence in the matter, his sentence must have effect to make a vacancy, be it never so wrong." For examples of decisions, other than those of a court, which have in modern times been treated as judicial decisions founding estoppels *per rem judicatam* reference may be made, for instance, to the decisions of arbitrators to whom the parties have entrusted the determination of some particular question (as to which see para. 26, *post*) and of (*e.g.*) the Chief Land Registrar in *In Re Freehold Land in Dances Way, West Town, Hayling Island, Hants*, [1962] 2 All E.R. 42, [1962] Ch. 490, C.A.

[4] See para. 65, *post.*

[5] See paras. 66 *et seq. post.*

[6] Such as the tribunals, constituted by statute for temporary purposes, whose decisions were the subject of the cases cited in notes 1, 2, 3, and 4 on p. 26, *post*, and the domestic tribunals referred to in para. 26, *post.*

first, English civil tribunals of the highest degree, whether technically denominated "superior" or not,[1] the following are tribunals which are deemed "judicial" in the sense already indicated, and whose decisions, therefore, by whatever name called,—judgments, orders, decrees, sentences, declarations, or what not,—have been held to be *res judicatae*, that is, conclusive and unimpeachable on the merits both before the tribunal pronouncing the decision, and before all others, and such that the party pleading the *res judicata* has always either succeeded, or, where he has failed, has failed on grounds not in any way negativing the status of the tribunals as "judicial"; the High Court of Parliament;[2] the House of Lords;[3] all superior courts of common law, whose decisions are conclusive both in those courts,[4] and also in Chancery courts,[5] Bankruptcy courts,[6] inferior common law courts,[7] and in any other court; all superior Chancery courts, whose decisions are unimpeachable on the merits both there,[8] and in any common law court,[9] Probate court,[10] or elsewhere; all superior matrimonial courts, whose decisions are binding, both in those courts,[11] and in any other, such as an equity court,[12] a superior court of

---

1 As to Courts which are "Superior Courts" see the provisions now contained in the Supreme Court of Judicature (Consolidation) Act 1925, ss. 18 (1) (the High Court), 26 (1) (the Court of Appeal) and of the Criminal Appeal Act 1907 (Court of Criminal Appeal) and the Courts-Martial (Appeals) Act 1951 (Courts-Martial Appeal Court).

2 "The judgment in the Exchequer Chamber betwixt the King and Mr Hampden" (in the *Ship Money Case* was held in *Lord Say's Case* (1639), Cro. Car. 524, to be "such a judgment" as "ought to stand until it is reversed in Parliament"—which it had not then been—"and none ought to be suffered to dispute against it", but, in the next year, the judgment having been so reversed by a Resolution of both Houses of Parliament (afterwards embodied in the statute 17 Car. 1, c. 14), it was held, in *Chambers* v. *Brumfeild* (1641), Cro. Car. 601 (an action for false imprisonment in which the defendant justified under the King's writ pursuant to such judgment), that, "it *having been resolved by Parliament* that the said writ and what was done by colour thereof was illegal, *the Court would no further dispute thereof*, but gave judgment for the plaintiff" (p. 601).

3 *Shedden* v. *Patrick* (1854), 1 Macq. 535, H.L.

4 The ordinary type of case, as to which there is no necessity to cite authorities.

5 *Re Bank of Hindustan, China, and Japan* (*Alison's Case*) (1873), 9 Ch. App. 1, at p. 25, 26.

6 But subject to the jurisdiction of the Court of Bankruptcy to go behind the judgment, as to which see paras. 45, 57, *post*.

7 *Cooke* v. *Rickman*, [1911] 2 K.B. 1125 D.C.

8 The authorities for this type of case, which is the ordinary one, are too numerous to be cited. Note that the Chancery Palatine Courts are "original" and (probably) "Superior" Courts: see *Peacock* v. *Bell* (1667), 1 Wms. Saund. 73, at pp. 74b–74d, which was a case involving the jurisdiction of the Chancery Court of the County Palatine of Durham; *London Corporation* v. *Cox* (1867), L.R. 2 H.L. 239 (per WILLES J., delivering the joint opinion of the judges summoned, at p. 257); *Re Connolly Brothers*, [1911] 1 Ch. 731, at p. 744. At any rate they are tribunals whose decisions bind all other courts: see *Horrocks* v. *Stubbs* (1896), 74 L.T. 58, C.A.

9 *Allason* v. *Stark* (1838), 9 Ad. & El. 255; *Collins* v. *Cave* (1858), 27 L.J. Ex. 146; *Langmead* v. *Maple* (1865), 18 C.B. N.S. 255; *Reichel* v. *Magrath* (1889), 14 App. Cas. 665, H.L.; *Bradshaw* v. *M'Mullan*, [1918] 2 I.R. 479.

10 *Spencer and Spencer* v. *Williams* (1871), L.R. 2 P. & D. 230.

11 The common type: not necessary to cite authorities.

12 *Perry* v. *Meddowcroft* (1846), 10 Beav. 122; *Harrison* v. *Southampton Corporation* (1853), 4 De G.M. & G. 137.

common law,[1] an inferior court of common law,[2] a Probate court,[3] or a criminal court;[4] all Testamentary courts (formerly ecclesiastical courts, now the Probate, Divorce, and Admiralty Division of the High Court, in its probate jurisdiction), whose decisions are conclusive both in those courts,[5] and in other civil courts,[6] though not in any criminal court;[7] the Admiralty Court, whose decisions are unimpeachable on the merits, both there,[8] and in any other civil court;[9] the Bankruptcy Court, whose adjudications of bankruptcy are conclusive in all courts;[10] the Court of Exchequer, whose decisions on revenue matters were, as long as this court existed, deemed conclusive in all courts;[11] and the Sovereign in Council, whose Order, in accordance with the advice of the Judicial Committee of such Council, concludes the parties in all courts.[12]

Local courts

23 Further, any local court of civil jurisdiction, established by charter, grant, prescription or custom, whether subsequently recognized or regulated by statute (as in many cases), or not, is deemed a tribunal, such that its decisions, if within its jurisdiction, and if otherwise conformable to the rules relating to estoppel by *res judicata*, are conclusive and binding upon the parties, or *in rem*, as the case may be, in that or any other court.[13] Thus, the Mayor's Court of London[14] is a tribunal whose judgments and orders, if made within its jurisdiction, are unimpeachable on the merits either there

[1] *Bunting* v. *Lepingwell* (1585), 4 Co.Rep. 29a; *Blackham's Case* (1709), 1 Salk, 290; *Da Costa* v. *Villa Real* (1773), 2 Stra. 960; *R.* v. *Wye Inhabitants* (1838), 7 Ad. & El. 761, at p. 764.

[2] *A fortiori* of the preceding note.

[3] *Meddowcroft* v. *Huguenin* (1844), 4 Moo. P.C.C. 386.

[4] *Duchess of Kingston's Case* (1776) 2 Smith, L.C. 13 Ed. 644.

[5] *Birch* v. *Birch*, [1902] P. 130, C.A.; see also *Re Langton, Langton* v. *Lloyd's Bank*, [1964] 1 All E.R. 749; [1964] P. 163.

[6] *Noell* v. *Wells* (1668), 1 Lev. 235; *Bouchier* v. *Taylor* (1776), 4 Bro. Parl. Cas. 708, H.L.—*Hargrave's Law Tracts*, 472; *Allen* v. *Dundas* (1789), 3 Term Rep. 125; *Thornton* v. *Curling* (1824), 8 Sim. 310; *Douglas* v. *Cooper* (1834), 3 My. & K. 378; *Barrs* v. *Jackson* (1845), 1 Ph. 582; *Whicker* v. *Hume* (1858), 7 H.L.Cas. 124; *Meluish* v. *Milton* (1876), 3 Ch.D. 27, C.A.; *Concha* v. *Concha* (1886), 11 App.Cas. 541, H.L.; *Beardsley* v. *Beardsley*, [1899] 1 Q.B. 746, D.C.

[7] *R.* v. *Vincent* (1721), 1 Stra. 481, which decided otherwise, was dissented from in *R.* v. *Gibson* (1802), Russ. & Ry. 343 n., and *Buttery's Case* (1818), Russ. & Ry. 342.

[8] *The Bellcairn* (1885), 10 P.D. 161, C.A.; *Kronprinz (Cargo Owners)* v. *Kronprinz (Owners) the Ardandhu* (1887), 12 App.Cas. 256, H.L.

[9] *Harris* v. *Willis* (1855), 15 C.B. 710; *Ballantyne* v. *Mackinnon*, [1896] 2 Q.B. 455, C.A.

[10] *Revell* v. *Blake* (1873), L.R. 8 C.P. 533, Ex. Ch.; *Re Foulds, Ex parte Learoyd* (1878), 10 Ch.D. 3, C.A.; *Boaler* v. *Power*, [1910] 2 K.B. 229, C.A.

[11] *Lord Say's Case* (1639), Cro.Car. 524, as to which see note 2, p. 22; *R.* v. *Matthews* (1797), 5 Price 202 n; *A-G.* v. *Wakefield* (1797), 5 Price 202, n; *A-G.* v. *Reynolds* (1804), 5 Price 203 n; *A-G.* v. *King* (1817), 5 Price 195; *Hart* v. *Macnamara* (1817), 4 Price, 154 n.

[12] *Farquharson* v. *Seton* (1828), 5 Russ. 45; *Venkata Narasimha Appa Row* v. *Court of Wards* (1886), 11 App.Cas. 660, P.C.; *Ram Narayan Singh* v. *Adhindra Nath Mukerji*, [1917] A.C. 100, P.C.

[13] For an exhaustive account of the Borough and Local Courts of Record in England, see 9 *Halsbury's Laws* (3rd edn.) pp. 486–572.

[14] Now the Mayor's and City of London Court (see 10 & 11 Geo. 5, cap. cxxxiv).

or elsewhere, as *e.g.*, in a superior court of common law,[1] or of equity.[2] In the first edition of this work a number of other ancient local courts were enumerated, which, as long as they existed (for they have now been abolished by statute, or have lapsed by desuetude), have been held to be tribunals capable of delivering decisions which, if complying with the above-mentioned conditions as to jurisdiction and otherwise, no party may be heard to controvert on the merits in any court of however high a degree.[3]

Statutory tribunals

24 A third class of civil tribunals accounted "judicial" in the sense indicated consists of what may be called "statutory tribunals", that is to say, tribunals which owe their existence and jurisdiction entirely to an Act of Parliament, or to a royal grant or charter having the same effect. The following are examples of this type of tribunal; a county court, whose decisions, within the limits of its jurisdiction, are unimpeachable on the merits unless and until reversed on appeal by such procedure and on such conditions as are authorized by statute, and are conclusively binding on the parties, not only in the county court itself,[4] but in all other courts, *e.g.* an inferior criminal court exercising civil jurisdiction,[5] or any superior court;[6] a court martial;[7] a naval court, within the meaning of the Merchant Shipping Act 1894;[8] a medical tribunal, such as the College of

---

1 *Magrath* v. *Hardy* (1838), 4 Bing. N.C. 782.

2 *Behrens* v. *Sieveking* (1837), 2 My. & Cr. 602.

3 1st Edn. p. 13; and reference may also be made to the exhaustive enumeration in 9 *Halsbury's Laws* (3rd Edn.) 486 *et seq*, mentioned above.

4 *Hacking* v. *Lee* (1860), 9 W.R. 70; *River Ribble Joint Committee* v. *Croston Urban District Council*, [1897] 1 Q.B. 251, D.C.

5 *Routledge* v. *Hislop* (1860), 2 E. & E. 549.

6 *Flitters* v. *Allfrey* (1874), L.R. 10 C.P. 29; *Webster* v. *Armstrong* (1885), 54 L.J.Q.B. 236; *Marginson* v. *Blackburn Borough Council*, [1939] 2 K.B. 426, C.A. at p. 438—"This seems to us to be a clear decision on the same issue between the same parties litigating in the present case, and establishes conclusively, albeit in the county court, in a claim by the dependents against the present plaintiff, that both were equally to blame."

7 *Hannaford* v. *Hunn* (1825), 2 C. & P. 148; *A-G. for Cape of Good Hope* v. *Van Reenen*, [1904] A.C. 114, P.C.

8 *Caine* v. *Palace Steam Shipping Co., Ltd.*, [1907] 1 K.B. 670, C.A. and *Hutton* v. *Ras Steam Shipping Co., Ltd.*, [1907] 1 K.B. 834, C.A. were cited to support the text in the first edition of this work. In the former the estoppel was abandoned for lack of identity of parties; in the latter it was sustained. But both of these cases seem to depend upon the wording of s. 483 (2) of the Merchant Shipping Act 1894, which provides that all orders made by a naval court under the powers given to it by the section shall in any subsequent proceedings be conclusive as to the rights of the parties. *In New South Wales* where the Navigation Act 1901 (N.S.W.) contains no such provision, the finding of a Marine Court of Inquiry exonerating the master of a ship from negligence was held by a majority of the High Court of Australia not to prevent the reventilation, in subsequent proceedings between master and owner, of the issue of the master's negligence: *Spain* v. *Union Steam Ship Co. of New Zealand, Ltd.* (1923), 33 C.L.R. 555 (H. Ct. of Aus.) at p. 563 per KNOX C.J. and STARKE J.

Physicians, or the General Medical Council;[1] judges appointed to try election petitions by the Parliamentary Elections Act 1868, whose "certificates" and "reports" are conclusive within the limits prescribed by the statute;[2] statutory compensation tribunals, whether sheriff and jury, or arbitrator, authorized by special Acts of Parliament, or the Lands Clauses Consolidation Act 1845, or other statutes, whose judgments, following on inquisitions and verdicts, or whose awards (as the case may be) are conclusive in every court;[3] a statutory arbitrator under Inclosure Acts;[4] Commissioners under the Metropolitan Commons Act 1866, with power to settle a scheme, and the limits of the property affected thereby;[5] any arbitrator under the Workmen's Compensation Acts 1897, and 1906;[6] the Chief Land Registrar in deciding, after hearing the parties, as to whether an entry shall be made upon the Register as to the existence of an overriding interest under the Land Registration Act 1925 and Rules made thereunder;[7] a "superintending architect", and "tribunal of appeal" established under various metropolitan building statutes;[8] a collegiate or scholastic authority exercising visitorial or other jurisdiction in virtue of its statutes or charter;[9]

---

1 *Groenvelt* v. *Burwell* (1699), 1 Ld. Raym. 454 (College of Physicians under patent of Henry VIII); *Hill* v. *Clifford*, [1907] 2 Ch. 236, C.A. (General Medical Council, acting under the Dentists Act 1878).

2 *Taunton Case, Waygood* v. *James* (1896), L.R. 4 C.P. 361; *Stevens* v. *Tillett, Norwich Case* (1870), L.R. 6 C.P. 147.

3 *R.* v. *Liverpool Corporation* (1768), 4 Burr. 2244; *R.* v. *Bagshaw* (1797), 7 Term Rep. 363; *R.* v. *Norwich and Watton Road Trustees* (1836), 5 Ad. & El. 563; *R.* v. *Nottingham Old Waterworks Co.* (1837), 6 Ad. & El. 355; *R.* v. *Swansea Harbour Trustees* (1839), 8 Ad. & El. 439; *Corrigal* v. *London and Blackwall Rail. Co.* (1843), 5 Man. & G. 219; *Taylor* v. *Clemson* (1844), 11 Cl. & Fin. 610; *R.* v. *London and North Western Rail. Co.* (1854), 3 E. & B. 443; *Chapman* v. *Monmouthshire Rail. and Canal Co.* (1857), 2 H. & N. 267; *Mortimer* v. *South Wales Rail. Co.* (1859), 1 E. & E. 375.

4 *Jacomb* v. *Turner*, [1892] 1 Q.B. 47; *Collis* v. *Amphlett*, [1918] 1 Ch. 232, C.A. But the estoppel was negatived in both these cases, because there was no jurisdiction to deal with the particular matters said to be the subject of it.

5 *Cook* v. *Mitcham Common Conservators*, [1901] 1 Ch. 387.

6 *Crossfield & Sons, Ltd.* v. *Tanian*, [1900] 2 Q.B. 629, C.A.; *Bailey* v. *Plant*, [1901] 1 K.B. 31, C.A.; *Sharman* v. *Holliday and Greenwood, Ltd.*, [1904] 1 K.B. 235, C.A.; *Blake* v. *Midland Rail. Co.*, [1904] 1 K.B. 503, D.C.; *Radcliffe* v. *Pacific Steam Navigation Co.*, [1910] 1 K.B. 685, C.A.; *Green* v. *Cammell, Laird & Co., Ltd.*, [1913] 3 K.B. 665, C.A.; *Dundee, Perth and London Shipping Co.* v. *Willcock* (1916), 9 B.W.C.C. 471, C.A.; *Smith* v. *Samuel Cutter & Sons, Ltd.*, (1932), 25 B.W.C.C. 408 C.A.

7 *In Re Freehold Land in Dances Way, West Town, Hayling Island, Hants*, [1962] 2 All E.R. 42; [1962] Ch. 490, C.A. In this case the determination of the Chief Registrar was held not to support a plea of *res judicata*, Lord EVERSHED M.R. and UPJOHN L.J. being of opinion that he had not finally determined the dispute between the parties; DIPLOCK, L.J. was of the contrary opinion. But all three Lords Justices clearly thought that the Registrar was a judicial tribunal whose determination could in a proper case support the plea.

8 *Spackman* v. *Plumstead District Board of Works* (1885), 10 App. Cas. 229, H.L.; *Lilley* v. *London County Council*, [1910] A.C. 1, H.L.; *London County Council* v. *Galsworthy*, [1918] A.C. 851, H.L.

9 *Philips* v. *Bury* (1694), Skin. 447 (Visitor of Exeter Coll. Oxon.); *R.* v. *Grundon* (1775), 1 Cowp. 315 (Master and Fellows of Queen's Coll. Camb.); *Doe* d. *Davy* v. *Haddon* (1783), 3 Doug. K.B. 310 (trustees of a school).

and occasional tribunals constituted for a temporary purpose, such as the Commissioners established, *circa* 1740, as a court of record, to determine disputes arising out of the destruction of house property by "the late dreadful fire" at Blandford,[1] the "Court of Claims" established by the statute 11 and 12 W. 3, sess. 2, c. 2,[2] Boundary Commissioners,[3] the Lords of the Treasury, invested by the statute 5 and 6 W. 4, c. 76, with appellate jurisdiction as to the amount of compensation to be paid by a corporation to the removed holders of offices within the borough, whose decisions on such question of amount, but not on any question of right, were held to be conclusive,[4] and the tribunals appointed by statute during the war of 1914–18 to hear and determine applications for certificates of exemption from military service.[5]

It was formerly accepted (and Mr Spencer Bower so stated the law in the first edition of this work) that Income Tax Commissioners under the Income Tax Acts were a tribunal whose decisions could give rise to estoppels between the parties;[6] but this is no longer held to be the case.[7] Indeed, as we shall later see in the special chapter dealing with this subject,[8] even when on appeal from an assessment of the Commissioners the Court gives a judgment *inter partes*, even that judgment will not now support an estoppel *inter partes* except in respect of the actual year or assessment as to which it relates.

Criminal courts exercising civil jurisdiction

25 A fourth class of civil judicial tribunal comprises all inferior criminal courts in the exercise of civil jurisdiction (justices sitting in petty or quarter sessions, as the case may be), whose orders or decisions, within the limits of their jurisdiction, are conclusive in all courts on the following

---

1 *Sollers* v. *Lawrence* (1743), Willes 413.

2 *Archbishop of Dublin* v. *Coote* (1849), 12 I. Eq. R. 251.

3 *Brisco* v. *Lomax* (1838), 8 Ad. & El. 198; *Evans* v. *Rees* (1839), 10 Ad. & El. 151.

4 *Sandwich Corporation* v. *R.* (1847), 10 Q.B. 571, Ex. Ch., at p. 579.

5 See *Langdon* v. *Richards* (1917), 33 T.L.R. 325, D.C., but here the Crown was precluded from setting up the estoppel, being itself estopped from doing so by conduct.

6 1st edn., p. 14. The following authorities are there cited: *Allen* v. *Sharp* (1848), 2 Exch. 352; *R.* v. *Income Tax Special Purposes Commissioners* (1888), 21 Q.B.D. 313, C.A.; *R.* v. *Bloomsbury Income Tax Commissioners*, [1915] 3 K.B. 768, D.C.

7 *Inland Revenue Commissioners* v. *Sneath*, [1932] 2 K.B. 362, C.A. ("The nature of the legislation for the imposition of taxes making it necessary that the statute should provide for some machinery whereby the taxable income is ascertained, that machinery is set going separately for each year of tax, and though the figure determined in one year is final for that year it is not final for any other purpose. It is final not as a judgment *inter partes*, but as the final estimate of a statutory estimating body. No *lis* comes into existence until there has been a final estimate of the issue which determines the tax payable. There can be no *lis* until the rights and duties are ascertained and thereafter questioned by litigation" per GREER L.J. at p. 386). *Cf. Patuck* v. *Lloyd* (1944), 26 T.C. 284 ("There is no such thing as *res judicata* in respect of the decisions of Income Tax Commissioners"—per Lord GREENE M.R. at p. 292).

8 See Chapter X, *post*.

questions of a civil or quasi-civil complexion: the legal settlement (original or derivative) of a pauper,[1] and (incidentally thereto) the validity of a pauper's marriage, or the legitimacy of his children,[2] questions of judicial separation and maintenance under the Summary Jurisdiction (Married Women) Act 1895,[3] affiliation questions,[4] questions as to the liability to repair an alleged highway,[5] questions as to the observance of the prescribed "building line", under the Public Health (Building in Streets) Act 1888;[6] questions as to the detention of, but not (except incidentally) the title to, goods under s. 40 of the Metropolitan Police Act 1839;[7] claims for wages under the Employers and Workmen Act 1875,[8] and the apportionment of paving expenses under the Metropolis Management Acts.[9]

Domestic tribunals

26 Lastly, every domestic forum, that is to say, any arbitrator, or arbitrators, or other person or body of persons (by whatever name called) who may be invested with judicial authority to hear and determine a particular dispute, or class of disputes, by the consent of the disputants, or by an order of court, or by a provision of a statute, is undoubtedly a "judicial

[1] *R.* v. *Kenilworth (Inhabitants)* (1788), 2 Term Rep. 598; *R.* v. *Lubbenham (Inhabitants)* (1791), 4 Term Rep. 251; *R.* v. *St. Andrew, Holborn* (1796), 6 Term Rep. 613; *R.* v. *St. Mary, Lambeth (Inhabitants)* (1796), 6 Term Rep. 615; *R.* v. *Rudgeley (Inhabitants)* (1800), 8 Term Rep. 620; *R.* v. *Corsham* (1809), 11 East 388; *R.* v. *Catterall* (1817), 6 M. & S. 83; *R.* v. *Wick St. Lawrence* (1833), 5 B. & Ad. 526; *R.* v. *Evenwood and Barony (Inhabitants)* (1843), 3 Q.B. 370; *R.* v. *Sow (Inhabitants)* (1843), 4 Q.B. 93; *R.* v. *Hartington Middle Quarter (Inhabitants)* (1855), 4 El. & Bl. 780; *Uxbridge Union* v. *Winchester Union* (1904), 91 L.T. 533, D.C.

[2] *New Windsor Parish* v. *White Waltham Parish* (1718), 1 Stra. 186; *Nympsfield Parish* v. *Woodchester Parish* (1742), 2 Stra. 1172; *R.* v. *Binegar* (1806), 7 East 377; *R.* v. *Wye* (1838), 7 Ad. & El. 761.

[3] *Pickavance* v. *Pickavance*, [1901] P. 60; *Stokes* v. *Stokes*, [1911] P. 195; *Hopkins* v. *Hopkins*, [1914] P. 282; *McGregor* v. *Telford*, [1915] 3 K.B. 237, D.C.; *Molesworth* v. *Molesworth*, [1947] 2 All E.R. 842. *Hopkins* v. *Hopkins (supra)* was overruled as to the principal point therein decided in the later case of *Land* v. *Land*, [1949] 2 All E.R. 218; [1949] P. 405, and the authority of *Pickavance* v. *Pickavance (supra)* considerably restricted; but they remain as authority for the proposition in the text.

[4] *R.* v. *Jenkin* (1736), Cas. temp. Hard. 301; *R.* v. *Machen* (1849), 14 Q.B. 74; *R.* v. *Buckinghamshire Justices* (1849), 18 L.J. M.C. 113; *R.* v. *Brisby* (1849), 18 L.J. M.C. 157; *R.* v. *Herrington* (1864), 12 W.R. 420; *R.* v. *Gaunt* (1867), L.R. 2 Q.B. 466; *R.* v. *Glynne* (1871), L.R. 7 Q.B. 16; *R.* v. *May* (1880), 5 Q.B.D. 382; *Anderson* v. *Collinson*, [1901] 2 K.B. 107, D.C.; *R.* v. *Seddon* (1916), 85 L.J. K.B. 806, D.C. *Cf. R.* v. *Sunderland Justices, Ex parte Hodgkinson*, [1945] 2 All E.R. 175; [1945] K.B. 502 D.C.; *Robinson* v. *Williams*, [1964] 3 All E.R. 12; [1965] 1 Q.B. 89 D.C.

[5] *R.* v. *Blakemore* (1852), 21 L.J. M.C. 60; *R.* v. *Haughton* (1853), 1 E. & B. 501; *R.* v. *Hutchings* (1881), 6 Q.B.D. 300, C.A.; *Heath* v. *Weaverham*, [1894] 2 Q.B. 108, D.C.; *North Eastern Rail. Co.* v. *Dalton Overseers*, [1898] 2 Q.B. 66, D.C.; *Wakefield Corporation* v. *Cooke*, [1904] A.C. 31, H.L.

[6] *Kinnis* v. *Graves* (1898), 78 L.T. 502, D.C.; *Jenkins* v. *Merthyr Tydvil Urban District Council* (1899), 80 L.T. 600, D.C.; *Balby-with-Hexthorpe District Council* v. *Millard* (1903), 68 J.P. 81, D.C.

[7] *Dover* v. *Child* (1876), 1 Ex. D. 172.

[8] *Hindley* v. *Haslam* (1878), 3 Q.B.D. 481.

[9] *Scott* v. *Lowe* (1902), 86 L.T. 421, D.C.

tribunal'', and its awards are as conclusive and unimpeachable (unless and until set aside on any of the recognized grounds) as the decisions of any of the constituted courts of the realm.[1]

Judgment of a lower court conclusive in a higher

27 It will be gathered from what has been stated, and on reference to the authorities cited, that the decision of the very lowest civil tribunal is, if conclusive at all, conclusive even in the very highest,[2] with this exception that, if a party fails in an inferior civil court on the sole ground of its want of jurisdiction, he is not liable to be met by a plea of estoppel in any subsequent proceedings which he may institute in respect of the same cause of action before a higher court invested with the jurisdiction which the inferior court lacked.[3]

28 The position of English criminal courts,[4] and of foreign courts,[5] as ''judicial tribunals'', will be discussed hereafter.

---

[1] *Doe d. Davy* v. *Haddon* (1783), 3 Doug. K.B. 310 (per Lord MANSFIELD C.J. at p. 312: ''the adjudication was in a domestic forum, and the merits of it cannot be entered into''); *Commings* v. *Heard* (1869), L.R. 4 Q.B. 669, where LUSH J. (at p. 673) said that there is no difference between an award and a judgment, as regards conclusiveness, and that in substance it makes no difference whether the tribunal is constituted by the sovereign power of the realm, or by the agreement of the parties, the principle and reason of the rule being the same in both cases, adding (at p. 674) that, though in strict technicality an award should be described as a ''bar'', and not as an estoppel, as had been observed by COLERIDGE J., at p. 312 of *Parkes* v. *Smith* (1850), 15 Q.B. 297, yet ''that I consider immaterial'', because an award, whatever phraseology be used, ''concludes the parties'', and ''precludes'' and ''prohibits'' either of them from contesting it on the merits, in which view there is no apparent reason why an award should not have been described outright as an ''estoppel'', and not merely as an ''estoppel quasi-of-record'', the timorous expression used by counsel at p. 672; *The Warwick* (1890), 15 P.D. 189; *Gueret* v. *Audouy* (1893), 62 L.J. Q.B. 633 (per LOPES L.J., at p. 637, and A. L. SMITH, L.J., at p. 640, though ''conclusive evidence'', and not ''estoppel'', was the expression used); *Re Newey* (1912), 107 L.T. 832, Div. Ct. On this last point, *cf.* the judgment of PEARSON L.J. in *Morrison, Rose & Partners* v. *Hillman*, [1961] 2 Q.B. 266, C.A. at p. 277. In *Ayscough* v. *Sheed Thomson & Co., Ltd.* (1923), 129 L.T. 429, C.A. BANKES L.J. said at p. 430 that ''An award made under such a submission is a bar to the action''. SCRUTTON L.J. used a similar phrase at p. 431. To these authorities there may be added *Fidelitas Shipping Company, Ltd.* v. *V/O Exportchleb*, [1965] 2 All E.R. 4 per DIPLOCK L.J. at p. 10: ''Issue estoppel applies to arbitration as it does to litigation. The parties, having chosen the tribunal to determine the disputes between them as to their legal rights and duties, are bound by the determination of that tribunal on any issue which is relevant to the decision of any dispute referred to that tribunal.''

[2] See generally the cases cited in the notes to paras. 22 *et seq.*, *ante*, and particularly *Lilley* v. *London County Council*, [1910] A.C. 1, H.L., where it was held that a certificate of a superintending architect under the London Building Act 1894 was binding on the House of Lords. In *Galbraith* v. *Neville* (1789), 1 Doug. K.B. 6 n, the Court of K.B. disclaimed any power to ''revise the judgment of the *lowest* courts of *foreign* countries where they have competent jurisdiction'' (per Lord KENYON C.J.). More recently the Court of Appeal has said in *Marginson* v. *Blackburn Borough Council*, [1939] 2 K.B. 426, at p. 438 ''This seems to us to be a clear decision on the same issue between the same parties litigating in the present case, and establishes conclusively, *albeit in the county court . . .*''

[3] *London Corporation* v. *Cox* (1867) L.R. 2 H.L. 239 (per WILLES J., advising the House of Lords, at p. 262). And see further the authorities cited in the footnotes to para. 40 *post*.

[4] See para. 65 *post*. [5] See paras. 66 *et seq. post*.

29 There are extremely few cases in which an English civil authority has been held not to be a "judicial tribunal", or (in other words) has been held absolutely incapable of making any order, pronouncement, or declaration having the effect of a *res judicata* under any circumstances, or for any purposes. The following, however, have been decided to be so incapable: a body, described as "the Lord Treasurer and other persons", assuming to make a so-called "decree", limiting the rights of the corporation of the City of Chester as against the County Palatine of Chester;[1] and justices acting under the Mental Deficiency Act 1913, and putting in force the limited powers thereby conferred upon them.[2]

The act of the Registrar-General, in re-registering as legitimate the birth of a child previously registered as illegitimate, after the marriage of the parents, is not a judicial act, and does not give rise to a plea of *res judicata*.[3] It was formerly thought that justices exercising jurisdiction in licensing matters were not a judicial tribunal,[4] but under the licensing legislation of today a different view has been taken of the matter.[5]

What is a judicial decision?

30 In order to establish a *res judicata* on which an estoppel may be founded, it must appear, not only that the person, or body of persons, pronouncing the deliverance constituted a judicial tribunal, but also that what was pronounced amounted to a judicial decision. There must have been both a *judex*, and a *judicium*,[6] which, for purposes of estoppel, means a *decision* or determination or adjudication of some question of law or fact, whether such decision takes the form of an express judicial declaration, or is necessarily involved in the command or prohibition which constitutes the judgment or judicial act in its coercive or operative aspect. Everything which answers to this description, by whatever name it may be called

---

[1] *Rogers* v. *Wood* (1831), 2 B. & Ad. 245, where it was held that the so-called "decree" was made not by the Court of Exchequer, but by a body compounded of some persons who were members of that court, and other persons who were not. "It was evidently, therefore", said Lord TENTERDEN C.J., at p. 256, "a proceeding before persons not forming any court known to the laws of this country", and the document, tendered in evidence, which purported to record the decision of this body, not only created no estoppel, but was not even evidence at all.

[2] *Newman* v. *Foster*, [1916] W.N. 369, D.C.

[3] *Jones* v. *Jones* (1929), 140 L.T. 647 (HILL J.).

[4] 1st Edn. of this work p. 17; the following cases were cited: *Smith* v. *Shann*, [1898] 2 Q.B. 347, D.C. (per WILLS J., at p. 350: "in no sense a decision, or the judgment of a court upon which an estoppel could be founded"). *Cp.* the following cases in which, though not cases of estoppel, it was held that justices, when sitting for licensing purposes, were not a judicial tribunal: *Royal Aquarium Society* v. *Parkinson*, [1892] 1 Q.B. 431, C.A.; *Boulter* v. *Kent Justices*, [1897] A.C. 556, H.L.; *Huish* v. *Liverpool Justices*, [1914] 1 K.B. 109, D.C. (cinematograph licence, under the Cinematograph Act, 1909); *Attwood* v. *Chapman*, [1914] 3 K.B. 275.

[5] *Jeffrey* v. *Evans*, [1964] 1 All E.R. 536; *R.* v. *East Riding Quarter Sessions Ex parte Newton*, [1967] 3 All E.R. 118; [1968] 1 Q.B. at p. 43, C.A.

[6] *Bradshaw* v. *M'Mullan*, [1920] 2 I.R. 412, H.L. per Lord SHAW at p. 424, 425.

(for different phraseology in this respect has been adopted by different tribunals, or by the same tribunal, at different stages in the history of our jurisprudence) is deemed a judicial decision;[1] and nothing which falls short of it (again, irrespective of nomenclature) is so deemed.

Instances of decisions amounting to res judicatae

31 It is easy to give instances of matters which will be at once recognized as, *prima facie*, falling within the above definition, such as judgments, orders, decrees, (in Scotland) decreets, sentences, "adjudications" (in bankruptcy), judicial "declarations", or (in Scotland) "declarators", and the like, whether the decision was of an issue of fact, or of both fact and law, or of a pure question of law,[2] and whether the judicial tribunal was exercising original or appellate jurisdiction,[3] and, in a case of a division of opinion between members of a tribunal exercising original jurisdiction, whether there was a majority in favour of the decision, or an equality of votes, if by the practice and usage of the particular tribunal, it was competent, in that court, to treat the result as a decision in favour of the party resisting the proceedings.[4]

Instances of decisions not amounting to res judicatae

32 So much is clear as to what is included in the definition of a judicial decision. Equally clear illustrations may be given of pronouncements which are either not decisions of anything in any sense, or, if decisions in a popular sense, are not judicial decisions, such as the following: a so-called

---

[1] See, generally, for the various terms employed in different courts to denominate their respective decisions, the cases cited in the notes to paras. 22–29, *supra*. The importance of the distinction between the jussive or prohibitive, and the declaratory, functions of a judgment or order is pointed out and illustrated in Chapter VI, paras. 186 *et seq.*, *post.*

[2] As in *Robinson* v. *Robinson* (1603), 5 Co. Rep. 32 b; *Hutt* v. *Morrell* (1849), 3 Exch. 240. *Cf.* the question of pure construction which came before the courts in the *Waring* cases referred to in more detail in para. 16, *ante*, viz. *In re Waring, Westminster Bank, Ltd.* v. *Awdry*, [1942] 1 All E.R. 556; [1942] Ch. 309, and on appeal, [1942] 2 All E.R. 250; [1942] 1 Ch. 426, C.A., which were made the subject of a plea of estoppel in *In re Waring, Westminster Bank, Ltd.* v. *Burton-Butler*, [1948] 1 All E.R. 257; [1948] Ch. 221.

[3] See paras. 62 *et seq.*, *post.*

[4] See *Kinnis* v. *Graves* (1898), 78 L.T. 502, D.C., where justices, being equally divided, instead of adjourning the case to a day when an uneven number of justices could be present, took the course of dismissing the information, and it was held (per WILLS J., at p. 504) that this constituted "a decision" that no offence had been committed, and therefore "a bar" to any subsequent information against the same party for the same offence. So also, where an application is made to the K.B., a rule having been granted by them, to make it absolute or to discharge it, and the judges are equally divided, a "decision" is arrived at by one of the judges (according to the ancient practice, the junior judge) withdrawing his judgment. Without such withdrawal, there could be no "decision". These observations, of course, have no application to proceedings and tribunals which are strictly of an appellate character. In any such case, if the court is equally divided, the appeal fails, the decision of the court appealed from remains the *res judicata*, and there is no "decision" at all emanating from the appellate court which has any independent effect as an estoppel. See paras. 62 *et seq.*, *post*, for the effect of an allowance of the appeal.

"sentence" which, on the face of the document recording it, does not even purport to be, or to incorporate by reference, anything in the nature of a decision;[1] an administrative report made to a State Department solely for its information and guidance, without any pretence to a judicial character;[2] a naked verdict, not followed by a judgment,[3] as distinguished from a verdict in certain statutory compensation cases, where the order in pursuance thereof is made by the statute a mere formality and ministerial act;[4] the finding of a judge or jury, even if followed by judgment, when that judgment has been set aside and a new trial directed;[5] a licensing or other purely administrative grant or order of justices;[6] a statutory

---

[1] *Obicini* v. *Bligh* (1832), 8 Bing. 335, an action on a so-called "sentence" of His Majesty's Vice-Admiralty Court of Malta, where the "document" said to record it did not set out the terms of the "sentence", though it contained a "monition" which purported to follow it, nor the terms of a "report of merchants" of which mention was made, nor did it purport to award any specific sum of money (per TINDAL C.J., at pp. 352–353, PARK J., at pp. 352–353, and ALDERSON J., at pp. 354–355).

[2] *Fracis, Times & Co.* v. *Carr* (1900), 82 L.T. 698, C.A., where the defendant set up, by way of estoppel, the report of a commission appointed by the Sultan of Muscat to inquire into the circumstances attending the seizure by the defendant, when in command of one of Her Majesty's gunboats, of the plaintiff's guns and ammunition on board a British ship. The "report" was submitted to and adopted by the Sultan. In it the Commission "reported" that the seizure was lawful. *Held* that since the inquiry and the report did not even purport to have been made for any other purpose than the information and guidance of the Sultan, and there had been no condemnation, forfeiture, or order or direction of any sort, commanding anything to be done or paid, there had been no judicial decision of anything (per VAUGHAN WILLIAMS L.J., delivering the judgment of the Court, at pp. 701, 702).

[3] *Re Dingle, Ex parte Butterfill, Ex parte Rashleigh* (1811), 1 Rose 192 (case of a verdict at Assizes which had not matured into a judgment, and which therefore Lord ELDON L.C. held to be *prima facie* evidence only); *Brisco* v. *Lomax* (1838), 8 Ad. & El. 198 (so stated by PATTESON J., at p. 213, and COLERIDGE J., at p. 215, as to the verdict of a jury summoned under a boundary Commission); *Bancroft* v. *Bancroft* (1864), 3 Sw. & Tr. 597 (per Sir CRESSWELL CRESSWELL, at p. 599, as to the verdict of a jury in a suit for judicial separation, which did not result in any judgment). In such cases the verdict is no more operative as a decision, than if a judge were to announce that he had found certain facts, and were to reserve his judgment on the legal result of the facts so found for further consideration and argument—a course often pursued by Lord ELDON. Obviously, such findings could not take effect as a decision until the judgment, or, if for any reason no judgment were ever delivered, at all.

But these observations (carried forward from the first edition of this work), valid no doubt in actions at law or in equity, are not completely applicable in divorce. There, where a verdict had been taken from a jury finding a party guilty of adultery, and a decree *nisi* made thereupon has been set aside, on the intervention of the Queen's Proctor, on the ground of subsequent conduct of the parties, a party found guilty of adultery by the jury may be estopped from relitigating that issue subsequently, even though no decree has resulted from the suit, provided that the grounds on which the decree had been set aside are grounds *dehors* the verdict: *Butler* v. *Butler*, [1894] P. 25 (a decision of which some criticism is made *post* in para. 365). And the decree *nisi*, and the finding of the court on which it is based, will not estop the Queen's Proctor from attacking the decree and the finding on the ground of the justice of the case—*Chalmers* v. *Chalmers*, [1930] P. 154.

[4] As in *R.* v. *Norwich and Watton Road Trustees* (1836), 5 Ad. & El. 563 (per PATTESON J., at p. 578, and WILLIAMS J. at p. 579).

[5] *Roe* v. *R. A. Naylor, Ltd.* (1918), 87 L.J. K.B. 958, C.A., and see Chap. V, para. 168, *post*, and cases there cited in footnotes to the text.

[6] But see the cases cited in footnotes 4 and 5 to para. 29, *supra*; the most recent decisions may involve some qualification of Mr Spencer Bower's original text.

"report" to which the statute does not give the effect of a judgment;[1] an order, containing no command or prohibition, but merely giving leave to a creditor in bankruptcy to withdraw his proof;[2] a file of proceedings in bankruptcy;[3] and a certificate (as distinct from a judgment) of Quarter Sessions, as to a pauper's place of settlement.[4] Decisions which, though in form judicial, are not in reality decisions at all, but *fabulae, non judicia*, by reason of collusion, will be considered at a later stage.[5]

33 So far, no difficulty arises. It is now necessary to traverse more debatable ground, and to examine whether, and under what conditions, the name of *res judicata* can properly be assigned to a termination of proceedings between litigants resulting from a voluntary withdrawal by one of the parties; to a judgment or order by consent, or by default; to a dismissal of an action or application; and to an appellate decision. These matters will now be considered in turn.

Termination of proceedings by voluntary withdrawal of party

34 Obviously, there is *prima facie* no "decision", in civil any more than in military warfare, where the attacking party sounds a retreat for strategic purposes. His retirement may indicate a perilous, or even disastrous, position for the moment, but there is no battle, and no "decision": indeed, his very object in declining the former is to escape the latter. This was the effect of the common law nonsuit, in which the plaintiff voluntarily withdrew from the contest at the trial for the express purpose of avoiding any judgment,[6] and reserving his liberty to bring a fresh action.[7] It is true that, in the Supreme Court, this ancient right of a plaintiff, and several analogous rights, both in law and in equity, to abandon his claim are either abolished or qualified;[8] but the authorities on the old practice are still

---

[1] *Stevens* v. *Tillett, Norwich Case* (1870), L.R. 6 C.P. 147 (per BOVILL C.J., at pp. 155–164, and WILLES J., at p. 172, as to a "report" of Election Judges under s. 11 (14) of the Parliamentary Election Act 1868).

[2] *Re Greaves, Ex parte Whitton* (1880), 43 L.T. 480 (per BACON V-C. at p. 481).

[3] *Re Bond, Ex parte Bacon* (1881), 17 Ch.D. 447, C.A. (per JAMES L.J. at p. 451).

[4] See *R.* v. *Lubbenham* (1791), 4 Term Rep. 251, where it seems to have been so considered, though it was recognized that the certificate might be conclusive against the parish granting it, not, however, as a *res judicata*, apparently, but as a representation.

[5] In Chapter XIII, para. 378, *post*.

[6] The old forms of the procedure indicate very clearly its character. The plaintiff was "called" (actually in the earliest times, and afterwards constructively), and then, in person, or by his counsel, he formally retired from the contest. The court did nothing and was not asked to do anything.

[7] *Almanson* v. *Davila* (1700), 1 Ld. Raym. 679; *Nesbit* v. *Rishton* (1839), 11 Ad. & El. 244, Ex. Ch. (per TINDAL C. J., at pp. 250, 251). Contrast *Re May* (1885), 28 Ch.D. 516, C.A., where it was vainly argued that the decision there was in the nature of a nonsuit (per BRETT M.R., at p. 518, explaining that in a nonsuit there is no verdict and no judgment of any sort).

[8] See *Fox* v. *Star Newspaper Co.*, [1900] A.C. 19, H.L. In this case, the plaintiff, on the trial before Lord RUSSELL C.J., claimed a right to elect to be nonsuited, so as to enable himself to

very useful as illustrations of the principle now under discussion, and, so far as regards the law administered in courts other than the Supreme Court, such as county courts, where the old common law non-suit is by rules made under the Statute expressly preserved,[1] they are also of practical interest.

In certain Commonwealth jurisdictions, too, where the common law procedure of non-suit is preserved, or where such a procedure is specially provided for by statute or rules of court,[2] the result of a non-suit will be to leave matters, so far as any plea of *res judicata* is concerned, precisely as they were before the action was commenced. Nothing has been decided as to the matters in dispute, except that they are, as between the parties, to remain at large.

Judgment of non pros. in criminal proceedings

35 For the same reason, the old judgment of *non pros.*, at common law, though nominally a decision, was always regarded as merely a formal regis-

---

bring a fresh action on the theory that there had been no "decision" against him, and, on its being held that he had no such right, declined to proceed any further, and the Judge thereupon directed a verdict for the defendants. This ruling was affirmed by the C.A., [1898] 1 Q.B. 636, where it was pointed out (per A. L. SMITH L.J., at p. 638) that the repeal by the R.S.C. 1883, of O. 41, r. 6, of the R.S.C. 1875 (providing that a nonsuit was to be equivalent to a judgment for the defendant) was not intended to revive the old nonsuit, and that O. 72, r. 2, of the R.S.C. 1883 (which preserved the old practice, where the new Rules were silent) had not this effect either, because the new Rules were not silent on this topic, but, by O. 26, r. 1, exhaustively provided for every species of voluntary abandonment by a party, wholly or in part, of his claim, counterclaim, or defence, under the name of "discontinuance" in its modern extended sense; and (per CHITTY L.J., at p. 639) that the party desirous of so withdrawing or abandoning his case as to entitle himself to bring a fresh action, free from any bar of *res judicata*, must now proceed under the last-cited Rule, or not at all, and, if he does not comply with the conditions as to time and notice thereby prescribed, he is no longer *dominus litis*, but is in mercy, and can only submit to the judgment of the court, or, in other words, to a judicial decision, unless the court otherwise orders, which will not be done except on terms, one of which may, and almost invariably will, be prohibition against bringing a fresh action. These views were supported in the House of Lords by Lord HALSBURY L.C., at pp. 19, 20, of the H.L. report, [1900] A.C. 19, in the following terms: "the sole question on this appeal is whether the old system by which a plaintiff at his own election could lose his writ, as it was said, and at his election bring another action for the same cause, is still a system which exists in our law, and I am very clearly of opinion that it does not. Our whole system has been changed, and I think that the reason why the word 'nonsuit' itself is not now to be found in the rules is that it was determined that the power of the plaintiff at the common law to claim a nonsuit, or the plaintiff in equity to dismiss his own bill at his own option, should no longer be permitted, and it is probable that the word 'discontinuance' was supposed to apply to both forms of procedure both at common law and in equity. Accordingly, by O. 26, r. 1, the only mode by which a plaintiff can submit to defeat is under that order". The rules of the old O. 26 are now carried forward, with some modification, in R.S.C. (1965) O. 21.

[1] C.C.R. Ord. 23 r. 3 (1).

[2] As in most, if not all, of the Australian State jurisdictions. *In New Zealand*: Code of Civil Procedure R. 272. A plaintiff may, at any time before judgment or verdict, elect to be non-suited, and the Court may nonsuit without his consent. "After a nonsuit the plaintiff shall not be debarred from proceeding again to trial on the same statement of claim, the costs of the first trial having been first paid".

tration of the fact that the plaintiff, by his want of prosecution, had voluntarily retired from the contest, and, therefore, in substance, not a judicial decision of any question or issue at all, or operative as a bar to a fresh action.[1]

Withdrawal of juror; discharge of jury

36 Similarly, the withdrawal of a juror, or the discharge of a jury, before verdict, does not ordinarily amount to, or involve, any decision;[2] but if it is made clear that the parties intended this proceeding to have the effect of finally terminating the litigation, there arises a bar to a fresh action, or at all events a right to invoke the inherent jurisdiction of the court to stay further proceedings, not so much on the ground of any *res judicata* as on a principle analogous to that of estoppel by conduct;[3] whence it follows that such right may itself be lost or waived by the conduct or inaction of the party entitled otherwise to exercise it.

Withdrawal of summons

37 On the same principle, in proceedings, whether of a strictly criminal, or of a civil or quasi-civil character, before a court of summary jurisdiction, the withdrawal of the summons by the complainant, because he has not complied, or recognizes that he cannot comply, with some statutory formality or condition, or with some rule of evidence, does not *per se* result in an adjudication either of guilt or innocence, and does not, therefore, rank as a *res judicata*, or *prima facie* constitute any bar to a fresh summons;[4] and the same result will follow even when the first summons is withdrawn in order to allow an allegation of a graver nature to be substituted for that contained in the original summons.[5] It was formerly thought that if the facts sufficiently showed that the withdrawal was intended as an

---

1 *Turton* v. *Hayes* (1720), 1 Strange 439; *Nesbit* v. *Rishton* (1839), 11 Ad. & El. 244, Ex. Ch. (per TINDAL C.J., at pp. 250, 251); *Re Orrell Colliery and Firebrick Co.* (1879), 12 Ch.D. 681 (per JESSEL M.R., at p. 682).

2 See *Harries* v. *Thomas* (1836), 2 M. & W. 32 (per Lord ABINGER C.B., at pp. 37, 38); *Thomas* v. *Lewis* (1836), 5 Dowl. 395 (per COLERIDGE J., at pp. 399, 400); *Burdon* v. *Flower* (1839), 7 Dowl. 786, at p. 788; *Norburn* v. *Hilliam* (1870), L.R. 5 C.P. 129; *Thomas* v. *Exeter Flying Post Co.* (1887), 18 Q.B.D. 822 (per DAY J., at p. 825, and WILLS J., at pp. 825, 826). Similarly in criminal cases, when a jury is discharged before verdict, there is no acquittal, or *res judicata*: *R.* v. *Charlesworth* (1861), 1 B. & S. 460 (per COCKBURN C.J., at p. 507).

3 As was the case in *Sanderson* v. *Nestor* (1826), Ry. & M. 402; *Everett* v. *Youells* (1832), 3 B. & Ad. 349; *Moscati* v. *Lawson* (1835), 1 Har. & W. 572; *Harries* v. *Thomas*, *sup*; *Gibbs* v. *Ralph* (1845), 14 M. & W. 804.

4 *R.* v. *Tyrone Justices*, [1912] 2 I.R. 44 (per PALLES C.B., at p. 48, and GIBSON J., at pp. 52, 53); *Davis* v. *Morton*, [1913] 2 K.B. 479 (per RIDLEY J. at pp. 484, 485, and PICKFORD and AVORY JJ., at p. 486); *R.* v. *Seddon* (1916), 85 L.J. K.B. 806, (per Lord READING C.J., at p. 807); *Williams* v. *Letheren*, [1919] 2 K.B. 262, where one of two summonses heard on the same day was withdrawn after, and not before, a conviction on the other—which was of course an *a fortiori* case (per BRAY J., at p. 269, and A. T. LAWRENCE J., at p. 270).

5 *Molesworth* v. *Molesworth*, [1947] 2 All E.R. 842—"It is clear to my mind that the question of wilful neglect to maintain has never been adjudicated on"; per Lord MERRIMAN P., at p. 844.

acceptance of, or a submission to, a decision, with a view to putting an end to the proceedings thereby, it could thereafter be set up as a bar;[1] but it is now clear that this view goes too far, and that the mere withdrawal of a summons will not in itself ever operate against the party withdrawing it, so as to estop him from making the same or a similar averment in future proceedings.[2]

38 The ancient practice in Chancery according to which a plaintiff was allowed to dismiss his own bill *before* the cause was set down for hearing, which corresponded roughly to the old common law judgment of "non-pros.", and, generally, the "discontinuance" of an action in its ancient and limited sense, was never accounted a "decision" of anything.[3] But, in the equity practice of former times, the dismissal by a plaintiff of his own bill *after* it had been set down for hearing had the same effect as a decision on the merits.[4] And, when the dismissal was by consent, in the sense that the party relying upon it as a bar was able to show beyond all reasonable doubt (the burden being on him of doing so), by such evidence as was available and admissible, that the consent was the outcome of a deliberate bargain, compromise, and release, and an intention on both sides to put an end to the litigation, the dismissal was always regarded as a *res judicata*.[5]

---

[1] 1st edn. p. 21, para. 30; *Hopkins* v. *Hopkins*, [1914] P. 282 was cited in support.

[2] *Land* v. *Land*, [1949] 2 All E.R. 218; [1949] P. 405, in which the ambit of the authority of *Pickavance* v. *Pickavance*, [1901] P. 60 is carefully limited, and *Hopkins* v. *Hopkins* (*supra*) overruled.

[3] See *Olmius* v. *Delany* (1744), 2 Stra. 1216, where "the defendant put in bail, which justified in court, and they were allowed. The plaintiff finding they were forsworn, and worth nothing, discontinued", and brought a fresh action, which the court held he was at liberty to do: *Re Orrell Colliery and Firebrick Co.* (1879), 12 Ch.D. 681, a case of a dismissal of an action for want of prosecution (per JESSEL M.R., at p. 682: "formerly a man could abandon his action by not taking any further steps in it, whether it was brought at common law, or in chancery. In the former case the defendant signed judgment of *non pros.*, which exactly described what had happened; in the latter case he would have the bill dismissed for want of prosecution, but in either case the plaintiff could bring a new action for the same matter, with this exception only, that in chancery, if the cause had been set down to be heard, the dismissal of the bill for want of prosecution was equivalent to dismissal on the merits, and was a bar to a new action"); *Massam* v. *Thorley's Cattle Food Co.* (1880), 14 Ch.D. 748, C.A. (per JAMES L.J., at p. 751, as to "the question whether there is anything in the nature of estoppel, or of a bar to the plaintiff's right to relief by reason of their having discontinued their former action against the company. . . . This is not a *res judicata*, nor can it be pleaded or dealt with as such"); *Magnus* v. *National Bank of Scotland* (1888), 57 L.J. Ch. 902 (dismissal of chancery action by consent before the cause was set down for hearing, which was held not to be a consent judgment,—as to which, see paras. 41 *et seq.*, *post.*—in substance, or even in form because the consent was to "an order on the application", and the application was to dismiss the bill, but was regarded as equivalent to a mere "discontinuance" in the old sense: per KAY J., at pp. 903, 904); *Fox* v. *Star Newspaper Co.*, [1900] A.C. 19, H.L. (per Lord HALSBURY L.C., at p. 19, as cited in note 8 on p. 32.

[4] See the observations of JESSEL M.R., in *Re Orrell Colliery and Firebrick Co.*, *sup.*, and of KAY J. in *Magnus* v. *National Bank of Scotland*, *sup.*, as cited, or referred to, in the last note.

[5] This was so stated by Lord HALSBURY L.C., at pp. 259, 260, Lord BRAMWELL, at p. 261, and Lord Herschell, at p. 262 of *Kronprinz* (*Cargo Owners*) v. *Kronprinz* (*Owners*); *The Ardandhu* (1887),

Discontinuance: dismissal for want of prosecution

39 "Discontinuance", in its modern sense, as regards civil proceedings in the Supreme Court, has been held to comprise not merely the ancient "discontinuance", but also all other possible forms and modes in which a party may express his voluntary withdrawal or abandonment of the whole, or a part, of his claim, counterclaim, or defence. He may still exercise the right of "discontinuance" in this comprehensive acceptation, without depriving himself of the further right to bring a new action, but only by the means, and within the periods, prescribed by the existing statutory rules of procedure.[1] If he fails to comply with these statutory requirements, he is not at liberty to "discontinue", and must submit to a judgment which will operate as a *res judicata*, unless he obtains an order of court, giving him leave to discontinue, and the court, in making such order, may impose terms, including the deprivation of the right to bring a fresh action, which, again, gives to the discontinuance the effect of a *res judicata*.[2]

Where a suit had been commenced by a purchaser for specific performance of an agreement for the sale and purchase of land, and the plaintiff was adjudicated bankrupt, his trustee in bankruptcy informed the defendant that proceedings would not be continued. Accordingly the action was dismissed by an order made by the Master. Subsequently a second suit for specific performance of the same agreement was commenced against the same defendant by one who set up that she was an undisclosed principal for whom the plaintiff had in reality been acting as agent in the transaction. On a preliminary application the defendant asked to have the statement of claim struck out on the ground that the cause of action was *res judicata*. It was held that the plea of *res judicata* could not be sustained, on the grounds,

---

12 App. Cas. 256, H.L. (a case of an order for discontinuance of the action pursuant to a written agreement between the solicitors); also by KAY J., at pp. 904, 905 of *Magnus* v. *National Bank of Scotland*, *sup*. In neither of these cases was the suggested bargain shown by such evidence as was available, and admissible, or by argument, to have been made, which fact, as was held in both cases, must be made out with the utmost clearness by the party relying on the estoppel.

[1] See R.S.C. (1965) O. 21 rr. 2–5, which are intended to be an exhaustive code on the subject, so far as regards the Supreme Court.

[2] See *Fox* v. *Star Newspaper Co.*, [1900] A.C. 19, H.L., as abstracted in note 8 on p. 32. Two years previously, in *Hess* v. *Labouchere* (1898), 14 T.L.R. 350, C.A., the plaintiff, in order to avoid answering certain interrogatories administered to him (the time for discontinuing without leave having expired), applied for such leave, which, on appeal, the C.A., disagreeing with the court below, thought fit to grant, annexing, however, the term (amongst others) that no fresh action should be brought. In *Robertson* v. *Purdey*, [1906] 2 Ch. 615, BUCKLEY J. (see pp. 618, 619) dealt in a similar manner with the plaintiff's application in a patent action, who, whilst it was pending, was advised of a defect in his specification which could not be "corrected" during such pendency, by reason of s. 19 of the Patents, Designs, and Trademarks Act 1883, and leave was refused except upon the terms of the plaintiff's being deprived of his liberty to bring a fresh action for the same infringement on the corrected specification.

inter alia, that the plea could not be founded on a dismissal for want of prosecution.[1]

40 Again, a decision by a tribunal that it has no jurisdiction to deal with the dispute between the parties, resulting in a withdrawal, not of the suit, by the parties or one of them, but of the tribunal from entering upon a consideration of it, cannot amount to a judicial decision such as will subsequently support a plea of *res judicata* upon the matters in dispute. The tribunal, in such circumstances, determines no more than that it has no jurisdiction, and, this being so, its decision or award does not, and cannot, determine the substance of the dispute itself.[2]

Consent judgments and orders

41 Any judgment or order which in other respects answers to the description of a *res judicata* is none the less so because it was made in pursuance of the consent and agreement of the parties.[3] It is true that, in such cases, the court is discharged from the duty of investigating, or (where the consent is given at a late stage in the proceedings) further investigating, the matters in controversy, and is not asked to, and does not, pronounce a judicial opinion upon any of such matters; but it is none the less true also that, at the joint request of the parties, the tribunal gives judicial sanction and coercive authority to what those parties have settled between themselves, and in that way converts a mere agreement which, except in certain special cases the subject of express statutory provision in that behalf,[4] could only operate as an agreement, and not as a bar, into a judicial decision on which a plea of *res judicata* may be founded. Accordingly, judgments, orders, and awards by consent have always been held no less efficacious as estoppels than other judgments, orders, or decisions,[5] though doubts

[1] *Pople* v. *Evans*, [1968] 2 All E.R. 743 at pp. 751–752 (UNGOED-THOMAS, J.).

[2] *London Corporation* v. *Cox* (1867), L.R. 2 H.L. 239, at p. 262; *Pinnock Brothers* v. *Lewis and Peat, Ltd.*, [1923] 1 K.B. 690 per ROCHE J. at p. 693. With this decision should be contrasted *Ayscough* v. *Sheed Thomson & Co., Ltd.* (1923), 129 L.T. 429, C.A., affirmed in the House of Lords in (1924), 131 L.T. 610, in which it was held that, although, if the point remained open, it might well be that the arbitrators had erred in deciding that the claim was out of time, yet they had actually determined the question, and until set aside their award must stand.

[3] "I cannot take the view that the matter is any the less finally determined by a judgment because that judgment is the result of an agreement"—per FINLAY J. at p. 125 of *Cohen* v. *Jonesco*, [1926] 1 K.B. 119 (reversed on appeal—[1926]2 K.B. 1—but this dictum not affected). "Their Lordships are clear that in relation to this plea of estoppel it is of no advantage to the appellant that the order . . . was a consent order"—per Lord BLANESBURGH, delivering the advice of the Privy Council in *Kinch* v. *Walcott*, [1929] A.C. 482, at p. 493.

[4] As, for instance, Sched. II, Clause (9) of the Workmen's Compensation Act 1906, which provided that a memorandum of an agreement for compensation, recorded in the prescribed register of the county court, should be "enforceable as a county court judgment". For an example of such a case, see *Manton* v. *Cantwell*, [1920] A.C. 781, H.L.

[5] See *Pearse* v. *Dobinson* (1865), 35 L.J. Ch. 110 (a case of two consent orders, which were recognized as standing in no different position from that of any other order, for purposes of the

have been occasionally expressed whether, strictly, the foundation of the estoppel in such cases is not representation by conduct, rather than *res judicata*.[1]

It must be observed, however, at this point, that the efficacy of a consent to found a *res judicata* may depend upon the capacity to consent of him who purports to do so.[2]

42 But, though consent judgments and orders are undoubtedly in every case (subject as above) decisions in the sense that the actual mandatory or prohibitive parts of the judgment or order are conclusively binding upon, not only the parties but the rest of the world, it may often be a matter of legitimate doubt and debate as to what, if any, particular questions or issues of right, title, or liability were, expressly or impliedly, the subject of the consent, and of the decision. For this purpose, as for all other purposes connected with the ascertainment of the subject-matter of a decision.[3] the court will closely examine all such evidence, if any, as is available and admissible, and, by the aid of such materials, will ascertain whether any and what adjudication of matters in dispute was expressed, or necessarily involved, in the actual decision assented to.[4] Any issue or question which is thus shown to have been recognized or taken by the parties as the subject of the litigation, and which appears fundamental to the judgment or order

---

doctrine of *res judicata*): *A-G.* v. *Dublin Corporation* (1841), 1 Dr. & War. 545 (plea confessing judgment); *Ennis* v. *Rochford* (1884), 14 L.R. Ir. 285; *Munster* v. *Cox* (1885), 10 App. Cas. 680, H.L.; *The Bellcairn* (1885), 10 P.D. 161, C.A., where it was held that a consent judgment was of such a binding nature between the parties that it could not afterwards be nullified, or set aside, by a subsequent consent order on a summons before the Registrar (per Lord ESHER M.R., at pp. 165, 166); *Thompson* v. *Moore* (1889), 23 L.R. Ir. 599 (consent order for perpetual injunction); *Re South American and Mexican Co., Ex parte Bank of England*, [1895] 1 Ch. 37, C.A. (per VAUGHAN WILLIAMS J., at pp. 44–46, in the Court below, and Lord HERSCHELL L.C., at p. 50, in the C.A.); *River Ribble Joint Committee* v. *Croston Urban District Council*, [1897] 1 Q.B. 251, (consent order of county court, declaring a statutory offence to have been committed, and commanding the defendants to execute works); *Great North-West Central Rail. Co.* v. *Charlebois*, [1899] A.C. 114, P.C. (though here, the consent order was inoperative as an estoppel, being defeated by the affirmative answer of illegality); *Haydock* v. *Goodier*, [1921] 2 K.B. 384, C.A. (consent award); *Cohen* v. *Jonesco*, [1926] 1 K.B. 119, as to which see note 3, p. 37. In *Kinch* v. *Walcott*, [1929] A.C. 482 consent orders in two actions (an action for conspiracy, and a counter-action for libel) whereby all the charges of conspiracy were withdrawn were held to found an estoppel *per rem judicatam* precluding the plaintiff from repeating the charges in another action.

1 See the observations of Lord SHAW at pp. 424–5 of *Bradshaw* v. *M'Mullan*, [1920] 2 I.R. 412, H.L.

2 For cases on the efficacy of a consent order or judgment where the consent was *ultra vires* of a company see *Great North West Central Rail. Co.* v. *Charlebois*, [1899] A.C. 114, P.C.; *In re Jon Beauforte (London), Ltd.*, [1953] 1 All E.R. 634; [1953] Ch. 131. For an infancy case see *Arabian* v. *Tuffnall and Taylor, Ltd.*, [1944] 2 All E.R. 317; [1944] K.B. 685—a merger case, but it is submitted that the same principles will be found applicable.

3 See Chapter VI, *post*.

4 As in *Cloutte* v. *Storey*, [1911] 1 Ch. 18, when NEVILLE J. at p. 26, and the Court of Appeal, affirming his judgment, at p. 33, examined the text of a deed of compromise which had been the subject of a court order.

agreed to, is deemed to have been thereby conclusively determined, so as to preclude any subsequent challenge.[1] Where, however, there are no such materials available as are above indicated, there is nothing which can operate as a decision of any particular question or issue, and neither party is estopped from disputing anything but the actual judgment or order itself.[2]

43 Where a judgment or order which fulfils all the requisites of a good *res judicata* has once been pronounced, a subsequent order merely embodying a compromise by the parties, on appeal, of their rights and liabilities so adjudged, or merely purporting to rescind or set aside by consent the former judgment or order, without the court being called upon to exercise its functions of review, or having any judicial cognizance of the unofficial reversal, is not a decision at all, and has no effect whatever on the first judgment, which remains the only *res judicata* binding on the parties.[3]

---

[1] This was the case in *Ennis* v. *Rochford*, *sup.* (issue of *devastavit* held to have been impliedly decided by the consent judgment); *Thompson* v. *Moore* (1889), 23 L.R. Ir. 599 (consent order for a perpetual injunction held to involve a decision both of the validity of the patent, and of its infringement: per Lord ASHBOURNE, L.C. (Ir.), at p. 661); *Re South American and Mexican Co., Ex parte Bank of England*, *sup.* (where, on reference to the pleadings, it clearly appeared that a question had been raised as to the validity of a certain agreement, which question, therefore, was held to have been a subject of the consent decision: per VAUGHAN WILLIAMS J., at pp. 46–48, in the Court below, and Lord HERSCHELL L.C., at pp. 48–50, in the C.A.): *River Ribble Joint Committee* v. *Croston Urban District Council*, *supra* (where the consent order, on the face of it, declared the exact question which it had been agreed should be taken to have been decided). *Kinch* v. *Walcott*, [1929] A.C. 482, in which the terms of settlement on which two actions were discontinued, being embodied in a consent order, were held to estop the parties.

[2] See *Goucher* v. *Clayton* (1865), 13 W.R. 336 (per WOOD, V.-C., at p. 337: "there appear to have been no pleadings in the action. Had there been an assertion of the validity of the patent on one side, and a denial on the other, the court would have held the defendants estopped by their submission. This, however, did not appear by the record"); *Great North-West Central Rail. Co.* v. *Charlebois*, [1889] A.C. 114, P.C. (where it was held,—see p. 124,—that the contract sought to be set aside was *ultra vires* the company, and illegal, and that a former consent judgment for the enforcement thereof did not operate to bar either party from afterwards asserting such illegality, because this particular question had not been put in issue, or brought to the notice of the court in the previous proceedings, both parties being then interested in assuming the validity of the contract, and in limiting the contest to the question of its construction, so that no decision on the former point was agreed to, or desired, or in fact pronounced).

The foregoing note is reproduced *verbatim* from the first edition of this work (pp. 24–5). See, however, *In re Jon Beauforte (London), Ltd.*, [1953] 1 All E.R. 634; [1953] Ch. 131, in which ROXBURGH J. was inclined to give a rather wider reading than Mr Spencer Bower to the decision of the Privy Council in *Great North-West Central Rail. Co.* v. *Charlebois* (*supra*).

[3] As in *Jenkins* v. *Robertson* (1867), L.R. 1 Sc. & Div. 117, H.L. In this case the council of a Scottish borough, "for behoof of the inhabitants and the public", had raised an action of a "popular" character for a declarator as to a public right of way, and had obtained a verdict at the trial. On the defenders obtaining a rule for a new trial, a compromise was entered into, whereby the pursuers abandoned their verdict, and paid the defenders' expenses, and a consent decree was drawn up, purporting to assoilzie the defenders, and otherwise giving effect to the arrangement. Afterwards a second action was raised, on behalf of the same "inhabitants and the public" for the same declarator, to which the defenders pleaded *res judicata*: but the House of Lords, reversing both the Lord Ordinary and the Court of Session, held that the decree consented to did not involve a declaration that no public right of way existed, and, therefore, no such declaration

Still less entitled to the name of "judicial decision" is an order which does not purport to embody any consent to an existing judgment, but merely records an undertaking by a party to allow judgment to be signed if at a future date he fails to comply with certain conditions,[1] or which is prefaced by an express declaration that no judgment on the matters in issue is pronounced, or desired by the parties.[2]

No res judicata *against parties not consenting*

44 Of course no consent judgment or order has the slightest operation or effect, whether by way of estoppel or otherwise, against any third person, or against any of the parties who is not shown to have consented.[3] Where a party, though cited in the proceedings and served, has not appeared at the hearing, and has taken no part therein, he will not be estopped by a judgment given by consent of the other parties, when the issue has not been really litigated, and the opposition has been "bought off" by the settlement.[4]

Whether there can be a judgment *in rem* by consent, at least in the absence of evidence properly adduced, disposing of the matters in dispute to the satisfaction of the court, may be doubted; and in any case where the court has purported to give such a judgment, it may be doubted whether it will be binding against the world, though the parties before the court may be estopped thereby *inter se*.

Bankruptcy

45 It should be observed here that the Bankruptcy Court, for the purpose of determining whether or not to make a receiving order against a debtor, under its statutory powers,[5] has jurisdiction in a proper (that is, a strong) case, to "go behind", or "go round", an existing judgment obtained against the debtor by consent,[6] as distinguished from a judgment

---

could be deemed to have been the subject of the consent, and it certainly did not amount to a decision of the question otherwise than by consent, for the court had "exercised no judicial function" (per Lord CHELMSFORD L.C., at p. 121, Lord ROMILLY, at pp. 122, 123, and Lord COLONSAY, at pp. 125, 126). Cp. *The Bellcairn* (1885), 10 P.D. 161, C.A., cited in note 5 on pp. 37–8, *ante* (per Lord ESHER, M.R., at pp. 165–6).

[1] Per PARKE B., at p. 947 of *Litchfield* v. *Ready* (1850), 5 Exch. 939.

[2] *Bradshaw* v. *M'Mullan*, [1920] 2 I.R. 412, H.L. (per Lord FINLAY, at p. 415, Lord ATKINSON, at p. 423, and Lord SHAW, at pp. 424, 425).

[3] See *Goucher* v. *Clayton* (1865), 13 W.R. 336 (per WOOD V.C., at p. 337); *Wytcherley* v. *Andrews* (1871), L.R. 2 P. & D. 327 (per Lord PENZANCE, at p. 329); *Munster* v. *Cox* (1885), 10 App. Cas. 680, H.L.: *The Bellcairn*, *sup.* (per COTTON L.J., and LINDLEY L.J., at p. 166); *Ritchie* v. *Malcolm*, [1902] 2 I.R. 403 (per ANDREWS J., at pp. 409–411, following *Wytcherley* v. *Andrews*, *sup.*).

[4] *Ritchie* v. *Malcolm* (*supra*) at p. 410.

[5] Section 7 of the Bankruptcy Act 1883 now s. 5 (3) of the Bankruptcy Act 1914.

[6] The following are cases in which the Bankruptcy Court went "behind", or "round" a consent judgment: *Re Blythe, Ex parte Banner* (1881), 17 Ch.D. 480, C.A. (a dishonest compromise

obtained after the issues have been fought out in a real trial.[1] And the court has the same power in determining whether the assignee must admit the judgment debt as a proved debt.[2] This, however, constitutes no exception to the rule that a consent judgment is as much a *res judicata* as any other; or, rather, it is an exception which proves the rule. The very use of the expressions "go behind", and "go round", presupposes the continued existence and conclusiveness of the former judgment. Outflanking assumes the impossibility of breaking through: the judgment stands as a *res judicata* until set aside, and this the court of bankruptcy has no jurisdiction to do, nor can it determine that there never was a debt due under the judgment.[3]

---

and extortion); *Re Lennox, Ex parte Lennox* (1885), 16 Q.B.D. 315, C.A. (though here it was the debtor himself who was applying for the receiving order, it was held that this did not deprive the Registrar of his discretion to examine the suspicious circumstances under which the supposed consent was given); *Re Hawkins, Ex parte Troup*, [1895] 1 Q.B. 404, C.A. (where the judgment was founded on a compromise which, though not fraudulent, was unfair and unreasonable); *Re Mead*, [1916] 2 I.R. 285 (practically a judgment by consent on the question of the debtor's infancy, having pleaded which, the debtor, at the trial, withdrew his plea, and it was held by the Irish C.A. that BOYD J. had rightly dismissed a debtor's summons taken out by certain creditors).

[1] At p. 323 of *Ex parte Lennox, sup.*, Lord ESHER M.R. expresses his view that some *prima facie* regard ought to be paid by the Court of Bankruptcy to a consent judgment, and his disagreement with each of the extreme views there contended for by the respective parties, (i) that no consent judgment ought to be taken any notice of at all in Bankruptcy, (ii) that any such judgment ought to have as much effect in Bankruptcy as in any other Court. At p. 484 of *Ex parte Banner, sup.*, JAMES L.J. acknowledges that, where there has been no consent, actual or implied, but, on the contrary, "a real fight between the parties", the court of bankruptcy has no more right than any other court to ignore a consent judgment. It was also held in *Re Flatau, Ex parte Scotch Whisky Distillers, Ltd.*, (1888), 22 Q.B.D. 83, C.A. (per Lord ESHER M.R., at p. 85, FRY L.J., at p. 86, and LOPES L.J., at p. 87) that the court of Bankruptcy ought not to examine the grounds and circumstances of a consent judgment except on a strong case of fraud, collusion, illegality, or the like, or a strong suspicion of such misconduct, calculated to prejudice the general body of creditors, and, further, that such court has no jurisdiction to go behind such a judgment at all where the issues have been fairly fought out in a trial, unless the alleged consent has not been strictly proved. Accordingly, in that case, the receiving order was made, and the judgment was not allowed to be canvassed or impeached. A similar decision, for the same reasons, was given in *Re Newey, Ex parte Whiteman* (1912), 107 L.T. 832, D.C. (where it was held that there had been no consent to the judgment, which was on an award with reference to a gaming debt), and also in *Re a Debtor* (1915), 113 L.T. 704, D.C. The dictum of BIGHAM J. in *In Re Van Laun, Ex parte Patullo*, [1907] 1 K.B. 155, at p. 163, approved by the Court of Appeal in [1907] 2 K.B. 23 ("no judgment recovered against the bankrupt, no covenant given by him or accounts stated with him, can deprive the trustee of this right. He is entitled to go behind such forms to get at the truth, and the estoppel to which the bankrupt may have subjected himself will not prevail against him") is *obiter*; in that case there was no judgment, but only an account stated. The liquidator of a company in liquidation appears to be in the same position as a Trustee in Bankruptcy as regards his powers and his duty to inquire into the consideration for a judgment debt—*Re Home and Colonial Insurance Co., Ltd.*, [1930] Ch. 102; it should be noted that this case also was based on an account stated, so that the dictum of MAUGHAM J. was therefore, when strictly read, *obiter* as to judgments. In New Zealand cf. *In re Sullivan* (1904), 7 G.L.R. 376.

[2] *Re Tollemache, Ex parte Revell* (*No.* 1) (1884), 13 Q.B.D. 720, C.A.

[3] *Re Vitoria, Ex parte Vitoria*, [1894] 2 Q.B. 387, C.A. (per Lord ESHER M.R., at pp. 389, 390).

Judgments and orders by default

46 A judgment or order by default is *prima facie* just as much a judicial decision in favour of the plaintiff as any other judgment or order, whether the default of the defendant was in appearance to the writ, or in pleading,[1] or in appearance at the trial or hearing,[2] or in prosecution of, or resistance to, an appeal.[3] Conversely, where a defendant has pleaded a plea in bar which, instead of replying to it, the plaintiff confesses, and taxes his costs, the result is deemed equivalent to a decision in favour of the defendant, which the plaintiff is estopped from afterwards disputing.[4]

47 As in the case of a consent judgment or order,[5] questions of the utmost importance may arise as to the precise issue or matter of fact or law (if any) which by express declaration or necessary implication, a default judgment or order has determined. Such a judgment or order will certainly found an estoppel as to something; but the question is what it is to be taken as concluding, and for what conclusions it is to stand; and the

---

1 See *Aslin* v. *Parkin* (1758), 2 Burr. 665 (per Lord MANSFIELD C.J., at p. 668: "there is no distinction between a judgment in ejectment by a verdict, and a judgment by default",—accordingly in an action for mesne profits the defendant was held concluded by a judgment in default which the plaintiff had recovered against "the casual ejector"); *Doe* v. *Huddart* (1835), 2 Cr.M. & R. 316 (but here the estoppel was not allowed, because the plaintiff had not pleaded it); *Wilkinson* v. *Kirby* (1854), 15 C.B. 430 (per JERVIS C.J., at p. 443, and CROWDER J., at p. 448); *Harris* v. *Mulkern* (1875), 1 Ex. D. 31 (where it was so stated by the Court of Exchequer, per CLEASBY B., at p. 35). "There is no doubt . . . that by the law of England . . . a default judgment is capable of giving rise to an estoppel *per rem judicatam*. The question is not whether there can be such an estoppel, but rather what the judgment prayed in aid shall be trusted as concluding and for what conclusion it is to stand"—per Viscount RADCLIFFE, delivering the report of the Judicial Committee in *Kok Hoong* v. *Leong Cheong Kweng Mines, Ltd.*, [1964] A.C. 993, P.C. at p. 1010. *In New Zealand, Tira Arika* v. *Sidaway*, [1923] N.Z.L.R. 158 (HOSKING J.), where a judgment entered by default ordering possession of premises, though obtained in circumstances which would have supported an application to set it aside, nevertheless stood until set aside, and while it stood supported an estoppel as to those issues which it necessarily decided between the parties as its foundation. As to the effect of setting aside a default judgment, see Chapter III, para. 84, *post*.

2 See *Nesbit* v. *Rishton* (1839), 11 Ad. & El. 244, Ex.Ch., where it was stated (per TINDAL C.J., at pp. 250–1) that default in appearing after joinder in demurrer, as distinct from default in appearing on the day given to join in demurrer (which was the case before the court), constituted, in the period when demurrers were allowed, a bar to a fresh action. In *Ker* v. *Williams* (1885), 29 Sol. Jo. 681, C.A., the dismissal of an action on default of appearance at the trial was held to be a "judgment" which "operated as an estoppel to the plaintiff" (per LINDLEY L.J. at p. 681).

3 See *Lockyer* v. *Ferryman* (1877), 2 App.Cas. 519, H.L., a case of a judgment given in the H.L. against an appellant who had made default in prosecuting his appeal; *Ram Narayan Singh* v. *Adhindra Nath Mukerji*, [1917] A.C. 100, P.C., a case of a judgment in the P.C. against respondents who had made default in appearance on the appeal, which was heard *ex parte*. The judgment was undoubtedly a *res judicata* whilst it stood, which was not for long, inasmuch as the respondents successfully petitioned the P.C. to set it aside on the ground that their default in appearance was procured by fraud.

4 As in *Newington* v. *Levy* (1870), L.R. 6 C.P. 180, Ex.Ch. (confession of plea of release by deed of composition); *Bennett* v. *Gamgee* (1877), 46 L.J. Q.B. 204, C.A. (confession of plea of liquidation by arrangement).

5 See paras. 41–44, *ante*.

result may be different from that flowing from a judgment by consent. For while, from one point of view, a default judgment may be looked at as only another form of judgment by consent,[1] and as such, as capable of giving rise to all the consequences of a judgment obtained in a contested action or with the consent or acquiescence of the parties, from another viewpoint a judgment by default may be thought to speak for nothing but the fact that a defendant, for unascertained reasons, negligence, ignorance, or indifference, has suffered judgment to go against him in the particular suit in question.[2]

48 It is certain that a judgment or order obtained by default, like one obtained by consent, will conclude finally between the parties (subject, however, to their rights of appeal, if any) the matters expressly decided by it—*i.e.* by the jussive, prohibitive, and declaratory parts of the formal judgment.[3] But it is not so clear how far a default judgment will give rise, as between the parties, to the more remote results of issue estoppel, such as will be the consequences of contested litigation. As will be seen in another chapter,[4] a judgment between parties in contested litigation will estop either from disputing against the other not only the actual issues of law and fact expressly established by the formal judgment ("cause of action estoppel") but also all issues of law and fact which, though not always expressly determined by the judgment, are necessarily to be deemed determined in favour of the successful party because their determination in his favour is a condition the fulfilment of which is necessary to support his cause of action ("issue estoppel").[5]

Possible criticism of the theory of res judicata as applicable to judgments by default

49 It is by no means clear exactly how far a judgment given by default will extend to such matters. It is a commonplace of decisions on *res judicata* to speak of the public interest which requires an end of litigation, and of the principle of justice pursuant to which *nemo debet bis vexari pro eadem*

[1] See *Re South American and Mexican Co., Ltd., Ex parte Bank of England*, [1895] 1 Ch. 37, at p. 45.

[2] Per Viscount RADCLIFFE delivering the report of the P.C. in *Kok Hoong*, v. *Leong Cheong Kweng Mines, Ltd.*, [1964] A.C. 993 P.C. at p. 1010.

[3] *New Brunswick Rail. Co.* v. *British and French Trust Corporation, Ltd.*, [1939] A.C. 1, H.L., where the default judgment in the first action certainly estopped the defendant from relitigating in the second the construction of the particular bond sued upon; *aliter*, however, for the reasons there appearing, in respect of the construction of other bonds of the same series—see the speech of Lord MAUGHAM L.C. at p. 21 and that of Lord WRIGHT at p. 35.

[4] See Chapter VI, *post*.

[5] For this statement of principle, and the terms "cause of action estoppel" and "issue estoppel" used in these senses, see the judgment of DIPLOCK L.J. in *Thoday* v. *Thoday*, [1964] P. 181, C.A. at pp. 197–9. Another statement of the principle may be found in the judgment of the Judicial Committee in *Hoystead* v. *Taxation Commissioner*, [1926] A.C. 155, P.C. at p. 170, where it is said that the principle extends to any point whether of assumption or admission that was in substance the ratio of and fundamental to the earlier decision.

causa.[1] But although it is evident that justice may be assisted by an estoppel founded on litigation satisfactorily contested between the parties, it is not so easy to see why the same result must necessarily attend on judgments given in default of appearance. There are many reasons why a party may allow judgment to go by default against him. The amount of the claim may be small; and he may not foresee the event in which his acceptance of a small liability now may result in a much larger one being subsequently forced upon him. The litigation may be inconvenient or expensive to contest; it may even be instituted in a foreign, or far-distant, court. Other pressing business may compete with what appears at the time to be unimportant litigation; the day of the court fixture may even simply be forgotten; and the amount involved may seem to be too small, or the dispute insufficiently important, to warrant the trouble and expense of an application for a rehearing. In any of such cases can it be said to be obvious, or necessary, or even just, that the first litigation should conclude for ever, in favour of him who signs a default judgment, issues perhaps having incomparably greater consequences in a subsequent action—issues which perhaps the defendant never saw, though doubtless they may have appeared in the pleadings?[2] It is on account of considerations such as these that in three modern cases[3] the highest authorities have sounded warnings against too ready an assumption that the consequences of default judgments, as regards issue estoppel, will always be held as extensive as those of judgments resulting from contested litigation.

New Brunswick Rail. Co., Ltd. v. *British and French Trust Corporation, Ltd.*

50 In *New Brunswick Rail. Co., Ltd.* v. *British and French Trust Corporation, Ltd.*[4] the House of Lords had to consider the effect, in subsequent litigation between the same parties, of a judgment by default which the respondent corporation had previously obtained against the appellant Railway Company. The first action had been brought for moneys due for principal and interest under a bond issued by appellant and held by respondent. It was for moneys due under one such bond only; and the statement of claim asked for judgment for principal and interest in the amount claimed, and for a

---

1 See Chapter I, where the theory supporting the doctrine is discussed.

2 As pointed out by Lord MAUGHAM L.C. in *New Brunswick Rail. Co.* v. *British and French Trust Corporation, Ltd.*, [1939] A.C. 1, H.L., a case examined in some detail in the text (para. 50, *post*). The particular observations are to be found at p. 21. *Cf.* the speech of Lord WRIGHT at pp. 38–9, and the judgment of the Judicial Committee per Lord RADCLIFFE in *Kok Hoong* v. *Leong Cheong Kweng Mines, Ltd.*, [1964] A.C. 993, P.C. at p. 1010.

3 *New Brunswick Rail. Co.* v. *British and French Trust Corporation*, [1939] A.C. 1, H.L.; *Kok Hoong* v. *Leong Cheong Kweng Mines, Ltd.*, [1964] A.C. 993, P.C.: *Carl-Zeiss-Stiftung* v. *Rayner and Keeler, Ltd.*, (*No.* 2), [1966] 2 All E.R. 536, H.L.

4 [1939] A.C. 1, H.L.

declaration construing the clause or clauses giving rise to the liability. The point in issue was whether the amount secured by the bond should be paid in gold or in sterling; both principal and interest were involved. The action was not contested, and the respondent (the lender) obtained judgment by default for principal and interest as in gold. The second proceedings concerned liability on a number of other bonds, part of the same issue, and in the same language, as the first. The House of Lords held that the first judgment gave rise to no estoppel. All their Lordships were agreed that the judgment in the first action, as to the construction of one bond only, determined a different question from what was decided in the second proceedings—*viz.* the construction of the others; it was held that the questions, though *similar*, were not *the same*, but in coming to their conclusion some of their Lordships permitted themselves some observations as to the effect of default judgments, and as to the different consequences which may follow from a default judgment, on the one hand, and from a judgment in a contested proceeding on the other. Lord MAUGHAM L.C., delivering the first speech, said:[1]

> "I do not think it necessary to express an opinion as to whether the alleged estoppel would have succeeded if the appellants had appeared in and contested the first action. But the judgment in that action, limited in form to a single bond, was pronounced in default of appearance by the defendants. In my view not all estoppels are 'odious'; but the adjective might well be applicable if a defendant, particularly if he is sued for a small sum in a country distant from his own, is held to be estopped not merely in respect of the actual judgment obtained against him, but from defending himself against a claim for a much larger sum on the ground that one of the issues in the first action (issues which he never saw, though they were doubtless filed) had decided as a matter of inference his only defence in the second action. My Lords, I think there is much to be urged in favour of the observation made by WILLES, J. in the case of *Howlett* v. *Tarte*,[2] though it may have been a little too widely expressed. He said:[3] 'It is quite right that a defendant should be estopped from setting up in the same action a defence which he might have pleaded but has chosen to let the proper time go by. But nobody ever heard of a defendant being precluded from setting up a defence in a second action because he did not avail himself of the opportunity of setting it up in the first action.' In my opinion we are at least justified in holding that an estoppel based on a default judgment must be very carefully limited. The true principle in such a case would seem to be that the defendant is estopped from setting up in a subsequent action *a defence which was necessarily, and with complete precision, decided by the previous judgment*; in other words, by the *res judicata* in the accurate sense."

[1] At p. 21.
[2] *Howlett* v. *Tarte* (1861), 10 C.B. N.S. 813.
[3] At p. 827.

Lord THANKERTON and Lord RUSSELL OF KILLOWEN, in short judgments, agreed with the judgment of the Lord Chancellor. Lord WRIGHT and Lord ROMER, however, went further; they were prepared to question whether the principles of issue estoppel had any applicability to default judgments at all. After adopting the reasoning upon which Lord MAUGHAM L.C. and Lord RUSSELL OF KILLOWEN had come to their conclusion (*viz.* that the questions were not *eadem questio*), Lord WRIGHT, who had introduced this part of his judgment with the remark that "several reasons" prevented the application of an estoppel to the facts,[1] went on to say:[2]

> "No authority has been produced in which a party has been held to be estopped from raising in a litigation an issue which he might have raised in a previous litigation in which he allowed judgment to go by default and omitted to raise the issue. The nearest analogy is the case of *Howlett* v. *Tarte.*[3] A defendant, sued for rent or a periodical payment under a building agreement, failed to plead issuably. His plea was struck out and judgment went against him for default of pleading under the procedure then current. He was sued for another instalment and by way of defence pleaded that the building agreement had been superseded by an agreement for a yearly tenancy which had been determined, so that the rent claimed was not due. It was held that he was not estopped. That decision has been explained as depending on the old system of pleading. But I think it depends on wider principles. I think it implies that default is not to be treated as an admission. WILLES J. said that the plea in the second action, which was by way of confession and avoidance, was consistent with the record. He said that the objection was a new device, which he thought should not be introduced. 'Nobody', he added, 'ever heard of a defendant being precluded from setting up a defence in a second action because he did not avail himself of the opportunity of setting it up in the first action'. It is enough for present purposes to treat this observation as limited to a case where judgment has gone by default, whether of appearance or pleading. In that sense I should accept these observations of WILLES J., one of the greatest common law judges. There are grave reasons of convenience why a party should not be held to be bound by every matter of fact or law fundamental to the default judgment. It is, I think, too artificial to treat the party in default as bound by every such matter as if by admission. All necessary effect is given to the default judgment by treating it as *conclusive of what it directly decides*. I should regard any further effect in the way of estoppel as an illegitimate extension of the doctrine, which in the absence of express authority I am not prepared to accept."

Lord ROMER's judgment proceeded principally on a consideration of the inquiry whether the questions in the two proceedings were the same. On the topic now under discussion, however, he said in stating his disagreement with the conclusion reached by the Court of Appeal:[4]

---

[1] [1939] A.C. 1, at p. 36.
[2] At p. 37.
[3] (1861), 10 C.B. N.S. 813.
[4] [1939] A.C. 1, at p. 41.

"Whether a judgment by default can ever be relied upon as *res judicata* and, if it can, whether the judgment alone is to be regarded, or whether the whole record of the proceedings may be looked at, are questions upon which I do not find it necessary to express my opinion."

Later Cases: Kok Hoong v. *Leong Cheong Kweng Mines, Ltd.*

51 *New Brunswick Rail. Co., Ltd.* v. *British and French Trust Corporation*[1] was decided in 1938; 25 years later the extent to which default judgments can be used to found an estoppel was considered by the Judicial Committee of the Privy Council (Lord RADCLIFFE, Lord MORRIS OF BORTH-Y-GEST and Lord GUEST) in *Kok Hoong* v. *Leong Cheong Kweng Mines, Ltd.*[2] In an action brought in Malaya for moneys due the defence had been taken that the transaction was one of money-lending; in a rejoinder to the statement of defence plaintiff set up an estoppel precluding this defence, founding it upon the fact that in an earlier action between the parties, claiming a previous instalment under the same contract, judgment had gone by default for the plaintiff. It was clear that if the money-lending defence had been good, and if it had been taken in the earlier action, judgment could not have gone for the plaintiff in that action. The plea of estoppel was disallowed by their Lordships, however, for the reason that the issue did not appear to them to be one which if raised in the earlier proceedings would have amounted to a direct traverse of what was there asserted—it was "more like a plea by way of confession and avoidance than a traverse".[3] It was therefore impossible to say that there was anything in the first judgment which (to use the language of Lord MAUGHAM in the *New Brunswick* case) "had necessarily and with complete precision concluded the issue in the second".[4]

Carl-Zeiss-Stiftung v. *Rayner and Keeler, Ltd.*, (*No.* 2)

52 The most recent decision of a Court of the highest authority, showing that the ferment of uncertainty is still working, is *Carl-Zeiss-Stiftung* v. *Rayner and Keeler, Ltd.*, (*No.* 2),[5] in which the House of Lords again had to consider the limits of issue estoppel when the judgment founding the estoppel was a default judgment. In that case, however, (as in the *New Brunswick* case) there were a number of other factors complicating the decision, and their Lordships' judgments, in which the estoppel was disallowed, were founded for the most part on the facts that the default judgment was a foreign judgment; that it was perhaps not a final judgment; and (most important

[1] [1939] A.C. 1, H.L.
[2] [1964] A.C. 993, P.C.
[3] At p. 1014.
[4] [1939] A.C. 1, at p. 21.
[5] [1966] 2 All E.R. 536, H.L.

of all) that there was not a sufficient identity of parties. It is plain, however, from their speeches in their Lordships' House that more than one of them was troubled about the practical difficulties arising from the application of the doctrine of issue estoppel to default judgments, and perhaps these difficulties are best summarised in the judgment of Lord REID[1] where he says:

> "The difficulty which I see about issue estoppel is a practical one. Suppose the first case is one of trifling importance, but it involves for one party proof of facts which would be expensive and troublesome; and that party can see the possibility that the same point may arise if his opponent later raises a much more important claim. What is he to do? The second case may never be brought. Must he go to great trouble and expense to forestall a possible plea of issue estoppel if the second case is brought? This does not arise in cause of action estoppel; if the cause of action is important, he will incur the expense; if it is not, he will take the chance of winning on some other point. It seems to me that there is room for a good deal more thought before we settle the limits of issue estoppel; but I have no doubt that issue estoppel does exist in the law of England, and if it does it would apply in the present case if the earlier judgment had been a final judgment of an English Court."

Statement of the principle to be applied

53 It seems clear from the judgments which we have been considering that while a default judgment will certainly estop the defendant from denying that the plaintiff is not entitled to the relief which it has awarded to him, it cannot be invoked to estop him by way of issue estoppel as to any question which is not *eadem questio*, using the words in their strictest sense. It is not enough to say that the questions are almost identical or almost certainly the same. They must be *eadem questio*. But if the identical question arising in the second action actually arose in the first, and has been or must necessarily be deemed to have been decided with complete precision one way or the other as the foundation of the default judgment signed by the plaintiff, then, at least while the judgment stands, that question is concluded between the parties. In *New Brunswick Rail. Co., Ltd.* v. *British and French Trust Corporation, Ltd.*[2] Lord MAUGHAM L.C. at least, and probably Lord RUSSELL OF KILLOWEN and Lord THANKERTON also, may be thought to have accepted this view. Lord RADCLIFFE in *Kok Hoong* v. *Leon Cheong Kweng Mines, Ltd.*[3] certainly so interpreted Lord MAUGHAM's judgment.[4] The same view seems to have been clearly accepted by Lord

---

[1] At p. 554: *cf.* Lord UPJOHN at p. 572.

[2] [1939] A.C. 1, H.L. at p. 21.

[3] [1964] A.C. 993, P.C.

[4] At p. 1012: "In their Lordships' opinions the *New Brunswick Rail. Co.* case can be taken as containing an authoritative reinterpretation of the principle of *Howlett* v. *Tarte* (1861), 10 C.B. N.S. 813 in simpler and less specialised terms. This reinterpretation amounts to saying that

UPJOHN in *Carl-Zeiss-Stiftung* v. *Rayner and Keeler, Ltd.*[1] But it must be remembered that Lord WRIGHT and Lord ROMER (in the *New Brunswick* case) may equally well be taken to have rejected this proposition, and it is possible that the true principle may still receive further clarification when in some later case the relevant question is again sharply posed in the Lords.

Default judgments as to the construction of documents

54 It may here be noticed that for the very reasons which dictate a strict limit being placed upon the applicability of the principles of issue estoppel to default judgments, it is undesirable that such judgments should in terms grant wider relief, or determine any more issues of fact or law, than may be absolutely necessary to give to a plaintiff the bare relief to which he may be entitled. It has been held particularly, in this regard, that it is undesirable for any declaration as to the true construction of a document to be included in the relief given on a motion of a judgment by default.[2]

55 It was at one time thought that in the course of deciding what matters were made the subject of estoppel by a default judgment, only the formal judgment itself in the first action could be looked at. In the first edition[3] of this work *Irish Land Commission* v. *Ryan*[4] was cited as possibly limiting the subjects of estoppel *per rem judicatam*, where the judgment was one by default, to matters "to be found on the face of the judgment itself". But the modern practice is to countenance an examination of the statement of claim, at least, "to see what it is that a plaintiff has set up in order to found the order that he has claimed", and to include as legitimate subjects of estoppel all those matters, shown to be fundamental to the claim, which must then appear necessarily and with complete precision to have been decided by the judgment.[5]

---

default judgments, though capable of giving rise to estoppels, must always be scrutinised with extreme particularity for the purpose of ascertaining the bare essence of what they must necessarily have decided, and, to use the words of Lord MAUGHAM L.C., they can estop only for what must 'necessarily and with complete precision' have been thereby determined."

[1] [1966] 2 All E.R. 536, at p. 572.

[2] *New Brunswick Rail. Co.* v. *British and French Trust Corporation, Ltd.* [1939] A.C. 1, H.L. But it is submitted that this admonition is perhaps worded rather too absolutely. An action duly constituted seeking a declaratory judgment as to construction, and that relief only, can hardly be stultified by defendant refusing to appear to argue the case. The counsel in their Lordships' judgments is, it is submitted, one of precaution only.

[3] Pages 27–8.

[4] [1900] 2 I.R. 565.

[5] *Kok Hoong* v. *Leong Cheong Kweng Mines, Ltd.*, [1964] A.C. 993, P.C. per Lord RADCLIFFE at p. 1013. *In New Zealand*, where defendants had not pleaded to a claim for a declaration declaring rescinded an agreement for sale and purchase of land and for an order for possession of the premises, and judgment and decrees were sealed by default accordingly, it was held on a subsequent action brought by the original defendants against the original plaintiffs, claiming performance of contract and in the alternative damages for fraud, that defendants were precluded by

Decrees by default in divorce

56 It has long been recognised in the divorce jurisdiction that a decree of divorce, where there has been no appearance of the respondent, will preclude the respondent from averring in subsequent nullity proceedings that the marriage was void as bigamous, notwithstanding that the question was never specifically traversed in the first suit, since the validity of the marriage must be regarded as fundamental to the prayer and to the decree;[1] and where a petitioner had obtained a decree nisi (afterwards made absolute) of divorce on the ground of adultery in an undefended suit, and had subsequently filed a separate petition against the co-respondent claiming damages, and the co-respondent filed a defence alleging connivance and conduct conducing adultery, it was held that he was estopped from denying adultery, and from raising the plea of connivance, which must be deemed necessarily decided against him, albeit by default, in the first proceeding. *Aliter*, however, with the plea of conduct conducing, which, being a discretionary bar only, was not to be deemed necessarily decided on the first petition.[2]

The effect of bankruptcy on default judgments

57 The observations which have already been made with reference to the treatment of consent judgments in bankruptcy apply, *mutatis mutandis*, to the treatment in bankruptcy of judgments by default: that is to say, the latter class of judgment, no less than the former, is a *res judicata* which cannot be set aside or impeached in the court of bankruptcy, but which that court, in the interests of the general body of creditors, can in a proper case, "go behind", or "get round", without affecting to disturb its status as a judicial decision.[3]

---

estoppel from proceeding on their averment that they had performed the contract on their part, since this was inconsistent with the allegation in the pleadings of the first action, essential as a foundation to the judgment entered therein, that there had been inexcusable failure to perform; but *aliter* as regards the allegations of fraudulent misrepresentation, which involved no such inconsistency—*Tira Arika* v. *Sidaway*, [1923] N.Z.L.R. 158.

[1] And this, even although in the case referred to the respondent was not aware, at the time of the first suit, that he had grounds for questioning the validity of the marriage—*Woodland* v. *Woodland (otherwise Belin)*, [1928] P. 169 per HILL J. at p. 172.

[2] *Hopkins* v. *Hopkins and Castle* (1933), 50 T.L.R. 99 (LANGTON J.).

[3] See para 45, *ante*, as to the mode of dealing with consent judgments in the Bankruptcy court. As to the similar practice in that court with reference to judgments by default, see the following cases, in all of which either a petition for adjudication was dismissed, or a receiving order refused, or a proof rejected, on the ground of strong circumstances of suspicion, notwithstanding the judgment: *Re Onslow, Ex parte Kibble* (1875), 10 Ch. App. 373 (infancy was the ground here: see the observations of JAMES L.J., at pp. 376, 377 as to the theory on which, and the conditions under which, the court of Bankruptcy will inquire into the consideration of a judgment by default); *Re Tollemache, Ex parte Revell* (1884), 13 Q.B.D. 720, C.A. (per BAGGALLAY L.J., at p. 724, who observes that *prima facie* the judgment is entitled to respect, and can only be inquired into when the circumstances are at least suspicious or special); *Re Tollemache, Ex parte Anderson*

Dismissals of actions or applications after hearing

58 When an action, or motion, or application, is dismissed by a judicial tribunal after a trial or hearing, it is often a question whether anything can be said to have been decided, so as to conclude the parties, beyond the actual fact of the dismissal. The answer to this inquiry depends upon whether, on reference to the record and such other materials as may properly be resorted to, the dismissal itself is seen to have necessarily involved a determination of any particular issue or question of fact or law, in which case there is an adjudication on that question or issue; if otherwise, the dismissal decides nothing, except that in fact the party has been refused the relief which he sought. The following are illustrations of the application of this principle to civil proceedings. It may be shown that the former action could not have been dismissed except on the supposition that some question of title was intended to be determined thereby;[1] but, *prima facie*, and in the absence of materials on which such a necessary inference can be established, a dismissal is not a decision of any question of title without an express declaration of the court.[2] A discharge of a rule to set aside a bond and warrant of attorney on the ground of non-compliance with certain statutory requirements has been held to carry with it a decision that all such statutory requirements have been duly complied with.[3] The dismissal of a petition under the National Debt Act 1870, on the ground of the failure of the petitioner (who claimed as legatee) to prove the identity of the owner of the stock with the testator who had bequeathed it,

---

(1885), 14 Q.B.D. 606, per Brett M.R., at pp. 609, 610, where the *prima facie* effect of the judgment is again referred to, and Cotton L.J., at p. 610); *Re Deerhurst, Ex parte Seaton* (1891), 64 L.T. 273, C.A. (per Lord Halsbury L.C., at p. 274); *Re Fraser, Ex parte Central Bank of London*, [1892] 2 Q.B. 633, C.A., where the default was in resisting an application under O. XIV, and where the debtor himself was the party who moved the court of Bankruptcy to go behind the judgment, and this though he had appealed from the judgment unsuccessfully to the C.A., which circumstances, however, were held to make no difference (per Lord Esher M.R., at pp. 635, 636, where, *inter alia*, he observes that "the court of Bankruptcy does not set aside the judgment. If I may use the expression, the court goes round the judgment"). It should be noted here that the power of "going round" a judgment or order is exercisable not only in Bankruptcy, but also in every other case in which a statute provides some new form of remedy, in considering applications for which any court is given the opportunity, and is under the duty therefore, in a proper case, of disregarding the judgment or order, as was recognized in two cases of a charging order under the Judgments Act 1838 (1 & 2 Vict. c. 110), ss. 14, 15, *viz. Re Onslow's Trusts* (1875), L.R. 20 Eq. 677 (per Hall V.C., at pp. 680, 681), and *Re Leavesley*, [1891], 2 Ch. 1, C.A.

[1] As in *Jones* v. *Nixon* (1831), You. 359.

[2] *Brandlyn* v. *Ord* (1738), 1 Atk. 571 (per Lord Hardwicke L.C.: "when the defendants plead a former suit, that the court implied there was no title when they dismissed the bill, is not sufficient; they must show it was *res judicata*, an absolute determination in the court that the plaintiff had no title"); *Bainbrigge* v. *Baddeley* (1847), 2 Ph. 705 (per Lord Cottenham L.C., at p. 710: "an order of dismissal is a bar only when the court has thereby determined that the plaintiffs had no title to the relief sought by the bill").

[3] *Greathead* v. *Bromley* (1798), 7 Term Rep. 455 (per Lord Kenyon C.J., at p. 456).

after an inquiry and certificate to this effect by the chief clerk to whom the Court had referred the issue, was held to be an "adjudication" against the petitioner on the question of the title to the stock, and not (as was vainly contended) a mere nonsuit, which decides nothing.[1] So also, a dismissal of a matrimonial suit in a colonial court was held to involve a decision on the absence of any title to relief, and none the less so because the then statutory law of the Colony, and therefore any court in the Colony, was inadequate to give such relief.[2] A refusal by a statutory tribunal to grant a certificate of exemption from military service in the war of 1914–18 was held conclusive of the applicant's liability to serve.[3] A decision of arbitrators that a claim was brought out of time, and that it could on this account not be considered by them, was held by the House of Lords to be a bar to an action in the courts on the same claim—and this notwithstanding that it appeared doubtful whether the decision of the arbitrators was sound in law—for "the appellant's claim has been dealt with by these arbitrators and their award is a bar to the action".[4] On the other hand, where an action has been dismissed on the sole ground that the particular court had no jurisdiction, there is no decision of the question in controversy, such as to estop the plaintiff from suing again in any court which has jurisdiction to entertain the suit;[5] but such a dismissal, while it will allow the dis-

---

[1] *Re May* (1885), 28 Ch.D. 516, C.A. (per BRETT M.R., at p. 518, and COTTON L. J., at p. 522).

[2] *Lemm* v. *Mitchell*, [1912] A.C. 400, P.C. at p. 405 is cited in the first edition to support the text. The judgment—it was an oral one—is in the respectful submission of the present author unconvincing; it seems at least to have been well arguable that the point decided in the earlier case was one of jurisdiction and no more.

[3] *Langdon* v. *Richards* (1917), 33 T.L.R. 325, D.C.

[4] Per Lord CAVE in *Ayscough* v. *Sheed Thomson & Co., Ltd.* (1924), 131 L.T. 610, affirming the decision of the Court of Appeal (BANKES, SCRUTTON, and ATKIN L.JJ.) reported in (1923), 129 L.T. 429.

[5] As in *Collins* v. *Cave* (1858), 27 L.J. Ex. 146 (a dismissal of a suit in chancery held to be no decision of either party's title or right, for "the plaintiff may have failed because he had no equity, which he would not have if he had a legal remedy": per MARTIN B., at p. 148. This case would, of course, have had a different result since the Judicature Acts, but it is still relevant as an illustration of the principle under discussion); *Waine* v. *Crocker* (1862), 3 De G.F. & J. 421 (per TURNER L.J., at pp. 431, 432); *Simpson* v. *Crowle*, [1921] 3 K.B. 243, D.C. (per BRAY J., at p. 243); *Pinnock Brothers* v. *Lewis and Peat, Ltd.*, [1923] 1 K.B. 690 (K.B.D. per ROCHE J.) in which an arbitrator to whom the dispute had been referred having decided that he had no jurisdiction, the court held plaintiff not precluded by this decision from proceeding with his common law claim for damages. *Cf.* the observations of WILLES J. at p. 262 of *London Corporation* v. *Cox* (1867), L.R. 2 H.L. 239 as to a plaintiff not being estopped from suing over again in a superior court when judgment has previously been given against him in an inferior court, and insisting that the judgment below "had turned, or must have turned on jurisdiction".

In New Zealand a special compensation court set up under the Public Works Act to award compensation for land compulsorily taken for public works had decided that certain matters included in the plaintiff's claim were outside its jurisdiction. It was held that this determination did not preclude the plaintiff from presenting a subsequent claim at Common Law to the Supreme Court in respect of these matters; for if the Supreme Court determined that it, and not the court of compensation, had jurisdiction over them, they had not been determined by the previous decision of the latter court.

But if, on the other hand, the Supreme Court determined that on the true construction of the

appointed party to prosecute his claim in a court having jurisdiction, will preclude him from reviving his claim before the tribunal which has formally refused jurisdiction.[1] A refusal of an application in a Scottish court to "reduce" a service on a person "as heir in special" is a decision against the applicant on the question of his legitimacy.[2] But where a party's plea of a marriage in answer to a suit for jactitation is rejected, there is no decision, or no final decision at all events, that the marriage is invalid.[3]

Where on a husband's petition for divorce on the grounds of adultery and desertion the trial judge had expressed the view that one act of adultery was proved, but had expressed no opinion as to the charge of desertion, and, declining to exercise his discretion in petitioner's favour, had dismissed his petition, and the final order recited that the husband had "sufficiently proved the contents of the petition" but that the court had refused to exercise its discretion in the petitioner's favour, wherefore it was dismissed, it was held that such a determination did not preclude the husband from repeating the charges of adultery which he had previously preferred in his Answer, in a later suit in which the wife was petitioner, since he had succeeded on that issue in the previous suit, nor from repeating the charge of desertion, since there had been no finding upon it; and the wife was not estopped from denying the charge of desertion for the same reason.[4] And so in all other cases where the result is no more than "not proven" there is no decision, or adjudication, of the non-existence of the unproven fact or right.[5]

The principle of *res judicata* is not applicable to the issue of greater

---

Statute the compensation court had jurisdiction, then at that point the claim must fail, since the compensation court must in such a case be taken, being seised of jurisdiction, to have refused relief in respect of such matters. "If it could not have been the subject of compensation, then the plaintiff would be entitled to succeed, and the award of the compensation court would not estop him, because the compensation court could not award upon subjects outside its jurisdiction . . . If it be the case that any of the items of the claim were properly subjects of compensation, and if it be the case that the President of the compensation court had decided erroneously on the point of law that they were not proper subjects of compensation, then the decision of the compensation court, even though erroneous, is final" per WILLIAMS J. in *Paterson* v. *Knapdale Road Board* (1892), 11 N.Z.L.R. 599.

[1] *R.* v. *Middlesex Justices, Ex parte Bond*, [1933] 1 K.B. 72; affirmed on appeal—[1933] 2 K.B. 1.

[2] *Shedden* v. *Patrick* (1854), 1 Macq. 535, H.L.

[3] *Duchess of Kingston's Case* (1776), 2 Smith, L.C. 13th edn. 644 (per DE GREY C.J., on behalf of himself and the other judges summoned to a *concilium* of the House of Lords, at p. 652).

[4] *Bernard* v. *Bernard*, [1958] 3 All E.R. 475 (BARNARD J.).

[5] As in *Moss* v. *Anglo-Egyptian Navigation Co.* (1865), 1 Ch. App. 108 (per Lord CRANWORTH L.C., at p. 114: "if the decree *must* have proceeded on the ground that there was no right to restrain the defendant, then the demurrer"—the ground of which was *res judicata*,—"was good: but that is not so; it might have proceeded upon a want of proof of some material fact in the case"); *Stevens* v. *Tillett* (1870), L.R. 6 C.P. 147 (per BOVILL C.J., at p. 165, and WILLES J., at pp. 172, 3); *R.* v. *Hutchings* (1881), 6 Q.B.D. 300, C.A. (per Lord SELBORNE L.C., at p. 306).

hardship as between landlord and tenant as raised by the Rent Acts, where an application for possession has failed on this ground. In such a case the failure is no bar to a subsequent application, for the relevant facts may alter at any time, and nothing is finally determined by the first decision except its own validity.[1] A dismissal of an action which can only succeed on establishing either fact *x* or fact *y*, may involve a decision negativing both of these facts,[2] but if the action is founded on *x* plus *y*, its dismissal does not, of necessity, carry with it a decision as to either *x*, nor *y*, since the action, for aught that appears from the dismissal itself, may have failed, because fact *x* had not been established, though fact *y* had been, or *vice versa*, or because neither fact had been established;[3] and the dismissal therefore, in such circumstances, does not preclude the unsuccessful plaintiff from suing again in another form of action, for the success of which proof of *x* only, or of *y* only, is sufficient.[4]

And it must be noticed that where a proceeding has been dismissed, no matter of fact expressly determined in the course of the dismissal will found an estoppel unless such a finding was necessary to the dismissal. So (in Australia) where in the first proceedings the court had accepted a plaintiff's submission that the resolution of a Municipal Council was valid, but had nevertheless proceeded to refuse plaintiff the relief which he sought, it was held that in a subsequent proceeding between the same parties the issue of the validity of the Council's resolution was not *res judicata*.[5]

Refusals of writs of habeas corpus

59 It was at one time generally considered[6] that, though an order granting a writ of *habeas corpus* was deemed an *in rem* decision[7] as to the right of the party to his liberty, yet a refusal to make an order *nisi*, or, if granted, to make it absolute, was (*in favorem libertatis*) not to be deemed a decision of the absence of such right, and that the applicant remained at liberty, the refusal notwithstanding, to make a fresh application, or a series of fresh

---

1 *Burman* v. *Woods*, [1948] 1 K.B. 111, C.A.

2 *Lockyer* v. *Ferryman* (1877), 2 App. Cas. 519, H.L., where, in a Scottish action for a declarator of marriage, on the ground of (i) a contract *per verba de praesenti*, or, alternatively (ii) a promise *subsequente copula*, the pursuer's claim had failed, and the rejection of the claim was treated as a decision that neither (i), nor (ii), had ever existed (per Lord CAIRNS L.C., at pp. 524, 525).

3 See *Re Allsop and Joy's Contract* (1889), 61 L.T. 213 (per CHITTY J., at p. 215); *Shoe Machinery Co.* v. *Cutlan*, [1896] 1 Ch. 667, where ROMER J., in the course of his observations at pp. 669–672, points out that, if (which, however, was not the case) the action for infringement of the patent had been dismissed, there would have been no implied decision either of the validity of the patent, or of its infringement, both of which the plaintiff was bound to establish in order to succeed.

4 See *Put and Hardy* v. *Rawsterne* (1682), T. Raym., 472.

5 *Vitosh* v. *Brisbane City Council* (1955), 93 C.L.R. 622 (High Ct. of Australia).

6 1st edition of this work, para 42. *Cf.* 11 *Halsbury's Laws* (3rd edn.) 49.

7 See Chapter VIII, *post*.

applications, without incurring any danger of the previous refusal being set up against him as a *res judicata*, to any and every court of competent original jurisdiction.[1] This widely-held belief was shaken, and its limits exposed, by a series of decisions in 1958–59;[2] and following thereon the matter has now been dealt with by Statute, from whose provisions it now appears that a refusal of an application for *habeas corpus* will have much the same effect, as regards *res judicata*, as a dismissal of any other type of application to the court.[3]

60 The principles above enunciated are applied, *mutatis mutandis*, to proceedings before courts of summary jurisdiction in the exercise of civil or quasi-civil jurisdiction conferred upon them by statute. Thus, in affiliation cases, the mere dismissal of the summons, and the refusal to make any order against the alleged father, is not, by itself, an adjudication that he is not the father.[4] The reason (which is now accepted as the only valid reason) for this is that the justices have no power to convict or acquit, but only to make, or refuse to make, an order for the maintenance of the alleged bastard, and, though an order cannot be made without deciding that the alleged father is so in fact, it can be refused without such refusal involving, of necessity, any decision on the issue of paternity,[5] or having

---

[1] *Ex parte Partington* (1845), 13 M. & W. 679, at pp. 683–4; *Cox* v. *Hakes* (1890), 15 App. Cas. 506, H.L., per Lord HALSBURY L.C. at pp. 514–5; Lord BRAMWELL at pp. 523–4; Lord HERSCHELL at pp. 527–8; and Lord FIELD at p. 543. In *Secretary of State for Home Affairs* v. *O'Brien*, [1923] A.C. 603, H.L. the judgment of Lord HALSBURY in *Cox* v. *Hakes* (*supra*) is cited and used to support the judgment of Lord DUNEDIN at p. 621 and of Lord SHAW OF DUNFERMLINE at pp. 637–8; the same rule was adopted and declared to be the law of Nigeria, as in England, by the Judicial Committee of the Privy Council in *Eshugbayi Eleko* v. *Nigeria Government* (*Administration Officer*), [1928] A.C. 459, P.C. But *in New Zealand* it has been held in *Ex parte Bouvy* (*No.* 2) (1900), 18 N.Z.L.R. 601 that any individual judge of the Supreme Court, in refusing a writ, exercises the whole jurisdiction of the Supreme Court, and hence that a refusal of a writ would operate as an estoppel. In *Australia* see *Wall* v. *R.* (*No.* 1) (1927), 39 C.L.R. 245 (High Court of Australia) and *Wall* v. *R.* (*No.* 2) (1927), 39 C.L.R. 266 (High Ct. of Australia).

[2] *Re Hastings* (*No.* 2), [1958] 3 All E.R. 625; *Re Hastings* (*No.* 3), [1959] 1 All E.R. 698—on appeal, [1959] 3 All E.R. 221, C.A.

[3] The Administration of Justice Act 1960, s. 14.

[4] As in *R.* v. *Jenkin* (1736), Cas. Temp. Hard., 301; *R.* v. *Machen* (1849), 14 Q.B. 74; *R.* v. *Buckinghamshire Justices* (1849), 18 L.J. M.C. 113 (where the defendant was not in a position to prove that the former dismissal was "on the merits"); *R.* v. *Harrington* (1864), 12 W.R. 420; *R.* v. *Gaunt* (1867), L.R. 2 Q.B. 466; *R.* v. *May* (1880), 5 Q.B.D. 382 (where the complainant and her witnesses did not appear, owing to an honest mistake as to the day fixed for the hearing); *McGregor* v. *Telford*, [1915] 3 K.B. 237, D.C. "Justices have no power to say that the defendant is not the father; they can only make an order in the nature of a non-suit"—per HUMPHREYS J. in the course of the argument in *R.* v. *Sunderland Justices, Ex parte Hodgkinson*, [1945] K.B. 502, at p. 503. *Cf.* per Lord PARKER C.J. in *Robinson* v. *Williams* [1965] 1 Q.B. 89 at p. 97: "I think that HUMPHREYS J. was only treating those proceedings as in the nature of a non-suit". In *New Zealand* this position is covered by statute—Destitute Persons Act 1910, s. 67; and see *Crozier* v. *Myers* (1915), 17 G.L.R. 583, 584 and *Tinney* v. *Ferrel*, [1958] N.Z.L.R. 114.

[5] See *R.* v. *Jenkin*, *supra*, per Lord HARDWICKE C.J., at p. 302; *R.* v. *Machen*, *supra*, per Lord DENMAN C.J., at pp. 79, 80.

any more effect as a *res judicata* than a nonsuit in an action.[1] The view formerly entertained that the reason and justification of the rule is to be found in the circumstance that the mother derives no right of appeal from the statute, whilst the putative father does, is now no longer accepted.[2] In the first edition of this work[3] the view was expressed that if it can be shown that in the first decision the dismissal "proceeded on the merits after a genuine contest" it will be deemed a judicial decision on the question of paternity in favour of the defendant. It is conceived, however, that this view must be revised on a consideration of later cases, and that the true view is that it is always open to an applicant whose case has been dismissed to make a fresh application to the justices,[4] but that they will be slow to reverse their own previous decision if only the same evidence is tendered as before.[5] It is clear, however, that in tendering fresh evidence on a second application the applicant will not be hampered by such rules as restrict the admission of new evidence in appellate courts to evidence not reasonably available in earlier proceedings.[6]

In the case of a summons on the ground of a matrimonial offence under the Summary Jurisdiction (Married Women) Act 1895,[7] a dismissal "on the merits" was held to be a decision which estops the complainant from afterwards taking out another summons based on the same matrimonial offence.[8] But a finding by a competent Court that desertion, on an earlier date, is not proved, will not be a bar to a finding, by another court, of desertion between the same parties at a later date.[9]

---

[1] Per Lord READING C.J. at pp. 240/242 of *McGregor* v. *Telford*, *supra*; *cf.* the observations of HUMPHREYS J. in the course of argument in *R.* v. *Sunderland Justices, Ex parte Hodgkinson*, [1945] K.B. 502, at p. 503.

[2] This theory was put forward in *R.* v. *Machen* (*supra*). It was dissented from by LUSH J. at p. 470 of *R.* v. *Gaunt* (*supra*) but adopted by him in the later case of *R.* v. *May supra* at p. 384. In *McGregor* v. *Telford*, [1915] 3 K.B. 237, D.C., Lord READING C.J. expressed the opinion that the reason suggested is a bad one, pointing out that having regard to s. 37 (2) of the Criminal Justice Administration Act 1914, which gives a right of appeal to the Quarter Sessions from a refusal to make the order, it has now become of importance, if not necessary, to dispose of the point, because if the theory in question be the sole justification of the rule, it is obvious that the law being altered as stated, the rule itself could no longer be supported. In *R.* v. *Sunderland Justices, Ex parte Hodgkinson*, [1945] K.B. 502, D.C. at p. 508 HUMPHREYS J. alluded to this dictum with some reserve, saying that he would express no opinion as to its correctness.

[3] 1st edn. p. 32 para. 43.

[4] *Robinson* v. *Williams*, [1965] 1 Q.B. 89 per Lord PARKER C.J. at p. 97: "All the cases show that there is no question of *res judicata* in such a case"; per WIDGERY J. at p. 100.

[5] *R.* v. *Sunderland Justices, Ex parte Hodgkinson*, [1945] K.B. 502 per OLIVER J. at p. 509; *Robinson* v. *Williams* [1965] 1 Q.B. 89 per WIDGERY J. at p. 100.

[6] *Robinson* v. *Williams*, [1965] 1 Q.B. 89 per Lord PARKER C.J. at pp. 98–100.

[7] Now repealed; the statutory provisions are now to be found in the Matrimonial Proceedings (Magistrates' Courts) Act 1960.

[8] *Stokes* v. *Stokes*, [1911] P. 195 (per EVANS P., delivering the judgment of himself and BARGRAVE DEANE J., at pp. 198–200), following *Finney* v. *Finney* (1868), L.R. 1 P. & D. 483 (per Lord PENZANCE at p. 484).

[9] *Froud* v. *Froud* (1920), 123 L.T. 176.

61 Criminal cases, strictly so called, are governed by the same canons and considerations. Thus, the dismissal of a summons, complaint, or charge by a court of summary jurisdiction, if expressly stated by the court, or shown by evidence properly receivable, to have proceeded upon a consideration of the merits, is a judicial decision of the innocence of the alleged offender,[1] and this is so, even in a case where the justices profess, or are proved, to have dismissed the charge on the ground of the insufficiency of the evidence adduced by the complainant, or some defect in the presentation of his case,[2] or on the ground that the accused was brought before them by some process not authorized by the law,[3] or on the ground of the non-observance of some statutory formality, if the justices had jurisdiction to convict notwithstanding the irregularity.[4] But where the dismissal did not purport to have been, or was not in fact, founded upon a consideration of "the merits", even in the largest and most liberal sense of that somewhat elastic expression, it is not deemed to involve, or necessarily to involve, any adjudication of the innocence of the accused. Thus, where the complainant deliberately absented himself from the court on the hearing of a summons for assault, having first given notice to the defendant of his intention to do so, and afterwards to sue for the assault in the

---

[1] As in *Kinnis* v. *Graves* (1898), 78 L.T. 502, D.C. (dismissal, after hearing evidence, of information for an offence under s. 3 of the Public Health (Buildings in Streets) Act 1888, being the erection of a building, the front of which projected beyond the building line: held to be a "decision" that the building did not so project as to constitute the alleged offence: per WILLS J. at p. 504). *In New Zealand, Bailey* v. *McCree & Son*, [1937] N.Z.L.R. 508 in which O'REGAN J. held that the dismissal of a prosecution by a stipendiary magistrate precluded the subsequent re-prosecution of the defendant on the same charges, the relevant period of time specified in the information being extended, but not so as to make the allegations relate to a materially different course of conduct. Contrast the case cited in note 2 on p. 58, *post*.

[2] *Ryley* v. *Brown* (1890), 62 L.T. 458, D.C. (where it appeared on the facts stated in the special case that the summons had been dismissed on the merits, for insufficiency of evidence, though the justices took upon themselves to say that they had not dismissed the summons on its merits, being evidently under the erroneous impression that a dismissal on the ground of "insufficiency of evidence" reduced the case to one of mere non-suit: per Lord COLERIDGE C.J. and Lord ESHER M.R. at p. 458). *Cf. R.* v. *Glynne* (1871), L.R. 7 Q.B. 16.

[3] *R.* v. *Brakenridge* (1884), 48 J.P. 293, D.C., where the justices dismissed a charge of night poaching, without considering whether the accused had committed the offence, on the ground that he was not properly before them at all, having been arrested without any legal justification whatever, and it was held that this was a judicial decision, though not "on the merits" in the narrowest sense of the expression (per Lord COLERIDGE C.J. and LOPES J., at p. 294).

[4] *Haynes* v. *Davis*, [1915] 1 K.B. 332, D.C., a case of a summons under the Sale of Foods and Drugs Act 1899, where no certificate of analysis had been served together with the summons on the defendant, as required by s. 19 (2) of the statute: held, however, that the dismissal was an adjudication of the defendant's right to be acquitted of the offence, for "in whatever way a person obtains an acquittal, whether it be by a verdict of the jury on the merits, or by some ruling on a point of law without the case going to the jury, he is entitled to protection from further proceedings" (per RIDLEY J., at p. 336), and the magistrates in this case, as had been already held in *Grimble & Co.* v. *Preston*, [1914] 1 K.B. 270, had jurisdiction to convict notwithstanding the non-observance of the formality in question (per AVORY J., at p. 337). Contrast the cases cited in notes 3 and 4, p. 58, *post*.

county court, and the defendant attended at the hearing and made a statement, and obtained a dismissal of the summons, and a statutory "certificate" thereof, it was held that the dismissal and "certificate" did not have the effect of a judicial decision that no assault had been committed;[1] and, similarly, where the dismissal proceeded on the ground that the summons on the face of it disclosed no such offence as alleged.[2] And, generally, where the indictment or summons is defective, or where there has been a non-compliance with some prescribed formality, the observance of which is a condition precedent to the jurisdiction of the tribunal to deal with the case at all, the dismissal of the charge on that ground is not a judicial decision of the innocence of the party, such as will support a plea of *autrefois acquit*,[3] any more than if in such a case the tribunal had convicted the accused, the conviction would amount to any adjudication of the guilt of the party on which a plea of *autrefois convict* could be based.[4]

Reversals by appellate tribunals

62 When a judicial tribunal of competent original jurisdiction has granted, or refused, the relief claimed in an action or other proceeding, and an appellate tribunal[5] reverses the judgment or order of the court of

[1] As in *Reed* v. *Nutt* (1890), 24 Q.B.D. 669, where it was held that, in the circumstances stated in the text, the defendant was not entitled to a "certificate" under s. 44 of 24 & 25 Vict. c. 100, which is only to be given where the dismissal was "upon the merits", unlike the corresponding section of the old statute, which did not contain these words (per Lord ESHER M.R., at p. 673, and Lord COLERIDGE C.J., at p. 674), and where (per Lord ESHER M.R., at pp. 673, 674) it was also held that it is proper in such cases to receive evidence as to how the "certificate" came to be given.

[2] *Jenkins* v. *Merthyr Tydvil Urban District Council* (1899), 80 L.T. 600, D.C., where the summons under s. 3 of the Public Health (Buildings in Streets) Act 1888, did not allege any previous notice by the local authority, without which there could be no statutory offence, and there was therefore nothing disclosed on the face of the summons which gave the justices jurisdiction (per LAWRANCE and CHANNELL JJ., p. 600). Contrast the case cited in note 1 on p. 57, *ante*.

[3] As in *R.* v. *Bitton* (1833), 6 C. & P. 92. *Cp.* the observations of AVORY J., at pp. 365, 366, of *R.* v. *Marsham*, [1912] 2 K.B. 362, D.C., who there says that, when the indictment is invalid, there is and can be no decision at all as to guilt or innocence, and therefore no *res judicata* on which a plea of *autrefois acquit* can be founded. See, also, for another illustration, *Williams* v. *Letheren*, [1919] 2 K.B. 262, D.C. (per BRAY J., at p. 269, and A. T. LAWRENCE J., at p. 270). As to the plea of *autrefois acquit* generally see Chapter XI, *post*.

[4] *R.* v. *Marsham*, *supra* (per Lord ALVERSTONE C.J., at p. 364, and AVORY J., at pp. 365, 366); *Bannister* v. *Clarke*, [1920] 3 K.B. 598, D.C. (per Lord READING C.J., at pp. 605–607). Contrast the case cited in note 4 on p. 57, *ante*. As to the plea of *autrefois convict* generally, see Chapter XXII, *post*.

[5] Instances of such appellate tribunals, whose decisions have the effect described in the text are the following: the Court of Appeal; the K.B.D. in its appellate jurisdiction; Parliament, a resolution of which was held to supersede the famous Ship Money judgment, and to estop the Crown from setting it up against the subject (*Chambers* v. *Brumfeild* (1640), Cro. Car. 601), just as, previously to the resolution, the judgment estopped the subject from impeaching it as against the Crown (*Lord Say's Case* (1639), Cro. Car. 524); the House of Lords (which tribunal, however, when granting relief denied in the court below, makes no "decision" itself, but remits the case to the court of first instance to make the "decision" which is declared by the House to be proper); Her Majesty in Council, who by Order gives effect to the report and advice of the Judicial Committee of the Privy Council (*Farquharson* v. *Seton* (1828), 5 Russ. 45; *Ram Narayan*

first instance, and either refuses the relief granted below, or grants the relief refused below, as the case may be, the former decision, till then conclusive as such, disappears altogether, and is replaced by the appellate decision, which thenceforth holds the field, to the exclusion of any other, as the *res judicata* between the parties.

63 Where, however, the appellate tribunal reverses, sets aside, or quashes a judgment or order, not on the ground that, having made within the jurisdiction of the tribunal appealed from, it was erroneous in law or fact, but on the sole ground that such tribunal had no jurisdiction to make it, or to entertain the question which it purported to decide, the result is that, from and after the reversal, there remains no judicial decision of that, or of any other question of law or fact, which can estop the parties from litigating again, since the judgment or order reversed, though as long as it stood it was a "decision", is pronounced to be a nullity, and the reversal, though a decision in a purely destructive and negative sense, in that it pronounces that nullity, is not so in the sense of deciding the question of right, title, or liability (whether civil or criminal) in dispute, which question is thenceforth in the same position as if it had never been heard or determined at all.[1]

64 It should be noted here that, as has already been explained,[2] where the so-called appellate "decision" is really nothing more than a mere

Singh v. *Adhindra Nath Mukerji*, [1917] A.C. 100, P.C.); the Court of Criminal Appeal (who, by s. 4 (2) of the Criminal Appeal Act 1907, "shall, if they allow an appeal against conviction, quash the conviction *and direct a judgment and verdict of acquittal to be entered*"); the Justices in Quarter Sessions, when quashing an order of the Petty Sessions as to a pauper's settlement, as in *R.* v. *Clint* (1841), 11 Ad. & El. 624 n., and *Heston Overseers* v. *St. Bride's Overseers* (1853), 1 E. & B. 583; and statutory appellate courts, such as the Tribunal of Appeal, under the London Building Act 1894 (57 & 58 Vict. c. ccxiii), when reversing the order of "the superintending architect", as in *London County Council* v. *Galsworthy*, [1918] A.C. 851, H.L.

[1] *Cross* v. *Salter* (1790), 3 Term Rep. 639 (reversal by Court of Arches of an adjudication of the Consistorial Court, as to the title to a pew, on the ground that the latter court had no jurisdiction to decide any question of title); *R.* v. *Drury* (1849), 3 Car. & Kir. 190 (per COLERIDGE J., at pp. 199, 200); *Conlin* v. *Patterson*, [1915] 2 I. R. 169 (where a conviction of a man for an offence against a certain statute had been quashed by the Irish K.B., and it was held that the quashing order was no adjudication at all, and could not be made the foundation of a plea of *autrefois acquit*, any more than the conviction itself could support a plea of *autrefois convict* (per PALLES C.B., at pp. 174, 175, and DODD J., at p. 177)). *Cp.* the observations of AVORY J., at pp. 365, 366 of *R.* v. *Marsham*, [1912] 2 K.B. 362, D.C. As to settlement cases, the following may be referred to: *R.* v. *St Andrew, Holborn* (1796), 6 Term Rep. 613 (where the quashing of an order of removal on the sole ground of a formal defect was held not to be, or to involve, any adjudication of the place of settlement of the pauper: per Lord KENYON C.J., at pp. 614, 615); *R.* v. *Wick St. Lawrence* (1833), 5 B. & Ad. 526 (where it was held that any such quashing order is *prima facie* not a "decision", concluding the parties, of any particular question, unless it appears by a special entry on the face of the order, which entry, however, the Quarter Sessions Justices are not compellable to make—see *R.* v. *Wheelock, Chester* (1826), 5 B. & C. 511,—that such question was intended to be adjudicated upon: per Lord DENMAN C.J., at pp. 533, 534, and PARKE J., at pp. 535, 536).

[2] See the cases cited in note 3 on p. 39, *ante*.

registration and record by the appellate tribunal of an agreement or compromise between the parties, without the mind of the tribunal having been brought to bear on the questions so compromised, and without its having exercised any judicial function in the matter, there is nothing which can be deemed, or operate as, a *res judicata*.

Criminal judicial decisions

65 For the purposes of estoppel, criminal decisions stand on very much the same footing as other judicial decisions; that is to say, any conviction or acquittal of, or any judgment or order for or against, a party on an indictment, information, summons, or complaint, pronounced by a court of competent jurisdiction, is conclusive in any subsequent proceedings between the same parties, in respect of the same offence, in any court, criminal or civil. The consequence of this is two-fold. The application of the principle of estoppel *per rem judicatam* against the Crown gives rise to the special plea of *autrefois acquit* upon arraignment; and at other stages of a criminal trial by indictment, and in summary proceedings, to a submission of *nemo debet bis vexari pro uno delicto*, having the same effect.[1] The application of the principle of merger, and of the maxim *transit in rem judicatam*, on the other hand, results in the plea of *autrefois convict*.[2] Each of these pleas is examined in detail in a separate subsequent chapter of this work.

Foreign judicial decisions

66 There was a period, at the close of the eighteenth, and beginning of the nineteenth, century, when, whether owing to the fierce patriotism and insular distrust of the foreigner which had been engendered by the long conflict with France, or to the English lawyer's professional homage to the sanctity of an English "Court of Record", and his comparative indifference to all other tribunals, many of our judges were disinclined to concede to the decision of a foreign tribunal any higher status than that of bare admissibility as *prima facie* evidence.[3] But, even in those days, dissentient voices

---

[1] The plea of *autrefois acquit* is dealt with in Chapter XI, *post*.

[2] The plea of *autrefois convict* is dealt with in a separate chapter (Chapter XXII) in Part II of this book. Though *autrefois acquit* is not infrequently accepted as being based on the same principle as *autrefois convict*, it is conceived, for reasons hereafter to be stated, to be a more logical course to deal with the latter in Part II of this work, as an instance of the adaptation to criminal procedure of the plea or bar of "former recovery" in civil proceedings.

[3] For instance, at p. 5 of *Walker* v. *Witter* (1778), 1 Doug. K.B. 1, Lord Mansfield C.J., after stating that "it had been admitted . . . on the part of the plaintiff that the judgment" there sued upon (which was that of a superior court in Jamaica) "was only *prima facie* evidence of the debt", proceeded to express his sense of the importance of "fixing accurately what a court of record is in the eye of the law", which "description is confined properly to certain courts in England, and their judgments cannot be controverted", but "foreign courts, and courts in England not of record have not that privilege", whence it followed that "their judgments are a ground of action everywhere, but they are examinable". The same opinion was afterwards expressed by

were not altogether wanting,[1] which, in the course of a generation or so, began to prevail; and it has now long been firmly established that, with certain exceptions to be noticed presently,[2] a foreign judicial decision, whether relied upon as the foundation of an action, or by way of bar or estoppel, is as conclusive, and is impeachable only on the same grounds, as a decision of any English tribunal.[3] The *dicta* of Lords MANSFIELD, CAMDEN, HARDWICKE, and BROUGHAM, which seem, in their literal acceptation, to indicate a different opinion, can be supported only on the theory that it was intended thereby to convey no more than that any foreign

---

him in *Herbert* v. *Cook* (1782), Willes, 37 n. So BULLER J., at p. 6a n. of *Galbraith* v. *Neville* (1789), 1 Doug. K.B. 6 n. ("the foreign judgment shall be *prima facie* evidence of the debt, and conclusive till it is impleaded by the other party"), and Lord CAMDEN L.C., at p. 710 of *Bayley* v. *Edwards* (1792), 3 Swan. 703. It is to be observed that in none of the above cases was the opinion cited necessary to the decision, and that in *Galbraith* v. *Neville*, *supra*, Lord KENYON C.J. very seriously doubted, whilst in *Bayley* v. *Edwards*, *supra*, PLUMER M.R. disagreed with Lord CAMDEN L.C. (see the next note).

[1] See, for example, the judgment of Lord NOTTINGHAM L.C., at pp. 326, 327 n. of *Cottington's Case* (1678), cited in 2 Swan. 326, one of a group of cases decided temp. Charles II, the reports of which are transcribed from Lord NORTHINGTON'S MSS. in a note appended to the report of *Kennedy* v. *Earl Cassilis* (1818), 2 Swan. 313. Later, in *Galbraith* v. *Neville*, *supra*, Lord KENYON C.J., at p. 6 n., expressed "very serious doubts respecting the doctrine laid down in *Walker* v. *Witter*, that foreign judgments are not binding on the parties here", and, at p. 712 of *Bayley* v. *Edwards*, *supra*, PLUMER M.R. associated himself with these doubts, and, indeed, stated his opinion to be that a foreign judgment is conclusive, and only to be falsified by showing error apparent.

[2] See paras. 71 *et seq. post.*

[3] See *Tarleton* v. *Tarleton* (1815), 4 M. & S. 20 (per Lord ELLENBOROUGH C.J., and BAYLEY J., at p. 22); *Martin* v. *Nicolls* (1830), 3 Sim. 458 (per KINDERSLEY V.-C., at pp. 461–465); *Bowles* v. *Orr* (1836), 1 Y. & C. Ex. 464 (per Lord LYNDHURST C.B., at p. 468, during the argument, and at p. 473, in his judgment); *Bank of Australasia* v. *Nias* (1851), 16 Q.B. 717 (per Lord CAMPBELL C.J., at pp. 735–738); *Reimers* v. *Druce* (1857), 26 L.J. Ch. 196 (per ROMILLY M.R., at pp. 198, 199), where reference is also made to the ancient, but now exploded, notion that a foreign judgment is somewhat less conclusive when sued upon than when set up as a bar); *Godard* v. *Gray* (1870), L.R. 6 Q.B. 139 (per BLACKBURN J., at p. 150); *Ellis* v. *M'Henry* (1871), L.R. 6 C.P. 228 (per BOVILL C.J., at p. 238); *Grant* v. *Easton* (1883), 13 Q.B.D. 302, C.A. (per BRETT, M.R., at p. 303); *Pemberton* v. *Hughes*, [1899] 1 Ch. 781, C.A. (per LINDLEY M.R., at pp. 793, 794). Modern *dicta* on the same subject may be found in *Carl-Zeiss-Stiftung* v. *Rayner and Keeler, Ltd.*, (*No.* 2), [1966] 2 All E.R. 536 per Lord REID at pp. 554–5 ("Next I must consider whether it makes any difference that the former judgment was the judgment of a foreign court. At one time foreign judgments were regarded as being only evidence and not conclusive; but at least since the decision in *Godard* v. *Gray* (*supra*) they have been regarded as equally conclusive with English judgments (subject to any difference there may be resulting from there being no merger of a cause of action in a foreign judgment). The same pleas, *e.g.*, fraud or lack of jurisdiction, are good against both"); per Lord HODSON at p. 560 ("The courts have moved a long way since the opinion was expressed by Lord BROUGHAM, L.C., in the Irish appeal of *Houlditch* v. *Marquess of Donegal* that the judgment of a foreign court in courts of this country is only *prima facie* evidence if liable to be averred against and not conclusive. The modern doctrine accepted since the decision of *Godard* v. *Gray* is that a foreign judgment may be pleaded and is conclusive. If this is so, I see no reason why the rule of estoppel *per rem judicatam* should not be applied, subject to the caution contained in Lord BROUGHAM'S observations in the *Houlditch* v. *Donegal* case as to the difficulties which arise from the differences in the course of procedure between one jurisdiction and another"); per Lord GUEST at p. 567; per Lord UPJOHN at p. 574 ("I accept at once that for the purpose of the doctrine of *res judicata* in general a prior foreign judgment may be just as effective as an English one").

decision can be impeached on the question of the jurisdiction of the tribunal over the cause or the parties.[1]

Mr Spencer Bower's original text[2] commented at this point that decisions of English Courts were no less impeachable upon the like grounds; but it may be pointed out that while in the case of a decision of an English Court jurisdiction is presumed until the contrary is shown, and, as regards such objections as fraud, the decision must stand until and unless by a judgment given in a substantive action it is set aside, in the case of a foreign decision the onus as to jurisdiction lies upon him who relies upon it as a *res judicata*, and such answers to the plea as fraud or public policy may be put forward in the action in which the judgment is set up, no separate substantive action to set the first judgment aside being necessary. In these respects there must be an essential distinction between the effects of an English, and a foreign, judgment.[3]

Theory of efficacy of foreign judgments

67 The theoretical justification of the doctrine according to which conclusive efficacy is given to the decisions of foreign tribunals is public policy in its widest sense, that is to say, the general advantage of the realm, as a member of the great family of nations whose lot it is to live together upon the earth, and who can only do so with comfort on the principle of mutual toleration and recognition which, by conserving the interests of civilization in general, is the only means of maintaining the mercantile security and welfare of each civilized state. In an earlier day it was well observed by the court, in an early action of trover for a ship and goods, which was defeated by proof of a sentence in the French Admiralty Court in favour of the defendant, that, "as we are to take notice of a sentence in the Admiralty here, so ought we of those abroad in other nations, and we must not set them at large again, for otherwise the merchants would be in a pleasant condition! For suppose a decree here in the Exchequer, and the goods happened to be carried into another nation, should the court abroad

[1] Thus, where Lord BROUGHAM, at pp. 477–479 of *Houlditch* v. *Marquess of Donegal* (1834), 2 Cl. & Fin. 470, spoke of a foreign judgment as being *prima facie* evidence, it is obvious from the context, and from the character of the authorities cited by him, that he meant no more than that a foreign judgment is impeachable on the ground of want of competent jurisdiction. This is the explanation accepted by Lord CAMPBELL C.J., delivering the judgment of the Queen's Bench, at p. 735 of *Bank of Australasia* v. *Nias*, *supra*.: "perhaps it was in contemplation of these modes in which a foreign judgment may be impeached that it has sometimes been said to be only *prima facie* evidence." And see the *dictum* of Lord HODSON quoted in note 3, p. 61, *supra* from *Carl-Zeiss-Stiftung* v. *Rayner and Keeler, Ltd.*, [1956] 2 All E.R. 536, H.L. at p. 560.

[2] 1st Edn. p. 38; and see upon this point Lord REID's judgment in *Carl-Zeiss-Stiftung* v. *Rayner and Keeler, Ltd.*, [1966] 2 All E.R. 536 at p. 555—"the same pleas—*e.g.* fraud, and lack of jurisdiction—are good against both" (*i.e.*, against English and foreign judgments).

[3] See the judgment of Lord WILBERFORCE in *Carl-Zeiss-Stiftung* v. *Rayner and Keeler, Ltd.*, (*supra*) at pp. 584–5, where he refers to fraud, public policy, and want of jurisdiction as matters in respect of which "foreign judgments retain their distinction from English judgments".

unravel this? It is but agreeable with the law of nations that we should take notice and approve of the laws of their countries in such particulars".[1]

And turning from mercantile transactions to questions of status, and particularly to matters of marriage and divorce, it has in recent years become increasingly apparent that while it is impossible to expect international uniformity in the domestic laws which govern these questions in particular states, yet considerations of convenience closely affecting subjects of our own state have proved compulsive towards a liberal recognition in our jurisdiction of the validity of marriages and divorces which Courts in other countries, accepting jurisdiction over the parties, have purported to recognise or dissolve. So long ago as 1678 on an appeal to the House of Lords from a decision of the Delegates affirming a sentence of the Court of Arches to the effect that the petitioner was precluded from asserting that his wife had another husband living by a sentence of divorce pronounced by the Archbishop of Turin, Lord NOTTINGHAM L.C., as the ground of dismissing the appeal, expressed a bold and broad view that "it is against the law of nations not to give credit to the judgment and sentences of foreign countries, till they be reversed by the law, and according to the form, of those countries wherein they were given. For what right hath one kingdom to reverse the judgment of another? And how can we refuse to let a sentence take place until it be reversed? And *what confusion would follow in Christendom, if they should serve us so abroad, and give no credit to our sentences?*".[2] Decrees pronounced by the court of the domicil of the parties have long been recognised almost without question in this country; and in more recent times the tendency has been to carry matters further, and to recognise decrees by courts of foreign jurisdictions in which the parties are not actually domiciled, if such decrees are made in circumstances which in this country would result in an English court assuming jurisdiction.[3] But the subject of *res judicata* and divorce in modern times will be dealt with, albeit shortly, in a separate chapter.[4]

The comity of nations

68 The "comity of nations" has been described not infrequently by eminent judges[5] as the basis and explanation of the practice which forbids

---

[1] *Hughes* v. *Cornelius* (1680), 2 Show. 232.

[2] *Cottington's Case* (1678), cited in 2 Swan. 326 n.

[3] See, for instance, *Travers* v. *Holley*, [1953] 2 All E.R. 794; [1953] P. 246, C.A.; *Indyka* v. *Indyka*, [1966] 3 All E.R. 583, and particularly the judgment of DIPLOCK L.J. at p. 587; and the judgments in the House of Lords (and perhaps particularly that of Lord Pearce) in the same case, on appeal to the House—[1967] 2 All E.R. 689.

[4] See Chapter XXII, *post*.

[5] *E.g.* Lord ELLENBOROUGH C.J., at p. 150 of *Power* v. *Whitmore* (1815), 4 M. & S. 141 ("the comity which is paid by us to the judgments of other courts abroad", and, again, "that principle of comity").

the examination of foreign decisions on the merits in the courts of this country. This expression was objected to as incorrect by Lord BROUGHAM,[1] and criticized as "loose" by BLACKBURN J.,[2] who preferred to state as the *ratio* of the doctrine the perhaps rather unsatisfactory formula (adopted from the two judgments of PARKE B.) that "the judgment of a court of competent jurisdiction over the defendant enforces a duty or obligation on the defendant to pay the sum for which judgment is given".[3] In so far as this dictum is extended to foreign judgments, it seems to give little guidance as to the nature and source of the supposed "obligation or duty". In the ordinary juridical meaning of the word there can be no obligation, that is to say, none that is enforceable by the courts of this country, "to pay the sum for which judgment is given" by a *foreign* tribunal except on the theory of unexpressed but well understood convention, which, by whatever name called, silently regulates the intercourse of nations in civil matters. In the general interests of civilization, every State, from considerations of practical convenience amounting almost to necessity, is constrained to give international currency to the civil decisions of every other State. This mutual deference and respect may, it is submitted, be not inaptly described as "international comity".[4]

But this opinion, expressed with characteristic vigour by Mr Spencer Bower in the first edition of this work,[5] must in the view of the present author be accepted with the reservation that, at least with regard to *res judicata* in marriage and divorce, the doctrine can hardly be satisfactorily explained on the basis of "comity" alone—nor yet on the basis of a tacit convention amongst the states of Christendom, as was in the first edition put forward as an alternative foundation for this extension of the doctrine. It must surely be based on nothing more or less than the convenience of citizens of our state, who, finding themselves the subjects for one reason or another of a decree of a foreign state which affects their marital status, at least in the jurisdiction where it is made, cannot with decency be left married in one part of the world and unmarried in another.[6] Although

---

1 At p. 530 of *Warrender* v. *Warrender* (1835), 2 Cl. & Fin. 488: "they"—the courts of this country—"can hardly be said to act from courtesy, *ex comitate*, but *ex debito justitiae*, and in order to explicate their own jurisdiction by discovering that which they are in quest of, and which alone they are in quest of, the meaning and intent of the parties".

2 At p. 159 of *Schibsby* v. *Westenholz* (1870), L.R. 6 Q.B. 155.

3 *Ibid.* *Cp.* his observations to the same effect at p. 140 of *Godard* v. *Gray* (1870), L.R. 6 Q.B. 139.

4 For the views of a more modern critic of "international comity" as the foundation of the recognition of foreign judgments, see the judgment of DIPLOCK J. in *Blohn* v. *Desser*, [1962] 2 Q.B. 116 at p. 123.

5 1st edn. p. 40.

6 This conclusion appears to be supported by the reasoning of Lord GREENE M.R. in *Baindail (otherwise Lawson)* v. *Baindail*, [1946] 1 All E.R. 342, C.A. at p. 347, ("Is it right that the courts of this country should give effect to a ceremony of marriage the result of which is to put the

such an unfortunate state of affairs must sometimes still be the ultimate result, for reasons so sound as to transcend the principle of convenience, yet there remains a great residuary group of cases in which convenience appears to be the ultimately prevailing consideration. It is now long since it became a commonplace of our divorce courts to accept the decisions of the courts of the jurisdiction where the parties are domiciled; but this has in recent times been extended so as to include the acceptance in England of decrees made in a jurisdiction in which the parties are not domiciled, but in circumstances which, if obtaining in this country, would persuade an English court to accept jurisdiction. More lately still it has been proposed to accept the decision of a Court of the jurisdiction whereof the parties are nationals.[1]

69 A "foreign" decision for the purposes of the rule as to the conclusiveness of foreign *res judicatae*, includes not only a decision of any judicial tribunal which is "foreign" in the popular sense of the word, but also that of any tribunal which, though within the British Commonwealth, is outside the English jurisdiction in its most strict and limited sense.[2] So,

---

respondent into such a position? It seems to me that effect must be given to common sense and decency"). *Cf.* DAVIES L.J. in *Russ (otherwise Geffers)* v. *Russ*, [1962] 3 All E.R. 193, C.A. at p. 204; and DIPLOCK L.J. in *Indyka* v. *Indyka*, [1966] 3 All E.R. 583, at p. 587 "It is, I apprehend, a well-established principle of public policy applied by English courts that, so far as it lies within their power to ensure it, the status of a person as married or single should be the same in every country which he visits, that is, that there should not be "limping marriages"; and if marriages are to be dissoluble at all, this involves deciding what courts we should recognise as having jurisdiction to dissolve them." And again on the same page; "Because the criteria adopted by the civilised countries of the world as the basis of their jurisdiction to dissolve marriages are so varied, there is no general rule of "comity" under which the courts of each country recognise the validity of decrees of dissolution of marriage pronounced by the courts of other countries. "Comity", at any rate in its strict sense, affords no guide as to the foreign courts whose jurisdiction to dissolve a particular marriage the English courts should recognise." *Cf.* the judgments in the House of Lords on appeal in the same case: [1967] 2 All E.R. 689, and particularly that of Lord PEARCE.

[1] *Indyka* v. *Indyka*, [1967] 2 All E.R. 689, H.L.

[2] In the first edition of this work, written before either the Statute of Westminster or the World War of 1939–45, there is a lengthy excursus, here omitted, to which footnotes exhibited numerous decisions in which it has been held, or the opinion has been expressed, that courts of different countries, within and without the British family of nations, are "foreign" courts for the purposes of this rule. Instances which may still be relevant are: (a) *Scotland*: *Houlditch* v. *Marquess of Donegal* (1834), 2 Cl. & Fin. 470; *Harvey* v. *Farnie* (1882), 8 App. Cas. 43, H.L. at p. 50. *Cf. Re Low, Bland* v. *Low*, [1894] 1 Ch. 147 C.A.; *Marchioness Huntley* v. *Gaskell* (1905), 2 Ch. 656; *Re a Bankruptcy Notice*, [1898] 1 Q.B. 383, C.A., (b) the *Isle of Man*: *Harris* v. *Quine* (1869), L.R. 4 Q.B. 653; *Harris* v. *Taylor*, [1915] 2 K.B. 580 (action on Manx judgment), (c) as to *British Colonies* the following cases are exhibited with annotations in a footnote in the first edition, but are here merely enumerated: *Houlditch* v. *Marquess of Donegal* (1834), 2 Cl. & Fin. 470; *Plummer* v. *Woodburne* (1825), 4 B. & C. 625; *Farquharson* v. *Seton* (1828), 5 Russ 45; *Henderson* v. *Henderson* (1843), 3 Hare 100; *Hunter* v. *Stewart* (1861) 4 De G.F. & J. 168; *Brasyer* v. *Maclean* (1875), L.R. 6 P.C. 398; *Caine* v. *Palace S.S. Co.*, [1907] 1 K.B. 670, C.A.; *Hutton* v. *Ras S.S. Co.*, [1907] 1 K.B. 834 C.A. The following cases were also enumerated in which Colonial judgments had been held conclusive when sued upon, or, if the action failed, the failure was due to some defect in proof independent of the circumstance that the decision was that of a

a fortiori, is a decision of a consular or other court exercising jurisdiction in a foreign state pursuant to a treaty between the states concerned,[1] and an award of a foreign domestic tribunal, if and when it has become enforceable according to the law of the state in which it was made.[2]

The court whose judgment is set up need not be the court of a Sovereign state, but may be the court of a member of a federation of states subject to a common rule—*e.g.* a court of one of the states of the United States of America, as distinct from the Federal Court of that country,[3] or a court of one of the States of Australia.[4]

70 It is scarcely necessary to add that any alleged foreign decision, if it is to have the same effect by way of estoppel as an English decision, must possess the same general characteristics as are required, in the latter case, to constitute it a decision at all in contemplation of law. Whenever any of these constituent elements has been wanting, the alleged foreign decision has been held wholly inefficacious for purposes of *res judicata*.[5]

71 It is proposed now to consider certain classes of foreign judicial decisions which, by way of exception to the general rule, are held inoperative, not only as estoppels, but even as *prima facie* evidence.

---

colonial court: *Walker* v. *Witter* (1778), 1 Doug. K.B. 1; *Galbraith* v. *Neville* (1789), 1 Doug. K.B. 6 n; *Sadler* v. *Robins* (1808), 1 Camp. 253 (but here the action failed, because the colonial judgment was not final); *Buchanan* v. *Rucker* (1808), 9 East 192 (but here held that the colonial court had no jurisdiction); *Hall* v. *Odber* (1809), 11 East 118; *Appleton* v. *Lord Braybrook* (1816), 2 Stark. 6 (where the action failed, but only because no proper proof of the record); *Henley* v. *Soper* (1828), 8 B. & C. 16; *Martin* v. *Nicolls* (1830), 3 Sim. 458; *Becquet* v. *MacCarthy* (1831), 2 B. & Ad. 951; *Obicini* v. *Bligh* (1832), 8 Bing. 335 (here action failed, because no jurisdiction over the party, and decision not final); *Robertson* v. *Struth* (1844), 5 Q.B. 941; *Henderson* v. *Henderson* (1844), 6 Q.B. 288; *Bank of Australasia* v. *Harding* (1850), 9 C.B. 661; *Bank of Australasia* v. *Nias* (1851), 16 Q.B. 717; *Frith* v. *Wollaston* (1852), 21 L.J. Ex. 108; *Ellis* v. *M'Henry* (1871), L.R. 6 C.P. 228; *Emanuel* v. *Symon*, [1908] 1 K.B. 302, C.A. (but here no jurisdiction over party, and action failed on that ground); *Gavin Gibson & Co., Ltd.* v. *Gibson*, [1913] 3 K.B. 379 (the like); *Robinson* v. *Fenner*, [1913] 3 K.B. 835.

[1] See *Dent* v. *Smith* (1869), L.R. 4 Q.B. 414 (Russian Consular Court at Constantinople); *Messina* v. *Petrococchino* (1872), L.R. 4 P.C. 144 (Greek Consular Court at Constantinople). And, for a case of a foreign court martial by treaty exercising jurisdiction in a foreign State over British subjects, see *R.* v. *Aughet* (1918), 13 Cr. App. Rep. 101, at pp. 103, 109.

[2] In *Merrifield, Ziegler & Co.* v. *Liverpool Cotton Association* (1911), 105 L.T. 97, EVE J. held, at pp. 103–105, that the award of the Bremen Cotton Association was absolutely binding on the parties as against the plaintiff's claim for a declaration that it was invalid, and, though he dismissed the defendant's counter-claim on the award, this was solely on the ground that, on the evidence, the award was shown not to have been final (pp. 105, 106). As to awards of colonial arbitrators, see s. 12 of the Administration of Justice Act 1920.

[3] As, the courts of the state of New York in *Colt Industries Inc.* v. *Sarlie* (*No.* 2), [1966] 3 All E.R. 85, C.A. per Lord DENNING M.R. at p. 87: "The relevant territory here is the State of New York".

[4] *E.g. Travers* v. *Holley*, [1953] 2 All E.R. 794; [1953] P. 264 C.A. (Supreme Court of New South Wales).

[5] As in *Price* v. *Dewhurst* (1838), 4 My. & Cr. 76; *Fracis, Times & Co.* v. *Carr* (1900), 82 L.T. 698, C.A. at pp. 701, 702. In *Carl-Zeiss-Stiftung* v. *Rayner and Keeler, Ltd.* (*No.* 2), [1967] A.C. 853; [1966] 2 All E.R. 536, the plea failed for lack of identity of parties, and, independently, because it was not shown that the foreign judgment was final and conclusive.

Penal judgments

72 In the first place, an exception is created by the long-established rule that "the Courts of no country execute the penal laws of another". As stated in a weighty judgment of the Privy Council, founded largely on judicial pronouncements of Chief Justice MARSHALL in the Supreme Court of the United States, "the rule has its foundation in the well-recognized principle that crimes, including in that term all branches of public law punishable by pecuniary mulct or otherwise, at the instance of the State Government, or of some one representing the public, are local in this sense, that they are only cognizable and punishable in the country where they were committed. Accordingly, no proceeding, even in the shape of a civil suit, which has for its object the enforcement by the State, whether directly or indirectly, of punishment imposed for such breaches by the *lex fori*, ought to be admitted in the Courts of any other country"[1], unless (it should be added) it be so provided by express treaty between the States concerned.[2] It is a corollary from this leading proposition that any decision of a foreign tribunal as to a purely local disqualification, or diminution of the status, of a subject of the foreign State is equally inoperative as an estoppel.[3] But the expressions "penal" and "penalty" when employed without qualification may be misleading. On the one hand, they may lead to too narrow a construction, for "penal" in this connotation has a wider sense than "punitive".[4] A judgment which has a restrictive effect—one whose effect is to alter the status of a party so as to "deprive him of a very valuable right" may be regarded as "penal" for the purposes of this rule. On the other hand the use of the word may lead to too wide a construction. For it might too easily be thought that the rule extends to "all proceedings for the recovery of penalties, whether exigible by the state in the interests of the community or claimed by private persons in their own interests", and it must also be remembered that "a proceeding, in order to come within the scope of the rule"—as to the purely local effect of penal decisions—

---

1 *Huntington* v. *Attrill*, [1893] A.C. 150, P.C. at pp. 156–157.

2 As in *R.* v. *Aughet* (1918), 13 Cr. App. Rep. 101.

3 *Worms* v. *De Valdor* (1880), 49 L.J. Ch. 261 (per FRY J., at pp. 261, 262); *Re Selot's Trust*, [1902] 1 Ch. 488 (per FARWELL J., at p. 492: "where the disability or the disqualification in question arises from the principles or customs or positive law of a foreign country, especially of a penal nature, it is not regarded by this court"). Both these cases related to the status of a "prodigue", and his adjudication as such by a French court. They were both referred to, and followed, by BUCKLEY J. in the Chancery Division, and by the Court of Appeal in affirming his decision, in *In re Langley's Settlement Trusts, Lloyds Bank Ltd.* v. *Langley*, [1961] 1 All E.R. 78; on appeal, [1962] 1 Ch. 541. There the order which the court refused to recognise in England was one of the Superior Court of California depriving a person, by reason of his physical, but not mental ailments, of contractual capacity.

4 Per BUCKLEY J. in *In re Langley's Settlement Trusts, Lloyds Bank Ltd.* v. *Langley*, [1961] 1 All E.R. 78 at p. 81. The judgment was affirmed on appeal: [1962] 1 Ch. 541. At p. 557 Lord EVERSHED M.R. gives some consideration to what "penal" means in this connection.

"must be in the nature of a suit in favour of the state whose law has been infringed. All the provisions of municipal statutes for the regulation of trade and trading companies are presumably enacted in the interest and for the benefit of the community at large; and persons who violate these provisions are, in a certain sense, offenders against the State law, as well as against individuals who may be injured by their misconduct. But foreign tribunals do not regard these violations of statute law as offences against the state, unless their vindication rests with the State itself, or with the community which it represents. Penalties may be attached to them, but that circumstance will not bring them within the rules, except in cases where these penalties are recoverable at the instance of the State, or of an official duly authorized to prosecute on its behalf, or of a member of the public in the character of a common informer. An action by the latter is regarded as an *actio popularis* pursued, not in his individual interest, but in the interest of the whole community".[1]

If the proceeding is in part "penal" in the above sense, and in part not, and if the penal is severable from the non-penal part, the foreign decision on the latter is conclusive, and, on the former, is not.[2] It is for the English court, and not for the foreign tribunal, to determine all questions as to the penal or non-penal character of the foreign decision relied upon.[3]

Judgments in aid of foreign revenue

73 It is submitted that a similar rule will apply to prevent an estoppel arising in respect of a foreign judgment whose effect is to enforce payment of revenue to a foreign state. It has long been settled that a claim by a foreign government for revenue will not be entertained in an English court,[4] and at least since the decision of the House of Lords in *Indian*

---

1 *Huntington* v. *Attrill*, [1893] A.C. 150, P.C. at pp. 156–8.

2 *Raulin* v. *Fischer*, [1911] 2 K.B. 93. This was an action on a French judgment in a proceeding of a criminal nature ("action publique") for reckless riding. In such criminal proceedings, however, French law allows the person injured to intervene as a "tiers partie", and to institute a claim for relief ("action civile") against the wrongdoer. The plaintiff in this case had so intervened, and had recovered damages, for which he now sued. HAMILTON J., at pp. 97–99, held that such a decision, if severable from the criminal decision, could be sued upon in this country, and, at pp. 99, 100, that in this case it was so severable.

3 *Huntington* v. *Attrill*, *supra.*, at p. 155; *Raulin* v. *Fischer*, *supra.*, per HAMILTON J., at p. 97. It appears from pp. 98, 99 of the report of the latter case that HAMILTON J. received, and acted upon, the evidence of experts in French law on the question.

4 "No country ever takes notice of the revenue laws of another", said Lord MANSFIELD in *Holman* v. *Johnson* (1775), 1 Cowp. 341 at p. 343; and he repeated this same observation in *Planche* v. *Fletcher* (1779), 1 Dougl. K.B. 251, at p. 253. These statements were *obiter*, but appear to have been accepted without question ever since as an authoritative statement of the law. "It has been settled, or at least considered as settled, ever since the time of Lord Hardwicke, that in a British court we cannot take notice of the revenue laws of a foreign state"—per ABBOTT C.J. (afterwards Lord TENTERDEN) in *James* v. *Catherwood* (1823), 3 Dow. & Ry. K.B. 190, at

Government v. *Taylor*[1] it has been apparent that even a judgment obtained abroad for a sum due by way of revenue will receive no recognition in this jurisdiction.[2]

Judgments outside the jus gentium

74 On the same principle foreign decisions on other matters which do not form part of the subject of the *jus gentium*, or of what may be called the accepted common law of nations, have no conclusiveness or currency in our courts. Thus, it was laid down by the Privy Council, in the case already referred to, again adopting the language of the Supreme Court of the United States, that "the rule that the courts of no country execute the law of another applies not only to prosecutions and sentences for crimes and misdemeanours, but to all suits in favour of the State for the recovery of pecuniary penalties for any violation of statutes for the protection of its revenue or other municipal laws, and to all judgments for such penalties".[3] So too, perhaps, in cases of civil liability pursuant to foreign statutes of purely local and domestic application.[4] Further, as stated by Dr Story in

---

p. 191. *Cf.* the judgment of TOMLIN J. in *Re Visser, Queen of Holland* v. *Drukker*, [1928] Ch. 877, at p. 883. Perhaps the first direct authority was *Sydney Municipal Council* v. *Bull*, [1909] 1 K.B. 7 (GRANTHAM J.).

[1] [1955] A.C. 491, H.L.

[2] *Indian Government* v. *Taylor* (*supra*), per Lord SIMONDS at p. 506. Lord SIMONDS regarded it as "axiomatic that the courts of one country do not regard the revenue laws of another, and therefore will not allow judgments for foreign taxes to be enforced". And he again adverted to the same topic in *Regazzoni* v. *K. C. Sethia* (1944), *Ltd.*, [1958] A.C. 301, H.L. at p. 318 when he said that *Indian Government* v. *Taylor* (*supra*) "shows beyond all doubt that an English court will not enforce the penal or revenue laws of another country at the suit of that country". *Cf. Peter Buchanan, Ltd. and McHarg* v. *McVey*, a decision of KINGSMILL MOORE J. in the High Court of Eire, approved by the Court of Appeal of Eire and reported in a note in [1955] A.C. 516 *et seq.* It was not reported in the Eire Reports, but received the commendation of Lord KEITH in the *Government of India* case at p. 510. At p. 526 it was said that "the courts of our country (Eire) will not enforce the revenue claims of a foreign country. . . . and even if a judgment for a foreign penalty or debt be obtained in the country in which it is incurred, it is not possible successfully to sue in this country on such judgment". *Cf.* the provisions of the Foreign Judgments (Reciprocal Enforcement) Act 1933, s. 2 (1) (b).

[3] *Huntington* v. *Attrill*, [1893] A.C. 150, P.C. at p. 157.

[4] *Re Macartney, Macfarlane* v. *Macartney*, [1921] 1 Ch. 522. This decision was severely criticised in the first edition of this work, in a special Appendix which has been omitted from this edition. The decision has not been overruled since Mr Spencer Bower wrote, and it appears to be accepted without undue reservation by the editors of the *Supreme Court Practice*, who write (1967 volume at p. 37) that the general principle is that "only judgments that rest upon principles of universal acceptation will be enforced". Some interesting observations on this or a closely cognate topic will be found in the judgments of the Court of Appeal in *British Nylon Spinners, Ltd.* v. *Imperial Chemical Industries, Ltd.*, [1953] Ch. 19. The case was not one of *res judicata*, but involved a consideration of the sort of conditions under which an English court would decline to recognise the validity of a foreign judgment, or the jurisdiction of the foreign court to make a decree. A sentence from the judgment of Sir RAYMOND EVERSHED M.R. may be cited, from p. 27: "I think it undesirable to say more, except to reaffirm the proposition that the courts of this country will, in the natural course pay great respect and attention to the superior courts of the United States of America, but I conceive that it is none the less the proper province of these courts,

his *Conflict of Laws*, in a passage which has been judicially adopted in our jurisprudence,[1] "personal disqualifications not arising from the Law of Nature, but from the principles and customary law of a foreign country, . . . are not generally regarded in other countries where the like disqualifications do not exist; hence the disqualifications resulting from heresy, excommunication, Popish recusancy, infamy and other penal disabilities, are not enforced in any other country except that in which they originate. They are strictly territorial, as the state of slavery will not be recognized in any country whose institutions and policy prohibit slavery".[2]

It may here be noticed that by the provision for the registration of foreign judgments contained in section 9 of the Administration of Justice Act 1920 it is especially directed that such a judgment may not be registered "if the judgment was in respect of a cause of action which, for reasons of public policy, or for some other similar reason, could not have been entertained by the registering court".

Foreign law a question of fact

75 Questions of foreign law are questions of fact, with this exception, that, in cases tried by a jury in England, it is provided by statute that any

---

when their jurisdiction is invoked, not to refrain from using that jurisdiction if they think it is their duty to do so for the protection of *rights which are peculiarly subject to the protection of the English courts*".

In a recent decision of the Court of Appeal—*In re Langley's Settlement Trusts, Lloyds Bank Ltd.* v. *Langley*, [1962] 1 Ch. 541—the Court of Appeal upheld a decision of BUCKLEY J. in which ([1961] 1 All E.R. 78) he had refused to recognise an order of the Superior Court of the State of California depriving the defendant of contractual capacity in that State. BUCKLEY J. held the order to be a "penal" one (see para. 72, *ante*); in the Court of Appeal the Lords Justices were not so positive about this, and while DANCKWERTS L.J. (at p. 560) was content to rest his decision on this ground, Lord EVERSHED M.R. at p. 557) preferred the ground afforded by the principle expounded in this para. of the text, while DONOVAN L.J. said plainly at p. 558: "From start to finish there is no reason, either in law or in equity, for depriving him of the valuable right which is his . . .", and later on the same page held that "*in the exercise of its discretion* the court should not in this case recognise the foreign status of incompetence."

[1] See para. 104 of Dr Story's treatise, cited, and approved, as part of the law of England, in *Worms* v. *De Valdor* (1880), 49 L.J. Ch. 261 (per FRY J., at p. 262); *Re Selot's Trust*, [1902] 1 Ch. 488 (per FARWELL J., at p. 492).

[2] Mr Spencer Bower's text proceeds: "Nor will the slightest effect or recognition be given in the courts of this country to foreign decision which are based upon, or pre-suppose, the validity of institutions or relations which are repugnant to the commonly-accepted principles and cardinal doctrines of Christendom, such as polygamy, or the dissolubility of marriage at the will and by the domestic sentence, of one of the spouses", and cites *R.* v. *Hammersmith Superintendent Registrar of Marriages, Ex parte Mir-Anwaruddin*, [1917] 1 K.B. 634, C.A. as his authority. But this decision has been by-passed on its special facts in later judgments, and it now appears clear that its true basis was that there was no judicial proceeding upon which the divorce therein set up could be said to be founded—see *Russ* v. *Russ (otherwise Geffers)*, [1962] 3 All E.R. 193 per WILLMER L.J. at p. 197. In the light of this decision Mr Spencer Bower's original text can hardly any longer be supported: *cf. Baindail (otherwise Lawson)* v. *Baindail*, [1946] 1 All E.R. 342; [1946] P. 122.

question as to the effect of the evidence given with respect to the law of any other country, applicable to the facts of the case, shall, instead of being submitted to the jury, be decided by the judge alone.[1] It follows that (except as stated) any question as to a foreign *res judicata* is one of fact, to be established by evidence, in the same way as any other issue of fact. Accordingly, the following have been held to be issues of fact, not of law: any question as to whether the foreign decision relied upon answers to the legal definition of a judicial decision, or as to whether there was any jurisdiction, in accordance with the law of the foreign state, to pronounce it;[2] or as to the operation and effect of a foreign decision, and as to its quality or class, for instance, whether it is regarded by the law of the foreign state as *in rem* or *inter partes* only,[3] final or interlocutory,[4] civil or criminal;[5] or as to the effect of an adjudication of personal disability, as in the case of a "prodigue" in French law;[6] or as to whether the judgment relied upon

---

[1] Supreme Court of Judicature (Consolidation) Act 1925, s. 102; County Courts Act 1934, s. 94. *Cf.* in New Zealand Judicature Amendment Act 1935, s. 4.

[2] See *Price* v. *Dewhurst* (1837), 8 Sim. 279 (per SHADWELL V.C., at p. 305), and, on appeal, (1838), 4 My. & Cr. 76 (per Lord COTTENHAM L.C., at p. 85), where evidence of practitioners in Danish law was received as to the alleged judicial functions of persons appointed as "incassators" or guardians by a will, with the result that the so-called "court" was found, as a fact, either not to constitute a judicial tribunal at all, or in any event, not to have any jurisdiction over the parties; *Fracis, Times & Co.* v. *Carr* (1900), 82 L.T. 698, C.A. (per VAUGHAN WILLIAMS L.J., at pp. 701, 702, who there pointed out that it was a question of fact to be established by evidence, whether the "inquiry" and "report" of persons appointed by the Sultan of Muscat were of a judicial nature or not); *R.* v. *Aughet* (1918) 13 Cr. App. Rep. 101, where evidence was received in the Criminal Court of Appeal as to the jurisdiction of a Belgian court martial to convict the prisoner of a lesser offence than that charged (*per Cur.*, at p. 107).

[3] *Castrique* v. *Imrie* (1870), L.R. 4 H.L. 414 (per Lord HATHERLEY L.C., at p. 443, and BLACKBURN J., at pp. 427, 429, 430, on behalf of the judges summoned to advise the House), as to the nature and effect of proceedings in a French court, and the determination of that court, in reference to a vessel; *Re Macartney, Macfarlane* v. *Macartney*, [1921] 1 Ch. 522 (French affiliation order: see pp. 523, 524, 526).

[4] See para. 178, *post*, and, particularly, *Nouvion* v. *Freeman* (1889), 15 App. Cas. 1, H.L. (per Lord HERSCHELL at pp. 6, 7); *Bouchet* v. *Tulledge* (1894), 11 T.L.R. 87 (per COLLINS J., at p. 88); *Merrifield, Ziegler & Co.* v. *Liverpool Cotton Association* (1911), 105 L.T. 97 (per EVE J. at pp. 105, 106); *Re Macartney, Macfarlane* v. *Macartney*, *supra*. In *Obicini* v. *Bligh* (1832), 8 Bing. 335, no evidence being offered as to the effect of the decision, the court could only infer the effect from the document itself, which, on the face of it, did not purport to be final. In *Carl-Zeiss-Stiftung* v. *Rayner and Keeler, Ltd.*, (*No.* 2), [1966] 2 All E.R. 536, H.L. the question of onus of proof was sharply posed in several of the judgments: see per Lord REID at p. 556; per Lord HODSON at p. 560; per Lord WILBERFORCE at p. 588.

[5] *Raulin* v. *Fischer*, [1911] 2 K.B. 93 (per HAMILTON J., at pp. 97–99), where it was held that the questions whether the foreign decision was of a civil or of a criminal character, or partly civil and partly criminal, and, in that case, whether the one part could be severed from the other, were, as already decided in *Huntington* v. *Attrill*, [1893] A.C. 150, P.C. (at pp. 155, 161), held to be questions for the English, and not for the foreign, court to determine, with the assistance, if necessary, of expert evidence, which, in fact, was resorted to by HAMILTON J. in that case, and without being in the least degree bound by any judicial opinions of the foreign tribunal.

[6] *Worms* v. *De Valdor* (1880), 49 L.J. Ch. 261 (per FRY J., at p. 262); *Re Selot's Trust*, [1902] 1 Ch. 488 (per FARWELL J., at p. 492). *Cf. In re Langley's Settlement Trusts, Lloyds Bank Ltd.* v. *Langley*, [1961] 1 All E.R. 78 where BUCKLEY J. had proved before him Californian law on a similar topic.

operates by the foreign law against the person, or the estate only, of the judgment debtor;[1] or as to how far the decision of one State in a foreign union of states is recognized by another state of that union;[2] or as to the effect of a foreign decision with respect to domicil according to the law of the State in which the foreign judgment was pronounced;[3] or as to the prerequisites of a valid sentence of divorce in the foreign state;[4] also any question as to the practice and procedure of the foreign tribunal, with reference to such matters as service of process,[5] rules of evidence,[6] or conditional appearance in an action;[7] and, lastly, where not ascertainable on the face of the proceedings, any question as to the grounds on which the foreign decision was based.[8] All such issues, like any other issue of fact, must be established by the appropriate—that is, the best,—evidence, which, in the case of foreign decisions, as in any other case of foreign law, will generally be the testimony of *jurisperiti*, not of *jurisprudentes*,—that is, of experts engaged in the actual practice of the law in question, not the treatises of jurists, however authoritative, except as expounded and illustrated orally by such experts.[9]

---

[1] *Re Low, Bland* v. *Low*, [1894] 1 Ch. 147, C.A., where the foreign (Scottish) judgment was proved, as a fact, to have the effect of operating on the party's assets only, and not on the party personally.

[2] *Armitage* v. *A.-G.*, [1906] P. 135 (per GORELL BARNES, P., at pp. 140, 141); *Cass* v. *Cass (otherwise Pfaff)* (1910), 102 L.T. 397 (per BIGHAM P., at p. 398).

[3] *Bater* v. *Bater*, [1906] P. 209, C.A. (per GORELL BARNES P., at pp. 213–217, COLLINS M.R., at p. 227, ROMER L.J., at pp. 233, 234, and COZENS-HARDY L.J., at p. 238).

[4] *Harris* v. *Taylor* (1914), 111 L.T. 564, per BRAY J., at p. 568, whose decision was affirmed by the C.A., [1915] 2 K.B. 580, C.A.

[5] See *Buchanan* v. *Rucker* (1808), 9 East 192; *Douglas* v. *Forrest* (1828), 4 Bing. 686; *Schibsby* v. *Westenholz* (1870), L.R. 6 Q.B. 155 (per BLACKBURN J., delivering the judgment of the Court, at p. 157); *Bergerem* v. *Marsh* (1921), 125 L.T. 630.

[6] *Scarpetta* v. *Lowenfeld* (1911), 27 T.L.R. 509, as to a rule of the Italian courts, excluding the evidence of the parties themselves, similar to that which prevailed in our jurisprudence until the middle of the 19th century. In *Robinson* v. *Fenner*, [1913] 3 K.B. 835, a rule of evidence in the Canadian courts justifying the rejection of certain testimony was "presumed" by CHANNELL J., at pp. 842–845, to exist, and to have been followed, but this was only because nobody seems to have disputed it.

[7] *Harris* v. *Taylor* (1914), 111 L.T. 564, per BRAY J., at p. 568, whose decision was affirmed, [1915] 2 K.B. 580, C.A.

[8] *Harris* v. *Quine* (1869), L.R. 4 Q.B. 653.

[9] *Re Selot's Trust*, [1902] 1 Ch. 488, per FARWELL J., at p. 492, disagreeing with the course adopted by FRY J. in *Worms* v. *De Valdor* (1880), 49 L.J. Ch. 261, who, though considering the similar question then before him to be one of fact, was content to rely, for evidence of the fact, solely upon works of authority in French law. But in *Brailey* v. *Rhodesia Consolidated, Ltd.*, [1910] 2 Ch. 95 WARRINGTON J. at p. 102 admitted the evidence of one who, though not residing in Rhodesia, was Reader in Roman-Dutch Law for the Incorporated Council of Legal Education, to prove Rhodesian law; and in *F. & K. Jabbour* v. *Custodian of Israeli Absentee Property* [1954] 1 W.L.R. 139 PEARSON J. came to his conclusion as to the law of Israel without the assistance of any expert at all; but counsel on both sides had agreed to this rather unusual course, the validity of which is discussed at page 147 of the judgment. See, further, *Perlak Petroleum Maatschappij* v. *Deen*, [1924] 1 K.B. 111, C.A. per SCRUTTON L.J., at p. 116. In *In re Langley's*

76 It should be noted here that the decision of a foreign court on any question of English law must be regarded as a foreign decision of fact, and, therefore, any misinterpretation or misapplication of English law by such foreign court can no more be impeached in our courts, when the decision is relied upon as a *res judicata*, than any other error of fact.[1]

Actions on judicial decisions

77 A judicial decision is, as has already been pointed out, conclusive when made the foundation of an action, no less than when it is set up as a bar. This conclusiveness of a judgment, when sued upon, may in the case of all judgments, English or foreign, be regarded as a manifestation of the principle of estoppel *per rem judicatam*; and in the case of an English (not a foreign) judgment it would seem equally to be a consequence of the principle of merger. The original cause of action being extinguished, and merged in the judgment, it is no longer relevant to question its merits, for *transiit in rem judicatam*; all that remains is the judgment, and no question of merit is left to be the subject of inquiry.

78 But it must be remembered that it is not every judicial decision which can be sued upon, and, obviously, where an action will not lie at all, no question of conclusiveness or estoppel will arise. It is necessary, therefore, to consider this question, and the common law and statutory rules relating thereto, as they affect, (a) judgments of English superior courts, (b) judgments of English inferior Courts, (c) orders of English superior courts, (d) orders of English inferior courts, (e) decisions of English domestic tribunals, and (f) foreign judicial decisions.

(*a*) *Actions on judgments of English superior courts*

79 One would suppose that *prima facie* any action on a judgment of an English superior court would be deemed such an abuse of the process, and so oppressive to the party, as to justify the prohibition of all such actions without special leave for good cause shown. But, as a matter of fact and history, it is not so. The general rule at common law has from the earliest times been, and still is, that an action will lie in an English superior court on a judgment of any such court, and the burden has always been on the defendant to show cause why in his case there should be an exception

---

Settlement Trusts, Lloyds Bank Ltd. v. *Langley*, [1961] 1 All E.R. 78 BUCKLEY J. received (p. 80) an affidavit by a Californian lawyer as to the legal effect in California of the order which was before the Court.

[1] Per BLACKBURN J., at p. 151 of *Godard* v. *Gray* (1870), L.R. 6 Q.B. 139.

to this general rule.[1] Illustrations of such actions are to be found in abundance.[2]

80 It is true that, by statute and otherwise, the party who unnecessarily and vexatiously sues on a judgment of an English superior court may be penalised in costs. Thus, by section 4 of the statute 43 Geo. 3, c. 46, it was provided that in an action on the judgment of any such court, the plaintiff, if successful, shall recover no costs, unless the judge thinks fit to so order.[3] But this statute clearly recognised the right of the party to sue upon the judgment, subject only to the risk of such deprivation of costs.[4] It has now been repealed, presumably because it was deemed unnecessary having regard to the much wider and more general discretion over costs, even in cases tried by a judge and jury, which is vested in the Supreme Court by the Judicature Acts, but the technical right to sue on the judgment still remains, and is recognised.[5]

81 It is submitted that at the present day there is no distinction between the judgment of a superior court of common law, and any other superior court, for the purpose of founding an action thereon. It is true that judicial opinions, to the effect that the decrees or judgments of a superior Court of Equity cannot be sued upon in a court of law, were in the last century pronounced by ABBOTT C.J., in a case of specific performance

---

1 Per Lord CAMPBELL C.J., at p. 807 of *Berkeley* v. *Elderkin* (1853), 1 E. & B. 805 ("*prima facie*, an action lies on the judgment of any court of competent jurisdiction"), and BRAMWELL B., at p. 815 of *Hutchinson* v. *Gillespie* (1856), 11 Exch. 798 ("I am not aware of any cases, except those of decrees in equity and judgments in county courts, in which it has been held that no action will lie upon the final order or judgment of a court for payment of a sum of money").

2 See, amongst others, *Erving* v. *Peters* (1790), 3 Term Rep. 685; *Mason* v. *Nicholls* (1845), 14 M. & W. 118; *Hebblethwaite* v. *Peever*, [1892] 1 Q.B. 124; *Jay* v. *Johnstone*, [1893] 1 Q.B. 189, C.A.; *Taylor* v. *Hollard*, [1902] 1 K.B. 676; *Shaw* v. *Allen* (1914), 30 T.L.R. 631.

3 Accordingly, the plaintiff was deprived of his costs, pursuant to this section, in *Mason* v. *Nicholls*, *supra*: *cf.* in the cognate case of *Pritchett* v. *English and Colonial Syndicate*, [1899] 2 Q.B. 428 C.A. where LINDLEY M.R. said of an action on a garnishee order: "If a person who has obtained a garnishee order brings an action upon it without any necessity he will run the risk of having it stayed as an abuse of the process of the court, and probably have to pay the costs".

4 See the judgment of the Court of Exchequer, at p. 119 of *Mason* v. *Nicholls*, *supra*: "the creditor clearly had a *right*, notwithstanding the Act, to bring an action on the judgment in the previous action, taking his risk of losing his costs in the present action, which the court was not in the practice of giving".

5 The statute of Geo. III was repealed by the Statute Law Revision Act 1890. The general discretion of the courts over costs, in virtue of the Judicature Acts, enables the judge, if he thinks fit, to order the plaintiff to pay the defendant's costs, and not merely to deprive him of his own costs, which was all that he could do under the repealed statute. In *Shaw* v. *Allen*, *supra*, at p. 632, LUSH J., in depriving the plaintiff of his costs, considered whether he ought further to make him pay the defendant's costs, and, though he decided that, in the circumstances of the case, he clearly ought not to take this course, it was not suggested by any one that he had not full discretion to do so, if he thought fit.

which at that date no court of common law could enforce,[1] by BRAMWELL B.,[2] and by BRETT M.R.;[3] but in recent times, when every court of law, within certain limits, is also a court of equity, the ground of these opinions —the then essential distinction between common law and equitable remedies—has disappeared, and, with it, the opinions themselves, which are no longer acted upon.[4]

82 If an action may be brought in a superior court on a judgment of any court of equally high degree, it follows *a fortiori* that an action will lie in an inferior court on a superior court judgment, subject to the like conditions and penalties as to costs and otherwise, except where expressly prohibited by statute. There is such an express statutory provision as regards county courts, whereby it is enacted that no action may be brought therein on any judgment of the High Court,[5] or even on any judgment of a county court which has been removed by *certiorari*, for the purposes of execution, into the High Court.[6]

(*b*) *Actions on judgments of English inferior courts*

83 At common law, there is no distinction for present purposes between judgments of an English superior court, and those of an English inferior court, or between judgments of a court of record and those of other courts. It has been distinctly held, or judicially recognised, that an action will lie on the judgment of any court of competent jurisdiction, of however humble a degree, under the same conditions, and subject to the

---

[1] At p. 55 of *Carpenter* v. *Thornton* (1819), 3 B. & Ald. 52, which was a suit in the K.B. on a decree of a court of equity for specific performance of an agreement to purchase an estate for £5500, and payment of the purchase money and the interest thereon computed by the Master in Chancery, whose report had been adopted by the Vice-Chancellor, and the taxed costs of the suit. The passage referred to runs as follows: "under the special circumstances of this case, I am at a loss to find anything like an implied contract. If there were merely a bill filed for an account, and, upon the balance, a precise sum of money was found to be due, which might originally have formed the subject of an action at law, a court of law might perhaps in that case have lent its aid to enforce such a decree. Here, however, it appeared by the declaration that the testator filed his bill for the specific performance of an agreement for the purchase of an estate, and the Vice-Chancellor decreed that the agreement should be specifically performed, and ordered that it should be referred to a Master in Chancery to compute the interest on £5500, or the residue of the purchase money, and to tax the plaintiff's costs". So BAYLEY J., at p. 56, said that "an action in a court of law must be on a legal obligation to pay, and the decree of a court of equity creates no such obligation". And to the same effect, HOLROYD and BEST JJ., at p. 58.

[2] In *Hutchinson* v. *Gillespie* (1856), 11 Exch. 798, at p. 815 ("for there is no implied promise to pay a mere equitable debt").

[3] In *Bailey* v. *Bailey* (1884), 13 Q.B.D. 855, C.A., at p. 859. *Cp.* BOWEN and FRY L.JJ., at p. 860.

[4] See *Seldon* v. *Wilde*, [1911] 1 K.B. 701, C.A., where a judgment of NEVILLE J. was successfully sued upon.

[5] County Courts Act 1934, s. 68. But by s. 39 of the Administration of Justice Act 1956 execution may, by leave of the county court, be obtained in the county court.

[6] County Courts Act 1934, s. 136.

same risks and penalties in costs and otherwise,[1] as an action on the judgment of a court of the highest degree.[2] Accordingly actions have been brought, without objection, upon judgments of ancient (not the modern statutory) county courts,[3] "courts of conscience",[4] manorial courts,[5] and borough and local courts of civil jurisdiction.[6]

84 Where, however, the inferior court is purely the creature of statute, the common law has nothing to say in the matter.[7] The statute alone must be examined to see whether an action on a judgment of the statutory inferior court is or is not expressly or impliedly prohibited. In the case of the county courts established by the County Courts Act 1846, such an examination resulted in a decision that the bringing of an action on the judgment of any such court was impliedly, though not expressly, prohibited[8]—a decision which, though it has been the subject of some criticism, has never been formally overruled.[9]

85 But, when it was found that the application of the above test had the effect of leaving a successful plaintiff in many cases without the means of obtaining full satisfaction of his judgment, by reason of the local or other limits of the inferior jurisdiction, the legislature came to the relief of the party to the following extent. Where the judgment debtor in any inferior court of record has no goods within the territorial limits of the jurisdiction, the judgment may be removed, for the purpose of execution, into a superior court,[10] and, when so removed for that purpose, it is as unimpeachable on the merits as it wouldbe if made the subject of an action.[11] By another

[1] See para. 80, *ante*.

[2] *Williams* v. *Jones* (1845), 13 M. & W. 628 (per POLLOCK C.B., and PARKE B., at p. 633, and ALDERSON B., at p. 634); *Berkeley* v. *Elderkin* (1853), 1 E. & B. 805 (per Lord CAMPBELL C.J., at p. 807: "*prima facie*, an action lies on the judgment of *any* court of competent jurisdiction"); *Hutchinson* v. *Gillespie* (1856), 11 Exch. 798 (per BRAMWELL B., at p. 815).

[3] As in *Williams* v. *Jones*, *supra*, which was an action on a judgment of "a county court of the Sheriff of the City of Carnarvon", one of the common law county courts which (per ALDERSON B., at p. 635) exercise "an ancient jurisdiction known to the common law"; *Read* v. *Pope* (1834), 1 Cr. M. & R. 302.

[4] As in *Coore* v. *Keneday* (1801), 3 Esp. 280.

[5] As in *Dawson* v. *Gregory* (1845), 7 Q.B. 756.

[6] As in *Hanmer* v. *White* (1844), 12 M. & W. 519 (Borough Court of Shrewsbury).

[7] The distinction is recognised by ALDERSON B., at p. 635 of *Williams* v. *Jones*, *supra*: "where it is a court created by statute or charter, it may be otherwise."

[8] *Berkeley* v. *Elderkin*, *supra*, where, at pp. 807–809, Lord CAMPBELL C.J. expressed the opinion that, a special mode of enforcing county court judgments being provided by the statute, only that statutory remedy was available.

[9] *Austin* v. *Mills* (1853), 9 Exch. 288, per POLLOCK C.B., stating, at p. 293, that the Court could not overrule the decision in *Berkeley* v. *Elderkin*, *supra*, "unless manifestly wrong", and this they were not prepared to say, though entertaining "doubts", which, however, "must be solved by a Court of Error". There has not as yet been any such solution.

[10] Judgments Act 1838, s. 22. See also Borough and Local Courts of Record Act 1872, s. 2.

[11] See *Simons* v. *Count de Wints* (1840), 8 Dowl. 646; *Williams* v. *Bolland* (1876), 1 C.P.D. 227 (per BRETT J., at p. 228: "when a judgment is removed from an inferior to a superior court

statutory provision the judgment of a county court for any sum not exceeding £20, exclusive of costs, where the judgment debtor has no goods at all, may be removed for execution to the High Court.[1]

(c) *Actions on orders of English superior courts*

86 The general rule of the common law was that no action will lie on any order of an English superior court,[2] except (probably) an order of such finality as to render it substantially equivalent to a judgment.[3] But, largely as a result of Rules of the Supreme Court introduced since the Judicature Acts, and particularly of O. 42 r. 24, since dropped in the revision of 1965 as otiose, the distinction in this regard between a judgment and an order has progressively diminished, until at the present day, in the words of the 1967 Annual Practice (p. 534) it is doubtful whether any distinction any longer exists. An order may now, in terms of the Rules, be enforced in the same manner as a judgment; but the courts have always applied the rule conservatively, and it is not competent for a party to sue (*e.g.*) upon orders of the Divorce Court,[4] or orders in proceedings of a

---

under this statute, it is only for the purpose of enabling the superior court to execute the judgment. No jurisdiction is given to the superior court *to inquire into the merits or into the regularity of the judgment in the court below*").

[1] County Courts Act 1934, s. 136.

[2] *Fry* v. *Malcolm* (1812), 4 Taunt. 705 (per Sir JAMES MANSFIELD C.J., at pp. 706, 707, and GIBBS J., at p. 707); *Carpenter* v. *Thornton* (1819), 3 B. & Ald. 52 (per HOLROYD J., at pp. 57, 58); *Patrick* v. *Shedden* (1853), 2 E. & B. 14 (per Lord CAMPBELL C.J., at pp. 21, 22); *Hookpayton* v. *Bussell* (1854), 10 Exch. 24 (per POLLOCK C.B., at p. 27: "we ought to guard against . . . new modes of *multiplying costs*"); *Dent* v. *Basham* (1854), 23 L.J. Ex. 161; *Furber* v. *Taylor*, [1900] 2 Q.B. 719, C.A., per A. L. SMITH L.J., at pp. 720, 721 ("prior to the Judicature Acts and the making of O. 42, r. 24, it was clear law that an action would not lie upon an order of a superior court, *as distinguished from a judgment*, the reason being that the person in whose favour the order was made could proceed by way of application to the court which made the order, and that to allow actions to be brought on such orders would tend to multiply actions unnecessarily"), and VAUGHAN WILLIAMS L.J., at p. 721 ("prior to the Judicature Acts, an action could not be brought upon the order of a superior court . . . *as distinguished from a judgment*, either in the court which made the order or in any other court").

[3] See *Ivimey* v. *Ivimey*, [1908] 2 K.B. 260, C.A. (per COZENS-HARDY M.R., at p. 263: "there may be a difference between an interlocutory order and a final order"); *Hutchinson* v. *Gillespie* (1856), 11 Exch. 798 (per MARTIN B., at p. 814, and BRAMWELL B., at pp. 815, 816).

[4] As was held in *Bailey* v. *Bailey* (1884), 13 Q.B.D. 855 (action on order for payment of alimony *pendente lite*: per BRETT M.R., at p. 859, and BOWEN and FRY L.JJ., at p. 860); *Robins* v. *Robins*, [1907] 2 K.B. 13 (action for arrears payable under order for permanent alimony; per JOYCE J., at p. 17); *Ivimey* v. *Ivimey*, *supra* (action on an order made against the husband to pay the wife's costs *pendente lite*, per COZENS-HARDY M.R., at pp. 262–4, and KENNEDY L.J., at pp. 265–6, pointing out that by O. 68, r. 1, of the R.S.C., divorce proceedings are expressly excepted from the operation of the rules generally, and, consequently, of O. 42, r. 24). Doubts were expressed by GODDARD L.J. in *Morse* v. *Muir*, [1939] 2 All E.R. 40; [1939] 2 K.B. 106 as to whether r. 81 of the Matrimonial Causes Rules 1937 did not give orders made in the Divorce Division the full force of judgments, notwithstanding these decisions; but in *Re Woolgar, Woolgar* v. *Hopkins*, [1942] 1 All E.R. 583; [1942] Ch. 318 SIMONDS J. held that the rule laid down in the older cases was still good law.

criminal nature,[1] as to which accordingly the old common law prohibition still obtains. Further, the exercise of such right as has been theoretically conferred by the Rules is in practice restricted within reasonable limits by the inherent jurisdiction of the court to prevent any abuse of its process, and the bringing of an action, in the absence of special circumstances justifying a resort to this form of procedure, instead of employing the ordinary means of enforcing the order by execution, is considered *prima facie* to constitute such an abuse.[2] It is for the party suing to establish the justification, and this he can only do by showing that complete satisfaction cannot be obtained except on a judgment in an action, as, for instance, where a judgment is a necessary foundation for proceedings in bankruptcy against an individual,[3] or for the winding up of a company,[4] and where, in such bankruptcy or liquidation, assets can be reached, and relief can be obtained, not otherwise available.

(d) Actions on orders of English inferior courts

87 At common law, no action will lie on any order of an English inferior court.[5] But such orders, when made by any inferior court in the

---

1 It was so recognised by the C.A. in *Godfrey* v. *George*, and in *Seldon* v. *Wilde* cited in note 3 *infra* though in each of those cases it was held that the order was not of a criminal nature.

2 *Pritchett* v. *English and Colonial Syndicate*, [1899] 2 Q.B. 428, C.A. (per LINDLEY M.R., at p. 435); *Furber* v. *Taylor*, [1900] 2 Q.B. 719, C.A. (per A. L. SMITH L.J., at p. 721). Accordingly, in *Ivimey* v. *Ivimey*, *supra*, where the party failed to show any justification for bringing the action, instead of resorting to the statutory remedies, cheaper and more expeditious, provided by rr. 179, 203 of the Divorce Rules and Regulations, it was held that there was no reason why the old common law rule should not apply (per COZENS-HARDY M.R., at pp. 262–264, and KENNEDY L.J., at pp. 265, 266).

3 As in *Re Boyd, Ex parte McDermott*, [1895] 1 Q.B. 611, C.A. (where the creditor's application in the Bankruptcy Court for leave to issue a bankruptcy notice against the debtor for non-payment of costs, the subject of an interlocutory order, had been dismissed on the ground that such a notice, by the then bankruptcy law, could only be issued on a final judgment); *Godfrey* v. *George*, [1896] 1 Q.B. 48, C.A. (where the plaintiff had unsuccessfully attempted to enforce by writ of attachment an order made upon a solicitor to pay the costs of an application to strike him off the rolls, and the action was here again held to be justified); *Seldon* v. *Wilde*, [1911] 1 K.B. 701, C.A. (a similar case to that last cited). It may be noted here that a bankruptcy notice may now be issued on a final order, as well as on a final judgment—see r. 1 (g) of the Bankruptcy Rules 1914, but interlocutory orders, to which alone probably the common law rule applies, are still unaffected.

4 As in *Pritchett* v. *English and Colonial Syndicate*, *supra*, which was an action on a garnishee order against a company, per LINDLEY M.R., at pp. 433, 434: "the avowed object of the plaintiffs was to put themselves in a position to wind up the company", which "had no assets in this country which could be reached by execution in the ordinary way on the garnishee order, but had property abroad which could be made available in the winding up, *and in no other way*",—since a winding up order cannot be made on a garnishee order,—"the plaintiffs cannot obtain payment without an action, and that is their justification for bringing it".

5 As was held in *Emerson* v. *Lashley* (1793), 2 Hy. Bl. 248 (per EYRE C.J., at p. 253, in an action on an interlocutory order for costs in the Mayor's Court); *Patrick* v. *Shedden* (1853), 2 E. & B. 14 (per Lord CAMPBELL C.J., at pp. 21, 22); *Furber* v. *Taylor*, [1900] 2 K.B. 719, C.A. (per A. L. SMITH L.J., at p. 721, and VAUGHAN WILLIAMS L.J., at pp. 721, 722, in an action on an interlocutory order of a county court for the payment of costs).

exercise of its ordinary jurisdiction, came to be regarded as enforceable in the same way as judgments by virtue of O. 25 r. 2 of the County Court Rules 1903 (now repealed). This rule was not reproduced in the Code of 1936; presumably it was thought unnecessary in view of the way in which the practice had developed, and in the light of the various relevant statutory provisions, which generally referred to "judgment or order"—*e.g.* section 120 of the County Courts Act 1959. But it was held under the old rule, and it is submitted still to be the law, that it is competent to sue on a county court order in a county court only, and not in the High Court.[1] But an order made by a county court, not in the exercise of its ordinary jurisdiction as such, but as a court of bankruptcy, stands on a different footing, and, as regards such orders, the effect of bankruptcy legislation has been to make them the legitimate subjects of an action in any court.[2]

(e) Actions on English arbitral decisions

88 An award has been defined as "the decision of one having a limited authority to determine those matters submitted to him by the parties, or . . . by a statute, and no other", and, more succinctly, as "the judgment of an inferior tribunal with limited authority".[3] Whether, strictly and technically, a "judgment" or not, it is at all events the "decision" of a judicial tribunal, on which an action would always lie: indeed, in early times, this was the only means of enforcing an award, and it was not until the period of Charles II that a practice sprang up of making the submission of the parties a rule of court, thereby rendering disobedience to the award a contempt of the court granting the rule.[4] The submission, however, was revocable without leave of the court, so that either party could deprive the other of the benefit of the new procedure, until the statute 3 & 4 W. IV, c. 42, when this blot was removed. Other improvements were introduced by the

---

[1] *Savill* v. *Dalton*, [1915] 3 K.B. 174, C.A. (per Lord Reading C.J., at pp. 180, 181, and Bray J., at pp. 186–188).

[2] By s. 103 of the Bankruptcy Act 1914, it is enacted that "a county court shall, for the purposes of its bankruptcy jurisdiction, in addition to the ordinary powers of the court, have all the powers and jurisdiction of the High Court, and the orders of the court may be enforced accordingly in manner prescribed", sc. by the Bankruptcy Rules, one of which (Rule 89 of the 1952 Rules) provides that every order of the Court (which s. 168 (a) of the Act of 1883, now s. 167 of the Act of 1914, defines as "the court having jurisdiction in bankruptcy") "may be enforced as if it were a judgment to the same effect". This, according to the C.A. in *Savill* v. *Dalton*, *supra* (per Lord Reading C.J., at pp. 181–183, and Swinfen Eady L.J., at pp. 184, 185) involves the necessary consequence that, in point of strict technicality, any order of a county court in its bankruptcy jurisdiction may be sued upon as much as any order of the High Court in its ordinary jurisdiction may be in virtue of the powers held to have been impliedly conferred by O. 42, r. 24, of the R.S.C.

[3] Per Blackburn J., at p. 229 of *Duke of Buccleuch* v. *Metropolitan Board of Works* (1870), L.R. 5 Exch. 221, Ex. Ch.

[4] *Ibid.*, per Blackburn J., at p. 230.

Common Law Procedure Act 1854,[1] and the codifying statute of 1889, now carried forward into the Act of 1950, to be considered presently. But in the meantime the right to sue on an award, whether as to matters submitted by the parties,[2] or as to matters referred to arbitration by a statute,[3] remained unimpaired, and was freely exercised, in the form of actions for the recovery of money awarded, or for specific performance of orders made by the arbitral tribunal.[4]

89 The Arbitration Act 1950, like its predecessor of 1899, recognizes and affirms the common law rule that awards are as conclusive and unimpeachable on the merits as any other judicial decision.[5] As regards the mode of enforcing an award, the only alteration made by the Act is to substitute for the old application to the court for a rule to compel payment of the sum awarded, or to attach the party for disobedience to the award, a more summary and convenient procedure by application in chambers for leave to enforce the award. But the ancient right to sue on the award still remains unaffected, in point of theory and technicality.[6] Accordingly, actions have from time to time since 1889 been brought on awards without objection on the score of jurisdiction,[7] but the exercise of this bare technical right has always been subject to the inherent jurisdiction of the court to prevent abuse of its process. Where special circumstances are shown

---

1 17 & 18 Vict. c. 125. By s. 5 of this statute an arbitrator was empowered to state his award in the form of a special case, and by s. 8 jurisdiction was for the first time conferred upon the court to remit the award to the arbitrator for reconsideration, instead of setting it aside,—a jurisdiction which was freely exercised, as in *Peterson* v. *Ayre* (1855), 15 C.B. 724, and *Mills* v. *Bowyers' Society* (1856), 3 K. & J. 66, but never upon any ground which would not, before the statute, have justified the court in setting aside the award, as was held in *Hodgkinson* v. *Fernie* (1857), 3 C.B. N.S. 189 (at pp. 201, 202, 204, 205).

2 *E.g.*, *King* v. *Bowen* (1841), 8 M. & W. 625.

3 Such as *Metropolitan District Rail. Co.* v. *Sharpe* (1880), 5 App. Cas. 425, H.L.

4 As in *Eads* v. *Williams* (1854), 4 De G.M. & G. 674 (where, however, the action failed on other grounds), and *Blackett* v. *Bates* (1865), 1 Ch. App. 117 (where it was recognised that such an action would lie, but the plaintiff was defeated because he could not establish that, if an agreement to the same effect as the award were being sued upon, the court would have had jurisdiction to order specific performance thereof).

5 Arbitration Act 1950, s. 16: "Unless a contrary intention is expressed therein, every arbitration agreement shall, where such a provision is applicable to the reference, be deemed to contain a provision that the award to be made by the arbitrator or umpire shall be final and binding on the parties and the persons claiming under them respectively."

6 By s. 26 of the Act "an award on an arbitration agreement may, by leave of the High Court or a judge thereof, be enforced in the same manner as a judgment or order to the same effect, and, where leave is so given, judgment may be entered in terms of the award". The effect of this provision is that *prima facie* it may be the subject of an action, as well as a process of execution. The leave of the court which must be sought is not a mere formality, or a matter of course. It may be refused in a proper case, as where the award is invalid on the face of it. The Master was held by the C.A., reversing the judge, to have rightly adopted this course in *Re Stone and Hastie*, [1903] 2 K.B. 463, C.A., and in *Re Colman and Watson*, [1908] 1 K.B. 47, C.A.

7 As in *United Kingdom Mutual S.S. Assurance Association* v. *Houston*, [1896] 1 Q.B. 567; *Davis* v. *Witney Urban District Council* (1898), 14 T.L.R. 433.

such as to justify an abstention from the cheaper and more expeditious, and a resort to the more costly and cumbrous, of the two alternative procedures there is no occasion for the interference of the court, and the action is allowed to proceed; as, for instance, where such action is the necessary foundation for the commencement of bankruptcy proceedings,[1] or where notice of an order giving leave to enforce the award cannot be served out of the jurisdiction on the party against whom the award has been made,[2] or where complicated questions arise gravely affecting the legality and validity of the award.[3] But, where no such special circumstances have been made to appear, the court, in the exercise of its above-mentioned large powers of control, has sometimes dismissed the action altogether.[4] It should be mentioned here that the court has jurisdiction to, and will, on an application for leave to enforce the award, where such special circumstances are shown, order judgment to be entered on the award as if an action had been brought on it, and the applicant were asking for judgment thereon.[5]

90 The above, and all other provisions of the Arbitration Act 1950, are by section 31 thereof applied to statutory arbitrations, except insofar as the particular statute authorising or requiring the arbitration contains provisions inconsistent with those of the general Act. It follows that a statutory award, where there is no such inconsistency, may be sued upon in the same manner and to the same extent, but subject to the same inherent jurisdiction of the court, as any award made pursuant to the voluntary submission of the parties.[6] An instance of such inconsistency may be found in an arbitration under s. 150 of the Public Health Act 1875, as to which it has been held that an award made thereunder is not enforceable under s. 31, the only remedy being that provided by s. 150 of the Public Health Act.[7]

(*f*) *Actions on foreign judgments*

91 In an earlier part of this chapter,[8] it has been pointed out that in law the term "foreign" is applied not merely to decisions of a foreign tribunal

---

[1] See *China Steam Navigation Co.* v. *Van Laun* (1905), 22 T.L.R. 26, where the avowed object was to make the defendant a bankrupt, which could not be done except upon a judgment in an action; *Re Newey, Ex parte Whiteman* (1912), 107 L.T. 832, D.C.

[2] As in *Rasch & Co.* v. *Wulfert*, [1904] 1 K.B. 118, C.A.

[3] As in *Re Boks & Co., and Peters, Rushton & Co.*, [1919] 1 K.B. 491, C.A.

[4] *Pedler* v. *Hardy* (1902), 18 T.L.R. 591; *May* v. *Mills* (1914), 30 T.L.R. 287.

[5] *Re a Bankruptcy Notice*, [1907] 1 K.B. 478, C.A.

[6] See *Hobbs* v. *Winchester Corporation* (1910), 79 L.J. K.B. 578, for an instance of an action on a statutory award (under s. 308 of the Public Health Act 1875), there being nothing in the section inconsistent with the provisions of the Act of 1889. The decision was reversed in the C.A.—see 79 L.J. K.B. 1123—but this point does not appear to have been affected.

[7] *Willesden Local Board* v. *Wright*, [1896] 2 Q.B. 412.

[8] See para. 69, *supra*.

in the popular sense, but to every decision of a court outside the English jurisdiction, though within the British Commonwealth. To actions on foreign decisions in the popular sense, it is obvious that no objection can be raised, founded on such considerations as generally render actions on English judgments oppressive and unreasonable. It is not a question here of a choice between alternative procedures. There is only one procedure by which the fruits of a foreign judgment can be secured in this country to the successful litigant, and that is the recovery of an English judgment in an English action. To sue here on a foreign judgment, in the sense of a non-British judgment, is therefore not merely a permissible but (except in the cases of judgments to which the Foreign Judgments (Reciprocal Enforcement) Act 1933—presently to be discussed—applies) the only permissible and practical course to adopt. But if a judgment is one which is capable of registration under this Act (see para. 99, *infra*) then by s. 6 thereof no proceedings can be entertained in any court of the United Kingdom for recovery of the sum payable, otherwise than by way of registration of the judgment pursuant to the Act.

92 All the considerations which are in this work set forth as relevant to the application of the doctrine of *res judicata* to foreign judgments are applicable to the case of a plaintiff who sues upon a foreign judgment in an English court, using it as a cause of action. To succeed he must prove the judgment itself, and must show, the onus of proof being upon him in respect of each requirement, (a) that the judgment is one of a foreign court having jurisdiction in the particular case (b) that it is final and (c) that it was made or given between the same parties as are now before the court.

These matters are all separately discussed elsewhere in this book, and nothing more need be said here especially, therefore, relating to the procedure of suing upon a foreign judgment; we will now pass to the special statutory provisions which in certain cases now render it unnecessary to commence a new action in order to enforce one.

Registration of foreign judgments

93 For something like a century efforts have been made to devise procedures whereby, by the use of some system of registration, judgments obtained in foreign courts may be rendered immediately effective in this country, without the necessity of having to sue thereon. Such a procedure offers considerable difficulties, for it will at once be apparent that while little objection can be taken to its being made available in respect of such judgments as (for example) judgments for commercial debts, other types of judgment may be open to exception on various accounts. But so long ago as 1868 the Legislature began the process of enabling registration of foreign judgments by the use of statutory procedures, and these will now be examined.

The Judgments Extension Act 1868

94 The first of the statutes was the Judgments Extension Act 1868, still in force, and operative reciprocally between the jurisdictions of England, Scotland, and (now) Northern Ireland,[1] a statute of which it was judicially observed that "the intention appears to have been to discourage the bringing of actions on such judgments, and to substitute for that mode of proceeding a shorter and more convenient mode of obtaining the same result".[2] This intention is achieved in the following manner. By s. 1, where any judgment has been obtained in any superior court of England or Northern Ireland for debt, damages, or costs, the proper officer of that court is empowered to give a certificate thereof to the successful party in one of the scheduled forms, and, on the production of such certificate to any superior court of Northern Ireland or England respectively, the officers of the latter court shall register it there; whereupon the effect of such judgment, certificate, and registration shall be the same as if the judgment had been obtained in the latter court. In s. 2 are similar provisions for the registration of English and Northern Irish judgments in Scotland, and s. 3 provides in like manner for the registration of Scottish decreets in England or Northern Ireland, with a special requirement in this case, as to notes of suspension or stay of execution in the Scottish Court, and (in s. 8) a further proviso that the Act is not to apply to any Scottish decreet pronounced *in absentia* in an action on an arrest *ad fundandam jurisdictionem*.[3] By s. 4, the court where any such certificate is registered shall have such control and jurisdiction over the certified and registered judgment as it has over its own judgments, but "in so far only as relates to execution under this Act". It will be observed that the above provisions do not absolutely abolish the right to sue on the judgment in question in any part of the United Kingdom other than that in which it was pronounced, but the exercise of this right in preference to the statutory alternative is subject to the important provision as to costs mentioned below. Accordingly, the statutory procedure has

---

[1] The Act was originally made applicable to the whole of Ireland, but no longer applies to judgments of the courts of the Republic of Ireland—see *Wakeley* v. *Triumph Cycle Co.*, [1924] 1 K.B. 214, C.A.; *Banfield* v. *Chester* (1925), 94 L.J. K.B. 805, C.A. Some of the cases referred to in the footnotes in this section are to be noticed as decided before the separation of the Irish jurisdiction.

[2] Per STIRLING L.J., at pp. 769, 770 of *Thompson* v. *Gill*, [1903] 1 K.B. 760, C.A.

[3] For this reason the Scottish decreet in *Re Low, Bland* v. *Low*, [1894] 1 Ch. 147, C.A., could not be extended.

nearly always been adopted.[1] In such cases, the judgment or decreet, and the certificate thereof, is as unimpeachable on the merits as any other *res judicata*, and, further, the registration cannot be set aside on any ground which attacks the judgment, unless and until the judgment has been set aside, and the certificate vacated, in the Court where the former was pronounced and the latter given.[2] The registration can be set aside only on grounds which affect the question of its regularity, as, for instance, that the certificate is not in accordance with the scheduled statutory form, or defective in omitting reference to matters of substance required by the statute to be stated therein.[3] In s. 6 is contained the significant provision above referred to that in every action on a judgment or decreet capable of being registered and extended, there shall be no costs, unless the judge so orders.[4]

95 The limits within which the operation of the statute is confined should be noticed. In the first place, the statute applies to judgments or decreets only, not to any other form of judicial decision. Secondly the statute is limited to judgments or decreets for debt, damages, or costs, it has no application to judgments for any other form of relief, though, as regards England and Northern Ireland only, there is a summary procedure provided by other legislation for the interchangeable enforcement of equitable judgments and decrees.[5] Lastly, the Act deals only with execution: it does not authorise any indirect mode of satisfying a judgment, such as a judgment summons,[6] or a bankruptcy notice.[7] On the other hand, a garnishee order,[8] and the appointment of a receiver,[9] have been held to be forms of "execution" within the Act.

---

1 *E.g.* an English judgment was registered in, and extended to, Ireland in *Bailey* v. *Welpley* (1869), I.R. 4 C.L. 243; *Part* v. *Scannell* (1875), I.R. 9 C.L. 426; *Johnstone* v. *Bucknall*, [1898] 2 I.R. 499. An Irish judgment was registered in, and extended to, England in *Re Watson*, [1893] 1 Q.B. 21, C.A. An English judgment was registered in, and extended to, Scotland in *Re Low, Bland* v. *Low*. [1894] 1 Ch. 147, C.A. A Scottish decreet was registered in, and extended to, England in *Re a Bankruptcy Notice*, [1898] 1 Q.B. 383, C.A.; *Thompson* v. *Gill*, *supra*.

2 *Bailey* v. *Welpley*, *supra*, at pp. 245, 246.

3 There are two scheduled forms, one applicable to a judgment for the plaintiff, in which there must be a statement as to service upon, and appearance by, the defendant, and the other applicable to a judgment for the defendant. In *Part* v. *Scannell*, *supra*, the registration was set aside, because the certificate of a judgment for the plaintiff omitted to state whether the defendant had appeared, or whether he had been served.

4 For an instance of a case where the judgment could not have been so registered, see *Re Low, Bland* v. *Low*, *supra*, as to the Scottish decreet therein referred to.

5 By ss. 5, 6 of the Crown Debts Act 1801 (41 Geo. 3, c. 90).

6 *Re Watson, Ex parte Johnston*, [1893] 1 Q.B. 21, C.A.

7 *Re a Bankruptcy Notice*, [1898] 1 Q.B. 383, C.A.

8 As in *Johnstone* v. *Bucknall*, [1898] 2 I.R. 499.

9 As in *Thompson* v. *Gill*, [1903] 1 K.B. 760, C.A.

The Inferior Courts Judgments Extension Act 1882

96 It will be noticed that the Act of 1868 relates only to judgments of superior courts extended to superior courts; but by the Inferior Courts Judgments Extension Act 1882, a similar code of procedure is established for the reciprocal enforcement of the judgments of inferior courts in the three parts of the United Kingdom, the terms "inferior court" and "judgment", as applied to England, Northern Ireland, and Scotland respectively, being carefully defined in the interpretation clause. The statute of 1882 contains the same restriction of its scope to judgments for debt, damages, or costs, and to execution, as the Act of 1868, and it visits any action on a registrable and extendable judgment with the like penalties in the matter of costs.

The Administration of Justice Act 1920

97 In 1920 somewhat similar statutory provisions were enacted, whereby judgments in other parts of the British dominions could be enforced in England, and vice versa, by means of a system of certification and registration. Any person who has obtained a judgment (or who by succession or assignment has become entitled to one) in any part of Her Majesty's dominions to which the Act applies may apply to the High Court within 12 months of the date of the judgment, or such further time as may be allowed, to have the judgment registered in the court.

For the procedure regulating this application the reader is referred to the Act itself; if registration is granted and the judgment is registered it is thereby given the same force and effect as a judgment obtained in the registering court on the day of registration.

The Foreign Judgments (Reciprocal Enforcement) Act 1933

98 The procedure was further extended thirteen years later by the provisions of the Foreign Judgments (Reciprocal Enforcement) Act 1933. This deals primarily with foreign, in the sense of non-British judgments; and its principle is that of reciprocity. When reciprocal arrangements have been made between Her Majesty's Government and the government of any given foreign state, it may be directed by Order-in-Council that Part I of the Act is to have reciprocal application between courts of this jurisdiction and specific courts exercising jurisdiction in the state in question.

Further Orders-in-Council may make the Act applicable to courts of Commonwealth jurisdictions outside England; and if and when any such Commonwealth jurisdiction is brought under the Act the provisions of the

Administration of Justice Act 1920 thereupon cease to apply to the Commonwealth jurisdiction so affected as from the date of such Order-in-Council.

99 As in the case of the Administration of Justice Act 1920, the procedure under the Foreign Judgments (Reciprocal Enforcement) Act 1933 is by application by the judgment creditor to the High Court. As to details of this procedure, the reader is referred to the Act itself. Two points, however, may be noticed. First, whereas under the Administration of Justice Act 1920 the court to which application was made was given a discretion whether to grant registration or not, under the Act of 1933 the court is required to order registration upon proof of the matters set out in the statute. Second, if the foreign judgment is one which may be registered under the Act, no proceedings for the recovery of the sum payable thereunder can be entertained in any court, superior or inferior, in the United Kingdom, otherwise than by way of registration of the judgment.

CHAPTER III

Proof of the Judicial Decision

Introductory

100 It is incumbent upon anyone setting up *res judicata* as a bar to the claim or defence (as the case may be) of the opposite party to establish (if disputed) that the particular decision relied upon was in fact pronounced as alleged, and that it is subsistent and effective at the time when the question is raised. It is of no avail, therefore, to prove that at the material date proceedings were pending, which afterwards matured into a judgment.[1] The material date is the time when the second action is heard; the easiest approach to the problem is to regard the decision in the first proceeding as conclusive evidence in the second.[2] It was at one time thought that a plea of *res judicata* could not be supported unless the earlier judgment had been given before the commencement of proceedings in the second action;[3] this theory is now exploded, and the plea of *res judicata* may be put forward up to the date of hearing of the second proceedings,[4] leave to amend the pleadings being granted if necessary, and if just, to this end.[5]

It was strenuously argued in one of the recent cases on the subject that even if a defendant might set up a plea of *res judicata* by virtue of a judgment given after the issue of the proceedings, a plaintiff must be in a worse position, and cannot be allowed to do so, on analogy with the principle that he cannot avail himself of any cause of action accruing after the date of commencement of the proceedings. But this argument was disallowed, and no difference is made between plaintiff and defendant in this regard.[6]

---

[1] *The Delta* (1876), 1 P.D. 393; *Houstoun* v. *Marquis of Sligo* (1885), 29 Ch.D. 448, at pp. 454–5.

[2] Per PEARSON L.J. in *Morrison, Rose & Partners* v. *Hillman*, [1961] 2 Q.B. 266, at p. 277.

[3] 15 Halsbury's Laws (3 Edn.) 211, para. 395; *The Delta* (1876), 1 P.D. 393; *Houstoun* v. *Marquis of Sligo* (1885), 29 Ch.D. 448, at pp. 454–5.

[4] *In re Defries, Norton* v. *Levy* (1883), 48 L.T. 703; *Bell* v. *Holmes*, [1956] 1 W.L.R. 1359, at pp. 1365–1366 per McNAIR J.; *Morrison, Rose & Partners* v. *Hillman*, [1961] 2 All E.R. 891; [1961] 2 Q.B. 266; *In the Estate of Langton* [1964] P. 163, C.A. per WILLMER L.J. at p. 168.

[5] *Morrison, Rose & Partners* v. *Hillman*, [1961] 2 Q.B. 266 at p. 277.

[6] *Ibid*: the point is raised in argument at p. 270, and is rejected by HOLROYD PEARCE L.J. at p. 276.

Conversely, if the decision relied upon has been set aside before the date of hearing in the second proceedings no *res judicata* is established.[1]

Evidence by which the fact of the decision, and its terms, must be established

101 The fact of the decision relied upon having been pronounced must be proved, as every fact must be, by the best evidence available. Obviously, where there exists an official "record",—which term is to be understood, not in its obsolete restricted sense,[2] but as embracing any and every kind of official document, or entry in any official book or roll, in which the judicial decisions of any court are lawfully recorded,—that record is the best, and accordingly, in general, the only, evidence by which the fact of the *res judicata* can be established.[3]

But the effect of the previous decision may be inferred satisfactorily from the pleadings, in which case of course formal proof of the record in the first cause will be unnecessary.[4]

102 The record is conclusive, not only as to the fact of adjudication, but as to the matters adjudicated upon, and the terms of the decision. It is in this sense, and to this extent, that certain ancient phrases and formulae, such as "the record proves itself", or "must be tried by itself", or is "of such uncontrollable verity as to admit no averment, plea, or proof to the contrary",[5] may be accepted.[6] Indeed, in this sense and to this extent, the conclusiveness of the record operates *in rem*, for it undoubtedly binds strangers, as well as parties.[7] It should be noted, however, that the party against whom the *res judicata* is set up is always at liberty to plead, by way of confession and avoidance, that the record relied upon as evidence of the

---

[1] So stated in the judgment of the King's Bench in *Noell* v. *Wells and Page* (1668), 1 Lev. 235. A judgment by default will support an estoppel until set aside—see para. 38, *supra*, and *Aslin* v. *Parkin* (1758), 2 Burr. 665, at p. 668; *Doe* v. *Huddart* (1835), 2 Cr. M. & R. 316; *Wilkinson* v. *Kirby* (1854), 15 C.B. 430, at p. 443; *Harris* v. *Mulkern* (1875), 1 Ex.D. 31, at p. 35. *In New Zealand, Tira Arika* v. *Sidaway*, [1923] N.Z.L.R. 158.

[2] Such as that given in Coke, Litt. 260a, where "recordum" is defined as "a memorial or remembrance in rolls of parchment of the proceedings and acts of . . . courts of record", and is distinctly stated not to include any memorial or remembrance in "the rolls of inferior, nor of any other courts which proceed not *secundum legem et consuetudinem Angliae*".

[3] *Dyson* v. *Wood* (1824), 3 B. & C. 449 (per ABBOTT C.J., at p. 451); *The Annie Johnson* (1921), 126 L.T. 614, P.C. ("the plea of *res judicata* cannot be entertained unless the record of the act of the court on which it is founded is forthcoming, or some valid reason is given why it cannot be produced").

[4] As was the case in *Bell* v. *Holmes*, [1956] 1 W.L.R. 1359, at p. 1367.

[5] Coke, Littl. 260a.

[6] *Noell* v. *Wells*, *infra*; *Reed* v. *Jackson* (1801), 1 East 354 (per Lord KENYON C.J., at p. 356).

[7] *Magrath* v. *Hardy* (1838), 4 Bing. N.C. 782 (per TINDAL C.J., at p. 796: "it is undoubtedly true, as a general rule, that no man can take any averment contrary to a record", and "that *not only parties and privies, but even strangers also*, are estopped to aver anything to the contrary").

decision has since been superseded by another record, or that it is a forgery.[1]

103 The record is conclusive not only as regards the decision which it purports to record, but also as to any other judicial act, or proceeding of the parties, which may be recited therein.[2] For instance, it is not permissible to controvert any facts stated in, or necessarily to be inferred from, the record as to the names, number, capacity, or qualification, of the jurors,[3] or of the justices,[4] taking part in the decision; the matters taken into consideration by the judicial tribunal;[5] the appearance of any of the parties at the trial or hearing;[6] the date of the pronouncement of the decision;[7] the compliance, or non-compliance, of the parties with any statutory requirement of notice;[8] the findings of the jury;[9] the capacity in which the plaintiff sued;[10] or, in a criminal case, the place in which the offence was committed.[11]

104 In the case of an adjudication by a judicial tribunal which is not required by statute to keep, and does not in fact keep, any official records of its decisions, the *res judicata* may be proved by other evidence, which

---

[1] *Noell* v. *Wells and Page* (1668), 1 Lev. 235, where, in support of an action of debt against an executrix, "the defendant pleaded never executrix; and on a trial the plaintiff produced the probate of the will in evidence. The defendant said that the will was not a true, but a forged will. And the Chief Justice, before whom it was tried, was of opinion that she could not give such evidence directly contrary to the seal of the Ordinary in a matter within his jurisdiction, whereupon a Case was made for the opinion of the court, . . . and upon motion the whole court held that it could not be given. But evidence may be given that the seal was forged, or was repealed, or that there were *bona notabilia*; for these confess and avoid the seal. But he cannot give in evidence that another was executor; or that the testator was not *compos mentis*, for these falsify the proceedings of the Ordinary in cases of which he is judge."

[2] *Ramsbottom* v. *Buckhurst* (1814), 2 M. & S. 565, per Lord ELLENBOROUGH C.J., at p. 567: "the judgment roll imports incontrovertible verity as to *all the proceedings which it sets forth* . . . *Every part* of the record, as long as it remains on the file of the court, must be taken to speak absolute verity". In this case the judgment roll set forth, in addition to the judgment itself, the award of an elegit thereon, and the return of the consequent inquisition.

[3] *Bowsse* v. *Cannington* (1610), Cro.Jac. 244; *Helbut* v. *Held* (1725), 2 Ld. Raym. 1414; *Irwin* v. *Grey* (1867), L.R. 2 H.L. 20 (per Lord CHELMSFORD L.C., at p. 23, and Lord CRANWORTH, at p. 24).

[4] *R.* v. *Carlile* (1831), 2 B. & Ad. 362 (per Lord TENDERDEN C.J., at pp. 367–369); *R.* v. *Tyrone Justices*, [1917] 2 Ir.R. 437 (per CAMPBELL C.J. (Ir.) at p. 441).

[5] *Corrigal* v. *London and Blackwall Rail. Co.* (1843), 5 Man. & G. 219 (per TINDAL C.J., at p. 248); *Mortimer* v. *South Wales Rail. Co.* (1859), 1 E. & E. 375.

[6] *Russell* v. *Smyth* (1842), 9 M. & W. 810 (per Lord ABINGER C.B., at pp. 817, 818, PARKE B., at p. 819, and ALDERSON B. at p. 820).

[7] *Trevivan* v. *Lawrance* (1703), 1 Salk. 276; 2 Ld. Raym. 1036, at p. 1048.

[8] *R.* v. *Liverpool Corporation* (1768), 4 Burr. 2244 (per WILLES J., at p. 2245: "if it had been properly set out that twenty days' notice was given pursuant to the Act, . . . the inquisition and judgment had been conclusive against the owner of the lands").

[9] *Keane* v. *O'Brien* (1871), I.R.5 C.L. 531.

[10] *Henderson* v. *Henderson* (1844), 6 Q.B. 288 (per Lord DENMAN C.J., delivering the judgment of the court, at p. 298).

[11] *R.* v. *Newton* (1855), 24 L.J. C.P. 148 (per JERVIS C.J., at p. 149, WILLIAMS J., at pp. 149, 150, and CROWDER J., at p. 150).

must be the next best. The old superstitious attitude towards "the record" vanished as soon as it came to be recognized that it is not that, but the decision, which creates the estoppel.[1]

105 Though the record, where there is one, proves conclusively the fact and the terms of the decision, it must first be proved itself in the manner prescribed or authorised by the statutory rules (if any) governing the particular case.

(1) *Records of English decisions*

106 Records of the superior courts are proved by production of office copies of the judgment or order.[2] Adjudications, and orders in bankruptcy[3] are established in accordance with the statutory provisions applicable in this regard.

107 Records of judgments and orders of inferior civil courts are proved, in the case of county courts, by the prescribed statutory means,[4] and, in the case of manorial, local, and other courts of record of civil jurisdiction, in accordance with the custom and practice of the particular court, as proved in evidence,[5] or the statute (if any) regulating its procedure.

108 Judgments and orders of the superior criminal courts are proved by production of copies of, or extracts from, the record, certified by the officer having the custody thereof, and otherwise in accordance with the several statutes.[6]

109 Convictions, or orders, or dismissals of charges, in a court of summary jurisdiction are proved by production of the register, or a certified extract therefrom, or, in the case of a dismissal, by a certificate thereof, and otherwise as prescribed by statutory rules, or authorised by the practice, of the particular court.[7]

---

[1] *Dyson* v. *Wood* (1824), 3 B. & C. 449 (per ABBOTT C.J., at p. 531); *Re May* (1885), 28 Ch.D. 516, C.A., per BRETT M.R., at p. 518, as cited in note 1 on p. 21, Chapter II, *ante*.

[2] See R.S.C. (1965) O. 38, r. 10; and 15 *Halsbury's Laws* (3rd Edn.) 364, 401.

[3] See Bankruptcy Act 1914, ss. 137–144.

[4] 15 *Halsbury's Laws* (3rd Edn.) p. 402; County Courts Act 1934, s. 23(2).

[5] Thus, in *Dawson* v. *Gregory* (1845), 7 Q.B. 756, an action on a judgment of a manorial court, the judgment was proved by the production of an entry or memorandum thereof in the books of the manor court, together with the evidence of the deputy steward, objected to, but admitted by COLTMAN J., as to the above being the proper mode of recording judgments according to the custom of the manor. *Cp.* para. 120 *post*, and the cases cited in the notes thereto, and see 15 *Halsbury's Laws* (3rd Edn.) 402.

[6] Evidence Act 1851, s. 13; *Richardson* v. *Willis* (1872), L.R. 8 Exch. 69; Criminal Procedure Act 1865, s. 6; Prevention of Crimes Act 1871, s. 18. *Cp.* 10 *Halsbury's Laws* (3rd Edn.) 432–433.

[7] Magistrates' Court Rules 1952 (S.I. 1952 No. 2190) r. 56.

110 As to orders, reports, and certificates in lunacy, it is provided by the Lunacy Act 1890,[1] that "every office copy of the whole of an order, or report confirmed by fiat purporting to be signed by a master, and sealed and stamped with the seal of the master's office, and every office copy of a certificate in lunacy that at all times, and on behalf of all persons, and whether for the purposes of this Act or otherwise, be admitted as evidence of the order, report, or certificate of which it purports to be a copy, without any further proof thereof".[2]

111 Awards pursuant to private arbitrations are proved by producing the original award, and for these reasons it is usual to produce, in addition, the submission to arbitration which is its foundation. The proof of awards made pursuant to statutory arbitrations is usually regulated by the particular statute regulating the arbitration, read in conjunction with the provisions of the Arbitration Act 1950.

(2) *Records of foreign decisions*

112 The record of a foreign judgment (in which term is to be included all judgments of Courts of Commonwealth jurisdictions outside the United Kingdom, including Colonial Courts) may be proved in the manner prescribed by the provisions of the Evidence Act 1851, a statute which is in the main declaratory of the common law procedure existing before its enactment.

---

[1] 53 Vict. c. 5.

[2] See s. 144 of the Act. By s. 107, provision is made for the transmission from England to Ireland, or from Ireland to England, of a transcript of the record of any inquisition, or writ of supersedeas, whereupon such transcript shall be entered of record in Ireland, or in England, as the case may be, and have the same effect as if it were the original record of proceedings instituted within such respective jurisdictions.

CHAPTER IV

Jurisdiction

Introductory

113 Competent jurisdiction is an essential condition of every valid *res judicata*,[1] which means that, in order that a judicial decision relied upon, whether as a bar, or as the foundation of an action, may conclusively bind the parties, or (in the case of *in rem* decisions) the world, it must appear that the judicial tribunal pronouncing the decision had jurisdiction over the cause or matter, and over the parties, sufficient to warrant it in so doing.[2]

114 A tribunal may exceed its jurisdiction either by embarking upon an inquiry outside its province, or, while confining its inquiry within the proper limits, by making an order in excess of its powers. In either case the result will be to nullify the decision as a *res judicata*; in the former case, by the effect of the events we have mentioned upon the declaratory part of the decision, and, in the second, by their effect upon its jussive or prohibitory provisions.[3]

115 The rule prescribing due jurisdiction as essential applies to every species of judicial decision, and of judicial tribunal, as already defined,[4] though, as will presently be explained, the burden of allegation and proof

---

1 "First, the decision must have been given by a competent tribunal"—per ROCHE J. in *Eastwood and Holt* v. *Studer* (1926), 31 Com. Cas. 251 at p. 256–257.

2 This is well illustrated by the decision of the High Court of Australia in *O'Keefe* v. *Williams* (1907), 5 C.L.R. 217, where a decision of the Land Court as to the ownership of land was held insufficient to support a plea of *res judicata* in a subsequent action for damages. At p. 227 GRIFFITH C.J. said ". . . the foundation of that plea is that the Land Court had jurisdiction to determine whether the piece of land was Crown land. There is no provision of the law cited to us that in any way supports that contention". And see, to the same effect, the judgment of ISAACS J. at p. 232.

3 Instances of courts making orders beyond their jurisdiction, though the subject matter of the inquiry was within that jurisdiction, may be found in *R.* v. *Willesden Justices, Ex parte Utley*, [1947] 2 All E.R. 838; [1948] 1 K.B. 397 (in which the justices had imposed a fine in excess of their jurisdiction); *R.* v. *London County Council, Ex parte, Entertainments Protection Association, Ltd.*, [1931] 2 K.B. 215 (a proceeding for a writ of *certiorari*, in which a writ was issued to quash a licence for Sunday entertainment granted by the County Council without jurisdiction); *In New Zealand, Stafford* v. *Porritt and Booth* (1911), 30 N.Z.L.R. 309; *Close* v. *Maxwell*, [1945] N.Z.L.R. 688; *Hereaka* v. *Prichard*, [1967] N.Z.L.R. 18, C.A.

4 See Chapter II, *ante*.

may be lighter, and the legal presumption of jurisdiction may be more readily made, in some classes of case than in others. It will be convenient, in this connection, to consider English, and foreign, judicial decisions separately.

116 English decisions group themselves into three main classes, *viz.* (1) decisions of English civil tribunals, other than arbitral: (2) awards of English arbitral tribunals, which present certain special features of their own: (3) decisions of English criminal tribunals.

Jurisdiction of English civil tribunals other than arbitral

117 As regards the burden of allegation and proof, there is a distinction between the judgments and orders of our superior courts,[1] and those of other English courts and tribunals. Every English judge is supposed to know the extent and limits of the jurisdiction of a superior court, and does not require to be specially informed on such matters. Therefore, as a general rule, it is not necessary for the parties relying upon the decision of a superior court as a *res judicata* to aver that the court had competent jurisdiction in that behalf, and the existence of such jurisdiction will be presumed in his favour,[2] unless and until the opposite party alleges some special matter (such as a statutory enactment) in virtue of which the superior court has been deprived of its general common law jurisdiction in the particular case, whereupon the onus is shifted on to the shoulders of the first party to allege with precision facts and circumstances which nevertheless invested the court with the jurisdiction of which otherwise it would have been divested. For instances, by a rule of the common law, confirmed by a declaratory statute,[3] no English court can entertain a suit against the ambassador or other diplomatic representative of a foreign sovereign, any more than it can a suit against that sovereign himself. In such a case it would obviously be incumbent on any party setting up an English judgment against such foreign sovereign or diplomatic representative, as an estoppel, to allege and establish that, by voluntary submission, the foreign sovereign, or, with his consent, his diplomatic representative, as the case may be, has brought himself with the jurisdiction.[4]

---

[1] Any court of a County Palatine is a superior court: *Peacock* v. *Bell* (1667), 1 Wms. Saund. 73; *London Corporation* v. *Cox* (1867), L.R. 2 H.L. 239 (per WILLES J., at p. 257).

[2] *Peacock* v. *Bell, supra*; *Read* v. *Pope* (1834), 1 Cr. M. & R. 302 (per Lord LYNDHURST C.B., at pp. 305–307); *London Corporation* v. *Cox, supra* (per WILLES J., at p. 259, citing and adopting "the rule for jurisdiction" stated in *Peacock* v. *Bell, supra*); *Scott* v. *Bennett* (1871), L.R. 5 H.L. 234 (per Lord CHELMSFORD, at pp. 248, 249, citing the first branch of the same rule).

[3] The Diplomatic Privileges Act 1708 (7 Anne, c. 12).

[4] As regards a foreign sovereign, see *Duff Development Co.* v. *Kelantan Government*, [1923] 1 Ch. 385, C.A. As to a diplomatic representative, by s. 3 of the above statute, it is declared and enacted that no court has jurisdiction to entertain a suit against any "diplomatic agent", whilst

118 An almost equally strong presumption will be made in favour of the jurisdiction of any English Court which, though not technically a superior court, is a court of ancient authority known to the common law, such as the pre-statutory county court,[1] or a tribunal constituted a court of record by statute or charter.[2] In such cases, though jurisdiction must be averred, it is sufficient to allege, in the most general terms, that the cause of action arose within the jurisdiction, without going into details; but the averment, however general, must be plain and unambiguous.[3]

119 In the case of decisions of inferior courts, the presumption is the other way. At a very early stage in the history of our jurisprudence, "the rule for jurisdiction" was laid down, in very uncompromising language, as follows:—"nothing shall be intended to be out of the jurisdiction of a superior court but that which specially appears to be so; and, on the contrary, nothing shall be intended to be within the jurisdiction of an inferior

---

he holds the office. It has been contended in two cases that it is open to the plaintiff to establish, if he can, that the diplomatic agent, with the consent of his Sovereign, voluntarily submitted to the jurisdiction. It was doubted by ASTBURY J., at p. 156 of *Re Republic of Bolivia Exploration Syndicate, Ltd.*, [1914] 1 Ch. 139, and by EVE J., at p. 138 of *Re Suarez, Suarez* v. *Suarez*, [1917] 2 Ch. 131, whether this can be done; but no one doubted that, if it can be done, the onus is on the plaintiff of proving with the utmost precision and detail how and when the court acquired a jurisdiction which is denied to it by the legislature. More recently, see *Dickinson* v. *Del Solar*, [1930] 1 K.B. 376; *R.* v. *A.B.*, [1941] 1 K.B. 454; *Empson* v. *Smith*, [1965] 2 All E.R. 881; [1966] 1 Q.B. 426.

[1] *Williams* v. *Jones* (1845), 13 M. & W. 628, an action on a judgment recovered in "a county court of the Sheriff of the City of Carnarvon", where it was held that the plaintiff need aver no more than that the cause of action arose within the jurisdiction, leaving the defendant to aver particular facts exempting him from such jurisdiction, per POLLOCK C.B., at p. 633, PARKE B., at p. 634, and ALDERSON B., at p. 635, who states, as the reason for so holding, that the county court of that day was "an ancient jurisdiction, known to the common law."

[2] Thus, in *Sollers* v. *Lawrence* (1743), Willes 413, where a party sued in debt on a decision of commissioners appointed by statute to determine disputes arising out of the destruction of house property by "the late dreadful fire" at Blandford, and constituted thereby a court of record, and it was held by the Court of Common Pleas, per WILLES C.J., at pp. 416–418, that a declaration alleging no more than that the statutory tribunal had jurisdiction in the matter was well pleaded, and that it was not necessary to aver in detail that the parties appeared, and submitted to the jurisdiction, or the like, for it will be intended, in the case of a statutory court of record, as in the case of a superior court at common law, that the court acted within their jurisdiction in every respect, and at every stage in the proceedings, unless anything appears on the record to the contrary.

[3] See *Read* v. *Pope* (1834), 1 Cr. M. & R. 302, an action on a judgment of one of the ancient county courts, in which it was held that a declaration averring merely that "the plaintiff had recovered the judgment within the jurisdiction of that court", without stating in plain terms that "the cause of action arose within the jurisdiction", was bad (per Lord LYNDHURST C.B., after consulting the other common law courts, at pp. 306, 307. So also, even in the case of a judgment of the judge of the then High Court of Admiralty, which was set up by the defendant as an estoppel to an action in the C.P. for collision in the Thames, a demurrer was allowed to a plea which, instead of averring that the Admiralty Court had jurisdiction to determine the question, in plain though general language, stated, with laborious obscurity, that "the merits" had already been determined by the Admiralty Court "after due proceedings", and "in due form of law", which might have meant anything: *Harris* v. *Willis* (1855), 15 C.B. 710.

court but that which is so expressly alleged".[1] The latter branch of this rule has been accordingly followed in considering the conclusiveness or otherwise of decisions pronounced by such tribunals as the Sheriff's Court of London,[2] the Mayor's Court of London,[3] or a statutory compensation tribunal.[4] It has even been held that, in an action on the judgment of an inferior court, it is of no avail to aver that the inferior court had jurisdiction in the matter, unless such an averment also appears upon the pleadings or record of proceedings in the inferior court,[5] and, *e converso*, that it is equally insufficient to point to such an averment in the record of the inferior court, without also alleging the jurisdiction of such inferior court over again in the court where the action on the judgment is brought.[6] It is now, however, held, notwithstanding the stricter views entertained in some of the earlier authorities, that this averment, whether in the original action,[7] or in the action on the judgment of the inferior court,[8] may be made in general terms, without setting out in succession all the facts and conditions upon the existence and satisfaction of which the jurisdiction depends.

---

[1] *Peacock* v. *Bell* (1667), 1 Wms. Saund. 73. *Cp.* the observations of the Judicial Committee at p. 463 of *Falkingham* v. *Victorian Railways Commissioner*, [1900] A.C. 452, P.C.

[2] *Mico* v. *Morris* (1685), 3 Lev. 234.

[3] So stated by WILLES J., delivering the opinion of the judges summoned, at p. 263 of *London Corporation* v. *Cox* (1867), L.R. 2 H.L. 239. At pp. 256–259, he points out the distinction between an inferior court of limited jurisdiction, such as the Mayor's court, and the "superior courts of general jurisdiction, of which the courts of Westminster are bound to take judicial notice", and, to the same effect, Lord CRANWORTH, at pp. 294, 295, and Lord WESTBURY, at p. 295.

[4] *R.* v. *Liverpool Corporation* (1768), 4 Burr. 2244.

[5] *Ibid.*, per Lord MANSFIELD C.J., at p. 2245 ("it ought to have appeared upon the inquisition"), and per WILLES J., at the same page ("we cannot enforce an inferior jurisdiction unless it be properly set out. If it had been properly set out that twenty days' notice was given pursuant to the Act . . . the inquisition and judgment had been conclusive against the owners of the lands").

[6] *Adney* v. *Vernon* (1684), 3 Lev. 243 (*per Cur.*, at p. 244); *London Corporation* v. *Cox* (1867), L.R. 2 H.L. 239 (per WILLES J., at p. 263: "not only must the declaration in the inferior court allege jurisdiction, but also in an action brought in the superior court upon a judgment of an inferior court, duly obtained, it must again be averred that the original cause of action arose within the jurisdiction of the inferior court, so that, on a traverse of that averment, the question of jurisdiction may be re-tried").

[7] See, for instance, *R.* v. *Bagshaw* (1797), 7 Term Rep. 363 (*per Cur.*, at p. 364); *R.* v. *Nottingham Old Waterworks Co.* (1837), 6 Ad. & El. 355 (per PATTESON J., at p. 370, WILLIAMS J., at p. 371, and COLERIDGE J., at pp. 371, 372); *R.* v. *Manchester and Leeds Rail. Co.* (1838), 8 Ad. & El. 413 (per Lord DENMAN C.J. at p. 426: not necessary that inquisition should state that notice to treat was given); *R.* v. *Swansea Harbour Trustees* (1839), 8 Ad. & El. 439 (per LITTLEDALE J., at p. 448: not necessary that fulfilment of each condition of the statutory jurisdiction should be separately set out on the record). With these contrast the earlier decisions here departed from, in which stricter views prevailed, and were carried to absurd lengths, such as *Read* v. *Pope*, *supra*, and *R.* v. *Norwich and Watton Road Trustees* (1836), 5 Ad. & E. 536 (as to notice to treat).

[8] Per WILLES J., in *London Corporation* v. *Cox*, *supra* as cited in note 6 *supra*.

120 Where the inferior court is alleged to have had jurisdiction over the cause and parties by custom, the burden is on the party setting up the decision of such court as a *res judicata* to prove by the appropriate evidence, the existence of the custom, as a fact,[1] and that the proceedings were in strict conformity with the custom so proved,[2] and further, if challenged on this point, to establish by argument that the custom is a reasonable one, in the sense that it is not in conflict with any elementary principle of justice.[3]

Cases in which the tribunal has decided on its own jurisdiction

121 Certain ancient cases, in which it was considered that the party relying on the decision of an inferior court need not aver the jurisdiction of that court, if its jurisdiction had been duly averred and established in the original proceedings, and that, in such circumstances, the decision itself precludes the parties from disputing the jurisdiction, as much as it precludes them from disputing the facts decided, have now clearly ceased to be law.[4] Other authorities, in which it has been held, or suggested, that in the exceptional circumstances there mentioned, the party was not subject to the burden imposed upon him by the general rule, serve merely to prove and illustrate that rule.[5]

---

[1] In *Williams* v. *Lord Bagot* (1825), 3 B. & C. 772, the custom of the lordship court of Ruthin, which was there in question, was proved by the written certificate of the steward of the court, set out at pp. 780–782, which, by *certiorari*, the K.B. had required him to prepare and furnish. In *Dawson* v. *Gregory* (1845), 7 Q.B. 756, the customary mode of entering judgments in a Manor Court was proved by the oral evidence of the deputy steward. In *London Corporation* v. *Cox. supra*, the London practice of foreign attachment was certified orally to the court by the Recorder of the City Corporation.

[2] This was alleged and proved in the cases cited in the last note.

[3] In *Williams* v. *Lord Bagot*, *supra*, the steward certified the practice there in question to be as follows: proceedings were initiated by issuing a summons and an attachment at the same time, and returnable at the same time, and judgment could be pronounced against a defendant, without personal service upon him either of the summons, or of the attachment. It was held that, this practice being a plain denial of elementary justice, no jurisdiction could be founded upon it (per BAYLEY J., at pp. 786, 787, HOLROYD J., at pp. 787, 788, and LITTLEDALE J., at pp. 788, 789). Similarly, in *London Corporation* v. *Cox*, *supra*, it was held that the London practice of foreign attachment was too unreasonable to support an averment of jurisdiction in the Mayor's Court.

[4] *London Corporation* v. *Cox*, *supra*, per WILLES J., at p. 264.

[5] At p. 263 of *London Corporation* v. *Cox*, *supra*, WILLES J. dealt with, and distinguished the rather curious case of *Briscoe* v. *Stephens* 1824), 2 Bing. 213, where, to an action for goods sold, the defendant pleaded estoppel by a former judgment given for him by an inferior court of record in an action against him by the plaintiff for the same causes of action, and the plaintiff, in his replication, denied the jurisdiction of the inferior court over either cause or parties, though he had himself resorted to it, and had obtained therein the relief prayed, and a demurrer to this replication was overruled. This was said by WILLES J., *ubi supra*, to have been a quite proper decision, and it is difficult to understand why the Court of Common Pleas exhibited "reluctance" to pronounce it, or why even WILLES J. described it as leading (at first sight) to a "paradoxical result". It would have been an extremely "paradoxical result" if the plaintiff had been suing on the judgment of the inferior court, but he was not, and the very reason of his suing in the superior court on the original cause of action was that his judgment in the inferior court was waste paper. At p. 305 of *Read* v. *Pope* (1834), 1 Cr. M. & R. 302, Lord LYNDHURST C.B. in the course of argument, suggests another type of case in which the party cannot be

122 These questions of the onus of allegation and proof, vital as they were as tests and guides at a time when the foundations of the doctrine now under consideration were being laid, are of less importance now that the structure has been completed, and the principle has been firmly established that, whenever it is made to appear, whether by reason of insufficient averment or proof of jurisdiction on the part of the party relying upon the decision as a *res judicata*, or as the result of a *prima facie* case of jurisdiction being displaced by affirmative evidence on the other side, that the tribunal was not competent to adjudicate on the particular question of law or fact which it purported to decide, the decision has no effect as a *res judicata*, and is controvertible on the merits, whether it be put forward as the basis of an action, or as a bar to a claim or defence. Of the application of this rule there are many illustrations. Judicial decisions of the following kinds have been held not to operate as *res judicatae*, or to conclude the parties:—a decision in a probate suit as to the disposition of the property the subject of a will, the Court of Probate having no jurisdiction to determine any such question;[1] decisions as to title pronounced by compensation and other tribunals invested by statute with jurisdiction to deal with certain specified matters other than questions of title;[2] decisions by tribunals acting under

---

expected to aver the jurisdiction of the inferior court, *viz.* where he is suing on that part of a judgment therein in his favour, he being then defendant, which ordered the costs of the action to be paid to him by the then plaintiff, because the very ground of the judgment in his favour with costs may have been that the inferior court had no jurisdiction. But this does not really constitute an exception to the rule: it would be the duty of the party in such a case to allege and establish that the inferior court had jurisdiction, on dismissing the action for want of jurisdiction, to order the costs to be paid to him.

[1] *Concha* v. *Concha* (1886), 11 App. Cas. 541, H.L. (per Lord BLACKBURN at p. 565: "the judge of the Probate Court had no jurisdiction to decide what was to be done with the residuary sum of the testator's property . . . This being so, . . . this is not a decision which would bind any one").

[2] *Cross* v. *Salter* (1790), 3 Term Rep. 639 (decision of ecclesiastical court as to the proprietary right to a pew not an estoppel, because no jurisdiction to deal with any question except the disturbance of a possessory right); *Sandwich Corporation* v. *R.* (1847), 10 Q.B. 571, Ex. Ch. (determination by the Treasury of a removed office-holder's right to compensation not an estoppel, they having jurisdiction only to hear appeals on the question of the amount of compensation: per WILDE C.J., at p. 579); *Archbishop of Dublin* v. *Coote* (1849), 12 I. Eq. Rep. 251, where it was held that a certain Irish "Court of Claims", established by statute to deal with forfeited lands, had no jurisdiction to determine whether any land had been forfeited or not, and, therefore, a decision by this court that the party's land had been forfeited did not estop him from afterwards asserting the contrary (per BRADY L.C. (Ir.), at pp. 267, 268); *R.* v. *London and N.W. Rail. Co.* (1854), 3 E. & B. 443 (statutory tribunal to assess compensation for land compulsorily taken, or injuriously affected, has no jurisdiction to determine questions of title, and its decision on any such question cannot take effect as a *res judicata*); *Chapman* v. *Monmouthshire Rail. and Canal Co.* (1857), 2 H. & N. 267 (the like); *Read* v. *Victoria Station and Pimlico Rail. Co.* (1863), 1 H. & C. 826, a similar case, where the Court of Exchequer, at pp. 838–840, expressed disagreement with the contrary view of Lord CAMPBELL C.J. on this point, in *Mortimer* v. *South Wales Rail. Co.* (1859), 1 E. & E. 375; *Horrocks* v. *Metropolitan Rail. Co.* (1863), 4 B. & S. 315 (the like); *Beckett* v. *Midland Rail. Co.* (1886), L.R. 1 C.P. 241 (the like: per ERLE J., at pp. 246, 247, and WILLES J., at p. 247); *Duke of Buccleuch* v. *Metropolitan Board of Works* (1870), L.R. 5 Exch. 221, Ex. Ch. (the like: per BLACKBURN J. at p. 227); *Dover* v. *Child* (1876),

the Inclosure Act 1845, as to the boundaries of, and titles to, lands, upon which questions the enactment does not empower such tribunals to adjudicate, their functions being limited to the making of awards and orders as to the allotment, exchange, and partition of lands;[1] decisions in bankruptcy express, or (as is usually the case) said to be implied, that the judgment on which the petition is based is good or bad, or that the judgment debt is valid, or invalid, or is sufficient, or insufficient, to constitute a good petitioning creditor's debt, or as to any similar matters, the jurisdiction of the Registrar on the hearing of the petition being strictly confined by statute[2] to the making of, or the refusal to make, a receiving order;[3] orders of a master in Chancery affecting to declare the rights of parties to administration proceedings, the functions of such masters being confined to the making of orders for the convenience of administration.[4]

Where the paternity of a child is in issue, a Registrar is not a court of competent jurisdiction to determine that issue by making an order under s. 26 (1) of the Matrimonial Causes Act 1950 for maintenance of the child. When such an order, therefore, has been made by a Registrar in the face of a husband's denial of paternity, the latter will not be precluded thereby from taking separate proceedings for a declaration as to the paternity of the child.[5]

123 Where the jurisdiction of a statutory tribunal is "contingent", as it has been termed, or conditional, it has to be considered to which of two possible classes the particular case belongs.

If the existence of a fact, or a state of things, is made by the statute a condition precedent to the jurisdiction of the tribunal, then, in order to render

---

1 Ex. D. 172, where it was held that a dismissal by a magistrate of a summons under s. 40 of the Metropolitan Police Act, 2 & 3 Vict. c. 71, if it was to be construed as involving a decision that the complainant had no title to the goods, was (so far) made without jurisdiction, and did not estop the party from afterwards asserting his title in an action for conversion (per KELLY C.B., at p. 175, and CLEASBY B., at pp. 175, 176).

1 *Jacomb* v. *Turner*, [1892] 1 Q.B. 47 (per COLLINS J., at pp. 51, 52); *Collis* v. *Amphlett*, [1918] 1 Ch. 232, C.A. (per SWINFEN EADY L.J., at p. 242: "the valuer had no jurisdiction to settle any question of title or boundaries", and, therefore, the award and map relied upon in that case was not "conclusive").

2 Bankruptcy Act 1883, s. 7, (2), (3), now s. 5 (3) of the Bankruptcy Act 1914.

3 *Re Vitoria, Ex parte Vitoria*, [1894] 2 Q.B. 387, C.A. (per Lord ESHER M.R., at pp. 389, 390, KAY L.J., at p. 391, and A. L. SMITH L.J., at p. 392); *King* v. *Henderson*, [1898] A.C. 720, P.C., where a colonial bankruptcy court having dismissed the creditor's petition, the debtor, in subsequent litigation with the creditor, set up, as an estoppel, not the decision itself, which he was entitled to do, but the record of the views which, in the course of his reasoned judgment, the judge had expressed on other questions which he had no jurisdiction to determine, and it was held that this record was not even admissible in evidence, much less effective as an estoppel (per Lord WATSON, delivering the opinion of the Judicial Committee, at pp. 729, 730); *Re Debtor, Ex parte Petitioning Creditor*, [1917] 2 K.B. 60, C.A. (per SCRUTTON L.J., at pp. 69–71).

4 *Thompson* v. *Thompson*, [1923] 2 Ch. 205 (per SARGANT J., at pp. 215, 216).

5 *Nokes* v. *Nokes*, [1957] P. 213. BARNARD J.'s decision (at p. 216) holding in favour of an estoppel, was reversed unanimously by the Court of Appeal (pp. 221 *et seq.*).

the decision of such tribunal binding and conclusive on the parties, it must be shown that the fact, or state of things, existed at the material date, and that the tribunal accordingly was empowered to decide as it did. If this is not shown, the decision will be one outside jurisdiction, and consequently without effect as a *res judicata*.[1] For where a statute has prescribed the subject-matter of the jurisdiction of an inferior court, and that court erroneously decides that it has jurisdiction, its decision cannot be effective to bestow upon itself a jurisdiction which the statute never gave; and a superior court may subsequently, on the same issue being raised in a later action, decide that there was no jurisdiction in the inferior court to deal with the matter in dispute, and accordingly may proceed to make such fresh adjudication between the parties as may be just. So where a Rent Tribunal had assumed jurisdiction on its own finding that the premises had been separately let since September 1st 1939, it was held competent—and indeed mandatory—for the county court to consider and deal with submissions that this finding of fact was erroneous and that the assumption of jurisdiction was accordingly unjustified.[2] So, too, (*in New Zealand*) where by the Fair Rents Act 1936 it was provided that:

> "Nothing in this Act shall apply with respect to any dwellinghouse . . . that has not been let as a dwellinghouse at any time since the 27th day of November 1935 . . ."

and the magistrate, in considering an application for possession as between landlord and tenant, held that the premises were protected by the Act, and refused an order for possession accordingly, the Supreme Court was held not precluded, in a subsequent action by landlord against tenant on the same facts, from reconsidering the question of jurisdiction; and, being of

---

[1] *Bunbury* v. *Fuller* (1853), 9 Exch. 111, at p. 140, per COLERIDGE J.—"Now it is a general rule that no court of limited jurisdiction can give its jurisdiction by a wrong decision on a point collateral to the merits of the case upon which the limit of its jurisdiction depends"; *R.* v. *Shoreditch Assessment Committee, Ex parte Morgan*, [1910] 2 K.B. 859, per FARWELL L.J. at p. 880; *R.* v. *Lincolnshire Justices, Ex parte Brett*, [1926] 2 K.B. 192, C.A. per ATKIN L.J. at p. 202—"Here is a collateral issue independent of the merits; no doubt the inferior court must give a decision upon it, but this decision being upon a point collateral to the main matter of complaint is open to review by the superior courts, and if a superior court decides that the matter of complaint arose outside the territorial limits, the result is that the inferior court had no jurisdiction". So, too, in *R.* v. *London, etc. Rent Tribunal, Ex parte Honig*, [1951] 1 K.B. 641, Lord GODDARD C.J. said at p. 645: "I have no doubt that we can review the collateral matter which the tribunal have decided, namely, the existence of a tenancy, as it is upon the existence of a tenancy that their jurisdiction depends". More recently still, see *Anisminic, Ltd.* v. *The Foreign Compensation Commission*, [1967] 2 All E.R. 986, C.A.

[2] *R.* v. *Judge Pugh, Ex parte Graham*, [1951] 2 K.B. 623, D. C. per Lord GODDARD C.J. at p. 629: "If the decision of an inferior court is pleaded as estopping a plaintiff from proceeding, the defendant must first adduce by his plea facts which will show that the inferior tribunal had jurisdiction, and the plaintiff can reply that there was no jurisdiction".

opinion on the facts that the premises were outside the provisions of the Act, from making an order for possession, notwithstanding the refusal of the magistrate to do so in the earlier proceedings.[1]

On the other hand the statute may expressly or by necessary implication constitute the tribunal the judge of the existence, or non-existence, of the fact, or state of things, and of the satisfaction or non-satisfaction, of the condition precedent; in such a case the decision of the tribunal on such a point is as much a *res judicata*, and as binding on the parties, as its decision on any other question within its jurisdiction to determine.[2]

124 The following rules as to the execution of judgments of inferior courts, being corollaries and illustrations of the principles already enunciated, seem not unworthy of notice in this place. It has been established that, where a party litigant complains that the judgment of an inferior court has been unlawfully executed against him, the opposite party, if he is minded to justify the alleged trespass on the ground of the unimpeachability of the judgments, and, therefore, of the warrant or process issued in execution thereof, must allege and prove the jurisdiction of the inferior court, and is answerable in damages if he fails to do so:[3] but a judicial or executive officer of the inferior court is protected if the pleadings, judgment, and other documents of record, purport to show jurisdiction on the face of them, whether in truth such jurisdiction existed, or not,[4] unless he is shown to have been aware of the absence of jurisdiction.[5]

---

[1] *Bethune* v. *Bydder*, [1938] N.Z.L.R. 1, C.A.

[2] Illustrations cited in the first edition are: *R.* v. *Income Tax Special Purposes Commissioners* (1888), 21 Q.B.D. 313 where it was held that having regard to the language of the statute—"proved to the satisfaction of the Commissioners"—it was not open to the court to revise their conclusion on fact; *R.* v. *Bloomsbury Income Tax Commissioners*, [1915] 3 K.B. 768 where the words were "if the surveyor discovers . . ."; *Spackman* v. *Plumstead District Board of Works* (1885), 10 App. Cas. 229, H.L.; *London County Council* v. *Galsworthy*, [1917] 1 K.B. 85, D.C. (per Lord READING C.J.) at pp. 91–94. More recently, *R.* v. *Ludlow, Ex parte Barnsley Corporation*, [1947] K.B. 634, in which Lord GODDARD C.J. held at p. 640, of the statutory tribunal whose jurisdiction was the subject of attack: "in other words Parliament may entrust the tribunal with the power of deciding whether or not they have jurisdiction, because they are empowered to decide the preliminary facts which alone will give it to them".

[3] *Adney* v. *Vernon* (1684), 3 Lev. 243; *Moravia* v. *Sloper* (1737), Willes, 30 (per WILLES C.J., delivering the judgment of the Court of Common Pleas, at pp. 34–36); *Ladbroke* v. *James* (1739), Willes, 199 (per WILLES C.J., at p. 201); *Herbert* v. *Cook* (1782), Willes, 37 n. (per Lord MANSFIELD C.J., at p. 37 n). The case of *Truscott* v. *Carpenter* (1697), 1 Ld. Raym. 229, is inconsistent with the above line of authorities and cannot now be accepted. The effect of the older authorities is summed up by WILLES J., delivering the opinion of the judges summoned at p. 263 of *London Corporation* v. *Cox* (1867), L.R. 2 H.L. 239, as follows: "the plaintiff isl iable to an action for executing the process of an inferior court in a matter beyond its jurisdiction, and cannot justify under such process whether he knows of the defect or not".

[4] *Lucking* v. *Denning* (1701), 1 Salk. 201 (per HOLT C.J., at pp. 201, 202).

[5] Per WILLES J., at p. 263 of *London Corporation* v. *Cox*, *supra*: "the judge and officer are liable to a civil action if they knew of the defect of jurisdiction".

Jurisdiction of English arbitral tribunals

125 When any dispute or difference between parties is made the subject of arbitration, the "arbitral tribunal" (by which expression is meant the single arbitrator, or the several arbitrators, or the majority of them, or the umpire, or other the person or persons appointed to adjudicate on the matters submitted) is undoubtedly a judicial tribunal,[1] and the doctrine of *res judicata* is accordingly applicable to its decisions, including the rules as to jurisdiction already enunciated. The judicial authority of the tribunal is constituted in some cases solely by the agreement and voluntary submission of the disputants; in others by an order of the court; in others, again, by, or pursuant to, a statute. A tribunal of the first kind alone is purely and strictly a *forum domesticum*: but tribunals of all three types may be described as domestic in the sense that, however created, they are not constituted Courts of the Realm, but exercise their functions merely as tribunals "d'occasion", or as unofficial judges appointed *ad hoc*. In the case of all these varieties of arbitral tribunal alike, where any award is relied upon as a *res judicata*, it must appear that such award, like any other judicial decision, was within the jurisdiction conferred.

It is obvious that if the contract or other document binding the parties to submit their disputes to arbitration specifies certain qualifications in the arbitrators, it is a condition of their jurisdiction that they possess these qualifications, and that a party who submits to their arbitration in ignorance of their lack of qualification will not be bound by the result.[2] *Aliter*, however, if with knowledge of the lack of qualifications of his nominee he has himself nominated the unqualified arbitrator and has proceeded with the arbitration; he will then be estopped (*in paiis*) from denying the nominee's qualifications, and will be bound by the award.[3]

In former times it was always held that, in an action on an award, the burden is on the plaintiff to allege that the award was in accordance with the submission.[4] But, whether the strictness of the old pleading rules would

---

[1] *Eastwood and Holt* v. *Studer* (1926) 31 Com. Cas. 251, per ROCHE J. at pp. 256–257.

[2] *Jungheim Hopkins & Co.* v. *Foukelmann*, [1909] 2 K.B. 948. And where two arbitrators, duly appointed and empowered under the submission to arbitration to appoint an umpire with certain specified qualifications, appointed an umpire without those qualifications, the parties were held not bound by the actions of their arbitrators in making the appointment, and the umpires' award was set aside—*Rahcassi Shipping Co., S.A.* v. *Blue Star Line, Ltd.*, [1967] 3 All E.R. 301 (ROSKILL J.).

[3] *Oakland Metal Co., Ltd.* v. *D. Benaim & Co., Ltd.*, [1953] 2 Q.B. 261; [1953] 2 All E.R. 650 (PARKER J.).

[4] See 2 Wms. Saund. 62, note 3: "an award or umpirage ought in pleading to be stated to have been made pursuant to the submission in form as well as in substance," At p. 231 of *Duke of Buccleuch* v. *Metropolitan Board of Works* (1870), L.R. 5 Exch. 221, Exch. Ch., BLACKBURN J. cites the above passage, and adds: "this is exactly for the same reason that jurisdiction must be averred in an action on the judgment of an inferior court".

be followed at the present day or not, and whether the party setting up the award as conclusive and unimpeachable would now be deemed bound to show jurisdiction, or the opposite party to show the absence of it, it is quite clearly established that, wherever the arbitral tribunal has exceeded the jurisdiction with which it has been invested by the agreement of the parties,[1] or by the order of the court, or by the statute, the award, so far from operating as a *res judicata*, is deemed an absolute nullity either in whole, or in part, as the case may be. "An award", in the language of BLACKBURN J.,[2] "is the decision of one having a limited authority to determine those matters submitted to him by the parties, or . . . by a statute, and no other. And from this it follows that, if that limited authority has not been pursued, and the arbitrator has awarded something beyond his authority, the award is *pro tanto* void, and, if the void part is so mixed up with the rest that it cannot be rejected, the award is void altogether, . . . And I think, both on authority and principle, this is a matter that may be pleaded as a defence to an action."

126 It will be seen from the concluding sentence of the passage above cited that, in the view of BLACKBURN J., supported by abundant authority, both prior and subsequent to the date of his judgment, absence or excess of jurisdiction is not merely a ground of a motion to set aside or remit the award,—which remedy raises no question of *res judicata*, since it presupposes that the award is binding unless and until so set aside or remitted, —but is also an answer to an action on the award (and it may be added, is also now an answer to the modern summary procedure for enforcing it), as well as to the setting up of the award as a bar,—which does necessarily involve the proposition that no arbitral decision can take effect as a *res judicata* unless made with competent jurisdiction.

127 The cases in which arbitral decisions, though made by arbitrators duly appointed[3] (by the parties, or as the case may be) have been held inconclusive and impeachable on the ground of want of jurisdiction naturally range themselves under three main heads, now to be examined.

---

1 The disputants may either extend the powers of the arbitral tribunal beyond, or confine them within narrower limits than, those of the common law jurisdiction of the courts. Thus, they may authorize or require the tribunal to decide the questions submitted to it on principles of honour, in preference to rules of law, where they conflict, as in *Re Newey* (1912), 107 L.T. 832, Div. Ct., or to receive evidence of a kind which would be inadmissible, or reject or disregard evidence of a kind which would be admissible, or even necessary, in a court of law.

2 At p. 229 of *Duke of Buccleuch* v. *Metropolitan Board of Works*, *supra*.

3 Where the arbitrators lack jurisdiction because ineffectually appointed, the award will of course be bad from this cause—*e.g.* where arbitrators were allowed to sit although (but not to the knowledge of the plaintiff) not qualified by the terms of reference, the plaintiff was held competent to object, even after the award, and the award was set aside: *Jungheim Hopkins & Co.* v. *Foukelmann*, [1909] 2 K.B. 948.

128 The first type of case is where the arbitral tribunal takes upon itself to hear and determine questions or issues other than those specified as the subjects of the arbitration in the written agreement or submission of the parties[1] or in the judicial order, or enactment,[2] from which the tribunal derives its authority and jurisdiction.

129 The second group comprises all those cases in which the arbitral tribunal assumes to make orders, and give directions, as to the execution of works and the like, which, though conceived by the tribunal to be ancillary to, and consequential upon, the main purpose of its decision, or otherwise convenient and equitable, do not in fact either expressly, or by reasonable implication, come within the powers with which the submission, the order, or the statute has invested it;[3] those in which the tribunal, or any member thereof, has delegated its, or his, judicial functions (as distinct from its functions of investigation, and the obtaining of evidence, information, and expert assistance) to a person not authorized as umpire or otherwise by the submission, the order of reference, or the statute (as the case may be), to pronounce any judicial decision whatever on the matters submitted, or in which the tribunal has disregarded the requirements of the instrument from which it derives its jurisdiction as to how, and by whom, the award is to be made and signed;[4] and those in which the tribunal has

---

[1] For instances, in cases of purely domestic arbitrations, see *Fisher* v. *Pimbley* (1809), 11 East 188 (per Lord ELLENBOROUGH C.J., at p. 192, and BAYLEY J., at p. 193: here absence of jurisdiction held proper subject of plea of "no award", sc. no valid award); *Bowes* v. *Fernie* (1838), 4 My. & Cr. 150 (per Lord COTTENHAM L.C., at pp. 158–162); *Jones* v. *Corry* (1839), 5 Bing. N.C. 187.

[2] For cases of statutory arbitrations, see *Beckett* v. *Midland Rail. Co.* (1866), L.R. 1 C.P. 241; *Re Dare Valley Rail. Co.* (1868), L.R. 6 Eq. 429; *Davis* v. *Witney Urban District Council* (1898), 14 T.L.R. 433, D.C.; on appeal, 15 T.L.R. 275, C.A.

[3] As in *Tomlin* v. *Fordwich Corporation* (1836), 5 Ad. & El. 147, where the tribunal directed repairs to be executed to the satisfaction of a person who was not an arbitrator; *Turner* v. *Swainson* (1836), 1 M. & W. 572, where the tribunal ordered works to be executed on a third person's land,—a case, it is true, of a successful motion to set aside the award, but, as observed by PARKE B., at p. 573, the excess of jurisdiction would equally have been a good defence to an action on the award; *Price* v. *Popkin* (1839), 10 Ad. & E. 139, where, again, arbitrators appointed to decide the issues in an action exceeded their jurisdiction by directing works to be executed (per Lord DENMAN C.J., at p. 141); *Re Green & Co. and Balfour, Williamson & Co.* (1890), 63 L.T. 325, C.A., where, the sole question submitted to the arbitrators being whether the goods answered to the warranty, the tribunal took upon itself, after deciding this question, to give directions as to payments, allowances, and the like (per COTTON L.J., at pp. 326, 327, and FRY L.J., at pp. 327, 328); *Pedler* v. *Hardy* (1902), 18 T.L.R. 591 (per CHANNELL J., at p. 592); *Re Stone and Hastie*, [1903] 2 K.B. 463, where the statutory tribunal had made orders which they were not authorised by the statute to make, and this excess of jurisdiction was held a good answer to a motion to enforce the award: *Leadbetter* v. *Marylebone Corporation*, [1904] 2 K.B. 893, C.A., where, a statutory award being set up as an estoppel, the estoppel was defeated on grounds similar to those on which the motion failed in the last cited case. Note that an order, without express authority, as to costs may be held bad, without affecting the residue of the award: *Cockburn* v. *Newton* (1841), 2 M. & G. 899.

[4] As in *Tomlin* v. *Fordwich Corporation*, *supra*; *Little, Roberts, and Mitchell* v. *Newton* (1841), 2 Man. & G. 351, where two arbitrators delegated their authority absolutely to a third person

received, or dispensed with, evidence, or has otherwise conducted the arbitration, in a manner not authorized by the submission or other instrument defining the extent of its powers.[1]

130 The third class consists of those cases in which the jurisdiction conferred upon the arbitral tribunal by the submission, order of reference, or enactment, is expressed therein to depend upon the doing of an act, the lapse of a period of time, the happening of an event, or the satisfaction of some other condition precedent, and the specified act, period, event, or condition has not been done, elapsed, happened, or been satisfied, before the tribunal assumes jurisdiction. In no such case can the award take effect as a *res judicata*[2] even though there be a statement on the face of the award that the condition on which the jurisdiction is contingent has been performed or satisfied; for an arbitral tribunal cannot give itself a jurisdiction which does not belong to it by such a finding contrary to the fact,[3] any

(per TINDAL C.J. at pp. 360–362); *Re Templeman and Reed* (1841), 9 Dowl. 962, where, the arbitral tribunal consisting of three arbitrators, two of them left the whole decision to the third; *Eads* v. *Williams* (1854), 4 De G.M. & G. 674, where the arbitrator, having sent another person to go down the mine and report to him, instead of inspecting it himself,—to which course, so far, there was no objection,—proceeded to delegate the whole of his judicial functions to that person, which he manifestly had no jurisdiction to do; *Whitmore* v. *Smith* (1861), 7 H. & N. 509, where the arbitrators delegated their duties to a third person, not as umpire, and agreed to surrender their opinions to his, and to be bound by his decision: *United Kingdom Mutual S.S. Association* v. *Houston & Co.*, [1896] 1 Q.B. 567, where, the reference being to three arbitrators, an award made by two only out of the three was held not binding for want of jurisdiction (per MATHEW J., at pp. 569, 570). In older and stricter days, it used to be held that, where the reference was to three arbitrators, or any two of them, any award signed by such two arbitrators at different times and places, and not *simul et semel*, was bad for want of jurisdiction: see *Wright* v. *Graham* (1848), 3 Exch. 131; *Wade* v. *Dowling* (1854), 4 E. & B. 44 (per COLERIDGE J., at pp. 50, 51, WIGHTMAN J., at pp. 51, 52, and ERLE J., at pp. 52, 53;) *Lord* v. *Lord* (1855), 5 E. & B 404 (appointment of umpire signed by both arbitrators, but not sitting together). This highly technical rule, however, in so far as it operated to invalidate the award, was not followed for long, and the sensible practice was adopted of sending the award back to the arbitrators for them to execute it *simul et semel*, thereby preserving its binding character: see *Peterson* v. *Ayre* (1855), 15 C.B. 724; *Anning* v. *Hartley* (1858), 27 L.J. Ex. 145.

[1] Such as the following: leaving it to one of the parties to discharge himself by his affidavit,—*Pedley* v. *Goddard* (1796), 7 Term Rep. 73; taking evidence by affidavit, when the submission required it to be taken orally,—*Banks* v. *Banks* (1835), 1 Gale 46; allowing the umpire to decide without having heard the evidence,—*Re Salkeld and Slater and Harrison* (1840), 12 Ad. & El. 767.

[2] See *The Warwick* (1890), 15 P.D. 189, where the rules of the association to which the parties belonged provided for arbitration in cases of collision between vessels owned by members of that association, and it was held that, there having been in fact no collision, as the association itself resolved, an award following an arbitration purporting to have been held in accordance with the rules was made without jurisdiction, and could not operate as an estoppel; *May* v. *Mills* (1914), 30 T.L.R. 287, where the condition of the jurisdiction was the existence of the relation of landlord and tenant between the parties at the time when the dispute arose, and COLERIDGE, J., being of opinion that this relation did not in fact exist at the above date, though the arbitral tribunal found that it did, held that the award was a nullity, as having been made without jurisdiction.

[3] See *May* v. *Mills*, *supra*, and the observations of Lord DENMAN C.J., at p. 143 (during the argument) of *Price* v. *Popkin* (1839), 10 Ad. & El. 139, and of ALDERSON B., at p. 350 of *Faviell (Farrill)* v. *Eastern Counties Rail. Co.* (1848), 2 Exch. 344 ("the extent of the arbitrator's jurisdiction could not be interpreted by his own judgment"). Cp. *A.-G. for Manitoba* v. *Kelly*, [1922] 1 A.C. 268, P.C., at p. 276.

more than, conversely, any finding or recital in the award, contrary to the fact, of the non-satisfaction of any condition precedent to the jurisdiction in respect of any question submitted can justify the arbitral tribunal in declining, or omitting, to adjudicate upon or deal with that question in the award.[1] DEVLIN J. has admirably summarised the principles which govern this aspect of arbitral jurisdiction. In his judgment in *Christopher Brown, Ltd.* v. *Genossenschaft Oesterreichischer*[2] he said:

> "It is clear that at the beginning of any arbitration one side or the other may challenge the jurisdiction of the arbitrator. It is not the law that arbitrators, if their jurisdiction is challenged or questioned, are bound immediately to refuse to act until their jurisdiction has been determined by some court which has power to determine it finally. Nor is it the law that they are bound to go on without investigating the merits of the challenge and to determine the matter in dispute, leaving the question of their jurisdiction to be held over until it is determined by some court which had power to determine it. They might then be merely wasting their time and everybody else's. They are not obliged to take either of those courses. They are entitled to inquire into the merits of the issue whether they have jurisdiction or not, not for the purpose of reaching any conclusion which will be binding upon the parties—because that they cannot do—but for the purpose of satisfying themselves as a preliminary matter whether they ought to go on with the arbitration or not. If it became abundantly clear to them, on looking into the matter, that they obviously had no jurisdiction as, for example, it would be if the submission which was produced was not signed, or not properly executed, or something of that sort, then they might well take the view that they were not going to go on with the hearing at all. They are entitled, in short, to make their own inquiries in order to determine their own course of action, and the result of that inquiry has no effect whatsoever upon the rights of the parties. That is plain, I think, from the burden that is put upon a plaintiff who is suing upon an award. He is obliged to prove not only the making of the award, but also that the arbitrators had jurisdiction to make the award. The principle *omnia praesumuntur rite esse acta* does not apply to proceedings of arbitration tribunals or, indeed, to the proceedings of inferior tribunals of any sort. There is no presumption that merely because an award has been made it is a valid award. It has to be proved by the party who sues upon it that it was made by the arbitrators within the terms of their authority, that is, with jurisdiction. Jurisdiction has to be proved affirmatively. If the plaintiff takes upon himself the burden of proving the award, and fails to prove that the arbitrators had jurisdiction, his action fails, and it is irrelevant whether the arbitrators thought or did not think that they had jurisdiction. Their finding is of no value to him. But if he proves that the arbitrators did have jurisdiction then he succeeds, and his success is not destroyed because the arbitrators themselves went into the matter and came to the same conclusion which, *ex hypothesi*, was the right one. In short, any view which is

[1] *Samuel* v. *Cooper* (1835), 2 Ad. & El. 752 (per Lord DENMAN C.J. at p. 757).
[2] [1954] 1 Q.B. 8, at pp. 12–13.

expressed by the arbitrators expressly or impliedly in the award, any finding which can be called a finding that they had jurisdiction does not make the award any better, and likewise does not make it any worse."

If in fact the condition of the jurisdiction existed, it is quite immaterial that nothing is said about it on the face of the award,[1]

131 There is, however, as has already been noticed, in relation to other tribunals of limited jurisdiction,[2] a type of case, not easily distinguishable from the class just described,[3] in which the jurisdiction of the arbitral tribunal is, by the instrument creating it, or by reasonable implication therefrom, made contingent, not upon the existence of a state of things in fact, but upon the decision of the tribunal that such a state of things exists, and where, therefore, the tribunal itself is made the final judge of its own jurisdiction, in the sense that its decision on this question is as conclusive and unimpeachable as its decision on any other matter submitted to its arbitrament. Thus, where "the claims of the plaintiff in the action" were by a judge's order referred to arbitration, and the plaintiff put forward at the hearing a claim which the defendant contended was not "a claim in the action", it was held that the arbitrator had jurisdiction to determine this question for himself, and that his decision thereon was incontrovertible.[4] Again, where disputes arising out of a trade contract had been submitted to arbitration, and the arbitral tribunal decided that there existed a certain trade custom which was applicable to the case before them, in the light of which the contract ought to be construed, the House of Lords rejected the contention of the unsuccessful party that the existence and applicability of the custom was a condition precedent to the jurisdiction, and held that this question was as much within the competency of the tribunal to decide, beyond the possibility of controversy, as any other question upon which they were called upon to adjudicate.[5]

---

[1] See *Davies* v. *Pratt* (*No.* 2) (1855), 17 C.B. 183 where the issues in the cause were referred by an order of the court to a barrister to decide as soon as he should have made his award concerning the issues in another action which had also been referred to him by an order of the court, and it was held that the fact that the arbitrator did not state that he had entered upon his duties at the prescribed time in no way affected the conclusiveness or validity of the award, there being no suggestion that in fact the arbitrator had not done his duty, and the presumption being that he had, and that the condition of his jurisdiction had been fulfilled (per JERVIS C.J., at p. 188).

[2] See para. 123, *ante*, and the illustrations given in note 2 on p. 100, *ante*.

[3] See the observations of BLACKBURN J., at p. 232 of *Duke of Buccleuch* v. *Metropolitan Board of Works* (1870), L.R. 5 Exch. 221, Ex. Ch. The difficulty of deciding whether a decision is one as to the existence of jurisdiction or one as to a matter within jurisdiction is well illustrated by the parallel cases of *Ayscough* v. *Sheed Thomson & Co., Ltd.* (1923), 129 L.T. 429 (affirmed by the H.L. on appeal, 131 L.T. 610) and *Pinnock Brothers* v. *Lewis and Peat, Ltd.*, [1923] 1 K.B. 690.

[4] *Faviell* (*Farrill*) v. *Eastern Counties Rail. Co.* (1848), 2 Exch. 344 (per POLLOCK C.B., at pp. 349, 350, ALDERSON B., at p. 350, and ROLFE and PLATT BB., at p. 351).

[5] *Produce Brokers Co., Ltd.* v. *Olympia Oil and Cake Co., Ltd.*, [1916] 1 A.C. 314, H.L. (per Lord PARKER, at p. 327). In this case the H.L. reversed the C.A., who only decided as they did because they conceived themselves bound by *Hutcheson & Co.* v. *Eaton & Son* (1884), 13 Q.B.D.

132 Where the form of the award is such as to make it clear that the arbitral tribunal has separately adjudicated upon separate matters, some of which were, and others were not, within its jurisdiction, so much of the award as purports to deal with the former is binding and conclusive, and the residue is a nullity: but where there is no separate decision of the several matters, as, for instance, when a lump sum is awarded, it is open to either party desirous of impeaching the award to establish, if he can, by extrinsic evidence that the arbitral tribunal did in fact take into consideration matters not within its *arbitrium*. In such cases, where the general jurisdiction to make an award of some kind on the matters submitted is not in question, the onus is on the party impeaching the award to show excess of jurisdiction, and not on the party suing upon or setting up, the award to show that the tribunal acted within its jurisdiction, as it is in cases where the jurisdiction of the tribunal to decide anything at all is challenged.[1] If this onus is discharged, the whole award is bad:[2] if, on the other hand, the attacking party fails to establish that the tribunal in fact took into account matters held to be outside its jurisdiction, or that matters found to have been taken into account were, in point of law, outside its jurisdiction, the whole of the award is good, and effective as a *res judicata*.[3] The onus is not discharged merely by proof that the

861, C.A., and *Re North Western Rubber Co. and Huttenbach & Co.*, [1908] 2 K.B. 907, C.A., with both of which the H.L. expressed their disagreement, as to the latter, conceding that the distinction between the two types of case had there been correctly stated, but thinking that the case before the C.A. had been placed by them in the wrong class. *Cf.*, again, the parallel cases of *Ayscough* v. *Sheed Thomson & Co., Ltd.* (1923), 129 L.T. 429 and *Pinnock Brothers* v. *Lewis and Peat, Ltd.*, [1923] 1 K.B. 690 referred to in note 3, p. 106, *ante*.

[1] The principle is stated by BLACKBURN J., at pp. 229, 230 of *Duke of Buccleuch* v. *Metropolitan Board of Works*, *supra*, and, particularly as regards the burden of proof, by Lord DAVEY, delivering the opinion of the P.C., at pp. 463, 464, of *Falkingham* v. *Victoria Railway Commissioners*, [1900] A.C. 452, P.C. See also *A.-G. for Manitoba* v. *Kelly*, [1922] 1 A.C. 268, P.C.

[2] As in *Tomlin* v. *Fordwich Corporation* (1836), 5 Ad. & El. 147; *Price* v. *Popkin* (1839), 10 Ad. & El. 139; *Beckett* v. *Midland Rail. Co.* (1866), L.R. 1 C.P. 241 (per ERLE J., at pp. 246, 247, and WILLES J., at p. 247). *Cp.* the compensation case of *Re Penny* (1857), 7 E. & B. 660, where the statutory tribunal, a sheriff's jury, was in substance, though not in name or form, an arbitral one. Here it was established by affidavit evidence—it did not appear upon the face of the inquisition or verdict,—that, in awarding a lump sum as compensation for the "injurious affection" of the claimant's lands under the Lands Clauses Acts, the jury had, on the direction of the under-sheriff, taken into consideration, amongst other matters, the fact that the claimant's premises would be "overlooked" by the railway, which was clearly beyond their jurisdiction, and the whole of the verdict was on that ground held bad (per Lord CAMPBELL, C.J., at pp. 668, 669).

[3] See *Duke of Buccleuch* v. *Metropolitan Board of Works* (1872), L.R. 5 H.L. 418, where it was proved by the oral evidence of the umpire that, in his estimate of the compensation payable, he had in fact taken into consideration the matter said to be beyond his jurisdiction under the statute, but the H.L., reversing the decision of the Exchequer Chamber, and restoring that of the Court of Exchequer, held that it had not been established that the matter in question was one with which the umpire was incompetent to deal. Conversely, in *Falkingham* v. *Victoria Railway Commissioners*, [1900] A.C. 452, P.C., the matters in question were admittedly matters which the tribunal had no jurisdiction to take into account, but it was not proved that the tribunal had in fact taken them into account.

arbitral tribunal heard evidence tendered by the parties on the matters in question, because the tribunal may have done so for the very purpose of ascertaining whether they were or were not, within the jurisdiction,—which, indeed, is their duty.[1] It is equally immaterial that the award contains no recital that the tribunal had not, or that it had, taken into consideration the matters said to be outside its jurisdiction: in the former case, if the award is otherwise shown to be unimpeachable on this ground, it is not rendered any the less so by the mere fact that, on the face of it, it does not appear that the arbitrator did not exceed his authority and duty, because this will be presumed in his favour:[2] in the latter case, on the other hand, if the award is otherwise shown to be impeachable in this respect, it is not rendered any the less so by the mere fact that, on the face of it, it does not disclose any examination of matters outside the jurisdiction, because this can be established *ab extra*.[3]

133 In every case where the arbitral tribunal is shown to have acted within, or is not shown to have acted in excess of, its jurisdiction, and all the other conditions of a good *res judicata* are established, and are not dis-established by any affirmative answer,[4] the award binds the parties and cannot be impeached by either of them either for error in law, or error in fact.[5] Jurisdiction, for this purpose, does not mean jurisdiction to give a correct decision only. It is true that, if error in law appears upon the face

---

[1] *Falkingham* v. *Victoria Railway Commissioners*, [1900] A.C. 452, P.C. at p. 464. *Cf.* the passage from the judgment of DEVLIN J. in *Christopher Brown, Ltd.* v. *Genossenschaft Oesterreichischer*, [1954] 1 Q.B. 8, cited in para 130, *supra*.

[2] *Falkingham* v. *Victoria Railway Commissioners*, *supra* at pp. 463, 464.

[3] Thus, in *Re Penny*, *supra*, cited in note 2 on p. 107, the fact was proved by affidavit, to the satisfaction of the court, who held that it was quite unnecessary that it should appear on the face of the proceedings (per WIGHTMAN and ERLE JJ., at p. 670, and CROMPTON J., at p. 671). So, also, in *Re Dare Valley Rail. Co.* (1868), L.R. 6 Eq. 429 (at p. 436). In *Duke of Buccleuch* v. *Metropolitan Board of Works*, *supra*, the oral evidence of the umpire, his award being silent on the point, was held admissible to prove what matters he had taken into account (per Lord CHELMSFORD L.C., at pp. 457, 458, and Lord CAIRNS, at p. 462).

[4] See Chapter XIII, *post*.

[5] See *Morgan* v. *Mather* (1792), 2 Ves. 15 (per Lord Commissioner WILSON, at p. 18); *Lancaster* v. *Hemington* (1835), 4 Ad. & El. 345; *Hagger* v. *Baker* (1845), 14 M. & W. 9; *Fuller* v. *Fenwick* (1846), 3 C.B. 705; *Hodgkinson* v. *Fernie* (1857), 3 C.B. N.S. 189 (per COCKBURN C.J., at p. 200, WILLIAMS J., at p. 202, and CROWDER J., at pp. 203, 204;) *Hogge* v. *Burgess* (1858), 3 H. & N. 293; *Duke of Buccleuch* v. *Metropolitan Board of Works* (1870), L.R. 5 Exch. 221, Ex. Ch. (per BLACKBURN J., at p. 231: "if the tribunal has jurisdiction, the decision of a point within its jurisdiction, or, as BRAMWELL B., in the court below expresses it, within its *arbitrium*, whether on the law or on the facts, cannot be reviewed except in a court having jurisdiction to sit as a court of appeal from that decision"); *Dinn* v. *Blake* (1875), L.R. 10 C.P. 388 (per BRETT J., at p. 391); *A.-G. for Manitoba* v. *Kelly*, [1922] 1 A.C. 268, P.C. (at pp. 281–283); *Champsey, Bhara & Co.* v. *Jivraj Balloo Spinning and Weaving Co.*, [1923] A.C. 480, P.C. (at pp. 486–488, where *Landauer* v. *Asser*, *infra*, cited in the next note, is distinguished). A robust note is furnished by the judgment of SCRUTTON L.J. in *Ayscough* v. *Sheed Thomson & Co. Ltd.* (1923), 129 L.T. 429 (subsequently affirmed in the Lords: 131 L.T. 610) at p. 431: "As I have frequently said, if people do not like the courts they should keep clear of them, and if they go to arbitrators they should stand by their decision and not try to upset it in the courts."

of the award, or in any memorandum or paper contemporaneously issued, and intended to form part of it, the award may be set aside, or remitted to the arbitral tribunal, on the motion of the party aggrieved,[1] except in cases where a specific question of law is expressly submitted, as such, for decision,[2] or where the tribunal is invested with authority to adjudicate upon a debt of honour, or other matter not cognizable by the courts of law;[3] it is also true that, for any mistake of fact, either apparent upon the face of the award, or to which the arbitrator himself calls attention in some memorandum, letter, notice or affidavit, whereby he seeks the aid of the court to set the matter right, the award may be remitted to the tribunal for the necessary rectification,[4] and that, even without any application to the court being made for that purpose, any arbitrator or umpire has now statutory authority of his own motion "to correct any clerical mistake, or

---

[1] As in *Kent* v. *Elstob* (1802), 3 East 18; *Ames* v. *Milward* (1818), 8 Taunt. 637; *Landauer* v. *Asser*, [1905] 2 K.B. 184, D.C. (though this case has been the subject of critical observations in the H.L., whereby its authority has been seriously shaken); *Ex parte Strabane Rural District Council*, [1910] 1 Ir.R. 135; *British Westinghouse Electric and Manufacturing Co., Ltd.* v. *Underground Electric Railway Co. of London*, [1912] A.C. 673, H.L.; *Parsons* v. *Brixham Fishing Smack Insurance Co.* (1918), 118 L.T. 600, D.C. (where LUSH and SANKEY JJ., at p. 603, distinguished *Re King and Duveen*, *infra*, cited in the next note). The exception, as to the error appearing on the face of the record, is reluctantly recognized as well-established in *Hodgkinson* v. *Fernie*, *supra* (per WILLIAMS J., at p. 202, and WILLES J. at p. 206), and, again, with the like reluctance, in *Champsey, Bhara & Co.* v. *Jivraj Balloo Spinning and Weaving Co. supra* (at p. 487).

[2] *Re King and Duveen*, [1913] 2 K.B. 32, D.C.; *Kelantan Government* v. *Duff Development Co.*, [1923] A.C. 395, H.L. (per Lord CAVE L.C., at pp. 408–412, and Lord PARMOOR, at pp. 416–418).

[3] *Re Newey, Ex parte Whiteman* (1912), 107 L.T. 832, D.C., where it was stated by PHILLIMORE J. that an award made by arbitrators on whom jurisdiction has been conferred to decide a gaming dispute is binding and conclusive in law, though the debt sought to be recovered is one of honour only, and not enforceable by action.

[4] As in *Rogers* v. *Dallimore* (1815), 6 Taunt. 111 (mistake admitted by arbitrator in a letter addressed to the parties); *Re Hall and Hinds* (1841), 2 Man. & G. 847 (figures subtracted which were obviously intended to be added); *Hutchinson* v. *Shepperton* (1849), 13 Q.B. 955 (admission by arbitrator in affidavit that he had omitted an item in the account); *Davies* v. *Pratt* (1855), 16 C.B. 586 (mistake in a name); *Gore* v. *Baker* (1855), 4 E. & B. 470 (where, as appears from a statement by DENMAN J. in *Dinn* v. *Blake*, *infra*, at p. 390, he having been the arbitrator in the earlier case, the facts were that, the issues in an action having been referred by the court, the arbitrator, instead of finding the issues distributively, by a pure act of inadvertence, made his award in a form which had the effect of giving all the costs to the plaintiff, though one of the issues had been found in his favour: on realising the unintended effect of what he had done, the arbitrator communicated with the parties by an explanatory letter, which was before the court, for the purpose of rectifying his error); *Mills* v. *Bowyers' Society* (1856), 3 K. & J. 66 (affidavits by the arbitrators, informing the court of their mistake: per WOOD V.C., at p. 74); *Flynn* v. *Robertson* (1869), L.R. 4 C.P. 324 (accidental omission, admitted both by the arbitrator, and by the parties). With the foregoing cases, contrast the following, in which the court declined to set aside or remit the award, in the absence of any admission by the arbitral tribunal, either to the court, or to the parties, that it had made the alleged mistake: *Phillips* v. *Evans* (1843), 12 M. & W. 309; *Leggo* v. *Young* (1855), 16 C.B. 626 (where the arbitrator had addressed a letter to one of the parties only, and this letter was in no sense an admission of any error, but merely an apologetic explanation of his reasons for deciding against him); *Holgate* v. *Killick* (1861), 7 H. & N. 418 (a somewhat similar letter to one of the parties only); *Dinn* v. *Blake* (1875), L.R. 10. C.P. 388.

error arising from any accidental slip or omission":[1] but the very existence of, and necessity for, these powers of setting aside, remitting, or correcting awards obviously involves the position that, unless and until so set aside, remitted, or corrected, the award, however wrong in law, or mistaken in fact, operates as a *res judicata*, and estops the parties from controverting it on the merits.

Jurisdiction of English criminal tribunals

134 The same jurisdiction rules apply to the decisions (whether strictly criminal, or quasi-civil) of English criminal tribunals. Thus, to take the simplest illustration, a judgment of acquittal pronounced by a criminal court which had no jurisdiction to convict, or to acquit, the accused is a nullity, and cannot be made the foundation of a plea of *autrefois acquit*, or constitute a bar to fresh criminal proceedings for the same offence.[2]

135 Where a court of summary jurisdiction is invested by statute with authority to pronounce decisions of a quasi-civil character, such as orders for payment of money to parties, or directions to execute works, as distinct from sentences of fine or imprisonment, there is the same, or even greater, necessity for examining the exact nature and limits of the statutory authority conferred, in order to ascertain whether the decision can rank as a *res judicata*. Thus, a court of summary jurisdiction is empowered by statute, on an affiliation summons, to make, or to refuse to make, an order for the maintenance of the bastard, but, in the latter event, it has no authority to decide that the party summoned is not the putative father of the bastard: accordingly a dismissal of the summons, even if it can be supposed to involve of necessity a decision negativing the alleged paternity (which it does not), is no bar to, or estoppel against, a fresh application by the woman for an affiliation order against the same person, because the court had no jurisdiction to pronounce such a decision even in express terms.[3]

---

[1] Arbitration Act 1950, s. 17: it is to be noted that the power is given subject to a contrary intention not being expressed in the arbitration agreement. As to what is not an "accidental slip or omission" and cannot be made the subject of amendment, see *Sutherland & Co.* v. *Hannevig Brothers, Ltd.*, [1921] 1 K.B. 336, D.C.

[2] For instance, where a grand jury had found a true bill without having sworn the witnesses who appeared before them, it was held that the indictment was bad, and that the judgment of acquittal on the trial thereof was wholly without jurisdiction, and a nullity: *R.* v. *Bitton* (1833), 6 C. & P. 92; *R.* v. *Chamberlain* (1833), 6 C. & P. 93.

[3] *R.* v. *Jenkin* (1736), Cas. temp. Hard., 300 (per Lord HARDWICKE C.J., at p. 302); *R.* v. *Machen* (1849), 14 Q.B. 74 (per Lord DENMAN C.J., at pp. 79, 80); *R.* v. *Harrington* (1864), 12 W.R. 420; *R.* v. *Gaunt* (1867), L.R. 2 Q.B. 466 (per BLACKBURN J., at pp. 469, 470, and MELLOR and LUSH JJ., at p. 470); *R.* v. *Seddon, Ex parte Hall* (1916), 85 L.J. K.B. 806 (per Lord READING C.J., at p. 807). See further *McGregor* v. *Telford*, [1915] 3 K.B. 237 where Lord READING C.J. at p. 241 said that the ground of the decision in *R.* v. *Machen* (*supra*) was that the dismissal

136 Similarly, the refusal by a court of summary jurisdiction to make an order upon a frontager, under s. 150 of the Public Health Act 1875, for payment to the local authority of his proportion of the expenses of paving or otherwise in connection with the road or street upon which he is a frontager, even on the assumption (quite unwarranted) that it must, or may, imply a decision that the road or street is a highway repairable by the inhabitants at large, cannot operate as a *res judicata*, because the court has no statutory jurisdiction to determine the status of the road or street, or to decide anything beyond the question whether an order of the nature above stated ought to be made upon the particular person, in the particular case, or not.[1] It is otherwise, of course, in the case of a private statute which, extending beyond the boundaries of general legislation on the subject, expressly empowers the court to adjudicate upon the question of the persons liable to repair the street.[2]

Jurisdiction of foreign judicial tribunals

137 If competent jurisdiction in the tribunal is a necessary condition of a valid English *res judicata*, it must, *a fortiori*, be so of a valid foreign *res judicata*. Accordingly, it is now well established that where a foreign decision,—which expression, as already explained,[3] means, for the purposes of this treatise, any judicial decision pronounced elsewhere than in England, and embraces, therefore, the decisions of Scottish, Northern Irish and colonial tribunals, and the like, and decisions of tribunals of the self-governing Dominions within the British Commonwealth as well as foreign decisions in the popular sense,—is relied upon as a *res judicata*, whether as a bar to a claim or defence, or (which is usually the case) as the foundation of an action,[4] it must appear that the foreign judicial tribunal had jurisdiction to pronounce the very decision which is so set up, and thereby to bind the parties, if the decision is *inter partes*, or the world, if it is *in rem*.

---

of an application under the Railway Acts was "in the nature of a non-suit". For more recent authorities, see *R.* v. *Sunderland Justices, Ex parte Hodgkinson*, [1945] K.B. 502 D.C. per HUMPHREYS J. in the course of argument at p. 503; per OLIVER J. at p. 509: *Robinson* v. *Williams*, [1964] 3 All E.R. 12; [1965] 1 Q.B. 89, D.C. *In New Zealand*, s. 67 of the Destitute Persons Act 1910 provides statutory authority for a similar rule; and see *Myers* v. *Bishop and Crozier* (1913), 33 N.Z.L.R. 159 (DENNISTON J.) and *Tinney* v. *Ferrel*, [1958] N.Z.L.R. 114 (GRESSON J.).

[1] *R.* v. *Hutchings* (1881), 6 Q.B.D. 300, C.A. (per Lord SELBORNE L.C., at p. 305).

[2] As in *Wakefield Corporation* v. *Cooke*, [1904] A.C. 31, H.L., where reliance was placed upon s. 31 of the Wakefield Corporation Act 1887, which in terms authorises and requires the justices to determine the question whether the street in which the works are to be executed is, or is not, repairable by the inhabitants at large, whereas s. 150 of the Public Health Act 1875, which was the enactment applicable to the case cited in the last note, confers no such jurisdiction (per Lord HALSBURY L.C., at pp. 34, 35, Lord SHAND, at p. 37, Lord DAVEY, at pp. 37, 38, and Lord LINDLEY, at p. 39).

[3] See Chapter II, *supra*.

[4] As to actions on foreign judgments, see Chapter II, *supra*.

Burden of allegation and proof

138 Where the foreign decision is set up as a bar, it has never been doubted that it is for the party so setting it up to allege the jurisdiction of the tribunal at least in general terms, and, if challenged, to establish it in detail.[1] But, in the case of an action on a foreign judgment, notwithstanding the absence of any sound reason for the distinction, the rule appears to be otherwise.[2] Here, according to the general practice, sanctioned by the best authorities, the onus would seem to be upon the defendant in such an action to point to any specific defect in the jurisdiction of the foreign tribunal, such as to excuse him from the discharge of the legal obligation which, *prima facie*, would be incumbent on him, to obey the judgment.[3]

139 As has already been pointed out, the question of the jurisdiction, or absence of jurisdiction, of a foreign judicial tribunal, is not one of law, but of fact, to be determined by expert and other evidence.[4]

"Competent jurisdiction"

140 "Competent jurisdiction" connotes two things: first, jurisdiction over the cause or matter adjudicated upon by the foreign tribunal, and,

---

[1] See *General Steam Navigation Co.* v. *Guillou* (1843), 11 M. & W. 877, where a plea of estoppel in virtue of a judgment recovered by the defendant against the plaintiff in a French court was held bad, on the ground that it contained no averment that the plaintiffs were subjects of France, or resident therein, or had otherwise brought themselves within the jurisdiction of the French Court (per PARKE B., delivering the judgment of the Court of Exchequer, at p. 894). But, if the fact of the jurisdiction be sufficiently averred, though in general terms, it is not necessary to set out in detail every step in the proceedings, and aver that the foreign court had jurisdiction in respect of each of such steps, in order to sustain the estoppel: *M'Leod* v. *Schultze* (1844), 13 L.J. Ex. 321 (per Lord ABINGER C.B., and PARKE B., at p. 324).

[2] *Reimers* v. *Druce* (1857), 26 L.J. Ch. 196 (per ROMILLY M.R., at p. 198).

[3] In *Sheehy* v. *Professional Life Assurance Co.* (1857), 3 C.B. N.S. 597, Ex. Ch., an action on an Irish judgment, WATSON B., at p. 618, said that "it was incumbent on the defendant to show that the proceeding which led to that judgment was without jurisdiction". In *Cowan* v. *Braidwood* (1840), 1 Man. & G. 882, an action on a decree of the Scots Court of Session, it was held that it is for the defendant to aver all the facts tending to show that the judgment is not binding (per MAULE J., during the argument, at p. 892). So, in the case of an action on a colonial judgment, it was held that the declaration need not state that the court had jurisdiction over the parties and cause: *Robertson* v. *Struth* (1844), 5 Q.B. 941, where a demurrer to the declaration, on the ground that it did not so state, was overruled (per Lord DENMAN C.J., and PATTESON, WILLIAMS, and WIGHTMAN JJ., at p. 944, and per PATTESON J., during the argument, at p. 942: "we presume that the judgment of a foreign court is correct. If you have any objection, ought it not to have been raised by plea?"). And, at p. 635 of *Williams* v. *Jones* (1845), 13 M. & W. 628, which was an action, not on a foreign judgment, but on that of an English inferior court, ALDERSON B., by way of illustration, observes that "if an action were brought upon the judgment of a foreign court, the defendant would be bound to allege that he did not reside within the jurisdiction of the court". On the other hand, it seems to have been considered in *Schibsby* v. *Westenholz* (1870), L.R. 6 Q.B. 155 (per BLACKBURN J., at pp. 161, 162), that the rule laid down by PARK B., as stated in note 1 *supra*, was no less applicable to cases of actions on the foreign judgment than to cases of estoppel.

[4] In Chapter II, para. 75, *ante*.

secondly, jurisdiction over the parties. It is of no avail to establish either of these, without the other.

Jurisdiction of the foreign tribunal over the cause or matter

141 If the foreign tribunal is not competent even to entertain the class of case to which the case adjudicated upon belongs, it is obvious that any suggestion of *res judicata* fails *in limine*, and that it is quite unnecessary to pursue the further inquiry, which otherwise would follow, as to the authority of the tribunal over the parties. Thus, no *res judicata* is established where a tribunal of a foreign belligerent state has, without jurisdiction, arrogated to itself authority to hear and determine cases of prize within the territorial limits of a foreign neutral state;[1] nor, where a colonial court, having statutory jurisdiction only to convict or acquit on a criminal charge of infringing Crown property, has impliedly decided a question of title;[2] nor, where a colonial revenue tribunal, having statutory authority to deal only with questions as to the amount of the assessment, has taken upon itself to decide that the property in respect of which the assessment was made was of a nature which, under the colonial taxing legislation, rendered it exempt from taxation of any kind.[3]

Jurisdiction of the foreign tribunal over the parties: (*a*) *Judgments* in rem

142 It is of no avail to establish the foreign tribunal's jurisdiction as regards the cause of action, unless it is also made to appear that the tribunal had jurisdiction over the parties litigant. When examining this question it is immediately necessary to distinguish between jurisdiction in actions *in rem* and jurisdictions in actions *in personam*. Whether a foreign judgment is one *in rem* or *in personam* is a question of fact.[4] An action *in rem* may be

---

[1] As in *The Flad Oyen* (1799), 8 Term Rep. 270 n., a case heard in the Admiralty Court, of an English ship captured by the French, carried into Bergen, and there condemned as prize by the French Consular Court, in which Sir W. SCOTT, after distinguishing such courts as those erected in Lisbon and other places pursuant to treaties between the States concerned, characterised "the act of the French court" as "a licentious attempt to exercise the right of war within the bosom of a neutral country", and indignantly protested against any attempt, such as he conceived the plea of *res judicata* before him to be, "to impose upon the court a sentence of a tribunal not existing in the belligerent country, but of a person pretending to be authorised within the dominions of a neutral country" (at pp. 271–273 n.); *Havelock* v. *Rockwood* (1799), 8 Term Rep. 268, in which the K.B. followed the last case, in relation to a sentence of the same Consular court (per Lord KENYON C.J., at p. 276, and GROSE J., at p. 277); *Donaldson* v. *Thompson* (1808), 1 Camp. 429, where, in relation to a sentence of condemnation pronounced by a prize commission sitting in Corfu under the authority of the Empire of Russia, Lord ELLENBOROUGH C.J., at pp. 431, 432, held that no effect could be given to the sentence of a tribunal which had no jurisdiction whatsoever, being that of a State which preserved the forms of independent neutrality, and was not "a co-belligerent".

[2] *A.-G. for Trinidad and Tobago* v. *Eriché*, [1893] A.C. 518, P.C., at pp. 522, 523. *Cp.* the cases cited in para. 122, *ante*, as to English tribunals.

[3] *Toronto Rail. Co.* v. *Toronto Corporation*, [1904] A.C. 809, P.C., at pp. 814–816.

[4] See note 3, p. 71, *ante*.

defined as one which is concerned with the status of persons or things, or one effecting, ordering, or recognising *contra mundum* a disposition of movable or immovable property.

Judgments *in rem* are more fully discussed in detail in a later chapter;[1] but in this place it should be observed that judgments *in rem*, whether concerned with the status of persons or things, or effecting, ordering or recognising *contra mundum* a disposition of specific movable or immovable property, generally derive their jurisdictional validity from the situation of those persons or things, or of that property, within the jurisdiction wherein the judgment is given. Such judgments, concerning themselves with status, must naturally, if they are to be effective at all, bind not only the immediate parties but all the world;[2] it makes little sense to speak of the status of a person unless that status is one to be generally accepted, and the same argument must be applicable to an order for the disposition (*e.g.* the sale of a vessel attached as prize) of movable or immovable property. No foreign court may give a judgment, afterwards to be supported as valid in a court of this country, directing or recognising the disposition of land outside its own jurisdiction, or effectively disposing of a chattel not on the date of the action situated within the jurisdiction of the court giving the judgment; but the courts of each country will have jurisdiction, as regards the subject matter of the action, over property situated within the jurisdiction. In such cases for the purposes of an action *in rem*, none of the requisites hereafter mentioned as necessary to support jurisdiction in actions *in personam* will be essential; for, the action being concerned with the status or disposition of property within the jurisdiction, the Courts of the jurisdiction will be recognised as endowed with authority to decide the matter in issue. While, therefore, service on or notice to the defendant must still be proved, the five requirements in *Rousillon* v. *Rousillon*[3] (to be discussed in paras. 144 *et seq.*, *infra*) are superfluous.[4]

Jurisdiction of the foreign tribunal over the cause of matter: actions in personam

143 In the case of actions *in personam* it must appear, in order to found jurisdiction, first, that at the commencement of the proceedings the party against whom the decision was given owed allegiance (permanent, or temporary) to the foreign state under the authority of which the tribunal exercised its judicial functions, and, secondly, that, being thus amenable to the foreign jurisdiction, he was in fact brought before the particular

[1] Chapter VIII, *post*.
[2] *Pemberton* v. *Hughes*, [1899] 1 Ch. 781, C.A., per LINDLEY M.R., at pp. 793, 794.
[3] (1880), 14 Ch.D. 351.
[4] See Chapter VIII, *post*.

tribunal in the particular case by such summons, citation, notice, or other proceedings as, according to the foreign practice, is requisite for that purpose. Each of these elements is an essential condition of jurisdiction; the party against whom the foreign judgment has been given has a good answer to a claim to enforce it in an English court, if he succeeds in negativing either the one or the other. If he was never in fact brought before the foreign court by the prescribed process, it does not signify how clearly amenable to the jurisdiction, by reason of his allegiance, he may have been, if and when so brought.[1] On the other hand, if he was not subject to the foreign jurisdiction, by reason either of permanent or temporary allegiance, at the date of the commencement of the proceedings, it does not matter how many citations or notices were served upon him, or how many opportunities were given him of defending himself, or how regular, in point of procedure, was the conduct of the foreign tribunal.[2]

The rules in Rousillon v. *Rousillon*[3]

144 The amenability of the party to the foreign jurisdiction exists in five different sets of circumstances any one of which is sufficient. These were stated by FRY J., in *Rousillon* v. *Rousillon*,[4] in a succinct list, which has been generally accepted and applied in subsequent authorities, as follows: "Where he"—the defendant—"is a subject of the foreign country in which the judgment has been obtained; where he was resident in the foreign country when the action began; where the defendant, in the character of plaintiff, has selected the forum in which he is afterwards sued; where he has voluntarily appeared; where he has contracted to submit himself to the forum in which the judgment was obtained". These five alternative conditions of the foreign jurisdiction over the party will now be separately examined.

It will first be useful, however, to notice that of the five possible bases for jurisdiction which we have mentioned, the last three arise from the positive selection of the jurisdiction, or from a voluntary submission to it, by the defendant, while the first two are independent of any such considerations. They enable an unwilling defendant, who will not agree to any jurisdiction,

---

[1] But see in this regard the discussion of substituted service in paras. 157–162, *post*.

[2] *Schibsby* v. *Westenholz* (1870), L.R. 6 Q.B. 155 (per BLACKBURN J., at p. 160); *Turnbull* v. *Walker* (1892), 67 L.T. 767 (per WRIGHT J., at p. 769); *Sirdar Gurdyal Singh* v. *Rajah of Faridkote*, [1894] A.C. 670, P.C. (at p. 683: "he was under no obligation to do so"—sc. to appear in the action—"by reason of the notice of the suits which he thus received, or otherwise, unless that court had lawful jurisdiction over him").

[3] (1880), 14 Ch.D. 351, at p. 371.

[4] For instance, in *Feyerick* v. *Hubbard* (1902), 71 L.J. K.B. 509, by WALTON J., at p. 510; in *Emanuel* v. *Symon*, [1908] 1 K.B. 302, C.A., by BUCKLEY L.J., at p. 309, and KENNEDY L.J. at p. 312; in *Phillips* v. *Batho*, [1913] 3 K.B. 25, by SCRUTTON J., at p. 29; in *Gavin, Gibson & Co., Ltd.* v. *Gibson*, [1913] 3 K.B. 379, by ATKIN J., at pp. 387, 388.

to be sued either where he is physically present, or in the State to which he owes allegiance. The necessity of postulating some competent jurisdiction which does *not* depend on the consent of the defendant is logically demonstrated by the reflection that without such a rule it would be possible for a claim, good in any jurisdiction where it might be pursued, to fail for lack of any jurisdiction competent to deal with it.[1]

Jurisdiction over parties: (1) Nationals of the jurisdiction

145 The first condition is the simplest of all, provided its basic proposition is not questioned. That basic proposition is that a subject of a foreign State owes permanent allegiance to that State in the exercise of all its functions including that of judicature. It has been generally accepted that the cases cited in the footnote[2] have been sufficient authority for it, and they are noted as such in the first edition of this work.[3] FRY J.'s five alternative bases of jurisdiction, including this one, were restated by BUCKLEY L.J. in *Emanuel* v. *Symon*[4] without modification, while in the same case KENNEDY L.J. without restating them, observed that "concerning the first four classes mentioned, no subsequent judgment has expressed any disagreement or doubt".[5] Six years later, in *Gavin Gibson & Co., Ltd.* v. *Gibson*,[6] ATKIN J. as he then was, said, of the first ground, but without deciding the matter (for it did not arise, since nationality in the required sense was not proved) of these two cases and of the earlier decision of BLACKBURN J. in *Schibsby* v. *Westenholz*[7] that:

> "It will be apparent that in none of the above cases was the defendant in fact a subject of a country where the judgment sued on was pronounced, nor was it claimed that he was, and the judicial expressions above referred to are therefore in the nature of obiter dicta. They are, however, of so great weight that I should probably feel compelled to follow them . . .".

More recently Sir RAYMOND EVERSHED, M.R. in *British Nylon Spinners, Ltd.* v. *Imperial Chemical Industries, Ltd.*[8] said:

> "On the other hand, there is no doubt that it is competent for the court of a particular country, in a suit between persons who are either nationals or subjects of that country or are otherwise subject to its jurisdiction, to make

[1] For this thought the writer is indebted to an article in (1967) 6 Melbourne University Law Review, p. 1, by Professor A. V. Levontin of the Hebrew University of Jerusalem.

[2] *Schibsby* v. *Westenholz* (1870), L.R. 6 Q.B. 155; *Rousillon* v. *Rousillon* (1880), 14 Ch.D. 351.

[3] 1st ed., p. 82–83.

[4] [1908] 1 K.B. 302, at p. 309.

[5] *Ibid.* at p. 312.

[6] [1913] 3 K.B. 379, at p. 388.

[7] (1870), L.R. 6 Q.B. 155.

[8] [1953] Ch. 19, C.A. at p. 25.

> orders in personam against one such party—directing it, for example, to do something or to refrain from doing something in another country affecting the other party to the action. As a general proposition, that would not be open to doubt."

But it is to be pointed out that every one of the decisions mentioned above deal with this basis of jurisdiction in passages which are *obiter*, and that there appears to be no authority directly deciding in terms that nationality, *without more*, will give a foreign court jurisdiction over one of its subjects, such that a judgment given pursuant thereto will have the force of *res judicata* in an English court. In the present writer's submission this justification of jurisdiction, if it should ever come to be tested in a court of the highest authority, would require careful re-examination in the light of modern conditions before it could be finally supported,[1] and the complexity of the concept of British nationality within the Commonwealth must be a factor which in itself might give rise to formidable difficulties in any case in which the point arose where the foreign Court was one within the British family of nations.[2]

If nationality be accepted as a basis for jurisdiction it is well established, notwithstanding some faint suggestions to the contrary in one or two of the earlier authorities,[3] that it is wholly immaterial whether the party was a native-born or a naturalised subject.[4]

---

[1] In *Blohn* v. *Desser*, [1962] 2 Q.B. 116, DIPLOCK J. said at p. 123: "There may be some doubt as to whether today it would be held that the jurisdiction exists in the first category of cases", referring to the one now under discussion. It may be noted, moreover, as some support to this argument that s. 4 (2) (a) of the Foreign Judgments (Reciprocal Enforcement) Act 1933 does not include nationality *simpliciter* as a basis for jurisdiction; and "jurisdiction" is prescribed by the statute as an essential prerequisite for registration. And in *Rossano* v. *Manufacturers' Life Insurance Co.*, [1963] 2 Q.B. 352 MCNAIR J. at p. 382 reflected on the difficulties of this foundation for jurisdiction, especially in cases where the "national" of the jurisdiction is not personally present within it, and is at the same time a national of another jurisdiction.

[2] As was long ago pointed out (*e.g.*) by ATKIN J. in the case mentioned in note 6 on p. 116, *ante*, at pp. 389–94. In testing jurisdiction in Divorce, however (where, as need not be pointed out, the question is one of jurisdiction *in rem*, not *in personam*; but on this point the difference may be slight) the House of Lords has in a recent case shown itself willing to accept the nationality of the parties as a basis of jurisdiction—*Indyka* v. *Indyka*, [1967] 2 All E.R. 689, H.L.

[3] See *Douglas* v. *Forrest* (1828), 4 Bing. 686, where BEST C.J. at pp. 702, 703, described the defendant's testator as subject to the jurisdiction of the Scottish courts, in respect of his being a Scotsman "born", leaving it at all events in doubt whether, if it had been otherwise, it might not have made a difference in his view, though he did not say so in so many words; *Turnbull* v. *Walker* (1892), 67 L.T. 767, where WRIGHT J., at p. 769, using a similarly dubious phrase, spoke of the defendants' not being subject to the jurisdiction of a New Zealand court because they were not "natives of New Zealand".

[4] *Phillips* v. *Batho, supra* (per SCRUTTON J., at p. 29); *Gavin, Gibson & Co., Ltd.* v. *Gibson, supra* (per ATKIN J., at pp. 385–394, pointing out at pp. 390–393, that the dicta referred to in the last note were not only not necessary to the decision, but did not even amount to a definite expression of opinion, in either case).

Jurisdiction over parties: (2) Persons within the jurisdiction

146 Though not a subject of the foreign state, and, therefore, not owing to it any permanent allegiance, a party may still be shown to have owed it temporary allegiance by proof that he was within its territorial limits at the date of the commencement of the proceedings which resulted in the foreign decision relied upon as a *res judicata*, in which event he is amenable to the foreign jurisdiction under the second class of case mentioned in Sir EDWARD FRY's list.[1] It is not necessary to establish that, at the above-mentioned material date, the party was what is called "ordinarily resident" or even strictly "resident" at all, in the foreign country: it is enough if it appears that, at the initiation of the proceedings, he was physically present therein, though merely on a visit to, or in the course of his travels through, the country; and, if this be proved, it is immaterial how soon before that date he arrived within, or how soon after it he passed outside, the territorial area of the foreign jurisdiction.[2] It may even possibly be sufficient to show that, at the material date, the party held a public office in the foreign State, though not physically present in the foreign country, on the theory that the tenure of such office may be deemed a kind of constructive residence.[3] This, however, is the utmost length to which any authority has gone, and, with the possible and very doubtful exception last mentioned, it is safe to say that, in order to bring the case within the class now under discussion, it is, on the one hand, necessary, and, on the other, sufficient, to establish that the party was corporally present in some part of the dominions of the foreign state at the commencement of the action; failing such proof, the foreign tribunal has no jurisdiction over any person not being a subject of the foreign state.[4]

---

[1] In *Rousillon* v. *Rousillon* (1880), 14 Ch.D. 351, at p. 371. It should be noted that for the purposes of enforcing a judgment under the Administration of Justice Act 1920 the statutory requirement as to this ground of jurisdiction is set out in s. 9 (2) (b) as that the defendant is "carrying on business or ordinarily resident" within the jurisdiction. In the case of the Foreign Judgments (Reciprocal Enforcement) Act 1933 the requirement of s. 4 is "if the judgment debtor, being defendant, was at the time of the institution of the proceedings *resident* in the foreign country, or, being a corporation, had its principal place of business in that country". A further clause extends the jurisdiction to cover the case where the defendant had an office or place of business in the foreign country, and the action was brought in respect of a transaction effected through or at such office or place. But mere momentary presence within the jurisdiction is insufficient.

[2] *Carrick* v. *Hancock* (1895), 12 T.L.R. 59 (per Lord RUSSELL C.J., at p. 60).

[3] It was said by Lord BROUGHAM, at p. 21 of *Don* v. *Lippmann* (1837), 5 Cl. & Fin. 1, and again, by the Court of Appeal in *Emanuel* v. *Symon*, [1908] 1 K.B. 302, C.A., that, on this theory, and on this alone, the decision in *Becquet* v. *MacCarthy* (1831), 2 B. & Ad. 951, may be supported.

[4] As was held in *Buchanan* v. *Rucker* (1808), 9 East 192 (per Lord ELLENBOROUGH C.J., at p. 194); *Cavan* v. *Stewart* (1816), 1 Stark. 525 (per Lord ELLENBOROUGH C.J., at pp. 529, 530), where, as in the last case, the defendant had never been in the colony; *Don* v. *Lippmann*, *supra*; *Schibsby* v. *Westenholz* (1870), L.R. 6 Q.B. 155 (per BLACKBURN J., at pp. 160, 162, 163); *Rousillon* v. *Rousillon*, *supra*; *Sirdar Gurdyal Singh* v. *Rajah of Faridkote*, [1894] A.C. 670, P.C. (at

The foregoing paragraph is reprinted from the first edition, and reflects the view of Mr Spencer Bower in 1924. To the present writer it would appear that this basis of jurisdiction, like the first, presents some difficulties under modern conditions brought about (for instance) by the speed and convenience of air travel; and it is submitted that future developments may possibly occasion some modifications of this ground of jurisdiction. As will be seen in the next paragraph, it is not the fact of the cause of action arising within the jurisdiction, but the presence of the defendant momentarily within it which constitutes this ground. Any momentary presence within the jurisdiction is deemed sufficient, without "residence" or domicil. Let us for the moment contemplate a possible illustration in the case of an English national, resident all his life in this country, who, while driving his car along an English road, collides with a vehicle driven by (say) a national of France. It may happen that a few weeks later he is paying a visit of a few days only (his first) to France; acquainted with this fact, the other party to the accident commences proceedings in France in respect of the accident in England. It seems hard logically to justify the extension of the principle in this paragraph to the point where the French court is endowed with jurisdiction to try the facts of this accident so as to bind the English party to it, and indeed, by hearing the dispute, to exclude the jurisdiction of the courts of this country.[1]

147 Just as, in the case where the party was present within the territorial limits of the jurisdiction at the material date, it is of no avail to establish that he was absent at some other date, however proximate thereto; so, in the converse case, where the party was not within these limits at the material date, it is equally useless to show that he was so at some other date, though, when resident or present in the foreign country on such other date, he may have entered into the contract (even one of partnership), or may have committed the wrong, which gave the opposite party his cause of action, or ground of complaint, in the foreign court.[2] It is

---

p. 683), where the defendant was not within the territory of the Indian native independent state in which the judgment sued upon had been pronounced at the date of the commencement of the proceedings; *Emanuel* v. *Symon*, *supra*, where the defendant was not resident in the colony at the material date; *Phillips* v. *Batho*, [1913] 3 K.B. 25, where the defendant had left British India before the proceedings were instituted (per SCRUTTON J., at pp. 29, 30).

[1] This criticism seems to the present author to be supported by the stricter terms in which this ground of jurisdiction is prescribed in the statutes referred to on p. 118, *ante*.

[2] At p. 161 of *Schibsby* v. *Westenholz*, *supra*, BLACKBURN J. left the question of whether it is enough to show that the party was resident within the jurisdiction at the time of incurring the obligation, though not at the time of the commencement of the foreign action, to be decided thereafter, if the occasion should arise. The occasion did arise, and the question was decided in the negative, in several subsequent cases, *viz.* *Turnbull* v. *Walker* (1892), 67 L.T. 767 (per WRIGHT J., at p. 769); *Sirdar Gurdyal Singh* v. *Rajah of Faridkote*, *supra*, at p. 683, where it is laid down that, for the purposes of the rule, it makes no difference whether the cause of action

now established, though at one time it was considered a moot point, that it is equally unavailing, for the purpose of showing foreign jurisdiction over a party not present in the foreign country at the material date, to prove that he then owned real property situate therein, in respect of which the matters in dispute had arisen at some previous date when he was within the territorial jurisdiction.[1]

Domicil as a ground of jurisdiction over parties

148 Domicil, though it has in one or two decisions been the subject of some unguarded mention as a basis for jurisdiction over parties,[2] is not a foundation of such jurisdiction. As has been seen, residence, or even less, may be a basis for jurisdiction, if the defendant is physically present in the jurisdiction at the time of the commencement of the proceedings; but domicil without physical presence is insufficient to support jurisdiction.

In some types of proceeding—*e.g.* in divorce—domicil may appear to be the foundation of jurisdiction; but it must be remembered that jurisdiction in divorce is governed by the rules relating to judgments *in rem*, which, differing entirely from those relating to judgments *in personam* (which we are now considering), will be considered in due course.[3]

Corporations: nationality and residence

149 The rules by virtue of which jurisdiction is deemed to be conferred on a foreign court by reason of (a) the nationality of the defendant or (b) his presence within the jurisdiction, are literally applicable, of course, only to natural persons. It is difficult to apply such conceptions as nationality literally to corporations; they do not owe natural allegiance as does a real person. But a corporation may be deemed to be a national of, and by

was in contract, or in tort; *Emanuel* v. *Symon*, [1908] 1 K.B. 302, C.A., per KENNEDY L.J., at p. 314, who there points out that the entering into a contract of partnership within the territorial limits of the foreign state, which was the case before the court, does not of itself confer jurisdiction upon the foreign court, any more than the making of any other contract within those limits.

[1] This question was left open by BLACKBURN J., at p. 163 of *Schibsby* v. *Westenholz*, *supra*, with a strong expression of doubt "whether the mere possession of property locally situated" in the foreign state would found jurisdiction over the person. It was stated by FRY J., at p. 371 of *Rousillon* v. *Rousillon* (1880), 14 Ch.D. 351, in very guarded language, that a sixth condition of a valid foreign *res judicata* might exist "possibly, if *Becquet* v. *MacCarthy* be right, where the defendant has real estate within the foreign jurisdiction in respect of which the cause of action arose whilst he was within that jurisdiction." But it has now been definitely established that, if intended to affirm such a proposition, and if not explainable on the theory stated in note 3 on p. 118, *ante*, *Becquet* v. *MacCarthy* (1831), 2 B. & Ad. 951, is *not* "right": see *Don* v. *Lippmann* (1837), 5 Cl. & Fin. 1 (per Lord BROUGHAM, at p. 23); *De Cosse Brissac* v. *Rathbone* (1861), 6 H. & N. 301, 308; *Sirdar Gurdyal Singh* v. *Rajah of Faridkote*, [1894] A.C. 670, P.C. at pp. 685, 686; *Emanuel* v. *Symon*, *supra* (per Lord ALVERSTONE C.J., at pp. 306, 307, BUCKLEY L. J., at pp. 309–312, and KENNEDY L.J., at p. 312).

[2] *E.g. Jaffer* v. *Williams* (1908), 25 T.L.R. 12 per BUCKNILL J. at p. 13.

[3] See Chapter XII, *post*, for some consideration of the rules as to jurisdiction in Divorce.

an extension of the same argument to be present in, the jurisdiction in which it was incorporated, on an analogy with the conception that a natural person owes a natural allegiance to, and has from birth a domicil of origin in the country in which he is born.[1]

A corporation, then, will be subject on this account to the jurisdiction of the courts of the country of incorporation; but a corporation may be regarded for the purposes of the rules as to jurisdiction as being resident *also* in any country in which it is carrying on business to a sufficient extent. But it is necessary to show, for this purpose, that the corporation is carrying on business to some substantial extent at some definite and reasonably permanent place in the jurisdiction; the mere presence of a salesman or representative, without more, is not sufficient.[2]

As for the members of a corporation which is itself subject to the jurisdiction: a member of such a corporation is not, by virtue of such membership and no more, subject to the jurisdiction. But if the Articles of Association, "statutes", or other instrument defining the constitution of the foreign corporation, be of such a character as to admit of a reasonable inference that, in becoming a party thereto, he contracted with the corporation, and its other *socii*, to submit any dispute to the foreign tribunal, then the jurisdiction of that foreign tribunal over him is established under another principle, to be considered presently.[3]

150 The rules hitherto examined, by which foreign jurisdiction is made to depend upon nationality or territoriality, may of course, like other rules of international common law, be displaced or modified by the express terms of a treaty between Her Majesty and a foreign state. Thus, during the world war of 1914–18, a treaty was made between Great Britain and Belgium, whereby the two States agreed to recognize the jurisdiction of the tribunals of one another's armies in the field, irrespective of all questions of the nationality of the accused, or of the territories in which the armies might be operating, and, on an indictment under the Offences against the Person Act 1861, to which the accused pleaded that he had previously been acquitted by a Belgian Court-Martial, established by the above treaty, of the same offences as those with which he was then being

---

[1] *Janson* v. *Driefontein Consolidated Mines, Ltd.*, [1902] A.C. 484, H.L. (all the judgments, but perhaps particularly that of Lord LINDLEY at p. 505); *A.-G.* v. *Jewish Colonisation Association*, [1901] 1 K.B. 123, C.A. at p. 135; *Gasque* v. *Inland Revenue Commissioners*, [1940] 2 K.B. 80, at p. 84.

[2] *Littauer Glove Corporation* v. *F. W. Millington* (1920), *Ltd.* (1928), 44 T.L.R. 746 (SALTER J.) and *cf.* the provisions of the Administration of Justice Act 1920 and of the Foreign Judgments (Reciprocal Enforcement) Act 1933 referred to in note 1 on p. 118, *supra*.

[3] In para. 155, *post*.

charged, it was held that, though but for the treaty it would not have been so, this tribunal was a court of competent jurisdiction over the accused, whose plea of *autrefois acquit* was accordingly sustained.[1]

Jurisdiction over parties: (3) *plaintiff in the foreign court*

151 The third possible case in which, according to Sir EDWARD FRY's list, foreign jurisdiction over the party may arise, is where the party, though owing no allegiance, permanent or temporary, to the foreign state, has elected to take the field against his opponent on the latter's own ground, by suing him in a court of the foreign State, in which case, if afterwards he is counter-attacked by his adversary in the forum so chosen by himself, he cannot be heard to complain that such forum had no jurisdiction to pronounce judgment against him.[2] Strictly, perhaps, this sort of case should be regarded as a variety of the fourth class, rather than as a class by itself.

Jurisdiction over parties: (4) *voluntary submission to the jurisdiction*

152 The fourth type of case referred to by FRY J. is that of a man who, owing no allegiance of any sort to the foreign state, and being under no compulsion to obey any summons issued by its judicial tribunals, nevertheless of his own free-will conforms to such a citation, appears in the foreign court, fights the action, and so submits to the jurisdiction.[3] It is obvious that by such conduct he deliberately precludes himself from denying the jurisdiction, as he otherwise might have done. Where the defendant thus "takes the chance of a judgment in his favour, he is bound".[4] Accordingly, whenever the voluntary appearance has been made out, the foreign court has always been held to have had competent jurisdiction over the defendant; but where it has not been proved that the defendant ap-

---

1 *R.* v. *Aughet* (1918), 13 Cr. App. Rep. 101, at pp. 108–109.

2 It was so stated by BLACKBURN J. at p. 161 of *Schibsby* v. *Westenholz* (1870), L.R. 6 Q.B. 155—a statement adopted by FRY J. at p. 371 of *Rousillon* v. *Rousillon* (1880), 14 Ch.D. 351. It does not appear that there is any actual decision on the point; in neither of the above cases were facts proved or admitted sufficient to raise the question.

3 This is an obvious and logical ground for jurisdiction, and it may be noticed that both the Administration of Justice Act 1920 and the Foreign Judgments (Reciprocal Enforcement) Act 1933 allow jurisdiction on this ground.

4 Per BLACKBURN J. at p. 162 of *Schibsby* v. *Westenholz supra*, citing *De Cosse Brissac* v. *Rathbone* (1861), 6 H. & N. 301 as his authority. A more recent instance is *Bergerem* v. *Marsh* (1921), 91 L.J. K.B. 80, where BAILHACHE J. held that the fact that the defendant had lodged an appeal in Belgium against the Belgian decision at first instance, and had appeared on the appeal by counsel (the appeal being dismissed) constituted a submission to jurisdiction.

In *Blohn* v. *Desser*, [1962] 2 Q.B. 116, DIPLOCK J. held at p. 123 that the appointment by an absentee principal of a resident agent to conduct business within the jurisdiction constituted, at least in the special circumstances of that case, an implied agreement with the public to submit to the jurisdiction of the courts of the country concerned. This seems to the writer, with respect, to be as far as any court has been willing to go in support of a submission on jurisdiction.

peared in fact, or, this having been proved against him, the defendant has succeeded in showing that his appearance was not voluntary, the assertion of the foreign jurisdiction has always failed.[1]

153 An appearance for the purpose of protecting property of the defendant then within the dominions of the foreign state, and challenging the jurisdiction of the foreign tribunal to seize or confiscate it, is obviously not a voluntary submission to the jurisdiction thus challenged;[2] but an appearance for the mere purpose of protecting, not existing, but possible future property, and general business interests, is voluntary.[3]

Appearance to object to the jurisdiction: appearance "under protest"

154 While it is certain that by voluntarily appearing before the foreign tribunal a party will give that tribunal jurisdiction to determine, as between him and other parties to the litigation, the substantive matters in dispute between them, yet the effect of such an appearance, if confined solely to disputing jurisdiction, is not quite so clear. It may be thought as a matter of logic, that merely to advance the contention of no jurisdiction should not necessarily result in any implication of the acceptance of jurisdiction, and that by such an appearance nothing can be deemed to be waived. In *Tallack* v. *Tallack and Broekema*,[4] for instance, Lord MERRIVALE P. says, of such an appearance:

> "The respondent's appearance to the petition was not an appearance to meet the present claim. I am not persuaded that an appearance to such a petition as the present, qualified at all stages of the case by a distinct and reasoned denial of the existence of jurisdiction, could with any propriety be regarded as a submission to the exercise of the jurisdiction so denied."[5]

---

[1] The voluntary appearance of the defendant was either proved by the plaintiff, or not sufficiently negatived by the defendant, and the *res judicata* was accordingly established, in the following cases of actions on foreign judgments: *Russell* v. *Smyth* (1842), 9 M. & W. 810 (per Lord ABINGER C.B., at pp. 817, 818, PARKE B., at p. 819, and ALDERSON B., at p. 820); *Sheehy* v. *Professional Life Assurance Co.* (1853), 13 C.B. 787 (per JERVIS C.J., and MAULE J., at p. 800, holding a plea bad which, whilst alleging want of jurisdiction, absence of notice, etc., was consistent with the defendant having in fact appeared). *Cp.* the cases cited in note 5, *infra*, and note 5 on p. 124, *post*. On the other hand, the fact of appearance was not established, and the foreign judgment accordingly was held not to operate as a *res judicata* in *Schibsby* v. *Westenholz* (1870), L.R. 6 Q.B. 155, where the non-appearance of the defendant in fact was admitted (per BLACKBURN J., at pp. 156, 162); *Rousillon* v. *Rousillon* (1880), 14 Ch.D. 351; *Turnbull* v. *Walker* (1892), 67 L.T. 767 (per WRIGHT J., at p. 769).

[2] *Simpson* v. *Fogo* (1860), 1 J. & H. 18 (per WOOD V.-C., at p. 27); *Schibsby* v. *Westenholz*, *supra* (per BLACKBURN J., at p. 162); *The Challenge and Duc d'Aumale*, [1904] P. 41. *Cp.* the analogous rule in the law of estoppel by representation that no such estoppel can be founded on involuntary statements or acts, as explained in the authors' *Law of Estoppel by Representation* (2nd Edn.) Chapter V, para. 100.

[3] *Voinet* v. *Barrett* (1885), 55 L.J. Q.B. 39, C.A. (per Lord ESHER M.R., at pp. 40, 41, COTTON L.J., at pp. 41, 42, and BOWEN L.J., at p. 42).

[4] [1927] P. 211 (Lord MERRIVALE, P.).

[5] At p. 222.

So, too, in the later case of *Re Dulles' Settlement* (*No.* 2), *Dulles* v. *Vidler*[1] it was held by the Court of Appeal that a party who had so appeared had not on the facts submitted to the jurisdiction, DENNING L.J. saying:

> "I cannot see how anyone can fairly say that a man has voluntarily submitted to the jurisdiction of a court, when he has all the time been vigorously protesting that it has no jurisdiction. If he does nothing and lets judgment go against him in default of appearance, he clearly does not submit to the jurisdiction. What difference in principle does it make, if he does not merely do nothing, but actually goes to the court and protests that it has no jurisdiction? I can see no distinction at all. I quite agree, of course, that if he fights the case, not only on the jurisdiction, but also on the merits, he must then be taken to have submitted to the jurisdiction, because he is then inviting the court to decide in his favour on the merits; and he cannot be allowed, at one and the same time, to say that he will accept the decision on the merits if it is favourable to him and will not submit to it if it is unfavourable. But when he only appears with the sole object of protesting against the jurisdiction, I do not think that he can be said to submit to the jurisdiction: see *Tallack* v. *Tallack*, per Lord MERRIVALE, P.".[2]

But, *contra*, it has been contended that a party, in appearing to protest against jurisdiction, necessarily submits to the foreign court the question of jurisdiction *vel non* on which he appears before it; and that if, so appearing, he finds this preliminary question decided against him, the result is that his protest has effectively conferred jurisdiction on the foreign court, whose decision *as to jurisdiction* is now *res judicata*. This was long thought to follow from *Harris* v. *Taylor*.[3] There, however, the question of jurisdiction was as to jurisdiction over the cause of action, not as to jurisdiction over the defendant; and in the later case of *Re Dulles*[4] the Court of Appeal distinguished it effectively on that ground. The effect of *Re Dulles* is that in a case where, without some voluntary appearance of the defendant which can be called in aid, the foreign court has no jurisdiction *in personam*, an appearance merely to protest against jurisdiction will not have the effect of conferring jurisdiction.

An appearance is not to be deemed involuntary by reason only of the fact that it was expressed to be "under protest" or "conditional". The use of such expressions by the defendant is vain as a prophylactic against the consequences of the act itself, which was none the less deliberate and intentional, with the view of getting the benefit of a judgment in his favour on the merits, if possible, merely because he, "saying he would ne'er consent, consented".[5] A similar rule, as to the prevalence of conduct over accom-

[1] [1951] Ch. 842, C.A.

[2] At p. 850.

[3] *Harris* v. *Taylor*, [1915] 2 K.B. 580, C.A.

[4] [1951] Ch. 842, C.A.

[5] *Boissière & Co.* v. *Brockner & Co.* (1889), 6 T.L.R. 85 (per CAVE J., at pp. 85, 86); *Harris* v. *Taylor*, [1915] 2 K.B. 580, C.A. (per BUCKLEY L.J., at pp. 587, 588, and BANKES L.J., at pp. 591, 592).

panying protests or reservations in words, obtains in the law of estoppel by representation.[1]

Jurisdiction over parties: (5) prior contract to submit to the jurisdiction

155 The fifth, and last, of the alternative means by which jurisdiction over the party may be established, as stated in Sir EDWARD FRY's list, is proof of the fact that the party, though not otherwise subject to the foreign jurisdiction, had expressly contracted beforehand to be bound by the decision of the foreign tribunal.[2]

156 A stipulation of this description need not necessarily be, or form part of, an express contract between litigant individuals. It is enough if, by a term of a contract *inter socios* constituted by the articles, or "statutes", or regulations of a foreign corporation, every members has agreed with the other members, and with the corporation, to submit all disputes, or all disputes of a specified character, to the jurisdiction of the foreign tribunal.[3] Such an agreement, however, will not be implied from the mere fact that the party alleged to have brought himself within the jurisdiction was a member of a foreign corporation, or partnership, the constitution of which does not expressly provide for such submission.[4]

Notice to the defendant as an essential of jurisdiction

157 If the party setting up the *res judicata* fails to show that in some one or more of the five ways indicated the opposite party had at the material date become amenable to the foreign jurisdiction, and liable, as such, to

---

[1] This topic is dealt with in Chapter VII, paras. 92–93, of the second edition of the authors' *Law of Estoppel by Representation*.

[2] As in *Feyerick* v. *Hubbard* (1902), 71 L.J. K.B. 509 (per WALTON J., at pp. 510–512); *Jeannot* v. *Fuerst* (1909), 100 L.T. 816 (per BRAY J., at p. 817). For a similar condition of the statutory right to the registration and enforcement of colonial judgments, see s. 9 (2), (c) of the Administration of Justice Act 1920. *Cf.* Foreign Judgments (Reciprocal Enforcement) Act 1933, s. 4 (2) (a).

[3] As in *Copin* v. *Adamson* (1875), 1 Ex.D. 17, C.A., where Lord CAIRNS L.C., at p. 18, described the statutes or articles of association of the French Société (the assignee of which was suing the defendant, a member thereof, on a French judgment) as an "agreement *inter socios*", and, at p. 19, expressed his opinion that "to all intents and purposes, it is as if there had been an actual and absolute agreement by the defendant." The first of the two replications, which alleged this agreement, was accordingly upheld on demurrer. On the other hand, the second replication, which did not set up the agreement, but relied solely on the fact that the defendant was a member of the Société, was held bad by a majority of the Court below, (1874), L.R. 9 Exch. 345, at pp. 355, 356, and, there being no cross-appeal on this point, it was not necessary for the C.A. to deal with it.

[4] See *Copin* v. *Adamson*, *supra*, as regards the second replication referred to at the end of the last note: *Emanuel* v. *Symon*, [1908] 1 K.B. 302, C.A. (per Lord ALVERSTONE C.J., at pp 307–309, and KENNEDY L.J., at pp. 313, 314, applying the principle laid down by the majority of the Court of Exchequer to the case of a partner in a firm, against whom it was vainly contended that from the fact of his membership alone an implication might be made of a contract to submit to the jurisdiction of the courts of the colony in which the firm carried on business).

obey the lawful citation of the foreign tribunal, there is no occasion for further inquiry; no foundation for jurisdiction is established. If, however, he so far succeeds, it is still open to the latter party to deny that he was ever brought before the court by due service of writ, notice, summons, or other process; or, if given notice of the proceedings, that he was given due and proper opportunity of appearing before the foreign tribunal and presenting his case. All questions such as whether or not the party was served, or otherwise given sufficient notice of the proceedings, or whether he was given an adequate opportunity to appear thereon and present his case, are questions of fact and evidence.[1]

158 If it is shown that, being otherwise subject to the jurisdiction of the foreign tribunal, the party now to be held liable was served with due notice of the proceedings, and had sufficient opportunity to appear before the tribunal and present his case, jurisdiction will be established.[2] If these essentials are not shown, then the foundation of jurisdiction is not established, and the plea of *res judicata* based on the foreign proceedings will fail[3]—except, however, in the case referred to in paragraph 152 above, where the defendant has in fact appeared and submitted to the jurisdiction. In such a case it is useless to inquire whether he was duly served in accordance with the procedure of the foreign court—he has by his appearance waived this requirement.

159 So much for the case where the defendant has been actually served with notice of the proceedings. Whether he can be satisfactorily held to have been duly brought before the foreign court whose jurisdiction is being questioned, in the absence of any *express* notice of the proceedings may be a doubtful matter. On the one hand it has many times been said that the requirement of natural justice makes it essential that the proceedings should have been brought to the actual notice of the defendant, and that he should have had due opportunity of appearing before the foreign tribunal and of presenting his case.[4] So, for instance, HORRIDGE J. in *Rudd* v.

---

[1] As explained in Chapter II, para. 75, *ante*.

[2] As in *Buchanan* v. *Rucker* (1808), 9 East 192; *Ferguson* v. *Mahon* (1839), 11 Ad. & El. 179; *Rousillon* v. *Rousillon* (1880), 14 Ch.D. 351; *Bergerem* v. *Marsh* (1921), 125 L.T. 630.

[3] See *Douglas* v. *Forrest* (1828), 4 Bing. 686; *Obicini* v. *Bligh* (1832), 8 Bing. 335; *Cowan* v. *Braidwood* (1840), 1 Man. & G. 882; *Sheehy* v. *Professional Life Assurance Co.* (1857), 3 C.B. N.S. 597, Ex. Ch.; *Schibsby* v. *Westenholz* (1870), L.R. 6 Q.B. 155 (here, however, the *res judicata* was not established, but only because the foreign court had no jurisdiction over the party at all; it was held, per BLACKBURN J., at p. 160, that the defendant had been properly served, according to the proved procedure of the foreign court): *Jeannot* v. *Fuerst* (1909), 100 L.T. 816.

[4] Per ATKIN L.J. in *Jacobson* v. *Frachon* (1927), 44 T.L.R. 103, at p. 105.

Rudd[1] declined to recognise a decree of divorce obtained by a husband in the State of Washington in the United States of America, when the only notice given to the wife of the American divorce proceedings was a registered letter posted to her in England, at her last known place of address, which had in fact never reached her, and an advertisement in the Seattle Weekly News, which she never in fact saw; and this notwithstanding the fact that these steps satisfied an order for substituted service duly made in the American court. But it may be argued (and perhaps this is particularly applicable to divorce proceedings) that if English courts having jurisdiction over the cause (in the case of divorce proceedings by reason of domicil) themselves allow substituted service as satisfactorily founding jurisdiction over the parties, should not they recognise the use of similar substituted service by foreign tribunals having, by reason of domicil, similar jurisdiction? So in *Boettcher* v. *Boettcher*[2] WALLINGTON J. recognised a decree made by a court of the state of Indiana, where service had been constructively effected by a newspaper advertisement in accordance with an order of the Indiana court, but in fact the proceedings had never been brought in time to the notice of the respondent. And in the later case of *Igra* v. *Igra*,[3] PEARCE J., as he then was, recognised a German decree made where the proceedings had been served only by substituted service, saying:[4]

> "In those circumstances it would be unfortunate if this court felt bound to reject its validity, with the result that the wife would have a married status in England and an unmarried status in Germany. It has long been accepted that the court of the domicile is the proper tribunal to dissolve a marriage. Its decisions should, as far as reasonably possible, be acknowledged by other countries in the interests of comity. Different countries have different personal laws, different standards of justice and different practice. The interests of comity are not served if one country is too eager to criticise the standards of another country, or too reluctant to recognise decrees that are valid by the law of the domicile."

It is easy to see that in divorce proceedings there may be much to commend the view of PEARCE J.; and for the reasons advanced in paragraph 68, *ante*, as to the real basis of the acceptability in this country of foreign decrees in divorce. So much inconvenience is caused by decrees of divorce being granted to parties in one country, yet not being available in another,

---

[1] [1924] P. 72. At p. 76, HORRIDGE J. said: "Notice, it was said, was immaterial, service having been effected according to the practice of that Court. I believe, however, that there must be a notice of the proceedings to the party to be affected by them before the proceedings can bind that party". But this case was one of jurisdiction *in rem*, and may be thought not to be a direct authority on the question of jurisdiction *in personam*.

[2] [1949] W.N. 83.

[3] [1951] P. 404.

[4] At p. 412.

that every possible effort, consistent with the requirement of natural justice, should be made towards uniformity. Different considerations may apply, however, to judgments not involving the status of persons *contra mundum*, but declaring or effecting only financial consequences between parties. Here no question arises of the inconvenience caused by conflicting decisions as to the status of persons. As has already been pointed out, it may now be regarded as very arguable, in the light of the most recent decisions, whether a judgment *by default* whereby A is adjudged by a foreign court to be liable to pay a sum of money to B should on principle, in every case, be acknowledged as a *res judicata* in this country;[1] and all the more when the proceedings are not *actually*, but merely notionally, brought to the notice of the defendant. In such a case it is submitted that, notwithstanding some earlier decisions, wherein a sterner attitude was favoured, for the future the Courts will tend rather to decline to give to a foreign decision the status in this country of a *res judicata* where the defendant has not both received actual notice of the proceedings, and, in addition, been afforded a sufficient opportunity of appearing before the tribunal and presenting his case.

Mr Spencer Bower's view

160 The foregoing passage is from the pen of the author of the second edition of this work, and differs distinctly from the view expressed by Mr Spencer Bower in the corresponding original text.[2] In the first edition the view was put forward that the test of jurisdiction was simply whether it was shown that the defendant was summoned to the foreign court "by such service of writ, notice, summons, or other process as is prescribed by the law of the foreign state". "Wherever it is made to appear" (so runs the text of the first edition) "that in the particular case the service was duly effected, or the notice given, and that the other preliminaries were duly observed, in accordance with the proved foreign procedure, the jurisdiction of the tribunal over the party in that particular case, assuming him to be subject to the jurisdiction in general, is established;[3] when the proof in this respect is defective, it is not".[4]

161 "It is wholly immaterial" (Mr Spencer Bower continued) "whether the proved foreign practice is, or is not, in accord with English practice, or with English views of what is just, convenient, and proper. If

[1] See Chapter II, paras. 49 *et seq.*, *ante*, where this topic is discussed.

[2] 1st Ed. paras. 137–140.

[3] The footnote in the first edition cites the cases set out in note 2 on p. 126, *supra*; with these cases should now be contrasted *Jacobson* v. *Frachon* (1927), 44 T.L.R. 103, C.A. and *Rudd* v. *Rudd*, [1924] P. 72.

[4] The note in the first edition cites the cases set out in note 3 on p. 126, *supra*.

the foreign procedure was duly followed, and the party was by allegiance (permanent or temporary), or otherwise, bound to recognise and conform to such procedure it does not matter how unjust or unreasonable, according to English habits of thought, such procedure may appear to be.[1] It has, indeed, from time to time, been vaguely suggested, under cover of such sonorous titles as 'natural', or 'universal', justice, that, even where the general jurisdiction over the party exists, our courts ought not to recognise, or give effect to, any foreign rule of practice purporting to bind a party on whom no service has been effected, other than substituted, or to whom no notice of the proceedings has been given, other than constructive. But, as will be explained hereafter in the proper place, any such view is wholly in conflict with both principle and authority''.

The present author in difference from Mr Spencer Bower: the statutory rules considered

162 With the views of Mr Spencer Bower, as expressed in the last two preceding paragraphs, the author of this second edition is not in complete agreement. It is submitted by him that the view of ATKIN L.J.[2] and of HORRIDGE J.[3] is now to be preferred. The climate of opinion seems to him to be changing; in 1968 the courts are no longer ready to recognise, so automatically as one hundred years ago, the validity of *every* foreign judgment *inter partes*. The change in attitude in respect of judgments by default has been marked;[4] and, as will presently be seen, a similar change has been evident in other aspects of the doctrine, especially in the field of issue estoppel[5] where, in particular, the applicability of general rules to foreign judgments has been questioned. The Courts are ready to have another look at the problem; and in the long run ATKIN L.J. may once again be proved to be right in principle, in the present instance as to his opinion that a foreign judgment pronounced without actual notice of the proceedings, and of sufficient opportunity to present a case, may amount to

---

[1] The note in the 1st Ed. reads: ''Accordingly the following foreign rules as to substituted, or constructive, service or notice, though in some cases not in accordance with English practice, were, on proof thereof by experts, given effect to by our courts in the following cases respectively: Scottish practice of proclamation of 'letters of horning', in *Douglas* v. *Forrest* (1828), 4 Bing. 686 (per BEST C.J., at pp. 701–703); Irish statutory mode of substituted service, in *Sheehy* v. *Professional Life Assurance Co.*, *supra* (per COLERIDGE J., at pp. 612, 613, ERLE C.J., at pp. 614, 615, CROMPTON J., and MARTIN B., at pp. 617, 618, and WATSON B., at pp. 618, 619), and *Crawley* v. *Isaacs* (1867), 16 L.T. 529 (per KELLY C.B., at pp. 530, 531, BRAMWELL B., at p. 531, and CHANNELL B., at p. 531); the French practice as to substituted service, in *Schibsby* v. *Westenholz*, *supra* (per BLACKBURN J., at p. 160), and *Jeannot* v. *Fuerst*, *supra* (per BRAY J., at pp. 817, 818). See also *Bergerem* v. *Marsh* (1921), 125 L.T. 630 (*ex parte* adjudication of bankruptcy in Belgian court, with liberty to the party to apply to set aside).''

[2] In *Jacobson* v. *Frachon* (1927), 44 T.L.R. 103, at pp. 104–105.

[3] In *Rudd* v. *Rudd*, [1924] P. 72.

[4] See Chapter II, paras. 49 *et seq.*, where this change in attitude is discussed.

[5] See Chapter VI, paras. 204 *et seq.*, in this regard.

such a denial of natural justice as to persuade an English court that the foreign tribunal pronouncing it did so without jurisdiction.

This conclusion seems to the writer to derive some support from the provisions of the two statutes to which we had occasion to refer in an earlier chapter in which the rules as to the enforcement of foreign judgments were examined. The Administration of Justice Act 1920 prescribes, as a matter precluding registration of a judgment for enforcement in this country, that "the judgment debtor was not served and did not appear in the original proceeding". Nothing is expressly said about substituted service; but it is submitted that this provision, read as a whole, contemplates actual, and not substituted, service. The Foreign Judgments (Reciprocal Enforcement) Act 1933 provides more explicitly, that registration must be set aside "if the judgment debtor, being the defendant in the original proceedings, did not (*despite service of process in accordance with the foreign law*) receive notice of the proceedings in sufficient time to enable him to defend them, and did not appear".

CHAPTER V

Finality

163 In order that a judicial decision,[1] whether of an English or of a foreign tribunal,[2] may operate as a *res judicata*, it must be final,[3] in the sense stated below. The burden of establishing this finality rests, in the first instance, upon the party who relies upon the decision, whether as the foundation of an action,[4] or in bar of his adversary's claim,[5] though in many cases, as will be explained later,[6] it is easily discharged, and thereupon the onus of impeaching the finality is cast upon the opposite party, if, indeed, it is not assumed by him at the outset.

---

[1] Which expression includes judgments, orders, declarations, decrees, certificates, etc., and also awards of domestic tribunals. See Chapter II, *ante*. In dealing with awards, the courts have been specially vigilant in requiring finality to be proved, the professed object of resort to arbitration being the saving of the expense of protracted litigation through a series of courts by referring the matters in dispute to a "*final* arbitrament and award".

[2] As to English, and foreign, judicial tribunals, see Chapter II, *ante*.

[3] See for instance *Eastwood and Holt* v. *Studer* (1926), 31 Com. Cas. 251, at pp. 256–7 per ROCHE J.—"secondly, where a decision of a competent tribunal is relied on as creating an estoppel and preventing a subsequent review of the matter, it is necessary that the matter should have been raised and controverted before the earlier tribunal and shall have been clearly, and finally, decided by it".

[4] *Nouvion* v. *Freeman* (1889), 15 App. Cas. 1, H.L. (per Lord HERSCHELL, at p. 9).

[5] *Plummer* v. *Woodburne* (1825), 4 B. & C. 625, where a plea of estoppel by a colonial judgment was held bad, for want of precision in averring that the judgment was final and conclusive (*per Cur.*, at p. 628, adopting "the reasons suggested by BAYLEY J.", at p. 627); *Behrens* v. *Sieveking* (1837), 2 My. & Cr. 602, where a judgment of the Mayor's Court was pleaded as an estoppel to a chancery suit (per Lord COTTENHAM L.C., at p. 603: "the defendant had to shew that . . . the result was conclusive", whereas here "the plea left the court in ignorance whether the proceedings in the Lord Mayor's Court were conclusive, even in that Court"); *Frayes* v. *Worms* (1861), 10 C.B. N.S. 149, where a Californian judgment was set up as a bar to an action for general average, and the plea was held bad on demurrer for not alleging that, by Californian law, the judgment was final (per ERLE C.J. at p. 153); *Harris* v. *Quine* (1869), L.R. 4 Q.B.653 (the like, as to a similarly defective plea of a Manx judgment in bar, per COCKBURN J., at p. 657). On the other hand, in *Langmead* v. *Maple* (1865), 18 C.B. N.S. 255, it seems to have been held that a plea of a chancery judgment in bar to an action for injury to the plaintiff's reversion, which did not allege finality, was good on demurrer, and was properly met by a replication of non-finality, which was held equally good on a cross-demurrer (per ERLE C.J., at pp. 265, 266, WILLIAMS J., at pp. 269, 270, and WILLES J., at pp. 270–272). It is impossible to reconcile this authority with the others here cited, except, perhaps, on the theory that the tribunals in the other cases were inferior, or foreign, courts, whereas here the decision was that of a superior court, the finality of which will be presumed, unless the contrary be shown.

[6] See para 178, *post*.

Meaning of "Finality"

164 A judicial decision is deemed final, when it leaves nothing to be judicially determined or ascertained thereafter, in order to render it effective and capable of execution, and is absolute, complete, and certain, and when it is not lawfully subject to subsequent rescission, review, or modification by the tribunal which pronounced it. This definition involves the existence of two distinct types of non-finality, which it is proposed to examine separately: one, in which the judicial decision on the face of it is imperfect, provisional, conditional, indefinite, or ambiguous, and the other in which the judicial decision, though *ex facie* purporting to be final, is, by the English, or (as the case may be) the foreign, law applicable, liable to be afterwards rescinded, re-opened, or varied by the originally adjudicating tribunal.

One test to be applied to *foreign* decisions, in order to determine whether they are "*final*", is to inquire whether the judgment is itself *res judicata* in the country where it was pronounced. This was made clear by Lord HERSCHELL in *Nouvion* v. *Freeman*,[1] and in more modern times the same test was again adverted to by Lord GUEST in his judgment in *Carl-Zeiss-Stiftung* v. *Rayner and Keeler, Ltd.*,[2] where he observed that

> "it would indeed be illogical if the decision were to be *res judicata* in England, if it were not also *res judicata* in the foreign jurisdiction."

Want of finality appearing on the face of the record

165 The simplest and most obvious illustrations of decisions which do not purport on their face to be other than temporary, provisional, or interlocutory are the following: an order made "until the trial of the action or further order", such as an interlocutory injunction, or an interim order for the preservation of property, or of the *status quo*,[3] though, if an interlocutory order as to the working out of the decision is contained in a judgment which finally declares the rights of the parties, the declaratory part

[1] (1889), 15 App. Cas. 1, H.L. at p. 9.

[2] [1966] 2 All E.R. 536, at p. 566. In that case Lord GUEST held that this requirement was not satisfied by the West German judgment set up as *res judicata*, and the plea failed, on this as well as on other grounds. In *Blohn* v. *Desser*, [1962] 2 Q.B. 116 (DIPLOCK J.) a submission of cause of action estoppel *per rem judicatam* against a partner in a firm, based on an Austrian judgment against the firm, failed for lack of finality, on its being shown that an Austrian judgment against a firm did not of itself impose final liability on the partners individually. If it was sought to impose individual liability upon them, additional proceedings were necessary, and in these, though the partners would be faced with issue estoppels as to matters finally decided in the earlier proceedings, they might raise new defences personal to the partners, which could not have been raised in the earlier litigation.

[3] *Pim* v. *Curel* (1840), 6 M. & W. 234 (per ALDERSON B., at p. 267: "the order amounts to no more than to direct the continuance, during the suit, of a certain state of things which existed at the time the order was made, without passing any judgment upon the facts, or upon the rights of the parties").

may be separately relied upon as *pro tanto* conclusive;[1] an order made "*pendente lite*", such as an order for alimony in the divorce court;[2] a decree nisi for divorce;[3] a judgment of a court of equity expressed to be "without prejudice to an action at law",[4] but not a judgment which merely reserves questions not then in issue,—an entirely unnecessary addition, which in no way qualifies the decision;[5] a judgment of a court of common law expressed to be subject to the decision of a court of equity;[6] or a purely interlocutory order for the payment of costs,[7] as, distinct from an order for costs forming part of a final judgment[8] or which otherwise can only be regarded as final.[9]

In a case decided in 1954 an originating summons for determination of

---

[1] As in *Peareth* v. *Marriott* (1882), 22 Ch.D. 182 (per COTTON L.J., at p. 193: "it is said that the direction for payment was only till further order, but it appears to me that it was only temporary as to the mode in which the payment was to be made, and the funds out of which it was to come. It was final as to the rights of the parties").

[2] See *Bailey* v. *Bailey* (1884), 13 Q.B.D. 855, C.A. (per GROVE J., at p. 857, and BRETT M.R., at p. 859); *Robins* v. *Robins*, [1907] 2 K.B. 13 (per JOYCE J., at pp. 16, 17).

[3] But notwithstanding that the suit never proceeded beyond the grant of a decree *nisi*, and even in a case where that decree was set aside on the intervention of the Queen's Proctor, a finding of adultery by a jury was held, in a case in which that finding was not impeached by the decision to set aside the decree, to estop the parties from relitigating the issue of fact involved: *Butler* v. *Butler*, [1894] P. 25. Some criticism of this decision will be found in a later chapter (Chapter XII) where decisions in matrimonial proceedings are examined.

[4] *Langmead* v. *Maple* (1865), 18 C.B. N.S. 255.

[5] *Rochester Corporation* v. *Lee* (1848), 1 Mac. & G. 467, at pp. 469, 470.

[6] As in *Jones* v. *Reynolds* (1836), 7 C. & P. 335.

[7] *Patrick* v. *Shedden* (1853), 2 E. & B. 14 (action on Scottish interim decreet for "expenses" incurred in successfully resisting the defender's appeal to House of Lords will not lie: per Lord CAMPBELL C.J., and WIGHTMAN J., at p. 22); *Sheehy* v. *Professional Life Assurance Co.* (1857), 2 C.B. N.S. 211 (the like as to interlocutory order for plaintiff's costs of resisting defendant's appeal to Irish appellate court: per CRESSWELL J., at p. 256); *Stephenson* v. *Garnett*, [1898] 1 Q.B. 677, C.A. (interlocutory order to tax costs in county court cannot be set up as a *res judicata* in bar of an action in the High Court for a declaration that the defendant had been released by the plaintiff, and for an injunction restraining him from proceeding further therewith: per A. L. SMITH L.J., at p. 680, CHITTY L.J., at p. 681, and COLLINS L.J., at p. 682). In *Hutchinson* v. *Gillespie* (1856), 11 Exch. 798, it is recognised that actions will not lie on mere interlocutory orders for payment of costs (per BRAMWELL B., at pp. 815, 816).

[8] As in *Russell* v. *Smyth* (1842), 9 M. & W. 810, an action on that part of a Scottish decree for divorce which had provided for the plaintiff's costs (per Lord ABINGER C.B., at p. 818). See also *Allnutt* v. *Mills* (1925), 42 T.L.R. 68 (interlocutory order as to title to sum paid into Court in part satisfaction pending final hearing of action).

[9] As in *Hutchinson* v. *Gillespie*, *supra*, where it was held that an order of the Judicial Committee of the Privy Council for the payment of an ascertained sum for costs was a final order, and that an action would lie thereon, per ALDERSON B., at pp. 810, 811 ("it has been argued that the order is not final, but it appears to me that it is. Looking at the nature of the proceedings it is so; for nothing remains to be done, so far as the present plaintiff's claim is concerned, except the carrying into effect of the order of the Judicial Committee of the Privy Council"), MARTIN B., at pp. 812–814, describing the order as one for the payment of a *fixed* sum of money, and, therefore, final, and BRAMWELL B., at p. 818, who considered the order to be final, because it was not subject to subsequent variation, or conditional. On an examination of this case, it is certainly difficult to understand why, for the excellent reasons above cited, the orders in *Patrick* v. *Shedden*, *supra*, and in *Sheehy* v. *Professional Life Assurance Co.*, *supra*, should not have been deemed equally final.

the validity of a charitable bequest had been argued upon the basis, common to all parties, that the matter fell to be determined as at the date of the death of the tenant for life; the court made an order directing further inquiries and ordering that the summons should stand over. On completion of the inquiries the accountants asked that the matter should be reargued on the basis that the relevant date was not as had been supposed, but was the date of death of the testatrix. A plea of *res judicata* was attempted, it being argued for the beneficiaries that this was a matter which had been conceded as an essential foundation for the order which had been made. It was held, however, that an order for further inquiries directing that the summons should stand over meanwhile was not an order having the attribute of finality necessary to found the plea.[1]

166 There is no finality in a judicial decision which does not order the payment of any specific sum, but only of a sum to be judicially determined, assessed, or computed, at a later stage by the tribunal itself or some officer, or person, or body of persons, acting by the authority of that tribunal, such as an English interlocutory judgment for damages to be assessed on a writ of inquiry, or by an official, or special, referee, or a foreign judgment for an amount to be ascertained on a report of merchants;[2] or, generally, in any judgment or order which expressly provides for calculation of amounts by an officer of the court,[3] or which directs a specific sum to be paid after deduction therefrom of an unspecified amount to be thereafter ascertained.[4] On the other hand, a judgment is final, not only when the sum to be paid is fixed and liquidated on the face of the record,[5] but also, where the sum is not liquidated in the judgment itself, but left to be determined by subsequent proceedings, if, and as soon as, it is so ascertained by the person and in the manner prescribed, whereupon the decision, till then interlocutory, becomes final, and proper to be set up as a *res judicata*.[6]

---

[1] *In Re Wright, Blizard* v. *Lockhart*, [1954] Ch. 347 (ROXBURGH J.); affirmed by the Court of Appeal at p. 357.

[2] *Obicini* v. *Bligh* (1832), 8 Bing. 335 (per TINDAL C.J., at pp. 351–353, PARK J., at pp. 352, 353, and ALDERSON J., at pp. 354, 355).

[3] *Carpenter* v. *Thornton* (1819), 3 B. & Ald. 52 (per ABBOTT C.J., at p. 55).

[4] *Sadler* v. *Robins* (1808), 1 Camp. 253, where an action on a decree of a colonial court of equity, ordering the defendant to pay to the plaintiff a certain sum of money, "first deducting thereout the defendant's costs *to be taxed*," was brought before any taxation (per Lord ELLENBOROUGH C.J. at pp. 254, 255).

[5] *Henderson* v. *Henderson* (1844), 6 Q.B. 288 (unconditional order of a colonial court of equity to pay an ascertained balance: *per Cur.*, at pp. 296–298). Cp. *Hutchinson* v. *Gillespie*, *supra*.

[6] *Henley* v. *Soper* (1828), 8 B. & C. 16, where a judgment had been given in a colonial court for the balance of a partnership account, to be ascertained by an arbitrator, and, the arbitrator having fixed the sum payable, an action was brought to recover this sum on the judgment which, originally interlocutory, had thus become final (per Lord TENTERDEN C.J., at p. 21, and HOLROYD J., at pp. 21, 22, distinguishing *Sadler* v. *Robins*, *supra*).

167 A judicial decision which on the face of it is not absolute, but expressed to be subject to a specified condition, such as a certificate of an officer of a court of equity which is stated to be subject to proof of title,[1] or an award directing one of the parties to pay a sum of money unless he discharges himself by affidavit,[2] or to execute works to the satisfaction of a third person,[3] is not a final decision on which a case of *res judicata* can be founded. Nor is a decision the record of which contains some express qualification, or limitation, which deprives it of even the appearance of absoluteness. Thus, during the time when suits for jactitation of marriage were within the exclusive jurisdiction of the ecclesiastical courts, it was the practice for the respondent, if so advised, to plead a marriage (in effect a plea of justification); if he failed to prove his plea, the sentence was not expressed in absolute terms, but in the form of a declaration that "the party has failed in his proof, and that the libellant is free from all matrimonial contract, *so far as yet appears*",—a declaration which, as was observed in the leading case on the subject of estoppel *per rem judicatam*,[4] left it open to the party to re-agitate the question afterwards in a new suit on fresh evidence, to which the carefully qualified sentence of the spiritual court could not be set up as an estoppel.

No issue estoppel from abortive trial

168 No finding of the court or of a jury of a trial which has proved abortive, a new trial having been directed, will give rise to a valid plea of estoppel.[5] And a decision of the court setting aside the verdict of a jury, or setting aside a judgment entered pursuant thereto, and directing a new trial, will not result in either party being estopped *per rem judicatam* by anything held on the facts in the judgment in which the new trial is ordered, for the judgment must be read as deciding no more than that, the first trial being unsatisfactory, the issues tried therein should be re-submitted to the court for fresh consideration.[6]

---

[1] As in *Mountcashell's Estate*, [1920] 1 I.R. 1 (certificate of chief clerk in Irish administration suit, as to ownership of lands, conditional upon title being shown: per Ross J., at p. 6).

[2] As in *Pedley* v. *Goddard* (1796), 7 Term Rep. 73 (per Lord KENYON C.J., at p. 77).

[3] As in *Tomlin* v. *Fordwich Corporation* (1836), 5 Ad. & El. 147.

[4] *Duchess of Kingston's Case* (1776), 2 Smith L.C. (13th edn.) 644 (per DE GREY C.J., delivering the opinion of himself and the other judges summoned to advise the House of Lords, at p. 761).

[5] *Roe* v. *R. A. Naylor, Ltd.* (1918), 87 L.J. K.B. 958, C.A. per SWINFEN EADY L.J. at p. 963—"This action was sent for a new trial, and the second trial superseded the first, and any finding in the first action was got rid of when the action was sent for a new trial".

[6] *Gray* v. *Dalgety & Co. Ltd.* (1916), 21 C.L.R. 509 (High Court of Australia). At p. 520 Sir SAMUEL GRIFFITH C.J. said: "But I never before heard it suggested that a grant of a new trial was a final decision upon any point except that the matter should be further investigated". So too, *in New Zealand*, *Lyons* v. *Nicholls No.* 3, [1958] N.Z.L.R. 755 C.A.

Defective awards

169 Another illustration of a judicial decision which is *ex facie* non-final is furnished on examining the law relating to the proceedings of a domestic forum. Here, an award which omits all reference to, and on the face of it, ignores any of the matters submitted to the arbitral tribunal by the instrument of reference, has always been held to be so apparently imperfect and defective as to deprive it of the capacity to rank as a *res judicata* which, if it had been apparently complete and definitive, would have belonged to it.[1]

Declaratory judgments

170 A judicial decision, however, is not deemed *ex facie* defective or imperfect, merely because it consists of a naked declaration of the rights and liabilities of the parties. Indeed, as regards English decisions, it is expressly provided by a statutory rule of practice[2] that a merely declaratory judgment or order may be made which shall be binding and conclusive on the parties, though no consequential relief be granted. Nor is a decision on one of several disputed points in a case, if otherwise final, rendered any the less so merely because it was separately pronounced at an earlier stage in the proceedings than the decision of the other points, or than is usual.[3] Nor can a decision be treated as wanting in finality, though appearing to be so on the face of it, if its apparent imperfection and incompleteness is due to the objecting party's conduct or tacit consent,[4] for in such a case the

---

[1] As in *Randall* v. *Randall* (1805), 7 East 81; *Mitchell* v. *Staveley* (1812), 16 East 58 (per Lord ELLENBOROUGH C.J., at p. 66); *Samuel* v. *Cooper* (1835), 2 Ad. & El. 752; *Re Tribe and Upperton* (1835), 3 Ad. & El. 295; *Bowes* v. *Fernie* (1838), 4 My. & Cr. 150; *Ross* v. *Boards* (1838), 8 Ad. & El. 290; *Price* v. *Popkin* (1839), 10 Ad. & El. 139; *Wilkinson* v. *Page* (1842), 1 Hare 276; *Richardson* v. *Worsley* (1850), 5 Exch. 613; *Williams* v. *Wilson* (1853), 9 Exch. 90 (per PARKE B., at pp. 100, 101); *Re Tidswell* (1863), 33 Beav. 213; *Re Becker, Shillan & Co. and Barry Brothers* (1920), 37 T.L.R. 101, D.C.; *Re O'Conor and Whitlaw's Arbitration* (1920), 88 L.J. K.B. 1242, C.A.

[2] Order 15, r. 16, of the R.S.C. (1965).

[3] *Dundas* v. *Waddell* (1880), 5 App. Cas. 249, H.L. (per Lord CAIRNS L.C., at pp. 262, 263, Lord HATHERLEY, at p. 264, Lord O'HAGAN, at pp. 269–271, and Lord BLACKBURN, at p. 271).

[4] As in *Henderson* v. *Henderson* (1843), 3 Hare 100, a partnership action, in which the defendant set up, in support of a demurrer to the bill for want of equity,—really by way of estoppel,—the judgment of a colonial court given in his favour, in answer to which the plaintiff argued that the whole of the issues had not been decided by the colonial court, but it was held that this was only because the plaintiff (then defendant) had deliberately refrained from putting forward his whole case in the colonial suit, as he ought to have done, and the decision must therefore be treated as if he had complied with his duty, and the demurrer was accordingly allowed (per WIGRAM V.C., at pp. 114–118). Cp. the following cases of awards: *Cockburn* v. *Newton* (1841), 2 Man. & G. 899 (where certain omitted matters had been treated by the parties in the course of the arbitration as having ceased to be in dispute: per TINDAL C.J., at p. 905, COLTMAN J., at p. 906, and ERSKINE J., at pp. 906, 907); *Rees* v. *Waters* (1847), 16 M. & W. 263 (where the party complaining of the omission in the award had neglected to bring the omitted matters to the notice of the arbitrators).

party is estopped by his act or omission from asserting the imperfection and inconclusiveness of the decision.[1]

Ambiguity and uncertainty

171 Finality cannot be attributed to a judicial decision, the terms of which, whether declaratory or directory, are so uncertain and ambiguous as to leave the parties in doubt as to the exact extent of their respective rights and liabilities, or as to the manner in which the decision is to be complied with, or enforced. The following are illustrations of decisions which have been held non-final on this ground: a verdict in an action of ejectment in respect of certain freehold and copyhold lands, the title to which was in question, finding that so many acres of the entire lands were freehold, and so many copyhold, without determining which of the parties had title to which;[2] an award directing a certain act to be performed either by A., or by B.;[3] an award whereby it was declared that one of the parties had been guilty of fraud towards the other, though it was also expressly found that he had no intention to mislead him,[4] an award which, one of the items of the claim having been admitted by the respondent, instead of reciting this fact and awarding the proper relief in respect of this item on the basis of the admission, made no reference to the matter at all, leaving the parties absolutely in the dark as to whether this particular head of claim might be taken to have been satisfied and discharged, or not;[5] in an action on the trial of which a verdict had been taken for the plaintiff for £3000 subject to a reference to a barrister, who was empowered to enter the verdict for either party, and also to determine what was to be done in respect of certain other matters in dispute, an award of such referee directing the verdict to be entered for the plaintiff, and that the defendant should pay to the plaintiff £260.12.6d. leaving it absolutely uncertain whether it was intended to reduce the amount of the verdict from £3000 to £260.12.6d., ignoring or awarding nothing in respect of the other matters in dispute, or to let the verdict stand for the £3000, and award the lesser sum in respect of the other matters;[6] an award directing payment of two alternative sums,

---

[1] This topic is dealt with in Chapter XIII, para 303, of the 2nd edition of the authors' *Law of Estoppel by Representation*.

[2] *Hardcastle* v. *Shafto* (1793), 1 Anst. 184 (per MACDONALD C.B., delivering the judgment of the Court of Exchequer in Equity, at p. 185).

[3] *Lawrence* v. *Hodgson* (1826), 1 Y. & J. 16 (per HULLOCK B., at p. 18).

[4] *Ames* v. *Milward* (1818), 8 Taunt. 637, per DALLAS C.J., at pp. 641, 642.

[5] *Re Robson and Railston* (1831), 1 B. & Ad. 723 (per Lord DENMAN C.J., who, at p. 726, said that such an award, so far from being final and definitive, would invite "no end of disputes").

[6] *Mortin (Martin)* v. *Burge* (1836), 4 Ad. & El. 973 (per Lord DENMAN C.J., and LITTLEDALE J., at p. 975).

without indicating any method or test whereby it could be determined which of the two was to be paid.[1]

Want of finality by reason that the decision of the judicial tribunal is subject to revision by the tribunal itself

172 The second of the two above-mentioned classes of non-final judicial decisions comprises every judgment or order which, though not purporting on the face of it to be other than final, is nevertheless, by the law of the State having jurisdiction in the particular case, liable to subsequent rescission, suspension, or modification at the hands of the judicial tribunal which pronounced it, as distinct from an appellate tribunal.

173 A familiar instance of this type is the kind of order which courts exercising jurisdiction in matrimonial causes and matters are empowered to make for periodical payments by the husband to the wife of alimony or allowances for maintenance:[2] an affiliation order for the payment by the putative father of periodical sums for the maintenance of the bastard;[3] and an award under the Workmen's Compensation Acts 1897, and 1906, directing weekly payments to be made by the employer to the workman as compensation for accidental injury. These orders are not expressed to be merely interlocutory or temporary—indeed, in the case of orders for "permanent" alimony (as distinguished from orders for alimony *pendente lite*, which, as already stated, belong to the first of the two main classes of non-final decisions), a term is used which positively suggests finality in one sense of the word: but, inasmuch as English, and (in some cases) foreign, law invests the court, after making the order, with continuous authority thenceforth to entertain any application made, or applications from time to time made, by the interested party for a fresh order extinguishing, reducing, or increasing the sums originally ordered to be paid, on proof of the altered circumstances of either or both of the parties, and to grant any such application which may appear to be warranted by the evidence, it is obvious that neither the original order, nor any subsequent order modifying it, can ever be considered as final, or treated as a *res judicata*. Where, how-

---

1 *Murray* v. *Dalton* (1920), 65 Sol. Jo. 155, D.C.

2 See for instance *Robins* v. *Robins*, [1907] 2 K.B. 13; *Wickins* v. *Wickins*, [1918] P. 282, C.A., *Harrop* v. *Harrop*, [1920] 3 K.B. 386.

3 *Re Macartney*, *Macfarlane* v. *Macartney*, [1921] 1 Ch. 522, where, in support of her claim to rank as a creditor in an administration action, the mother of an illegitimate child, of whom the testator was the putative father, set up, as a *res judicata*, an order of a Maltese Court condemning the testator's estate to pay to the claimant a half-yearly alimentary allowance of a certain sum; but, it being proved by the evidence of experts that the Maltese Court had power to determine the affiliation allowance at any subsequent date on being satisfied that the husband was no longer in need of it, it was held that the order was not final, and the claim was accordingly disallowed (per ASTBURY J., at pp. 531, 532).

ever, a statute which, in one section, empowers the tribunal to rescind or vary its original decision, indicates, in another section, by the use of plain and unqualified language, the intention of the legislature that the original decision is to be regarded as final and binding, unless and until so rescinded or varied, there is no reason why it should not take effect as a *res judicata*, as soon as it is pronounced, notwithstanding its liability to future revision.[1]

Whether a decision of the Chief Land Registrar directing, after hearing the parties, the cancellation of a note on the Register as to the existence of an overriding interest in the land, but at the same time declining to direct an entry on the Register that the land was free from the encumbrance alleged, was a final determination of the rights of the parties such as to give rise to a plea of *res judicata*, was debated in 1962 before the Court of Appeal in *In Re Dance's Way, West Town, Hayling Island*.[2] DIPLOCK L.J. thought that the matter was *res judicata* unless and until the Registrar's decision had been altered on appeal; but Lord EVERSHED, M.R. and UPJOHN L.J. were of the contrary opinion.[3]

Judgments by default

174 Notwithstanding what is above written it is clear that a judgment obtained by default, like one obtained by consent, is to be regarded for the purposes of the doctrine of *res judicata* as a final judgment;[4] and this is so notwithstanding that by the Rules of Court it is open to the defendant at any time to move for its rescission upon cause being shown in that regard. Unless and until steps are taken to set it aside, it is to be taken, if it is a judgment of an English court, to be a final judgment. The same rule will not apply unqualifiedly, however, to foreign judgments, which will at least be closely scrutinised in this as in other regards in a case where jurisdiction has been assumed without any appearance of the defendant. In such a case it must be for him who sets up the estoppel to prove the finality of the foreign judgment which he invokes.[5]

---

[1] *Austin* v. *Mills* (1853), 9 Exch. 288, where it was held that an order made in a county court established by the County Courts Act 1846 (9 & 10 Vict. c. 95), was a final order, as expressly enacted by s. 89, and, therefore, operated as a *res judicata*, notwithstanding that, by s. 100 of the statute, any such order might afterwards be rescinded or varied by the county court judge who made it (*per Cur.*, at p. 293).

[2] [1962] Ch. 490, C.A.

[3] Lord EVERSHED M.R. at p. 505; UPJOHN L.J. at p. 507; DIPLOCK L.J. at p. 509.

[4] The applicability of the doctrine to default judgments is of long standing: *In Re South American and Mexican Co., Ex parte Bank of England*, [1895] 1 Ch. 37 C.A. per VAUGHAN WILLIAMS L.J. at p. 45; *Kok Hoong* v. *Leong Cheong Kweng Mines, Ltd.*, [1964] A.C. 993, J.C. per Lord RADCLIFFE at p. 1010. *In New Zealand*, *Tira Arika* v. *Sidaway*, [1923] N.Z.L.R. 158 per HOSKING J. at pp. 163–164. As for judgments by consent, see para. 179, *post*.

[5] See para. 178, *infra*.

Foreign judgments

175 Many, indeed most, foreign judgments, whether expressed in terms of finality or not, are, in accordance with the positive law of the foreign State, subject to being re-opened and reviewed by the tribunal from which they issued, on the prescribed steps being taken by the interested party within the prescribed time. Any such judgment, so long as there exists the bare possibility of its being thus re-opened and revised, or replaced by a final and definitive judgment, can only be regarded as provisional or interlocutory and, cannot operate as a *res judicata*. The principal illustration of such a non-final foreign judgment is the Spanish "remate" judgment which was the subject of investigation by the House of Lords in a case which is recognised as the leading modern authority on this question. It was there established by the evidence of experts that the Spanish law provides for two distinct forms of judgment in civil causes, the one being termed "remate" or "executive", and the other, "plenary" or "declaratory". The essential differences between the two kinds of judgment, and the proceedings resulting therein, respectively, are stated by Lord HERSCHELL in the case referred to as follows. "In an action of this nature" (an "executive" action) "only a very limited number of defences can be raised by the person sued", such as waiver, payment, etc. But "it is open to either of the parties . . . to sue in the same court in another form of action, which is called a declaratory or plenary action . . . In such a plenary action, to which either of the parties may have recourse, every defence which may be available is open as well as every consideration establishing the ground of action; and such a plenary action may be instituted by either of the parties to the executive action; that is to say, the party against whom the decision has been pronounced in the executive action, be he plaintiff or defendant, is at perfect liberty to sue in a plenary action for the purpose of obtaining a declaration of the rights of the parties; and in such a plenary action the fact that a judgment has been delivered in an executive action cannot be set up as at all affecting the rights of the parties, either in the way of proof or of title to succeed in the plenary action. The same points which have been decided in the executive action can again be raised in the plenary action, as well as other questions which were not open in the executive action. No effect is given, in the court in which it was pronounced and in which afterwards the plenary judgment may be pending, to the judgment in the executive action as being *res judicata* and as finally concluding the rights of the parties upon any point whatever".[1] In this state of the Spanish law, it was held that a "remate" judgment presented all the characteristics of a

---

[1] At pp. 6, 7, of *Nouvion* v. *Freeman* (1899), 15 App. Cas. 1, H.L.

purely provisional, and no characteristic of a final, decision, and, accordingly, the plaintiff in that case was not allowed to set up such a judgment as a *res judicata*, precluding any inquiry into the merits, whilst it was still open to the defendants to institute plenary proceedings, the effect of which would be to paralyse the executive judgment.[1] As regards French judgments, it was proved in a case of the year 1890, that the French law then in force (whatever it may be now) provided that any judgment became void automatically in six months, unless in the meantime it had been executed, or the utmost efforts had been used to effect execution: and, though it was not put expressly as one of the grounds of his decision, FRY J. inclined to the view that such a judgment could not be sued upon in this country if the above-mentioned condition had not been complied with,[2] which involves, as a corollary, the proposition that such a judgment cannot be sued upon in an English court before the expiration of the period limited, by a plaintiff who has not satisfied the condition, because the decision is as yet in a state of suspended animation. The French law as to judgments by default has been proved to be this. If, at any time before execution the defendant enters an "opposition", the default judgment is entirely superseded, fresh proceedings are instituted, and an entire re-hearing takes place on the merits, the judgment on which is a final, and the only final, decision. Accordingly the default judgment is not final, but provisional only, as long as the defendant is entitled to enter an "opposition".[3] The dictum of one of the judges in an earlier case,[4] to the effect that a French judgment which can be reopened by an "opposition" is none the less final on that account, unless and until it be so reopened, is contrary to the later authorities,[5] and must be regarded as unsound.

A question may well arise, in the case of a foreign country with a federated constitution, as to which is the "country" in which the foreign judgment must be regarded as final. In *Colt Industries Inc.* v. *Sarlie* (*No.* 2),[6] the question arose with regard to a final judgment of a court of the State of New York, upheld by the Supreme Court of that state whether it could be regarded as "final" in the "country" of its origin, when not all of the separate States of the American Federation so regarded it. It was held that the test was simply whether in the State of New York the judgment was regarded as final. The relevant question was not whether such a judgment would be recognised throughout the other states of the United States of

---

[1] *Nouvion* v. *Freeman* (1899), 15 App. Cas. 1, H.L. (per Lord HERSCHELL, at pp. 6, 7, 9–11, Lord WATSON, at pp. 12, 13, Lord BRAMWELL, at p. 14, and Lord ASHBOURNE, at pp. 17, 18).

[2] At p. 370 of *Rousillon* v. *Rousillon* (1880), 14 Ch.D. 351.

[3] *Bouchet* v. *Tulledge* (1894), 11 T.L.R. 87 (per COLLINS J., at p. 88).

[4] By ERLE C.J., at pp. 367, 368 of *Vanquelin* v. *Bouard* (1863), 15 C.B. N.S. 341.

[5] *Nouvion* v. *Freeman*, *supra*: see the references to the relevant passages in note 1, p. 140, *supra*.

[6] [1966] 3 All E.R. 85, C.A. per Lord DENNING M.R. at p. 87.

America but whether "the courts of this country should recognise, to the extent of pronouncing judgment upon it, a judgment of a court of competent jurisdiction, namely, the Supreme Court of New York".[1]

The difficulties with which an English court is faced when it is not satisfactorily shown whether in the jurisdiction in which the earlier decision was pronounced that decision would be regarded as finally deciding the issue between the parties, is clearly shown in the judgments in the Lords in *Carl-Zeiss-Stiftung* v. *Keeler and Rayner, Ltd.*[2] There Lord REID said:

> ". . . it seems to me to verge on absurdity that we should regard as conclusive something in a German judgment which the German court themselves would not regard as conclusive. It is quite true that estoppel is a matter for the *lex fori*, but the *lex fori* ought to be developed in a manner consistent with good sense. The need to prove whether the West German law would permit these issues to be re-opened there appears to have escaped the notice of the appellant's advisers, and your Lordships are left in considerable difficulty".

His Lordship did not expressly resolve the difficulty as to onus of proof on the point, being content to say that he "did not dissent" from what had been said in some of the other judgments. Some obscurity, and not a little difficulty, still seems to surround the point.

176 When the conditions precedent to a valid plenary action, or rehearing on an "opposition", are satisfied in accordance with the foreign law, the judgment which results from such proceedings is a new final judgment, not a confirmation of the first judgment.[3] On the other hand, as soon as the prescribed time has expired, without the party having taken the necessary steps to re-open the litigation, the "executive", or default, judgment, till then provisional, becomes final and absolute.[4]

177 The award of a foreign arbitral tribunal is not of itself a final foreign judgment, or, indeed, a judgment at all, if by the law of the foreign State, it only becomes so on the granting of an enforcement order by one of the established tribunals of that state.[5]

---

[1] *Colt Industries Inc.* v. *Sarlie* (*No.* 2), [1966] 3 All E.R. 85, C.A., per DAVIES L.J. at p. 88. *Cf.* RUSSELL L.J. on the same page: "I regard the possible attitude of sister states in the United States of America on the question of present enforceability within their jurisdictions of the judgment as entirely irrelevant in the present case."

[2] [1966] 2 All E.R. 536, H.L. at p. 555.

[3] See, again, *Nouvion* v. *Freeman*, *supra* (per Lord HERSCHELL, at pp. 6, 7); *Bouchet* v. *Tulledge*, *supra* (per COLLINS J. at p. 88), in which case the question whether the French judgment pronounced on the reopening of the case after the "opposition" was a new and independent judgment, or a mere confirmation of the previous judgment in default, was of vital importance, having regard to the defendant's plea of the Statute of Limitations).

[4] As in *Jeannot* v. *Fuerst* (1909), 100 L.T. 816 (per BRAY J., at p. 818).

[5] *Merrifield, Ziegler & Co.* v. *Liverpool Cotton Association* (1911), 105 L.T. 97 (per EVE J., at pp. 105, 106, who in reference to a German award which the defendants set up as a *res judicata*,

178 The law and practice of the foreign tribunal as to the finality or non-finality of its judgments must be proved, as a fact, by the proper evidence,[1] like any other question of foreign law.[2] Strictly, as has already been stated, the burden of establishing the finality of the foreign decision is upon the party who asserts that it is a *res judicata*.[3] It would seem, however, to be not unusual, at all events in the case of an action on the foreign judgment, to treat the onus as being shifted as soon as the party relying upon the foreign judgment has produced an instrument which, on the face of it, records a decision which does not purport to be other than final, the opposite party thereupon taking upon himself the duty, if only in his own interests, of proving the foreign law in virtue of which the judgment may be shown not to possess that quality of finality which *ex facie* appears to belong to it.[4]

Judgments by consent

179 A judgment is not the less final because it is a judgment entered by consent of the parties. Such a judgment is as much a final judgment as one resulting from a contested hearing.[5]

Irrelevancy of questions of appealability and execution

180 A judicial decision, otherwise final, is not the less so merely because it is appealable. If it is incapable of revision by the court which pronounced it, it is final in that court, which is all that is required to be

---

counterclaiming for its enforcement, held, solely on the ground stated in the text, that such counterclaim was bad, although he had dismissed the plaintiff's claim for a declaration that the award was invalid).

[1] See the cases cited in notes 1 on p. 140, 2 and 3 on p. 141, and 5 on p. 142, where the evidence was given orally. In *Re Macartney, Macfarlane* v. *Macartney*, [1921] 1 Ch. 522, the written opinion of an expert in Maltese law was (presumably by consent) received in evidence, without any examination of witnesses.

[2] See Chapter II, para. 75, *ante*.

[3] "It is for the defendants to show the estoppel, and to prove it they must establish as a matter of German law that the judgment is finally conclusive"—per Lord HODSON in *Carl-Zeiss-Stiftung* v. *Rayner and Keeler, Ltd.*, [1966] 2 All E.R. 536, H.L. at p. 560.

[4] See the cases cited in notes 1, p. 140; 2, 3, 4, p. 141 and 5, p. 142. So Lord HODSON, in *Carl-Zeiss-Stiftung* v. *Rayner and Keeler, Ltd.*, [1966] 2 All E.R. 536, H.L. at p. 560–561, after stating the strict legal burden as set out in footnote 3 above, went on to say that "although defendants had failed by express evidence to prove finality, yet for my part I think it would be legitimate to rely on the assumption commonly made in English courts that in the absence of evidence of foreign law it is to be taken to be the same as English law, and to hold that the judgment relied on for the estoppel is final and conclusive". But Lord WILBERFORCE in the same case would have disallowed the estoppel on the ground that it had not been satisfactorily shown that the foreign judgment was conclusive between the parties (p. 588); and Lord REID at p. 556 "did not dissent" from his view. Lord GUEST at p. 566 rested his decision on the burden of proof. The better view appears to be that the burden lies, as a matter of law, upon him who sets up the estoppel, and that failure to discharge it will result in the estoppel being disallowed.

[5] *Cohen* v. *Jonesco*, [1926] 1 K.B. 119 per FINLAY J. at p. 125. The judgment was reversed on appeal, but this dictum does not appear to have been affected.

shown, and it is wholly immaterial that it is capable of being rescinded or varied by some other court invested with competent appellate jurisdiction in that behalf.[1]

181 Equally erroneous, as is now well established, is the exactly opposite contention, which was raised at one time, not without some judicial countenance, that a decision is wanting in finality when it is *not* appealable, as in the case of affiliation orders under the statutes which gave no right of appeal to the mother,[2] and certain colonial judgments not the subject of appeal to the Privy Council.[3]

182 It has sometimes been contended that, though a decision is none the less final because it is appealable, and though if the right of appeal is not exercised, or intended to be exercised, the decision is on the same footing as if it had been confirmed on appeal,[4] nevertheless it makes a difference if the decision, besides being appealable, is actually under appeal at the time when it is set up as a *res judicata*. This contention is wholly unfounded.[5] It should be here noted, however, that the special statutory procedure for the registration and summary enforcement of colonial judgments cannot be

---

[1] See *Nouvion* v. *Freeman* (1889), 15 App. Cas. 1, H.L. (per Lord HERSCHELL, at pp. 10, 11, and Lord BRAMWELL, at p. 15); *Wakefield Corporation* v. *Cooke*, [1904] A.C. 31, H.L. (per Lord HALSBURY L.C., at p. 36). *Colt Industries Inc.* v. *Sarlie (No. 2)*, [1966] 3 All E.R. 85, C.A. per Lord DENNING M.R. at p. 86.

[2] One of the grounds of the decision in *R.* v. *Machen* (1849), 14 Q.B. 74, was that the statutes, 7 & 8 Vict. c. 101, and 8 Vict. c. 10, gave no appeal to the mother, though they did to the alleged father (per Lord DENMAN C.J., at pp. 79, 80). This was assumed (without argument or discussion, because the case before the court was of a different character, and was distinguished) to be a valid reason for holding that the dismissal of an affiliation summons is not final, in *Stokes* v. *Stokes*, [1911] P. 195 (per EVANS P., at pp. 197, 198). But the doctrine was seriously doubted by LUSH J., at p. 470 of *R.* v. *Gaunt* (1867), L.R. 2 Q.B. 466 ("nor do I quite see why, because there is no appeal, the decision should not be conclusive"), and it was definitely condemned in *McGregor* v. *Telford*, [1915] 3 K.B. 237, D.C. (per Lord READING C.J., at pp. 240, 241). Note, however, the reserve with which HUMPHREYS J. appears to have treated this dictum in *R.* v. *Sunderland Justices, Ex parte Hodgkinson*, [1945] K.B. 502, at p. 508. This conception, or one very like it, may have some validity in the field of issue estoppel; but its effect there is not truly founded on lack of finality, but on the impossibility of discerning what was actually decided. The relevancy of appealability in this connection is alluded to in Chapter VI, paras. 211 and 215, *post*.

[3] In *Henderson* v. *Henderson* (1843), 3 Hare 100, WIGRAM V.C., in deciding that the colonial judgment there set up as an estoppel was not the less final because it was liable to be reversed on appeal by the Privy Council, suggested, at p. 118, that it might have been otherwise if there had been no such right of appeal. But this rather faint suggestion was considered quite untenable in *Bynoe* v. *Bank of England*, [1902] 1 K.B. 467, C.A. (per COLLINS M.R., at pp. 470, 471, holding that a conviction is none the less final and conclusive, because it is not the subject of appeal).

[4] *Allen* v. *Sharp* (1848), 2 Exch. 352 (per PARKE B., at p. 366); *R.* v. *Bloomsbury Income Tax Commissioners*, [1915] 3 K.B. 768, D.C. (per AVORY J., at p. 790).

[5] *Doe* v. *Wright* (1839), 10 Ad. & El. 763 (per Lord DENMAN C.J., at p. 783); *Harris* v. *Willis* (1855), 15 C.B. 710; *Scott* v. *Pilkington* (1862), 2 B. & S. 11 (per COCKBURN C.J., at p. 41); *Marchioness of Huntley* v. *Gaskell*, [1905] 2 Ch. 656, C.A. (per COZENS-HARDY L.J., at p. 667).

resorted to if an appeal from the judgment is, at the time of the application to register, either pending or intended.[1]

183 It is equally irrelevant to the question of finality that execution of the judicial decision has been stayed by order of the court[2] or that the judgment creditor has forborne, or neglected, to levy execution.[3] Nor, on the other hand, is the decision deprived of its finality by the mere fact that it has been executed, as has been held in the case of a conviction for the non-repair of a highway, where the prosecutor had executed the judgment by the exaction of the fine imposed.[4]

---

[1] Administration of Justice Act 1920, s. 9, (2), (e). The provisions of the Foreign Judgments (Reciprocal Enforcement) Act 1933 are different. Section 1 (3) of that Act provides that a judgment shall be deemed final and conclusive notwithstanding that an appeal may be pending against it, or that it may still be subject to appeal. By section 5 (1) it is provided that the fact that such an appeal is pending, or that the applicant is entitled to appeal and intends to do so, is a ground for an application to set aside registration on such terms as may be thought fit.

[2] *Hall* v. *Odber* (1809), 11 East 118 (per Lord ELLENBOROUGH C.J., at pp. 123, 124, and LE BLANC J., at pp. 125, 126).

[3] *Doe* v. *Wright, supra.*

[4] *R.* v. *Inhabitants of Haughton* (1853), 1 E. & B. 501 (per Lord CAMPBELL C.J., at p. 515).

CHAPTER VI

The Subject Matter of the Judicial Decision

Identity of subject matter essential

184 It is of the essence of all estoppels that there shall be two statements of the same fact exhibiting *inter se* an essential contradiction or discrepancy;[1] the result of the application of the doctrine of estoppel is always that the earlier statement is to be taken as the truth, precluding an assertion of the later. There can be no estoppel *per rem judicatam* unless a substantial discrepancy is shown to exist between the *res judicata* and the case set up in the subsequent proceedings; and no such discrepancy can be shown to exist unless these two relate to *the same* subject matter.

185 It follows that, in strictness, the burden is on the party setting up the estoppel of alleging and establishing this identity of subject-matter—that is to say, that his opponent is seeking to put in controversy and re-agitate some question of law, or issue of fact, which is the very same question or issue which has already been the subject of a final decision between the same parties by a tribunal of competent jurisdiction.[2] Where there

---

[1] The same discrepancy is an essential ingredient of estoppel by representation—see the authors' *The Law of Estoppel by Representation* (2nd Edn.) Chapter IV.

[2] As to the *onus allegandi*, see *Behrens* v. *Sieveking* (1837), 2 My. & Cr. 602 (plea not alleging identity of subject-matter held bad: per Lord COTTENHAM L.C., at p. 603); *Moss* v. *Anglo-Egyptian Navigation Co.* (1865), 1 Ch. App. 108 (per Lord CRANWORTH L.C., at pp. 114–116); *Robinson* v. *Robinson* (1877), 2 P.D. 75, where a wife, petitioning for divorce, moved to strike out so much of the respondent's answer as alleged, by way of countercharge, her adultery with one Furber and with unknown persons, on the ground that a former suit by the husband against her, alleging adultery by her with Furber, and with one Petrococchino, had been dismissed with costs; but no replication, or affidavit even, averring identity of either subject-matter, or parties, having been filed, the motion failed (per HANNEN P., at p. 77); *Ripley* v. *Arthur & Co.* (1902), 86 L.T. 735, C.A., where the plaintiff moved to attach the defendant for breach of an injunction, for which he had obtained a judgment in default of pleading, restraining the defendants from dealing in a certain class of goods alleged to be colourable imitations of the plaintiff's goods, but the plaintiff's affidavit contained no direct averment that the class of articles said to have been

are no pleadings or particulars, the identity of the subject matter of the two decisions must be established by evidence.[1]

"Decision" can have two meanings

186 The term "decision" imports a twofold function of judicature, and, therefore, is a term *ancipitis sensus*. It may, with equal propriety, be used to denote either the judicial act, or the judicial declaration, of the tribunal—either the grant (or refusal) of the relief and remedy prayed—or on the other hand the determination of a question of law, or issue of fact, in contest between the parties. For purposes of the doctrine of "former recovery", as will be explained in the proper place hereafter,[2] it is only a decision in the sense of a judicial act which is of importance: for the purposes of estoppel *per rem judicatam*, strictly so called, it is only a decision in the sense of a judicial declaration or opinion which is to be considered.[3]

187 There is a type of judicial decision the formal record of which contains an express declaration of right or liability, or an express finding or recital of fact, with or without an accompanying grant, or refusal, of consequential relief: on the other hand, there is another type, the formal record of which consists of nothing but a pronouncement of the relief which the tribunal has thought fit to grant, or of the fact that the tribunal has refused to grant any relief. These two types, involving, as they do, very different considerations, demand separate treatment.

Express judicial declarations

188 Where the record of the decision—by which is meant the formal record of the judgment or order bearing the seal of the court or other proper authentication—contains in its text an express declaration of the judicial opinion of the tribunal on any question of law, or its finding on any issue of fact, whether by way of preface to the jussive, or prohibitive, part of the decision, or standing by itself, and unaccompanied by any grant of consequential relief, a form of judgment or order sanctioned by various statutes in certain specified classes of case, and in Scotland by the law relating

---

dealt with by the defendants in breach of the injunction was the same as the class which he was thereby prohibited from manufacturing and selling, and, on this ground, it was held that no case of *res judicata* had been made out (per VAUGHAN WILLIAMS L.J., at p. 736). As to the *onus probandi*, see the cases cited in the notes to this section, *passim*.

[1] See para. 216, *infra*.

[2] See Part II, Chapter XV, *post*.

[3] *Outram* v. *Morewood* (1803), 3 East 346 (per Lord ELLENBOROUGH C.J., at p. 354: "it is not the recovery, but the matter alleged by the party, and upon which the recovery proceeds, which creates the estoppel. The recovery itself . . . is only a bar to the future recovery of damages for the same injury, but the estoppel precludes parties and privies from contending to the contrary of that point, or matter of fact, which having been once distinctly put in issue by them, . . . has been, on such issue joined, solemnly decided against them").

to actions of declarator,[1] and now, generally, by the existing English rules of practice,[2] there is no difficulty whatever in ascertaining the subject-matter of the decision,[3] unless, of course, the declaration or finding is expressed in such ambiguous or indefinite terms as to make it impossible to say what was declared or found, or that any question or issue was decided at all.[4] And, the subject-matter of the first decision being readily and certainly ascertainable, there will be no difficulty in deciding whether the question previously decided is identical with that which is the subject of later litigation. If it is, there will be an estoppel in the later litigation; if not, there will be no estoppel. The consequences of this type of judgment, therefore, do not need further consideration in this chapter.

Inferential judicial determinations of disputed questions of law or fact to be deduced from formal judgment or order

189 But where the particular question as to which it is desired to found a plea of *res judicata* in the second proceeding is not the subject of any express declaration or finding appearing on the face of the formal record, questions of considerable difficulty and nicety may arise.[5] The problem which presents itself in all such cases is this. From a judicial decision which, on the face of the record, purports to do no more than to register a command,

---

[1] See some of the cases cited in note 3, *infra*.

[2] Order 15, r. 17.

[3] See *Shedden* v. *A.-G.* (1860), 30 L.J. P. M. & A. 217 (Scottish judgment in action of "declarator" as to the pursuer's legitimacy,—a form of action which was sanctioned for the whole of the United Kingdom by the Legitimacy Declaration Act 1858); *Mackintosh* v. *Smith* (1865), 4 Macq. 913, H.L. (Scottish "declarator" of pursuer's sanity); *Taunton Case, Waygood* v. *James* (1869), L.R. 4 C.P. 361 (declaration and certificate of election judges as to the validity or voidness of a parliamentary election, under the Parliamentary Elections Act 1868); *Stevens* v. *Tillett* (1870), L.R. 6 C.P. 147 (the like); *Dundas* v. *Waddell* (1880), 5 App. Cas. 249 (declaration, separately made at an early stage of the proceedings, before deciding any other point, or any question of relief, as to the rights and liabilities of the heritors *inter se*, in a Scottish action of "augmentation" raised by the minister of a parish against the heritors); *Shoe Machinery Co.* v. *Cutlan*, [1896] 1 Ch. 667 (separate declarations, first, as to validity of a patent, and then as to its infringement); *River Ribble Joint Committee* v. *Croston Urban District Council*, [1897] 1 Q.B. 251, D.C. (declaration by judge of county court that an offence had been committed against the Rivers Pollution Prevention Act 1876); *Badar Bee* v. *Habib Merican Noordin*, [1909] A.C. 615, P.C. (declaration by a colonial court "on the construction of the testator's will, as to the destination of funds released from the operation of" certain trusts created thereby).

[4] As in *Bernardi* v. *Motteux* (1781), 2 Doug. K.B. 575 (equivocal foreign prize sentence); *Dalgleish* v. *Hodgson* (1831), 7 Bing. 495, where the express findings of fact which prefaced the decision of a foreign prize court were considered so wanting in precision and clearness that no estoppel could be founded on them (per TINDAL C.J., at pp. 504, 505); *Hobbs* v. *Henning* (1864), 17 C.B. N.S. 791 (the like: per ERLE C.J., at pp. 822–825); *Harris* v. *Taylor*, [1915] 2 K.B. 580, C.A. (ambiguous and contradictory recitals in two judgments of a Manx Court as to whether, and in what sense, the defendant had "appeared": per BUCKLEY L.J., at pp. 588, 589, and PICKFORD L.J., at p. 590).

[5] The thought is echoed by SOMERVELL L.J. recalling this sentence in the text of the first edition, in *Re Koenigsberg, Public Trustee* v. *Koenigsberg*, [1949] Ch. 348, at p. 363—"I think this is particularly true of procedure by way of originating summons".

prohibition, or other judicial act, or at least is silent as to the required determination of contested questions of law, or issues of fact, what, as regards these, may legitimately be inferred?

This is a problem which poses nice questions, and its consideration may be prefaced by the observation that two separate species of the genus of estoppel *per rem judicatam* spring from such judicial decisions. Even a judgment which on the face of the sealed record does no more than decree or refuse certain relief will by virtue of the judgment necessarily affirm or deny the existence of some cause of action. The decision as to the existence or non-existence of this cause of action will give rise to a "cause of action estoppel". But many of such decisions will also necessarily include, either expressly or impliedly, as an essential and fundamental step in the process of their production, some lesser determinations of questions of fact or law. These determinations *may* give rise to "issue estoppels".

Cause of action estoppel

190 The term "cause of action estoppel", which may first have been used by DIPLOCK L.J. in *Thoday* v. *Thoday*,[1] signifies the estoppel which arises between parties by reason of a judgment given in favour of one and against the other with respect to the cause of action set up in the first proceedings. It is the simplest estoppel *per rem judicatam*; *res judicata* in its most essential form. Its operation prevents a party to an action from asserting or denying as against the other party the existence of a cause of action the non-existence or existence of which has been determined by a court of competent jurisdiction in previous litigation between the same parties or their privies. The very existence of the cause of action in the second proceeding has in such a case actually been the subject of a precise adjudication between the parties or their privies in the first proceeding, and it must be taken to have been decided, Yea or Nay, once and for all. *Interest rei publicae sit finis litium.*

Issue estoppel

191 It is when the decision relied on in the earlier proceedings is less than a determination as to the existence of a cause of action, that difficulties begin to arise. The former judgment, as delivered, will generally determine the existence or non-existence of some cause of action set up in the first proceedings, but in such a case it is invoked, in the later proceedings, not as so doing, but as determining, as an essential and fundamental step in the logic of the judgment, without which it could not stand, some lesser issue which is necessary to establish (or demolish) the cause of action set up

[1] [1964] 1 All E.R. 341; [1964] P. 181, C.A.

in the second. The term *issue estoppel* to cover estoppel by issues determined in some earlier proceeding, which necessarily and fundamentally form the very basis of the judgment delivered, was apparently first coined by HIGGINS J. in Australia in 1921, in his (dissenting) judgment in the High Court of Australia in *Hoysted* v. *Taxation Commissioner*.[1] It was taken up by DIXON J. in the same court nearly twenty years later[2] and later again (still in Australia) by FULLAGAR J. in *Jackson* v. *Goldsmith*.[3] It finally achieved the feat of successful transplantation to the English jurisdiction, Lord DENNING, M.R. and DIPLOCK L.J. in the Court of Appeal,[4] and finally the Lords of Appeal in Ordinary[5] accepting it as a useful addition to the terminology of the subject.

DIPLOCK L.J. thus defined it in *Thoday* v. *Thoday*[6]

> "The second species, which I will call 'issue estoppel', is an extension of the same rule of public policy. There are many causes of action which can only be established by proving that two or more different conditions are fulfilled. Such causes of action involve as many separate issues between the parties as there are conditions to be fulfilled by the plaintiff in order to establish his cause of action; and there may be cases where the fulfilment of an identical condition is a requirement common to two or more different causes of action. If in litigation on one such cause of action any of such separate issues whether a particular condition has been fulfilled is determined by a court of competent jurisdiction, either on evidence or on admission by a party to the litigation, neither party can, in subsequent litigation between them on any cause of action which depends on the fulfilment of the identical condition, assert that the condition was fulfilled if the court has in the first litigation determined that it was not, or deny that it was fulfilled if the court in the first litigation determined that it was."

Much of the balance of the text of the present chapter will be devoted to an elaboration of this economical statement of the doctrine.

The same, and different, causes of action

192 Cause of action estoppel is applicable solely to the case where the *same* cause of action is alleged in successive proceedings. It is a reciprocal

---

1 (1921), 29 C.L.R. 537 (H. Ct. of Aus.) at p. 161. The appellant's name is spelled *Hoysted* in the Australian, *Hoystead* in the English, reports of the litigation. HIGGINS J. dissented from the majority in the High Court, whose judgment was later reversed in the Judicial Committee—[1926] A.C. 155—their Lordships expressly adopting the propositions in the judgment of HIGGINS J.

2 In *Blair* v. *Curran* (1939), 62 C.L.R. 464 (H. Ct. of Aus.) at p. 531.

3 (1950), 81 C.L.R. 446 (H. Ct. of Aus.) at p. 466.

4 In *Fidelitas Shipping Co.* v. *V/O. Exportchleb*, [1965] 2 All E.R. 4; [1966] 1 Q.B. 630, C.A.

5 In *Carl-Zeiss-Stiftung* v. *Rayner and Keeler, Ltd.*, [1966] 2 All E.R. 536, H.L.; per Lord REID at p. 552, Lord HODSON at p. 560, Lord GUEST at p. 565, Lord UPJOHN at p. 572, and Lord WILBERFORCE at p. 583.

6 See *Thoday* v. *Thoday*, [1964] P. 181, C.A. per DIPLOCK L.J. at pp. 197–198.

estoppel, and operates both as an estoppel *per rem judicatam* and conversely by way of *merger*. The maxim *transit in rem judicatam* prevents a successful plaintiff from re-asserting in a second proceeding the cause of action which he has already made the subject of a judgment in the first. This is the operation of the doctrine of merger. On the other hand the maxim *interest rei publicae sit finis litium* denies the unsuccessful defendant the opportunity of relitigating a case which he has already lost. This is estoppel *per rem judicatam*. (And the case of plaintiff and defendant may be reversed when the opposite circumstances obtain.) But where one cause of action has been the subject of final adjudication between parties, those determinations of particular issues which are its essential foundation, without which it could not stand, may be used as the basis of issue estoppels between the same parties when *another* cause of action altogether is set up.[1] Thus where two motor vehicles collided, and by reason of the collision a third party suffered damage, and on an action by the third party against both drivers for damages, in which each driver claimed contribution from the other, the court held both to blame, this finding was sufficient to found an estoppel on a different cause of action altogether when one driver sued the other for damage which he himself had suffered arising directly out of the accident.[2]

Evolution of the doctrine

193 There is nothing new about issue estoppel, except (it has been said)[3] its name—and even that, as has been pointed out above, now goes

[1] Early examples are *Da Costa* v. *Villa Real* (1733), 2 Stra. 960 (per Lord HARDWICKE C.J.); *Hitchin* v. *Campbell* (1772), 2 Wm. Bl. 826, where the first action was for trover, and the second for money had and received (*per Cur.*, at p. 831: "in this second action there arises the same question of property. The first action has determined the goods not to be the assignee's. He shall not now try whether the money produced by those goods is his or no"); *Bouchier* v. *Taylor* (1776), Hargrave's Law Tracts, p. 472, per Lord MANSFIELD, as cited in note 3 on pp. 156–7, *post*; *Heston Overseers* v. *St. Bride Overseers* (1853), 1 E. & B. 583 (immaterial that the one proceeding related to the removal, and the other to the maintenance, of the pauper, the fact in controversy being the same: per Lord CAMPBELL C.J., at p. 586); *Routledge* v. *Hislop* (1860), 2 E. & E. 549 (question the same, *viz.* whether a servant's dismissal was justified or not, though the first proceeding was an action for damages, and the second a summons for wages before a magistrate under a statute: *per Cur.*, at pp. 555, 556); *Sopwith* v. *Sopwith* (1860), 2 Sw. & Tr. 160 (question of the husband's adultery the same, though, in the one case, the wife was petitioning for judicial separation, and, in the other, the husband was claiming restitution of conjugal rights: per Sir CRESSWELL CRESSWELL, at pp. 163–9); *Doglioni* v. *Crispin* (1866), L.R. 1 H.L. 301 (identity of subject-matter established, "although the objects of the suits in the two countries were in some degree different": per Lord CHELMSFORD L.C., at p. 311).

[2] *Marginson* v. *Blackburn Borough Council*, [1939] 1 All E.R. 273; [1939] 2 K.B. 426; and see for other examples Chapter IX, where the running-down cases are considered in greater detail. *Cf. Blair* v. *Curran* (1939), 62 C.L.R. 464 (H. Ct. of Aus.) and *Re Koenigsberg, Public Trustee* v. *Koenigsberg*, [1949] 1 All E.R. 804; [1949] Ch. 348. *In New Zealand* note *Wilson* v. *Matheson*, [1955] N.Z.L.R. 927, at p. 930.

[3] By Lord REID in *Carl-Zeiss-Stiftung* v. *Rayner and Keeler, Ltd.*, [1966] 2 All E.R. 536, H.L. at p. 552.

back fifty years. It must be conceded, however, that the doctrine has undergone much development during the last quarter of a century, attaining an importance to which it hardly seemed earlier to pretend. But its origins are respectably traceable back for nearly two hundred years, and the judicial pronouncement usually resorted to for a correct statement of the rule is the opinion of the judges, delivered to the House of Lords by DE GREY C.J., in the *Duchess of Kingston's Case*;[1] but it may be doubted whether the judgment of the Court of Queen's Bench, delivered by COLERIDGE J. in the case of *R.* v. *Hartington, Middle Quarter (Inhabitants)*,[2] is not, in point of precision and lucidity at all events, a preferable exposition and guide. In the latter case it was laid down that "the judgment" relied upon as a *res judicata* "concludes, not merely as to the point actually decided, but as to a matter which it was necessary to decide, and which was actually decided, as the groundwork of the decision itself, though not then directly the point at issue", or (as it is expressed in another passage) is "conclusive evidence not merely of the facts directly decided, but of those facts which are . . . necessary steps to the decision", in the sense that they "are so cardinal to it that, without them, it cannot stand". It is recognised that "unless they are necessary steps, the rule fails and they are collateral facts", but the court indicates its dissent from the sweeping proposition that, in every case, "the judgment can be evidence only of the very fact actually decided"—a proposition which is characterised as "a construction of the language of the celebrated judgment in the *Duchess of Kingston's* case which will not square with several decisions". On the whole, it is conceived that the rule may compendiously, but safely, be stated in the following form. *Where the decision set up as a* res judicata *necessarily involves a judicial determination of some question of law or issue of fact, in the sense that the decision could not have been legitimately or rationally pronounced by the tribunal without at the same time, and in the same breath, so to speak, determining that question or issue in a particular way*,[3] *such determination, even*

---

1 (1776), 2 Smith L.C. (13th edn.) 644, at p. 645: "neither the judgment of a court of concurrent or exclusive jurisdiction is evidence of any matter which came collaterally in question, though within their jurisdiction, nor of any matter incidentally cognizable, nor of any matter to be inferred by argument from the judgment". Neither of the last two expressions in this constantly cited passage seem quite happily chosen. A matter expressly, or by necessary implication, adjudicated upon, is none the less a *res judicata*, because only "incidentally cognizable": and every matter which is not the subject of express declaration must be "a matter to be inferred from the judgment", the only question and criterion being whether the inference is legitimate in the sense, and for the reason, stated in the text, or not.

2 (1855), 4 E. & B. 780, at pp. 794–7.

3 *Hoystead* v. *Taxation Commissioner*, [1926] A.C. 155, P.C. This case, though no longer a recognised authority on estoppel in revenue cases (see *Caffoor* v. *Income Tax Commissioner*, [1961] 2 All E.R. 436; [1961] A.C. 584, P.C.), contains a valuable exposition of the general principles governing issue estoppel. At page 170 Lord SHAW, delivering the advice of the Board, said, "It is seen from this citation of authority that if in any court of competent jurisdiction a decision is

though not declared on the face of the recorded decision, is deemed to constitute an integral part of it as effectively as if it had been made so in express terms:[1] *but, beyond these limits, there can be no such thing as a* res judicata *by implication.*

194 The rule has been applied in a variety of instances, of which the following may be selected as illustrations. The condemnation of goods for offences against the revenue has always been held to involve of necessity a decision of all facts without which there would have been no jurisdiction to condemn the goods, so as to estop the offender from disputing them in any information afterwards filed against him.[2] Affiliation orders, as has been explained and illustrated in Chapter II, necessarily presuppose a finding of the paternity of the bastard, but a refusal to make such an order does not involve a decision negativing such paternity, because the refusal may have been made on other grounds.[3] An order of justices for the removal of a pauper is conclusive as to a variety of matters which are "necessary steps" to the order, as will be fully expounded at a later stage, but not as to matters which were not essential to justify the order.[4] In an action by a company for calls, where a verdict was taken for the plaintiffs subject to a special case, which submitted for the opinion of the court the specific question whether the defendant was or was not a shareholder, and judgment was

---

reached, a party is estopped from questioning it in a new legal proceeding. But the principle also extends to any point, whether of assumption or admission, which was in substance the ratio of and fundamental to the decision". At p. 171 their Lordships deal with an argument raised in defence that "the admission and assumption of joint ownership made in the former case between the parties were upon a matter which was only incidentally or collaterally related to the point actually discussed and litigated," and decided that "it was not merely incidental or collateral to the question so decided . . . it was fundamental to it".

[1] In *Jaeger Co., Ltd.* v. *Jaeger* (1929), 46 R.P.C. 336 SANKEY L.J. said at p. 349; "The best statement of *res judicata* is probably that to be found in the *Digest of the Laws of Evidence* by the late Mr Justice STEPHEN. He says in the 41st Article: 'Every judgment is conclusive proof as against parties and privies of facts directly in issue in the case, actually decided by the court, and appearing from the judgment itself to be the ground on which it was based; unless evidence was admitted in the action in which the judgment was delivered, which is excluded in the action in which that judgment is intended to be proved.' Now it will be observed that there are three conditions laid down there: the facts (1) directly in issue in the case; (2) actually decided by the court; and (3) appearing from the judgment itself to be the ground on which it was based. That does not mean the mere formal judgment as drawn up, but the judgment as delivered."

[2] *Scott* v. *Shearman* (1775), 2 Wn. Bl. 977 (per BLACKSTONE J., at p. 978: "I take this condemnation to be conclusive evidence . . . not only with respect to the goods themselves, but every other collateral remedy for taking them"); *R.* v. *Matthews* (1797), 5 Price 202, n. (condemnation of boat for having smuggled goods on board held conclusive evidence of the smuggling of the goods, and of the ownership of the boat, as well as of the forfeiture of the bond given by the defendant that the boat should not be employed in smuggling); *A.-G.* v. *Wakefield* (1797), *ibid.* (condemnation of paper held conclusive evidence that it was liable to duty, and had left the defendant's mill before it had been charged, and an account taken by the officer); *A.-G.* v. *Reynolds* (1804) *ibid.*, p. 203 n. (condemnation of pieces of calico held conclusive evidence that the pieces had not been measured, marked, and stamped by the officer of excise before being printed).

[3] Chapter II, para. 60, *ante*.

[4] See Chapter VIII, para. 256, *post*.

given for the defendant on the case so stated, it was held that this judgment, having regard to the special case on which it purported to have been pronounced, was necessarily at the same time a decision that the defendant was not a shareholder in the company,[1] because "the special case raised only one single question for the opinion of the court", though it was recognised that it would have been otherwise "if the special case had left it open to the court to decide in favour of the defendant upon several grounds".[2] An allowance of a creditor's claim in respect of a lien on certain debentures of a company in liquidation necessarily involves a decision that the debentures are valid.[3] A conviction of the inhabitants of a township or other local district for non-repair of a road is a decision that the road is a highway, because otherwise there would have been no jurisdiction to convict; but an acquittal of inhabitants on such an indictment does not in the least involve a decision that the road is not a highway, because it may have proceeded upon other grounds, such as failure to prove the non-repair, or the like.[4] For the same reason, on an application by a local authority for an order for payment of a frontager's rateable contribution to the expenses of the repair and upkeep of a road or street, a decision in favour of the respondent does not involve a decision that the road or street is a highway repairable by the inhabitants at large, or negative the liability of the defendant *ratione tenurae*, such a finding not being a "necessary step" to the decision.[5] A judgment for damages in an action for trespass to land necessarily affirms the plaintiff's right to possession, but does not necessarily involve a decision as to title;[6] whilst, conversely, a judgment for the plaintiff in ejectment, though presupposing, as its basis, a decision of title, is not inferentially a decision as to any purely possessory question or issue, such as length of occupation, value of the premises, and the like.[7] A judgment in a probate suit does not involve any decision as to the domicil of the

---

[1] *Re Bank of Hindustan, China, and Japan, Alison's Case* (1873), 9 Ch. App. 1 (per MELLISH L.J., at pp. 25, 26: see also the observations of Lord SELBORNE L.C., at p. 25).

[2] *Ibid.*, per MELLISH L.J., at p. 26.

[3] *Cox* v. *Dublin City Distillery Co., Ltd.* (*No.* 3), [1917] 1 I.R. 203, where a declaration, made in previous litigation, and affirmed ultimately by the H.L. in *Dublin City Distillery, Ltd.* v. *Doherty*, [1914] A.C. 823, H.L., that the plaintiff was entitled to a lien on certain debentures, was held tantamount, by necessary implication, to a decision that such debentures were valid (per RONAN L.J., at pp. 224–229).

[4] *R.* v. *Haughton Inhabitants* (1853), 1 E. & B. 501 (per Lord CAMPBELL C.J., at p. 514).

[5] *R.* v. *Hutchings* (1881), 6 Q.B.D. 300, C.A. (per Lord SELBORNE L.C., at p. 305): *North Eastern Rail. Co.* v. *Dalton Overseers*, [1898] 2 Q.B. 66, D.C. (per WILLS J., at pp. 73, 74). See, further, Chapter II, *ante*.

[6] *Outram* v. *Morewood* (1803), 3 East 346 (per Lord ELLENBOROUGH C.J., delivering the judgment of the Court of K.B., at p. 357).

[7] *Aslin* v. *Parkin* (1758), 2 Burr. 665 (per Lord MANSFIELD C.J., at p. 668). *In Australia*, *Burnham* v. *Carroll Musgrove Theatres, Ltd. and Victoria Arcade, Ltd.* (1928), 41 C.L.R. 540 (H. Ct. of Aus.), affirming the judgment of the Full Court of New South Wales, per FERGUSON J., reported in (1928), 28 N.S.W. S.R. 169.

testator.[1] An order made by a master in an administration action for the transfer of funds to a particular account is not an inferential declaration of rights.[2] A judgment (in which the court pronounced against the will on the ground of incapacity of the testator) in an action for probate in solemn form brought against a certain defendant (with others) in which the pleadings averred that she was the widow of the testator, the action proceeding on this basis to judgment, did not estop the same parties from alleging against the defendant in a subsequent action that she had never been lawfully married to the testator.[3] An agreement to pay compensation in respect of an accident, registered under the Workmen's Compensation Acts, was held to estop the employer from contending that he was not liable to pay compensation *inter vivos* in respect of that accident; but not from contending, on the subsequent death of the claimant, that his death was due to an independent cause, and did not arise from the accident at all.[4] On an application for production of documents by a company, the court, in the first proceedings, held that the order, though obtainable upon a proper application, should be refused in a particular case, on the ground that the documents sought were insufficiently specified; upon a second application, properly specifying the documents, it was sought to re-argue the point whether the order could be made, and a plea of *res judicata* was raised. It was held by the Court of Appeal that the earlier decision, that it was competent to make an order, could not preclude the company from relitigating the point, for its resolution (against the company) was not necessary to the earlier decision (which was in the company's favour).[5] So, too, (*in Australia*) where in a suit between a fruit merchant and the Commonwealth Government it had been contended for the plaintiff that a statutory provision was *ultra vires* of the Commonwealth legislature, and this contention had been disallowed by the High Court, which, however, had given

---

[1] *Concha* v. *Concha* (1886), 11 App. Cas. 541, H.L. (per Lord HERSCHELL L.C., at pp. 550–552, and Lord BLACKBURN, at pp. 563–565).

[2] *Thompson* v. *Thompson*, [1923] 2 Ch. 205 (per SARGANT J., at pp. 213–215).

[3] *In the Estate of Park, Park* v. *Park*, [1954] P. 89 (KARMINSKI J.) at pp. 94, 95; the case went to appeal (*ibid*, p. 112) and the substantive judgment of KARMINSKI J. was affirmed. The estoppel point does not appear to have been argued in the Court of Appeal.

[4] *Cleverley* v. *Gas Light and Coke Co.* (1907), 24 T.L.R. 93.

[5] *Penn-Texas Corporation* v. *Murat Anstalt* (*No.* 2), [1964] 2 Q.B. 647, C.A. per Lord DENNING M.R. at p. 660. It was pointed out by Lord DENNING that it was impossible to regard the company as estopped as if by a "decision" on a point on which the company could not appeal—for no decision had been given against the company. "One of the tests in seeing whether a matter was necessary to the decision, or only incidental to it, is to ask: could the party have appealed from it? If he could have appealed, and did not, he is bound by it. See *Badar Bee* v. *Habib Merican Noordin*, [1909] A.C. 615, at p. 623, P.C. by Lord MACNAGHTEN. If he could not have appealed from it (because it did not affect the order made) then it is only an incidental matter, not essential to the decision, and he is not bound: See *Concha* v. *Concha* (1886), 11 App. Cas. 541, at p. 552, per Lord HERSCHELL". *Cf.* the dicta of DIXON J. in *James* v. *Commonwealth* referred to in note 1, p. 156, *infra*.

judgment in the action for the plaintiff on other grounds, it was held, in a later action between the same parties, that the plaintiff was not thereby estopped from readvancing his contention that the provision was *ultra vires*, for, since he had succeeded on other grounds in the first action, it could not be said that the decision on the validity of the statute was necessary to the judgment; moreover, had he wished to appeal against the decision of the High Court on the point of *ultra vires*, he would have been unable to do so, since he had in fact succeeded in his action, judgment having been given in his favour.[1] A certificate made by an officer of the court in the course of an action, if it is not necessary to the ultimate decision of the court, is not deemed a part of that decision, or involved therein.[2] The jurisdiction of the courts ecclesiastical, spiritual, or Christian (as they were variously called), in purely civil matters has now been abolished; but the authorities as to the effect of the sentences of these courts, whilst that jurisdiction existed, whether in matrimonial causes, or in suits for the administration of the estates of deceased persons, are still valuable as illustrations of the canons of construction now under consideration:[3] indeed, this line of cases

---

[1] *James* v. *Commonwealth* (1935), 52 C.L.R. 570 (H. Ct. of Aus.). "Although the Court rules that he was wrong upon his first ground, he is not estopped, because the decision passed in his favour. He could not appeal from the court's ruling. It was, so to speak, a ruling in the air as far as he was concerned"—per RICH J. at p. 584. "In one sense it is true that the question was decided against him. He submitted the contention to the Court which announced an opinion that he was wrong; but that opinion was not translated into a decree or order, because upon an independent contention he succeeded. There was no judgment from which he could seek special leave to appeal, none which estopped him".—per DIXON J. at pp. 590–591. These dicta of DIXON J. may be compared with those of Lord DENNING M.R. in the preceding note.

[2] *Mountcashell's Estate*, [1920] 1 I.R. 1 (per ROSS J., at pp. 5, 6).

[3] In *Blackham's Case* (1709), 1 Salk, 290, an action for trover, the defendant having proved that the goods in question belonged to Jane B. in her lifetime, and that he had taken out letters of administration to her estate on her decease, the plaintiff set up a marriage between himself and Jane a few days before her death, and the defendant replied estoppel, in that the Spiritual Court, by the grant of the above-mentioned letters of administration to him, had determined the right to the goods to be in him, for that court could not have made the grant except upon the supposition that there had been no such marriage as alleged; but it was held that this was a merely "collateral matter", and not absolutely necessary to the decision (per HOLT C.J., on pp. 290, 291: "a matter which has directly been determined by their sentence cannot be gainsaid: their sentence is conclusive in such cases, and no evidence shall be admitted to prove the contrary; but that is to be intended only in the point directly tried; otherwise it is if a collateral matter be collected or inferred from the sentence, as in this case"). Herein HOLT C.J., though stating the principle quite correctly, would appear to have made a rather glaring misapplication of that principle. His decision is inconsistent with, and must, it is conceived, be taken to have been overruled by two subsequent authorities, *Bouchier* v. *Taylor* (1776), Hargrave's Law Tracts, 472, H.L., and *Barrs* v. *Jackson* (1845), 1 Ph. 582. The former of these two cases was decided in the same year as, and about six weeks before, the *Duchess of Kingston's Case* (1776), 2 Smith L.C. (13th edn.) 644. The report in 4 Brown P.C., 708, is a mere register of the result in the H.L., as were all Brown's parliamentary reports (no reporting in either House being at that time permitted), though it is a valuable record of the arguments and judgments in the court below. For the purpose of the arguments and speeches in the House of Lords, resort must be had to the work cited above, Hargrave's "Collection of Tracts relating to the Law of England from Manuscripts, published in 1787", at pp. 499 *et seq*, whereof is an essay from the editor's own pen "concerning the effect of sentences of courts ecclesiastical, . . . when pleaded, or offered in evidence, in the courts

includes that which is usually regarded as the leading authority on such questions. Other classes of case, equally illustrative of the principles on which a decision of a question not directly or expressly determined, may legitimately be inferred, are those relating to orders in lunacy,[1] decisions of statutory tribunals, such as the General Medical Council,[2] and the judgments and sentences of English and foreign admiralty tribunals.[3]

Judgments by consent: bare dismissals: reversals on appeal

195 Questions as to the conditions under which a judicial decision on any matter of law or fact may properly be deemed to be involved in judgments or orders by consent[4] or in decisions of bare dismissal,[5] or of reversal on appeal,[6] have already been fully examined.

Judgments by default

196 In the first edition of this work little distinction was made between judgments obtained by default and any other type of judgment, as regards

---

temporal'', founded on the notes made by him as junior counsel for the prosecutors in the *Duchess of Kingston's Case*, *supra*, which decided, *inter alia*, ''that a sentence in the Spiritual Court against a marriage in a suit of jactitation of marriage is not conclusive evidence, so as to stop the council for the Crown from proving the marriage in an indictment for polygamy''. At pp. 473–476 n. of this essay, he sets out the Case and Reasons of the appellant (for whom also he had acted as junior counsel) in *Bouchier* v. *Taylor*, *supra*, and at pp. 472–475, gives an abstract of the facts, and states the ground of the decision of the House of Lords therein, as follows:—''in that case Alice Merchant, as first cousin, and Dr Bouchier, as first cousin once removed, had been competitors in the Prerogative court for administration to . . . an intestate; and A.M. dying during the suit, her executors became parties, and a sentence was at last pronounced, declaring that they had failed in proving her next of kin, and therefore directing administration to be granted to Dr B. Several years after, Taylor, who was A.M.'s residuary legatee, and not a party to the suit about administration, filed a bill in chancery against Dr. B. for a distribution, and, though he had pleaded the sentence, the present Master of the Rolls granted an issue to try whether A.M. was next of kin, and his order was confirmed by the Lord Chancellor''—Lord BATHURST. ''But Dr B. appealed to the Lords; and before them two points were made: one being, whether the sentence of the ecclesiastical court was not conclusive; the other'' . . . (immaterial hereto). ''On the hearing, the decree was reversed on both grounds, without the least opposition by the Lord Chancellor, or any other Lord. And Lord MANSFIELD, who was the only speaker on the subject, in his reasons against the decree, was clear that the sentence was conclusive, notwithstanding the difference, in point of objects, between the two suits; and that the court of chancery, in exercising its concurrent jurisdiction as to distribution, was concluded by sentences of the spiritual court in granting administration, and not at liberty to re-examine the points decided in the exercise of that peculiar jurisdiction''. This case was followed in *Barrs* v. *Jackson* (1845), 1 Ph. 582, where the circumstances were substantially identical, by Lord LYNDHURST L.C., who held, at pp. 587, 588, that the case before him was indistinguishable from *Bouchier* v. *Taylor*, *supra*, and (at pp. 588, 589) essentially distinguishable from *Blackham's Case*, *supra*, whilst recognizing the soundness of Lord HOLT C.J.'s exposition of the rule therein, as above cited, and also (see pp. 585, 586) from the *Duchess of Kingston's Case*, *supra*, the doctrine of which he accepted and applied.

[1] See para. 267 *post*, notes 1 and 2.

[2] See para. 267 *post*, note 3.

[3] See para. 274, paras. 282 *et seq. post*.

[4] See Chapter II, paras. 41 *et seq. ante*.

[5] See Chapter II, paras. 58 *et seq. ante*.

[6] See Chapter II, paras. 62 *et seq. ante*.

their consequences in founding an estoppel.[1] It is clear that a judgment obtained by default is a final judgment, such as will give rise to an estoppel *per rem judicatam*; and this notwithstanding that it may be vacated by the court, on proper terms, on the application of the defendant.[2] But the extent of the estoppel to which such a judgment will give rise must be very carefully limited. The true principle would seem to be that in such a case the defendant is estopped from setting up, in a subsequent action, any matter of defence which was "necessarily and with complete precision" decided against him by the previous judgment by default.[3] The limits prescribed by this principle will be strictly observed; and the courts will scrutinise such judgments with extreme particularity in order to avoid implying, as having been decided by a judgment by default, any more than is necessarily involved by reason of the fact that judgment has been obtained.[4]

The dangers and injustices inherent in too ready an application of the doctrine of issue estoppel to default judgments are so obvious that it is remarkable that they escaped notice for so long. When the first edition of this work was published, *Howlett* v. *Tarte*[5] was almost the sole authority to emphasise the difficulties which stood in the way of extending the full application of the doctrine to these judgments. There, WILLES J. said:[6]

> "It is quite right that a defendant should be estopped from setting up in the same action a defence which he might have pleaded but has chosen to let the proper time go by. But nobody ever heard of a defendant being precluded from setting up a defence in a second action because he did not avail himself of the opportunity of setting it up in the first action."

This was possibly too-widely expressed;[7] but in a recent case in the Lords it has been acknowledged that the statement of WILLES J. was not far from the truth. In *New Brunswick Co.* v. *British and French Trust Corporation*[8] Lord MAUGHAM L.C. after citing from *Howlett* v. *Tarte* the passage quoted above said:

---

[1] Pages 26–28: p. 108.

[2] *Huffer* v. *Allen* (1866), L.R. 2 Exch. 15. The point is taken for granted in the Lords in *New Brunswick Rail. Co.* v. *British and French Trust Corporation, Ltd.* (*infra*). In New Zealand, *Tira Arika* v. *Sidaway*, [1923] N.Z.L.R. 158 (HOSKING J.).

[3] *New Brunswick Rail. Co.* v. *British and French Trust Corporation, Ltd.* [1939], A.C. 1, H.L. per Lord MAUGHAM L.C. at p. 21, approving, though with reservations as to whether the principle was therein too widely expressed, the observations of WILLES J. in *Howlett* v. *Tarte* (1861), 10 C.B. N.S. 813, at p. 827.

[4] *Kok Hoong* v. *Leong Cheong Kweng Mines, Ltd.*, [1964] A.C. 993, P.C. per Lord RADCLIFFE at p. 1012.

[5] (1861), 10 C.B. N.S. 813.

[6] At p. 827.

[7] *New Brunswick Rail. Co.* v. *British and French Trust Corporation, Ltd.*, [1939] A.C. 1, H.L. per Lord MAUGHAM L.C. at p. 21.

[8] [1939] A.C. 1, H.L.

"In my opinion we are at least justified in holding that an estoppel based on a default judgment must be very carefully limited. The true principle in such a case would seem to be that the defendant is estopped from setting up in a subsequent action a defence which was necessarily, and with complete precision, decided by the previous judgment; in other words, by the *res judicata* in the accurate sense".[1]

In the same case Lord RUSSELL OF KILLOWEN recalled the broad statement from the judgment of Lord SHAW in *Hoystead* v. *Taxation Commissioner*[2] and said:

"It is true that in the judgment of the Judicial Committee in the case of *Hoystead* v. *Taxation Commissioner* the following passage occurs: 'It is seen from this citation of authority that if in any court of competent jurisdiction a decision is reached, a party is estopped from questioning it in a new legal proceeding. But the principle also extends to any point whether of assumption or admission, which was in substance the ratio of and fundamental to the decision'. These no doubt are wide words, but they relate to a case of estoppel by a judgment in contested proceedings; and I am not prepared to extend them to the case of a default judgment on a claim under contract A, followed by an action under a similarly worded contract B."[3]

Lord WRIGHT was inclined to be even more cautious in applying the doctrine. He too quoted the dictum of WILLES J. which has been cited above; but he then proceeded:

"It is enough for present purposes to treat this observation as limited to a case where judgment has gone by default, whether of appearance or pleading. In that sense I should accept these observations of WILLES J., one of the greatest Common Law judges. There are grave reasons of convenience why a party should not be held to be bound by every matter of fact or law fundamental to the default judgment. It is, I think, too artificial to treat the party in default as bound by every such matter as if by admission. All necessary effect is given to the default judgment by treating it as conclusive of what it directly decides. I should regard any further effect in the way of estoppel as an illegitimate extension of the doctrine, which in the absence of express authority I am not prepared to accept."[4]

The judgments in the *New Brunswick* case were to form the subject of further comment in a still later case before the Judicial Committee. In *Kok Hoong* v. *Leong Cheong Kweng Mines, Ltd.*[5] Lord RADCLIFFE, delivering the judgment of the Committee, expressly followed with approval the dictum of Lord MAUGHAM, L.C. above cited, and concluded that:

---

1 At p. 21.

2 [1926] A.C. 155, P.C.

3 [1939] A.C. 1, H.L. at p. 28.

4 At pp. 37–38.

5 [1964] A.C. 993, P.C. There are also some observations in the judgments of the Lords in the later case of *Carl-Zeiss-Stiftung* v. *Rayner and Keeler, Ltd.*, [1966] 2 All E.R. 536, H.L. (though this was not concerned with judgment by default). Reference may be made to the observations

> "In their Lordships' opinion the *New Brunswick Rail. Co.* case can be taken as containing an authoritative reinterpretation of the principle of *Howlett* v. *Tarte* in simpler and less specialised terms. This reinterpretation amounts to saying that default judgments, though capable of giving rise to estoppels, must always be scrutinised with extreme particularity for the purpose of ascertaining the bare essence of what they must necessarily have decided and, to use the words of Lord MAUGHAM L.C., they can estop only for what must 'necessarily and with complete precision' have been thereby determined."[1]

It is abundantly clear on principle, and supported by the authorities which have been mentioned, that there may be good reasons why a judgment may be allowed to go by default in circumstances in which neither private justice nor convenience, nor state policy, can recommend *sit finis litium*. The fact that a judgment has been taken by default may signify no more than that the defendant for unascertained reasons, negligence, ignorance, or indifference, has suffered judgment to go against him; if no more than this is known there may be grave and obvious dangers in a rule precluding the defendant from re-opening on another occasion, perhaps of very different significance, whatever issues can be discerned as having been involved in the judgment obtained by default.[2]

Questions omitted to be raised in the earlier proceedings

197 Whenever it is shown that the *party against whom a judicial decision is ultimately pronounced* omitted to raise by pleading, argument, evidence, or otherwise some question, or issue, or point which he could have raised in his favour by way of defence or support to his case without detriment to his position or interests in the pending, or in future, proceedings, and which, therefore, it was his duty (in a sense) to have then raised, the adverse general decision, though it contains no express declaration to that effect, is deemed to carry with it a particular adverse decision on the question, issue, or point so omitted to be raised, just as much as if it had been expressly raised by the party, and expressly determined against him. And this is so whether the question or issue is simply passed over through inadvertence, or is made the subject of express or implied assumption or admission.

The decision generally cited as the prime authority on this principle is that of Sir JAMES WIGRAM, V-C. in *Henderson* v. *Henderson*[3] so long ago as 1843.

---

of Lord REID as to the circumspection to be observed in the case of a foreign judgment (to which much the same considerations apply as are applicable to judgments by default) at p. 554, and Lord UPJOHN expressly refers to Lord MAUGHAM's dicta at p. 572.

[1] [1964] A.C. 993 at p. 1012. [2] *Ibid.* at p. 1010.

[3] (1843), 3 Hare 100 at pp. 114–115. For a very recent case in which omission to raise a point formed the basis of an estoppel see *Fidelitas Shipping Co., Ltd.* v. *V/O. Exportchleb*, [1965] 2 All

"In trying this question I believe I state the rule of the court correctly when I say that, where a given matter becomes the subject of litigation in, and of adjudication by, a court of competent jurisdiction, the court requires the parties to that litigation to bring forward their whole case, and will not (except under special circumstances) permit the same parties to open the same subject of litigation in respect of matter which might have been brought forward as part of the subject in contest, but which was not brought forward, only because they have, from negligence, inadvertence, or even accident, omitted part of their case. The plea of *res judicata* applies, except in special cases, not only to points upon which the court was actually required by the parties to form an opinion and pronounce a judgment, but to every point which properly belonged to the subject of litigation, and which the parties, exercising reasonable diligence, might have brought forward at the time."

These words have been cited and followed over and over again in many subsequent decisions of the highest authority. It was made clear in *Hoystead* v. *Taxation Commissioner*[1] in 1926 that the principle applies to matters of admission as well as matters of omission which were fundamental to the judgment ultimately pronounced. Lord SHAW delivering the judgment of the Judicial Committee said:[2]

"In the opinion of their Lordships it is settled, first, that the admission of a fact fundamental to the decision arrived at cannot be withdrawn and a fresh litigation started, with a view of obtaining another judgment upon a different assumption of fact; secondly, the same principle applies not only to an erroneous admission of a fundamental fact, but to an erroneous assumption as to the legal quality of that fact. Parties are not permitted to begin fresh litigations because of new views they may entertain of the law of the case, or new versions which they present as to what should be a proper apprehension by the court of the legal result either of the construction of the documents or the weight of certain circumstances. If this were permitted litigation would have no end, except when legal ingenuity is exhausted. It is a principle of law that this cannot be permitted, and there is abundant authority reiterating that principle. Thirdly, the same principle—namely, that of setting to rest rights of litigants, applies to the case where a point, fundamental to the decision, taken or assumed by the plaintiff and traversable by the defendant,

---

E.R. 4 per DIPLOCK L.J. at p. 14. For an Australian case in which the point assumed was held not to found an estoppel see *Vitosh* v. *Brisbane City Council* (1955), 93 C.L.R. 622 (High Ct. of Aus.) at p. 628; it must be regarded as a borderline case, its basis being that the point which was assumed by both parties was not truly fundamental to the substantive decision.

[1] *Hoystead* v. *Taxation Commissioner*, [1926] A.C. 155, P.C. at pp. 165–166. The authority of this decision as to the principle to be followed in successive revenue cases was destroyed by the later decision of the Privy Council in *Caffoor* v. *Income Tax Commissioner*, [1961] 2 All E.R. 436; [1961] A.C. 584, which may be taken as overruling it. But the case retains its authority as a statement of the general principles governing issue estoppel.

[2] *Hoystead* v. *Taxation Commissioner*, [1926] A.C. 155, P.C., cited *supra* in the text: this decision was specifically used as the basis for the judgment of DIPLOCK L.J. in the Court of Appeal in the later case of *Fidelitas Shipping Co., Ltd.* v. *V/O. Exportchleb*, [1965] 2 All E.R. 4, at p. 14.

has not been traversed. In that case also a defendant is bound by the judgment, although it may be true enough that subsequent light or ingenuity might suggest some traverse which had not been taken. The same principle of setting parties' rights to rest applies and estoppel occurs''.

But though this rule is generally applicable to judgments in contested actions, even where judgment has been given by consent, or pursuant to admissions, it will not necessarily be rigorously applied in every case; for it has always been accepted that ''special circumstances'' may conceivably arise, of sufficient merit to exclude its operation.[1] This modification of the absolute application of the rule has particular effect in the case of judgments obtained by default; for it has been said that a difference is perceptible between a judgment which has ''gone by default, whether of appearance or of pleading'' and one where the unsuccessful party has ''appeared in the proceedings and contested either the issue or the (substantive) decision'', though he make the essential admission in the course of such a proceeding.[2]

198 In accordance with these principles, it has been held that, where a defendant, sued in the character of executor or administrator, omits to plead *plene administravit*,[3] or, having so pleaded, fails to adduce evidence which would have supported such a plea,[4] or where a plaintiff will not contest a plea of release by a deed of composition, but, on the contrary,

---

[1] *Henderson* v. *Henderson* (1843), 3 Hare 100, where in the often-quoted passage in which the rule is stated, Sir James WIGRAM V.-C. particularly qualifies it with the words ''except in special cases''. These words were particularly noticed by Lord MAUGHAM L.C. in his judgment in *New Brunswick Rail. Co.* v. *British and French Trust Corporation*, [1939] A.C. 1, H.L. at p. 21. See also the judgment of Lord DENNING M.R. in *Fidelitas Shipping Co., Ltd.* v. *V/O. Exportchleb* (*supra*) (''this is not an inflexible rule'').

[2] *New Brunswick Rail. Co.* v. *British and French Trust Corporation, Ltd.*, [1939] A.C. 1, H.L. per Lord WRIGHT at p. 38. *Cf.* Lord RUSSELL OF KILLOWEN at p. 28. See further *Kok Hoong* v. *Leong Cheong Kweng Mines, Ltd.*, [1964] A.C. 993, P.C. at p. 1012.

[3] *Erving* v. *Peters* (1790), 3 Term Rep. 685 (per BULLER J., at p. 693: ''if an executor may plead *plene administravit*, and neglect to do so, I see no difference between such a case and one where he does so plead, and the plea is found against him''); *Palmer* v. *Waller* (1836), 1 M. & W. 689.

[4] See *Jewsbury* v. *Mummery* (1872), L.R. 8 C.P. 56, Ex. Ch. Here the plaintiff having recovered judgment against the defendant, as executor, after the arbitrator, to whom the issue of *plene administravit* had been referred, had found this issue for the plaintiff, sued the defendant again, alleging that the judgment was unsatisfied, and suggesting a *devastavit* by the defendant of goods which had come to his hands at the date of judgment. The defendant pleaded that the acts complained of as a *devastavit* had been done with the plaintiff's concurrence and leave, in answer to which the plaintiff, at the trial, relied upon the above judgment as an estoppel, and it was held that, ''if the defendant could have shown before the arbitrator that, though assets had come to his hands, he had parted with them under circumstances which precluded the plaintiff from alleging that they had not been duly administered, clearly that would have been a defence under the plea of *plene administravit*'' (per KELLY C.B., at p. 60), but that, not having attempted to raise this point in evidence, the defendant was estopped from disputing the arbitrator's finding, or the judgment consequent thereon (per BLACKBURN J., at pp. 61, 62, and ARCHIBALD J., at p. 62).

elects to confess the plea, and takes judgment for his costs,[1] or where a defendant, in an action for infringement of a patent, having pleaded the invalidity of the patent for want of novelty, omits to bring to the notice of the court a certain previous specification which would have tended to show anticipation,[2] a judgment against the party responsible for such omission or neglect imports an adverse decision against him on the particular point which he has thus omitted or neglected to plead, or to support by evidence. So, if a plaintiff obtains relief of a certain character on certain aspects of the case, but omits to press for relief of another character on another aspect, a general adverse decision necessarily involves a decision that the plaintiff is not entitled to the latter, any more than to the former, kind of relief,[3] and, *a fortiori*, if a plaintiff complains of the infringement of his right to go upon one of the banks of a river for certain purposes on the expressly pleaded ground of a prescriptive right to use both banks for such purposes, a dismissal of the action involves a decision that he is not entitled to the right claimed in respect of either bank.[4] Again, in a Scottish action of declarator of marriage on two distinct grounds, one of which the pursuer attempted, but failed, to establish, and the other he did not attempt to prove, it was held that a judgment for the defender imported a decision against the pursuer on the second, as much as on the first, of the two grounds.[5]

And where a petitioner had obtained a decree of divorce on the ground of adultery in an undefended suit, and subsequently filed a separate petition against the co-respondent wherein he claimed damages, and the co-respondent thereupon filed a defence alleging connivance and conduct conducing, it was held that he was estopped by reason of the decree having been made absolute from denying the fact of adultery and from raising the plea of connivance which, being an absolute bar, was deemed to have been the subject of a decision in the first proceeding.[6]

In *Australia* the omission of a wife to ask for maintenance for a child

---

1 *Newington* v. *Levy* (1870), L.R. 6 C.P. 180, Ex. Ch.

2 *Shoe Machinery Co.* v. *Cutlan*, [1896] 1 Ch. 667 (per ROMER J., at p. 672).

3 In *Blake* v. *O'Kelly* (1874), 9 I.R. Eq. 54, it was so stated, at pp. 56, 57, by CHATTERTON, V.-C. (Ir.), but in that case the estoppel failed because the defendant was sued in a totally different character from that in which he had been sued to judgment in the former proceedings (per CHATTERTON V.-C., at pp. 57, 58).

4 *Long* v. *Gowlett*, [1923] 2 Ch. 177 (per SARGANT J., at pp. 193, 194).

5 *Lockyer* v. *Ferryman* (1877), 2 App. Cas. 519, H.L., where the pursuer had, in the action for a declarator, alleged both a contract *per verba de praesenti*, and a promise *subsequenti copula*, the former of which he had attempted, but failed, to prove, and on the latter of which he offered no evidence, and it was held that he was as much estopped from renewing the latter, as he was from reasserting the former, allegation (per Lord CAIRNS L.C., at pp. 524, 525).

6 *Hopkins* v. *Hopkins and Castle* (1933), 50 T.L.R. 99. *Aliter*, however, as regards a plea of conduct conducive; for this plea, raising only a matter which would have been a discretionary bar in the first proceeding, was not necessarily decided between the parties by reason of the grant of a decree absolute in divorce.

about to be born (where paternity was denied) when consenting in the Supreme Court of New South Wales to a decree for judicial separation on which there was an order by consent by which she received no maintenance for herself or the other children of the marriage (custody of whom was given to the husband) was sufficient to preclude her from making application before a magistrate for a maintenance order for the child after birth, though it would have been competent for her, by virtue of a right reserved to her by the statute, although the matter was *res judicata*, to have applied in the Supreme Court for a variation of the original order.[1]

Similarly, where, on the trial of an interpleader issue, a trustee in bankruptcy contended that a deed of assignment executed by the bankrupt was invalid on one specific ground, and judgment was given against him, the judgment was held to involve a decision negativing the invalidity of the deed not only on the single ground put forward, but also on other specific grounds which the trustee at the date of the former proceedings was in a position to, but did not, set up.[2] And, where a local authority had consented to an adverse order in respect of the pollution of a river, the order was held to preclude the local authority from afterwards setting up, as an excuse for non-compliance therewith, certain matters which it might have raised in the first instance by litigation, instead of voluntarily submitting.[3]

Where an action for conspiracy (which can be maintained on it being shown either that the defendants agreed together to do an unlawful act, or that they agreed to do a lawful act by unlawful means)[4] had failed because the acts proved were not unlawful, on a second action being brought, in which it was alleged that, though the acts were lawful, the agreement was to do them by unlawful means, it was held by the Court of Appeal that the second action could not proceed, for though the second alternative support for the cause of action had not been the subject of any express decision in the first action, it was an issue which was so clearly part of the subject matter of the litigation, and so clearly could have been raised, that it would be an abuse of the process of the court to allow a new proceeding to be commenced in respect thereof.[5]

---

[1] *Brown* v. *Brown* (1905), 3 C.L.R. 373 (H. Ct. of Aus.).

[2] *Re Hilton*; *Ex parte March* (1892), 67 L.T. 594, per VAUGHAN WILLIAMS L.J. at p. 595.

[3] *River Ribble Joint Committee* v. *Croston Urban District Council*, [1897] 1 Q.B. 251, D.C. (per WILLS J., who, at p. 256, says that it would be "contrary to all principle to allow the defendants now to urge reasons for not obeying it which might have been set up at the time the order was consented to").

[4] *Mulcahy* v. *R.* (1868), L.R. 3 H.L. 306, at p. 317 per WILLES J.; *Crofter Handwoven Harris Tweed Co., Ltd.* v. *Veitch*, [1942] A.C. 435 H.L. per Lord WRIGHT at p. 461.

[5] *Greenhalgh* v. *Mallard*, [1947] 2 All E.R. 255, C.A. per SOMERVELL L.J. at p. 257. EVERSHED L.J. was of the same opinion. This statement of principle was cited with approval in the Court of Appeal in the following year in *Wright* v. *Bennett*, [1948] 1 All E.R. 227 per TUCKER L.J. at

199 When it is laid down, as it is in the earlier cases, that a general adverse decision imports also a particular adverse decision on any traversable allegation made by the successful party which his opponent has omitted to traverse, it is important to note that, according to the more recent authorities, an allegation may be "traversable", for the purposes of the rule, not only when it is express and direct, but also when it is reasonably implied. Thus, in an action on an agreement for a lease, the plaintiff must be supposed to be alleging both the subsistence and the validity of the agreement, which implied allegation, being traversable, the defendant omits to traverse at his peril—the peril, that is, of a judgment in the plaintiff's favour being deemed to carry with it an affirmation of the validity, as well as the making, of the agreement, so as to preclude the defendant in any subsequent litigation with the plaintiff in respect of the same agreement from setting up that it was invalid by reason of its not having conformed to the requirements of s. 4 of the Statute of Frauds.[1] Following this authority, in a case where a defendant had omitted to plead that there was no consideration for the agreement sued upon, raising only a plea of payment, and judgment had been recovered by the plaintiff, the defendant was held estopped from afterwards setting up the former contention, just as much as if he had pleaded it, and the specific point had been expressly determined against him.[2] A similar estoppel, for the like reasons, has been held to operate against a defendant who, in proceedings under the old O. XIV, had neglected to raise the objection that the writ was issued before the due date of the bill of exchange sued upon.[3] And where, in an inquiry before a master as to the indebtedness of a husband to his wife's estate, a certificate was given of nett indebtedness, BUCKLEY J. held that this precluded the husband from contending, in subsequent proceedings, that certain lands the farming of which was the subject-matter of the original investigation were lands, not of the wife, but of a partnership wherein the husband was a partner, for this was a matter which ought reasonably to have been included in the first inquiry.[4]

p. 230; but in that case the court preferred, on the particular facts before it, not to go to the length of invoking the doctrine of *res judicata*; and made an order striking out the statement of claim in the second action, using the inherent jurisdiction of the court to dismiss or strike out frivolous or vexatious claims. In the later case of *Re a Debtor* (*No.* 472 *of* 1950), [1958] 1 All E.R. 581 the Court of Appeal, while not disapproving of the course adopted in *Greenhalgh* v. *Mallard*, yet found the first decision was not such as to be regarded as disposing of the issue in the second proceedings.

[1] *Humphries* v. *Humphries*, [1910] 2 K.B. 531, C.A. (per FARWELL L.J., delivering the judgment of the court, at pp. 534–537).

[2] *Cooke* v. *Rickman*, [1911] 2 K.B. 1125, D.C. per BRAY J. at pp. 1128–1129, and BANKES J. at pp. 1129–1130, following *Humphries* v. *Humphries*, *supra*.

[3] *Stirling & Co.* v. *North* (1913), 29 T.L.R. 216, following *Humphries* v. *Humphries*, *supra*.

[4] *Public Trustee* v. *Kenward*, [1967] 2 All E.R. 870 (BUCKLEY J.). At pp. 874–875 the learned judge said: "The parties, and particularly the defendant, had, however, every reason to understand that the inquiry was directed to discovering any sort of claim which he could put forward

200 On the other hand, where there was no duty on the party to raise the question at issue, or to set up the case, which in fact he did not bring to the notice of the tribunal, or where he could not have done so without detriment, or the reasonable possibility of detriment, to his legal position or interests, a general decision against him does not necessarily involve an adverse decision on that particular question, issue, or case. For instance, from a judgment for an account of tithes "subtracted", no implication can be made of a decision against the defendant that a particular *modus* of no more than a certain amount has existed from time immemorial, merely because the defendant omitted to make this case, he being in no way called upon to do so;[1] a judgment for the recovery of the price of goods or work, to which the defendant might have pleaded the inferiority of the goods or work in reduction of the price, but was not bound to do so, and (before the Judicature Acts) could not have done so without prejudicing his right to complete remedy and relief, was held not to carry with it a decision negativing the plaintiff's negligence, merely because the defendant had not so pleaded;[2] the fact that an employer sued in the county court for wages refrained from setting off a claim for damages against the workman for wrongfully injuring materials, in the reasonable belief that it would be more to his advantage to resort to his statutory remedy under the Employers and Workmen Act 1875, and afterwards to raise the claim for damages in a court of summary jurisdiction, does not render a judgment for the workman in the county court an implied decision that the workman had not wrongfully damaged his employer's materials;[3] and, generally, the omission of a party to plead affirmative matters which if pleaded, would not have conflicted with any traversable allegation made on the other side, such matters, for example, as release, confession and avoidance, and the like,

---

to reduce or counterbalance his indebtedness to his wife's estate, whether it would in strictness then be called a present right of set-off or not. On these grounds I think that as he did not then put forward this claim he is now barred from doing so on the ground that the matter is in fact *res judicata*".

1 *Collins* v. *Gough* (1785), 7 Bro. Parl. Cas. 94, at p. 99.

2 *Rigge* v. *Burbidge* (1846), 15 M. & W. 598; *Davis* v. *Hedges* (1871), L.R. 6 Q.B. 687, where the ground of the decision was that, though the defendant had an option to plead the inferiority of the goods, or the work, as a defence, there was no obligation on him to do so, and it would be unjust to impose such a duty upon him, if he conceived it to be for his advantage to set up an independent claim for damages, rather than raise the point in a form which would not result in adequate relief (per BLACKBURN and HANNEN JJ., at pp. 688–691), though the court was careful to disclaim any intention of disparaging the authority of those cases which decide that, where the party could have raised the question *without detriment to himself*, his omission to do so may create an estoppel against any reagitation of that question (per BLACKBURN and HANNEN JJ., at pp. 691, 692, and LUSH J., at p. 693).

3 *Hindley* v. *Haslam* (1878), 27 W.R. 61 (*per Cur.*, at p. 62; "the question raised before the justices was never brought before the County Court judge, and the respondents were not bound to raise it before him").

does not entitle the opposite party to treat a general judgment in his favour as a decision in his favour on the particular affirmative matter.[1]

201 And indeed, wherever a plaintiff has two separate causes of action (though they arise out of the same transaction) as distinct from several remedies for one cause of action,[2] he is not generally under any duty to set up both in the first proceedings which he may institute. As will later be seen, if he sets up one cause of action only, and is successful, he is not thereby precluded by the operation of the doctrine of merger from proceeding subsequently on the other;[3] and the same result will attend if he fail in his first proceedings—he may thereafter, notwithstanding such failure, proceed independently on the separate and independent cause of action which has not yet been litigated. He is under no duty by which he is compelled to join all his available causes of action in the first proceedings.[4]

202 The desirability of keeping the application of the doctrine within the limits stated in the preceding paragraphs is strikingly illustrated in the case of an originating summons for an interpretation of a will or for

---

[1] *Howlett* v. *Tarte* (1861), 10 C.B. N.S. 183, an action for rent under a building agreement, to which the defendant pleaded a plea of confession and avoidance (by the substitution of an agreement from year to year for the agreement sued upon), and the plaintiff, by his replication, set up a judgment recovered by him in a former action for rent under the same building agreement, by which the defendant had pleaded various defences, but not the present plea, and it was held that the defendant was not estopped (per WILLIAMS J., at p. 826: "if the defendant had attempted to put on the record a plea which was inconsistent with any traversable allegation in the former declaration, there would be an estoppel. But the defence set up here is quite consistent with every allegation in the former action. The plea admits the agreement, but shows by matter *ex post facto* that it is not binding upon the defendant"). With this case contrast *Humphries* v. *Humphries*, [1910] 2 K.B. 531, C.A., cited in note 1 on p. 165, where the principle of the former authority was adopted, explained, and applied, but where, the allegation being traversable, unlike averments of release, or pleas of Gaming, and similar Acts, it was held that there was an estoppel (*per Cur.*, at pp. 535–537).

The text of the above note is reproduced *verbatim* from the first edition of this work (1924). *Howlett* v. *Tarte* was subsequently carefully examined in the judgment of the Privy Council per Lord SHAW in *Hoystead* v. *Taxation Commissioner*, [1926] A.C. 155, P.C. at pp. 168–169. Its basis was found to lie in the niceties of the old rules of pleading. ("While the rules against double pleading were in force, it would have led to much injustice if a suitor who had two answers to a claim, or two replies to a defence, but was prevented from raising more than one, was deemed to have admitted that he had no other answer or reply than that to which he had to confine himself, and this is the *ratio decidendi* of the two cases (*viz. Howlett* v. *Tarte* and *Carter* v. *James*) on which reliance was placed for the respondent. Thus explained they in no way derogate from the general principles of law".)

[2] The distinction is adverted to by Lord ATKIN in *United Australia, Ltd.* v. *Barclays Bank, Ltd.*, [1941] A.C. 1, H.L. at pp. 27–28.

[3] See Chapter XX, *infra*; *Brunsden* v. *Humphrey* (1884), 14 Q.B.D. 141; *Marginson* v. *Blackburn Borough Council*, [1939] 1 All E.R. 273; [1939] 2 K.B. 426.

[4] *In New Zealand, Thompson and Taylor* v. *Ross*, [1943] N.Z.L.R. 712 per CALLAN J. at p. 719. In this case a plaintiff, who had failed in one action based on innocent misrepresentations preceding a contract for the sale and purchase of land, whereupon he claimed rescission of the contract, was not precluded thereby from instituting a second action based on breach of warranty to the same effect as the representations previously alleged. But note the recent decision of the S. ct. of Canada in *Cahoon* v. *Franks* (1967), 63 D.L.R. (2d) 274 referred to in a note to para. 453, *post*.

directions thereunder where there has previously been another originating summons in which the point now raised, though not specifically placed before the court, has been close to the argument, or even assumed in the course of it.[1] The court will be cautious in such a case, and will be reluctant to restrict the rights of the beneficiaries by the application of the principle of estoppel *per rem judicatam*[2] unless the same point has been actually decided in the first proceedings,[3] or is necessarily to be implied in the earlier decision by virtue of the duty of the party now to be estopped to raise it therein.[4]

203 It must be remembered that only when the decision is adverse to the party omitting to plead any particular matter, either generally, or on the issues which were in fact raised, can any implication of an adverse decision on such particular matter be made. If the decision, generally, or on the issues raised, was in favour of such party, the admission implied from his failure to plead the particular matter, however effective for the purposes of the then proceedings, is of no effect or value whatsoever in any subsequent litigation between the parties.[5]

Ignorance of the matter previously omitted

204 If the party, though omitting to bring to the notice of the judicial tribunal some fact or matter which he desires to establish or raise in subsequent litigation, can show that at the time of the former proceedings he

---

1 *Re Koenigsberg, Public Trustee* v. *Koenigsberg*, [1949] Ch. 348, C.A. per SOMERVELL L.J. at p. 362.

2 *Ibid.*, per EVERSHED L.J. at p. 364.

3 As in *Re Waring, Westminster Bank* v. *Burton-Butler*, [1948] Ch. 221, from which *Re Koenigsberg supra*, is expressly distinguished on this very point at p. 358 by SOMERVELL L.J.

4 *Re Koenigsberg, Public Trustee* v. *Koenigsberg*, [1949] Ch. 348, C.A. per SOMERVELL L.J. at p. 363.

5 In *Boileau* v. *Rutlin* (1848), 2 Exch. 665, PARKE B., delivering the judgment of the court, at p. 681, lays down the rule as follows: "the facts actually decided by an issue in any suit cannot be again litigated between the same parties, and are evidence between them, *and that conclusive* . . .; and so are the material facts alleged by one party which are directly admitted by the opposite party, or *indirectly admitted by taking a traverse on some other facts, but only if the traverse is found against the party making it*". In a previous case of *Carter* v. *James* (1844), 13 M. & W. 137, where to an action of debt on a bond, the defendant had pleaded an usurious agreement, which the plaintiff had not traversed in his replication, though he took a traverse on another plea, and judgment was given for the defendant, it was nevertheless held that the plaintiff was not estopped from setting up, in a second action to recover the same debt, that the agreement was not usurious (per ALDERSON B., at pp. 147, 148). This decision is obviously inconsistent with the rule afterwards laid down by PARKE B., and, at p. 241 of *Hutt* v. *Morrell* (1849), 3 Exch. 240, POLLOCK C.B. intimates a very strong doubt as to its soundness: "I find", he there says, "at the end of that case, a note in my own handwriting: *Quaere*, whether in this case the rule was brought to the notice of the court that, *when the plaintiff replies to one part of the plea, and thus admits the other, if the issue be found for him, the admission avails nothing*; *but, if the issue be found against him, and there be judgment, he is estopped as to both*". This entry is all the more significant, as coming from one who was a party to the decision in *Carter* v. *James, supra*.

The text of the above note is copied *verbatim* from the first edition of this work; but as to

was not only in fact, but also excusably, ignorant thereof, and that such fact or matter, if then proved, would have altered the whole aspect of the case, he is entitled to claim that no estoppel by implied *res judicata* shall take effect, or other adverse inference of any kind shall be made against him, by reason of such omission.[1] Such an answer to an *exceptio rei judicatae* is known to Scottish jurisprudence as *res noviter veniens ad notitiam*, or as a new *medium concludendi*. If any of the above elements be wanting the estoppel remains unaffected: if, for instance, there never was any newly discovered fact of the nature alleged,[2] or if the fact was newly discovered only in the sense that the party "newly" realised its importance as constituting an additional element in proof or disproof of an issue determined by the judicial decision,[3] or if the party had at the date of the former proceedings actual knowledge of the fact,[4] or might by the exercise of reasonable diligence have acquired knowledge thereof;[5] or, if the fact is not shown to have been, not merely material, but of such vital and essential materiality that its establishment must have altered the whole aspect of the case.[6]

When, however, the decision itself was that the former action had been prematurely brought,[7] or was expressed in such a form as (in effect) to promise a reconsideration of the question in dispute on the procurement of fresh evidence, as in the case of a sentence in the old suit for jactitation of

---

Carter v. *James* the reader is referred to the discussion of this decision in the judgment of the Privy Council per Lord SHAW in *Hoystead* v. *Taxation Commissioner*, [1926] A.C. 155 J.C. at pp. 168–169, a note of which appears in footnote 1 on p. 167, *supra*.

[1] The best statement of this rule is to be found in the following three House of Lords cases: *Lockyer* v. *Ferryman* (1877), 2 App. Cas. 519, H.L. (per Lord CAIRNS L.C., at pp. 525–527, Lord HATHERLEY, at p. 527, and Lord SELBORNE, at p. 528); *Phosphate Sewage Co.* v. *Molleson* (1879), 4 App. Cas. 801, H.L. (per Lord CAIRNS L.C., at pp. 814, 815, Lord HATHERLEY, at pp. 816–819, and Lord BLACKBURN, at pp. 819–822); *Boswell* v. *Coaks* (*No.* 2) (1894), 86 L.T. 365 n., H.L. (per Lord SELBORNE, at pp. 366). For a good illustration of a case of *res noviter veniens ad notitiam* which satisfied all the requirements stated in the text, see *Stevens* v. *Tillett*, *Norwich Case* (1870), L.R. 6 C.P. 147 (per BOVILL C.J., at pp. 155, 164, 165, WILLES J., at pp. 170, 171, 174, 175, and KEATING J., at pp. 177, 178).

[2] As in *Boswell* v. *Coaks*, *supra*.

[3] As in *Greathead* v. *Bromley* (1798), 7 Term Rep. 455; *Phosphate Sewage Co.* v. *Molleson*, *supra* (per Lord CAIRNS L.C., at pp. 814, 815, and Lord HATHERLEY, at pp. 816–819).

[4] As in *Greathead* v. *Bromley*, *supra* (per Lord KENYON, C.J., at p. 546); *Lockyer* v. *Ferryman*, *supra* (per Lord CAIRNS L.C., at pp. 524–527); *Phosphate Sewage Co.* v. *Molleson*, *supra*.

[5] As in *Shoe Machinery Co.* v. *Cutlan*, [1896] 1 Ch. 667 (per ROMER J., at p. 672). Contrast *Stevens* v. *Tillett*, *supra*, where the new "corrupt practices" alleged could not reasonably have been known to the party at the time of the former proceedings, having been disclosed in the evidence given before a Royal Commission which was not appointed until after that date.

[6] See the citations from the three House of Lords cases which are given in note 1 above.

[7] As in *Palmer* v. *Temple* (1839), 9 Ad. & El. 508 (per Lord DENMAN C.J., at p. 521, who points out that the ground of the decision set up as a *res judicata* was "that the action was prematurely brought, *viz.* before the contract was rescinded, and before the defendant had disabled himself from completing it", and, therefore, "the former judgment forms no obstacle to the recovery, now that that event has taken place").

marriage, negativing the existence of the marriage "so far as yet appears", there is obviously an unanswerable case of *res noviter ad notitiam veniens.*[1]

Foreign judgments

205 The same principles were, in the older cases,[2] applied to foreign judgments pronounced as the result of litigation in which one of the parties had failed to bring to the notice of the foreign tribunal some question, issue or matter which, without prejudice to his interests he might (and therefore should) have then and there raised. It appears doubtful, however, how far these earlier decisions will in future be followed, for it has become fashionable to hesitate before giving to foreign decisions the full force of *res judicata* in our courts, if they have been pronounced on anything less than a fully-argued case. In *Carl-Zeiss-Stiftung* v. *Rayner and Keeler, Ltd.*[3] the Lords showed a remarkable divergence of opinion as to whether a foreign judgment could be used as a foundation of issue estoppel, and, if so, how far. Lord REID posed the difficulties which lie in the way of a whole-hearted application of the doctrine when he said:[4]

> "The difficulty which I see about issue estoppel is a practical one. Suppose the first case is one of trifling importance but it involves for one party proof of facts which would be expensive and troublesome; and that party can see the possibility that the same point may arise if his opponent later raises a much more important claim. What is he to do? The second case may never be brought. Must he go to great trouble and expense to forestall a possible plea of issue estoppel if the second case is brought? This does not arise in cause of action estoppel: if the cause of action is important, he will incur the expense; if it is not, he will take the chance of winning on some other point. It seems to me that there is room for a good deal more thought before we settle the limits of issue estoppel: but I have no doubt that issue estoppel does exist in the law of England, and if it does it would apply in the present case if the earlier judgment had been a final judgment of an English court.
>
> Next I must consider whether it makes any difference that the former judgment was the judgment of a foreign court. At one time foreign judgments were regarded as being only evidence and not conclusive; but at least since the decision in *Godard* v. *Gray* (1870), L.R. 6 Q.B. 139 they have been regarded as equally conclusive with English judgments (subject to any difference there may be resulting from there being no merger of a cause of

---

[1] As in the *Duchess of Kingston's Case* (1776), 2 Smith, L.C. (13 edn.) 644 (per DE GREY C.J., at p. 651).

[2] The authorities cited in the first edition, in support of a more stringently-worded statement of principle, are *Henderson* v. *Henderson*, (1843), 3 Hare 100 (per WIGRAM V.-C., at pp. 114–118); *Godard* v. *Gray* (1870), L.R. 6 Q.B. 139 (per HANNEN J., at p. 154); *Ellis* v. *M'Henry* (1871), L.R. 6 C.P. 228 (*per Cur.*, at p. 238); *Re Trufort, Trafford* v. *Blanc* (1887), 36 Ch.D. 600 (per STIRLING J., at pp. 616, 617).

[3] [1966] 2 All E.R. 536, H.L.

[4] At pp. 554–555.

action in a foreign judgment). The same pleas, *e.g.*, fraud or lack of jurisdiction are good against both. It would seem that the only plea which may be available against foreign judgments alone is perversity, if *Simpson* v. *Fogo* (1863), 1 Hem. & M. 195 was rightly decided. In that case Sir WILLIAM PAGE WOOD, V.C., at p. 246 refused to give effect to a judgment of the Supreme Court of Louisiana. There was no question of perversity in the ordinary sense of obstinately or dishonestly shutting one's eyes to what one knows to be right. The Supreme Court had applied what they believed to be their common law, but it was at variance with a generally accepted rule of private international law, which required foreign (in this case, English) law to be applied in the circumstances of that case. Sir WILLIAM PAGE WOOD, V.C., at p. 247 called this 'a perverse and deliberate refusal to recognise the law of the country by which title has been validly conferred'. I shall have to return to this case later.

I can see no reason in principle why we should deny the possibility of issue estoppel based on a foreign judgment, but there appear to me to be at least three reasons for being cautious in any particular case. In the first place, we are not familiar with modes of procedure in many foreign countries, and it may not be easy to be sure that a particular issue has been decided or that its decision was a basis of the foreign judgment, and not merely collateral or *obiter*. Secondly, I have already alluded to the practical difficulties of a defendant in deciding whether even in this country he should incur the trouble and expense of deploying his full case in a trivial case: it might be most unjust to hold that a litigant here should be estopped from putting forward his case because it was impracticable for him to do so in an earlier case of a trivial character abroad with the result that the decision in that case went against him."

His view may be summarised as being that it is possible to found an issue estoppel on a foreign judgment, but extreme caution should be used in scrutinising both the judgment and the procedure by which it was obtained. Lord HODSON,[1] Lord UPJOHN,[2] and Lord WILBERFORCE[3] agreed, expressing similar conclusions each in his own words. The necessity for caution was emphasised by each of them. Lord GUEST went so far as to conclude that a foreign judgment was ineffective as the foundation of issue estoppel. He said:[4]

"There are, in my view, moreover, considerations of policy and expediency which make it undesirable that the doctrine of issue estoppel should be introduced in the case of foreign judgments. There has been no case in which it has been applied in England and while, perhaps, not all estoppels are odious, considerable caution, in my view, should be exercised before the principle is extended any further. In operating issue estoppel it may be necessary, in order to ascertain what issues have been inferentially or incidentally decided,

---

1 At p. 560.
2 At p. 574.
3 At pp. 584–585.
4 At p. 567.

to look, not only at the judgment, but also at the pleadings and, it may be, at the evidence. We are not familiar in this country with the practice and procedure in foreign countries, and it may be a matter of considerable nicety in certain cases to find out what issues were determined and whether they were incidental or collateral to the main decision.''

The result must be as proposed by Lord REID: that while a foreign judgment, if final and founded upon an acceptable procedure, may found an issue estoppel, extreme caution is desirable in scrutinising both substantive and adjectival aspects of the foreign decision before accepting it as the basis of an estoppel *per rem judicatam*.

The same question

206 In the preceding paragraphs we have considered the nature of the determinations which may be discovered to have been included—expressly or impliedly—in the substantive decision in the first proceedings. We now pass to a discussion of the proposition that, whatever the determination which is found to have been made in the first proceedings *the same question* must arise in the later, as arose in the earlier, proceedings, if an estoppel is to be established.

In the first edition of this work several pages[1] of the text were directed, in introducing this aspect of the doctrine of issue estoppel, to the proposition that—

> ''for this purpose, identity of subject matter means not only *eadem res*, but also *eadem quaestio*,—not only identity of subject matter in a physical sense, but identity of subject matter in a juridical sense. These two forms of identity, neither of which is sufficient without the other, demand separate consideration''.[2]

In this respect it was suggested that the common law doctrine carried forward the same principles as the Roman law from which it had taken its origin.[3]

It is the view of the author of this edition that the two questions which seemed to Mr Spencer Bower to be separate are now better regarded as only one—*viz.*: Is the question to be decided in the second proceedings the same as was contested in the first? If it is not, then there can be no estoppel.

207 The aspect of this question which seemed to the original author to require a separate inquiry as to ''physical identity'' in the *res* is still relevant, but only as part of the larger question. It has been held, for instance,

---

[1] First edition pp. 115–119.
[2] First edition pp. 115–116.
[3] The original author's excursus on *The Doctrine of Res Judicata in Roman Law* is reproduced in this edition as Appendix B.

that the construction which the Court has in one proceedings placed on a contract between the parties will not found an estoppel precluding any other construction being placed in later proceedings on another, but distinct, contract made between them in identical terms.[1] This may be said (following Mr Spencer Bower) to be because the two contracts are physically different, in that they are written on different pieces of paper; but the present author would prefer to say that it is because the two contracts will not necessarily have been executed in the same circumstantial context, and that therefore the construction to be placed upon them is not *necessarily* the same question in each case, even though it may be highly probable that it will be the same. The difficulty to which Mr Spencer Bower's proposition may lead is well demonstrated by the sadly conflicting judgments of RICH J. and DIXON J. on the one hand, and of STARKE J. on the other in the High Court of Australia in *Blair* v. *Curran*[2] (it may be said at once that all three Judges agreed on the substantive result in the case; but they disagreed on the estoppel point involved). In *Blair* v. *Curran*[2] the Court had held in earlier proceedings that the construction of a particular clause in a will was as stated in the judgment, in which a question was decided as to the

---

[1] This was the position in *New Brunswick Rail. Co.* v. *British and French Trust Corporation, Ltd.*, [1939] A.C. 1, H.L. A series of mortgage bonds, printed in identical terms, secured principal and interest. The question was whether interest was to be paid in sterling or in gold. In the first action respondent had sued appellant on one bond of which it was the holder, claiming interest as in gold. Appellant did not appear, and respondent took judgment for the amount claimed by default. Respondent subsequently sued appellant for interest (a subsequent instalment) as in gold on the same bond and on 992 other bonds of the same series. It was held by the House of Lords that though appellant was estopped by the first judgment as to the construction of the bond which had been the subject of that action, the estoppel did not extend to the construction of the other 992 bonds of the same series. Lord WRIGHT said at p. 35:

> "It may be that where a matter of fact or law has been adjudicated upon by the court on the same instrument and with regard to the same facts and between the same parties, an estoppel arises in regard to that matter, at least in a case where the party estopped has appeared in the proceedings and either contested the issue or has contested the particular decision. This is not *res judicata* in the sense that the judgment binds the parties, but it is based on analogous principles. The decision of the court, it was said, should not be disputed by parties to it in a matter which was fundamental to the decision, though it was not the decision itself".

His Lordship then observes that there is a strong reason for refusing the estoppel; it was true that the default judgment expressly declared that in the case of one bond an amount was due which must have been calculated as in gold, but "there was no issue before the court on any or all of the 992 bonds now sued on. The construction of each and any of these bonds was not a controversial issue in the previous action". With this ground Lord ROMER expressly agreed; and it is the respectful opinion of the author that these views were thoroughly sound, for however likely it may be that the same construction will be found to govern two documents in identical language, it does not follow that in *all* circumstances this will inevitably be so. Mere probability will not support an estoppel in these circumstances. In the words of Lord MAUGHAM L.C. in the same case at pp. 19–20. "The doctrine cannot be made to extend to presumptions or probabilities as to issues in a second action which may be, and yet cannot be associated beyond all possible doubt to be, identical with those raised in a previous action".

[2] (1939), 62 C.L.R. 464 (H. Ct. of Aus.). In contrast with the case discussed in the previous note, *Blair* v. *Curran* concerned itself with successive actions on the construction of the same text in the same will.

distribution of certain property affected by the clause construed by the Court. In later proceedings the disposal of other property by the *same words in the same clause* of the will was the subject of dispute. DIXON J. and RICH J. held in favour of estoppel *per rem judicatam*—DIXON J. by a process of reasoning which has been adopted in the present text;[1] RICH J. expressly in spite of "the difference in subject matter" which he thought he perceived[2] in the two questions successively before the court. STARKE J. on the other hand "could not assent to the applicability of the principle (of estoppel) in cases where the subject matter of the litigation was not the same".[3] (He thought, however, notwithstanding his refusal to sustain an estoppel, that it would be so "incongruous" in this case to have held differently from the first judgment that it should be followed.) It is submitted that in this case the real question to which all the members of the Court should have addressed themselves was simply whether the question to be decided was the same; DIXON J., asking himself this question, decided that it was. The difficulty which beset the other two judges could have been clarified had it been suggested that the *res* which had to be the same was perhaps not the property to be affected, but the paper-writing containing the clause under construction. If this were the same, there was perhaps the physical identity which Mr Spencer Bower looked for; but it is submitted, as at the beginning of this paragraph that the proper inquiry is simply whether the *same question* arises in both proceedings.

208 Where the question in the second proceedings is not *eadem quaestio* as that decided in the first, there can be no estoppel. Thus, to take first the class of civil decisions, a party against whom judgment has been given, when suing in a particular representative character, is not estopped from afterwards, in a different representative character, suing the same person, because the two proceedings do not raise the very same question.[4] Trover, or conversion, is not the same cause of action as trespass, and does not require precisely the same kind and degree of proof to support it, and, therefore, a judgment for the defendant in an action based on one of these two causes of an action does not preclude the plaintiff from afterwards suing the same defendant on the other.[5] An adverse decision in former proceedings, not purporting to adjudicate upon the validity of a certain will,

---

[1] At pp. 531–533.

[2] At p. 502.

[3] At p. 510.

[4] *Robinson's Case* (1603), 5 Co. Rep. 32 b; *Overton* v. *Harvey* (1850), 9 C.B. 324 (per CRESSWELL J., at p. 336, during the argument); *Hacking* v. *Lee* (1860), 9 W.R. 70 (per COCKBURN C.J., at p. 71). See also Chapter VII, *post*.

[5] *Lacon* v. *Barnard* (1626), Cro. Car. 35; *Put and Hardy* v. *Rawsterne* (1682), T. Raym. 472. The first of these was a merger case and, as such, is cited in Chapter XX; see para. 452, 2, p. 374, *post*.

which was an element in the case, was held not to preclude the party against whom judgment was given from impugning such validity, as against the same party, in subsequent proceedings;[1] and a decision that a clause in a will is not void for vagueness or uncertainty is not inconsistent with, and, therefore, creates no estoppel against a subsequent contention that the same clause offends against the perpetuity rule.[2] A "declarator" in Scottish proceedings that, during a certain period, a certain person was *compos mentis*, is not in the least incompatible with, or contradicted by, a subsequent assertion on the part of one sued for illegal detention of the person as a lunatic during that period that his acts were warranted by statutory authority.[3] A decision in bankruptcy proceedings that certain royalties were the bankrupt's personal earnings, though it estops the trustee from afterwards setting up that they were not, does not preclude him from raising the quite distinct question as to whether the royalties were, or were not, in excess of what was required for the maintenance of the bankrupt and his family, and, therefore, to the extent of that excess, divisible amongst the general body of creditors pursuant to the statutory law of bankruptcy.[4] A judgment, in an action for injury to the plaintiff's reversion by breaches of certain repairing covenants in an underlease during the subsistence thereof, whereby it was adjudged that the underlessee was liable to the underlessor in a certain sum as damages for such injury, does not preclude the underlessor from claiming, on the expiration of the underlease, as damages for breach of a covenant therein to deliver up the premises in good repair on such expiration, the amount required to put the premises into the covenanted state of repair, less the amount previously awarded.[5] A judgment in the old ecclesiastical court repelling the "libel", in which a husband had libelled his wife for adultery, was held not to estop the husband, when afterwards sued by the wife for restitution of conjugal rights, from pleading a "responsive allegation" setting up the same adultery, because of the essential difference in the degree and strength of the

---

[1] *Bainbrigge* v. *Baddeley* (1847), 2 Ph. 705 (per Lord LANGDALE M.R., at p. 709). Contrast with this case *Beardsley* v. *Beardsley*, [1899] 1 Q.B. 746, D.C. (per BRUCE J., at p. 749: "the question decided was the validity of the will; the issue of fact is the same, whether the will relates to real or to personal property").

[2] *Kennedy* v. *Kennedy*, [1914] A.C. 215, P.C. (per Lord PARKER, delivering the opinion of the Judicial Committee, at p. 220).

[3] *Mackintosh* v. *Smith and Lowe* (1865), 4 Macq. 913, H.L. (per Lord WESTBURY L.C., at p. 918, Lord CRANWORTH, at p. 919, and Lord CHELMSFORD, at pp. 923, 924, pointing out that, if the defenders in the action had acted pursuant to statutory licence and authority, it did not matter how sane the pursuer may then have been; whilst, if they had not so acted, it did not matter how insane he may then have been).

[4] *Re Graydon, Ex parte Official Receiver*, [1896] 1 Q.B. 417 (per VAUGHAN WILLIAMS L.J., at pp. 420–422.

[5] *Ebbetts* v. *Conquest* (1900), 82 L.T. 560, D.C. (per BIGHAM J., at p. 572).

proof required in the two suits, evidence insufficient to establish the claim to relief in the first case not being necessarily inadequate to sustain the "responsive allegation" in the second,[1] and so, where a wife, suing for judicial separation on the ground of cruelty, was absolved from the adultery charged against her by the husband in a cross-suit, the husband was held not estopped from afterward suing his wife for divorce on the ground of this adultery.[2]

In New Zealand, where in a prosecution for breach of the provision of Income Tax Acts, instituted by the Commissioner of Inland Revenue personally, (there being therefore complete identity as to parties) the taxpayer had been acquitted on a criminal charge of wilfully making a false return of income, such an acquittal was held no bar to a civil claim for unpaid tax by the Commissioner against the taxpayer, based upon an allegation that the return was fraudulent or wilfully misleading; for not only were the issues not identical, but the fact that the onus of proof varied between the two proceedings was in itself fatal to the constitution of an estoppel.[3]

Where on an action by a wife for instalments of maintenance under a deed of separation, the husband pleaded by way of defence an alleged act of adultery, but failed to prove it to the satisfaction of the Court, with the result that the wife obtained judgment for the amount of the instalment due, the husband was held not precluded by this judgment from setting up, as a defence to a subsequent action for instalments falling due later, other acts of adultery of which he had no knowledge, and therefore did not set up, and in fact had no opportunity of setting up, in the first proceeding. He was estopped only from setting up, as a defence to the second action, the same act of adultery the allegation as to which had been dismissed in the first action.[4] Where as between wife and husband a charge of cruelty before and up to a certain date has been dismissed by justices as unproved, there is no estoppel whereby the wife is in subsequent proceedings precluded from leading the same evidence (with further evidence as to a subsequent period) to substantiate cruelty before and up to a subsequent date;

---

[1] *Moore* v. *Moore* (1840), 3 Moo. P.C.C. 84 (at pp. 86, 87).

[2] *Bancroft* v. *Bancroft and Rumney* (1864), 3 Sw. & Tr. 597 (per Sir CRESSWELL CRESSWELL, at pp. 598, 599).

[3] *Maxwell* v. *Inland Revenue Commissioner*, [1962] N.Z.L.R. 683, C.A. The question of the difference between the issues was dealt with by GRESSON P. at p. 696; by NORTH J. at p. 703 and by CLEARY J. at p. 709. The point as to onus of proof was not noticed by GRESSON P.; NORTH J. mentioned it at p. 702, but did not decide it; at p. 709 CLEARY J. seems to regard the difference in onus as fatal. *Cf.* in the same jurisdiction, *In Re a Medical Practitioner*, [1959] N.Z.L.R. 784, where the same point is made in the joint judgment of NORTH and CLEARY JJ. at p. 817.

[4] *Ord* v. *Ord*, [1923] 2 K.B. 432, D.C. "In order to see what he must admit the truth of, one has always to see what was the precise question, the precise point, that has been decided"—per LUSH J. at p. 440.

for what may be insufficient to support the first allegation may serve as a valid introduction to the evidence supporting the later, and different, allegation.[1] "The conduct which is alleged to amount to persistent cruelty can only be judged in the light of the whole course of conduct, and the mere fact that at an earlier stage, when the conduct was only partly completed, a court has adjudged that at that point it does not amount to persistent cruelty, does not shut that evidence out for ever."[2]

In *Wright* v. *Bennett*[3] a plaintiff, having failed in an action in which he claimed damages for fraudulent misrepresentation against two defendants and damages for negligence against one of them, began a second action against the same defendants, covering substantially the same ground as the first, but based on an allegation of fraudulent conspiracy. On an application by the defendants to have the statement of claim struck out on the ground that the action was frivolous and vexatious, an order striking it out was made on the ground that the repetitive nature of the allegations was an abuse of the process of the court. TUCKER L.J. and COHEN L.J. (with whom WROTTESLEY L.J. concurred) declined—in the present writer's respectful view quite correctly—to go so far as to say that a plea of *res judicata* must have succeeded if the action had gone on; in this respect the case was distinguished from *Macdougall* v. *Knight*[4] in which an earlier judgment for defendant on a claim for libel in respect of certain selected passages in a pamphlet published by defendant was held to estop the same plaintiff from alleging in a later action that other passages in the same pamphlet were libellous, the question being in each case the same—*viz.* was the pamphlet as a whole libellous?[5]

A decision declining an order for possession of premises protected by rent restriction legislation, on the ground that the balance of hardship does not warrant the making of an order, will not bar further proceedings between the same parties in respect of the same premises at a later date; for the factors contributing to hardship may change.[6] And a decision the foundation of which was a finding that it had not been proved that respondent was a gipsy was held to be no bar to the litigation in subsequent proceedings of the different question whether he was a gipsy on a later date.[7] And, generally, there can be no *eadem quaestio*, and, therefore, no estoppel by

[1] *Richards* v. *Richards*, [1953] P. 36 (Lord MERRIMAN P.).

[2] *Molesworth* v. *Molesworth*, [1947] 2 All E.R. 842 at pp. 843–844.

[3] [1948] 1 All E.R. 227, C.A.

[4] (1890), 25 Q.B.D. 1, C.A.

[5] For a New Zealand decision expressly resting on this distinction see *Thompson and Taylor* v. *Ross*, [1943] N.Z.L.R. 712 per CALLAN J. at p. 719.

[6] *Burman* v. *Woods*, [1948] 1 K.B. 111, C.A.: *In New Zealand*, *Macdonald* v. *Fyson*, [1948] N.Z.L.R. 669 (CHRISTIE J.).

[7] *Mills* v. *Cooper*, [1967] 2 All E.R. 100 (Q.B.D.).

res judicata, unless everything in controversy in the proceedings where the question of estoppel is raised was also in controversy in the litigation which resulted in the judicial decision relied upon as an estoppel.[1]

Perhaps the most striking illustration of the nicety involved in the inquiry as to *eadem quaestio* is to be found in the contrasting decisions in *Hoystead* v. *Taxation Commissioner*[2] in 1926 and *New Brunswick Rail. Co.* v. *British and French Trust Corporation*[3] in 1939. One was a decision of the Judicial Committee; the other of the Lords. In *Hoystead's* case both actions were concerned with the construction of the same statutory provisions with regard to the same words in the same will; the estoppel was sustained. In *New Brunswick Rail. Co.* v. *British and French Trust Corporation, Ltd.*[3] the court was concerned with a series of bonds all in identical texts. One of them had been construed in an earlier proceeding between the same parties. It was held that it was not sufficient to show in the later proceeding that the bonds were in identical language; the Lords held that this did not necessarily result in their being given an identical construction. Lord MAUGHAM, L.C. said:

> "If an issue has been distinctly raised and decided in an action, in which both parties are represented, it is unjust and unreasonable to permit the same issue to be litigated afresh between the same parties or persons claiming under them; *but in my view the doctrine cannot be made to extend to presumptions or probabilities as to issues in a second action which may be, and yet cannot be asserted beyond all possible doubt to be, identical with those raised in the previous action.* In the earlier action here the only relevant issue was as to the true construction of the only bond then sued upon; and an allegation that other bonds of the same issue were in precisely the same form would have been irrelevant and improper. In fact, however, the statement of claim contained no such allegation. Nor is it true to assert that all the bonds of such an issue are necessarily in the same terms. The issue of construction in the second action could indeed be proved in the second action to be *similar* to that decided in the first; but it related to a different cause of action based on other bonds and could not be asserted to be the same issue. Moreover, it is a matter of common knowledge that such bonds are often issued at different dates and in different countries, matters which might well have a possible

---

[1] *Moss* v. *Anglo-Egyptian Navigation Co.* (1865), 1 Ch. App. 108, 114–116. *In New Zealand, In Re Westlake, Public Trustee* v. *Westlake*, [1940] N.Z.L.R. 887 (MYERS C.J.) in which, although the declaration made in the first proceedings (as to the vesting of shares in an estate) purported to be in general terms, yet it appeared on inquiry that the contingency on which the second proceedings turned was one which had never been made the subject of any argument in the first proceedings, which had been directed exclusively, by all concerned therein, to the rights of the beneficiaries upon the happening of a completely different contingency: MYERS C.J. had no difficulty, after citing the text as it appears on this page, in holding that the matter in controversy in the second proceedings was not in controversy in the first, and that therefore no estoppel resulted.

[2] [1926] A.C. 155, P.C.

[3] [1939] A.C. 1, H.L.

bearing on their true construction. The defendants in the first action, in special circumstances, might themselves have been estopped from contending as against the plaintiffs for the more limited construction of bond No. 3300 then sued upon, while there might have been no such estoppel as regards the 992 bonds."[1]

This illustration will perhaps of itself suffice to show the care which must be taken to see that the two issues in the two proceedings are the *same* and not merely *similar*;[2] but many other illustrations of the same fastidious approach by the courts are to be found in the Reports. The subtleties of the running-down cases, to be considered in a later chapter, afford many illustrations of the same point.

Questions of law and fact

209 Questions as to whether the point expressly determined by, or necessarily involved in, the judicial decision is, or is not, in substance the same as the point raised in the subsequent proceedings, are questions of law.[3] On the other hand, any question as to the physical identity of the subject-matter, and, in that special class of case where it can only be determined by oral evidence, any question as to what was actually decided by the judicial tribunal in the former proceedings, is a question of fact.[4]

The determinations must be fundamental, not collateral

210 Even when in one way or another it can be demonstrated that the court has *expressly* determined, in the earlier proceeding, the same issue as is now in dispute, an issue estoppel will not by any means always be the result. Only determinations which are necesssary to the decision—which are fundamental to it and without which it cannot stand—will found an issue estoppel. Other determinations, without which it would still be possible for the decision to stand, however definite be the language in which they are expressed, cannot support an issue estoppel between the parties between whom they were pronounced. The authority for the rule

---

[1] At p. 20.

[2] The Australian case of *O'Donel* v. *Road Transport and Tramways Commissioner* (1938), 59 C.L.R. 744 (H. Ct. of Aus.) is perhaps the high-water mark of the cases which decline an estoppel on this ground. There a decision in the earlier proceedings awarding workers' compensation during a period of incapacity by reason of the blindness sustained in an industrial accident was held not to estop the employer, in later proceedings for further payments during a subsequent period of incapacity, from alleging that the blindness of the worker during the subsequent period arose from a different cause, in respect of which he was under no liability.

[3] As in *Robinson* v. *Robinson* (1603), 5 Co. Rep. 32 b., and, generally, such of the cases cited in the foregoing notes to this chapter as were decided on demurrer.

[4] Such questions were accordingly left to the jury in *R.* v. *Sheen* (1827), 2 C. & P. 634 (per Burrough J., at pp. 639, 640), and in *R.* v. *Tancock* (1876), 13 Cox C.C. 217. *Cp.* the observation of Maule J., at p. 336 of *Overton* v. *Harvey* (1850), 9 C.B. 324, and those of Vaughan Williams L.J., at p. 736 of *Ripley* v. *Arthur & Co.* (1902), 86 L.T. 735, C.A.

as above set out is ancient, and it may be traced back as far as a dictum of Lord HOLT in *Blackham's Case*;[1] and a passage from the judgment of Sir L. J. KNIGHT BRUCE, V.C. in *Barrs* v. *Jackson*[2] is frequently cited as one of the principal authorities. This decision was reversed on appeal;[3] but the statement of principle of the Vice-Chancellor is not generally regarded as being affected by the appellate judgment. He said:

> "... generally the judgment, neither of a concurrent nor of an exclusive jurisdiction is conclusive evidence of any matter which came collaterally in question before it, though within the jurisdiction, or of any matter instantly cognizable, or of any matter to be inferred by argument by the judgment; and that a judgment is final only for its proper purpose and object",[4]

and then went on to say in the passage most usually quoted:

> "But it is, I think, to be collected that the rule against re-agitating matter adjudicated is subject generally to this restriction, that, however essential the establishment of particular facts may be to the soundness of a judicial decision, however it may proceed on them as established, and however binding and conclusive the decision may as to its immediate and direct object be, those facts are not all necessarily established conclusively between the parties, and that either may again litigate them for any other purpose as to which they may come in question, provided the immediate subject of the decision be not attempted to be withdrawn from its operation so as to defeat its direct object."[5]

These dicta have been endorsed over and over again in later authorities In *R.* v. *Hartington, Middle Quarter (Inhabitants)*[6] COLERIDGE J. expressed the principle as being

> "The judgment concludes, not merely as to the point actually decided, but as to a matter which it was necessary to decide, and which was actually decided, as the groundwork of the decision itself, though not then directly the point at issue".

Again, Lord SHAW delivering the judgment of the Judicial Committee in *Hoystead* v. *Taxation Commissioner*[7] said

> "The former judgment was pronounced by the Australian Courts under that section (s. 38 (7) of the Land Tax Assessment Act). It was not merely incidental or collateral to the question so decided, that the appellants were

---

[1] (1709), 1 Salk 290.

[2] (1842), 1 Y. & C.C.Ch. Cas. 585.

[3] (1845), 1 Ph. 582.

[4] (1842) 1 Y. & C.C.Ch. Cas. 585, at p. 595.

[5] *Ibid.*, at p. 597–598.

[6] (1855), 4 E. & B. 780, at pp. 794–797.

[7] [1926] A.C. 155. See also *Thoday* v. *Thoday*, [1964] P. 181 per DIPLOCK L.J. at p. 198. See, *in New Zealand*, *Hutchison* v. *Muldrock* (1911), 30 N.Z.L.R. 336, where COOPER J. declined to allow an estoppel, holding that the previous proceeding had decided only a "mere collateral question".

joint owners. It was fundamental to it. Unless it had been decided that under the settlement Mr Campbell's children had a beneficiary interest in land or income 'in such a way as they are taxable as joint owners' they could not have been taxed at all."[1]

Perhaps the judgment given in the High Court of Australia in *Blair* v. *Curran*[2] may be allowed to complete the citations by which the text of this paragraph may be supported. STARKE J. in that case said:

"It is well settled that a judgment concludes not merely the point decided but matters which were necessary to decide and which were actually decided as the groundwork of the decision itself though not then directly the point at issue and that a judgment is conclusive evidence not merely of the facts directly decided but of those facts which are necessary steps to the decision—so cardinal to it that without them it cannot stand."[3]

DIXON J., after citing the judgment of Lord SHAW to which we have already referred in *Hoystead* v. *Taxation Commissioner* said:

"In the phraseology of Lord SHAW, 'a fact fundamental to the decision arrived at' in the former proceedings and 'the legal quality of the fact' must be taken as finally and conclusively established (*Hoystead* v. *Taxation Commissioner*). But matters of law or fact which are subsidiary or collateral are not covered by the estoppel. Findings, however deliberate and formal, which concern only evidentiary facts and not ultimate facts forming the very title to rights give rise to no preclusion. Decisions upon matters of law which amount to no more than steps in a process of reasoning tending to establish or support the proposition upon which the rights depend do not estop the parties if the same matters of law arise in subsequent litigation."[4]

How to distinguish the fundamental from the collateral

211 "The difficulty in the actual application of these conceptions", continued DIXON J.,[5] in the judgment to which we have been referring, "is to distinguish the matters fundamental or cardinal to the prior decision or judgment, or necessarily involved in it as its legal justification or foundation, from matters which, even though actually raised and decided as being in the circumstances of the case the determining considerations, yet are not in point of law the essential foundation or groundwork of the judgment". In order to make this essential distinction one has always to inquire with unrelenting severity—is the determination upon which it is sought to found

---

[1] [1926] A.C. 155, P.C. at p. 171.

[2] (1939), 62 C.L.R. 464 (H. Ct. of Aus.).

[3] *Ibid.*, at p. 510.

[4] *Ibid.*, at p. 532. *Cf.* CHITTY J. in *Re Allsop and Joy's Contract* (1889), 61 L.T. 213, at p. 215: "It is new to me that on the doctrine of estoppel either side can rely upon the reasons which the learned judge gives for his coming to a conclusion upon any points".

[5] *Ibid.*, at p. 533.

an estoppel so fundamental to the substantive decision that the latter *cannot stand* without the former. Nothing less than this will do. Even where this inquiry is answered satisfactorily, it is suggested by DIXON J. that there is still another test to pass, *viz.*, whether the determination is the "immediate foundation" of the decision as opposed to merely "a proposition collateral or subsidiary only, *i.e.* no more than part of the reasoning supporting the conclusion". It is well settled that a mere step in reasoning is insufficient.[1] What is required is no less than the determination of law, or fact, or both, fundamental to the substantive decision.

One practical quick test which has been suggested as not infrequently suggesting the correct answer is: was it possible to appeal against the determination which it is now proposed to use as the foundation of an estoppel? It is not suggested that this is a criterion which will decide the question in all cases; but it is often a useful test to apply. There are many determinations of law, or fact, or mixed law and fact, contained in judgments—and even in judgments remarkable for their conciseness—as to which it is impossible for him against whom they were determined to institute any appeal. This topic is more fully discussed in a later paragraph to which the reader is referred.[2] Here it is sufficient to say that if there can be no effective appeal against the particular determination it is impossible to regard it as fundamental to the judgment. But this is not the only test; the inquiry must always be—is the determination such that without it the judgment cannot stand?

The determinations may be of fact or of law

212 The determinations which will found an issue estoppel may be determinations of pure law, or findings of fact, or decisions of mixed fact and law. An example of the first is to be found in cases where the question determined in the first proceedings has been the construction of a document or statute whose construction also comes up for determination between the same parties in the second proceedings. Such was the decision in *Hoystead* v. *Taxation Commissioner*[3], where the question decided in the first proceedings depended fundamentally upon the construction of a section of a revenue statute as applied to the text of a will. It was admitted in the first proceedings that the beneficiaries under the clause were by the operation of the text of the will constituted joint owners within the special meaning of this term in the statute. When the same point arose for determination in the second proceedings the estoppel was sustained. In *New*

[1] See *Re Allsop and Joy's Contract* (1889), 61 L.T. 213.
[2] See para. 215, *post.*
[3] [1926] A.C. 155, P.C.

Brunswick Rail. Co., Ltd. v. *British and French Trust Corporation*[1] the determination in the first proceedings was again one of construction, and as such a matter of law. But, as the documents in which the text was contained were different, the questions were held not identical, notwithstanding the identical wording of the provisions. *Blair* v. *Curran*[2] was another case where the estoppel was as to a question of law. In *Re Waring, Westminster Bank* v. *Burton-Butler*[3] which has been discussed in detail in another connection, the question was again the construction of a will.

In the running-down cases,[4] on the other hand, the issues decided in the first proceedings, which it is sought to make the subject of an estoppel in the second, have generally (as might be expected) been issues of fact, or at least issues of mixed law and fact with the factual element predominant. Such a case was *Marginson* v. *Blackburn Borough Council*[5] where the question was one of negligence or no negligence. In *Jones* v. *Lewis*[6] BANKES L.J. expressly observed that the doctrine was applicable to a point of law, or of one of mixed law and fact. In *Fidelitas Shipping Co., Ltd.* v. *V/O. Exportchleb*[7] the question was again one of mixed law and fact, this time the decision of an arbitrator.

What materials, other than the formal record of the judgment or order, may be resorted to

213 It has been said, and the statement has been often repeated,[8] that for the purpose of ascertaining the subject matter of the decision relied upon as *res judicata*, in general only the record (in the formal sense) of the judgment or order itself can be examined. Where an express declaration as to any particular question or issue appears on the face of the record of a formal judgment,[9] or where "from the judgment itself the actual grounds of the decision can be clearly ascertained" there is no necessity for further search; but it is not in general permissible, where there is no such express declaration in the formal record, to examine "what was said by the judges" —in delivering their judgments—"for the purpose of discovering what

---

1 [1938] 4 All E.R. 747; [1939] A.C. 1, H.L.
2 (1939), 62 C.L.R. 464 (H. Ct. of Aus.).
3 [1948] 1 All E.R. 257; [1948] Ch. 221 (JENKINS J.).
4 For a detailed consideration of these cases see Chapter IX, *post*.
5 [1939] 1 All E.R. 273; [1939] 2 K.B. 426, C.A.
6 [1919] 1 K.B. 328, C.A. at pp. 344–345.
7 [1965] 2 All E.R. 4, C.A. per DIPLOCK L.J. at p. 13.
8 *E.g.* in the first edition of this work at p. 113.
9 These express declarations on the face of the record are not usual, except where they are part of the relief specifically prayed, in our jurisprudence, but, in the form of reasons attached to a "jugement motivé", they constitute an invariable, if not obligatory, part of French, and other foreign, judicial decisions. See, for examples, *Dalgleish* v. *Hodgson* (1831), 7 Bing. 495; *Reimers* v. *Druce* (1857), 26 L.J. Ch. 196; *Hobbs* v. *Henning* (1864), 17 C.B. N.S. 791.

were the real grounds of their decision".[1] The inconvenience, to say the least of it, of adopting such a practice, is obvious, particularly in any case where a judicial tribunal has consisted of two or more persons.[2] It is legitimate, however, to look at the report of a judgment as delivered to ascertain, not what the fundamental grounds of the decision actually were, but what they were not, for the purpose of negativing a contention that some one particular ground was the only possible and necessary basis of the decision.[3]

214 Notwithstanding the categorical statement of principle set forth in the foregoing paragraph, which has been reproduced with only minor modifications from the first edition of this work, the general rule has been relaxed somewhat in some of the modern cases, and the trial judge's "judgment" or "reasons for judgment" looked at; not, however, to ascertain what matters of detail he decided against the party now sought to be estopped, but to ascertain what determinations forming steps in his decision can *not* be regarded as fundamental to the decision itself. By such a process of exclusion it is sometimes possible to conclude that one of a number of apparently possible alternative grounds for a decision was necessarily, in the event, actually its foundation.[4]

---

[1] The statement in the first edition was categorical, and the words "in general" have been inserted in the statement of principle by the present writer. In the first edition the following decisions were cited in a footnote as the basis of the text: *Re Bank of Hindustan, China, and Japan; Alison's Case* (1873), 9 Ch. App. 1 (per MELLISH L. J., at pp. 25, 26). This rule was rigidly observed in *Waine* v. *Crocker* (1862), 3 De G. F. & J. 421; *Re Allsop and Joy's Contract* (1889), 61 L.T. 213 (per CHITTY J., at p. 215); *Ballantyne* v. *Mackinnon*, [1896] 2 Q.B. 455, C.A. (*per Cur.*, at p. 462); *R.* v. *Brixton Prison Governor, Ex parte Savarkar*, [1910] 2 K.B. 1056, C.A. (per VAUGHAN WILLIAMS L.J., at pp. 1071, 1072, MOULTON L.J., at pp. 1075, 1076, and BUCKLEY L.J., at pp. 1077, 1078); *Jones* v. *Lewis*, [1919] 1 K.B. 328, C.A. (per BANKES L.J., at pp. 344, 345, and WARRINGTON L.J., at pp. 351, 352).

[2] Mr Spencer Bower's original footnote reads: "In any such case, if the decision is that of a majority only, or if the tribunal is equally divided, or if each member arrives at the same decision by totally different reasoning, or if (*nefandum dictu*!) Minos should permit himself the caustic declaration that he agrees with the decision of his brother Æacus on the grounds stated by his dissentient brother Rhadamanthus, whose reasons are to be deemed conclusive?"

[3] The original text ran "it is legitimate however to look at the report of a judgment as *orally* delivered . . .", and there was a corresponding limitation in the text of the earlier part of the paragraph. It is submitted, however, that there can be no difference in this regard between oral and written "judgments". *Ord* v. *Ord*, [1923] 2 K.B. 432 was a case, decided just before the publication of the first edition, where the court examined the text of the oral judgment of the judge, who had given the earlier decision; *Marginson* v. *Blackburn Borough Council*, [1939] 1 All E.R. 273; [1939] 2 K.B. 426 is a case where the Court of Appeal, expressly approving and following the practice apparently adopted in *Ord* v. *Ord*, and referring back to *In Re Graydon Ex parte Official Receiver*, [1896] 1 Q.B. 417, called for the written decision of the county court judge in the earlier proceeding (though, in the court below, LEWIS J. had expressly refused to look at it) in order to see by the process of exclusion mentioned in the text "what was the question of law or fact which was decided". See also the cases referred to in the next note.

[4] An instance is *Marginson* v. *Blackburn Borough Council*, [1939] 1 All E.R. 273; [1939] 2 K.B. 426 referred to in the preceding note. In the later running-down case of *Randolph* v. *Tuck*, [1962] 1 Q.B. 175, at p. 183, LAWTON J. followed the same course; he looked not only at the

215 At first sight it might perhaps be thought less than logical, when endeavouring to ascertain "the subject matter of the judicial decision", to

---

pleadings but also at the notes of evidence taken in the county court and at a note taken by the solicitors, or by counsel, of the (oral) findings of the county court judge. *In Australia* in *Jackson* v. *Goldsmith* (1950), 81 C.L.R. 446, while it is not clear from the report exactly what was in fact looked at on the appeal, the point was expressly referred to by FULLAGAR J. in his judgment—a dissenting one, but not on this point—at p. 467; "Where the plea is of *res judicata* only the actual record is relevant; where the plea is of issue estoppel, any material may be looked at which will show what issues were raised and decided. *Reasons given for the judgment pronounced are likely to be particularly important*: see *Ord* v. *Ord* and *Marginson* v. *Blackburn Borough Council*".

Some of the decisions cited above are running-down cases, a highly specialised field for the application of the doctrine, which in this work has been thought worthy of a chapter to itself (Chapter IX, *post*). But other decisions are available to demonstrate the same tendency. In *Patchett* v. *Sterling Engineering Co., Ltd.* (1953), 71 R.P.C. 61, a patent case, the question arose in the Court of Appeal whether a claim set up in a later proceeding was *res judicata* by virtue of an earlier; the Court of Appeal had no hesitation in examining the "judgment" of ROXBURGH J., who had decided the first contest. True, that was an extraordinary case; a claim and counterclaim coming on for hearing together had proceeded before ROXBURGH J. only as far as the completion of the evidence on the claim, when the vacation intervened, and ROXBURGH J. gave judgment on the claim only, leaving the counterclaim to be litigated later. When the matter came on again it was before another judge, and on appeal from DANCKWERTS J., who heard the counterclaim, it was contended that the issues on the counterclaim had become *res judicata* by reason of the decision of ROXBURGH J. The Court of Appeal, thoroughly disapproving of the procedure, nevertheless examined ROXBURGH J.'s "judgment" notwithstanding the express submission of counsel that "the court will look only at the proceedings of the formal order, and cannot take into account the learned judge's reasons".

> "As a general rule" (said JENKINS L.J. delivering the judgment of the Court of Appeal) "We believe it to be the case that in applying the principle of *res judicata* the judge's reasons cannot be looked at for the purpose of excluding from the scope of his formal order any matter which, according to the issues raised on the pleadings and the terms of the order itself, is included therein: (*cf. In re Bank of Hindustan, China and Japan, Alison's case* (1873), 9 Ch. App. 1, at p. 26). But where (as here) a judge, taking the unusual course of trying an action "separately from a counterclaim, prefaces the reasons he gives for dismissing the action with a statement to the effect that he leaves open, for consideration when the counterclaim is tried, the bearing of some particular fact or facts on the counterclaim, it seems to us that it would be wholly unreasonable in the face of that express reservation to treat the formal order of dismissal as precluding the plaintiff from raising such fact or facts as parts of his defence to the counterclaim".

The substantive decision of the Court of Appeal was reversed in the Lords—[1955] A.C. 534; their Lordships found it unnecessary to decide whether the plea of *res judicata* could have been successfully asserted before DANCKWERTS J. on the counterclaim. Viscount SIMONDS said at p. 542 that he was glad that the case had fallen to be decided on its merits, for in the circumstances of the particular case he would have been very reluctant to apply the ordinary rules of *res judicata*. At p. 541 he said:

> "So far as the action was concerned, an order was made whereby it was dismissed with costs, and that was all. And it is clear that whatever else your Lordships may look at in the event of a plea of *res judicata* being raised, you are at least entitled to know what were the issues raised in the pleadings in the action; and you know therefore that the respondent failed to establish his right to remuneration under any heading of claim or to rectification of the 1944 agreement."

A New Zealand decision of relevance is *Thompson and Taylor* v. *Ross*, [1943] N.Z.L.R. 712. There, CALLAN J. asked for the point to be specially argued, and after hearing argument expressly followed the course adopted at the Court of Appeal in *Marginson* v. *Blackburn Borough Council* (*supra*), and looked at his own written reasons for judgment in earlier proceedings, as well as at the notes of evidence there taken, "in order to ascertain exactly what was in issue between the parties in the earlier case, and how what was then in issue between them was decided".

refrain from examining the "judgment" or "reasons for judgment" containing the judge's own statement of what he found as fact, or held as the law, as between the parties with regard to their dispute; but a little reflection will show that by no means everything which he found as a fact or held as the law, in the first proceedings, will estop the parties in the second —but only those decisions which were fundamental and necessary to his determination of the substantive dispute. To recall the statement of principle from the judicial pen of COLERIDGE J., set out in an earlier paragraph,[1] the question as to findings or decisions not expressly set out in the formal record (*i.e.* the sealed judgment or order) is as to what matters were necessary to decide, and actually decided, as the groundwork of the decision itself. Not every finding of fact in a judge's judgment, not every issue of fact determined by a judge or jury, is *res judicata* between the parties in later proceedings. Thus, a decision of fact or law *against* the party in whose favour the substantial dispute was ultimately decided will not found an estoppel in a later proceeding; and this because it cannot have been necessary to the substantive decision. It is merely collateral, clearing the way perhaps to the point where a substantive decision can be given, but not fundamental or necessary to the decision itself. Moreover, it would be not only illogical but unjust to make it the foundation of a subsequent estoppel; for, the substantive decision being in his favour, no appeal is available on such a collateral decision to the person against whom it was given. And a similar argument may apply to cases where, of several available factual grounds alternatively advanced as the basis of a cause of action, the court (or a jury in issues put to it) has determined more than one *in favour of* the party who ultimately succeeds on the main issue. No estoppel can be founded on any one of the findings, for it is obvious that the party failing on such issues cannot appeal on any of them separately. In order to succeed on an appeal he must succeed on *all* the issues, and if the finding on even one of them be good this will be fatal to an appeal on any of the others. It would therefore be unjust to regard the findings of fact on each issue separately as estopping the parties in later proceedings. The parties will indeed be estopped by the result of the trial as to the existence and incidence of the cause of action resting upon the issues, but individually the detailed findings will be regarded as collateral findings, not properly founding an estoppel.[2]

---

1 Para. 210, *ante*; the reference is to *R.* v. *Hartington, Middle Quarter Inhabitants* (1855), 4 E. & B. 780, at p. 794–795.

2 *Penn-Texas Corporation* v. *Murat Anstalt* (*No.* 2), [1964] 2 Q.B. 647, C.A. At p. 660 Lord DENNING M.R. said: "Note that there was no application by the English company for leave to appeal, for the simple reason that there was nothing for them to appeal against. No order had been made against the English company". A little later (on the same page) he proceeded, "Would

Australian Consolidated Press, Ltd. v. *Uren*[1]

216 It has been stated in terms in the preceding paragraph that a decision of fact or law *against* a party in whose favour the substantive dispute was ultimately decided will not found an estoppel in a later proceeding, and this because it cannot as a matter of logic have been necessary to that ultimate substantive decision, which has been given in spite of, and not because of it. Moreover it has been observed that the substantive decision being in his favour, no appeal is available on such a collateral decision to the person against whom that collateral decision was given, and that for this reason also the collateral decision cannot found an estoppel. But while it is submitted by the present writer that this last statement is unexceptionable, it must now be noticed that a recent decision of the Judicial Committee appears to ignore the principle above expounded. This is *Australian Consolidated Press, Ltd.* v. *Uren*,[1] of which we must now make some examination.

---

the English company in a subsequent case be bound by the master's ruling? Clearly not. The English company would not be bound by a ruling from which they could not appeal. I think that Mr Caplan is right. In my opinion a previous judgment between the same parties is only conclusive on matters which were essential and necessary to the decision. It is not conclusive in other matters which came incidentally into consideration in the course of the reasoning: see the *Duchess of Kingston's case* (1776), 2 Smith L.C. 13th edn. 644, at p. 645 and *R.* v. *Hutchings* (1881), 6 Q.B.D. 300, C.A. One of the tests in seeing whether a matter was necessary to the decision, or only incidental to it, is to ask: could the party have appealed from it? If he could have appealed and did not, he is bound by it, see *Badar Bee* v. *Habib Merican Noordin*, [1909] A.C. 615, at p. 623 P.C. per Lord MACNAGHTEN. If he could not have appealed from it (because it did not affect the order made) then it is only an incidental matter, not essential to the decision, and he is not bound: see *Concha* v. *Concha* (1886), 11 App. Cas. 541, H.L. at pp. 541–542 per Lord HERSCHELL". See further *Lake* v. *Lake*, [1955] 2 All E. R. 538; [1955] P. 336, C.A. in which a husband petitioned for divorce on the ground of cruelty and adultery. The Commissioner found adultery proved, but found that it had been condoned, and dismissed the petition. The wife sought to appeal against the finding of adultery; but it was held that there was nothing in the order against which an appeal could lie, since the petition, in accordance with her submissions, had been dismissed. See further (*in Australia*) *James* v. *Commonwealth* (1935), 52 C.L.R. 570 (H. Ct. of Aus.). In that case in a suit between a fruit merchant and the Commonwealth Government it had been contended for the plaintiff that a statutory provision was *ultra vires* of the Commonwealth Legislature. This contention had been disallowed by the High Court which, however, had given judgment in the action for the plaintiff on other grounds. It was held in a later action between the same parties that the plaintiff was not thereby estopped from re-advancing his contention that the provision was *ultra vires* for, since he had succeeded on other grounds in the first action it could not be said that the decision on the validity of the statute was necessary to the judgment; moreover had he wished to appeal against the decision of the High Court on the point of *ultra vires* he would have been unable to do so since he had in fact succeeded in his action, judgment being given in his favour. "Although the court ruled that he was wrong upon his first ground he is not estopped, because the decision passed in his favour. He could not appeal from the court's ruling. It was so to speak a ruling in the air so far as he was concerned."—per RICH J. at p. 584. "In one sense it is true that the question was decided against him. He submitted the contention to the court which announced an opinion that he was wrong; but that opinion was not translated into a decree or order and could not be, because upon an independent contention he succeeded. There was no judgment from which he could seek special leave to appeal, none which estopped him."—per DIXON J. pp. 590–591.

[1] [1967] 3 All E.R. 523, P.C.

In this case, at the original hearing (in Australia) a defendant against whom judgment had been given on trial moved the Full Court for an order setting aside the verdict obtained against him, and directing a new trial of all the issues in the action. Only partially successful in the Full Court of New South Wales, defendant appealed further to the High Court of Australia, before whom it obtained an order granting to it all the relief which it sought. This notwithstanding, it subsequently sought before the Judicial Committee of the Privy Council a review of the *reasons* given in the High Court in the course of the judgments delivered by its members, in which the law had been stated, on one particular point, *against* the successful appellant, the appeal succeeding, however, *in toto*, on other grounds. The Judicial Committee, for reasons which it is now to be submitted were inadequate, allowed argument on the matter, and heard appellant's appeal in a case where, on the substantive question in dispute, it had totally succeeded in the court below.

It is necessary here to mention only some of the questions which in this complicated piece of litigation were decided in the High Court and in the hearings leading up to that court.[1] At the trial a jury had awarded heavy damages for libel on each of four separate counts in which four separate publications were pleaded. An application by defendant for an order setting aside the verdict, and directing a new trial on all issues, or alternatively on the question of damages only, succeeded, as to the issues of damages only, before the Full Court of New South Wales.[2] All the judges in that court were of opinion (a) that the trial judge had erred in directing the jury, on the particular facts of the case, that an award of exemplary damages would be competent, and (b) that the verdicts on the four counts "reflected prejudice engendered by inflammatory advocacy exceeding permissible limits."[3] Two of the judges, however, (HERRON C.J. and WALLACE J.) were of opinion that the new trial should be limited to the issue of damages on each of the four counts; WALSH J., dissenting on this point, thought that the new trial should include the issue of liability as well as the issues as to quantum of damage.

Defendant appealed to the High Court of Australia[4] against the decision

---

[1] The decision is a notable one for several distinct reasons, one of which may be noticed here—*viz.* that the Judicial Committee decided that the principles restrictive of the award of exemplary damages enumerated by Lord DEVLIN in *Rookes* v. *Barnard*, [1964] 1 All E.R. 367; [1964] A.C. 1129, H.L. were not applicable *at common law* in Australia. A future generation may see in this decision the abandonment by the Privy Council of any claim to be the moderator, as between various jurisdictions in the British Commonwealth, of the common law.

[2] (1965), 83 N.S.W. (W.N.) (Part 2) 229.

[3] Per MENZIES J. in the High Court of Australia on appeal—(1966), 40 A.L.J.R. 143, at p. 144.

[4] The report of the appeal to the High Court may be found in (1966), 40 A.L.J.R. 143.

of the majority on the question on which the Full Court had differed, and asked for an order in the form advocated by WALSH J.—*i.e.* one for a new trial on the issue of liability as well as on the issues of damage. Plaintiff cross-appealed. The High Court allowed defendant's appeal, and set aside the whole verdict in the court of trial, directing a new trial on the issues both of liability and of quantum on each of the four counts. In the course of their judgments the members of the High Court[1] all expressed views as to the competency of the Court to award exemplary damages. The judges of the High Court held unanimously that the classes of cases in which exemplary damages may be awarded in defamation actions in Australia are not limited to the categories specified by Lord DEVLIN in *Rookes* v. *Barnard*;[2] but a majority went on to hold that, though this was so, yet (in agreement with the Full Court of New South Wales in the result) the case was on the facts not one in which it was open to the jury to find that the foundation for exemplary damages had been laid. On the other alternative ground the High Court upheld the Full Court of New South Wales in deciding, by a majority, that the same result should follow as a result of the unduly inflammatory advocacy which had characterised the presentation of plaintiff's case. But, in this regard in disagreement of the majority of the Full Court of New South Wales, and in accord with the dissenting (in this respect only) judgment of WALSH J., a majority of the High Court held that the new trial should not only be on all four counts, but should include issues of liability as well as those of damages.

At this point it will be seen that defendant had now been granted all that it had asked of the Court, and it would appear that there was nothing left against which it could appeal. Before the Full Court of New South Wales defendant had asked (1) that the verdict be set aside (2) that a new trial should be directed (3) that this should be on all four counts and (4) that questions of both liability and quantum should be retried. The Full Court of New South Wales had granted its prayers Nos. 1, 2, and 3, but had refused its fourth prayer limiting the new trial to damages. Before the High Court prayer No. 4 was all that was left to form the subject of an appeal by the defendant.

In the High Court of Australia[3] defendant succeeded on the fourth and last prayer. Plaintiff's cross-appeal was dismissed. The result was complete success for defendant; yet defendant was less than completely satisfied. It had succeeded on what appeared to it to be the wrong ground. For a new trial, in which plaintiff could ask for exemplary damages if the evidence was such as to support such an award, perhaps had its dangers.

[1] There were five—MCTIERNAN, TAYLOR, MENZIES, WINDEYER, and OWEN JJ.

[2] [1964] A.C. 1129, H.L.

[3] The appeal is reported at (1966), 40 A.L.J.R. 143.

There might be different evidence upon such a second trial. And so it came about that defendant, having succeeded *in toto* in its appeal, but for reasons which appeared to it to have their disadvantages, sought leave to appeal to the Judicial Committee in an attempt to ask that court to amend, not the result, but the reasons for it, in the course of which the court before which the new trial could come might receive some direction, advantageous to the defendant, as to the applicability of Lord DEVLIN's now famous judgment in *Rookes* v. *Barnard*.[1]

The Judicial Committee, on an interlocutory application in this regard, granted leave to appeal; and the substantive appeal was subsequently heard before a Judicial Committee differing in personnel from that which had granted leave. At the hearing the appeal was dismissed, the Judicial Committee holding that the reasons given by the judges of the High Court in their judgments were correct in principle, and that in Australia the restrictions set out in Lord DEVLIN's speech had no validity. It is here submitted that in principle there was no room for hearing this appeal, for the reasons which have been given in preceding paragraphs in the text of this book.[2] There was nothing left to form the subject of any appeal. Appellant had already succeeded in obtaining everything which it had asked. The absurdity, it is respectfully suggested, of entertaining an appeal may be demonstrated by contemplating what would have been the Order recommended by their Lordships if this appeal had succeeded. It would not have been asked by defendant, in such an event, that the substantive order made in the court below should be varied in any respect whatever. While it is clear that *convenience* was served by the procedure followed, principle seems, with respect, to have been allowed to go by the board. It is to be observed that the members of the Committee which heard the appeal were obviously exercised in the matter; they excused themselves for their action in hearing the appeal by explaining that they had been directed to hear it by an Order-in-Council of Her Majesty, made upon the recommendation of a different Judicial Committee on the earlier application for leave. It is this earlier order, therefore, to which exception must respectfully be taken in this chapter; and it is here submitted that the order granting leave to appeal was one which cannot be sustained in principle.

217 Documents, other than the official sealed record of the judgments (at all times examinable), and the judge's "judgment" or "reasons for

---

[1] [1964] A.C. 1129, H.L.

[2] Para. 215: para. 211, *supra*. *Cf.* the decisions cited in note 2 on pp. 186–7: that of HODSON L.J. in *Lake* v. *Lake*, [1955] P. 336, C.A. at p. 346 is particularly worth notice as Lord HODSON was one of the Judicial Committee which granted leave, apparently without difficulty, in *Uren's* case.

judgment" (which may be referred to, but only for the purposes set out in detail in the preceding paragraphs) which have at various times been examined, in cases of *res judicata*, for the purpose of ascertaining whether any, and, if so, what questions of law or issues of fact must necessarily have been determined in order to justify the actual decision, comprise the following: the pleadings,[1] and also the preamble or introduction to any order directing issues;[2] a special case;[3] in Ireland, a report by the trial judge to the court, according to the Irish practice, which in the timeof Lord MANSFIELD prevailed in England also;[4] special findings of the jury in answer to questions left to them by the trial judge;[5] the notes or transcript of evidence, in courts where this is officially taken down and placed upon the file;[6] in an equity case, entries in the registrar's book.[7] *In New Zealand*, where on a second originating summons asking for a declaration as to the event in which the shares given under a will would indefeasibly vest it was sought to raise an estoppel on the answer given by the court in earlier proceedings between the same parties, and it was contended, in opposition to the estoppel, that the contingency forming the basis of the first argument was different from that forming the basis of the second, and that the same question consequently never arose on the two proceedings, the court looked at the record of the first proceedings and particularly at the originating summons in which the questions were formulated, and then went so far as to have regard to the argument advanced by counsel in the earlier proceedings, a summary of which was apparently available.[8] In another New Zealand case in the first suit plaintiff sued an incorporated company for specific performance of an agreement to grant a lease. In the Supreme Court specific performance was refused on the ground of uncertainty. Plaintiff appealed; in the Court of Appeal it was held that the agreement was sufficiently certain, but an entirely new point was raised by the court

---

[1] As for instance in *Mangena* v. *Wright*, [1909] 2 K.B. 958 per PHILLIMORE J. at pp. 974–975.

[2] *Robinson* v. *Duleep Singh* (1878), 11 Ch.D. 798, C.A., for "in order to determine what the decree really decides, it is essential to see what were the rights which were in dispute between the parties" (per JAMES L.J., at p. 813).

[3] As in *R.* v. *Sow Inhabitants* (1843), 4 Q.B. 93 (special case stated by Quarter Sessions in a question of settlement of pauper): *Re Bank of Hindustan, China, and Japan*; *Alison's Case* (1873), 9 Ch. App. 1 (where the *res judicata* was the decision of one specific question, and one only, submitted for the opinion of the court by the special case which the parties had agreed to state); *Ryley* v. *Brown* (1890), 62 L.T. 458, D.C. (grounds of decision appearing in case stated by magistrates).

[4] As in *Houstoun* v. *Marquis of Sligo* (1885), 29 Ch.D. 448, C.A. (per COTTON L.J., at p. 458).

[5] As in *Macdougall* v. *Knight* (1890), 25 Q.B.D. 1, C.A. and *Want* v. *Moss* (1894), 70 L.T. 178, P.C. at p. 179.

[6] "It is often necessary to see what the evidence before the court at the previous trial was in order to see what the precise facts were that cannot afterwards be disputed"—per LUSH J. in *Ord* v. *Ord*, [1923] 2 K.B. 432, at p. 442.

[7] *Re Allsop and Joy's Contract* (1889), 61 L. T. 213, at p. 215.

[8] In *Re Westlake, Public Trustee* v. *Westlake*, [1940] N.Z.L.R. 887 (MYERS C.J. at p. 892).

itself—*viz.* that the transaction amounted to a distribution of capital, and accordingly was *ultra vires*. The new point was argued, and was decided against plaintiff; the appeal was consequently dismissed, but on a ground not raised by the pleadings, or in the court below. When subsequent proceedings raised the invalidity of the same agreement for a lease, the question arose as to what had been decided at the first hearing. It was held that it was necessary in the second proceedings to look at the memorandum from the Court of Appeal which had raised the new point for argument, and to the reasons for judgment in the Court of Appeal, in order to see what had not been decided, and what was fundamental in dismissing the appeal—which certainly was *not* any degree of concurrence with the grounds given in the court below for its original decision to refuse specific performance.[1] In the case of judgment and orders by consent,[2] or by default,[3] and also in cases of dismissal of an action or refusal of an application,[4] as has been fully explained and illustrated in earlier chapters, it is absolutely essential to refer to the pleadings or affidavits of the parties, if the judgment or order is in a naked and general form, in order to ascertain what, if any, decision of particular questions or issues, was impliedly consented or submitted to by the party against whom such consent or default judgment or order was made.

Moreover, the pleadings in the second proceedings may furnish admissions from which the matters determined in the first proceedings may be ascertained satisfactorily.[5]

Even oral evidence has, in a proper case, been received for the purpose of determining the grounds of the earlier decision, and the intention of the tribunal therein to adjudicate, or not to adjudicate, upon any suggested specific question or issue.[6]

Issue estoppel and arbitration

218 Issue estoppel arises from issues decided as the fundamental basis of an award in arbitration proceedings, as it does to issues determined in litigation.[7] The parties, having chosen their tribunal (or having been deemed—*e.g.* by statute—to have done so) to determine the disputes be-

---

[1] *Jenkins* v. *Tileman (Overseas), Ltd.*, [1967] N.Z.L.R. 484 (MOLLER J.).

[2] See Chapter II.

[3] See Chapter II.

[4] See several of the cases cited in the notes to Chapter IV, *ante*.

[5] As was the case in *Bell* v. *Holmes*, [1956] 1 W.L.R. 1359, at p. 1367.

[6] See *Flitters* v. *Allfrey* (1874), L.R. 10 C.P. 29, at pp. 40–42, where oral evidence was admitted to ascertain the questions which the judge determined as the groundwork of his formally recorded judgment; *cf. Ord* v. *Ord*, [1923] 2 K.B. 432 at pp. 439–444.

[7] Per DIPLOCK L.J. in *Fidelitas Shipping Co., Ltd.* v. *V/O. Exportchelb*, [1965] 2 All E.R. 4, C.A. at p. 10.

tween them as to their legal rights and duties, are bound by the determinations of that tribunal on any issue fundamental to its substantive decision. Moreover, where the matters to be determined by the arbitrator are themselves simply the answers to questions of fact, the answers of the arbitrator to such questions being the very questions which he is called upon substantively to determine, will become *res judicatae* in a manner closely analogous to the constitution of cause of action estoppel.

Taxation and rating cases

219 Questions of assessment from one year to another in taxation and rating cases form an interesting exception to the principles of issue estoppel, by which they are not governed. They are *sui generis* in this regard, and issues involved in the determination of a question *inter partes* as to liability for tax or rates in one year, or on the fixing of one assessment list, even though the question determined be fundamental to liability, will not form the basis of an estoppel *inter partes* in other and subsequent proceedings in which the assessment for that year or that list is not involved.[1] The taxation and rating cases will be found separately discussed in a later chapter of this work devoted exclusively to this topic.[2]

But taxation and rating cases, though they must be regarded as *sui generis*, and on this account outside the operation of the ordinary rules as to estoppel *per rem judicatam*, nevertheless furnish some excellent illustrations of the impossibility in any case of arguing from one year to the next on account of the possible change of circumstance which may have intervened. A good example is *Edwards* v. *"Old Bushmills" Distillery Co., Ltd.*[3] (decided before it was finally clear that an estoppel could not arise) where the House of Lords affirmed a decision of the Court of Appeal of Northern Ireland, deciding that a decision of the High Court between the same parties, ruling that certain operations were in one year capital operations, did not finally conclude the matter, when similar operations were being assessed in the following year—for there might be differences in circumstances which could lead to a different assessment.

Criminal decisions: autrefois acquit

220 The general principles of issue estoppel are applicable, under another name, to English criminal decisions. In order to establish a plea of *autrefois acquit* which, as is explained in another chapter,[4] is in substance

[1] *Caffoor* v. *Income Tax Commissioner*, [1961] A.C. 584, P.C. at pp. 599–600, expressly disproving in this regard *Hoystead* v. *Taxation Commissioner*, [1926] A.C. 155, P.C. *Cf. Broken Hill Pty., Ltd.* v. *Broken Hill Municipal Council*, [1926] A.C. 94, P.C.

[2] See Chapter X, *post*.

[3] (1926), 10 T.C. 285, H.L.

[4] Chapter XI, *post*.

neither more or less than a plea of estoppel *per rem judicatam* under another name, based on the same theory, and subject (perhaps with some slight qualifications) to the same rules, it must appear that the offence of which accused was acquitted was in substance identical with the offence charged in the second proceedings. Wherever this substantial identity is established the plea prevails; where it is not the plea will fail.

The criterion of this identity was for some time a matter of some difficulty, and did not by any means appear clearly from the decided cases. This obscurity was clarified by the speeches in the Lords (and particularly that of Lord MORRIS) in 1964 in *Connelly* v. *Director of Public Prosecutions*.[1] This case, and the propositions of law which seem to be its result, will be found fully discussed in Chapter XI, *post*.

Criminal decisions and issue estoppel

221 Apart from the application of the formal plea of *autrefois acquit* to prosecutions by indictment, and from the analogous application of the maxim *nemo debet bis vexari pro eadem causa* to other types of criminal proceedings, there remains a further application of the principle of estoppel *per rem judicatam* to criminal proceedings—*viz.* the effect of issue estoppel in cases where, the plea of *autrefois acquit* being inappplicable, it can yet be submitted that the prosecution now embarked upon is inconsistent with some finding of the court express or necessarily implied in a previous proceeding.[2] Where this is the submission made, it is not possible for the accused to avail himself of the relaxation of the rules as to identity of subject matter which Lord MORRIS' dicta give to those who pleaded *autrefois acquit*; he must, it is submitted, show the same exact degree of identity of subject matter as is necessary for any other plea of issue estoppel.[3]

Where a new trial has been directed

222 In jurisdictions such as Australia and New Zealand, where the Court of Appeal has power, in allowing an appeal and quashing a conviction, to direct a new trial of the accused, the question will sometimes arise, where there are a number of separate but connected counts in one indictment, on some of which the accused has been acquitted, whether, on his retrial on the other counts or counts, an issue estoppel arises in his favour in respect of the counts on which he has been acquitted. This is something quite different from a plea of *autrefois acquit*, for the charges on which he has been acquitted are of offences different from the one of which a new

---

[1] [1964] 2 All E.R. 401; [1964] A.C. 1254, H.L.

[2] This is discussed in more detail in paras. 323 *et seq.*, *post*.

[3] *Mills* v. *Cooper*, [1967] 2 All E.R. 100 is an example of the court refusing to consider a submission of issue estoppel because the questions were not identical in the two proceedings.

trial has been directed. A case decided in the High Court of Australia in 1948[1] poses the problem. An information against W. and his wife charged three offences—(1) manslaughter of B., (2) conspiracy with B. and P. to procure the unlawful miscarriage of B., and (3) conspiracy with P. to defeat the course of public justice. The jury found both accused not guilty on the first two counts, but guilty on the third count. On appeal the Court of Criminal Appeal of South Australia quashed the conviction on the third count, on the ground of inconsistency between the verdicts; and in quashing the conviction on the third count the court directed (as it had power to do) the acquittal of the accused on this count, observing[2] that it would be useless from a practical point of view to order a new trial, because a jury upon the new trial would have to be told that "as between the Crown and the accused it had been conclusively established" (that is by the acquittals) "that they" (that is W. and his wife) "did not kill Mrs B., and further that they did not conspire with P. and Mrs B. to procure her miscarriage". The Crown sought the leave of the High Court of Australia to appeal against this decision, principally on the ground that the proposition which has just been cited was bad law. In refusing leave to appeal (which the High Court did, exercising its discretion on the facts of the case) two of the judges adverted to what had been said on the point of estoppel in the Full Court. LATHAM C.J. thought it was so far from the mark that, for himself, he would have granted the Crown leave to appeal. "I am not aware", he said,[3] "of any authority which shows that an acquittal conclusively establishes more than that some element, which often it would be quite impossible to identify, which is necessary to constitute the offence charged, has not been proved."

DIXON J., who was one of the majority refusing leave, observed that there was little authority as to the application of the principles of issue estoppel to criminal cases. He might have added, but did not, that this may be because the point arises principally, if not solely, in jurisdictions in which the Court of Criminal Appeal has, and exercises, the power to order a new trial. DIXON J. said:[4]

> "Whilst there is not a great deal of authority upon the subject, it appears to me that there is nothing wrong in the view that there is an issue estoppel, if it appears by record of itself or as explained by proper evidence, that the same point was determined in favour of a prisoner in a previous criminal trial which is brought in issue on a second criminal trial of the same prisoner. That seems to be implied in the language used by WRIGHT J. in *R.* v. *Ollis*[5] which in effect I have adapted in the foregoing statement. Such a question

---

[1] *R.* v. *Wilkes* (1948), 77 C.L.R. 511 (H. Ct. of Aus.)
[2] *Ibid.*, on p. 515.
[3] *Ibid.*, on p. 515.
[4] *Ibid.*, on p. 518.
[5] [1900] 2 Q.B. 758, at p. 769.

must rarely arise because the conditions can seldom be fulfilled which are necessary before an issue estoppel in favour of a prisoner and against the Crown can occur. There must be a prior proceeding determined against the Crown necessarily involving an issue which again arises in a subsequent proceeding by the Crown against the same prisoner. The allegation of the Crown in the subsequent proceeding must itself be inconsistent with the acquittal of the prisoner in the previous proceeding. But if such a condition of affairs arises I see no reason why the ordinary rules of issue estoppel should not apply. Such rules are not to be confused with those of *res judicata* which in criminal proceedings are expressed in the pleas of *autrefois acquit* and *autrefois convict*. They are pleas which are concerned with the judicial determination of an alleged criminal liability and in the case of conviction with the substitution of a new liability. Issue estoppel is concerned with the judicial establishment of a proposition of law or fact between the parties. It depends upon well-known doctrines which control the relitigation of issues which are settled by prior litigation. However, it is not necessary for us to determine any such question upon the present application. It is a question, as I have said, about which in criminal matters there is little authority.''

Divorce

223 The principles of issue estoppel have only a limited and special application in the divorce jurisdiction; for in that jurisdiction it has to be constantly borne in mind that the court has a duty, based upon public policy, itself to investigate the facts. The ''adversary system'' of litigation has only limited operation in the divorce courts, in which, for instance, it is not enough that a respondent may admit or concede a matrimonial offence sufficient to found a grant of a decree; public policy requires the court to be satisfied that the offence was in fact committed, and in this respect it has an inquisitorial function which does not generally pertain to courts in Commonwealth jurisdictions.

For this reason, while a finding of *acquittal* of a specified matrimonial offence on a given occasion, shown to be fundamental and necessary to a decision refusing relief in the divorce jurisdiction, will generally estop the party against whom it is given from setting up the same offence (on the same occasion) in another subsequent proceeding between them, yet a positive finding in one proceeding that an offence has been committed will not generally estop the party so found guilty from denying the same offence (on the same occasion) in a later proceeding—for the court, in the second proceeding, is required itself to be satisfied of guilt, and public policy is stultified by any estoppel whose effect will be to stifle a defence on the facts. This distinction was referred to by WILLMER J. in *Bright* v. *Bright*[1] where he said:

---

[1] [1953] 2 All E.R. 939; [1954] P. 270.

"I think that that argument rests on a misapprehension and on a failure to distinguish between an estoppel as against a party charged with an offence and an estoppel against a party putting forward a charge against the opposite party. It is one thing to say that the respondent is not estopped from denying charges made by the petitioner; that is to say, that the petitioner cannot in this court get relief simply because the respondent is estopped from denying the charges. In that case, the public interest no doubt does intervene to see that relief is not improperly obtained by a petitioner merely through some technical rule. But it is quite another thing to say that a petitioner, who is the party bringing the charges, is entitled to persist in repeating allegations which have already been the subject of previous proceedings, and which have already been determined against him or her, merely to obtain relief for himself or herself. In such circumstances, as I see it, no interest of the public is infringed by saying that the petitioner is estopped *per rem judicatam* from repeating allegations which have previously been the subject of judicial determination. On the contrary, there is abundant authority for the proposition that in such cases the doctrine of estoppel applies with its full force in this court as in any other court."

But the divorce cases have been thought worthy of a short chapter to themselves, in which they may be found more fully discussed than is convenient here.[1]

---

[1] See Chapter XII, *post*.

CHAPTER VII

Parties: I—Judicial Decisions in Personam

224 There are two separate and distinct types of judicial decision; one, the ordinary type which purports to determine the rights, liabilities and interests only of the parties litigant, and the other the kind which, though incidentally affecting the immediate parties, has for its primary object the final determination of the status of a person or thing, and which, therefore, is conclusive upon the world at large. Decisions of the former class are usually termed decisions *in personam*, or *inter partes*, while those of the latter are known as decisions *in rem*. It is obvious that these two forms of judicial decision involve different rules and considerations as to parties, and require separate examination. In this chapter it is proposed to deal with the first of the two classes—judicial decisions *inter partes*. In Chapter VIII consideration will be given to judicial decisions *in rem*.

225 A judicial decision *inter partes* operates as an estoppel, in favour of, and against, parties and privies only, not third persons or strangers.[1]

---

[1] See *Duchess of Kingston's Case* (1776), 2 Smith L.C. (13th Edn.) 644 (per DE GREY C.J., on behalf of the judges summoned to advise the House, at pp. 644–645); *Gray* v. *Lewis* (1873), 8 Ch. App. 1035 (per MELLISH L.J., at pp. 1059, 1060: "it unquestionably is not the general rule of law that a judgment obtained by A. against B. is conclusive in an action by B. against C. On the contrary, the rule of law is otherwise . . . a judgment *inter partes* is conclusive only between the parties and those claiming under them"); *R.* v. *Hutchings* (1881), 6 Q.B.D. 300, C.A. (per Lord SELBORNE L.C., who, at p. 304, speaks of "the principle on which the limitation of estoppel *per rem judicatam* depends, that *res inter alios acta alteri nocere non potest*").

An interesting decision which at first sight seems to support the view that a party to a decision *inter partes* may be estopped against one not a party to it is *Re Savoy Estate, Ltd., Remnant* v. *Savoy Estate, Ltd.*, [1949] 2 All E.R. 286; [1949] Ch. 622. R. sued the company for the possession of furniture allegedly lent by her: she set up her title to the furniture, alleging that it was a gift to her from F. The action failed because she could not prove her own title. F.'s executors then sued the company (collusively) for the furniture. The company set up that it belonged to R., but the Court of Appeal held it estopped from so doing. There are passages in the judgment of JENKINS L.J. indicating that this estoppel is based on *res judicata*; but it is here submitted that the case when properly construed is one of election.

Burden of proof of identity of party or privies

226 Since there can be no estoppel by *res judicata* unless the claim, defence, or other matter set up by the person sought to be estopped is in conflict with the *res judicata*, and since there can be no such conflict unless the parties, or their privies, in the one proceeding are the same as the parties, or their privies, in the other, where both proceedings are *in personam*, it follows that in all cases of this class the onus is on the person asserting the estoppel to establish identity of parties, or privies. Whenever this burden has not been discharged, in the case of any English civil decision *inter partes*, the estoppel has been negatived.[1] Any question of physical identity of persons is one of fact.[2]

227 The only parties to English criminal decisions are, where the offence is indictable, the Crown and the prisoner, and, where the offence is punishable summarily, the complainant and the respondent. It follows that a judgment of conviction or acquittal, though, as will be explained at a later stage, conclusive evidence *in rem* of the fact of conviction or acquittal, and also *prima facie* evidence *in rem* of the guilt or innocence of the accused, is not conclusive evidence of such guilt or innocence, except as between the Crown and the prisoner, or (as the case may be) the complainant and the respondent, in any subsequent proceedings, civil or criminal, unless the legislature has expressly provided otherwise, as it has in the case of certain classes of offence punishable summarily.

But this paragraph is perhaps to be read subject, as regards the plea of *autrefois acquit*, to the view expressed in a later part of the text[3] *viz.* that notwithstanding the strict rule as to identity of parties, this particular plea may possibly be available in some cases in which, though the prosecutor be different, it appears that the accused has been acquitted of the same offence.[4]

---

[1] Old cases are *Reed* v. *Jackson* (1801), 1 East 354; *Lady Wenman* v. *Mackenzie* (1855), 5 E. & B. 447 (per COLERIDGE J. at pp. 458–459). Later cases cited in the first edition are: *Mercantile Investment and General Trust, Co.* v. *River Plate Trust Loan and Agency Co.*, [1894] 1 Ch. 578 (per ROMER J. at p. 594); *Re Bowling and Welby's Contract*, [1895] 1 Ch. 663, C.A. per Lord HALSBURY L.C. at pp. 667–668, LINDLEY L.J. at pp. 671–672 and A. L. SMITH L.J. at p. 673; *Young* v. *Holloway*, [1895] P. 87 per JEUNE P. at pp. 89–90; *Re Lart, Wilkinson* v. *Blades*, [1896] 2 Ch. 788 (per CHITTY J. at pp. 794–795; *Anderson* v. *Collinson*, [1901] 2 K.B. 107, D.C. (per Lord ALVERSTONE C.J. at p. 109). To these may now be added; *Fernando* v. *Gunatillaka*, [1921] 2 A.C. 357, P.C. at p. 364; *Harper* v. *Dick, Kerr & Co.* (1921), 124 L.T. 438 per Lord STERNDALE M.R. at p. 439; *Ellerman Lines* v. *Read* (1927), 44 T.L.R. 7 (per MACKINNON J. at p. 8). *In Australia*, *O'Keefe* v. *Williams* (1907), 5 C.L.R. 217 (H. Ct. of Aus.) per GRIFFITH C.J. at p. 228. For a case in which the submission of an estoppel failed when based on a foreign judgment for lack of identity of parties see *Blohn* v. *Desser*, [1962] 2 Q.B. 116 at p. 124 (DIPLOCK J.).

[2] See *Russell* v. *Smyth* (1842), 9 M. & W. 810 (per Lord ABINGER C.B., at p. 818, and PARKE and ALDERSON BB., at p. 819). Here the personal identity was proved by "abundant evidence".

[3] See Chapter XI, para. 319, *post*.

[4] And see the New Zealand case *In Re a Medical Practitioner*, [1959] N.Z.L.R. 784, C.A. discussed in some detail in para. 233, *post*.

Foreign decisions

228 The rule as to parties and privies applies equally to all such foreign decisions as are not decisions *in rem.*[1]

Actions in personam: who are deemed parties

229 For the purposes of estoppel *per rem judicatam*, a "party", in proceedings *in personam*, means not only a person named as such, but also one who intervenes and takes part in the proceedings, after lawful citation, in whatever character he is cited to appear, or who, though not *nominatim* a party, insists on being made so, and obtains the leave of the court for that purpose.

There is a further rule, peculiar to the Probate jurisdiction, that he is also a "party" for the purposes of estoppel *per rem judicatam* who, being cognisant of proceedings, and of the fact that a party thereto is professing to act in his interests, allows the battle to be fought by that party, intending to take the benefit of his championship in the event of success.[2] This rule has its basis in the right of any person claiming an interest in the estate of a deceased person to intervene in Probate suits.

230 Among the reported decisions is an interesting judgment of DU PARCQ L.J. sitting as an additional judge of the King's Bench Division as to

---

[1] As in *Shedden* v. *A.-G.* (1860), 30 L.J. P.M. & A. 217 (per Sir CRESSWELL CRESSWELL, at pp. 229, 230); *Cammel* v. *Sewell* (1860), 5 H. & N. 728, Ex. Ch. (per COCKBURN C.J., at p. 741); *Simpson* v. *Fogo* (1863), 1 Hem. & M. 195 (per WOOD V.C., at p. 224); *Cox* v. *Dublin City Distillery Co.* (*No.* 2), [1915] 1 I.R. 345, cited in note 2 to para. 231, p. 202. The fact that the plaintiff was not a party to the earlier proceedings which were set up as giving rise to a *res judicata* was the true ground of the decision in *British Nylon Spinners, Ltd.* v. *Imperial Chemical Industries, Ltd.*, [1953] Ch. 19, C.A.—see the judgment of Sir RAYMOND EVERSHED M.R. at p. 25 and the decision of DANCKWERTS J. at the next stage of the proceedings at [1954] 3 All E.R. 88, pp. 91–92—"It is impossible for me to accept the conclusions of the United States Court as findings of fact binding in this action against the plaintiff company which was not a party to the American proceedings". See further the still more recent judgments in the House of Lords in *Carl-Zeiss-Stiftung* v. *Rayner and Keeler*, [1966] 2 All E.R. 536, H.L. in which their Lordships' refusal to allow an estoppel founded on proceedings in West Germany was grounded on a lack of identity between parties per Lord REID at p. 550, 556; per Lord HODSON at p. 561; per Lord GUEST at p. 566; per Lord UPJOHN at p. 572. Lord WILBERFORCE had no quarrel with the same principle, but at p. 586 dissented on the facts.

[2] See *In the Estate of Langton*, [1964] P. 163, C.A. per WILLMER L.J. at p. 169: "The principle relied on is that any interested person who is cognisant of the proceedings, and has the opportunity to intervene, is bound by the result and cannot be allowed to re-open the matter". So, too, DANCKWERTS L.J. at p. 175, and DIPLOCK L.J. at p. 178. Earlier cases, cited in the first edition of this work are *Emberley* v. *Trevanion* (1860), 4 Sw. & Tr. 197, at pp. 197, 198; *Collier* v. *Walters* (1873), L.R. 17 Eq. 252, at p. 268; *Wytcherley* v. *Andrews* (1871), L.R. 2 P. & D. 327, at 329; *Young* v. *Holloway*, [1895] P. 87, at pp. 89–90; *Re Lart, Wilkinson* v. *Blades*, [1896] 2 Ch. 788, at pp. 794–795; *Beardsley* v. *Beardsley*, [1899] 1 Q.B. 746, at p. 749; *Ritchie* v. *Malcolm*, [1902] 2 I.R. 403, at pp. 409–11; *Badar Bee* v. *Habib Merican Noordin*, [1909] A.C. 615, at p. 622. *Cf.*, as a modern authority, *Abuakwa* v. *Adanse*, [1957] 3 All E.R. 559 P.C., applying the dictum of Lord PENZANCE in *Wytcherley* v. *Andrews*, *supra*.

the effect of an order annulling bankruptcy as an estoppel against a creditor who had not proved in the bankruptcy, and therefore can hardly be regarded as an actual party to the bankruptcy proceedings.[1] A bankrupt persuaded one of his creditors not to prove in the bankruptcy, promising to pay the debt in full privately in due course. The bankruptcy having resulted in the payment in full of all the proved debts, an application was made to the court for an order annulling the adjudication, and an order was made accordingly. Subsequently, on the creditor claiming for his debt, a plea of estoppel was raised against him; and it was held that he was estopped by virtue of the order annulling the bankruptcy from contending that his debt, with all the other debts of the bankrupt, had not been paid. Du Parcq L.J. said:[2]

> "It is plain that the court will only make an order annulling an adjudication in bankruptcy under that head of the sub-section when it is clearly and conclusively proved that the debts have been paid in full. It is not sufficient now, though it was sufficient under the earlier law, that the creditors should all consent to the annulment of the adjudication. It is necessary to prove that the debts of the bankrupt have been paid in full. I look at that order, which of course is an order of the High Court of Justice, and find that it is recited there as the ground upon which the adjudication was annulled that it appeared to the court that all the debts of the debtor had been paid in full. If the plaintiff had come forward and said: 'There is owing to me a sum of £852. 15*s*.6*d*. or indeed any sum, then unless it was shown that he was wrong and his debt had been paid, and paid in full, the order of the court annulling the adjudication would never have been made. I think it is true to say that for the purposes of considering whether there is an estoppel one must treat the plaintiff here as having been a party, I do not say to the application to annul, but to the bankruptcy proceedings. His position was that he knew that a receiving order had been made. He knew that it was his duty under the Act, if he desired to claim that he was a creditor, to lodge a proof, and he must be taken to have known that, because he cannot urge ignorance of the law on his own behalf. He knew the result of the bankruptcy proceedings might be a receiving order and an adjudication, and further that if there were an adjudication there might subsequently be an annulment. It was open to him by proving to prevent any annulment of the receiving order on the ground that all debts had been paid, and I think that on the general principles of estoppel by record he is just as much estopped after that order of annulment from coming into another branch of the High Court of Justice and contending that after all a debt was due to him as if there had been a judgment to the opposite effect to that for which he now contends in this same Division of the High Court."

This may be regarded as an interesting example of a party being estopped in later proceedings because, though not an actual party to an earlier

[1] *John* v. *Mendoza*, [1939] 1 K.B. 141; du Parcq. J.
[2] At pp. 146–147.

proceeding, he was deemed to have been one. It is submitted with great respect, however, that the judgment goes too far, and that if the result of du Parcq J.'s decision can be justified on the facts, it must be on some ground other than estoppel by record. For, in the first place, how can it be said that the plaintiff in the second action was a "party" either to the adjudication proceedings or to the annulment proceedings? He chose to turn his back on both. His refusal to participate may have had some consequences properly flowing from the law of bankruptcy; but it is submitted that he cannot properly be deemed a party to either proceedings so as to estop him *per rem judicatam* on his later claim from contending that his debt had not been paid.

231 A judicial decision *inter partes* operates as an estoppel in favour of, or (as the case may be) so as to bind, the principal, or master, of any party who, by his direction, raises a question of title,[1] and, in the case of a "representative" or "test" action, all members of the class, whom a party purports to represent therein, or all persons who have given their consent (embodied in an order of the court) to be bound by the result thereof,[2] but not those who, though alleged to be so represented, insist and establish that they are not, and that such allegation is unfounded and fraudulent. And, where A. is jointly, and only jointly, liable with B., to

---

[1] In *Kinnersley* v. *Orpe* (1780), 2 Doug. K.B. 517, which was an action to recover a statutory penalty for taking fish from a fishery of which the plaintiff claimed to be the owner, the defendant being the servant of one Cotton, a rival claimant of the fishery, it was proved that the plaintiff had previously sued to judgment a servant of the same Cotton for trespass to the same fishery, whereupon C. at once gave notice to the plaintiff that he would raise the question again by directing another servant of his to fish, and the defendant by C.'s direction did so fish, which was the grievance complained of. At the trial, the plaintiff produced the record of the former judgment, which Perryn B. held to be conclusive evidence, on the ground that, though the two defendants were not the same, they were both acting as the servants, by the direction, and under the title, of the same master or principal. It is conceived that this ruling was correct. It is true that the Court of K.B. granted a new trial, one of the two grounds being (per Buller J., at p. 517) "that the record in the former case, though admissible evidence, was not conclusive", but this expression of opinion, not being the only ground, and, therefore, not necessary to the decision, is not authoritative, and, it is submitted, is contrary to principle, and wrong.

[2] As in *Cox* v. *Dublin City Distillery Co.* (*No.* 3), [1917] 1 I.R. 203, where the class of second-debenture holders in the company, whom certain of them were by order of the court appointed to represent, were held to be estopped by a former decision in *Dublin City Distillery, Ltd.* v. *Doherty*, [1914] A.C. 823, H.L., from disputing that D. was entitled to a lien on the second debentures, this class having been represented in the previous litigation by the trustee of the deed securing the debentures (per O'Brien L.C. (Ir.), at pp. 322–324, and Ronan L.J., at pp. 234–236), and it being proved that the trustee, though he had put in no defence, and judgment had been given against him for default of pleading, had nevertheless requested the liquidator to appeal to the House of Lords, and fight the second debenture holders' battle (per O'Brien L.C., at p. 218). With this case should be contrasted *Cox* v. *Dublin City Distillery Co.* (*No.* 2), [1915] 1 Ir.R. 345, in which it was held that certain persons claiming the benefit of the estoppel created in favour of Doherty by the above decision of the House of Lords were not entitled thereto, not being parties to the former action, which so far as the plaintiff therein was concerned, did not purport to be either a test, or a "representative", action (per Cherry L.J., at pp. 366, 367, Palles C.B., at pp. 372, 373, and Molony L.J., at pp. 377, 378).

X., and X. has unsuccessfully sued A. alone, the former judgment in favour of A. operates for the benefit of B. also, if,—and the burden of establishing this is on B.,—the judgment proceeded on some ground common to A. and B., and not upon some ground purely personal to A., such as infancy, bankruptcy, or the like.[1]

232 A party who, though identical in name, litigates in different characters in the two proceedings, is, in contemplation of law, and in the correct sense of the civilians, two separate and distinct *personae*;[2] so that a decision for, or against, a man who appears in a representative character, is not conclusive in favour of, or (as the case may be) against, the same man appearing in subsequent proceedings as an individual, or in a different representative character.[3] But where in a Probate suit a person is deemed a

---

[1] *Phillips* v. *Ward* (1863), 2 H. & C. 717, where, to an action on an attorney's bill of costs, the defendant pleaded, by way of estoppel, that the work was done on the joint retainer of himself and one B., and that the defendant had previously sued B. unsuccessfully for the same causes of action, without alleging that B. had recovered judgment on a ground common to both of the then defendants, and the plea was held bad on demurrer, the court, however, distinctly recognizing that if the above averment had been made, the estoppel would have been well pleaded (per POLLOCK C.B., at p. 720, BRAMWELL B., at pp. 720, 721, and CHANNELL B., at p. 721).

[2] See Appendix B, *post*.

[3] *Bainbrigge* v. *Baddeley* (1847), 2 Ph. 705 (parties in the two suits litigating in different characters: per Lord COTTENHAM L.C., at pp. 709, 710); *Overton* v. *Harvey* (1850) 9 C.B. 324 (where, at p. 336, to a question was put, *arguendo*, by counsel,—"suppose a first action brought by a person as executor, but it turned out that he now claimed by letters of administration?", and CRESSWELL J. replied, —"in that case he would be a different person"); *Blake* v. *O'Kelly* (1874), 9 Ir.R. Eq. 54 (the case of a defendant sued as an accounting party in the former proceedings, and judgment against him in that character, whereas in the second action he was sued as a fraudulent donee: per CHATTERTON V.-C. (Ir.), at pp. 57, 58); *Leggott* v. *Great Northern Rail Co.* (1876), 1 Q.B.D. 599, where the plaintiff sued as administratrix of her deceased husband, to recover damages for personal injuries caused to the deceased, *during his lifetime*, by the defendant's negligence, whereby his estate had been diminished, and it was held that the defendants were not estopped from disputing the alleged negligence by a judgment recovered against them by the same person for compensation for the loss occasioned to her by the death of her husband under Lord Campbell's Act, because she was then litigating in a totally different right and capacity (per MELLOR J., at pp. 604, 605, and QUAIN J., at pp. 606, 607); *Poulton* v. *Adjustable Cover and Boiler Block Co.*, [1908] 2 Ch. 430, C.A. (one against whom, as an individual, judgment had been given in an action for infringement of a patent, held to be litigating in a different capacity when afterwards applying for a revocation of the patent, as a member of, and representing, the public: per BUCKLEY L.J., at p. 440); *Manton* v. *Cantwell*, [1920] A.C. 781, H.L., where Lord BIRKENHEAD L.C., at p. 788, and Lord FINLAY, at p. 791, expressed an opinion, though it was not necessary to the decision, that a widow of an alleged workman injured by an accident resulting in his death, who claimed compensation for herself and children, as "dependants", under the Workmen's Compensation Act 1906, was not entitled to insist that the employer was estopped from asserting that the deceased was not a workman by a previous order, or an agreement taking effect as an order, made under the statute on the application of the deceased during his lifetime, whereby the employer admitted his liability to pay him the agreed weekly payments during his incapacity, because the widow was applying for compensation in an independent statutory character and right, wholly distinct from that of a personal representative of the deceased at common law; *Marginson* v. *Blackburn Borough Council*, [1939] 1 All E.R. 273; [1939] 2 K.B. 426, C.A. In this case a car belonging to M. in which he was being driven by his wife collided with a bus driven by an employee of the Corporation. As a result of the accident M.'s wife was killed, he was injured, both vehicles were damaged, and two houses belonging to third

party to earlier proceedings by the application of the rule adopted in the Probate jurisdiction (whereby he who has stood by, having the opportunity to intervene, and has not done so, is deemed a party)[1] it does not matter whether in the second proceedings he appears in a different capacity; if, having the opportunity to intervene in the first proceedings, he has stood by and refrained from joining in them, he will later be bound by the result in all the capacities which he was capable of assuming on the earlier occasion.[2]

Conversely, two persons distinct in name, but substantially identical in title and interest, constitute in law one and the same party for the purposes of estoppel by *res judicata*, as for all others.[3]

233 In an interesting case before the Court of Appeal of New Zealand[4] an application for Certiorari had been made in respect of proceedings taken in the name of the Solicitor-General for New Zealand (pursuant to an express statutory provision in this regard) before the New Zealand Medical Council, a statutory body, for the removal of the name of the respondent from the roll of medical practitioners on the ground of conduct infamous in a professional respect. It was common ground that, on being prosecuted on indictment on a charge of indecent assault in respect of identically the same conduct as was now alleged, the practitioner had been found not guilty by a jury, and had been acquitted. It was sought in the second proceedings to set up an issue estoppel by which the Solicitor-General would be precluded from advancing against the practitioner the same conduct, and the same charge, as those in respect of which he had been acquitted. In answer to this submission it was contended *inter alia* that the parties to the two proceedings were not the same. This argument was accepted by the Court of Appeal of New Zealand; though the first prosecution was

---

parties were damaged. The householders sued both M. and the Corporation in the county court in respect of their damage, alleging that each was responsible for the negligence of the driver of his vehicle. M. and the Corporation exchanged contribution notices, and the Corporation also sought to recover from M., under a third party notice, the damage sustained by its bus. The county court each held that each driver was equally blameworthy. In a subsequent action M. sued the Corporation for (a) personal injury and damage to his car (b) (as administrator of his wife) for damages for her loss of expectation of life and (c) (again as such administrator) for compensation under the Fatal Accidents Act. *Held* by the Court of Appeal (the Contributory Negligence Act not yet being enacted) that the finding of the county court judge that the drivers were equally blameworthy precluded M. from proceeding on his first claim; but that the second and third claims, being made by him in a different capacity (as administrator of his wife's estate) were unaffected by estoppel.

1 See para. 229, *supra*.

2 *In the Estate of Langton*, [1964] P. 163, C.A., approving in this regard *Beardsley* v. *Beardsley*, [1899] 1 Q.B. 746.

3 See *Aslin* v. *Parkin* (1758), 2 Burr. 665 (per Lord MANSFIELD C.J., at p. 668); *Ex parte Harper, Re Bremner* (1875), 10 Ch. App. 379 (per JAMES L.J., at p. 381).

4 *In Re a Medical Practitioner*, [1959] N.Z.L.R. 784, C.A.

brought in the name of the Crown, and the second in the name of Her Majesty's Solicitor-General, there was not in the circumstances the identity of parties[1] necessary to found an estoppel. NORTH and CLEARY JJ., in giving their joint judgment said:[2]

> "In our opinion, neither the object of s. 43c(6) nor the nature of the duty thereby imposed on the Solicitor-General fairly warrants a conclusion that, in carrying out that duty, the Solicitor-General is serving a Crown purpose and thereby representing the Crown so as to make proceedings before the Council Crown proceedings. The object was to ensure that a responsible and independent person would put the proceedings in motion before the Council, and so obviate criticism of the kind made in the courts before the Act was amended in 1957 that the tribunal set up to inquire into the conduct of a practitioner should not take any part in the preferment of the charge which it was to hear. The making and presentation of a charge before the domestic tribunal possessing disciplinary powers is not to be assimilated to the prosecution of offences against the public, which is plainly a Crown function. The preferment of such a charge might equally well have been entrusted to some other person who was not a Crown servant at all. The nature of the duty requires that the Solicitor-General act merely in a ministerial capacity to take the action recommended by the Committee, with no independent discretion allowed to him in the initiation or continuance of that action. In any later proceedings that may be taken by way of application to the court, it is clear that the party is the Council and not the Crown. These features distinguish the duty of the Solicitor-General under this statute from the position of the Law Officers of the Crown in Crown proceedings, where the Crown decides whether the proceedings will be instituted and may at any stage put an end to them. This is so also in the case of proceedings *ex relatione*, and, even in the case of criminal proceedings, the Crown may stay them. In the present case, the duty of the Solicitor-General is not associated with any interest of a Government Department or with the advancement of protection of a Crown function. In view of this, and having regard to the purpose of the Medical Practitioners Amendment Act 1957 and the limited and transitory duty thereby imposed on the Solicitor-General, we think this is one of the somewhat rare cases where a statutory duty has been imposed upon a Crown servant otherwise than for a Crown purpose.
>
> Mr Cooke also advanced an argument that, on the facts of this particular case, the complaint was in fact instigated by a Crown Solicitor and could for this reason be described as a Crown proceeding. We do not think it necessary to say more on this point than that there is no finding to this effect in the judgment appealed from, and we do not think there is evidence from which this Court should or could infer that the complaint was so instigated.
>
> We therefore think that the appeal must be allowed with costs as proposed by the President."

---

[1] Per GRESSON P. at p. 806; per NORTH and CLEARY JJ. at pp. 817–818.

[2] At pp. 819–820.

Departments of State

234 No attention was given in the first edition of this work to the position of the great departments of Government as liable to estoppel by *res judicata*; but the topic has become one of interest, and is bound in due course to give rise to litigation of importance. Is the Attorney-General, for instance, when joined in litigation pursuant to the provisions of one statute, bound by a decision previously given against him in other litigation at the suit of the same parties, pursuant to another? And if so, will this estoppel enure against other Departments of State—*e.g.* against those who collect income tax? This question was posed by UPJOHN J. in *Vernon* v. *Inland Revenue Commissioners*[1] on an appeal from a decision of the Special Commissioners of Income Tax affirming an assessment of the Commissioners of Inland Revenue refusing exemption from income tax on the ground that the trusts upon which the income was received were not charitable. It was attempted by the trustees to submit that the Commissioners were estopped by reason of the fact that on two earlier applications to the court, to both of which the Attorney-General was party, it had been decided (a) on the first application, that the capital should be settled on certain charitable trusts and (b) on the later application, that a scheme submitted as carrying out the charitable trusts should be approved. UPJOHN J. pointed out that before the plea could succeed it would be necessary to hold (a) that the Attorney-General was estopped from denying that the scheme ultimately sanctioned was one for a charitable trust and (b) that this estoppel bound not only the Attorney-General, but the Commissioners as well. The matter was decided (against the submission of estoppel) on the first point, and the decision is not helpful as to how far, if at all, one Department of State may be estopped by a decision given against another, except as an illustration of the way in which the question may arise.

It is submitted that with the passing of time the development of the activities of the Departments of State will make it increasingly necessary to use circumspection in holding that one Department of State is bound by any estoppel which may validly arise against another, and that it may be too much of a generalisation to submit that in such circumstances "the Crown" is estopped by the previous judgment.

Suretyship and indemnity

235 Where one recovers judgment against another, who thereupon sues a third person for indemnity or contribution under a contract of suretyship or other contract whereby such third person has agreed to in-

[1] [1956] 3 All E.R. 14.

demnify the judgment debtor, the judgment cannot, merely by reason of such contract of suretyship or indemnity, be set up as binding upon the third person, he being neither a party, nor a privy, to the judgment.[1] It is true that, in a case of this kind, it has been laid down that "if a demand be made which the person indemnifying is bound to pay, and notice be given to him, and he refuse to defend the action, in consequence of which the person indemnified is obliged to pay the demand, that is equivalent to a judgment, and estops the other party from saying that the defendant in the first action was not bound to pay the money":[2] but, on a careful examination of the terms in which the above ruling is expressed,—a ruling which has been approved in later authorities[3]— it is clear that it was not intended to suggest that this type of case raises any question of estoppel *per rem judicatam* at all, the "estoppel" there referred to being an election (implied from conduct and inaction) by the indemnifying party that he was content to treat the judgment in the first action as binding upon himself, though in fact and law, he not being a party thereto, it was not so.

Natural and artificial persons

236 "Person", for the purposes of the rules now under discussion, means an artificial, as well as a natural, person. It therefore comprises corporations, whether aggregate,[4] or sole, such as the Crown, which can take advantage of, and is bound by, any estoppel *per rem judicatam*, as much as any of the Queen's subjects.[5]

Criminal proceedings: Divorce

237 It is to be observed here that, in the case of an indictment, the Crown is the only "actor", whoever may be the person on whose prosecution it indicts, and, therefore, that the identity or non-identity of the

---

[1] *Pritchard* v. *Hitchcock* (1843), 6 Man. & G. 151, a case of a guarantee of a bill of exchange (per TINDAL C.J., at p. 167, COLTMAN J., at p. 168, and MAULE J., at pp. 168, 169); *King* v. *Norman* (1847), 4 C.B. 884, a case of a guarantee of credit and fidelity (*per Cur.*, at p. 898); *Gray* v. *Lewis*, *Parker* v. *Lewis* (1873), 8 Ch. App. 1035, a case of implied contract of indemnity (per MELLISH L.J., at pp. 1059, 1060).

[2] Per BULLER J., at p. 377 of *Duffield* v. *Scott* (1789), 3 Term Rep. 374.

[3] Notably by PARKE J., at pp. 408, 409 of *Smith* v. *Compton* (1832), 3 B. & Ad. 407, and again, when PARKE B., at p. 501 of *Jones* v. *Williams* (1841), 7 M. & W. 493.

[4] See several of the cases cited in the notes to this Chapter. Unincorporated public bodies, such as overseers of the poor, and the like, sometimes called "quasi-corporations", may also be deemed parties, or at least privies: see the cases cited in note 5, p. 209, *post*.

[5] See *A.-G. for Trinidad* v. *Eriché*, [1893] A.C. 518, P.C.; and see the separate chapters in this work on *autrefois acquit* and *autrefois convict*. Interesting questions as to identity of parties sometimes arise in cases where the Crown is made a party to one suit, and some Law Officer of the Crown (*e.g.* the Att.-Gen. or the Solr.-Gen.) is a party to the other. For illustrations see paras. 226 and 227, *ante*.

named prosecutors in the two proceedings is wholly immaterial.[1] Similarly, in matrimonial causes, if the spouses between whom a marriage is sought to be dissolved are the same in the two suits, it is immaterial that the question of the petitioner's adultery or misconduct is raised by the co-respondent in one of them, and by the Queen's Proctor in the other.[2]

Infants

238 An infant, by his next friend or other proper representative, can take the benefit, and must bear the burden, of an estoppel,[3] and if he has sued, or has been sued, by his next friend in the former proceedings, and, in the subsequent proceedings, having in the meantime attained his majority, he appears as a person *sui juris*, he is still the same party.[4]

Plaintiff or defendant

239 It makes no difference, where identity of parties is established, that in the proceedings resulting in the decision set up as *res judicata*, the party was a plaintiff, claimant, or petitioner, and, in the subsequent proceedings, is attempting to controvert the decision by way of cross-bill, counterclaim, set-off, "responsive allegation" (in divorce suits), or any other form of cross-claim or affirmative defence, or *vice versa*.[5]

---

1 *Petrie* v. *Nuttall* (1856), 11 Exch. 569, an action for trespass to land, to which the defendant pleaded that the land was a public highway, and, further, by rejoinder, that the plaintiff was estopped from asserting the contrary by a previous verdict and judgment of conviction against him on an indictment for obstructing such highway. The plea of estoppel was held bad on demurrer, per ALDERSON B., at pp. 575, 576: "it is essential to an estoppel that it be mutual, so that the same parties and privies may both be bound and take advantage of it. *The Crown and subject were the parties to the indictment*, and, therefore, it was not between the two parties to this action". It appears from p. 571 that identity of the parties was attempted to be established by an averment in the rejoinder that "the defendant was one of the prosecutors of the indictment", —a contention which was disposed of by the above observation of ALDERSON B.

2 *Conradi* v. *Conradi* (1868), L.R. 1 P. & D. 514 (per Lord PENZANCE, at p. 521: "I am not . . . pressed by the argument that the adultery in the former suit was alleged by the co-respondent who is no party to this suit, whereas in this suit it is alleged by the Queen's Proctor, for, by whomsoever the petitioner's adultery was alleged in the former suit, that adultery was declared and adjudged to have been proved in a decree pronounced between the very parties who, so far as the question of divorce is concerned, are the sole parties to this suit").

3 See *Gregory* v. *Molesworth* (1747), 3 Atk. 626 (per Lord HARDWICKE L.C., at p. 627); *Don* v. *Lippmann* (1837), 5 Cl. & Fin. 1 (infant by his "tutor" in Scottish action); *Shedden* v. *Patrick* (1854), 1 Macq. 535, H.L. (infant by factor *loco tutoris* appointed by the Scottish court); *Vaughton* v. *Bradshaw* (1860), 9 C.B. N.S. 103 (infant by his father as next friend).

4 *Venkata Narasimha Appa Row* v. *Court of Wards* (1886), 11 App. Cas. 660, P.C.

5 As in *Kinsey* v. *Kinsey* (1754), 2 Ves. Sen. 577; *Eastmure* v. *Laws* (1839), 5 Bing. N.C. 444; *Geils* v. *Geils* (1852), 1 Macq. 36, 255, H.L.; *Webster* v. *Armstrong* (1885), 54 L.J. Q.B. 236. In *Marginson* v. *Blackburn Borough Council*, [1939] 1 All E.R. 273; [1939] 2 K.B. 426 (a running-down case) the parties had been co-defendants in the earlier action, in which their respective responsibilities for the accident were assessed by the county court on a third party notice issued by one defendant against the other; but this finding of the county court was sufficient to preclude the plaintiff in the later action from proceeding on a claim for damages for personal injury which had not been the subject of any claim in the earlier litigation.

Persons affected who are not parties

240 It may happen that one who is not a party to a suit at all may in the event find his rights determined, or limited at least to some extent, by the result of litigation between other parties. But this is not the result of estoppel; it is merely a consequence of his being compelled in circumstances of the particular case to take matters as he finds them. So (*in Australia*) where as between parties of whom the Commissioner of Taxation was not one, the Court had determined the rights of ownership to property of certain beneficiaries with the result that in law they were not entitled to specified exemptions from taxation (though this point did not arise in the litigation) it was held in later proceedings between some of the parties and the Commissioner (a) that no question of estoppel arose against these parties in favour of the Commissioner when he assessed them on the basis indicated by the judgment, since he was not a party to these first proceedings (b) but nevertheless the Commissioner was bound in law to assess the taxpayers in relation to their rights as they actually existed; and that these rights had in the event been determined by the previous judgment.[1]

Who are deemed privies

241 Estoppel *per rem judicatam* operates for, or against, not only the parties, but also those who are privy to them in blood, title, or interest.[2]

242 There is a dearth of authority as to who are privies so as to be bound by a *res judicata*.[3] Privies include any person who succeeds to the rights or liabilities of the party upon his death[4] or insolvency[5] or who is otherwise identified with his or her estate or interest;[6] but it is essential that he who is later to be held estopped must have had some kind of interest

---

1 *Executor Trustee and Agency Co. of South Australia* v. *Deputy Federal Commissioner of Taxes* (1939), 62 C.L.R. 545 (High Ct. of Aus.) per LATHAM C.J. at pp. 562–3; per DIXON J. at p. 570.

2 Per Lord REID in *Carl-Zeiss-Stiftung* v. *Rayner and Keeler, Ltd.* (No. 2), [1966] 2 All E.R. 536, H.L. at p. 550. The text of this paragraph, as it appeared in the first edition of this work, is noticed with apparent approval by Lord GUEST in the same case at p. 566 where he says: "Privies have been described as those who are privy to the party in estate or interest (*Spencer Bower* at p. 130). Before a person can be privy to a party there must be community or privity of interest between them".

3 Per Lord GUEST in *Carl-Zeiss-Stiftung* v. *Rayner and Keeler, Ltd.* (*supra*) at p. 566.

4 Instances of liability of representatives of deceased to the estoppel are:—*Douglas* v. *Forrest* (1828), 4 Bing. 686 (executors); *Don* v. *Lippmann* (1837), 5 Cl. & Fin. 1 (personal representative in Scottish action); *Holland* v. *Clark* (1842), 1 Y. & C. Ch. Cas. 151 (administrator); *Reimers* v. *Druce* (1857), 26 L.J. Ch. 196 (executors); *Ennis* v. *Rochford* (1884), 14 L.R. Ir. 285 (executors). In the following, the representative of the deceased took the benefit of the estoppel: *Bouchier* v. *Taylor* (1776), 4 Bro. Parl Cas. 708 (residuary legatee); *Whittaker* v. *Jackson* (1864), 2 H. & C. 296 (devisee).

5 *Douglas* v. *Forrest, supra* (assignees entitled to the benefit of the estoppel); *Re South American and Mexican Co., Ex parte Bank of England*, [1895] 1 Ch. 37, C.A. (liquidator of company liable to the estoppel).

6 The following were cases of liability to the estoppel: *R.* v. *Blakemore* (1852), 21 L.J. M.C. 60 (privy in estate); *Re Allsop and Joy's Contract* (1889), 61 L.T. 213 (successor in title); *A.-G. for*

in the previous litigation or its subject matter.[1] A person may be a privy who, though not a party, has given faith to the decision as a *res judicata*, and has acted thereon in the litigation, as for instance an incumbrancer who has obtained stop orders on the fund which is the subject of the decision.[2]

And it has been suggested[3] that the doctrine may be extended so as to include the case where a party against whom a previous decision has been pronounced may employ a servant or agent or engage a third party to do something which infringes the right established in the earlier litigation, thus raising the whole matter again in his interest; it would be unjust to allow the successful party so to be vexed by relitigating the original question by means of the device of putting forward a third party.

It is not enough to found an estoppel that a relationship such as that of principal and agent should exist as between the party to the earlier action and him whom it is sought to estop in the later, if this relationship is not such as to require recognition by the person whom it is sought to estop; the relationship must be such as to have validity *vis-à-vis* the party to be estopped in the later action. So in *Pople* v. *Evans*[4] where C. was the undisclosed agent of P. in entering into an agreement for sale and purchase, and, still without disclosing this relationship, sought against E. an order for specific performance, and failed, this did not estop P. from seeking an order in a later action; for though as between P. and C. the relationship was that of principal and agent, this was not such a relationship as was capable of recognition by E.,[5] and hence was not such a relationship as could found privity for the purpose of *res judicata*.

Where privity of estate is set up as the foundation of estoppel *per rem judicatam*, the title relied on to establish such privity must have arisen after the judgment on which the *res judicata* is based, or at least after the commencement of the proceedings in the course of which that judgment was given.[6]

Trinidad v. *Eriché*, [1893] A.C. 518, P.C. (identical in title and interest); *North Eastern Rail. Co.* v. *Dalton Overseers*, [1898] 2 Q.B. 66, D.C. (successors of highway authority); *O'Connor* v. *O'Connor*, [1916] 2 I. R. 148 (successor in title to land); *Jones* v. *Lewis*, [1919] 1 K.B. 328, C.A. (overseers of poor for the time being liable to the same estoppel as their predecessors, but here it was held that nobody was estopped: per BANKES L.J., at p. 345). For cases where the benefit of the estoppel was taken by the privy, see *Re Allsop and Joy's Contract*, *supra* (successors in title on both sides); *O'Connor* v. *O'Connor*, *supra* (undertenant).

[1] Per Lord REID in *Carl-Zeiss-Stiftung* v. *Rayner and Keeler, Ltd.*, [1966] 2 All E.R. 536 H.L., at p. 550.

[2] *Re Eyton, Bartlett* v. *Charles* (1890), 45 Ch.D. 458 (per CHITTY J., at pp. 460–2).

[3] Per Lord REID in *Carl-Zeiss-Stiftung* v. *Rayner and Keeler, Ltd.* (*supra*) at p. 550.

[4] *Pople* v. *Evans*, [1968] 2 All E.R. 743 (UNGOED-THOMAS J.).

[5] For it had not been disclosed at the essential time, and this non-disclosure itself gave rise to special rights against P. or C., on the part of E., at the election of the latter—*Allan* v. *F. O'Hearn & Co.*, [1937] A.C. 213.

[6] *Pople* v. *Evans* (*supra*) at p. 746.

It is an essential of privity of *interest* that the privy must claim under or through the person of whom he is said to be a privy. So it was held in a recent decision of the High Court of Australia that a judgment in favour of the driver of a car on a negligence claim in which contributory negligence had been alleged against him as a plaintiff was not available to his notional employer so as to found an estoppel in the employer's favour on the same issue against him who had been defendant in the first action; for the employer had no interest in the first action, nor did he in any sense claim under or through the employee in the second.[1]

243 The following are illustrative cases in which persons, admittedly not parties, have been held not to be privies either, but strangers to the estoppel. A landlord is not deemed a privy of a tenant who instituted the former proceedings without his direction or sanction, and cannot take the benefit of a judgment recovered therein by such tenant for injury to his reversionary interest.[2] Where an order has been made fixing a fair rent, as between tenant and landlord only, under the Land Law (Ireland) Act 1881, a mortgagee of the land, who has not adopted the tenancy, is not bound by the order as a privy of the landlord.[3] Children, not claiming through or under their mother in her character as administratrix of their deceased father, but solely as next of kin to certain renouncing next of kin, are not privies of the deceased, and cannot set up as an estoppel in their favour any judgment obtained by their mother in that character in an administration suit.[4] A person who has merely given financial assistance to a party does not thereby become his privy,[5] nor is a purchaser of land the subject of litigation, where the land itself is not bound by the judgment, deemed a privy of any party to such litigation and judgment.[6]

Identical question differently answered as between different parties

244 Generally the same question does not arise in two sets of proceedings which are not between the same parties; as will be seen in another chapter, the questions whether A. was negligent in the same highway

---

[1] *Ramsay* v. *Pigram* (1968), 42 A.L.J.R. 89 per Sir GARFIELD BARWICK, C.J. and WINDEYER J. At the time of going to press the case had not yet been reported in the Commonwealth Law Reports.

[2] *Lady Wenman* v. *Mackenzie* (1855), 5 El. & Bl. 447 (per COLERIDGE J., delivering the judgment of the court, at pp. 458, 459).

[3] *Clarke* v. *Hall* (1888), 24 L.R. Ir. 316, per Lord ASHBOURNE L.C. (Ir.), at p. 319, and FITZGIBBON L.J. (Ir.), at p. 320).

[4] *Spencer* v. *Williams* (1871), L.R. 2 P. & D. 230 (per Lord PENZANCE, at pp. 236, 237).

[5] See *Mercantile Investment and General Trust Co.* v. *River Plate Trust Loan and Agency Co.*, [1894] 1 Ch. 578 (per ROMER J., at pp. 594, 595).

[6] *Re Bowling and Welby's Contract*, [1895] 1 Ch. 663, C.A. (per Lord HALSBURY L.C., at pp. 667, 668, LINDLEY L.J., at pp. 671, 672, and A. L. SMITH L.J., at p. 673).

accident quoad X. and quoad Y., while very similar, are not necessarily *identical* questions. But there may be a type of question which when asked of one litigant as regards A. is identical with the same question asked of him as regards B. An example is the construction of a document or a statute as it affects (say) trustees and a beneficiary A., and of the same passage in the same document or statute affecting the same trustees as against beneficiary B., where A. and B. are mentioned in the document or statute, not by name, but as members of a class between whom no distinction is made. It would seem here that an interpretation of a document or statute contained in a judgment to which A., and not B., is a party, will not bind B., who may thereafter, in other proceedings, contend for a different and more favourable construction as regards himself.[1]

---

[1] And he may succeed: *In re Waring*; *Westminster Bank* v. *Burton-Butler*, [1948] Ch. 221 (JENKINS J.), where the facts were as stated in the text.

CHAPTER VIII

Parties: II— *Judicial Decisions in Rem*

245 A judicial decision *in rem* is one which declares, defines, or otherwise determines the status of a person, or of a thing, that is to say, the jural relation of the person, or thing, to the world generally,[1] and therefore is conclusive for, or against, everybody, as distinct from those decisions which purport to determine the jural relation of the parties only to one another, and their personal rights and equities *inter se*, and which, therefore, are commonly termed decisions *in personam*.

246 Neither of the above expressions, adapted from the formulary terminology of Roman jurisprudence, and the distinction there drawn between a *jus in rem*, and a *jus in personam*,[2] is very happily chosen. "In rem" is obviously inappropriate in its strict literal sense of "against a thing",[3] and, if we understand the phrase as meaning—"directed to, or operating upon, a subject-matter", it is unfortunate that *res* in this sense must be made to include *persona*, the antitheton of *res* in its physical meaning. It would, perhaps, have conduced to clearness, though the old terminology is so firmly established as to render any attempt to alter it now somewhat pedantic, if decisions *in rem*, and *in personam*, had been respectively named decisions *inter omnes*, and *inter partes*—the latter expression has, indeed, been occasionally used by high judicial authorities[4]—from the beginning.

---

[1] *Minna Craig Steamship Co.* v. *Chartered Mercantile Bank of India, London and China*, [1897] 1 Q.B. 460, C.A.

[2] See Appendix B, *post*.

[3] The only instances of a judgment strictly *against* a thing in any system of jurisprudence are the ancient Athenian and Roman sentences of outlawry against the instrument by which a crime had been committed, and its expulsion beyond the border, or the Jewish committal of the scapegoat to the wilderness, if such an order can be described as a judicial decision at all.

[4] For instance, in *Katama Natchier* v. *Rajah of Shivagunga* (1863), 9 Moo. Ind. App. 543 (at p. 601); *Castrique* v. *Imrie* (1870), L.R. 4 H.L. 414 (per BLACKBURN J., at p. 435); *Gray* v.

247 Since a decision *in rem* estops anyone in the world from disputing it, and enables anyone in the world to take advantage of it, it follows that a person relying upon a decision of this kind as a *res judicata* is not concerned with any question of identity of parties or privies. Or, to put it another way, if there is any onus upon him of establishing such identity, he discharges it by showing that the decision is *in rem*, for the whole world is a party to every such decision.[1] It is scarcely necessary to add that, in order to make out an estoppel *in rem*, all the other conditions of a valid estoppel *per rem judicatam* of any kind must be satisfied, for, as will be seen hereafter,[2] decisions *in rem* occupy in other respects no privileged position over other judicial decisions.

248 "The world",—a rather loose expression,—whom a decision *in rem* is said to affect, means, in the case of an English decision, all persons subject to the jurisdiction of the English courts, and in certain cases of a criminal complexion, all Her Majesty's subjects:[3] in the case of a foreign decision, it means the subjects of all civilised states. It has been said[4] that where the decision determines matrimonial status, "the world" will include the subjects of the states of Christendom only; but this is perhaps an outmoded statement of principle, and the reader is referred to such discussion of this topic as will be found in Chapter XII, *post*.

249 It would appear impossible in principle to obtain a judgment *in rem* by consent of the parties before the court; for not only they but the world will be bound if a valid judgment *in rem* is pronounced. The better view would appear to be that a judgment on a matter which would, if propertly litigated, result in a judgment *in rem*, will have force only *inter partes* if the processes of the law are short-circuited and judgment purports to be given by consent.[5]

250 It is proposed to consider separately, in the following order: (1) English decisions which determine the status of a person; (2) the like foreign decisions; (3) English decisions which determine the status of a thing, and (4) the like foreign decisions.

Lewis, *Parker* v. *Lewis* (1873), 8 Ch. App. 1035 (per MELLISH L.J., at p. 1060); *R.* v. *Hutchings* (1881), 6 Q.B.D. 300, C.A. (per Lord SELBORNE L.C., at p. 304); *Re Allsop and Joy's Contract* (1889), 61 L.T. 213 (per CHITTY J., at p. 215).

[1] As was said in terms by Lord MANSFIELD C.J., with reference to one class of *in rem* decisions, in *Bernardi* v. *Motteux* (1781), 2 Doug. K.B. 575 (at p. 580: "all the world are parties to a sentence of a court of admiralty").

[2] See para. 273, note 1, *post*, p. 229.

[3] *Castrique* v. *Imrie* (1870), L.R. 4 H.L. 414. But on this topic see paras. 265 *et seq. post*.

[4] *E.g.* in the first edition of this work at p. 133.

[5] See *Ritchie* v. *Malcolm*, [1902] 2 I. R. 403. *Cf. Jenkins* v. *Robertson*, (1867), 1 Sc. & Div. 117, H.L.

English decisions which determine the status of a person

251 The status of a person, capable of determination by an English judicial decision *in rem*, includes his domestic, matrimonial, corporate, professional, financial, parliamentary, official, or other civic rights or position *vis-à-vis* the world in general, as illustrated in the ensuing paragraphs.

252 An English criminal decision is conclusive *in rem* as to the *fact of the conviction, or of the acquittal*, as the case may be; for it determines whether the status of the accused is that of a convict, or not: but, as will be shewn hereafter,[1] it is not conclusive *in rem* to any further extent.

253 A decision, on the return to a writ of *habeas corpus*, that there is no legal ground or justification for the arrest or detention of the applicant, and an order that he be discharged from custody, is a determination of the applicant's right to his liberty, and of the legality of his discharge, which is conclusive upon all subjects of the Queen,[2] both at common law, and under the provisions of the Habeas Corpus Act 1679 (31 Car. 2, c. 2), which declares and confirms the common law.[3] It was for long considered, on the other hand, that a refusal to grant the writ effected no estoppel of any kind, and that after refusal by one court to grant the writ the applicant could renew his application in another court.[4] This anomalous position has now been rectified by statute, and the refusal of an application for a writ of *habeas corpus*, though perhaps not efficacious *in rem*, has much the same consequences as regards the applicant as the refusal of any other type of application.[5]

254 Sentences, decrees, and judgments, in matrimonial causes and matters, pronounced in this country by a tribunal of competent jurisdiction, as to the existence and validity,[6] or as to the nullity or dissolution,[7] of a marriage, are decisions which determine the domestic status of the spouses, or alleged spouses, and are, therefore, conclusive *in rem*. This is so, even if the judgment or decree does not contain any specific determination of matrimonial status, if a determination of matrimonial status was

---

[1] In paras. 265 *et seq.*, *post.*

[2] *Cox* v. *Hakes* (1890), 15 App. Cas. 506, H.L. (per Lord HALSBURY L.C., at p. 514). See further, *Secretary of State* v. *O'Brien*, [1923] A.C. 603, H.L. But since 1960 an appeal has lain from a Divisional Court to the House of Lords against the issue of a writ of *habeas corpus* even in a criminal matter: Administration of Justice Act (1960) s. 15. *Cf.* (*In Australia*) *Wall* v. *R.* (*No.* 1) (1927), 39 C.L.R. 245 and *Wall* v. *R.* (*No.* 2) (1927), 39 C.L.R. 266 (H. Ct. of Aus.).

[3] *Cox* v. *Hakes* (1890), 15 App. Cas. 506, H.L. per Lord HALSBURY L.C. at p. 515.

[4] See first edition of this work, paras. 42, 216: *cf. XI Halsbury's Laws of England* (3rd Edn.) 49.

[5] See para. 59, *ante*, and notes thereto.

[6] *Brownsword* v. *Edwards* (1750), 2 Ves. Sen. 243 per Lord HARDWICKE L.C. at p. 245.

[7] *Bunting* v. *Lepingwell* (1585), 4 Co. Rep. 29a; *Meddowcroft* v. *Huguenin* (1844), 4 Moo. P.C.C. 386.

necessarily the basis upon which the decree proceeded.[1] But, unless all the conditions of a valid estoppel by *res judicata* of any kind be satisfied, the decision is no more conclusive against the world than, on a similar defect in proof, any other decision would be between the parties; if, for instance, there is no direct declaration of matrimonial status, and no determination thereof is necessarily involved in the decision, then, on principles enunciated at an earlier stage, there can be no estoppel.[2] So also, if the decision is wanting in finality.[3]

A decree in the Divorce jurisdiction declaring the legitimacy of children recited as children of the marriage, while binding as *res judicata* upon the parties to the suit, will not have the force of a judgment *in rem*; hence, even though such a decree may establish the legitimacy of the named children as between petitioner and respondent, it cannot do so as between (*e.g.*) them and other children who were not parties to the suit.[4]

---

[1] *Woodland* v. *Woodland*, [1928] P. 169 per HILL, J.

[2] *Brownsword* v. *Edwards* (1750), 2 Ves. Sen. 243, where, at p. 245, Lord HARDWICKE L.C., referring to a case of *Hicks* v. *Harris* (1693), 12 Mod. Rep. 35, in which he had been of counsel for one of the parties, said that "in that cause, during life of the father and mother, there had been a proceeding against both of them in the Consistory Court of Lincoln for living together in fornication, and sentence given against them. On the trial that sentence was offered in evidence to prove that they were not married: the whole court were of opinion that it could not be given in evidence . . . but they held that, if it had been a sentence on the point of marriage on a question of the lawfulness of the marriage, it, being a sentence of a court of proper jurisdiction, might have been given in evidence", and that such a sentence, in the absence of any proof of collusion, "'binds all the world''; *Needham* v. *Bremner* (1866), L.R. 1 C.P. 583, an action for necessaries supplied to the defendant's wife when living apart from him, to which the defendant set up, as an estoppel, an alleged finding in a divorce suit that his wife had been guilty of adultery. It appearing, however, on production of the record, that in this suit the defendant's petition for divorce had been dismissed on the ground that he also was found to have committed adultery, it was held that the plea of estoppel failed (per ERLE C.J., at p. 585: "the judge of the Divorce Court has not altered the status of the parties. The woman still continues the wife of the defendant. The case does not fall within the class of cases referred to, where the sentence put an end to the relation of husband and wife. There is nothing here but the mere verdict of a jury, binding as between the parties to the suit, but not as between other parties who come to litigate the same question").

[3] *Duchess of Kingston's Case* (1776), 2 Smith L.C. (13th Edn.) 644, per DE GREY C.J., at p. 665. And, generally, as to finality, see Chap. V, *ante*.

[4] So, where a wife had obtained a decree in divorce from her husband, the proceeding being undefended, on a petition which alleged that A was a child of the marriage, and the decree had awarded the petitioner-wife the custody of A, the husband was held estopped, as against the wife, from contesting the paternity of A in subsequent separate proceedings for maintenance. But on a later petition for a declaration of legitimacy presented by A twenty-five years afterwards, to which the husband and his other children were cited as respondents, it was held by WILLMER L.J., sitting as an additional judge in the Divorce Division, that the custody order in the original decree of divorce did not amount to a determination of legitimacy binding *in rem*, and consequently that it did not bind the other children of the marriage, who had not been parties to the divorce proceedings: *B.* v. *A.-G.*, (*N.E.B. intervening*), [1965] P. 278 (P.D.). "It seems to me", said WILLMER L.J. at p. 284, "that it would be absurd to suppose that, because a maintenance order may be embodied in the same document as that which determines the status of the parties, it is, therefore, to be regarded as an order binding *in rem*. I do not see why an order for custody should be regarded any differently; that is to say, as anything other than an order binding only the parties to the suit."

255 Where a receiving order has been made against a debtor, or an order adjudging a debtor bankrupt, pursuant to the statutory law of bankruptcy for the time being, the order obviously affects his financial status, and, therefore, whilst it stands, would probably be conclusive *in rem* at common law, and certainly is made so by statute, so as to estop not only the debtor,[1] but also everyone else from disputing the fact of the order having been made, and the date thereof,[2] and the fact of the act of bankruptcy on which the order was founded having been committed by the bankrupt, and the date of such act, for the purpose of fixing the date to which the title of the trustee relates back.[3]

256 The law relating to settlements of paupers, now outmoded, abounds in illustrations of the topic under discussion. In the older authorities dealing with this department of our jurisprudence, it was held that a decision of justices declaring a pauper to be settled in a certain parish, or an order for the removal of a pauper from one parish to another (which necessarily involved a decision that his settlement was in the latter parish), was conclusive against the world in general, and not merely against the parishes concerned, as to the fact that the order was made, and that the legal settlement of the pauper was in the parish in which he was adjudged to be settled or to which he was ordered to be removed.[4]

257 A judgment of ouster on a *quo warranto* would seem, on principle, a decision affecting the corporate status of the person against whom the judgment was given, and, therefore, a judgment *in rem*, but there is no direct decision to this effect. In one case, where the parties were not the same, it was held that, on this ground, such a judgment, though evidence, was not conclusive, but, in another case, where equally the parties were not the same, the judgment was held to be conclusive, which is tantamount to holding it to be a decision *in rem*.[5]

---

[1] *Boaler* v. *Power*, [1910] 2 K.B. 229, C.A. (per FARWELL L.J., at p. 232).

[2] Bankruptcy Act 1869, s. 10, the construction of which was the subject of the case cited in the next note. This section was substantially reproduced in the Act of 1883, and, again, in the Bankruptcy Act 1914, s. 173 (2): "the production of a copy of the London Gazette containing any notice of a receiving order, or of an order adjudging a debtor bankrupt, shall be conclusive evidence *in all legal proceedings* of the order having been *duly* made, and of its date".

[3] *Ex parte Learoyd, Re Foulds* (1878), 10 Ch.D. 3, C.A. (per JAMES L.J., at pp. 7–9, BAGGALLAY L.J., at pp. 9, 10, and THESIGER L.J., at p. 11).

[4] The first edition contains a lengthy discussion of the pauper cases, which has been omitted in this text, as have the footnotes and the cases cited in support. Those who find an interest in the topic are referred to the first edition pp. 135–136.

[5] *R.* v. *Hebden* (1738), Andr. 388; *R.* v. *York Corporation* (1792), 5 Term Rep. 66 (per BULLER J. on p. 76).

258 Sentences of deprivation of a collegiate office,[1] or of expulsion from a college,[2] pronounced by the authorities having jurisdiction in that behalf, since they affect the academical or corporate status of the person deprived or expelled, are decisions *in rem*.

259 The certificate of election judges on the hearing of a parliamentary election petition as to the validity or invalidity of an election is, both at common law and by statute, a decision *in rem*, since it purports to adjudicate upon the parliamentary and political status of the candidate declared to have been, or not to have been, duly elected.[3] On the other hand, the election judges' statutory "report" as to the prevalence or otherwise of bribery at the election, and as to the complicity, or non-complicity, of any candidate therewith, is not at common law, nor is it made by the statute, a judicial decision *in rem*, or indeed a judicial decision at all.[4]

260 An order for the expulsion, deprivation, or degradation of a member of a profession, made by a body of persons invested by statute with disciplinary jurisdiction over the members of that profession, such as an order of the General Medical Council erasing the name of a member from the register on the ground of his professional misconduct, is a decision

---

[1] *Philips* v. *Bury* (1694), Skin. 447. This is the best and fullest report of the case, Skinner having been (see p. 491) counsel for the defendant in the H.L. Other reports are 1 Ld. Raym. 5; Comb. 265; Holt 715; 1 Show. 360; 4 Mod. 106. The question here arose, amongst others, whether a sentence of the Bishop of Exeter, in his character of Visitor of Exeter Coll. Oxon., whereby he deprived the defendant of his office as Rector of the College, was conclusive on everybody, or not. The majority of the Court of K.B. held that it was not, but the House of Lords allowed the plaintiff's appeal, and agreed with the dissentient judgment of HOLT C.J., which is set out at pp. 475–491, and is also interjected in 2 Term Rep. 346. This they did "without giving any reasons", though "the Bishop of Worcester, Stillingfleet, spoke very earnestly against the sentence of a Visitor's being examinable", as we are told by the reporter at p. 512. The judgment of HOLT C.J. must, therefore, be resorted to for the grounds of the ultimate decision. That part of it which relates to the question of the conclusiveness of the Visitor's sentence is at pp. 477–482.

[2] *R.* v. *Grundon* (1775), 1 Cowp. 315, an indictment for assault upon the prosecutor, a fellow-commoner of Queen's Coll. Cambr. in turning him out of the College gardens. The accused justified under a sentence of expulsion pronounced against the prosecutor by the Master and Fellows of the College. It was held by the Court of K.B. that WILLES J. was "extremely right" in rejecting the evidence tendered by the prosecutor at the trial for the purpose of impugning the legality of the sentence, on the ground that "this expulsion by the Master and residential Fellows must be taken *by everybody* to be a right sentence until avoided or set aside by the Visitor, who is the sole judge" (per Lord MANSFIELD C.J., at p. 322).

[3] *Waygood* v. *James* (1869), L.R. 4 C.P. 361 (per BOVILL C.J., at pp. 365, 366, MONTAGUE SMITH J., at p. 371, and BRETT J., at p. 372); *Stevens* v. *Tillett* (1870), L.R. 6 C.P. 147, as cited in the next note. It was pointed out in these cases that the common law principle is confirmed by s. 11 (13) of the Parliamentary Elections Act 1868.

[4] *Stevens* v. *Tillett*, *supra*, per BOVILL C.J., at pp. 155–164, and WILLES J., at p. 172, who there point out that, whilst the determination and certificate of the judge as to the validity or voidness of the election is final and conclusive on everybody, both at common law, and in virtue of the enactment cited in the last note, no such finality or conclusiveness attaches either at common law, or by s. 11 (14) of the Act of 1868, to the "report" therein mentioned.

which obviously affects the professional status of the person whose name is so erased, and is accordingly conclusive *in rem* as to the fact of the order having been made, and also (perhaps) as to the impliedly decided fact that the acts proved against the member constitute professional misconduct, within the meaning of the statute,[1] but, as will be shewn presently, not to any further extent.[2]

261 A judgment of declarator in a Scottish "public action", a form of proceeding founded on the *popularis actio* of Roman law,[3] but unknown to the common law of England,[4] is (as the name imports) a judicial decision to the benefit, and to the burden, of which the whole of the Scottish public is respectively entitled, and subject.[5]

262 An order for the revocation of a patent is conclusive *in rem*, in so far as it determines the extinction of the *res* (the patent), but not as to the grounds of the revocation.[6]

Two classes of decisions falling short of decisions in rem

263 Of judicial decisions which have been *unsuccessfully* contended to be *in rem* decisions, and which it is now convenient to notice by way of illustrative contrast to the foregoing exemplification of decisions which have been held to operate as such, there have been said[7] to be two classes or degrees. On the one hand there is the type of decision which is not even admissible as evidence of anything at all (except of course that the decision was pronounced) for or against any person who is not a party or privy. On the other hand it has been said[7] that there is a type of decision (intermediate

---

[1] *Hill* v. *Clifford*, [1907] 2 Ch. 236, C.A. (per COZENS-HARDY M.R., at p. 245, GORELL BARNES P., at p. 252, and BUCKLEY L.J., at p. 257; but it is suggested in para. 268, *post* that there may be doubt, since the decision of the Court of Appeal in *Hollington* v. *F. Hewthorn & Co.* and in the light of the legislation proposed at the date of going to press, how far *Hill* v. *Clifford* would now be followed to establish an estoppel as to anything beyond the mere fact of de-registration, with its consequent provisional disqualification.

[2] See para. 268, *post*.

[3] See Appendix B, *post*.

[4] *Shedden* v. *A.-G.* (1860), 30 L.J. P.D. & A. 217 (*per Cur.*, at p. 231,—so stated); *Jenkins* v. *Robertson* (1867), L.R. 1 Sc. & Div. 117, H.L. (per Lord ROMILLY, at p. 121, and Lord COLONSAY, at p. 124). There are certain English statutes, however, such as the Legitimacy Declaration Act 1858, which provide for such a form of action, as to legitimacy of children, validity of marriages, and the like. See *Shedden* v. *A.-G.*, *supra*, and *Armitage* v. *A.-G.*, [1906] P. 135.

[5] *Jenkins* v. *Robertson*, *supra*, where it was conceded that if, in the public action of declarator, there had been a judicial decision, after a contest, against the pursuer, it would have bound the public at large whom the pursuer represented (per Lord CHELMSFORD L.C., at p. 121, and Lord COLONSAY, at p. 124), but the compromise and consent order relied upon was held not to have amounted to a judicial decision of any kind.

[6] *Poulton* v. *Adjustable Cover and Boiler Block Co.*, [1908] 2 Ch. 430, C.A. (per MOULTON L.J. at p. 439).

[7] In the first edition of this work, at pp. 138 *et seq.*, *Hill* v. *Clifford*, [1907] 2 Ch. 236 is cited as the principal authority. It is doubted below (paras. 265 *et seq.*) how far there is room for the

between that just described and the class of decisions *in rem* in the strict sense of the term) which, though not conclusive *in rem*, is *prima facie* evidence *in rem*, and if not rebutted, becomes uncontradicted and sufficient evidence as against the world at large.[1] Each of these will now be briefly considered.

The first class considered

264 The first of the above classes is illustrated by the following. A winding up order against a company is not an order *in rem*, and does not estop a stranger from contesting the validity of the order, or the jurisdiction of the court to make it.[2] "A judgment is not a judgment *in rem* because, in a suit by A. for the recovery of an estate from B., it has determined an issue concerning the status of a particular person or family".[3] The verdict of a jury on a coroner's inquisition as to the cause of a person's death is no evidence whatever, for or against anyone, as to the guilt or innocence of any person inculpated by such verdict.[4] A refusal to make an affiliation order, or a quashing on appeal of such an order is, as regards anyone except parties and privies, *res inter alios acta*, and, therefore, not admissible evidence in support of an averment that the respondent is not the father of the bastard.[5] Indeed a refusal on the part of justices to make an order is not even *res judicata* between the parties, but is a decision "in the nature of a non-suit" not barring a further application by the mother.[6]

A finding or declaration made in an action between borrower and lender, in an action for moneys lent, that the lender is a "banker" and therefore not a "money-lender" within the meaning of section 6 of the Moneylenders' Act 1900[7] is one made *inter partes* on the evidence submitted; as between the parties it is *res judicata*, but it does not follow that if in some other case between some other parties the evidence is more completely or more closely probed the result will be the same.[8]

---

second class of decisions there referred to, since the decision of the Court of Appeal in *Hollington* v. *F. Hewthorn & Co., Ltd.*, [1943] K.B. 587; but legislation proposed at the date of going to press may re-establish the validity of Mr Spencer Bower's original text.

1 *Hill* v. *Clifford*, [1907] 2 Ch. 236 is cited in the first edition in support of the text: see note 1 above.

2 *Re Bowling and Welby's Contract*, [1895] 1 Ch. 663 (per Lord HALSBURY L.C. at pp. 667, 668, LINDLEY L.J., at pp. 671, 672, and A. L. SMITH L.J., at p. 673).

3 *Katama Natchier* v. *Rajah of Shivagunga* (1863), 9 Moo. Ind. App. 543 at p. 601.

4 *Bird* v. *Keep*, [1918] 2 K.B. 692, C.A. (per SWINFEN EADY M.R. at pp. 698–700 and BANKES L.J. at pp. 703–704).

5 *Anderson* v. *Collinson*, [1901] 2 K.B. 107, D.C. (per Lord ALVERSTONE C.J., at p. 109).

6 *Robinson* v. *Williams*, [1964] 3 All E.R. 12; [1965] 1 Q.B. 89.

7 Section 6 provides: "The expression 'money-lender' in this Act shall include every person whose business is that of money-lending . . . but shall not include . . . any person *bona fide* carrying on the business of a banker".

8 *United Dominions Trust, Ltd.* v. *Kirkwood*, [1966] 1 All E.R. 968 per DIPLOCK L.J. at p. 992.

The decision in Hollington v. *F. Hewthorn & Co., Ltd.*

265 It has never been contended, at least in recent times, that the record of a conviction will estop the person convicted, as against the rest of the world (the Crown excepted) from denying his guilt of the offence charged.[1] But it was for long supposed that though not available with the effect of a judgment *in rem* to support the proposition that the accused was in fact guilty of the crime of which he has been convicted, a conviction will amount nevertheless to *prima facie* proof thereof.[2] This was the view expressed in the first edition of this work,[3] and it appeared, at the time when that edition was published, to be supported by the weight of then existing authority.[4] There was much that could be urged as logically supporting this result, and indeed not a little to support the view that a conviction should prove guilt in favour of all the world, with all the force of estoppel; for on a first consideration of the matter, it may be difficult to understand why, if a judgment of conviction is conclusive *in rem* as to the fact of conviction, it is not also conclusive *in rem* as to the guilt of the convicted person, which is necessarily determined as between him and the Crown, and hence (it may be supposed) in favour of the public by his conviction.

But while at first sight it may seem logical that a conviction in due form should estop him who has been convicted from denying his guilt thereafter, weighty reasons have always been apparent, urging some caution in this respect. Before the establishment of the Court of Criminal Appeal the only effective way in which a man wrongly convicted might ultimately prove his innocence was through a libel action, in which he could once again litigate the facts; and though the establishment of the Court of Criminal Appeal has diminished somewhat the force of this argument, yet it remains valuable to a person unjustly convicted to have the right, in civil

---

[1] *Petrie* v. *Nuttall* (1856), 11 Exch. 569 (per ALDERSON, PLATT, and MARTIN BB., at p. 576); *Castrique* v. *Imrie* (1870), L.R. 4 H.L. 414 (per BLACKBURN J., at p. 434); *Leyman* v. *Latimer* (1878), 3 Ex.D. 352, C.A. (per BRAMWELL L.J., at p. 354); *Ballantyne* v. *Mackinnon*, [1896] 2 Q.B. 455, C.A. (*per Cur.*, at p. 462, adopting the statement of BLACKBURN J. in *Castrique* v. *Imrie, supra*); *Caine* v. *Palace S.S. Co.*, [1907] 1 K.B. 670, C.A. (per COZENS-HARDY L.J., at p. 677, and FARWELL L.J., at p. 683); *In the Estate of Crippen*, [1911] P. 108. In a more recent case, *Hollington* v. *F. Hewthorn & Co., Ltd.*, [1943] K.B. 587, C.A., it was not attempted to argue that a conviction set up an estoppel except between the prisoner and the Crown; and the concession of counsel was accepted as good law in the judgment of the Court of Appeal.

[2] *Petrie* v. *Nuttall* (1856), 11 Exch. 569 per ALDERSON B. at p. 576; *Prince of Wales etc. Co.* v. *Palmer* (1858), 25 Beav. 605 per ROMILLY M.R. at p. 608; *In the Estate of Crippen*, [1911] P. 108 per EVANS P. at p. 115.

[3] First edition (1924) para. 227, where the contrary view is dubbed "unjust and ridiculous", "a further extravagance".

[4] To the cases cited in footnotes 1 & 2, *supra*, there were added in the two years following on the publication of the first edition of this work two further decisions—*Partington* v. *Partington and Atkinson*, [1925] P. 34 and *O'Toole* v. *O'Toole* (1926), 42 T.L.R. 245. Both of these two decisions, together with *In the Estate of Crippen* (*supra*) were expressly overruled by the Court of Appeal in *Hollington* v. *F. Hewthorn & Co., Ltd.*, [1943] K.B. 587, at p. 601.

proceedings supervening upon his release from prison, to challenge afresh the evidence upon which he was convicted.

Moreover is any grave harm done by allowing him to do so? It may be "convenient" that a plaintiff in a civil action in damages should be able to produce the conviction of his defendant on a charge (for instance) of negligent driving as proof of negligence; but, though this must possibly cheapen litigation for plaintiffs, can it be said to be unjust to allow the truth to be re-investigated on the civil claim, in which matters much more important to the parties may be involved? And it must be admitted that no principle requires the court to have regard, in the later civil proceedings, to a conviction obtained between different parties, in criminal proceedings, except in proof of the fact (if it be relevant) that the accused was in fact convicted. All these matters were agitated before the Court of Appeal in 1943 in *Hollington* v. *F. Hewthorn & Co., Ltd.*,[1] in which Mr A. T. DENNING K.C., (later Lord DENNING M.R.) appeared for the appellant to argue that the *prima facie* rule should be applied—*viz.* that proof of the conviction should be admitted as *prima facie* evidence of guilt.[2] His submissions fell upon deaf ears. The court accepted the view that once the argument for a complete estoppel fails—and it cannot succeed because the parties are different, even if it can be said that the issues are the same—it is of little use to speak of *prima facie* proof, since, when the defendant has challenged the propriety of the conviction, the court, on the subsequent trial, must necessarily proceed to re-try the criminal case in order to see what ought to be the result on the evidence now adduced.[3] *Prima facie* proof must mean proof until something better *contra* turns up; but how is the evidence of witnesses called in court for the defendant, and heard *viva voce*, to be evaluated against, and compared with, a record of conviction written on a piece of paper and given the status of *prima facie* proof, when it is supported by no witnesses at all? The difficulty of comparison is at once seen to be formidable.[4]

266 *Hollington* v. *F. Hewthorn & Co., Ltd.*,[5] stood from 1943 till 1968 as firm authority for the proposition that there could be no halfway house between a decision *in rem*, estopping him found guilty in criminal proceed-

---

[1] [1943] K.B. 587, C.A., GODDARD L.J. delivered the judgment of the court, which consisted (see [1943] 2 All E.R. 35) of Lord GREENE M.R., and GODDARD and DU PARCQ L.JJ.

[2] It was not attempted to argue that the record of the conviction set up an estoppel, though the parties were different. This was abandoned at p. 589, and the court so held at p. 601.

[3] At p. 595.

[4] *Hollington* v. *F. Hewthorn & Co., Ltd.*, [1943] K.B. 587 C.A.: "It ought not to be admitted as *some* evidence of a fact which must have been found, owing mainly to the impossibility of determining what weight should be given to it without retrying the former case"—per GODDARD L.J. at p. 596.

[5] [1943] K.B. 587, C.A.

ings from denying his guilt thereafter, whoever might be his accuser in later proceedings, and a decision *in personam*, estopping him only against the Crown from denying such guilt, and operating as a decision *in rem* only as to the fact of conviction and no more. The possibility of steering between these two extremes and accepting a conviction, not as an estoppel *inter alios*, but as *prima facie* evidence of the facts on which it was founded had apparently been finally rejected. But sound though the conclusion in *Hollington* v. *F. Hewthorn & Co., Ltd.*, may have been in principle, it has been subjected to persistent criticism; and among its most effective critics (as the event has shown) has been Lord DENNING M.R., who has continued to recall the argument which as counsel he unsuccessfully submitted before GODDARD L.J. When in the Court of Appeal, in 1966, *Hollington's* case was brought to mind, he vigorously criticised GODDARD L.J.'s judgment delivered twenty-five years before, and said:

> ". . . there is a strange rule of law which says that a conviction is no evidence of guilt, not even *prima facie* evidence. That was decided in *Hollington* v. *F. Hewthorn & Co., Ltd.* I argued that case myself, and did my best to persuade the court that a conviction was evidence of guilt. But they would not have it. I thought that the decision was wrong at the time. I still think that it was wrong. But in this court we are bound by it. It means that when anyone publishes a story about a crime, he is in peril of being sued for libel. In the action he cannot rely on the conviction as proof of guilt. He has to prove it all over again, if he can."[1]

And again in *Barclay's Bank, Ltd.* v. *Cole*,[2] only a few months later, Lord DENNING again said:

> "He wishes to canvass again his guilt or innocence, but this time before a jury in a civil case. There is too much of this sort of thing going on: *Hinds*, *Goody*, *Rondel*, and now (the defendant). It is made possible by the unfortunate decision of this court in *Hollington* v. *F. Hewthorn & Co., Ltd.*, where it was held that a conviction in a criminal court cannot be used as evidence, not even *prima facie* evidence, in a civil case. I hope it will soon be altered. See what it means here. In order to be able to bring this civil action Barclay's Bank had first to make sure that (the defendant) was prosecuted in the criminal court: see *Smith* v. *Selwyn*. Now after seeing him duly prosecuted and convicted, they are asked to prove his guilt all over again in this civil suit."[3]

His observations, moreover, were echoed by his brother Lords Justices, and it began to be apparent that the stage was being set for the repeal of the rule in *Hollington* v. *F. Hewthorn & Co., Ltd.* either by judicial or by legislative process.

---

[1] *Goody* v. *Odhams Press, Ltd.*, [1967] 1 Q.B. 333, C.A. at p. 339.
[2] [1967] 2 Q.B. 738, C.A. [3] At p. 743.

267 The consequence of all this has been legislation adopting the recommendations of the Fifteenth Report of the Law Reform Committee, under the chairmanship of Lord Pearson, which was presented to Parliament in September 1967; these were enacted into law by the Civil Evidence Act 1968. The text of the Report, and of the relevant provisions of the Act, are to be found in Appendices to this work,[1] and the effect of the new statute may be briefly summarised as follows:

(1) In any civil proceedings the fact that a person has been convicted of an offence before any court in the United Kingdom, or by a Court Martial there or elsewhere, is admissible in evidence for the purpose of proving, when to do so is relevant, that he committed that offence, and this whether he was convicted on a plea of guilty or after trial, and whether or not he is a party to the later proceedings.[2]

(2) But the effect of proving the conviction is only that the person convicted is to be taken to have committed the offence *unless the contrary is proved*. It is now, as before, open to the convicted person to disprove his guilt by evidence led in this regard to displace the presumption raised by the statute.[3]

It may be commented, that the difficulty in such a case in weighing the pros and cons in the second proceeding will be enormous, for one side may rely simply on the presumption raised by the conviction, while the other sets out to rebut the presumption by evidence. The difficulty will be particularly apparent when the trial of the second proceeding is before a jury. The prospect of such a situation has always constituted one of the arguments which have stood effectively in the way of the repeal of the rule in *Hollington* v. *F. Hewthorn & Co., Ltd.*; [4] but formidable as the object may be, it has been thought better to face it than to allow the state of affairs to continue which called forth Lord DENNING's strictures in the cases to which we have referred above.[5]

(3) A similar rule is to apply to a finding of adultery in matrimonial proceedings, and to an adjudication of paternity in affiliation proceedings. Again, in these cases, the findings in the first proceeding will result in a presumption being raised, which is rebuttable by evidence

---

[1] The Civil Evidence Act 1968 is printed as Appendix C at p. 417, *post*; the text of the Fifteenth Report of the Law Revision Committee appears as Appendix D at p. 421 *post*.

[2] Civil Evidence Act 1968, s. 11 (1).

[3] *Ibid.*, s. 11 (2).

[4] [1943] K.B. 587 C.A. The difficulty referred to in the text is expressly discussed by GODDARD L.J. at p. 596, in the passage quoted in note 4 on p. 222, *ante*.

[5] *Goody* v. *Odhams Press, Ltd.*, [1967] 1 Q.B. 333, C.A. at p. 339, *Barclays Bank Ltd.* v. *Cole*, [1967] 2 Q.B. 738, C.A.

in this regard called in the second proceeding, of sufficient weight to rebut the presumption.[1]

(4) Where the second proceeding is a defamation action a special rule obtains, and in such cases the conviction of the plaintiff in the first proceeding is conclusive evidence that he has committed the offence of which he was found guilty.[2]

This provision effectively disposes of the possibility, in the future, of cases like *Goody* v. *Odhams Press, Ltd.*[3] and *Barclays Bank, Ltd.* v. *Cole.*[4] It may be regretted by some that the legislation has deprived a person wrongly convicted of a method of demonstrating, after his punishment is served, that he was innocent despite his conviction; but the scandal which followed upon the prosecution of several libel actions in the present decade, ingeniously founded upon the legal possibilities inherent in *Hollington* v. *F. Hewthorn & Co., Ltd.* have been sufficient to persuade the Legislature that the new Act may be the lesser of two evils.

It is to be noticed that the provisions of the Civil Evidence Act 1968 are restricted to cases where the first decision is either (a) a conviction for a criminal offence in a court of the United Kingdom (b) a conviction before a Court Martial (c) a finding of adultery or (d) an adjudication of paternity. The old rule must be taken still to obtain in all other cases. There may be instanced, as an illustration, the case of a conviction in a Commonwealth Court outside the United Kingdom.

There have in fact from time to time been other instances of decisions wherein judgments or verdicts of guilt, though not in criminal courts, have been held to be evidence of the facts supporting the judgment or verdict in later proceedings *inter alios*. Thus it has been held that the verdict or finding of a jury on an inquisition in lunacy,[5] or the order of a master in lunacy

---

[1] Civil Evidence Act 1968, s. 12. The authority of *Partington* v. *Partington and Atkinson* [1925] P. 34 and *O'Toole* v. *O'Toole* (1926), 42 T.L.R. 245, expressly overruled by the decision in *Hollington* v. *F. Hewthorn & Co., Ltd.*, may now be taken as restored, at least approximately, if not exactly, by the new legislation.

[2] *Ibid.*, s. 13.

[3] [1967] 1 Q.B. 333, C.A.

[4] [1967] 2 Q.B. 738, C.A.

[5] *Sergeson* v. *Sealey* (1742), 2 Atk. 412; *Faulder* v. *Silk* (1811), 3 Camp. 126 (per Lord Ellenborough C.J., at p. 126); *Prinsep and East India Co.* v. *Dyce Sombre* (1856), 10 Moo. P.C.C. 232, at p. 234; *Hill* v. *Clifford*, [1907] 2 Ch. 236, C.A., per Cozens-Hardy M.R., at pp. 244, 245, who there states, after referring to the appendix to the case before the House of Lords in *Van Grutten* v. *Foxwell*, [1897] A.C. 658, H.L., that it appears therefrom, though the point is barely noticed in the report (at p. 660), that the C.A. had in that case held that the invalidity of a certain disentailing deed of 1835 as against a party thereto was not established *in rem* by the mere production of the record of a finding of an inquisition of 1845 that the party had been a lunatic since the year 1833, but that such record constituted *some* evidence of his lunacy as against third persons, which it was for them to rebut.

under the Lunacy Act 1890, reciting that, in his judgment, the person affected by the order was then of unsound mind, though not so found by inquisition, is admissible evidence *in rem* of the fact of the lunacy;[1] that an order of the General Medical Council, erasing the name of a medical practitioner from the register, is *prima facie* evidence *in rem* of the fact that he was guilty of the professional misconduct on the ground of which his name was so erased;[2] that the finding of a jury summoned under a Boundary Commission is admissible evidence *in rem* on any question as to what was the true boundary between certain lands or estates, and the like;[3] and that an order cancelling the certificate of a mercantile marine officer for negligence, made by a tribunal holding an inquiry under the Merchant Shipping Acts, is *prima facie* evidence *in rem* of the fact that the officer was guilty of the negligence with which he was charged.[4]

After the decision in *Hollington* v. *F. Hewthorn & Co., Ltd.*[5] it was generally considered that these cases must be the subject of some reassessment in the light of that decision. It does not appear that they are touched in any way by the provisions of the Civil Evidence Act 1968, and it would seem likely that the principle in *Hollington* v. *F. Hewthorn & Co., Ltd.* will still be applicable to them, precluding any inference being drawn from the earlier case to the later.

268 It has never (or perhaps it is more correct to say hardly ever)[6] been seriously suggested that a verdict of acquittal should have the force either of an estoppel establishing innocence affirmatively in the face of all the world, or even that such a verdict should be accepted as *prima facie* evidence establishing such innocence in later proceedings *inter alios*. Many reasons will at once occur to the reader for this; not least, the difference in the onus of proof in civil and criminal proceedings.[7] It was not proposed, in

---

1 *Harvey* v. *R.*, [1901] A.C. 601, P.C., at p. 611.

2 *Hill* v. *Clifford*, *supra* (per COZENS-HARDY M.R., at p. 245, and GORELL BARNES P. at p. 252).

3 *Brisco* v. *Lomax* (1838), 8 Ad. & El. 198 (per PATTESON J., at p. 212, and COLERIDGE J., at pp. 214, 215).

4 *Caine* v. *Palace S.S. Co.*, [1907] 1 K.B. 670, C.A. (per COZENS-HARDY L.J., at p. 677, and FARWELL L.J., at p. 683). This class of case is referred to by GORELL BARNES P., at pp. 251, 252, of *Hill* v. *Clifford*, *supra*. *In Australia*, *Spain* v. *Union Steamship Co., Ltd. of New Zealand, Ltd.* (1923), 33 C.L.R. 555 (H. Ct. of Aus.).

5 [1943] K.B. 587 C.A.

6 GODDARD L.J. in *Hollington* v. *F. Hewthorn & Co., Ltd.* (*supra*) did indeed say "If a conviction can be admitted not as an estoppel, but as *prima facie* evidence, so ought an acquittal".

7 *Helsham* v. *Blackwood* (1851), 11 C.B. 111. (Obviously the view of the court, though not necessary to decide the point.) The logic of this proposition has been defended in considered decisions of the High Court of Australia, where it has been pointed out that to extend the principles of estoppel to give an acquittal the force of a judgment *in rem* would amount to judicial legislation having remarkable and far-reaching consequences. Reference may be made to the judgment of ISAACS J. in *R.* v. *Seery* (1914), 19 C.L.R. 15 (H. Ct. of Aus.) at p. 18. Later, in *Helton* v. *Allen* (1940), 63 C.L.R. 691 (H. Ct. of Aus.) where it was sought to set up an acquittal on a charge of murder as an estoppel in favour of the accused when later he was made a party to

the report of the Law Reform Committee, that the existing rules should be altered in this regard, nor is the law on this point changed by the provisions of the Civil Evidence Act 1968.

Foreign decisions which determine the status of a person

269 Foreign decisions *in rem* take a wider range than English. In order to establish that a foreign decision operates *in rem* in this country, it must be shewn, not only that the decision is deemed an *in rem* decision in the particular foreign state,—which is a question of fact,[1] like all other questions of foreign law,[2]—but also that it is such as to determine the status of a person, or of a thing, so as to conclude "the world", in the largest sense of that term, that is to say, the community of civilized States who by tacit consent, if not by positive treaty, recognize the principles of private international law, and all the subjects of those States. Only a decision having such extra-territorial efficiency can rank as a decision *in rem* in Her Majesty's Dominions, whether it affects the status of a person, which alone concerns the present discussion, or that of a thing, which will be dealt with in its proper place hereafter.

270 Of foreign, that is to say, non-English,[3] judicial decisions determining the status of a person which operate *in rem* in England, the most important are those relating to the Christian status of marriage, which has been judicially defined as "a voluntary union of one man with one woman".[4]

---

civil proceedings, it was held that this acquittal could not so operate. The judgment of DIXON, EVATT and MCTIERNAN JJ. after stating that:

> "his acquittal cannot operate as an estoppel. The plaintiff in the present proceedings is not bound by it as decisive of his innocence. Nor indeed do we think that it would be admissible against her as an evidentiary fact".

went on to say:

> "The only ground upon which the acquittal of Helton could exclude the operation of the rule is that, the rule being one of public justice, it ought not on grounds of public justice to be extended to a case where the claimant has been absolved in the criminal jurisdiction from the material crime. In other words, it may be said that to retry as a civil issue the guilt of a man who had been acquitted on a criminal inquest is so against policy that a rule drawn from public policy ought not to authorize it. There is, however, no trace of any such conception in the history of the principle that by committing a crime no man could obtain a lawful benefit to himself. To qualify the rule in the manner suggested would, we think amount to judicial legislation. It is much more than the application of settled principle to an instance hitherto unforeseen or not adverted to in the general formulation of the rule. We are, therefore, of opinion that the appellant Helton is not entitled as a matter of law to a verdict and judgment in his favour."

[1] *Castrique* v. *Imrie* (1870), L.R. 4 H.L. 414 (per BLACKBURN J., at pp. 429–430).

[2] See Chapter II, para. 75 *ante*.

[3] As to the juridical meaning of "foreign" see Chapter II, para. 69, *ante*.

[4] *R.* v. *Hammersmith Superintendent Registrar of Marriages, Ex parte Nir-Anwaruddin*, [1917] 1 K.B. 634, C.A. (per A. T. LAWRENCE J., at p. 652). In this case, at p. 642, Lord READING

The topic of estoppel *per rem judicatam* in Divorce, whether that estoppel be *inter partes* or against the world is considered in a separate chapter devoted to the subject.[1]

271 Foreign decisions as to the legitimacy or illegitimacy of a person domiciled within the foreign state, or as to the rights of inheritance of an illegitimate child there domiciled, are conclusive *in rem* in this country.[2] So also is an express declaration of the paternity of a bastard made by a foreign tribunal having competent jurisdiction to make such a declaration.[3]

272 A foreign decision, which does not determine the status of a person, in the international sense, though such status may be affected for purely local, municipal, or national purposes, or which does not establish, or entirely alter, such status, is not operative *in rem* in England. Thus, the adjudication of a man as a "prodigue" by a French court, the effect of which is to preclude him from dealing with his property, and from suing in the French courts without the intervention of a "conseil judiciaire", but not to deprive him of any other of his civil rights, is not a decision which binds the English public, or prevents the "prodigue" from suing in the English courts, whatever may be its effect in French, for the reason that "the disability, or the disqualification, arises from the principles or customs or positive law" of the particular foreign state, like the disabilities imposed by various states at various times upon heretics, recusants, or slaves, and for the further reason that in such a case the status is prejudically affected in certain respects only, and is not extinguished, or entirely changed.[4]

And in a recent decision the Court of Appeal[5] upheld BUCKLEY J's refusal[6] to recognise as effective in this country an order of the Superior Court of the State of California which by appointing (pursuant to the Probate Code of that State) a guardian of a physically-disabled person, had under the law of that State thereby deprived the protected person of contractual capacity.

C.J. doubted whether our courts could take any notice of a Mahomedan matrimonial decision. But times are changing, and with this judgment cf. *Russ* v. *Russ*, [1962] 1 All. E.R. 649; on appeal, [1962] 3 All E.R. 193.

1 Chapter XII, *post*.

2 *Doglioni* v. *Crispin* (1866), L.R. 1 H.L. 301 (per Lord CHELMSFORD L.C., at p. 311, and Lord CRANWORTH, at pp. 314, 315); *Re Trufort, Trafford* v. *Blanc* (1887), 36 Ch.D. 600 (per STIRLING J., at pp. 609–611).

3 *Re Macartney, Macfarlane* v. *Macartney*, [1921] 1 Ch. 522 (per ASTBURY J., at p. 532).

4 *Worms* v. *De Valdor* (1880), 49 L.J. Ch. 261 (per FRY J., at pp. 261, 262); *Re Selot's Trust*, [1902] 1 Ch. 488 (per FARWELL J., at p. 492).

5 *In Re Langley's Settlement Trusts, Ltd.*; *Lloyds Bank, Ltd.* v. *Langley*, [1962] Ch. 541.

6 The decision of BUCKLEY J. is reported in [1961] 1 All E.R. 78.

English decisions determining the status of a thing

273 Any English judicial decision which operates upon a thing (in the physical sense) by effecting a disposition of it, is said to determine the status of the thing, and such decision accordingly may be set up by, or against, any member of the English public, as conclusive *in rem*, whereas any decision which determines, not the disposition of the thing, but solely the personal rights, liabilities, equities, and interests of the parties *inter se* in relation to the thing, concludes those parties only, or their privies. It must be remembered, however, that, in order to establish that a decision operates *in rem*, whether it be one which determines the status of a person, or that of a thing, all other conditions of a valid estoppel *per rem judicatam* must be satisfied, no less than where the decision is *inter partes*.[1]

Admiralty decisions

274 In accordance with the above principle, English Admiralty decisions, in so far as they purport to make a disposition of the vessel, are decisions *in rem*,[2] but only as to the point actually determined thereby. Thus, a declaration, in a salvage suit, that a maritime lien attached to the vessel to the extent of the salvage awarded, was held to be a decision *in rem* of the existence and validity of such lien, but not a decision *in rem* that the vessel was lost by the perils insured against.[3]

Streets and roads

275 Similarly, a declaration by a tribunal having competent jurisdiction to make it that a street or road is, or that it is not, repairable by the inhabitants at large, determines the status of the street or road, and, therefore, operates *in rem*.[4] But a mere dismissal of a summons to compel payment by a party, *ratione tenurae*, of his rateable share of the expenses of repairing a road, is not an implied decision that the road is repairable by the

---

[1] *Ballantyne* v. *Mackinnon*, [1896] 2 Q.B. 445, C.A., *per Cur.*, at p. 462: "as to a judgment being only conclusive as to the point decided, there is no distinction between a judgment *in rem*, and a judgment *in personam*, except that, in the one, "the point" adjudicated upon (which in a judgment *in rem* is always as to the status of the *res*) is conclusive against all the world as to that status, whereas, in the other, "the point", whatever it may be which is adjudicated upon, it not being as to the status of the *res*, is only evidence between parties or privies".

[2] *Duckworth* v. *Tucker* (1809), 2 Taunt. 7 (sentence of a British Prize Court, condemning a vessel "as lawful prize of His Majesty", held conclusive *in rem*, so as to estop anyone in the world from disputing not only the fact that the vessel was captured, but also that it was captured by the naval forces of this country, and not wholly, or in part, by those of any ally: (per Sir James MANSFIELD C.J., at pp. 34, 35, LAWRENCE J., at pp. 35, 36, and CHAMBRE J., at p. 36); *Ballantyne* v. *Mackinnon*, *supra* (so stated, *per Cur.*, at p. 462).

[3] As in *Ballantyne* v. *Mackinnon*, *supra* (*per Cur.*, at pp. 462, 463).

[4] *Wakefield Corporation* v. *Cooke*, [1904] A.C. 31, H.L. (per Lord HALSBURY L.C., at pp. 35–37, Lord DAVEY, at p. 37, and Lord ROBERTSON, at pp. 38, 39).

inhabitants at large, or, as such, conclusive *in rem*; nor, indeed, would an express declaration to that effect so operate, unless the tribunal had jurisdiction to make such declarations.[1]

The Inclosure Acts

276 Decisions under Inclosure Acts[2] determine the status of the lands to which they relate, and accordingly conclude the world at large, so far as regards any allotment, exchange, or partition directed thereby, but not as to any question of pre-existing title to any of such lands.[3]

The London Building Act 1894

277 A certificate of the superintending architect, or of the "tribunal of appeal", pursuant to the London Building Act 1894[4], fixing the building line of a street or road, is, for like reasons, a decision *in rem*.[5]

Probate decisions

278 English testamentary decisions are conclusive *in rem* to the following extent. The probate of a will operates to estop the world in general from disputing that the instrument admitted to probate was a will, validly executed according to the laws of this country, where the testator was domiciled, and that the testator was of sound disposing mind when making it, and uninfluenced by fraud or coercion, and that the person named therein as executor was entitled to that office.[6] Similarly letters of administration are conclusive *in rem* as to the fact of the grant thereof,[7] and so also is a decision in administration proceedings that one of two competing applicants for the grant is, and that the other is not, entitled thereto, as next of

---

1 *R.* v. *Hutchings* (1881), 6 Q.B.D. 300, C.A. (per Lord SELBORNE L.C., at p. 303); *Heath* v. *Weaverham Overseers*, [1894] 2 Q.B. 108, D.C.; *North Eastern Rail. Co.* v. *Dalton Overseers*, [1898] 2 Q.B. 66, D.C.

2 See, for instance, s. 105 of the Inclosure Act 1845, which enacts, as to any award made thereunder, that "every allotment, exchange, partition, direction, matter, and thing set forth in such award as aforesaid shall be binding and conclusive on all persons whatsoever".

3 *Jacomb* v. *Turner*, [1892] 1 Q.B. 47 (per COLLINS J., at pp. 51, 52); *Collis* v. *Amphlet*, [1918] 1 Ch. 232, C.A. (per SWINFEN EADY L.J., at p. 242, and WARRINGTON L.J., at p. 251).

4 57 & 58 Vict. cap. ccxiii.

5 *Lilley* v. *London County Council*, [1910] A.C. 1, H.L. (per Lord LOREBURN L.C., at pp. 2, 3, and Lord MACNAGHTEN, at p. 3); *London County Council* v. *Galsworthy*, [1917] 1 K.B. 85, D.C.

6 *Noell* v. *Wells* (1668), 1 Lev. 235 (*per Cur.* at pp. 235, 236); *Allen* v. *Dundas* (1789), 3 Term Rep. 125 (per ASHHURST J., at p. 129, BULLER J., at pp. 130–132, and GROSE J., at pp. 132, 133); *Thornton* v. *Curling* (1824), 8 Sim. 310 (per Lord COTTENHAM L.C., at pp. 311–313); *Douglas* v. *Cooper* (1834), 3 My. & K. 378 (per LEACH M.R., at p. 382); *Allen* v. *M'Pherson* (1847), 1 H.L. Cas. 191 (per Lord LYNDHURST, at pp. 207–214, Lord BROUGHAM, at pp. 222–227, and Lord CAMPBELL, at pp. 232–238); *Whicker* v. *Hume* (1858), 7 H.L. Cas. 124 (per Lord CHELMSFORD L.C., at pp. 143, 144); *Melhuish* v. *Milton* (1876), 3 Ch.D. 27, C.A. (per JAMES L.J., at p. 33); *Birch* v. *Birch*, [1902] P. 130, C.A. (per COZENS-HARDY L.J., at pp. 137, 138).

7 So stated in *Blackham's Case* (1709), 1 Salk. 290 (per HOLT C.J. at p. 290).

kin.[1] But, in accordance with principles already expounded, any such decision is not conclusive *in rem*, or at all, except as to the point actually decided:[2] thus, it is not conclusive on a question "what part of the contents of the will is effectual, and in what way the court shall determine on the property",[3] or, generally, on any question of the administration of the estate of the deceased, or as to the law (depending on the domicil of the deceased) under which the administration is to proceed.[4]

Tax decisions

279 Judgments declaring the legality, or the illegality, of a tax, affecting as they do both the financial and the political status of all subjects of the Crown on whom the tax is imposed, are manifestly decisions *in rem*. The most striking reported illustration of the conclusiveness *in rem* of decisions affecting the public revenue is a case in which the legality of the famous Ship Money judgment, pronounced by a majority of the Exchequer Chamber in *R.* v. *Hampden*, was vainly sought to be questioned by Lord SAYE, in an "action for trover and conversion of three oxen, taken for three pounds, five shillings, assessed by the sheriff of Lincoln upon the plaintiff towards the finding of a ship". At the trial, "upon demurrer at the bar, Holbourn being ready to argue, BANKS, Attorney-General, moved that he might not be permitted to argue any of the matters contrary to the judgment of the Exchequer Chamber betwixt the King and Mr Hampden. Holbourn offered to argue that anyone who was not a party to the former judgment in the Exchequer Chamber may be permitted to argue against it. But BRAMPSTON C.J., JONES and BERKELEY JJ., . . . said that such a judgment ought to stand until it is reversed in Parliament, and none ought to be suffered to dispute against it".[5] The judgment in *Hampden's Case*, as the Exchequer Chamber seems to have anticipated, was very shortly afterwards "reversed in Parliament" by a Resolution of both Houses, embodied in 17 Car. 1, c. 14, whereupon not only was everybody "suffered to dispute against it", but no one was suffered to dispute for it, as was held in a

---

1 *Bouchier* v. *Taylor* (1776), 4 Bro. Parl. Cases 708; *Barrs* v. *Jackson* (1845), 1 Ph. 582, at pp. 587–588.

2 As in *Blackham's Case*, *supra*, per Lord HOLT C.J. at pp. 290–291. *Cf.* the observations of Lord LYNDHURST L.C. at pp. 588–589 in *Barrs* v. *Jackson*, *supra*.

3 *Thornton* v. *Curling*, *supra* (per Lord COTTENHAM L.C., at pp. 313–314).

4 *Whicker* v. *Hume*, *supra* (per Lord CRANWORTH, at pp. 156, 157, and Lord WENSLEYDALE, at pp. 165, 166).

5 *Lord Say's Case* (1639), Cro. Car. 524. The judgment *was* afterwards "reversed in Parliament" by a Resolution of both Houses, which was thereafter embodied in the statute 17 Car. 1, c. 14. The tables were thus completely turned, and not only was anyone "suffered to dispute against" the Hampden judgment, but no one was "suffered to dispute" for it.

case,[1] following closely upon the reversal, which, if the reversal can be deemed a judicial decision, is an apt illustration of the conclusiveness *in rem* of a declaration of the illegality of a tax, just as the former authority is of the conclusiveness *in rem* of a declaration of the legality of a tax. On the same principle, a condemnation of goods by the Exchequer for offences against the revenue is conclusive, not only as between the Crown and the offender on a subsequent information,[2] but also as against all the subjects of the Crown, both as to the fact of the condemnation and forfeiture, and also as to the existence of all such facts and conditions as rendered the goods liable to forfeiture, and constituted the offence.[3] But an order upon the offender to pay penalties for the offence, or so much of a conviction as consists of such an order, is not deemed a decision which determines the status of the goods, or which, therefore, concludes anyone but the Crown and the particular offender.[4]

Status of property under the Rent Acts

280 It has sometimes been said that the Rent Acts operate *in rem* and not *in personam* as determining whether or not premises are within those Acts; but this does not mean that judgments declaring that premises are within, or outside, the acts are judgments *in rem* binding upon all the world. They are judgments only *inter partes*, and those not parties to the judgments may accordingly subsequently dispute the validity of any such determination.[5]

Foreign decisions which determine the status of a thing

281 A foreign decision which determines the status of a thing, in the sense already indicated, is as conclusive *in rem*, both in the foreign country

[1] *Chambers* v. *Brumfeild* (1641), Cro. Car. 601, an action for false imprisonment against the then Lord Mayor of London, who attempted to justify under the Ship Money judgment: ("it having been resolved by Parliament that the said writ, and what was done by colour thereof, was illegal, the court would no further dispute thereof, but gave judgment for the plaintiff").

[2] As in *R.* v. *Matthews* (1797), 5 Price 202 n.; *A.-G.* v. *Wakefield* (1797), *ibid.*; *A.-G.* v. *Reynolds* (1804), 5 Price 203 n.; *A.-G.* v. *R.* (1817), 5 Price 195, where, however, the offence, the subject of the information, not being the same as that for which the goods were condemned, there was no estoppel (per RICHARDS C.B., at p. 214); *Hobbs* v. *Henning* (1865), 17 C.B. N.S. 791 (*per Cur.*, at p. 823).

[3] *Scott* v. *Shearman* (1775), 2 Wm. Bl. 977 (per BLACKSTONE J., at p. 978: "I take this condemnation to be conclusive evidence against all the world . . . not only with respect to the goods themselves, but every other collateral remedy for taking them"); *Hart* v. *Macnamara* (1817), 4 Price 154 n., per GIBBS C.J., as cited in the next note.

[4] *Hart* v. *Macnamara*, *supra*, where, in an action for the price of rum, the defendant relied upon the record of a condemnation of the rum as conclusive evidence of the fact that the rum was adulterated, and also upon the record of a conviction for penalties against the plaintiff, and "GIBBS C.J. held that the record of the condemnation was admissible, being *in rem*, but he refused to admit the record of conviction for penalties, as it was *in personam*, and it was not evidence in any case in which the parties were different".

[5] *Lazarus-Barlow* v. *Regent Estates Co., Ltd.*, [1949] 2 All E.R. 118; [1949] 2 K.B. 465, C.A.

and in this, as an English decision determining the status of a thing is in England. In order to determine whether the foreign decision does, or does not, determine the status of a thing, "the inquiry is, first, whether the subject-matter was so situated as to be within the lawful control of the State under the authority of which the court sits; and, secondly, whether the sovereign authority of that State has conferred on the court jurisdiction to decide as to the disposition of the thing, and the court has acted within its jurisdiction. If these conditions are fulfilled, the adjudication is conclusive against all the world",[1] and, in the language of Dr Story, in the case of "proceedings *in rem* as to moveable property, within the jurisdiction of the court pronouncing the judgment", in any country, "whatever it settles as to the right or title, or whatever disposition it makes of the property by sale, revendication, transfer, or other act, will be held valid in every other country".[2]

282 The "thing" of which the status is adjudicated upon by a foreign tribunal, is usually a vessel, as to which decisions of foreign admiralty courts, whether sitting in their ordinary capacity, or in prize, have always been held conclusive upon the world, such courts having, to quote Dr Story again, "a rightful jurisdiction" in such proceedings, "whether they be causes of prize, a bottomry, or salvage", which is "founded on the actual or constructive possession of the subject-matter".[3]

283 Thus, an order of a foreign court of admiralty for the attachment and sale of a vessel, in accordance with the maritime law of the foreign State, to satisfy a *bona fide* holder of a bill of exchange drawn by the master upon the owners for disbursements, is "conclusive everywhere and upon everybody",[4] the intention and effect of the order being to assert jurisdiction over, and to change the property in, the ship.[5] But, when no title is made to the ship, and the order merely disposes of a party's interest in her, by way of execution, or where the order is merely for the attachment and sale of the ship for the benefit of the general body of creditors on the insolvency of the owners, there can be no estoppel *in rem*.[6]

---

[1] *Castrique* v. *Imrie* (1870), L.R. 4 H.L. 414 (per BLACKBURN J., at p. 429).

[2] *Conflict of Laws* para. 792, cited by BLACKBURN J., at p. 428 of *Castrique* v. *Imrie*, *supra*.

[3] *Ibid.*, cited by BLACKBURN J., at p. 429 of *Imrie* v. *Castrique*, *supra*.

[4] *Castrique* v. *Behrens* (1861), 3 E. & E. 709 (per CROMPTON J., delivering the judgment of the court, at p. 722). *Minna Craig S.S. Co.* v. *Chartered Mercantile Bank of India London and China*, [1897] 1 Q.B. 460 C.A. per Lord ESHER M.R. at p. 465; per LOPES L.J. at p. 467; per CHITTY L.J. (semble) at p. 468.

[5] *Castrique* v. *Imrie* (1870), L.R. 4 H.L. 414 (per BLACKBURN J., delivering the opinion of all the judges summoned except CLEASBY B., at pp. 429–432, Lord HATHERLEY L.C., at pp. 442–445, and Lord CHELMSFORD, at p. 447).

[6] *Simpson* v. *Fogo* (1863), 1 Hem. & M. 195 (per WOOD V.-C. at pp. 224, 243).

284 The sentences of the admiralty courts of a foreign state, sitting in prize, whereby a vessel is condemned as lawful prize of that State, are as conclusive *in rem* in all countries, in respect of any question expressly, or by necessary implication, adjudicated upon thereby, as is any other decision of a foreign maritime court which orders the arrest, sale, or other disposition of a vessel. In such cases the question of estoppel usually arises in actions on policies of marine insurance, where the plaintiff alleges the loss of the ship by one of the perils insured against, *viz.* capture, and the defendant sets up the assured's breach of his warranty of neutrality, which breach he contends that the plaintiff is estopped from disputing by the foreign decision that the vessel was an enemy ship, and not a neutral, for otherwise she could not have been condemned as "lawful prize",—a decision which, since the parties can never be identified in such a case, must necessarily take effect *in rem*, or not at all.

285 The doctrine of the conclusiveness of a foreign prize decision is of very gradual growth.[1] Its introduction at the end of the eighteenth, and beginning of the nineteenth, centuries was exceedingly distasteful to Lords THURLOW, KENYON, and ELLENBOROUGH, who expressed, in unmeasured and flamboyant terms, their antagonism to the "overstrained comity" which conceded to the sentences of tribunals of a belligerent State any evidentiary effect at all in this country.[2] Mercantile opinion in time broke down the opposition of these recalcitrant spirits, who, however, while yielding a reluctant submission to the pressure, set to work, in a manner very characteristic of our jurisprudence in some stages of its development, to undermine the unpalatable doctrine by the invention of subtleties and refinements which was carried to such lengths as to excite the just condemnation of Lord ELDON.[3] It may be that an exaggerated deference to the strongly felt, and strongly expressed, views of these early opponents is responsible for the description, which is even now to be found in text-books and in certain judicial deliverances, of the doctrine under discussion, in its application to foreign prize-court decisions, as "anomalous" and

---

[1] *Castrique* v. *Imrie*, *supra* (per BLACKBURN J., at p. 434).

[2] See, for example, the observations of Lord KENYON C.J., at pp. 695, 696, of *Geyer* v. *Aguilar* (1798), 7 Term Rep. 681, and those of Lord ELLENBOROUGH C.J., at p. 431 of *Donaldson* v. *Thompson* (1808), 1 Camp. 429 ("I am by no means disposed to extend the comity which has been shewn to these sentences of foreign admiralty courts. I shall die, like Lord Thurlow, in the belief that they ought never to have been admitted").

[3] At pp. 454–456 of *Lothian* v. *Henderson* (1803), 3 Bos. & P. 499, H.L., where he expressed the view that, whatever sound objections there may have been to its introduction in the first instance, it was then too late to reject the doctrine, considering the large number of contracts, and the vast amount of shipping afloat, on the faith of it, and he deprecated the attempts made in such cases as *Bernardi* v. *Motteux* (1781), 2 Doug. K.B. 575, to whittle it away by refinements, and suggested that possibly this class of authority, as to which see para. 287, note 2, p. 236, *post*, might yet be susceptible of review,—a pious hope which has not been realized.

"exceptional",[1] for, without some such explanation, it is very difficult to understand exactly what it is which is supposed to constitute the anomaly or exception. Be this, however, as it may, it is now well established, in accordance with the first principles of the doctrine of *res judicata* in general, that a foreign prize decision binds the world as to every point which it professes to determine directly and unequivocally, or which, by necessary inference, is "within" the decision, that is to say covered by it.[2] The ordinary form of a foreign prize sentence is that such and such a vessel was captured by the naval forces of the State to which the prize tribunal belongs, and is accordingly condemned as lawful prize of that State. Such a form of sentence necessarily involves a decision, which is conclusive *in rem*, on the question of prize in fact, and on the question of who were the ship's captors, and the like,[3] and, by necessary inference from the use of the word "lawful", it is also a decision that the captured vessel was an enemy, and not a neutral, ship.[4]

286 But, in order that a foreign prize decision may take effect as an estoppel *in rem* or at all, it is essential that all the constituents of estoppel *per rem judicatam* of any kind be established. For instance, there is no estoppel if the foreign tribunal had no jurisdiction in prize over the vessel, as was held to be the case when the tribunal of the belligerent State assumed to exercise judicial authority in prize within the limits of a neutral State, or even within those of a State which was still *de jure*, and in form, an independent neutral state, though, owing to the pressure of enemy forces, it could scarcely be called so *de facto*.[5]

---

1 *Castrique* v. *Imrie* (1870), L.R. 4 H.L. 414 (per BLACKBURN J., at p. 434); *Ballantyne* v. *Mackinnon*, [1896] 2 Q.B. 455, C.A. (*per Cur.*, at p. 462).

2 *Bernardi* v. *Motteux*, *supra* (per Lord MANSFIELD C.J., at p. 580: "all the world are parties to a sentence of a court of admiralty", and "the sentence, *as to that which is within it*, is conclusive upon all persons"); *Christie* v. *Secretan* (1799), 8 Term Rep. 192 (per Lord KENYON C.J., at p. 196); *Dalgleish* v. *Hodgson* (1831), 7 Bing. 495 (per TINDAL C.J., at p. 504: "the sentence of a foreign Court of Admiralty is binding upon all parties and in all countries as to the fact upon which the condemnation proceeded, *where such fact appears upon the face of the sentence, free from doubt and ambiguity*"); *Hobbs* v. *Henning* (1864), 17 C.B. N.S. 791 (*per Cur.*, at p. 824).

3 *Duckworth* v. *Tucker* (1809) 2 Taunt. 7, a case of an English prize decision—see note 3, p. 229, to para. 274, *ante*—but the observations for a general application to prize sentences of all countries.

4 *Geyer* v. *Aguilar* (1798), 7 Term Rep. 681 (per Lord KENYON C.J., and ASHHURST, GROSE, and LAWRENCE JJ., at p. 697); *Bolton* v. *Gladstone* (1809), 2 Taunt. 85, Ex. Ch. (per Sir JAMES MANSFIELD C.J., at pp. 94, 95: "if the court were at liberty to look out of the sentence, there is very little doubt but that the sentence was wrong, and that the ship and cargo were Danish, as warranted; but, if we are not at liberty to look out of the sentence, it is very little material what were the circumstances on which that sentence was given. In several cases, sentences of foreign courts have been held not to be conclusive evidence on this head, because on the face of them it has appeared, perhaps inadvertently, that the ships were condemned, not because they were enemy's property, or not neutral, but on some collateral matter, . . . but such authorities do not apply to any cases where the courts have determined, as here, to condemn the vessel *as not being neutral*").

5 *Donaldson* v. *Thompson* (1808), 1 Camp. 429 (per Lord ELLENBOROUGH C.J., at pp. 431, 432). Generally, as to "competent jurisdiction", see Chap. IV, *ante*.

287 So also, where the fact or point which the world at large is said to be precluded from controverting is not of necessity involved in the foreign prize decision, or is indefinitely and ambiguously expressed, or is mere matter of inducement and preamble, then, in accordance with principles already expounded,[1] the world at large is not estopped, even if the parties are, from disputing that fact or point. Thus, if it appears that the condemnation of the vessel may possibly have proceeded on the ground of some breach of purely national, or municipal, or internal regulations or instructions, and not necessarily, and unequivocally, on the ground of a breach of international law, or the enemy character of the vessel, the prize decision has no extra-territorial efficacy *in rem*, or otherwise.[2] Again, in a case where the foreign sentence was not expressed in the usual form, and the vessel was condemned, not "as lawful prize", but "forasmuch as the true destination of the vessel was the English Islands", it was held that the declared ground of the condemnation (or the principle of *expressum facit cessare tacitum*) left no room for the inference of non-neutrality which otherwise would have been drawn, and, therefore, in no wise precluded the owners from denying, as against the underwriters, any breach of their express warranty that the vessel was American.[3]

288 Where the underwriters have contracted themselves out of the benefit of the estoppel by an express term of the contract of insurance pursuant to which they undertook to pay the policy moneys, whatever the foreign prize court might decide, on the assured proving the vessel's neutrality by production of certain special evidence, all possibility of estoppel disappears.[4]

---

[1] See Chapters V and VI, *ante*.

[2] *Bernardi* v. *Motteux* (1781), 2 Doug. 575; *Christie* v. *Secretan* (1799), 8 Term Rep. 192; *Pollard* v. *Bell* (1800), 8 Term Rep. 434; *Bird* v. *Appleton* (1800), 8 Term Rep. 562; *Price* v. *Bell* (1801), 1 East. 663; *Fisher* v. *Ogle* (1808), 1 Camp. 418; *Dalgleish* v. *Hodgson* (1831), 7 Bing. 495; *Hobbs* v. *Henning* (1864), 17 C.B. N.S. 791. The first edition of this work contains at p. 151 an elaborate footnote analysing these decisions, the details of which have been omitted in this edition.

[3] *Calvert* v. *Bovill* (1798), 7 Term Rep. 523 (per Lord KENYON C.J., at p. 526, and LAWRENCE J., at p. 527).

[4] *Lothian* v. *Henderson* (1803), 3 Bos. & P. 499, H.L. (per Lord ELDON L.C., at pp. 546, 547, and Lord ALVANLEY, at p. 547). See para. 387, Chapter XIII, *post*.

CHAPTER IX

Particular Applications of the Doctrine of Res Judicata: I—Running-Down Cases

Introductory

289 Having considered in sufficient detail the principal essentials of an estoppel *per rem judicatam*, we shall in this and the following three chapters consider some applications of the doctrine to particular cases. The first of the topics thus to be considered is a group of decisions in running-down cases.

290 Running-down cases demonstrate perhaps more readily than any other class of case the difficulties inherent in determining whether the question decided in one proceeding is indeed identical with the question to be decided in another. These difficulties do not at once appear in cases in which two persons, and two only, are concerned as the drivers of two colliding vehicles and as the subsequent litigants; but the presence of a passenger, or of a bystander who is injured, or of a third person whose property is damaged, may reveal them, and in such cases the question is to be posed—is the negligence which has been the subject of one action the same as the negligence which is pleaded as the subject of the other?

Marginson v. *Blackburn Borough Council*

291 A detailed consideration of seven cases[1] decided in the years 1938–66 will serve to demonstrate how difficult is the question which

[1] *Marginson* v. *Blackburn Borough Council*, [1939] 1 All E.R. 273; [1939] 2 K.B. 426, C.A.; *Jackson* v. *Goldsmith* (1950), 81 C.L.R. 446 (H. Ct. of Aus.); *Bell* v. *Holmes*, [1956] 3 All E.R. 449 (McNair J.); *Edwards* v. *Joyce*, [1954] V.L.R. 216 (Sup. Ct. of Victoria; Sholl J.): *Clyne* v. *Yardley*, [1959] N.Z.L.R. 617 (Sup. Ct. of N.Z.; Shorland J.); *Randolph* v. *Tuck*, [1961] 1 All

must be answered. In *Marginson* v. *Blackburn Borough Council*,[1] the first of the cases to be the subject of this study, M. was the owner and his wife the driver of a car in which M. was travelling as a passenger. The pleadings in the subsequent litigation alleged that the husband was the principal or employer of the wife as regards the conduct of the vehicle. The car in which husband and wife were travelling came into collision with a bus driven by B., a servant of the defendant Corporation, in the course of his employment. By reason of the collision the Corporation's bus ran into and damaged two shops belonging to P., a neighbouring property-owner. In one vehicle M.'s wife, the driver, was killed, and M. himself injured; the other vehicle (the Corporation's bus) was seriously damaged. In the first action P. sued M. and the Corporation in negligence for the damage done to his buildings and the goods therein. In their defences M. and the Corporation each alleged that the damage was due solely to the negligence of the servant or agent of the other. Furthermore, M. and the Corporation each served a third-party notice on the other, claiming indemnity or contribution in respect of the damages claimed by P.; and each of them put in a defence to the third-party notice of the other denying liability, denying the other's right to indemnity or contribution, and alleging that the damage sued for was caused solely by the negligence by the other's servant or agent. In addition the Corporation, in its third-party notice, claimed £66.16.0d. against M. in respect of damage alleged to have been done to its bus by the negligence of Mrs M. The date of the case is particularly to be borne in mind; it was decided in 1938–9, after the passing of the Law Reform (Miscellaneous Provisions) Act 1934, but before the enactment of the Law Reform (Contributory Negligence) Act 1945. Though a contribution notice was effective, accordingly, to apportion between the defendants any damages awarded in favour of P. against either or both of them as might be just and equitable having regard to the respective degrees of responsibility of the two defendants for the damage caused, no procedure was available to apportion their responsibility as regards the damage done to their own vehicles, in respect of which, as between the two owners, the contributory negligence of either driver, if established, constituted a complete defence to a claim by him against the other of them. In respect of the Corporation's claim for damages to the bus, therefore, the establishment by M. of contributory

E.R. 814; [1962] 1 Q.B. 175 (LAWTON J.) and *Wood* v. *Luscombe*, [1964] 3 All E.R. 972; [1966] 1 Q.B. 169 (STREATFEILD J.). To these must now be added an eighth decision, only just appearing in the Reports as this work was in the press—*Ramsay* v. *Pigram* (1968), 42 A.L.J.R. 89. It is not at the date of writing yet reported in the Commonwealth Law Reports. This case is briefly noticed in a short appendix at the end of this chapter (*post*, page 257).

[1] [1939] 1 All E.R. 273; [1939] 2 K.B. 426, C.A.

negligence on the part of the bus driver would amount to a complete defence. The county court judge, on the issues before him, found: (a) that Mrs M.'s negligence was a cause of the damage to P.'s property, (b) that the negligence of B. (the Corporation's driver) was also a cause of the same damage, (c) that they were answerable for the damage due to P.'s property in equal shares, (d) that, as between M. and the Corporation, the damage to the Corporation's bus was caused equally by Mrs M.'s negligence and by the contributory negligence of the bus driver. He therefore dismissed the Corporation's claim against M. for damage to the bus.

In subsequent proceedings M. sued the Corporation on three causes of action—(a) on his own behalf, for damages for personal injuries which he himself had sustained in the accident, (b) as his wife's personal representative, in respect of her pain and suffering, before her death, pursuant to the Law Reform (Miscellaneous Provisions) Act 1934, (c) as administrator of his wife's estate on behalf of the persons entitled (*viz.* himself and his daughter) for compensation for her death under Lord Campbell's Act. A plea of estoppel *per rem judicatam* was entered. The decision of Lewis J. at first instance is a classic demonstration of confusion between the principles governing issue estoppel and those governing merger in judgment.[1] But in the Court of Appeal the court rightly applied only the principles governing issue estoppel, to the exclusion of those governing merger. It was held in the Court of Appeal that as regards the first claim (*viz.* that in which M. claimed personally in negligence against the Corporation for damages for personal injury) that M. was precluded by issue estoppel from proceeding, since it had already been adjudged between the same parties, suing or sued in the same right, that "in the matter of the negligence alleged in the driving of the two motor vehicles . . . both parties were to blame";[2] but as regards the second and third claims the plea of issue estoppel was dismissed, since, although these were claims on causes of action vested in M., yet they were vested in him as a different person. In respect of these claims M. was suing as administrator of his wife's estate, or as her personal representative, and it was in fact a mere accident that it was he, and not another, in whose name the claim was to be brought. No difficulty is raised by the dismissal of the plea of issue estoppel in these two cases, and this part of the decision will not be the subject of further discussion in this chapter.[3] Further reference will be made below, however, to the first claim made by M., and to the decision of the Court of Appeal that M. was

---

1 [1938] 2 All E.R. 539.
2 In the judgment of the court per Slesser L.J. at p. 437.
3 The topic of Parties has been fully discussed in Chapter VII, *ante*.

precluded from proceeding with it by the issue estoppel created by the decision of the county court in the earlier case.

292 This decision, when it was first reported, appeared to be a straightforward instance of the proposition that where there are two parties only to litigation arising from the collision of two vehicles driven by the parties or their agents, a decision in one action between them as to the existence or non-existence of negligence on the part of either driver as a cause of the accident will estop either of them from contending, in a subsequent action, for a different result, notwithstanding that the causes of action alleged in the two proceedings may be different. But subsequent criticism has revealed possible flaws in this summary of the effect of the decision, and the problems revealed by this criticism must now be discussed.

293 If the question at issue between M. and the Corporation in the first of the two proceedings had been, "Whose acts or omissions caused the collision between the two vehicles?", and if it appeared that the answer which the court gave to this question was fundamental to the judgment which it gave *inter partes*, and that the judgment could not stand without it, then it would be clear that the answer given by the county court was, "Both were equally to blame", and that if the same question were asked in the second proceedings an estoppel would preclude a different answer.

But was this really the question answered in the first proceedings, or in the record? It may be thought that the real questions posed and decided in the first proceedings were "Was the damage to the Corporation's bus caused by the negligence of Mrs M., and, if so, was it contributed to by the contributory negligence of the Corporation's driver?" Both halves of this question received the answer "Yes". It is apparent that these answers were indeed fundamental to the judgment given in the county court. But it is submitted that in the second proceedings the questions were: "Was the personal injury sustained by M. caused by the negligence of the Corporation's driver, and if so was it contributed to by the contributory negligence of Mrs M., M.'s agent, or by the contributory negligence of M. himself?" These, it is submitted, were not questions identical with those answered in the first proceedings, for negligence as the basis of a claim in tort, and contributory negligence, constituting a complete defence thereto before the Act of 1945, are different things. The result of the first decision in *Marginson's* case, taking into account not only the result, but the words of the judgment, would be substantially justified by a finding of fact that the Corporation bus driver, though not negligent in the breach of any duty which he owed to any other driver on the road, had not taken due care for the safety of his own vehicle.[1] But proof of such a fact, it is submitted, would be irrelevant to the second proceedings, for a finding that the driver of the bus has failed in his duty to himself or to the Corporation does not necessarily make him negligent as regards M. and Mrs M., two other persons in the roadway.[2] And even before *Nance* v. *British Columbia Electric Rail. Co., Ltd.*[3] it could not have been said with certainty that a breach of a duty to take care for his own safety or that of his bus was not all that had been held against the bus driver in the first proceedings. Similarly the finding of the county court in the first proceedings that Mrs M. had been negligent *vis-à-vis* the Corporation's driver—*i.e.* had failed in some material respect in the duty of care which she owed to him—does not necessarily result in the conclusion that she was in default in any material respect as regards any duty of care which she owed to her husband, or that he had contributed by some breach of duty owed to himself to his own injuries—and these are the only duties the breach of which would support a defence of contributory negligence to a claim by him for personal injury against another. In answer to such a claim only a breach by him or his agent of a duty to take care for his preservation, and not the breach of a duty to other users of the road, would give rise to the defence of contributory negligence as such a defence was constituted before the passing of the Act of 1945. Neither *Bourhill* v. *Young*[4] nor *Nance* v. *British Columbia Rail. Co., Ltd.*[5] had been decided in 1939, however, and the Court of Appeal may be excused, as the law of negligence was then understood, for simplifying the question considered in the first action, as in effect they did, to "Whose negligence (*vis-à-vis* everybody) caused this collision?"

Johnson v. *Cartledge and Matthews*

294 The earliest critic of *Marginson* v. *Blackburn Borough Council* appears to have been CASSELS J. who, in *Johnson* v. *Cartledge and Matthews*,[6] decided

---

[1] Indeed it was soon to be decided by the Privy Council in *Nance* v. *British Columbia Electric Rail. Co., Ltd.*, [1951] A.C. 601, P.C. that this is the only proper basis for a finding of contributory negligence—per Viscount SIMON, delivering the advice of their Lordships at p. 611.

[2] *Bourhill* v. *Young*, [1943] A.C. 92, H.L. pre Lord PORTER at p. 113—"Before any decision on quantum of damage is required, it has first to be determined whether the cyclist was guilty of any negligence towards the appellant. 'The law takes no cognisance of carelessness in the abstract. It concerns itself with carelessness only where there is a duty to take care, and where failure in that duty has caused damage': per Lord MACMILLAN in *Donoghue* v. *Stevenson*. It is not enough to say that the cyclist was guilty of negligence towards someone". And at p. 116 of the same case—"In the case of a civil action there is no such thing as negligence in the abstract; there must be neglect in the use of care towards a person to whom the defendant owes a duty of observing care". *Cf.* the judgment of Lord RUSSELL OF KILLOWEN at pp. 101–102.

[3] [1951] 2 All E.R. 448; [1951] A.C. 601, P.C.

[4] [1943] A.C. 92, H.L.

[5] [1951] 2 All E.R. 448; [1951] A.C. 601, P.C.

[6] [1939] 3 All E.R. 654 (CASSELS J.).

in the same year, distinguished it and declined to uphold an estoppel in a short judgment which it is not proposed to discuss in any detail here.

Jackson v. *Goldsmith*

295 The possible criticism of the decision in *Marginson's* case which is adumbrated in the preceding passage in the text gains in emphasis when the next of the cases is considered—*Jackson* v. *Goldsmith*,[1] a decision of the High Court of Australia in 1950. As will be seen, that court, in circumstances very different from those in *Marginson's* case, disallowed the plea of estoppel, differentiating the questions asked in the two sets of proceedings by a process of reasoning very similar to that suggested above. The High Court, however, uttered no word of disagreement with the actual result of *Marginson's* case, the only judge in the majority group who mentioned that decision contenting himself with distinguishing it as on a very different set of facts, in which only the duties of the parties *inter se*, and not their duty of care to a third party, arose.[2]

The facts in *Jackson* v. *Goldsmith* were as follows. J., the owner and driver of a motorcycle on which W. was being carried as a passenger, collided with a car owned and driven by G. In the first of the proceedings which ensued G. sued J. in the District Court, claiming damages in negligence for damage done to his car. It is important to notice at this point that in 1950 the old Common Law rules as to contributory negligence still obtained in New South Wales, and that in that jurisdiction the contributory negligence of a plaintiff was at that time a complete defence. J. pleaded the contributory negligence of G. as a defence. The decision of the District Court on G's claim against J. was that the accident was caused by J's negligence only, and that G. was not guilty of contributory negligence, and G. recovered judgment accordingly for the damages proved. In the second proceedings W, J's passenger, sued him (J.), but not G., for damages for personal injury; J. joined G. as a third party, alleging that G.'s negligence had materially contributed to the collision, and claiming under the Law Reform (Miscellaneous Provisions) Act 1946 (N.S.W.) to be entitled to recover either contribution or a complete indemnity from him in respect of any verdict which W. might recover. In a plea to this notice G. pleaded that J. was precluded from re-litigating his liability to contribute, since

[1] (1950), 81 C.L.R. 446 (H. Ct. of Aus.). It has been convenient simply to notice at this point, as part of the historical narrative, the decision of CASSELS J. (at the Nottingham Assizes) in *Johnson* v. *Cartledge and Matthews*, [1939] 3 All E.R. 654. CASSELS J. perceived the essential difficulty, and declined to allow the estoppel contended for: but the decision is not examined in any detail in the text, since his use of the words 'this is not the same *damage*' serve rather to obscure than to illuminate a discussion of the difficulty which he undoubtedly discerned.

[2] WILLIAMS J. at p. 462.

the matter of G.'s liability to J. was *res judicata*, all questions of negligence between them having been concluded in G.'s favour in the first action, in which the District Court had found J. negligent and G. not guilty of contributory negligence. It was held by the High Court of Australia that there was no issue estoppel by which J. was precluded by the findings of the District Court in the first action from proceeding by way of contribution notice against G. in the second action, for the reason that the questions were different in the two actions.

296 Once again in this case the confusion between merger in judgment and issue estoppel clouded the arguments of counsel—but not the judgments of the members of the High Court. It was recognised in the judgments that the fact that the causes of action were different in the two proceedings was quite irrelevant to the crucial question *viz.* whether the *issue* was the same. The issue in the first action (so far as the decision in that action could be relevant to the issue in the second) was held to be simply whether or not G. was guilty of contributory negligence amounting to a defence to G.'s plea of J.'s negligence causing the collision. This was, so the court held, not the same as the question whether G. was in breach of a duty to take care owed to W. It will be sufficient to quote from the judgment of LATHAM C.J. which reflects the opinion of the majority of the court. He said:[1]

> "In the District Court the issue was whether Goldsmith had been guilty of contributory negligence, that is, had he contributed to the injury to Jackson[2] (sic) by either—(1) carelessness with respect to his own safety; or (2) breach of a duty which he owed to Jackson to take care? What was decided was that Goldsmith was not guilty of contributory negligence. This decision therefore negated the following propositions: (1) that Goldsmith contributed to his own injury by carelessness for his own safety; (2) that he contributed thereto by negligence consisting in a breach of a duty owed by him to Jackson to take care.[3]
>
> In the third party proceedings in the Supreme Court the question is whether Goldsmith is liable in respect of the injury done to White by reason of a breach of a duty to take care which he owed to White. The proceedings in the District Court did not determine whether there was any breach by Goldsmith of a duty which he owed to White. Neither proposition (1) nor proposition (2) is a determination of the issue in the third party proceedings.

---

[1] At p. 455.

[2] Clearly an error; the text should read "to himself". The first claim had been made by Goldsmith against Jackson, in respect of the damage to Goldsmith's car, and there was no counterclaim.

[3] It will be remembered that at this time *Nance* v. *British Columbia Electric Rail. Co., Ltd.*, [1951] A.C. 601 had not yet been decided. The duality of LATHAM C.J's proposition does not, it is submitted, in any way affect the logic of his reasoning. Indeed, in adopting exactly the same reasoning MCTIERNAN J. at p. 458 bases his decision on the narrower ground.

> Therefore the decision in the District Court does not estop Jackson from alleging that Goldsmith was guilty of a breach of a duty which he owed to White."

Three of the other members of the court gave judgment along similar lines, though it appears possible that a majority would have interpreted the finding in the first case simply as a finding that G. was not in breach of a duty owed to *himself* to take care; but this point does not affect in any way the logic of the judgments. FULLAGAR J. dissented, but on a point of pleading.

297 It is submitted that this case was correctly decided. Whereas in *Marginson* v. *Blackburn Borough Council* the Court of Appeal made no distinction between the duty the breach of which was the subject of the decision in the first action and the duty the breach of which was alleged in the second, in *Jackson* v. *Goldsmith* the High Court recognised that the duties which J. & G. owed respectively to W., the passenger of one of them, might be different from the duty of care which each owed to the other. Negligence is not a matter which can be discussed *in vacuo*; it consists of a breach of a duty of care owed in certain circumstances to a given person, and the duty may differ from person to person. Hence it follows that a decision as to one duty cannot estop the parties when in any subsequent proceedings the breach of another is alleged, even though in fact it may, and generally will, turn out to be the case that there is little or no difference between the duties in the two proceedings.

Three points are particularly to be noticed about *Jackson* v. *Goldsmith*. First, like *Marginson* v. *Blackburn Borough Council*, it was decided before the passing (in this case in New South Wales) of the Contributory Negligence Act. Contributory negligence was still a complete defence, and the considerations arising from the text of the Contributory Negligence Act, which had importance in the later cases, still did not arise here. In the second place, no-one suggested that the decision in *Marginson* v. *Blackburn Borough Council* was not correct. That case was mentioned in the judgment only of one judge in the majority group—WILLIAMS J.—and he was content to distinguish it on the facts without any examination of the question whether the same principles upon which the High Court declined to sustain the estoppel might not also have been applicable to the facts in *Marginson's* case when the latter were examined in detail. It is also to be noticed (and this will more clearly be seen when *Edwards* v. *Joyce*[1] and *Clyne* v. *Yardley*[1] come to be considered) that the failure of the estoppel in *Jackson* v. *Goldsmith* is not to be attributed to the fact that in one of the sets of proceedings

---

[1] *Edwards* v. *Joyce*, [1954] V.L.R. 216 (SHOLL J.); *Clyne* v. *Yardley*, [1959] N.Z.L.R. 617 (SHORLAND J.). These two decisions are considered in the text, *infra*.

an additional party was joined. The question on which an estoppel was invoked was one exclusively between the two parties to the first action. The reason for the failure of the estoppel was that as between the same parties a different question had arisen.

Bell v. *Holmes*

298 The third of the decisions to be examined is that of McNAIR, J. in *Bell* v. *Holmes*[1] in 1956. The date is again particularly to be borne in mind, for it is to be noticed that this case, and all those which follow, are governed by the provisions of the Contributory Negligence Act. *Bell* v. *Holmes* was an oral decision given at first instance at Leeds Assizes, and the learned judge expressly acknowledged that he had not had the opportunity of giving consideration to the report of *Jackson* v. *Goldsmith*, though this case had been mentioned to him through the industry of counsel. B's taxi-cab had come into collision with H.'s vehicle. In the first action E., a passenger in H.'s vehicle, sued B. and H. for damages for personal injury. Each denied negligence, and each blamed the other for the accident. Though no formal contribution notices were issued by either defendant against the other, the matter of contribution between them was dealt with by the trial judge by consent, and McNAIR J. held, for the purposes of the second proceedings, that this question of contribution had been dealt with in the first proceedings in every way as if contribution notices had been formally served. It was adjudged that B. should contribute five-sixths of the damages and H. one-sixth. The damages were duly paid in these proportions, pursuant to the judgment.

In the second proceedings B. sued H. for damages in respect of the personal injuries sustained by him in the collision. The facts resembled those in *Jackson* v. *Goldsmith* in that in one set of proceedings the drivers were suing and sued *inter se* while in the other a third party sued one or both; but in the Australian case the drivers litigated first and the passenger sued afterwards, while in *Bell* v. *Holmes* the reverse was the case. It is submitted that this distinction is unimportant. McNAIR J. began his oral judgment with an expression of regret that the matter had to be determined at Assizes, without the time for deliberation which would have been desirable. He held that an estoppel precluded the second action, as a question so similar as to be almost identical had been decided in the first. He said:

> "A further point was taken of this nature. It was said that the issues in the County Court action and the issues in the present action were not the same because in the County Court action the matter in issue between Miss Elsworth and the two defendants to that action was whether or not there had been a

[1] [1956] 3 All E.R. 449.

breach of their respective duties towards her, whereas in the present action the question was whether there had been a breach of the duties: (i) owed by the defendant to the plaintiff, and (ii) owed by the plaintiff to the defendant. Those are different legal issues of course, in a sense, but I do not feel that the fact that they are technically different should prevent effect being given to the plea of estoppel in a case where, having examined the pleadings in the County Court action and compared them with the pleadings in the present action, I am satisfied that the issues of fact, and the evidence to support them in respect of liability, would be identically the same. In *Ord* v. *Ord*, [1923] 2 K.B. 432, at p. 443 LUSH, J., quoted this passage from the judgment of Lord WESTBURY, L.C. in *Hunter* v. *Stewart* (1861), 4 De G.F. & J. 168, at p. 178):

> 'One of the criteria of the identity of two suits, in considering a plea of res judicata, is the inquiry whether the same evidence would support both.'

Furthermore, it seems to me that as the County Court judge's decision on the material matter in the present action was as to the apportionment of the responsibility which rested on the two defendants in that action, that question is identical with and would be supported by the same evidence as the issues in this action if it were allowed to go to trial."

He distinguished *Jackson* v. *Goldsmith* (which decision he admittedly had not read *in extenso*) by saying that:

> "It seems to me that there is a distinction between that case and this, as in the Australian case the judgment which it was sought to set up as an estoppel was a judgment in an action between two only of the three parties here involved in the collision, and I can well understand that the introduction of an additional party might operate to destroy the conclusiveness of the judgment given in the earlier action."

299 It is suggested that *Bell* v. *Holmes*, if it is to be distinguished from *Jackson* v. *Goldsmith*, must be distinguished on another ground—*viz*. that the Contributory Negligence Act 1945, as well as the Law Reform Act of 1935, was by this time in force in England. It can be argued that the parallel wording of Section 6 of the Law Reform Act and of Section 1 of the Contributory Negligence Act had the effect of making the questions which arose in the two actions the same. The words of the Law Reform Act, if read into the record of the first proceedings, give to the apportionment order made on E.'s action the effect of deciding that it was just and equitable that B. should assume five-sixths, and H. one-sixth, of the responsibility for the injury sustained by E., H.'s passenger. If the words of Section 1 of the Contributory Negligence Act are similarly applied to the second action, the question there arising may be seen to be: In what proportions is it just and equitable that B. and H. should assume responsibility for the injury sustained by B. in the collision? MCNAIR J. found these to be "almost identical" questions. So they were: but were they *necessarily identical*? This is a question which we must reserve for consideration later in the text.[1]

Edwards v. *Joyce*

300 In the meantime, in the Supreme Court of Victoria, SHOLL, J. had decided *Edwards* v. *Joyce*.[2] N. and E. were passengers in a car driven by Mrs W., which collided with a truck owned by L. and F. and driven by their servant J. N. and E. were injured and Mrs W. killed. In the first proceedings, N., one of Mrs W.'s passengers, sued J. and also W., as executor of his deceased wife, for negligence in respect of the personal injuries which she had sustained. W. issued a third party notice claiming indemnity and contribution under the Wrongs (Tortfeasors) Act 1949. A verdict was entered for N. against both J. and W., and the proportions in which they were held responsible *inter se* for N.'s damages was fixed at three-fourths for J. and one-fourth for W. In the second proceedings E., the other passenger in Mrs W.'s car, sued J. and his employers in respect of the personal injuries which she had sustained. She was out of time to join W. as a defendant, but both J. and his employers issued third party notices against W. as Mrs W.'s executor claiming indemnity and contribution in respect of any damages awarded against them. Pleadings on the third party notices were directed, and W. claimed that the issue raised against him by J. and by L. and F., his employers, was the same as that already determined in his favour (in the ratio one-fourth to three-fourths) in the action brought by N., and that both J. and his employers were estopped by the result of that action from contending that the proportions in which any damages should be borne should be other than those of one-fourth to three-fourths.

SHOLL J. held that L. and F. were not in any case to be estopped by the result of earlier proceedings to which they were not parties, nor, (as he held) privies.[3] As regards J., he held that no estoppel arose, applying *Bourhill* v. *Young* (*supra*) and *Jackson* v. *Goldsmith* (by which decision he was of course bound). It may be questioned, however, whether he was correct in concluding that the latter case was directly in point. In *Jackson* v. *Goldsmith* it will be remembered that a distinction was made between a decision that, as between drivers, one of them was not guilty of contributory negligence, and a decision as to the respective degrees of responsibility of the same two drivers as regards injuries suffered by a passenger of one of them. In

---

[1] See pp. 305 *et seq. infra*.
[2] [1954] V.L.R. 216 (Supreme Ct. of Victoria; SHOLL J.).
[3] This topic is to be found more fully discussed in Chapter VII, *ante*.

Edwards v. *Joyce*, however, no question of contributory negligence as between the two drivers had arisen in the first proceedings; what was decided in the first proceedings in that case, was the proportion in which it was just and equitable that the two drivers should bear the responsibility for any damages awarded to N., a passenger of one of them. It might seem (so it is now submitted) that this question was necessarily identical with the question in the second proceedings *viz.* in what proportion it was just and equitable that the two drivers should bear the responsibility for the damages suffered by E., another passenger in the same car, and that it is inconceivable that the proportion should be different in the two cases. No submission of contributory negligence on the part of either of the passengers can possibly complicate the matter, for, if either was contributorily negligent, his claim would thereby be diminished before any question of contribution as between the two drivers arose, and it would be only as regards the net claim that the proportions of responsibility would fall to be decided. It is theoretically possible, but practically difficult, to distinguish between the issues of liability as regards the claims of the two passengers in the same car; and it is therefore submitted that *Edwards* v. *Joyce* was too meticulously decided, and that in view of the statutory provisions by reference to whose text the question between the parties is to be determined, *Bell* v. *Holmes* may be the better authority.

Clyne v. *Yardley*

301 The next case to be considered is *Clyne* v. *Yardley*[1] a case decided by SHORLAND J. at first instance in the Supreme Court of New Zealand in 1959. The judgment was in writing, and bears the marks of a careful consideration of all the authorities which have already been examined. A collision occurred between a car owned and driven by C., and one owned by W., and driven by Y., his son, but not in the course of agency or employment. In the first action C. sued Y. in the Magistrate's Court for the damage to C.'s car, alleging negligence, and obtained judgment for £205.14.6d., less a contribution of one-fourth for contributory negligence on his own part.[2] On the same day, in another and separate action, W. sued C. for damage done to his car and obtained judgment for the full amount claimed, £206.9.0d. It will be noticed that, Y. not being W.'s servant or agent, no plea of his contributory negligence could be effective in these proceedings to lessen W.'s claim. In subsequent proceedings C. sued Y. under Section 17 of the Law Reform Act 1936, (N.Z.) claiming to recover by way of contribution three-fourths of the total sum of £206.9.0d.

[1] [1959] N.Z.L.R. 617.
[2] New Zealand's Contributory Negligence Act as passed in 1947.

for which judgment had been recovered against him in the second of the first two actions. It was argued on a question of law before trial that Y. was precluded by issue estoppel from contending by way of defence that his share of the responsibility for the damage done to W.'s car was other than three-fourths. SHORLAND J. held Y. estopped from contending that his share of responsibility was other than three-fourths. He based his decision on *Hoystead* v. *Federal Taxation Commissioner*,[1] and *Blair* v. *Curran*,[2] and said:[3]

> "The important point for present purposes, which I take to be established by the authorities so far dealt with, is that the principle in its application extends to a point of fact which was, in substance, the ratio of and fundamental to the decision. If this is the law, then those points of fact which were the ratio of and fundamental to the decision of the magistrate in his determination in the prior action brought by Clyne against David Yardley for damages in respect of the damage done to Clyne's car, wherein he decided that the collision was caused by negligence on the part of them both, and further, that it was (pursuant to s. 3 of the Contributory Negligence Act 1947) just and equitable having regard to Clyne's share in the responsibility for the damage, that the damage suffered by Clyne should be reduced by 25 per cent, having been litigated to conclusion between Clyne and David Yardley, must now be taken as finally and conclusively established between these two parties."

In so deciding he followed *Marginson* v. *Blackburn Borough Council*[4] and *Bell* v. *Holmes*[5] and declined on the facts of the case before him to follow *Jackson* v. *Goldsmith*[6] and *Edwards* v. *Joyce*[7]; he did not find the question in the two proceedings before him tainted with the same lack of identity as formed the basis of the two Australian decisions. He realised, as had SHOLL J. in *Edwards* v. *Joyce*, that there was an essential cleavage in principle between *Marginson's* case and *Jackson's* case, and that the difference in the decisions in these cases was not due, as MCNAIR J. had thought, to the introduction of a third party, but to a difference on the essential question as to whether the issues of negligence in the two sets of proceedings were distinguishable. On this point he said:[8]

> "although there are differences and distinctions between *Marginson's Case* and *Jackson's Case*, I find the two decisions in the final analysis to be irreconcilable. If the view adopted by the majority in the High Court that the duty of care upon the driver of a motor-vehicle is to be taken as a separate duty and

---

[1] [1926] A.C. 155, P.C. at p. 166.
[2] (1939), 62 C.L.R. 464.
[3] At page 621.
[4] [1939] 1 All E.R. 273; [1939] 2 K.B. 426.
[5] [1956] 3 All E.R. 449.
[6] (1950), 81 C.L.R. 446.
[7] [1954] V.L.R. 216.
[8] (1959) N.Z.L.R. 617 at p. 626.

issue in respect of each person or object encountered, then the finding of the County Court in *Marginson's* case that Mrs Marginson had been guilty of failure to exercise reasonable care to avoid coming into collision with the bus and thereby in breach of the duty owed to the Borough and to the owners of the dwellinghouses, the identical duty of care which she owed to her husband as her passenger was a different issue from the one decided in the County Court. Nevertheless the Court of Appeal held that Marginson was estopped by the prior decision, because he was the principal answerable for her negligence and met by the defence of contributory negligence in respect of his personal claims against the Borough.''

Left with the choice between *Marginson* v. *Blackburn Borough Council* (*supra*) and *Jackson* v. *Goldsmith* (*supra*), SHORLAND J. followed the former. Recognising that ''the principle of issue estoppel . . . extends to every point of fact which was put in issue and which was in substance the ratio of and fundamental to the decision'', he concluded that the charges of negligence in running-down litigation could without undue difficulty be broken down into a number of detailed allegations of fact, and that the findings of the court in respect of these in earlier proceedings could form the subject of a series of issue estoppels in subsequent litigation between the same parties. These findings of detailed fact in the earlier proceedings, he thought, must necessarily be accepted by the parties in later litigation as a sort of official narrative of what had taken place.

302 It has already been submitted in another passage in this work[1] for the reasons there to be found, that estoppel in running-down cases, as in other cases, goes no further than what DIXON J. has called ''those ultimate facts which form the ingredients of the cause of action''.[2] On this view of the principle governing issue estoppel, the parties will be estopped by a finding of negligence in one action which relates as between the same parties to the very duty the breach of which is alleged in the second action; but will not be estopped by any finding as to the factual particulars in detail on which that allegation of negligence is based. If the test proposed by DIXON J. is to be accepted, it is submitted that SHORLAND J. was wrong in preferring *Marginson's* case to *Jackson's* case; but the acceptability of DIXON J.'s test will be adverted to again at the conclusion of this chapter.

It may be thought possible, nevertheless, to justify the decision in *Clyne* v. *Yardley* as good on its own facts. In the circumstances of that case it was indeed possible to say that the closest approximation to absolute accuracy, if not with mathematical certainty, that the fundamental facts previously

---

[1] The topic is discussed in Chapter VI, *ante*.

[2] In *Blair* v. *Curran* (1939), 62 C.L.R. 464 (H. Ct. of Aus.) at p. 532.

found against the driver and constituting negligence in respect of the duty owed by him to the opposing driver must also constitute negligence on the part of such driver in respect of any duty which he owed to the owner of the opposing driver's car. In both cases, his duty was no more, and no less than to exercise such care as is reasonable to avoid a collision with the incoming car. If this analysis of the factual situation be acceptable, then SHORLAND J. was right in the decision to which he came, and this notwithstanding the decision in *Jackson* v. *Goldsmith*, for the latter decision was clearly distinguishable as on a set of facts in which the issues of negligence were different.

But in attempting to justify the decision in *Clyne* v. *Yardley* as a matter of "common sense", solacing ourselves with the comfortable reflection that the duty owed by each of two car drivers, approaching each other, to the other of them must be the same in nearly every case, must we not ultimately become conscious of the nagging objection that the issues of negligence in the two cases, though nearly always the same, will not necessarily be so in *every* case? Principle is principle: and once *identity* of issues is departed from in the interests of "robust common sense", it becomes impossible to draw the line. Does the maxim *interest rei publicae sit finis litium* have any validity at all, where the issues are not *necessarily identical*? This is a hard question; yet it is submitted that it admits of only one final answer, *viz.*, the conclusion that, tempting as it is to justify *Clyne* v. *Yardley* on the grounds of common sense, the case was wrongly decided in law.

Randolph v. *Tuck*

303 *Randolph* v. *Tuck*[1] was a case decided at first instance by LAWTON J. in 1961. A car owned and driven by T. collided with one owned by A.P. Ltd. and driven by S., its servant. R., a passenger in T.'s car, was injured, as was T. himself also. In the first proceedings T. sued A.P. Ltd. and S. in the West London County Court for damages for the personal injuries which he received in the collision. Judgment was given for both defendants. There was no appeal. In the second proceedings R. (T.'s passenger) sued T. and S., and also A.P. Ltd., for damages for the injuries received by him. S. and A.P. Ltd. issued a contribution notice against T., seeking a complete indemnity. LAWTON J. held that R. was entitled to judgment against all the defendants, and apportioned the responsibility as equal between T. and S. The question was then argued as a matter of law, whether issue estoppel arising from the first proceedings did not preclude T. from contending that he should not give S. and his employers a complete indemnity. LAWTON J., after considering all the authorities which we have examined above,

---

[1] [1961] 1 All E.R. 814; [1962] 1 Q.B. 175.

thought that he was not bound by *Marginson* v. *Blackburn Borough Council*,[1] which dealt only with two parties and their claims *inter se*. He preferred *Jackson* v. *Goldsmith* to *Bell* v. *Holmes*, and followed the Australian cases; he considered and rejected *Clyne* v. *Yardley*, though accepting that the point which SHORLAND J. decided was the same as that which came before him.

The reasons on which LAWTON J. founded his judgment are to be found in the following passage:[2]

> "The validity of the second submission depends on the second and third defendants establishing that in the County Court action, there was put in issue and decided the precise question, the precise fact which arises in these third-party proceedings: see *Ord* v. *Ord*, [1923] All E.R. Rep. 206, at p. 210; [1923] 2 K.B. 432, at p. 440, per LUSH J. What was the precise question, the precise fact which was put in issue and decided in the County Court action? In my judgment it was that the damage suffered by the first defendant was caused, not by any breach of duty owed to him by the third defendant, but by his failure to take proper care for his own safety. In the action before me, the question in issue and for decision was whether the damage suffered by the plaintiff had been caused by any breach of duty owed to her by the defendants Tuck and Steele or either of them. The nature and extent of their duty to her may have been similar to the nature and extent of their duty to each other, but, if I understand *Bourhill* v. *Young*, [1942] 2 All E.R. 396; [1943] A.C. 92, they were separate and distinct duties, not two aspects of a general duty which, as motorists, they owed to all road users and which the County Court judge had decided had not been broken by the first defendant, Steele. The issue whether these defendants, or either of them, were in breach of their respective duties to the plaintiff was never before the County Court. The fact that issues in two actions are similar does not raise an estoppel: see *Broken Hill Proprietary Co.* v. *Broken Hill Municipal Council*, [1925] All E.R. Rep. 672; [1926] A.C. 94 and *New Brunswick Rail Co.* v. *British and French Trust Corporation, Ltd.*, [1938] 4 All E.R. 747; [1939] A.C. 1, in which Lord ROMER said [1938] 4 All E.R. at p. 770; [1939] A.C. at p. 43:
>
> > 'It is no doubt true to say that, whenever a question has in substance been decided, or has in substance formed the ratio of, or been fundamental to, the decision in an earlier action between the same parties, each party is estopped from litigating the same question thereafter. However, this is very different from saying that he may not thereafter litigate, not the same question, but a question that is merely substantially similar to the one that has already been decided.'
>
> Now that these defendants have each been adjudged to have been in breach of duty to the plaintiff, a further question arises between them as to the extent of their respective responsibilities for the damage suffered by the plaintiff. This issue was never before the County Court, and was not substantially the same as that which was. The County Court action was concerned with causation, whereas I have had to consider both causation and blameworthiness

---

[1] [1939] 1 All E.R. 273; [1939] 2 K.B. 426, C.A.

[2] [1962] 1 Q.B. 175, at page 184 of the report.

—and the factor of blameworthiness may have an important bearing on the extent of responsibility: see *Stapley* v. *Gypsum Mines, Ltd.*, [1953] 2 All E.R. 478; [1953] A.C. 663 and *Cavanagh* v. *London Transport Executive*, *Times*, 1956, Oct. 23. It follows, so it seems to me, in principle, and in the absence of any binding authority, that the second and third defendants have not established an estoppel by record. On broadly similar facts the High Court of Australia, in *Jackson* v. *Goldsmith* ((1950), 81 C.L.R. 446), and the Appellate Division of the Supreme Court of the State of New York, in *Neenan* v. *Woodside Astoria Transport Co.* (1932), 256 New York Supp. 38, held that no estoppels were raised."

Wood v. *Luscombe*

304 Before proceeding to a criticism of the reasoning of LAWTON, J. let us notice the last, in point of time, of the running-down cases. This is *Wood* v. *Luscombe*[1] another Assizes decision, this time of STREATFEILD, J. W. was a pillion passenger on a motor cycle, of which S., his son, was the driver: the cycle collided with another motor cycle driven by L. on a straight road, but in fog. L. sued S. for damages for personal injuries. PHILLIMORE, J. held both parties equally to blame for the collision, and gave judgment for half the amount claimed. In the second action W. sued L., and L. joined S. as a third party. As between W. and L. the claim was settled, and judgment was entered for an agreed amount as between them in the second proceedings; but the respective responsibilities of the defendant and the third party for the agreed damages remained for argument. L. contended that S. was estopped by the earlier decision of PHILLIMORE, J. S. contended that the issue was a different one, and that there was no estoppel. It will be seen that the material facts are identical with those in *Randolph* v. *Tuck*. They are similar, moreover, to those in *Clyne* v. *Yardley*[2] except that the third party who made his appearance in the intermediate proceedings was the owner of one of the vehicles, while in *Wood* v. *Luscombe* he was a passenger. But in the final proceedings the question was the same in all these cases—as between the two drivers (whose responsibilities *inter se* for the damage to one of the vehicles had been determined in the earlier case) was the proportion of their respective degrees of responsibility to another party the same as that of their responsibilities to each other? STREATFEILD J. followed *Marginson* v. *Blackburn Borough Council*,[3] *Bell* v. *Holmes*[4] and *Clyne* v. *Yardley* (*supra*). As to *Randolph* v. *Tuck*[5] the headnote in [1966] 1 Q.B. 170 contains at p. 171 the statement: "*Randolph* v. *Tuck*

[1] [1964] 3 All E.R. 972; [1966] 1 Q.B. 169.
[2] [1959] N.Z.L.R. 617 (Sup. Ct. of N.Z.).
[3] [1939] 1 All E.R. 273; [1939] 2 K.B. 426, C.A.
[4] [1956[3 All E.R. 449.
[5] [1961] 1 All E.R. 814; [1962] 1 Q.B. 175.

distinguished". It is not said, however, on what ground it was distinguished, and nothing is to be found on this subject in the text of the report. "I find myself in disagreement with the judgment of LAWTON J.", said STREATFEILD J.;[1] no more. The decision of the High Court of Australia in *Jackson* v. *Goldsmith*[2] is not mentioned except in a footnote; STREATFEILD J. dismisses "the Australian and American cases" as something decided in a foreign jurisdiction, of which it is not necessary to say why he passes them over, preferring the English authorities with their demonstrable defects.

305 It will be seen when the cases stated above are considered that all of them except two—*Marginson* v. *Blackburn Borough Council*[3] and *Jackson* v. *Goldsmith*[4] are decisions of judges at first instance, many of them given under the pressure of conditions at Assizes. Until some English Court of high authority has the opportunity (and takes it) of giving deliberate consideration to the conflict demonstrably existing between *Marginson* v. *Blackburn Borough Council* and *Jackson* v. *Goldsmith*, and of stating clearly which is correct in principle, and why, the position as to estoppel in running-down cases in English courts must remain regrettably obscure. It is here suggested that principle must ultimately lead to the vindication of *Jackson* v. *Goldsmith*, and of the decisions of CASSELS J.,[5] and LAWTON J.,[6] and to the abandonment of *Marginson* v. *Blackburn Borough Council*, *Bell* v, *Holmes*, and *Wood* v. *Luscombe*. For it seems impossible, since the decision of the House of Lords in *Bourhill* v. *Young*[7] to revert to the principle that negligence is the breach of a duty owed "to the world at large" and to deny that it must not always be tested "by asking with reference to each of several complainants 'Was the duty owed to him or her?'."[8] "It is not enough to say the cyclist was guilty of negligence towards some one".[9]

But if this be so, and if negligence is always to be considered as a duty owed by one specified person, in given circumstances, to another specified person or persons, then it seems impossible to accept the basis of *Marginson* v. *Blackburn Borough Council*, in which the Court of Appeal was content to regard the determination of the county court in the first case as being that "both parties were to blame in the driving of the two motor vehicles"; and if there be validity in this conclusion, and the question determined by

---

[1] At p. 176 of the report.
[2] (1950), 81 C.L.R. 446.
[3] [1939] 1 All E.R. 273; [1939] 2 K.B. 426, C.A.
[4] (1950), 81 C.L.R. 446 (H. Ct. of Aus.).
[5] In *Johnson* v. *Cartlege and Matthews*, [1939] 3 All E.R. 654. The decision is noticed in footnote 1, p. 242, *supra*.
[6] In *Randolph* v. *Tuck*, [1961] 1 All E.R. 814; [1962] 1 Q.B. 175.
[7] [1943] A.C. 92 (H.L.).
[8] Per Lord PORTER at p. 117 of the report.
[9] Per Lord WRIGHT at p. 113 of the report.

the County Court is examined, it will be seen that it must involve two special questions—(a) whether Mrs Marginson was negligent in driving her vehicle, in failing to discharge the duty of care which she owed to the on-coming bus, and (b) whether the corporation's bus driver took due care *for the safety of his own bus.* To these two questions the court gave the answer "Yes". It seems impossible, except by one of the devices mentioned below, to translate this finding into one that the Corporation's driver failed to discharge a duty of care which he owed to Mrs Marginson.

306 But, as has been pointed out in the course of discussing the decisions, there remain two ways in which it still might be possible to restore *Marginson* v. *Blackburn Borough Council* and to avoid the consequences which logically follow from accepting *Jackson* v. *Goldsmith* and *Randolph* v. *Tuck*. These involve respectively giving to the finding in the first proceedings a broader, or a narrower, significance than is proposed above. The broad view was the one taken by the Court of Appeal in *Marginson* v. *Blackburn Borough Council*. There the finding of the County Court in the first proceedings was not analysed in the Court of Appeal for the purpose of ascertaining whose was the duty and to whom the first finding related; all that was said of the first finding was that "in the matter of alleged negligence in the driving of the motor omnibus and motor car both parties were to blame". If the question can be looked at as broadly as this, many estoppels could be sustained which break down under the kind of analysis to which they were subjected in *Jackson* v. *Goldsmith* or *Randolph* v. *Tuck*. But it is submitted that an example will readily show the impossibility of maintaining this argument. Let the first action arising from the collision of two cars driven by A. and B. respectively be an action by A. against B. for personal injuries. The facts show that B. drove his vehicle in gross disregard of his duty of care to other road users, including A., while A. drove his vehicle exercising all care which he owed to other road users, including B. But A., though he had a safety belt in his vehicle which he had been specifically advised by his passenger to fasten, shortly before the accident, had declined to take this precaution; and moreover all his injuries were found to be such that had the belt been fastened they would not have been sustained. The contributory negligence of A. is pleaded as a defence to the claim. On these facts the court finds B. negligent and A. guilty of contributory negligence solely on the ground of failing to fasten his belt; the responsibility for the injuries is apportioned equally between them. A. obtains judgment against B. for half the damage proved or, before the Contributory Negligence Act, fails in his action. B. then sues A. for damage to his vehicle. May it be said that "the blame for the accident" has been the subject of the earlier decision? Clearly not—yet this is *Marginson* v. *Blackburn Borough Council*. It is submitted that this example illustrates clearly the impossibility of maintaining the "broad view" as one applicable generally to issues arising in running-down cases.

307 SHORLAND J. in *Clyne* v. *Yardley*[1] was the protagonist of the narrow view. He saw clearly that there was a conflict between *Marginson* v. *Blackburn Borough Council* and *Jackson* v. *Goldsmith*, but sought to justify the former case, not on the broad view, but because the finding of negligence, on being broken down into more detailed findings of facts constituting negligence, gave rise, in his opinion, to a sort of official factual evaluation of the accident, which he thought must bind the parties. In the eyes of supporters of this argument the issues of negligence, when examined, may establish (*e.g.*) that one driver was driving too fast, or insufficiently far over, or with an insufficient look out, and this finding of fact will estop him from contending to the contrary in other proceedings. But it is submitted this argument overlooks the fact that when it is said that the speed was *too* fast or the look out *insufficient* these very terms necessitate reference to the persons by whom and to whom the duty is owed, and the surrounding circumstances. It may be actionable negligence to be insufficiently far over as regards A., a blind man carrying a white cane advertising his blindness, while the same position in the road would not be sufficient to convict the driver of negligence as regards B., a person in full possession of his senses, who has given a signal that he has observed the approach of the oncoming car.

Again, where the parties and the issues are the same, a finding in an action between A. and B. that A. was *negligent* will constitute a finding of "ultimate fact", and an estoppel may be founded upon it; but it is submitted that the same result will not follow from a finding that (for instance) A. was driving insufficiently far over on his correct side of the road, or at an excessive speed, or without a proper lookout. In the ordinary case a group of some such allegations will appear in the pleadings against him. If one, and one only, is found against him there could be an argument that this is a finding so essential to the ultimate decision of the case that it must estop him: but if more than one is found against him at first instance (as almost invariably happens) there is at once grave difficulty, for in the event of his wishing to dispute the decision of the court on any such finding (*e.g.* on the ground that there is no evidence to support it) he has no appeal thereon, but only an appeal against the finding of negligence as a whole. If on such an appeal there be one ground on which he fails to upset the court's finding of

[1] [1959] N.Z.L.R. 617.

negligence, he is helpless to appeal against any of the other special findings, for an appellate court will not concern itself to revise these findings, when the judgment in the case as a whole would not be affected by such a revision. On each such separate detailed finding, therefore, he is without any effective appeal, and the very *Ratio* of estoppel is diminished at once, if it does not entirely disappear. For these reasons it is submitted that DIXON J. was abundantly right when he said that an estoppel can be founded only on "ultimate findings" and that it can never be based on detailed findings of evidentiary fact.[1] None of the findings on sub-allegations of fact supporting a conclusion of negligence is "ultimate" because it cannot be said of any of these that it is a matter *necessarily* decided by the *judgment*, which may rest on some one or more of the other findings supporting a conclusion of negligence.

Conclusion

308 If the ultimate result of applying pure principle to the decisions is as is above submitted, the consequence must be that there can be but few estoppels sustained in running-down cases, on which the facts almost always demonstrate such a variety of duties that it becomes impossible to reason with *certainty* from one of them to the next. This may be so; the answer, it is submitted, is that it is not enough that the duties are very similar, or that they are probably the same. If they cannot be demonstrated to be *identical* an estoppel cannot be founded.[2]

APPENDIX

Ramsay v. *Pigram*

Since the text of Chapter IX went to press, the author has received copies of the judgments of the members of the High Court of Australia in yet another running-down case in this series of decisions—*Ramsay* v. *Pigram*,[3] decided in July 1968. These judgments appear to support the conclusions reached in the text of this chapter.

The facts in *Ramsay* v. *Pigram* were satisfactorily simple, in that there were only two vehicles, and only one person in each vehicle, concerned in the collision which was the origin of the litigation. No third party was

1 In *Blair* v. *Curran* (1939), 62 C.L.R. 464 (H. Ct. of Aus.) at p. 532.

2 The reader is referred again to the judgment of LAWTON J. in *Randolph* v. *Tuck*, [1962] 1 Q.B. 175, at p. 184–185, and to the *dictum* of Lord ROMER in *New Brunswick Rail. Co.* v. *British and French Trust Corporation*, [1939] A.C. 1, H.L. at p. 43, quoted therein, cited *in extenso* in the text of para. 303, *supra*.

3 *Ramsay* v. *Pigram* (1968), 42 A.L.J.R. 89. At the time of going to press the decision was not yet reported in the Commonwealth Law Reports.

injured or suffered damage. One vehicle was driven by a police constable, P.C. and one by a private driver, P. In the first action P.C. sued P. in negligence for damages in respect of the personal injuries suffered by P.C. in the accident. P.'s defence alleged contributory negligence on the part of P.C. The action was tried before a judge and jury. The jury found (a) that the accident and injuries sustained by P.C. had been brought about by the negligence of P., and (b) that P.C. had not been guilty of contributory negligence. In a subsequent action P. sued N.D. (the Nominal Defendant who is by statute sued on behalf of the Crown when an action is brought in New South Wales in respect of alleged negligence by a Crown servant) in negligence for damages for the injuries suffered by P. in the collision. N.D. by way of defence sought to plead that P. had no cause of action, setting up a plea of *res judicata* in this regard. To this plea P. demurred (demurrer procedure is still available in New South Wales Courts, which adhere to the pre-Judicature Act practice). On the demurrer N.D. contended that the issue of the negligence of P.C. had been necessarily and precisely determined in favour of P.C. and against D. when in the earlier action P.C. had been acquitted of contributory negligence, and that he (N.D.) was entitled, as the privy of P.C., to the benefit of an estoppel established by the earlier judgment.

The High Court of Australia (Sir GARFIELD BARWICK C.J., and McTIERNAN, KITTO, TAYLOR and WINDEYER JJ.) unanimously dismissed the plea of estoppel. They held that the police constable and the Nominal Defendant were not privies one of the other, such that a verdict and judgment against one of them must bind the other. But they also considered as a separate point whether, if these two had been held to be privies, the question to be decided in the second action was the same as that already decided in the first; and they held (unanimously) that it was a different question. Sir GARFIELD BARWICK C.J. said:

> "The issue between the parties to the District Court action might be expressed as being whether the injury to that plaintiff was, as between those parties, wholly caused by the negligent act of the respondent: but in so far as contributory negligence was asserted by the respondent, the case involved what were really two subsidiary issues, subsidiary upon an issue whether the respondent was in relation to that injury in breach of his duty to that plaintiff to exercise reasonable care. The subsidiary issues were, one, did that plaintiff contribute to the incident out of which his injury arose by an act of his own done without proper care for his own safety and, two, did some act of that plaintiff in breach of his duty to the respondent to take reasonable care contribute to the occurrence of that incident, for the duties of the users of the road in this respect are mutual. . . .
>
> So expressing the issues in the District Court action, it will be seen that no

issue of breach of the Government's duty to the respondent was involved. Whilst it is no doubt true that rarely will there be any practicality in drawing the distinction in an action for personal injuries between the duty of the principal and that of the agent where the suggested cause of the injury is the act of that agent, it is none the less of importance on occasions, of which I think this is one, to maintain and observe the distinction. . . . . Thus, though the act in question be the same in each case and, if you will, though I think it not to matter, the evidence establishing it be the same, the issues raised in each case are not, upon a proper analysis, identical. In the District Court what was involved in the defence of contributory negligence was, *inter alia*, the police officer's personal duty towards the respondent. In this action it is a breach of the Government's duty towards the respondent which is alleged. For lack of the necessary identity in the issues, the appellant's plea in this action, in my opinion, was demurrable."

At the time of going to press this decision has only just appeared in the Reports, and it is not possible in this edition to do more than briefly notice its result. It is clear that as between P.C. and P. the issue of P.C.'s breach of any duty of care owed by him to P. was precisely decided, in favour of P.C., in the first proceedings. If therefore P.C. and N.D. had been held privies, and the estoppel in favour of P.C. had been available to N.D., then in the second proceeding P. must have been precluded from alleging a breach by P.C. of *his own* duty to P. But it is always possible that in a given set of circumstances the duty of care which P.C. owed to P. and the duty of care which the Crown owed to him might not prove to be co-extensive; and in respect of any duty outside the area of co-extent no estoppel could stand in the way of a claim by P. in the second action ("It will be seen", said Sir GARFIELD BARWICK C.J., in the passage which we have just quoted, "that no issue of breach of the Government's duty to the respondent was involved").

It must be remembered that this was a demurrer application. No particulars of negligence had to be pleaded under the New South Wales procedure. In a jurisdiction using the post-Judicature Act procedures, particulars of negligence must be given. In any such jurisdiction it would have been possible for N.D. to insist on particulars of the negligence upon which P. relied, and, having obtained them (always on the assumption that he could rely on the argument as to privity which was essential), to demonstrate that all the issues of negligence raised by the statement of claim were necessarily and precisely determined against P. by the earlier proceedings. But this argument was not available to N.D. under the New South Wales procedure, where the necessary particulars could not be obtained at this stage of the action. Accordingly the distinction between the duties of care owed by P. to P.C. and to the Crown, respectively, afforded P. good ground in that jurisdiction for disposing of the plea of estoppel.

CHAPTER X

Particular Applications of the Doctrine of Res Judicata: II—Taxation and Rating Cases

309 It is now settled law that decisions on questions of land tax, income tax and rating assessments constitute an important exception to the general rules as to *res judicata*, and that such decisions given in regard to one year's tax or rates, or as to given rating or assessment lists, do not give rise to estoppels binding the parties in respect of another year's tax or rates, or a later assessment list.[1] In the first place such decisions often involve taking into account facts which change in some degree from year to year, and on this account alone it is impossible to hold the parties estopped from one year to another.[2] "The assessment seems inherently to be of a passing nature".[3] But it has long been clear that there are other grounds for excluding any estoppel on principle, for such decisions, at least when made at an administrative level, cannot be regarded as decisions made by a judicial tribunal in the course of resolving a true *lis inter partes*.[4] Hence while such decisions may, and generally will, be conclusive *inter partes* as regards the actual assessment made, or the actual list fixed,[5] yet they will not estop either party when the same question arises on another year's assessment, or on the fixing of a subsequent list. A decision of the Special

---

1 *Caffoor* v. *Colombo Income Tax Commissioners*, [1961] A.C. 584, P.C. at pp. 599–600.

2 *Edwards* v. *"Old Bushmills" Distillery Co. Ltd.* (In Liq.) (1926), 10 T.C. 285, H.L. per Viscount CAVE L.C. at p. 299.

3 Per Lord HANWORTH M.R. in *Inland Revenue Commissioners* v. *Sneath*, [1932] 2 K.B. 362, C.A. at p. 383, this sentence being incorporated in the judgment of Lord RADCLIFFE in *Society of Medical Officers of Health* v. *Hope*, [1960] A.C. 551, H.L. at p. 563.

4 Per Lord HANWORTH M.R. in *Inland Revenue Commissioners* v. *Sneath*, [1932] 2 K.B. 362, C.A. at p. 382; per GREER L.J. in the same case at pp. 385–386; per ROMER L.J. at p. 391.

5 *Inland Revenue Commissioners* v. *Sneath*, [1932] 2 K.B. 362, C.A. per Lord HANWORTH M.R. at pp. 383–384; *Broken Hill Proprietary Co.* v. *Broken Hill Municipal Council*, [1926] A.C. 94, P.C. per Lord CARSON at p. 100—"No doubt as regards that year the decision could not be disputed."

Commissioners in one year will on this account not found an estoppel when the same point arises between the same parties in a subsequent year.[1]

310 But not only decisions at an administrative level, but also those given by courts of competent general jurisdiction fall within the exception to the general rule, and no estoppel can be founded upon them when the same point is raised again in another year of assessment, or in respect of a list other than that fixed in the original decision. This will be so even in cases where there is a formal admission that no material circumstance has in the meantime changed.[2] The reason appears to be because the question of the liability of the taxpayer for the subsequent year's tax or rate is not to be regarded as the same question as that of his liability for the first.[3] What might in other types of case be regarded as *eadem quaestio* is not so to be regarded in taxation and rating cases, which are *sui generis* in this regard.[4] This principle, though now firmly established, was for long in some doubt, and formed the subject of a remarkable conflict between two decisions of the Judicial Committee of the Privy Council, the subject of argument in the same year, and reported in the same volume of the Reports. In the first of these it was decided that an earlier decision of a court of competent jurisdiction did not, and in the second that it did, estop the parties from re-litigating the original issue of liability for taxation.

The Broken Hill Case: Hoystead v. *Taxation Commissioner*

311 *Broken Hill Proprietary Co., Ltd.* v. *Broken Hill Municipal Council*[5] was heard in July 1925, and judgment was delivered on November 10th in the same year by Lord Carson, the Committee consisting of Viscount Cave L.C., Lord Carson, Lord Blanesburgh and Duff J. The question at issue was the construction of a section in a statute providing the basis for an assessment of rating value, and the earlier decision on this question of construction had been given by the High Court of Australia on appeal. It was held that the construction given to the section by the High Court as regards the assessment for the earlier year did not estop the parties from

[1] *Inland Revenue Commissioners* v. *Sneath*, [1932] 2 K.B. 362, C.A.; *Patuck* v. *Lloyd* (1944), 26 T.C. 284, at p. 292, C.A.; *Cf. Society of Medical Officers of Health* v. *Hope*, [1960] 1 All E.R. 317; [1960] A.C. 551, H.L.

[2] *Society of Medical Officers of Health* v. *Hope*, [1960] 1 All E.R. 317; [1960] A.C. 551, H.L.

[3] *Broken Hill Proprietary Co.* v. *Broken Hill Municipal Council*, [1926] A.C. 94, P.C., per Lord Carson at p. 100—"The present case relates to a new question—namely the valuation for a different year and the liability for that year. It is not *eadem quaestio*, and therefore the principle of *res judicata* cannot apply."

[4] *Caffoor* v. *Colombo Income Tax Commissioners*, [1961] A.C. 584, P.C. per Lord Radcliffe at p. 599; *cf. Society of Medical Officers of Health* v. *Hope*, [1960] A.C. 551, H.L. per Lord Radcliffe at p. 563.

[5] [1926] A.C. 94, P.C.

re-litigating the same question on a subsequent year's assessment. In the same year *Hoystead* v. *Taxation Commissioner*[1] was decided. It was heard in October 1925, while their Lordships were still considering their judgment in the *Broken Hill* case, but judgment was not given till December 17th, some five or six weeks after judgment in that case had been delivered. In *Hoystead's* case the judgment was that of Lord SHAW, and the Judicial Committee consisted of Lord SHAW, Lord SUMNER, Lord PHILLIMORE, Lord DARLING, and Lord SALVESEN. There the question was again one of the construction—in this case of the language used in a will—which had been assumed in argument by both parties, rather than decided, in the High Court of Australia, but as an essential basis for the decision of that court as to the assessment of land tax in a given year. Their Lordships held that the implied decision of the High Court on the point in the first judgment, though it had not been the subject of argument, but had been conceded rather than argued, nevertheless formed an essential part of the basis of the judgment, and therefore estopped the parties from putting forward a different construction of the same document on a dispute relating to a later year's assessment.

Society of Medical Officers of Health v. *Hope*

312 The conflict between these two decisions stood unresolved until 1960–1, and in the intervening period many textbooks cited both cases without furnishing any satisfactory synthesis.[2] But in 1960 came the decision of the House of Lords in *Society of Medical Officers of Health* v. *Hope*.[3] In 1951 a local Valuation Court had decided that a certain hereditament owned by the appellant Society was exempt from rates under Section 1 of the Scientific Societies Act 1843. In 1956 a new valuation list was settled, and the Society's hereditament appeared thereon as rateable. The Society thereupon claimed exemption; the valuation officer objected to the claim. The local Valuation Court decided the matter favourably to the Society. On appeal a formal admission was made by the valuation officer that there had since 1951 been no change in any material circumstance. The Lands Tribunal rejected the Society's submission that the matter was the subject of an estoppel *per rem judicatam* by virtue of the earlier decision of the local Valuation Court, on facts which were *ex hypothesi* identical. On appeal the Court of Appeal, MORRIS L.J. and WYNN-PARRY J. (SELLERS L.J. dissenting), agreed that the doctrine of *res judicata* was inapplicable. MORRIS

[1] [1926] A.C. 155, P.C.

[2] See for instance the note in 15 *Halsbury's Laws* (3rd edn.) 182 footnote (d), where both cases are cited in the same footnote without any mention of the direct conflict between them.

[3] [1960] 1 All E.R. 317; [1960] A.C. 551.

L.J. expressly followed the *Broken Hill* case; SELLERS L.J. (dissenting) followed *Hoystead's* case, while WYNN-PARRY J. distinguished the latter. In the Lords it was finally laid down that "it is not in the nature of a decision given on one rate or tax that it should settle anything more than the bare issue of that one liability, and that, consequently, it cannot constitute an estoppel when a new issue of liability to a succeeding year's rate or tax comes up for adjudication. The question of this liability is a 'new question'."[1]

Why a "new question"?

313 The precise process of reasoning upon which it can be said that this result was founded was still left less than perfectly clear by the judgments in *Hope's* case. Lord RADCLIFFE had put forward two bases for his conclusion that the two questions were not *eadem quaestio*. He acknowledged that the matter fell to be decided on principles not applicable in other cases in which the doctrine of *res judicata* could be invoked. He said:[2]

> "To say that the issue of liability to one year's rate is not the same subject-matter as the issue of liability to another year's, or that the one cause of action is different from the other is, perhaps, rather an arbitrary way of disposing of the appellant's case. There are legal contexts, in trespass or recurring claims for rent, for example, in which much the same might be said and yet is it not impossible for an estoppel to arise. The reason why, when you are dealing with rates and taxes, the difference of subject-matter is treated as being so important seems to lie in two considerations which, as I read the authorities, are peculiar to their particular field.
>
> One consideration is that the jurisdiction of the tribunal to which the decision belongs by the administrative scheme is a limited one. It is limited in the sense that its function begins and ends with that of deciding what is to be the assessment or liability of a person for a defined and terminable period. "The assessment seems inherently to be of a passing nature".[3] For the purpose of arriving at its decision the tribunal may well have to take account of, and form its own opinion on, questions of general law; it may even have necessarily to consider one or more of such questions: but in either case the view adopted with regard to them is incidental to its only direct function, that of fixing the assessment. For that limited purpose it is a court with a jurisdiction competent to produce a final decision between the parties before it: but it is not a court of competent jurisdiction to decide general questions of law with that finality which is needed to set up the estoppel *per rem judicatam* that arises in certain contexts from legal judgments."

---

[1] Per Lord RADCLIFFE at p. 562.

[2] At p. 563.

[3] This quotation is from the judgment of Lord HANWORTH in *Inland Revenue Commissioners* v. *Sneath*, [1932] 2 K.B. 362 at p. 383.

This was one of the considerations to which he subscribed: the other[1] was the special position of the valuation officer, surveyor, or equivalent official or committee, to whom, he said, the term "party" to a "*lis*" can be applied only with some reservations.

Lord KEITH OF AVONHOLM preferred to put the grounds for his concurrence in different words, possibly involving a different process of reasoning. He said:[2]

> "What we are faced with here is an administrative act of a public official, the valuation officer, against which the party affected has a right of appeal, to the local valuation court, with further appeals to higher courts. The valuation officer has a public duty to perform by making periodically every five years a valuation list of all hereditaments, with certain exceptions, in his rating area. He must necessarily reconsider and revise the previous valuation list. He has no personal interest in any appeals taken against his valuations, and has a duty to hold the scales as fairly as he can among the ratepayers affected, the occupiers of the various hereditaments. The general body of ratepayers is constantly changing. With each quinquennium the revaluations will affect a new body of ratepayers. I doubt if the valuation officer owing such a duty to an ever-changing body of ratepayers can be regarded as always the same party in the sense in which that expression is used for the application of the rule of *res judicata*. What if the appellant society changes its habitat, and moves into another rating area with a different valuation officer?
>
> I emphasise these aspects of the functions of a valuation officer under the statute, for they lead to what I regard as the true answer to the submission for the appellants, which is that a public officer in the position of the respondent cannot be estopped from carrying out his duties under the statute. The case is, I think, *a fortiori* of the judgment of a Board of the Privy Council in *Maritime Electric Co., Ltd.* v. *General Dairies, Ltd.*[3] where it was held, in the circumstances of that case, that a public utility company could not be estopped from carrying out its duty under a statute. It has been said on other occasions that there is no estoppel against a statute."

Lord RADCLIFFE, then, said (a) the limited nature of the jurisdiction of the court which decides taxation matters will in itself suffice to prevent its decisions becoming the basis of *res judicata* in later cases; (b) in any case can there be said to be a true *lis* between the same parties? Lord KEITH OF AVONHOLM found the second of these reasons relevant, but he fused it with the principle of the law of estoppel which has always prevented an estoppel from being raised so as to hinder the carrying out of a statutory duty.

Caffoor v. *Colombo Income Tax Commissioners*

314 There can be little quarrel, in the view of the present writer, with Lord KEITH's reasoning, or with the second of the grounds put forward by Lord RADCLIFFE, and the two will be found to be inter-connected. The

[1] [1960] A.C. 551, at p. 565. [2] At p. 568.
[3] [1937] 1 All E.R. 748; [1937] A.C. 610, P.C.

taxing or rating official has a statutory duty, not only to the objector but to all other taxpayers; and a decision in a taxing case affects not only the objector, but in some degree, perhaps very small, all other taxpayers. It is contrary to the basic principles of the law of estoppel that the obligation to administer the law according to its tenor which is placed upon every assessor of taxes should be hindered, qualified or stultified by any estoppel, or that the interest of any taxpayer should in any degree whatsoever be capable of being affected by any estoppel raised by or against any other taxpayer. For these reasons there appears to have been good ground for supporting the decision of the Privy Council in the *Broken Hill* case, and for rejecting that in *Hoystead* v. *Federal Taxation Commissioner*. But this final definite step was not expressly taken until the following year. In 1961 in *Caffoor* v. *Colombo Income Tax Commissioners*[1] the Privy Council was compelled to choose between its two former decisions. The Committee on this occasion comprised Lord MORTON, Lord RADCLIFFE (who had delivered the leading judgment in *Hope's* case), Lord MORRIS and Mr L. M. D. DE SILVA. It was at once apparent that the first ground upon which Lord RADCLIFFE had relied in *Hope's* case was of little relevance in establishing the essential principle. The decision in *Hoystead's* case could not be disapproved on the ground of any restricted jurisdiction in the court which had pronounced the first decision; it was a decision of the High Court of Australia. Some other ground had to be found.[2] The Board found itself content with the proposition that taxation and rating assessments were decisions *sui generis*, to which the principles ordinarily governing judgments *inter easdem partes* were not applicable. But this, it was added, was not necessarily a matter for regret. Their Lordships expressly adopted the principle laid down in the *Broken Hill* case and expressly disapproved *Hoystead* v. *Federal Taxation Commissioner*,[3] adding that:

> "It may be that the principles applied in these cases form a somewhat anomalous branch of the general law of estoppel *per rem judicatam*, and are not easily derived from or transferred to other branches of litigation in which such estoppels have to be considered; but in their Lordships' opinion they are well established in their own field, and it is not by any means to be assumed that the result is one that should be regretted in the public interest."[4]

Stamp duty in connected transactions

315 Though decisions on questions arising on one annual assessment of one year's rates or income tax will give rise to no estoppel when the same

---

[1] [1961] A.C. 584, P.C. [2] See pp. 597–599.

[3] At p. 600: "Their Lordships are of opinion that it is impossible for them to treat *Hoystead's* case as constituting a legal authority on the question of estoppels in respect of successive years of tax assessment."

[4] At pp. 599–600.

question arises in a subsequent year, on the authority of the cases above cited it has been held in *Australia* that the same result will not follow when a series of connected transactions covering the same facts are assessable at different dates for stamp duty, or death or gift duty. In such a case it may be that a decision as to the effect of one of the documents in the series will estop the taxpayer, or the revenue authorities, from asserting, when another document in the same series is presented for assessment, that duty is assessable on the second document inconsistently with the decision given in the earlier litigation between the same parties.[1]

---

[1] *Queensland Trustees, Ltd.* v. *Stamp Duties Commissioner* (1956), 96 C.L.R. 131 (H. Ct. of Aus.).

CHAPTER XI

Particular Applications of the Doctrine of Res Judicata: III—The Plea of Autrefois Acquit

Introduction

316 *Autrefois acquit* is the special plea by virtue of which the principles of estoppel are applied by the criminal law[1] to preclude a second prosecution of an accused person for a crime in respect of which he has been acquitted in previous proceedings.[2] The plea is one of great antiquity. In *Coke's Institutes*[3] the plea of "*auterfoitz acquite*" is stated to be a defence to a further charge "of the same felony", and in *Blackstone*[4] it is said that

---

[1] It was said by WRIGHT J. at the conclusion of his often-quoted judgment in *R.* v. *Ollis*, [1900] 2 Q.B. 758, C.C.R. at p. 771 that "the defence of *autrefois acquit* never seems to have been rested on the law of estoppel", and *cf.* the same view expressed by CROMPTON J. in the course of argument in *R.* v. *Haughton (Inhabitants)* (1853), 1 E. & B. 501, at p. 506. But these *dicta* cannot prevail against the strong current of modern authority which clearly identifies the doctrine of *autrefois acquit* with that of estoppel, though perhaps as an anomalous case. In *Connelly* v. *Director of Public Prosecutions*, [1964] 2 All E.R. 401; [1964] A.C. 1254, H.L. all the Lords of Appeal treated the plea as a plea of *res judicata* in a criminal case—see, for instance, the speech of Lord DEVLIN at p. 1356; "The doctrine of *res judicata* occupies the same place in the civil law as the doctrine of *autrefois* does in the criminal". And in Australia in *R.* v. *Wilkes* (1948), 77 C.L.R. 511, DIXON J. at p. 519 referred twenty years ago to the rules of *res judicata* "which in criminal proceedings are expressed in the pleas of *autrefois acquit* and *autrefois convict*". Cf. *in New Zealand* in *Re a Medical Practitioner*, [1959] N.Z.L.R. 784, C.A. per GRESSON P. at p. 806: "The principle of *res judicata* is applicable both in criminal law and in civil law; indeed the doctrine of *autrefois acquit* or *autrefois convict* in criminal law is but an expression of *res judicata*—the application to a criminal matter of the doctrine of estoppel *per rem judicatam*".

[2] The law as stated in this and the succeeding paragraphs is the common law of England. In some Dominion jurisdictions the extent and operation of the plea are governed by statute, and what is here said must in such jurisdictions be read as subject to the statutory provisions. In New Zealand, for instance, the statute law will be found in the Crimes Act 1961, sections 357 *et seq*. These provisions apply equally to summary proceedings before a stipendiary magistrate—Summary Proceedings Act 1957 sections 3 and 8. In Australia a somewhat similar position obtains—see, *e.g.* Crimes Act 1900 (N.S.W.) section 399.

[3] *Coke Inst.* Part III p. 213.

[4] *Blackstone, Commentaries* (1769) Book IV, p. 329. See also *Hale's Pleas of the Crown* (1778) Vol. II, p. 240; *Hawkins' Pleas of the Crown* 8th edn. (1824) p. 515.

> "The plea of *autrefoits acquit*, or a former acquittal, is founded on this universal maxim of the Common Law of England, that no man is to be brought into jeopardy of his life, more than once, for the same offence."

The plea is generally said to be founded upon the maxim "*nemo debet bis vexari pro eadem causa*";[1] but the use of a Latin maxim has perhaps served at times to obscure both the limits of the doctrine and the principle upon which it is based. Whether a man is *bis vexatus* who is subjected to a second set of proceedings, when an earlier proceeding has resulted in his acquittal on the charges then preferred against him, may become a nice question in particular circumstances.[2] And, again, what precise meaning is to be given to *eadem causa*?[3] These considerations have led to questions as to the accuracy of the proposition with which this paragraph commences. Is the plea of *autrefois acquit* a plea of estoppel *per rem judicatam*, or is it, as some judges[4] have ventured to suggest, something quite distinct?

Mr SPENCER BOWER, in the first edition of this work, was clearly of the opinion that *autrefois acquit* was nothing more or less than a manifestation, in the field of criminal law, of the plea of estoppel *per rem judicatam*.[5] To that view the present writer will adhere[6]—with the reservation, however, that in its application to the criminal law the doctrine of estoppel is seen to undergo some modifications made expedient by the nature of the subject matter. It will be seen, for instance, that it is not necessary, in order that the doctrine should apply, that the parties should have the same degree of identity as is essential to support an estoppel *per rem judicatam* in a civil action; and, when the nature of the *vexatio* comes to be considered, it will be seen that on the topic of identity of issues there are also special rules. The views expressed by WRIGHT J. in *R.* v. *Ollis*[7] and by CROMPTON J. in the course of argument in *R.* v. *Haughton*[8] are accordingly rejected in this work, in which *autrefois acquit* is treated as a plea of estoppel *per rem judicatam*, subject, however, to such modifications of the general rules applicable to estoppel as will be found set out below.

Autrefois acquit contrasted with autrefois convict

317 On the very threshold of the discussion it is to be observed that there is a crucial distinction, as to the nature of the plea, between pleas of

---

[1] *Broom's Legal Maxims* 10th edn. p. 223.

[2] This topic is dealt with in para. 329, *infra*.

[3] In *Connelly* v. *Director of Public Prosecutions*, [1964] A.C. 1254 Lord HODSON asks at p. 1331: "What is meant or involved in the words 'the same crime'? It is in the answer to this question that so much difficulty has arisen."

[4] See footnote 1, p. 267, *ante*.

[5] 1st edn. para. 51.

[6] The view is supported by all modern authority, and reference may be made to the *dicta* cited in footnote 1, p. 267, *ante*.

[7] [1900] 2 Q.B. 758.

[8] (1853), 1 E. & B. 501.

autrefois acquit and *autrefois convict*,[1] though the two are often spoken of in the same breath.[2] *Autrefois acquit*, summarised in the maxim *nemo debet bis vexari pro eadem causa*, is a species of estoppel by which, as in other cases of estoppel, one party (in this case the Crown) is precluded, as against the other, from asserting the contrary (in this case the guilt of the accused) of something which has been determined in previous proceedings between them. *Autrefois convict*, on the other hand, which is usually said to depend upon the maxim *nemo debet bis puniri pro uno delicto*, is not a manifestation of the doctrine of estoppel as it is presented in Part I of this volume, but is akin to merger as it is treated of in Part II; it is an application to criminal proceedings of the maxim *transit in rem judicatam*. By its operation one party to concluded proceedings (in this case the Crown) is precluded as against the other from re-asserting, in fresh proceedings, the same facts as have served in earlier proceedings as the foundation of a judgment (in this case the conviction of the accused) in which the rights of the successful party have become merged. While, therefore, the plea of *autrefois acquit* will be considered in this chapter, the plea of *autrefois convict* will be postponed for consideration in Part II of this work.[3]

Autrefois acquit and issue estoppel

318 As noticed in an earlier chapter,[4] the doctrine of estoppel *per rem judicatam* may manifest itself through an estoppel precluding the parties to an earlier proceeding from challenging the decision itself (an estoppel *per rem judicatam*) or, while leaving that decision itself unchallenged, from challenging findings which may be demonstrated to have been fundamental to it, though these may not have been expressed therein (issue estoppel). So, the doctrine of *autrefois acquit* may be used to preclude the Crown not only from reasserting the guilt of the accused in respect of a crime of which he has been acquitted, but, in cases where no such reassertion is made, from asserting facts the denial of which is to be seen as fundamental to the former acquittal, even though no mention of them is made in the previous finding of the court. This is the application of issue estoppel to the plea of *autrefois acquit*, and it will be dealt with in some particularity in a later paragraph.[5]

---

[1] See the judgment of Lord Pearce in *Connelly* v. *Director of Public Prosecutions*, [1964] A.C. 1254, at p. 1365.

[2] Though the basic principles on which the two pleas rest are distinct, the tests by which their availability is determined have much in common. So in the case now regarded as the *locus classicus* on *autrefois acquit*—*Connelly* v. *Director of Public Prosecutions* (*supra*) Lord Morris, making the principal speech in the House of Lords, is to be found importing into his series of propositions one—the fifth—which on examination is clearly referable exclusively to the doctrine of *autrefois convict*.

[3] It is considered in Part II, Chapter XXII, *post*.

[4] Chapter VI, *ante*.

[5] Para. 332, *infra*.

Parties

319 It is fundamental to estoppel *per rem judicatam* that the parties to the two sets of proceedings be the same, and that they sue or be sued in the same right. On the plea of *autrefois acquit* it is apparent that the accused will always be one party to both sets of proceedings, and on that side therefore there can never be any difficulty as to identity. On the side of the prosecution, however, the matter may be less self-evident; but it has come to be accepted that though the prosecutors be different in the different proceedings the second prosecutor will be bound by the result of the first proceeding, at least where in either case the prosecution may be said to be in truth by or on behalf of the Crown. This has long appeared to follow, in the case of a plea of *autrefois convict*, from such decisions as *R.* v. *Walker*[1], *R.* v. *Miles*,[2] and *Wemyss* v. *Hopkins*;[3] and it is difficult to see how a different principle can apply to *autrefois acquit*.[4] There would not appear to be a case reported where, on the failure of one private prosecutor to secure a conviction, the plea has been successfully set up against a second different private prosecutor; but it is conceived that the rule as to identity of parties would in such a case be relaxed so as to make the plea available, and that the effect of any verdict of acquittal presented by a competent court on a lawful charge and after a lawful trial has been correctly described by Lord MACDERMOTT, delivering the report of the Judicial Committee in *Sambasivam* v. *Public Prosecutor, Federation of Malaya*,[5] as being "that the person acquitted cannot be tried again for the same offence". So, too, NORTH and CLEARY JJ. in a case heard before the New Zealand Court of Appeal[6] said—

> "It is not necessary to show that the parties to the two proceedings are strictly identical. It would seem proper that, once there has been a prosecution according to law for an offence, the maxim should apply to precluding any further prosecution for the same offence, whether or not the second prosecution be set in motion by the same informant."

and they cited in support of this conclusion the cases, decided on the plea of *autrefois convict*, which have been referred to earlier in this paragraph.

---

1 *R.* v. *Walker* (1843), 2 Mood. & R. 446.

2 *R.* v. *Miles* (1890), 24 Q.B.D. 423.

3 *Wemyss* v. *Hopkins* (1875), L.R. 10 Q.B. 378.

4 In the New Zealand case of *In re a Medical Practitioner*, [1959] N.Z.L.R. 784, C.A. GRESSON P. points out at p. 806 that "the plea of *autrefois acquit* can operate when there are different prosecutors in the two proceedings".

5 [1950] A.C. 458, P.C. at p. 479.

6 *In re a Medical Practitioner*, [1959] N.Z.L.R. 784, C.A. at p. 813.

Connelly v. *Director of Public Prosecutions*[1]

320 This case, in which much of the law as to the plea of *autrefois acquit* can now conveniently be found, came before the House of Lords in 1964. The accused had been charged on two indictments, one presenting a charge of murder, the other robbery with aggravation. Had it not been for the rule of practice in *R.* v. *Jones*[2] it might in the circumstances have been thought proper to join both counts in the alternative in one indictment, for the facts were the same; but the rule forbidding any alternative count (save, impliedly, manslaughter) to be joined in any indictment charging murder, precluded this course. The trial of the accused proceeded on the indictment charging murder, and the alternative indictment was held over after the accused had pleaded Not Guilty upon it. The accused was convicted of murder on the first indictment. He appealed to the Court of Criminal Appeal. In that court he successfully submitted a plea of misdirection by the learned trial judge. As a result the conviction was quashed, and a verdict of acquittal was entered on the charge of murder. After some procedural vicissitudes the accused was tried, on the same facts, on the alternative indictment for robbery with violence, and he was convicted. He had set up the plea of *autrefois acquit* before his second trial, and this had been rejected, by a jury empanelled expressly to try this issue, on the direction of the trial judge. The verdict of this jury, and the direction on which it was based, were upheld by the Court of Criminal Appeal and (unanimously) in the House of Lords. In the course of the speeches their Lordships made a number of valuable observations on the principles governing the plea of *autrefois acquit*.

It is clear that the doctrine upon which the plea rests cannot be interpreted so generally as to lead to the result that, when a man has been prosecuted upon a given set of facts, and acquitted on charges formulated in respect of them, he is thereafter protected from all further criminal proceedings in respect of the same facts. Mere abstract considerations of fairness might perhaps so suggest; but as Lord Reid points out in his short introductory speech in *Connelly's* case, the law has taken a more restricted view than this, and "many generations of judges have seen nothing unfair in holding that the plea of *autrefois acquit* must be given a limited scope".[3] A number of propositions will now be examined, taken principally from

---

[1] [1964] 2 All E.R. 401; [1964] A.C. 1254, H.L.

[2] [1918] 1 K.B. 416, C.C.A. "The proper course in a case like this is to have two indictments so that the second charge may be subsequently tried if the charge of murder fails and it is thought desirable to proceed upon the second charge". This direction was expressly overruled in *Connelly* v. *Director of Public Prosecutions* (*supra*).

[3] [1964] A.C. 1254, H.L. Lord Reid's observations may be found at p. 1295.

the speech of Lord MORRIS in *Connelly's* case, in which the scope of the doctrine in its modern form is more particularly defined.

321 *A man cannot be tried for a crime in respect of which he has previously been acquitted.* This is the first of the propositions with which Lord MORRIS prefaces his speech in *Connelly's* case.[1] It is a proposition rooted in the tradition of the Common Law, now so obvious as to need no elaboration. *Blackstone*, after remarking in the passage which we have already cited that by virtue of the plea "no man is to be brought into jeopardy of his life, more than once, for the same offence" adds that "it is to be observed, that the pleas of *autrefoits acquit* and *autrefoits convict*, or of formal acquittal, and former conviction, must be a prosecution for the same identical act and crime."

It is clear, then, as a starting point for our consideration of the doctrine, that an acquittal on a charge of any given crime serves as a complete defence to a further charge against the same person of the same crime on the same facts. This is as far as the doctrine went in its earliest form;[2] but it must be remembered that the modern conception of issue estoppel was unknown to the author of the Institutes, or of the Commentaries, in its present developed form; and (as we shall presently see) it is no longer true to say that the narrow statement of the doctrine which serves as Lord MORRIS's first proposition is a sufficient definition of the whole extent of its application. In modern times the plea will extend, as we shall see, so as to afford a shield against cognate charges distinct from, but sufficiently connected—in accordance with propositions now to be stated—with the original charge on which the prisoner has been acquitted.

322 *A man cannot be tried for a crime in respect of which he could on some previous indictment have been convicted.* This is the second of Lord MORRIS's propositions in *Connelly* v. *Director of Public Prosecutions.* Not only is the plea available in respect of any repetition of the actual charge of which the accused has previously been acquitted; he is also protected on counts on which the jury could have convicted him in the earlier proceedings, even though he was not in them made the subject of a formal acquittal on such counts.[3] What is principally referred to is of course cases such as murder

---

[1] The nine propositions are set out *seriatim* at pp. 1305–1306.

[2] Subject to this: that *Blackstone* was prepared to concede that an acquittal on a charge of murder was a bar to a subsequent charge of manslaughter. See note 1, p. 273, *post*, and text to which it is appended.

[3] [1964] A.C. 1254, H.L. per Lord MORRIS at p. 1311: "My Lords, the authorities to which I have referred show that the plea of *autrefois acquit* has availed if the charge contained in a later indictment is one of which a man could have been convicted on the trial of the earlier indictment."

and manslaughter; so long ago as the time of *Blackstone*[1] it was already generally acknowledged that a man acquitted of murder was protected against a subsequent charge of manslaughter on the same facts, for the jury could have convicted him of manslaughter in their verdict, instead of presenting a verdict of acquittal of murder; and *Hale*[2] includes *petit treason* as in similar case. In more modern times it has become recognised that the doctrine will similarly extend to cover charges of criminal attempts in the second proceedings, where the accused has already been previously acquitted of the actual crime. This is because on the first indictment (in which the principal crime was charged) it was competent for the jury, if they thought the full crime was not proved, yet to convict of an attempt if they thought fit to do so;[3] their refusal to present such a verdict, and their presentation instead of a verdict of acquittal, is therefore accepted as a bar to a subsequent charge of attempting. And there are other cases in which the jury is authorised by statute, or the Common Law, to acquit the accused of the offence of which he is charged, and to convict him of some other offence of less degree. In such cases, if the jury return a verdict of acquittal, the judgment following the verdict, whereby the accused is acquitted of the major offence, is deemed to carry with it a judgment of acquittal on the minor offence also.[4]

Some slight improvement to the wording of Lord MORRIS's proposition may be respectfully suggested at this point. It is submitted that it might have been preferable so to state the rule as to make it clear that the plea will not protect the accused in a subsequent proceeding from a charge on which the jury deliberately refrained from delivering any verdict at all, though it would have been competent for them to have convicted if they had rendered a verdict. Where, for instance, the accused is charged with larceny and with the alternative of receiving, if he is convicted of larceny it is usual for no verdict to be taken on the receiving charge. If, on an appeal from his conviction for larceny on the ground of misdirection by the trial judge, the accused has his conviction quashed in the Court of Criminal Appeal, and it then appears that the proper charge was after all one of receiving, there will, it is submitted, be no bar to trying him subsequently on that count; for though he "could have been convicted" on the first indictment on this charge, the failure of the jury to convict him was not due to their returning

---

1 Blackstone, *Commentaries* (1769), Book IV, 330.

2 *Hale, Pleas of the Crown* (1778), Vol. II, p. 245. See also *Hawkins' Pleas of the Crown* 8th edn. (1824), Book II, p. 578.

3 Criminal Procedure Act 1851, s. 9. *In New Zealand*, Crimes Act 1961, s. 337. *Cf.*, in Australia, Crimes Act 1900 (N.S.W.) s. 427.

4 Examples may be found noticed in *Archbold's Criminal Pleading Evidence and Practice* 35th edn. at para. 574. *In New Zealand* the point is provided for by the Crimes Act 1961 s. 339; *cf.* in New South Wales the Crimes Act 1900, ss. 425 and 426.

impliedly a verdict of acquittal on the count, but to their refraining from making any finding on the matter.[1]

323 The third principle enunciated by Lord MORRIS in *Connelly* v. *Director of Public Prosecutions* is: *The same rule applies if the crime in respect of which the prisoner is being charged is in effect the same, or is substantially the same, as either the principal or a different crime in respect of which he has been acquitted or could have been convicted or has been convicted.*

It may be respectfully observed of this proposition that it lacks both the high authority to support it and the clarity of expression in its definition which characterised both propositions I and II. But this criticism will be found to be answered when the propositions which succeed proposition III are considered. The matter is not left to be decided according as whether charges may be "in effect the same" or "substantially the same"—phrases which are possibly taken from *R.* v. *Kendrick and Smith*.[2] In the propositions which succeed proposition III a test is proposed, by which it is to be decided whether the crime charged in the second proceedings is "in effect the same" or, "substantially the same"; and we will now proceed to consider the definition of this test, and the authorities on which it is supported.

The test as to the availability of the plea

324 *The true test as to whether the plea is available is whether the evidence which is necessary to support the second indictment or the facts which constitute the offence charged in it would have supported a conviction in the first indictment on some count on which it was competent for the jury to find the accused guilty.*

This, with some slight amendment to the phraseology, is the fourth of Lord MORRIS's propositions in *Connelly* v. *Director of Public Prosecutions*;[3] and again, on this proposition, it is necessary to point out that there must be excepted the case where the jury, though it was open to them on the earlier indictment to convict of the crime now charged, yet failed to do so, not because they must be taken as having impliedly acquitted the accused, but because they put the charge on one side, coming to no conclusion upon it, in consequence of having found a verdict of guilty on some other alternative charge.

---

[1] *R.* v. *Barron*, [1914] 2 K.B. 570 affords an illustration of the same kind of situation. In that case there had been two indictments against the accused. One charged him with sodomy with a boy, the other with gross indecency with the same boy. Only one set of depositions was taken. The accused was tried on the first indictment and was convicted. On appeal the Court of Appeal quashed the conviction for wrongful admission of evidence. The accused was then tried on the second indictment, and pleaded *autrefois acquit*. The plea was disallowed; it is submitted that it would have been allowed if the accused had been charged with two offences in the alternative on one indictment.

[2] (1931), 144 L.T. 748. It may be mentioned that this was a case of a plea of *autrefois convict*.

[3] [1964] A.C. 1254, H.L. at p. 1305.

If this exceptional case be omitted from consideration, then it will be true to say that in cases where the evidence now put forward, or the facts necessary to support the charge now preferred, would have supported a conviction in the earlier proceedings on some count on which the accused was in the event acquitted, either expressly or impliedly, the plea of *autrefois acquit* will be available to him. *Aliter*, however, if the evidence now put forward, or the facts necessary to support the charge now preferred, would not have supported a conviction in the earlier proceedings, either on a count actually in the indictment or as to a charge on which, in the indictment as drawn, it would have been competent for the jury to have convicted.

In *R.* v. *Vandercomb and Abbott*,[1] where an indictment for breaking and entering and theft had been presented, and accused had been acquitted thereon, a plea of *autrefois acquit* was disallowed by all the judges of England sitting together, on a subsequent indictment on which the same accused was charged in respect of the same transactions with breaking and entering the same premises with intent. It was observed that the proof of breaking and entering with intent, with which crime accused was charged in the second proceedings, would not by itself without more have supported a conviction for breaking and entering and theft; the plea was therefore not sustainable. This decision was noticed favourably, and indeed followed, in *Connelly* v. *Director of Public Prosecutions*;[2] it may be pointed out, however, that the same circumstances can hardly be repeated under modern procedure, in which it would be proper for a prosecutor to prefer in the alternative all the offences which the Crown submitted as supported by the evidence to be adduced; moreover it will be recollected that at the time of the decision in *Vandercomb and Abbott's* case such modern statutory provisions as the Criminal Procedure Act 1851 and the Larceny Act 1916 were not yet enacted.

Again in *R.* v. *De Salvi*[3] accused was indicted upon a charge of wounding with intent to commit murder. He was acquitted. The victim subsequently died, and the accused was indicted for murder. Since murder can be committed without any intent to murder the facts necessary to support a conviction on the second indictment would not necessarily have supported a conviction on the first; hence the plea failed.

The record of the earlier conviction

325 *On a plea of autrefois acquit the accused is not to be restricted to a comparison of the indictments; he may prove by evidence if necessary such facts as may*

---

[1] *R.* v. *Vandercomb and Abbott* (1796), 2 Leach 708.
[2] [1964] 2 All E.R. 401; [1964] A.C. 1254, H.L.
[3] *R.* v. *De Salvi* (1857), 10 Cox C.C. 481 n.

demonstrate the identity between persons, transactions and offences charged which is requested to sustain the plea. This is the sixth of the propositions enunciated by Lord MORRIS in *Connelly's* case. The fifth has been omitted, since it will be found to relate exclusively to the plea of *autrefois acquit.* So, if a man be convicted for the murder of A.B. and acquitted, and be subsequently indicted for the murder of C.D., he may plead *autrefois acquit* and show by evidence that A.B. was the same person as C.D. The court will not be confined to an examination of the record, but the reality of the matter will be considered.[1]

Lord MORRIS cites little direct exact authority for this sixth proposition. There can be little doubt that the proposition states the law correctly in the light of modern legal philosophy; but exactly how far it will be taken in practice will remain to be seen as cases arise for its application. It will be interesting to consider under this head the cases where in Australia the same question has been considered, in relation to a point not precisely the same—*viz.* the validity of the plea of issue estoppel in criminal prosecutions. For a note of these the reader is referred to paragraph 337, *infra*.

326 *It is the substantial identity of the crime charged in each of the two proceedings that is the criterion, and it is immaterial whether the facts under examination, or the witnesses to be called, in the later proceedings are the same as those in the earlier proceedings.*[2]

This is the seventh of Lord MORRIS's propositions. The facts under examination and the witnesses to be called may be identical;[3] yet the crime charged in the second indictment may still be one of which it is not possible for the accused to have been convicted on the first indictment. Unless this test is complied with the plea of *autrefois acquit* cannot be available.[4]

---

1 *Connelly* v. *Director of Public Prosecutions*, [1964] A.C. 1254, H.L. per Lord MORRIS at p. 1307.

2 The words "substantial identity" are here used by the author of this text as a short convenient phrase covering Lord MORRIS's longer but more accurate phraseology—"Whether the crime or offence charged in the later indictment is the same or is in effect or is substantially the same as the crime charged (or in respect of which there could have been a conviction) on the former indictment". The phrase used above in the text is used by Lord READING C.J. in *R.* v. *Barron*, [1914] 2 K.B. 570, at p. 575.

3 Lord REID's judgment is to a similar effect. At p. 1295 he says "I cannot disregard the fact that with certain exceptions it has been held proper to try a man a second time on the same criminal conduct where the offence charged is different from that charged at the first trial".

4 Examples are given under proposition II, para. 322, above. See, for examples of the failure of the plea, *R.* v. *Barron*, [1914] 2 K.B. 570; *R.* v. *Ollis*, [1900] 2 K.B. 758; *R.* v. *Miles* (1909), 3 Cr. App. Rep. 13; *R.* v. *Kupferberg* (1918), 13 Cr. App. Rep. 166. *Cf.* on a plea of *autrefois convict* *R.* v. *Kendrick and Smith* (1931), 144 L.T. 748, *Cf.* again the facts in *Connelly* v. *Director of Public Prosecutions* (*supra*), a case in which there were two indictments in the first place, and it had been impossible for the accused to have been convicted of robbery, on the first indictment, only because of the procedural requirement that no other charge could be joined in one indictment with a charge of murder.

When and how may the plea of autrefois acquit be put forward

327 *Autrefois acquit*, exactly regarded, is found to be not a doctrine, but a plea alternative to the plea of "guilty" or "not guilty" which the accused may put forward when arraigned.[1] (If this *special plea* be found against him, he may then still plead "not guilty" to the charge preferred.) If the plea is put forward on arraignment the normal procedure upon it is that the Crown must either admit it, in which case the prisoner will be discharged, or answer it by way of replication, which is done by filing a notice to the effect that the plea is denied. In this event the question of the validity of the plea is tried by the jury; but the judge may, and often will, direct them firmly as to the verdict which they should find on the facts put forward.[2] If the issue is found against the accused he is then called upon to plead generally to the charge preferred.[3]

This is not to say, however, that the plea *or its equivalent* may not be put forward by an accused when its availability appears only after arraignment, and even in the course of trial. And a similar position obtains in summary prosecutions. In such cases the plea, or its equivalent, may be raised as justice may require in the course of the prosecution; it will then be for the court to decide upon it. So Lord MORRIS states as the ninth of his propositions in *Connelly* v. *Director of Public Prosecutions*.[4] *Apart from cases where indictments are preferred and where pleas in bar may therefore be entered, the fundamental principle applies that a man is not to be prosecuted twice for the same crime.*

In *Flatman* v. *Light*[5] (an appeal to the King's Bench Division from proceedings before Justices) Lord GODDARD C.J. said of a summary prosecution:

> "In common justice and fairness, if during the course of a case it turned out that a man had been previously convicted or acquitted of the same offence with which he was then charged the court would, of course, allow him to plead it and would give effect to that plea. When a case is before justices I doubt very much whether it is right to say that a plea that a man has been already acquitted or convicted of a previous offence is in any strictness a plea of *autrefois acquit* or *autrefois convict*, because those pleas are pleas which have to be pleaded formally, because they form part of the record of the court.

---

[1] It is "sufficient for any defendant to state that he has been lawfully . . . acquitted"—Criminal Proceedings Act 1851, s. 28; Archbold's *Criminal Pleading Evidence and Practice* 34th ed. paras. 446 *et seq*; *Connelly* v. *Director of Public Prosecutions*, [1964] A.C. 1254 per Lord MORRIS at p. 1303.

[2] The direction given by JOHN STEPHENSON J. to the jury trying the issue of *autrefois acquit* in *Connelly* v. *Director of Public Prosecutions* is an example of a firm direction. Its terms were referred to by Lord MORRIS at p. 1298; *cf.* the judgment of Lord DEVLIN at p. 1339—"STEPHENSON J. directed the jury to reject the plea".

[3] See the judgment of Lord GODDARD C.J. in *Flatman* v. *Light*, [1946] K.B. 414, at pp. 418–419.

[4] [1964] A.C. 1254, H.L. at p. 1306.

[5] [1946] K.B. 414, at p. 419.

They ought to be pleaded in writing and then a replication is pleaded by the prosecution. When a case is being dealt with by a court of summary jurisdiction I think it is true to say that what the court must do is to give effect to the maxim *Nemo debet bis vexari pro una et eadem causa*. I do not think it is technically *autrefois acquit*, but that does not matter."

So, too, in *Connelly* v. *The Director of Public Prosecutions*[1] Lord HODSON said:

"It is clear that the plea may be raised at any time either as a plea in bar to the second indictment or at any stage in the proceedings. In this case the appellant raised the plea in bar to the indictment of robbery after the Court of Criminal Appeal had quashed his conviction for murder and directed judgment and verdict of acquittal to be entered. He failed in his plea, but raised it again on his trial for robbery before NIELD J., and again before the Court of Criminal Appeal on his unsuccessful appeal to that court. It has not been contended before your Lordships that he was then or is now too late to take the point that he was by reason of the result of the first trial *autrefois acquit* of the robbery. The point may not arise until the second trial has taken place where, as in *Sambasivam* v. *Public Prosecutor*, *Federation of Malaya*,[2] the prosecution on a second trial rely on a statement made by the accused not put in evidence at the first trial which impugns the verdict of acquittal pronounced in the first trial. In that case Lord MACDERMOTT, delivering the judgment of the Board, pointed out that the verdict of acquittal is binding and conclusive in all subsequent proceedings between the parties to the adjudication."

In *Sambasivam* v. *Public Prosecutor*, *Federation of Malaya*,[2] as Lord HODSON points out in his speech, the point did not arise until a very late stage in the trial, and indeed not completely until the stage of appeal.

Previous acquittal in a foreign Court

328 The plea of *autrefois acquit* will be available even though the previous acquittal took place in a foreign jurisdiction, provided that the acquitting court was one competent to try the charge.[3] While it seems that this is clear law in cases where there has been an actual acquittal on the same charge as is now presented, it does not seem to have been decided how far the principle will extend as regards previous acquittals in a foreign jurisdiction where these have been not as to the actual offence subsequently charged, but of some cognate offence.

The nature of the second proceeding

329 It was suggested in an earlier paragraph[4] that the phrase *bis vexatus* might serve to obscure, rather than to clarify, the precise limitations of the

[1] [1964] A.C. 1254, H.L. at p. 1331.

[2] [1950] A.C. 458, P.C. at pp. 472–473 and pp. 479–480.

[3] *R.* v. *Roche* (1775), 1 Leach 134, and the case of *R.* v. *Hutchinson* referred to in a note thereto.

[4] Para. 316 *supra*.

operation of the doctrine of *autrefois acquit*. It will never operate, it is submitted, unless the first proceeding has been a prosecution on a criminal charge, the result of which has been acquittal. But the nature of the second proceeding is susceptible of rather more critical examination. It is of course established that if the second proceeding is a criminal prosecution wherein a crime is charged, be it felony or misdemeanour, the accused can be said (provided other essentials are complied with) to be *bis vexatus* if he has been prosecuted in an earlier proceeding; and this whether in both proceedings the prosecution has been for misdemeanour, or for felony, or whether felony has been charged in one and misdemeanour in the other.[1] But if the accusation in the second proceeding, while of conduct amounting to a criminal offence, is not put forward as supporting a prosecution for a crime in a criminal court, is he who is so accused *bis vexatus*?

The question will not arise where the second accusation is simply an averment in civil proceedings, *e.g.* to support a claim for damages. If a man has been prosecuted for assault, and acquitted, such a verdict cannot operate to preclude the complainant from claiming damages for assault in a subsequent civil action. This must be so for a variety of reasons as *e.g.* the two proceedings are between different parties, and the rule laid down (but as to a conviction) in *Hollington* v. *F. Hewthorn & Co.*[2] must apply; again, the onus of proof being different in civil and criminal proceedings, there would be grave difficulty in equating the result of the first proceeding with the question raised in the second.

The second proceeding, however, may be of an intermediate nature—*e.g.*, proceedings in which no claimant seeks an award of damages or other comparable remedy, and where the only relief sought is a consequence which may be regarded by the accused as penal. An example is readily found in an inquiry instituted by the disciplinary authority of a professional body, with a view to the expulsion of one against whom conduct infamous in a professional respect is alleged. In such a case it may be that the conduct alleged is no more and no less than conduct in respect of which the accused person has already been acquitted by a criminal court on a criminal charge. Neither a conviction nor an acquittal before a criminal court on a criminal charge will bar the use of the same conduct before such a tribunal on an application to suspend or expel; for the purpose of the proceeding is not

---

[1] Indictments Act 1915, s. 4 and Sched. 1 r. 3; *Connelly* v. *Director of Public Prosecutions*, [1964] A.C. 1254, H.L. per Lord DEVLIN at p. 1350–1351.

[2] [1943] 2 All E.R. 35; [1943] K.B. 587. Notwithstanding that the rule in *Hollington* v. *F. Hewthorn & Co., Ltd.* has now to a considerable extent been abrogated by statute, the common law rule disallowing estoppels where the parties are different in the two proceedings still applies with full force to the case where there has been an acquittal in the first proceedings; for such cases are left unaffected by the provisions of the Civil Evidence Act 1968—see Appendices C, D, *post*.

to punish the practitioner for the commission of an offence as such, but to exercise disciplinary power over the members of a profession so as to ensure that their conduct conforms to the standards of the profession.[1] Having observed that such appeared to be the basis of the "professional cases", NORTH and CLEARY JJ. in the New Zealand case *In Re a Medical Practitioner*[2] conclude on this topic by saying:

> "The Council may be concerned with many kinds of conduct which cannot constitute offences punishable by law, such as improper advertising, the commission of adultery with a patient, and unethical practices; when it becomes concerned with conduct which constitutes an offence, it is not for the purpose of punishing that conduct as an offence against the public, which is the purpose of the criminal law, but because it is conduct which may show that the practitioner concerned is no longer fit to continue to practise the profession. We think, therefore, that, before the Council, the respondent would not again be in jeopardy, and would not be subject to a second "vexatio", for the offence—the offence against the criminal law—of which he was acquitted. In the course of the argument, we were not referred to any case in which the maxim or the pleas of *autrefois acquit* or *autrefois convict* had succeeded except before a Court or judicial tribunal claiming jurisdiction to punish the offence charged as being a breach of the criminal law; and we do not think the operation of the maxim can be extended beyond that ambit."

The plea as now understood implies a necessity to include all charges in the first indictment upon which conviction may be sought.

330 Though a different rule has long obtained in some Dominion jurisdictions,[3] in which it has never been deemed unfair, but indeed in the interests of justice, in proper circumstances to retry in a second proceeding a person who has already undergone one trial, it has only recently been thought fair in this country ever to subject an accused person to a second

---

[1] Reference may be made to *In Re Weare*, [1893] 2 Q.B. 439, C.A.; *Allinson* v. *General Council of Medical Education and Registration*, [1894] 1 Q.B. 750, C.A.; *Ziems* v. *Prothonotary of the Supreme Court of New South Wales* (1957), 97 C.L.R. 279 (High Court of Australia); *In Re a Medical Practitioner*, [1959] N.Z.L.R. 784, C.A.

[2] [1959] N.Z.L.R. 784 C.A. at p. 814. *Cf.* the judgment of GRESSON P. at p. 800: "The exercise by the Medical Council of its powers is not by way of punishment, but rather to enforce a high standard of propriety and professional conduct. My conclusion is therefore that the proceedings before the Medical Council were neither criminal nor quasi-criminal".

[3] *E.g. in New Zealand* it has been within the powers of the Court of Criminal Appeal, ever since its institution in 1945, in quashing a conviction on the ground, for instance, of misdirection, to direct a new trial; the Court of Appeal possessed the same power, on a case stated, before the institution of the present Court of Criminal Appeal. In practice the direction of a new trial is the normal result of a successful appeal on a ground such as misdirection. The Court of Criminal Appeal has, in the alternative, the power to substitute a verdict of acquittal for the conviction which is quashed, and this is done where justice seems to require it; but this course is followed in only a small number of cases.

trial. From the time of the passing of the Criminal Appeal Act 1907, Parliament refused for more than half a century to sanction a retrial in respect of the same offence after a verdict of guilty had been quashed on any ground by the Court of Criminal Appeal; the policy of the law has recently undergone a change in this regard.[1] But notwithstanding its reluctance to sanction new trials on the same charge pursuant to decisions of the Court of Criminal Appeal, it is clear from the decisions that the law has never seen anything unfair in allowing an accused person who has been acquitted by a jury to be re-tried on a *different charge*, in respect of the same transactions as form the foundation of the previous proceedings, if on the first proceedings it was not open to the jury to convict on the facts now put forward as the basis for the second charge. So Lord MORRIS says in his seventh proposition in *Connelly's* case:[2] *What has to be considered is whether the crime or offence charged in the later indictment is the same or is in effect or is substantially the same as the crime charged (or in respect of which there could have been a conviction) in a former indictment; and it is immaterial that the facts under examination or the witnesses being called in the later proceedings are the same as those in earlier proceedings.*

But this proposition has a corollary. In *Connelly* v. *Director of Public Prosecutions* Lord REID[3] expressed the view that the Indictments Act 1915 was probably designed to ensure that all charges arising out of the same facts be contained in one indictment, thus preventing a series of indictments and trials on substantially the same facts. In murder cases, however, it was until recently the practice, following *R.* v. *Jones*,[4] not to include any other charge with one of murder in the same indictment. This led to the set of facts in *Connelly's* case, in which an accused found guilty of murder by a jury, and successfully appealing to the Court of Criminal Appeal on the ground of misdirection, found himself able to submit, on being subsequently indicted on the same facts for armed robbery, that he had been *autrefois acquit*. The fact that the jury could not have convicted him of armed robbery decided the matter against him and the plea was disallowed.

It follows that the prosecutor ought always to combine in one indictment all the charges which he intends to prefer, arising out of one transaction.[5] If he does not do so, then after an acquittal on the first proceeding subsequent charges should be entertained only if (a) his omission to include the

---

[1] The Criminal Appeal Act 1964 s. 1 now empowers the Court of Criminal Appeal to direct a new trial under certain circumstances.

[2] [1964] A.C. 1254, H.L. at p. 1306.

[3] At p. 1296. *Cf.* Lord DEVLIN at p. 1347.

[4] [1918] 1 K.B. 416.

[5] *Connelly* v. *Director of Public Prosecutions*, [1964] A.C. 1254, H.L. per Lord REID, at p. 1296; per Lord MORRIS at p. 1313; per Lord DEVLIN at p. 1350; per Lord PEARCE at p. 1367.

charges was for just reason in accordance with proper practice or (b) the accused has accepted without demur the omission to combine the charges.[1] It is submitted that if this rule of practice should in the future be disregarded, with the result that an accused person finds himself in subsequent proceedings facing a charge which ought to have been included (perhaps in the alternative) in the first indictment, he may be able to avail himself of the discretion of the court which is referred to in the next paragraph, and to have the second proceedings stayed as unjust.

Discretion of the court to stay second proceedings

331 In *Connelly* v. *Director of Public Prosecutions* it was argued on behalf of the appellant that, even if a plea of *autrefois acquit* was not strictly tenable, the discretion of the Court should have been exercised to stay the second proceedings as unfair and unjust.[2] This plea did not commend itself on the merits to their Lordships, who saw nothing unfair to the appellant, on the facts in that particular case, in his being charged with robbery when his acquittal on the earlier charge of murder was due to what might be described as a technical accident. But the question of whether there was a discretion, which the court in a more meritorious case might have exercised, is one on which their Lordships found themselves in some difference. Lord DEVLIN[3] and Lord PEARCE[4] were clearly of the opinion that the Court would have a wide inherent discretion to stay proceedings where these were demonstrated to be unfair to the accused. Lord REID agreed that there must be a discretion in the case of "anything that savours of abuse of process".[5] Lord MORRIS[6] on the other hand (and Lord HODSON[7] agreed with him) thought that it was of little help to inquire "in some vague and imprecise way" whether the second prosecution was "unfair"; and they felt that the only test must be (as perhaps was implicit too in Lord REID's speech) whether the prescribed practice had been followed on presenting the indictment.

> "I consider (Lord MORRIS said) that if a charge is preferred which is contained in a perfectly valid indictment which is so drawn as to accord with what the court has stated to be current practice, and which is presented to a court clothed with jurisdiction to deal with it, and if there is no plea in bar which can be upheld, the court cannot direct that the prosecution must not proceed."

---

1 Per Lord REID at p. 1296; *cf.* Lord DEVLIN at p. 1352.

2 The existence of a discretion had been assumed by Lord READING C.J. in *R.* v. *Barron*, [1914] 2 K.B. 570, at p. 575.

3 *Connelly's* case, *supra*, at p. 1352.

4 At p. 1361 *et seq.*

5 At p. 1296.

6 At p. 1299.

7 At p. 1334 *et seq.*

In view of the division between their Lordships, and in view of the fact that the point does not appear to have been one necessary for the ultimate decision to which the House came, the exercise of the inherent discretion of the court may perhaps be regarded as a matter still capable of some discussion in a case in which it is crucial. But the extent of the division between their Lordships may not be as great as might at first appear. All appear to have agreed that, as Lord PEARCE said "the court has an inherent power to protect its process from abuse"; the question on which they differed was whether such a discretion would enable a judge, confronted with an indictment drawn in accordance with prescribed practice, charging a crime to which *autrefois acquit* could not validly be pleaded, and presented by a prosecutor insisting on his right to proceed, to order that the proceedings should be stayed. The view of Lord MORRIS and of Lord HODSON was that the courts being at that stage bound by the rule in *R.* v. *Jones*, the first indictment was perfectly regular, and in accordance with the practice actually prescribed by the Court of Criminal Appeal; and the second likewise. No rule of practice therefore having been infringed by either indictment, it was not to be said "in some vague and imprecise way" to have been unfair that appellant should not have been tried on the second indictment. But Lord MORRIS and Lord HODSON did not go so far as to say that they would not use the inherent power of the court if in a future case it is found that the plea of an accused has been stultified by the failure of a prosecutor to include all proper charges in the former indictment, contrary to directions given in *Connelly's* case. It is therefore rather to the exercise than to the existence of the discretion that their Lordships are ultimately seen to have been in some difference.

Issue estoppel in criminal cases: Introductory

332 There will be cases where the plea of *autrefois acquit* will not be available, because the crime with which an accused is charged in the later proceedings is not the crime of which he was acquitted in the earlier, nor one of which the court was in the earlier proceedings competent to convict him; nor yet was the crime of which he was acquitted in the earlier proceedings one on which he could have been convicted on the facts or evidence now to be put forward. Yet the verdict of acquittal in the earlier proceedings may possibly have had, as its necessary foundation as a matter of logic, a finding the consequence of which is that he must be acquitted on the charge in the later proceedings. This is not *autrefois acquit*; for the accused is not able to show an acquittal of the same or substantially the same crime. All he can show is a finding of fact, express or implied, in the first

verdict, from which it follows that, if the prosecutor in the second proceedings is bound thereby, the result must be an acquittal.[1] Such an argument amounts to no less than the application of the principles of issue estoppel to criminal proceedings, and the doctrine regulating their application is expressed in the eighth of Lord MORRIS's propositions in *Connelly* v. *Director of Public Prosecutions*,[2] which is as follows: *Apart from circumstances under which there may be a plea of autrefois acquit a man may be able to show that a matter has been decided by a Court competent to decide it, so that the principle of res judicata applies.*

It is obvious that it will only seldom happen that an acquittal on any charge will lead with the necessary certainty to any satisfactory formulation of the issues or findings on which the jury must necessarily have based their conclusion.[3] The cases in which issue estoppel will be available, though *autrefois acquit* will fail, will accordingly be rare. There must be a prior proceeding determined against the Crown, necessarily involving an issue which again arises in a subsequent proceeding by the Crown against the same prisoner. The allegation of the Crown in the subsequent proceeding must itself be inconsistent with the acquittal of the prisoner in the previous proceeding. But if such a state of affairs arises it would seem at least arguable that the ordinary principles of issue estoppel should apply;[4] and

---

1 Lord DEVLIN (who does not agree that issue estoppel can be extended to criminal proceedings) states the proposition lucidly thus in his speech in *Connelly* v. *Director of Public Prosecutions*, [1964] A.C. 1254, at pp. 1343–1344: "The difference between issue estoppel and the *autrefois* principle is that while the latter prevents the prosecution from impugning the validity of the verdict as a whole, the former prevents it from raising again any of the several issues of fact which the jury have decided, or are presumed to have decided, in reaching their verdict in the accused's favour". In *Sealfon* v. *United States* (1948), 332 U.S. 575 the plea of double jeopardy was abandoned, but the plea of issue estoppel succeeded.

2 [1964] A.C. 1254, H.L. at p. 1306.

3 So in *R.* v. *Ollis*, [1900] 2 Q.B. 758—one of the earliest cases where this topic is touched upon—WRIGHT J. said at p. 769: "Nor can there be an estoppel of record or quasi-record unless it appears by record of itself, or as explained by proper evidence, that the same point was determined in the first trial which was in issue in the second trial. But in this case the record of the first trial would show no more than a general verdict of not gulty." In *Connelly* v. *Director of Public Prosecutions* the acquittal in the first trial had been by direction of the Court of Criminal Appeal, on a submission of misdirection, after the jury had found a verdict of guilty; there was obviously no material for the foundation of issue estoppel in favour of the accused. So, too, in the N.S.W. case of *Brown* v. *Robinson*, [1960] S.R. (N.S.W.) 297, where it proved impossible for the same reason to obtain any foundation for issue estoppel. In *Sealfon* v. *United States* (1948), 332 U.S. 575, where the plea of issue estoppel succeeded, the headnote refers to "the unique circumstances of this case". But it may be easier to found an issue estoppel where the earlier proceedings have been before (*e.g.*) Justices; in *Mills* v. *Cooper*, [1967] 2 All E.R. 100 it was apparent that a particular issue had been determined in favour of the accused in the first proceedings; but the estoppel failed because the question whether he was a gipsy on the first date proved to be different from the same question asked at a later date.

4 *R.* v. *Wilkes* (1948), 77 C.L.R. 511 (H. Ct. of Aus.) per DIXON J. at pp. 518–519. *Cf. R.* v. *Walker* (1843), 2 Mood. & R. 446 for an early case in which the Court was clearly on the threshold of the doctrine.

this now appears to be settled as a result of *Connelly* v. *Director of Public Prosecutions.*[1]

If the doctrine is made to apply, its result will be the disallowance of an accusation inconsistent with a finding shown to have been fundamental on the first occasion. It was expressly stated by Lord MACDERMOTT, delivering the report of the Judicial Committee in *Sambasivan* v. *Public Prosecutor, Federation of Malaya*,[2] that a verdict of acquittal pronounced by a competent court on a lawful charge and after a lawful trial is binding and conclusive in all subsequent proceedings between the parties to the adjudication. "The maxim *res judicata pro veritate accipitur*", said Lord MACDERMOTT,[3] "is no less applicable to criminal than to civil proceedings". In *Sambasivan's* case their Lordships reported their opinion that a conviction should be quashed, because the jury had not been directed that in considering the fact before them they were precluded from accepting the possibility that the accused might have been guilty of the offence (a different one, but relevant when considering the facts) charged in the first proceedings on which he had been acquitted. So, too, in several Australian cases it has been made clear that in that jurisdiction the principle of issue estoppel will be available so as to preclude the Crown in the second proceedings upon any issue which could not be found consistently with the verdict in the first.[4] This is in accordance with the cardinal principles of issue estoppel which require the second tribunal "to treat an issue of fact or law as settled once and for all between the parties if it is distinctly raised and if the judgment pronounced implies its determination necessarily as a matter of law."[5]

It is to be noted that the dicta upon which reliance has been placed in the foregoing text all refer to findings in the first proceeding being binding *upon parties thereto* in the second proceeding. Issue estoppel is binding, in the second proceeding, on the parties to the first; and the general relaxa-

---

[1] [1964] A.C. 1254, H.L. Lord MORRIS adverted to the availability of issue estoppel in criminal proceedings in his eighth proposition on p. 1306. Lord HODSON accepted the applicability of issue estoppel at pp. 1333–1334, and Lord PEARCE at p. 1364 and at p. 1368. Lord DEVLIN (see below) did not approve; the judgment of Lord REID is silent on the matter. It would appear that Lord PARKER L.C.J. so late as March 1967 had doubts as to the availability of issue estoppels in criminal cases, notwithstanding the views of their Lordships in *Connelly's* case as noted above—*Mills* v. *Cooper*, [1967] 2 All E.R. 100, at p. 103.

[2] [1950] A.C. 458, P.C.

[3] At p. 479.

[4] *Mraz* v. *R.* (*No.* 2) (1956), 96 C.L.R. 62 (H. Ct. of Aus.) at p. 68: "On any subsequent indictment the Crown will be precluded on any issue which could not be found consistently with the negative of the proposition. For the Crown is as much precluded by an estoppel by judgment in criminal proceedings as is a subject in civil proceedings—*Sambavisam* v. *Public Prosecutor of Malaya*".

[5] *Mraz* v. *R.* (*No.* 2) (1956), 96 C.L.R. 62, (H. Ct. of Aus.) at p. 70; *cf. Brown* v. *Robinson*, [1960], S.R. (N.S.W.) 297, 301.

tion of the rule as to identity of parties which characterises the application of the maxim *nemo debet bis vexari pro eadem causa*[1] will not, it is submitted, be so readily accorded to a plea of issue estoppel in criminal cases. Indeed, it has been expressly stated in one decision of the New Zealand Court of Appeal that the same identity as to parties will be required in criminal as in civil proceedings when a plea of issue estoppel is raised.[2]

But as has been pointed out above, it will be seldom only that a plea of issue estoppel will be available in a criminal prosecution, because of the fact that the previous verdict of acquittal, in the very nature of acquittals, is not usually couched in such terms as to make it possible to know whether it involves the particular determination on which in the second proceedings accused proposes to place reliance.[3] This was the determining factor in *Connelly's* case; the accused in the very nature of the result of the first proceedings (in which the Court of Criminal Appeal had directed an acquittal after the jury had brought in a verdict of guilty of murder) could take the matter no further than that on some ground or other the Crown's case had failed. In these circumstances "no more could be said than that for one reason or another the accused was not guilty of murder and not guilty of manslaughter".[4]

Issue estoppel recognised by Connelly's case

333 It is important, however, notwithstanding the comparative rarity of the occasions on which the plea of issue estoppel may arise in criminal cases in which no plea of *autrefois acquit* can be made to apply, to recognise that the doctrine is available, and that it has been recognised to be available both in the courts of this country and in other Commonwealth jurisdictions[5] and indeed in the United States[6] as well. Lord MORRIS, Lord HODSON and Lord PEARCE expressly gave their approval to it in *Connelly's*

---

[1] See para. 319, *supra*.

[2] *In Re a Medical Practitioner*, [1959] N.Z.L.R. 784, C.A.; in the judgment of GRESSON P. at p. 806 and in the joint judgment of NORTH and CLEARY JJ. at p. 812, pp. 817–818.

[3] *Connelly* v. *Director of Public Prosecutions*, [1964] A.C. 1254, H.L. per Lord MORRIS at p. 1322; *cf.* Lord PEARCE at p. 1368.

[4] Per Lord MORRIS at p. 1322. *Cf.* Lord HODSON at p. 1334: "This argument breaks down because one cannot in this case say that the only issue before the jury on the murder trial is whether or not the appellant was there. The issue of intent to murder was also an issue in the case, and there is no way of establishing any separate issue in his favour, either by looking at the verdict of the jury or by looking at the judgment of the Court of Criminal Appeal which reversed the verdict. The reversal was not of any specific issue or finding of fact but of the verdict of guilty of murder, and more than that cannot be read into it".

[5] *In Australia* in *R.* v. *Wilkes* (1948), 77 C.L.R. 511, and *Mraz* v. *R.* (*No.* 2) (1956), 96 C.L.R. 62; *in New Zealand* the point was adverted to, but not decided, in *In Re a Medical Practitioner*, [1959] N.Z.L.R. 784 where the second proceeding was not a criminal prosecution.

[6] *Sealfon* v. *United States* (1948), 332 U.S. 575 (Supreme Court S.C.T. of U.S.A.).

case;[1] and it must be remembered that it had already received the imprimatur of the Judicial Committee in *Sambasivan* v. *Public Prosecutor, Federation of Malaya*,[2] long before. Only Lord DEVLIN stands out with a definite view against its application.

Lord Devlin's view

334 It may be interesting in conclusion to summarise Lord DEVLIN's view.[3] He denies that issue estoppel is available in criminal cases. Notwithstanding its distinct recognition both in the United States and in Australia, he would not have similar recognition accorded by the law of this country. There is "no trace whatsoever" he says (passing over *R.* v. *Ollis*,[4] and distinguishing the dictum of Lord MACDERMOTT in *Sambasivan's* case[5]) "of its application to criminal matters". The difficulty in its application to criminal trials is that as a rule there is no determination by the jury of separate issues, and so their conclusion on any particular issue can be reached only by a subtle analysis of the general verdict. How subtle that analysis can become is demonstrated by such cases as *Mraz* v. *R.*[6] In *Connelly* v. *Director of Public Prosecutions* the conception of issue estoppel led to the highly unreal submission that the appellant had been notionally acquitted of robbery, whereas the facts were that the jury had been convinced (it turned out on a wrong direction of the law) of all the elements of his guilt. For these reasons Lord DEVLIN would have confined the plea of *autrefois acquit* within its orthodox limits, and, denying any extension by way of issue estoppel, he would have protected the interests of prisoners by recognising the court's final discretion to stay proceedings where considerations of fairness demanded such a course.

May issue estoppel be used against the accused?

335 These arguments against the application of issue estoppel to criminal proceedings are indeed formidable; but a final objection raised by Lord DEVLIN appears more formidable still. Estoppels are in their nature reciprocal, and if it is to be accepted that the prosecution may be precluded by issue estoppel based upon an earlier verdict from making a fresh accusation against the accused on a different charge, because of a fundamental inconsistency between such a charge and the formal verdict, can the prosecution be denied resort to the same course as a means of convicting a

---

[1] See footnote 1 on p. 285, *supra*.
[2] [1950] A.C. 458, P.C.
[3] *Connelly's* case, [1964] A.C. 1254, H.L. at pp. 1344 *et seq.*
[4] [1900] 2 Q.B. 758.
[5] [1950] A.C. 458, P.C.
[6] (1956), 96 C.L.R. 62 (H. Ct. of Aus.).

prisoner in later proceedings where the formal verdict is shown to be inconsistent with his innocence? No-one has yet contended that this should be the result of the application of issue estoppel to criminal proceedings. Yet it is hard to resist the conclusion that it should be so. If an accused (for instance) is convicted of an assault intended to cause grievous bodily harm and actual bodily harm and his victim subsequently dies, it is clear that the accused can then be indicted afresh for murder. But is the judge to direct the jury that the only question of fact for their consideration is whether the deceased died as a result of the injuries he received in the course of the assault?[1] For it might be said that all allegations of the assault and the intent with which it was made have been concluded for ever against the accused upon the first verdict by the process of issue estoppel. This is taking matters a long way; yet it appears to be at least a logical result of the unrestricted application of the principles of issue estoppel to criminal procedure and Lord DEVLIN's note of warning may yet be echoed in courts of high authority if this difficult point comes up for essential consideration.

Synthesis of the opposing views in Connelly's case

336 None of the other Lords of Appeal would go with Lord DEVLIN, and his objection to the use of the doctrine of issue estoppel may be taken to have been overborne by the majority. But it must be noted that the result of either view will in practice be much the same. Lord DEVLIN would compel the prosecutor to join all charges in one indictment, on which on any view of the facts it could be proposed to rely; the result would be the protection of the accused, in the event of a verdict of acquittal, from any further conceivable *vexatio*, through the strict application of the orthodox doctrine of *autrefois acquit*. If the prosecution ignored the rule of procedure requiring all to be staked on the first prosecution, then the wide discretion which Lord DEVLIN would give to the court would ensure, by enabling a stay of proceedings, that justice was done. Others of the Lords of Appeal, while regarding so wide a use of discretion as advocated by Lord DEVLIN as too vague to be countenanced, would achieve the same result by recognising the extension of the operation of the plea of *autrefois acquit*, through the application of the supplemental doctrine of issue estoppel to criminal proceedings, thus in effect enlarging the ambit of the principal doctrine to cover much the same kind of case as was contemplated in Lord DEVLIN's speech.

---

[1] The facts postulated are not dissimilar from those of *R.* v. *Friel* (1890), 17 Cox C.C. 325, referred to in Lord MORRIS's speech in *Connelly's* case at p. 1319. But the question supposed in the text did not arise.

What may be looked at to ascertain the Issues?

337 In the application of issue estoppel to civil cases it is clear that not only may the judgment in the first proceeding be looked at, but the whole record of that proceeding, including the pleadings, the transcript of the evidence, the written issues placed before the jury and their answers thereto, and the transcript of the summing up of the trial judge if the proceeding has been before a jury; and, where the matter has been tried before a judge alone, the written judgment (if any) read by him. All these are available in order to determine with the necessary precision exactly what was in fact decided betweeen the parties.[1] There is as yet little, if any, authority in this country on the question of how far the same rules are applicable to criminal procedure. In the trial of a criminal charge before a jury the crucial documents, in the case of an ordinary appeal against conviction before a Court of Criminal Appeal, are generally thought to be the transcript of the summing-up of the trial judge, the transcript of the notes of evidence, and if they are available (and they seldom are) any accurate record of the way in which Counsel put the case to the jury. Which of these may be used on a submission of issue estoppel in a criminal proceeding? It is as yet too early to say.

Connelly's case was, of course, one in which the decision in the earlier proceedings was the bare judgment of the Court of Criminal Appeal setting aside the conviction of the accused. Had the decision of acquittal resulted from the verdict of a jury it might have been permissible to endeavour to ascertain what issues had been left to them for determination. There seems to be no reported decision in this country in which the court, in considering what was necessarily decided by a formal verdict of acquittal, has examined and taken into account (for instance) the summing-up of the trial judge, in order to see what were the real issues which the jury were called upon to resolve. In certain Australian cases, however, such a course has been followed. *Mraz* v. *R.* (*No.* 2)[2] was a case the framework of which was not unlike that of *Connelly* v. *Director of Public Prosecutions.*[3] The accused was in the first proceedings found guilty of manslaughter by the jury, but this verdict was set aside on appeal, and a judgment of acquittal entered in substitution. The accused was thereupon tried for rape. He raised the plea of *autrefois acquit* and (the matter raised by the plea being reserved) upon his conviction for rape argued the plea before the High Court. It could not be contended that the plea was one of *autrefois acquit* in its strict sense, but the matter was argued exclusively as one of issue

---

[1] See Chapter VI, *ante.*

[2] (1956), 96 C.L.R. 62 (H. Ct. of Aus.).

[3] [1964] A.C. 1254, H.L.

estoppel. The Court had little hesitation in examining the transcript both of the evidence and of the trial Judge's summing-up.

So too in the later case of *Brown* v. *Robinson*[1] the Full Court of New South Wales examined the typed transcript of the evidence (there was no summing up, the jury having acquitted, without leaving the box, before the defence was entered upon in the first proceedings) in order to see what the allegations of fact were which had been made against the accused. All in vain; for, as will usually be the case, the examination of the evidence still left the court unable to determine which of the allegations of fact essential for the Crown's case had been rejected by the jury as insufficiently proved.

In the *United States* case of *Sealfon* v. *United States*[2] the Supreme Court of the United States found no difficulty in considering the verdict of the jury in the first case in the light of the text of the direction given to the jury by the trial judge. In this case the search for light proved more successful, and it became apparent, when the text of the direction was examined, that the issues before the jury in both proceedings were in fact the same; the plea of issue estoppel was upheld.

---

[1] [1960] S.R. (N.S.W.) 297 (Full Court of N.S.W.).
[2] (1948), 332 U.S. 575 at p. 579.

CHAPTER XII

Particular Applications of the Doctrine of Res Judicata: IV—Estoppels Per Rem Judicatam in Matrimonial Proceedings

Introduction

338 In this chapter it is proposed to examine in some detail two aspects of the principles of estoppel *per rem judicatam* as they apply in matrimonial proceedings; the chapter is divided into two sections accordingly. In Section I questions of jurisdiction will be discussed, and an examination will be made of the principles by which it is to be determined how far foreign decisions in matrimonial affairs will be accepted in this country as decisions *in rem* governing the status of the parties.

In this part of the text we shall not be concerned with issue estoppel, or indeed with estoppel *inter partes*; the question under examination—and it is often a most important question—is whether a previous decision of a foreign court declaring or altering the matrimonial status of the parties subsequently litigating in this country has determined the matter *in rem* so as to preclude further dispute upon it.

Section II of this chapter discusses a quite different topic. We are not there to be concerned with foreign decisions, but exclusively with the decisions of English courts, as to which it is proposed to consider how far the ordinary rules of issue estoppel *inter partes* are applicable in matrimonial disputes in this country. It will be seen in the course of this discussion that because of the injection by statute into the functions of the court, in its divorce jurisdiction, of an inquisitorial duty, peculiar to matrimonial litigation, the ordinary rules as to issue estoppel are of only limited application, and, as regards certain questions, may fail altogether.

SECTION I: FOREIGN DECREES AS RES JUDICATAE

Jurisdiction of foreign courts in matrimonial cases

339 *Res judicata* presupposes jurisdiction in the adjudicating tribunal. A foreign decree, if it is to be recognised in this country, must proceed from a court of competent jurisdiction. The essential grounds which must in normal types of litigation be established to found jurisdiction over parties, if it is sought to have the judgment of a foreign court recognised in this country, have been dealt with in an earlier chapter.[1] But matrimonial cases are in this respect in a class by themselves; and in the following paragraphs it is proposed to examine the essentials of jurisdiction over parties in various types of matrimonial litigation. Those to be discussed will be (a) proceedings for divorce, and (b) proceedings for nullity or for declarations of validity of marriage.

It will readily be seen that jurisdiction in such cases can never depend, as it may in litigation having only pecuniary consequences between the parties, on such matters as consent or contract; the judgments or decrees which proceed from these types of litigation are judgments *in rem*,[2] and the jurisdiction of the court must be founded on such matters as the nationality, the domicil, or the residence of those whose status is to be affected, or at least of one of them, within the jurisdiction, at the time of the commencement of the proceedings[3] or of the judgment or decree. The types of litigation which have been mentioned will now be considered.

Jurisdiction in divorce cases

340 It was for long an inflexible rule in this country that a decree of divorce pronounced in a foreign jurisdiction (in which term is of course included all jurisdictions outside England)[4] will be entitled to recognition in this country only if pronounced by a Court of the jurisdiction within which the parties are domiciled, both at the time of filing and at the time of

---

[1] Chapter IV, *supra*.

[2] As to decrees of divorce, see *Pemberton* v. *Hughes*, [1899] 1 Ch. 781, at p. 793; *Bater* v. *Bater*, [1906] P. 209, C.A. at p. 228. As to decrees of nullity see *Salvesen* (*or von Lorang*) v. *Administrator of Austrian Property*, [1927] A.C. 641, H.L. at p. 655, at p. 663.

[3] Per Lord Reid in *Indyka* v. *Indyka*, [1967] 2 All E.R. 689, at p. 693.

[4] See para. 69 *supra*.

hearing of the petition.[1] The effect of this rule is that divorce proceedings must be brought in the country in which the husband is domiciled, for in English law the domicil of wife and husband is necessarily always the same, the wife automatically assuming her husband's domicil.[2] The rule worked much injustice; for while it left it open to a husband to petition for divorce in the courts of whatever might be the jurisdiction in which he was domiciled, in confidence that any decree would be recognised as valid in this country, the wife was in a much more difficult position, since she could petition with the same result only in the jurisdiction in which the husband was domiciled—which might be thousands of miles away from her own actual place of residence. Deserted wives were therefore at a considerable disadvantage. This injustice has been the subject of remedial legislation in most Commonwealth jurisdictions, and today it is a commonplace of the substantive law in some of these jurisdictions,[3] though not in our own,[4] that a wife's domicil may be, or may be deemed to be, different from that of her husband.

341 The general requirement that the parties must be domiciled in England is still retained as the general basis of jurisdiction for divorce causes in English courts.[5] Where the husband is petitioner, his domicil in this country is a *sine qua non* of jurisdiction; but the requirement has been

---

[1] It is suggested in some texts that domicil at the time of filing the petition is sufficient—see also the dictum of Lord REID in *Indyka* v. *Indyka* referred to in note 3 at p. 292; but it may be doubted whether the jurisdiction will persist if thereafter, but before hearing, the domicil of the petitioner is lost; *Le Mesurier* v. *Le Mesurier*, [1895] A.C. 517, at pp. 539–540, *Bater* v. *Bater*, [1906] P. 209 at p. 217 and *Simons* v. *Simons*, [1939] 1 K.B. 490, at p. 499 all speak of domicil at *both* times. As to the mode of proof of foreign domicil, see the *Practice Direction*, [1968] 1 All E.R. 400.

[2] *A.-G. for Alberta* v. *Cook*, [1926] A.C. 444, P.C. at p. 465; *Indyka* v. *Indyka*, [1967] 2 All E.R. 689, H.L. per Lord REID at p. 693 (see note 4, *post*); per Lord MORRIS at p. 706; per Lord PEARCE at p. 711.

[3] For instance in New Zealand, where by section 3 of the Matrimonial Proceedings Act 1963 it is provided that *for the purposes of the Act* the domicil of a married woman, wherever she was married, shall be determined as if she was unmarried. The Australian provisions are cast rather on the English model, and do not appear to confer a separate domicil on the wife. The sequence of the statutory provisions in Canada, New Zealand, and the Australian States is noticed by Lord WILBERFORCE in his judgment in *Indyka* v. *Indyka*, [1967] 2 All E.R. 689 at p. 724. It is observed by Mr B. C. GOULD in a thoughtful essay on this subject in *The A. G. Davis Essays in Law* (1965: London; Butterworths) at p. 34 that the application of *Travers* v. *Holley*, [1953] P. 246 to the provisions of the New Zealand legislation may produce some interesting results.

[4] *Indyka* v. *Indyka*, [1967] 2 All E.R. 689, H.L. per Lord REID at p. 693: "I accept for the purposes of this case the present doctrine of English law that during the subsistence of a marriage the wife cannot have a domicil different from that of the husband. This rule may (or may not) be "the last barbarous relic of a wife's servitude" (per Lord DENNING M.R. in *Gray* (*otherwise Formosa*) v. *Formosa*, [1963] P. 259, at p. 267) but to alter it might have repercussions, and I think that this matter had better be left to Parliament".

[5] *Le Mesurier* v. *Le Mesurier*, [1895] A.C. 517; *Armytage* v. *Armytage*, [1898] P. 178, at p. 185; *Bater* v. *Bater*, [1906] P. 209; *Dunne* v. *Saban*, [1954] 3 All E.R. 586; [1955] P. 178 (DAVIES J.); *Indyka* v. *Indyka*, [1967] 2 All E.R. 689 H.L. per Lord REID at p. 693; per Lord MORRIS at p. 705; per Lord WILBERFORCE at p. 718.

relaxed in the case of wives who petition for divorce, to meet the exceptional cases referred to in the preceding paragraph. By s. 18 (1) (a) and (b) of the Matrimonial Causes Act 1950 it is provided that a wife may petition for divorce if—

> "the wife has been deserted by her husband, or the husband has been deported from the United Kingdom under any law for the time being in force relevant to the deportation of aliens, and the husband was immediately before the desertion or deportation domiciled in England",

or if the wife, notwithstanding that her husband is not domiciled in England, is resident in England at the date of the commencement of the proceedings and has been so resident for the three years immediately preceding. If either of these conditions is complied with, the court proceeds to hear the petition, and to deal with it in accordance with the law which would be applicable to the proceedings if the parties were domiciled in England.

The rule in Travers v. *Holley*

342 The statutory provisions mentioned in the preceding paragraph do not, of course, directly affect foreign decrees; but these provisions and those which preceded them have acquired a special relevance to foreign decrees by virtue of decisions which have laid down the principle that where a decree in divorce has been granted in a foreign jurisdiction to a petitioner-wife not domiciled in the jurisdiction, then, although the requirement as to domicil is not complied with, that decree will be recognised in the courts of this country if the case is one in which, if the wife had been resident in this country, instead of in the foreign jurisdiction, the Courts of this country would have assumed jurisdiction under the statute to hear her petition for divorce.

This extension of the principles of the English statute law, to invest the decrees of foreign jurisdictions with validity in this country, was rendered logically necessary by the principles of comity and convenience to which reference has already been made in an earlier chapter. If it is good enough for Parliament to provide that English courts should assume a divorce jurisdiction in favour of a deserted wife left within this jurisdiction, although the parties are not domiciled in this country, should not considerations of comity and convenience require the recognition of like decrees made in foreign jurisdictions?[1] Thus in *Travers* v. *Holley*,[2] HODSON L.J. said:

---

[1] In *Indyka* v. *Indyka*, [1967] 2 All E.R. 689, H.L. Lord REID said at p. 695: "The argument must be that whenever Parliament requires the court to exercise a new jurisdiction, it thereby requires or authorises the court to recognise the validity of a further class of foreign decrees which the courts would previously not have recognised."

[2] *Travers* v. *Holley*, [1953] P. 246, C.A.

"It seems to me, therefore, that Parliament has cut the ground from the argument put forward on behalf of the husband. If English courts will only recognize foreign decrees of divorce where the parties are domiciled in the territory of the foreign court at the time of the institution of proceedings, because that is the jurisdiction which they themselves claim, what is the situation when the courts of this country arrogate to themselves jurisdiction[1] in the case of persons not domiciled here at the material date? It must surely be that what entitles an English court to assume jurisdiction must be equally effective in the case of a foreign court."

Indyka v. *Indyka*[2]

343 *Travers* v. *Holley*[3] was decided by the Court of Appeal in 1953. For the next fourteen years it was the subject of much discussion, and of some criticism. In Victoria the Full Court refused to follow it.[4] It was said—and with some considerable justification, if legal logic was to be regarded as the deciding factor—that if domicil was to be regarded as the sole true basis of jurisdiction, then the fact that exceptions had been made in favour of deserted wives by an English statute could not affect the jurisdiction of a foreign court so as to increase it. But these considerations of legal logic had to be balanced against those of comity and of convenience[5] which we have mentioned. In 1967 in *Indyka* v. *Indyka*[2] the validity of the rule in *Travers* v. *Holley*[3] was expressly challenged before the House of Lords; their Lordships unanimously approved the decision[6] and applied it. In approving what was done in *Travers* v. *Holley*, however, they declined to accept in a restrictive way the process of reasoning on which that decision had been based by the Court of Appeal, and preferred to regard *Travers* v. *Holley* as an example of a class wider than had been contemplated in that Court. It was thought by at least a majority of their Lordships that this class must include all cases where the parties are shown to have a "real and substantial connection"[7] with the country whose courts have granted a decree. In the case before them, their Lordships accepted the nationality

---

[1] A phrase which has sometimes raised judicial eyebrows in later decisions. Thus in *Mountbatten* v. *Mountbatten*, [1959] P. 43 at p. 81. DAVIES J. respectfully thought that HODSON L.J. had been "a little hard on the Courts"; and in *Indyka* v. *Indyka*, [1967] 2 All E.R. 689 Lord REID points out at p. 695 that the Courts were "required by Parliament" to exercise the jurisdiction.

[2] *Indyka* v. *Indyka*, [1967] 2 All E.R. 689, H.L. The facts of this important case are to be found set out in para. 345 *post*.

[3] *Travers* v. *Holley*, [1953] P. 246, C.A.

[4] *Fenton* v. *Fenton*, [1957] V.L.R. 17, referred to as a "powerful judgment" by Lord MORRIS in *Indyka* v. *Indyka*, [1967] 2 All E.R. 689, at p. 706.

[5] Lord REID would have nothing to do with "comity" in *Indyka* v. *Indyka* (*supra*) at p. 696; in the same case Lord PEARCE is perhaps nearer the mark when he speaks at p. 708 of "the point of view of public policy and common sense".

[6] Lord REID at p. 693; Lord MORRIS at p. 707; Lord PEARCE at pp. 714–715; Lord WILBERFORCE at p. 727; Lord PEARSON at p. 729.

[7] Per Lord MORRIS at p. 708; Lord WILBERFORCE at p. 727; Lord PEARSON at p. 727; and Lord PEARCE at pp. 714–715 is clearly of the same opinion.

of the parties as a ground of jurisdiction, available to give validity in an English court to a foreign decree in divorce.

Limits of the rule in Travers v. *Holley*

344 *Travers* v. *Holley*, the result, if not the entire reasoning of which, is supported by *Indyka* v. *Indyka*, recognised the validity in England of a decree granted by a foreign court to a wife who, though not domiciled in the jurisdiction granting the decree, nevertheless would have qualified in England to invoke the Divorce jurisdiction, if able to show in England those qualifications as to residence which were actually hers in the foreign jurisdiction. Once these qualifications are shown it will not matter that such qualifications would not, according to the law of the foreign country concerned, give grounds for jurisdiction, and that in fact jurisdiction was assumed on some other ground unrecognised in England,[1] or that the divorce itself was granted on some substantive ground unrecognised by English law, as long as it was a ground sufficient in the country where the decree was granted.[2]

It is clear that the indulgence available by virtue of the rule in *Travers* v. *Holley* is available to wives only, and never to a husband, even by way of cross-petition.[3] The rule which gives validity to a decree granted on a wife's petition does not proceed on the basis of a notional domicil in the foreign jurisdiction being attributed to the wife, but purely on the residential qualification which, if possessed in this country, would have entitled her to petition in this jurisdiction notwithstanding that she had no English domicil. In *Mountbatten* v. *Mountbatten*[4] the husband's domicil of origin was English; though he and his wife had for several years been resident in the state of New York, it was shown that he had quite deliberately retained his domicil of origin throughout. The wife began proceedings in New York for a divorce on the ground of cruelty, desertion, and adultery. It was clear that if she had continued these proceedings, and had been successful, her New York decree would have been good in England by virtue of

---

[1] *Robinson-Scott* v. *Robinson-Scott*, [1957] 3 All E.R. 473; [1958] P. 71 (KARMINSKI J.); *Arnold* v. *Arnold*, [1957] P. 237, at p. 252. The judgment of KARMINSKI J. in *Robinson-Scott* v. *Robinson-Scott* was expressly approved by Lord REID in *Indyka* v. *Indyka supra* at p. 695; both the cases cited above receive Lord PEARCE's approval in the same case at p. 716. At first there was a tendency (*e.g.* in *Dunne* v. *Saban*, [1954] 3 All E.R. 586; [1955] P. 178) to require that the provision under which the foreign court assumed jurisdiction should be closely similar to that obtaining in Fngland (see the observations of Lord REID in *Indyka* v. *Indyka supra* at p. 694); but this has clearly disappeared in the later decisions. For a more recent case still, see *Brown* v. *Brown*, [1968] 2 All E.R. 11.

[2] *Arnold* v. *Arnold*, [1957] 1 All E.R. 570; [1957] P. 237; *Manning* v. *Manning*, [1958] 1 All E.R. 291; [1958] P. 112; *Indyka* v. *Indyka*, [1967] 2 All E.R. 689, H.L. per Lord MORRIS at p. 706.

[3] *Levett* v. *Levett and Smith*, [1957] 1 All E.R. 720; [1957] P. 156, C.A.

[4] [1959] 1 All E.R. 99; [1959] P. 43 (DAVIES J.).

the decision in *Travers* v. *Holley*.[1] But she abandoned these proceedings. She went to Mexico, where after a short period of residence she obtained a decree. The Mexican proceedings could not be deemed valid in England by the simple application of the rule in *Travers* v. *Holley*, for the wife's residence in Mexico was not long enough. But it was sought to apply the rule in *Armitage* v. *A.-G.*,[2] by which divorces are recognised as valid in this country, even if granted in a country where the parties are not domiciled, if the country of domicil would recognise the decree actually granted as valid. The country of domicil in *Mountbatten* v. *Mountbatten*[3] was England. It was argued for the wife, however, that the rule in *Travers* v. *Holley*[1] entitled her to claim a notional New York domicil, and on the basis of this domicil, and invoking the rule in *Armitage* v. *A.-G.*,[2] to claim validity for the Mexican divorce. DAVIES J. held against this contention; he rejected the argument that *Travers* v. *Holley*[1] gave the wife a notional domicil, and held that it did no more than extend to her a wife's indulgence, whereby jurisdiction was recognised as validly exercised in a foreign country in certain events, on the ground of residence only.[4]

The importance of the cases cited in this paragraph as setting limits upon the rule in *Travers* v. *Holley* is now greatly lessened in view of the extension of recognition of foreign decrees which must follow on the decision of the Lords in *Indyka* v. *Indyka*.

Nationality as a basis for jurisdiction in divorce

345 Nationality, for long entirely overlooked as a basis for the recognition of the jurisdiction of foreign courts in divorce, has been elevated into a ground of jurisdiction co-equal, or almost co-equal, with domicil, by the decision of the House of Lords in 1967 in *Indyka* v. *Indyka*.[5] There a decree of divorce had been granted by a Czechoslovakian Court to a wife who was a Czechoslovakian national, and who had lived all her life (including of course her matrimonial life) in Czechoslovakia. She and her husband—also a Czechoslovakian national—had been parted during the world war, and, to make a long story short, the husband had in 1946 acquired an English domicil which he subsequently retained. The wife divorced the husband in Czechoslovakia in 1949 on the ground of "deep disruption of matrimonial relations", a ground valid in that jurisdiction. Relying on the validity of this divorce, the husband married again in England in 1959. When in 1964 his second wife instituted proceedings for divorce against

[1] [1953] 2 All E.R. 794; [1953] P. 246, C.A.

[2] [1906] P. 135.

[3] [1959] 1 All E.R. 99; [1959] P. 43 (DAVIES J.).

[4] "DAVIES J. rightly refused to apply the principle of *Armitage* to the wife's Court of residence" —per Lord PEARCE in *Indyka* v. *Indyka*, [1967] 2 All E.R. 689, H.L. at p. 717.

[5] [1967] 2 All E.R. 689, H.L.

him, he pleaded as a defence his first marriage, which he said was still subsisting and undissolved. The questions of the subsistence of the first marriage, and of the validity of the Czechoslovakian divorce, were crucial in the second proceedings. It was obvious that since the husband had acquired an English domicil in 1946, an English court must hold his wife to be domiciled in this country in 1949 (the year of the divorce); the validity *in rem*, therefore, of the divorce could not be sustained on the ground that it was granted by a foreign Court of a jurisdiction in which the wife was actually domiciled. It was for this reason sought to invoke the authority of *Travers* v. *Holley*,[1] using the arguments which have been discussed in the preceding paragraphs in the text. It could not be suggested, and was not, that the husband had ever deserted his first wife—the divorce was not granted on any allegation of desertion, and indeed LATEY J., at first instance, found as a fact that there had been no desertion by the husband. It was therefore impossible to invoke the "deserted wife" provision of the statute by which to support *Travers* v. *Holley*, and the husband was compelled to submit that *Travers* v. *Holley* would support the divorce simply because his wife had been resident in Czechoslovakia for three years before the divorce was granted. One difficulty about this argument was that at the time of the decree in Czechoslovakia the section of the Matrimonial Causes Act by which this jurisdiction arose in England had not yet been passed into law; and in the court of hearing LATEY J. held that this fact prevented the argument from succeeding. The Court of Appeal (Lord DENNING M.R. and DIPLOCK L.J., RUSSELL L.J. dissenting) reversed this decision. The House of Lords unanimously affirmed the majority decision of the Court of Appeal.

346 In doing so the House set the stage for one of its rare pieces of legislation. Not content with holding on narrow grounds that the Court of Appeal had been right in applying *Travers* v. *Holley*, notwithstanding that the English legislation did not pass into law until after the divorce in Czechoslovakia, the House proceeded to review the whole of the law relating to the recognition of foreign decrees. All of their Lordships recalled that the rule that domicil alone could be regarded as supporting jurisdiction in divorce was judge-made law. Adverting to the authorities by which the judgments in *Le Mesurier* v. *Le Mesurier*[2] were supported, they noticed that the passage in *Bar on Private International Law* on which the advice of the Judicial Committee rested, when examined, reads:

---

[1] [1953] 2 All E.R. 794; [1953] P. 246, C.A.
[2] *Le Mesurier* v. *Le Mesurier*, [1895] A.C. 517.

> "A decree of divorce therefore, pronounced by any other Judge than a Judge of the domicil *or nationality* is to be regarded in all countries as inoperative."

but the words "or nationality" seem to have received no subsequent attention. After reviewing the question, all their Lordships giving judgment in *Indyka* v. *Indyka*,[1] except Lord REID, who left the matter open,[2] were of the opinion that the Czechoslovakian decree should be supported on the independent ground that the parties to it were at the time of the proceedings Czechoslovakian in nationality. And all their Lordships favoured an extension of recognition of foreign decrees, most of them, as has been explained, on the rather vague basis of a sufficient connection between the parties and the country granting the decree, of which connection nationality may be regarded as an eminent example.

Since *Indyka* v. *Indyka*,[1] therefore, the position may be taken to be that the courts of the country whereof the matrimonial parties are nationals at the date of divorce proceedings between them will be recognised in an English court as having jurisdiction in divorce, concurrent with the jurisdiction of the courts of the country in which the husband is domiciled; and moreover, in cases where the parties are neither nationals of nor domiciled in the country of the decree, an English court may recognise the decree if a sufficient connection is shown between the parties and the jurisdiction invoked.

Limits of the rule in Indyka v. *Indyka*

346A It is certain, as has been remarked above, that the result in *Travers* v. *Holley* was approved in *Indyka* v. *Indyka*, and that the Lords indicated that not only was that decision right, but that it should be regarded only as an example of a wider recognition of foreign decree to be accorded by English courts than had been thought possible previously. But the limits of the wider recognition henceforth to be accorded to foreign decrees was left not clearly defined. This was acknowledged by more than one of their Lordships, but the fact did not seem to give them undue concern.[3] It is respectfully observed by the present writer that it seems less than completely satisfactory for the highest appellate court, exercising a quasi-legislative function, to declare that the recognition to be given to foreign decrees in the future should be wider than that accorded in the past, and to lay it down that the principle formerly obtaining is not to be regarded as the true criterion, without proposing some new limits or criteria by which inferior courts may in the future be guided. But this is the

---

[1] [1967] 2 All E.R. 689, H.L.

[2] At p. 703.

[3] See per Lord MORRIS at p. 708; per Lord PEARCE at p. 716; per Lord WILBERFORCE at p. 727; per Lord PEARSON at p. 729.

position as it is left by *Indyka* v. *Indyka*, and it seems that a series of cases at a lower level will require to be decided[1] before practitioners can advise their clients, in what may be regarded as borderline cases, whether their foreign decrees will or will not be recognised in English courts.

There appears as yet[2] to be no decision in which a decree obtained by a husband in a foreign jurisdiction has been recognised by the courts in this country where the husband has not at the time of obtaining the decree been domiciled in the courts in the country of the court which granted it. But though, as has been pointed out above, there is no room for a husband to take advantage of the rule in *Travers* v. *Holley*,[3] it is submitted that it is now possible to contend that a husband, not domiciled in the foreign jurisdiction granting a decree, may seek under the decision in *Indyka* v. *Indyka* to have his foreign decree recognised by an English Court, praying in aid (*e.g.*) the fact that both parties are nationals of the country whose Court have assumed jurisdiction.

Residence as a basis for jurisdiction for divorce: the "matrimonial home"

347 Residence alone, of however long standing, not amounting to domicil, can never be recognised in an English court as a proper foundation entitling a foreign court to exercise jurisdiction to grant a decree in divorce. This has always been so held; and in *Indyka* v. *Indyka* the matter is alluded to by Lord WILBERFORCE[4] and by Lord PEARSON.[5] Both of them posed the question whether something less than domicil, but more than casual residence, could be acceptable, but neither was willing to go further than was necessary in the case before them. Lord REID[6] went further. Being brought to the view that domicil no longer provided a completely satisfactory test of jurisdiction, he was willing to consider "reviving the old conception of the matrimonial home" as a basis of the recognition of jurisdiction. It will be interesting to see how far this suggestion will influence the trend of further judicial legislation on this subject.

---

[1] They are already beginning to make their appearance in the Reports—*e.g. Angelo* v. *Angelo*, [1967] 3 All E.R. 314; *Peters (otherwise Petrovic)* v. *Peters*, [1967] 3 All E.R. 318; *Brown* v. *Brown*, [1968] 2 All E.R. 11.

[2] June 1968.

[3] *Levett* v. *Levett and Smith*, [1957] 1 All E.R. 720; [1957] P. 156 C.A.

[4] *Indyka* v. *Indyka*, [1967] 2 All E.R. 689, H.L. Lord WILBERFORCE says at p. 726 "As regards the second of these (possibilities), although it may be possible without any change in the law by Parliament for a judicial decision to allow recognition generally to decrees based on the non-domiciliary residence of the spouses, to do so in the present context appears to me to go further than is justified by the considerations advanced before us."

[5] Lord PEARSON at p. 731 "As to the validity in England of divorces granted in other countries on the basis of a merely residential qualification, I feel that there is a difficulty".

[6] At p. 702.

Fraud: denial of natural justice

348 All the rules which have been discussed above are subject to the overriding requirement of the English Divorce Courts that substantial justice shall have been accorded the parties in the foreign proceedings. If it should appear that natural justice has not been observed,[1] or (as may be the same thing) that the decree is tainted by fraud going to the matter of jurisdiction,[2] the decree of the foreign Court will be refused recognition.[3]

Jurisdiction in nullity suits: A: Domicil of the parties

349 The exact definition of the essentials for recognition of a decree of nullity pronounced by a foreign court has proved a matter of some difficulty.[4] The judgment or decree of a foreign court in proceedings wherein the validity of a marriage is in dispute will found a plea of *res judicata* in courts of this jurisdiction if the parties were at the time of the foreign proceedings domiciled in the foreign jurisdiction in question.[5] Moreover, the rule in *Armitage* v. *A.-G.*[6] applies to nullity suits, and a decree of nullity obtained in a foreign country in which the parties are not domiciled will be recognised in England if it would be recognised as valid in the country where the parties are domiciled.[7]

Jurisdiction in nullity suits: B: Residence of the parties

350 Since the same provision in the Matrimonial Causes Act 1950 gives to wives, living apart from their husbands, the same exceptional position in instituting nullity proceedings as is given to them in divorce proceedings, for the same reasons as we have expressed above, the courts of this country will recognise a decree of nullity made on a wife's application in a jurisdiction in which she is not domiciled but in which she has residential

---

[1] *Pemberton* v. *Hughes*, [1899] 1 Ch. 781, C.A., per Lord LINDLEY M.R. at p. 790; *Macalpine* v. *Macalpine*, [1958] P. 35 per SACHS J. at p. 43: "It is thus clear that there is an unbroken line of statements of high authority that a foreign decree of divorce obtained in proceedings the course of which ran contrary to natural justice is to be treated as a nullity".

[2] *Macalpine* v. *Macalpine* (*supra*) where fraud was found by SACHS J. as a fact at p. 45; *Middleton* v. *Middleton*, [1966] 1 All E.R. 168; [1967] P. 62 (CAIRNS J.).

[3] "Recognition should, however, always be subject to the proviso that the foreign decree is not vitiated by fraud nor contrary to natural justice"—per Lord MORRIS in *Indyka* v. *Indyka*, [1967] 2 All E.R. 689, at p. 706. *Cf.* in the same case per Lord PEARCE at pp. 715–716.

[4] See the judgment of Lord GREENE M.R. in *De Reneville* v. *De Reneville*, [1948] P. 100, C.A. at p. 109.

[5] *Salvesen (or von Lorang)* v. *Administrator of Austrian Property*, [1927] A.C. 641, H.L. at p. 663, p. 671; *De Reneville* v. *De Reneville* [1948] P. 100, C.A. per Lord GREENE M.R. at p. 109; *Ross Smith* v. *Ross Smith*, [1963] A.C. 280, H.L. at p. 304 per Lord REID. *In New Zealand*, section 82 of the Matrimonial Proceedings Act 1963 provides by statute for recognition if one or both of the parties was domiciled within the jurisdiction at the time of the decree.

[6] [1906] P. 135.

[7] *Abate* v. *Cauvin* (*formerly Abate otherwise Cauvin*), [1961] 1 All E.R. 569; [1961] P. 29 (LLOYD-JONES J.). *In New Zealand*, see Matrimonial Proceedings Act 1963 section 82 (1) (b) (vi).

qualifications which, if proved, in England would give the English court jurisdiction.[1]

The position is perhaps more doubtful where *both parties* are actually resident, but are not domiciled, in the jurisdiction whose courts pronounce the decree of nullity. But it is submitted that since English courts assume jurisdiction in petitions for nullity where both parties (as distinct from the petitioner only) are actually *bona fide* resident in this country at the date of the commencement of the suit,[2] a corresponding qualification as to residence in the foreign country assuming jurisdiction will suffice to support a decree of nullity pronounced in the court of such a country.[3]

Jurisdiction in nullity suits: C: Locus celebrationis

351 Where the parties, though not domiciled nor ordinarily resident within the foreign jurisdiction whose court pronounces the decree, yet have made application to that court in virtue of their marriage ceremony having been performed in that jurisdiction, it is probable that the courts of this country will recognise a decree, provided that the declaration of nullity is sought, and made, on the ground that the marriage is void *ab initio*;[4] for who can say better than the country in which the marriage was celebrated whether the ceremony constituted a valid marriage? But this rule will not extend to decrees sought and made on the ground that the marriage, though not absolutely void, was voidable by the petitioner; if a decree is to be recognised when made by a foreign court on such a ground, domicil will be essential to found jurisdiction.[5]

Fraud: Denial of natural justice in nullity cases

352 A rule that a sentence of nullity pronounced by a foreign court of competent jurisdiction will be recognised in this country is not of universal application;[6] and there is a residual discretion, which has been freely exercised where the circumstances require it, to refuse recognition of such a decree where it appears that substantial justice has not been done in the foreign country.[7]

---

1 *Merker* v. *Merker*, [1963] P. 283, at pp. 296–297.

2 *Ramsay-Fairfax (otherwise Scott-Gibson)* v. *Ramsay-Fairfax*, [1956] P. 115, C.A.; *Ross Smith* v. *Ross Smith*, [1963] A.C. 280, H.L. per Lord COHEN at p. 311.

3 *In New Zealand*, section 82 of the Matrimonial Proceedings Act 1963 provides that a decree shall be recognised if jurisdiction has been exercised on the basis of two years' residence by one or both parties.

4 *Corbett* v. *Corbett*, [1957] 1 All E.R. 621; *Merker* v. *Merker*, [1963] P. 283, at p. 296. *In New Zealand* see Matrimonial Proceedings Act 1963 section 82 (1) (b) (v).

5 This would appear to follow from *Ross Smith* v. *Ross Smith*, [1963] A.C. 280, H.L.

6 *Ramsay-Fairfax* v. *Ramsay-Fairfax*, [1956] P. 115 C.A. per HODSON L.J. at p. 135; *Gray (otherwise Formosa)* v. *Formosa*, [1963] P. 259 C.A. per DONOVAN L.J. at p. 270.

7 *Formosa* v. *Formosa supra*; *Lepre* v. *Lepre*, [1963] 2 All E.R. 49; [1965] P. 52 (Sir JOCELYN SIMON P.).

SECTION II—ISSUE ESTOPPEL IN MATRIMONIAL LITIGATION

Introduction

353 A decision in the divorce jurisdiction may be a decision *in rem*,[1] but often is not;[2] and even those judgments and decrees in divorce which as to parts thereof are judgments *in rem* may, as to other matters dealt with therein, be decisions *inter partes* only.[3] In the remaining part of this chapter it is proposed to put aside further consideration of judgments *in rem* in divorce, as *ex hypothesi* binding on all the world while they stand; we shall now pass on to consider the applicability of the rules of issue estoppel *inter partes* to those judgments, or parts of judgments, in divorce, which have not the effect of judgments *in rem*.

Issue estoppel of limited application in matrimonial cases

354 The solemn determination of an issue of law or fact by a court of competent jurisdiction, as a necessary fundamental step in its substantive decision, will in general preclude the same parties, through the operation of the doctrine of issue estoppel, from asserting to the contrary in subsequent litigation.[4] This doctrine has only limited application in the Divorce jurisdiction. The reason is to be found in the basic language of the Divorce Acts, which provide that the court shall be "under a duty to inquire into the facts" as a condition of granting relief, or must find it "proved", or "be satisfied" that a matrimonial offence has been committed. The court is enjoined, moreover, to "inquire into" any countercharge made by a respondent against a petitioner for relief.[5] When therefore the question before the court in the later proceedings is whether a matrimonial offence has been committed, no *affirmative* finding by a court in earlier proceedings as to the commission of such matrimonial offence can bind the second court,

---

1 *Pemberton* v. *Hughes*, [1899] 1 Ch. 781, at p. 793 (Divorce); *Bater* v. *Bater*, [1906] P. 209, C.A. at p. 228 (Divorce); *Salvesen* (or *von Lorang*) v. *Administrator of Austrian Property*, [1927] A.C 641, H.L. at p. 655, 663 (Nullity).

2 *Needham* v. *Bremner* (1886), L.R. 1 C.P. 583; *Conradi* v. *Conradi* (1868), L.R. 1 P. & D. 514, at pp. 518–519.

3 An instance is noticed in *B.* v. *A.-G.*, [1965] P. 278. The point is referred to in footnote 2 to para. 368, *post*.

4 See chapter VI, *ante*.

5 Section 4 of the Matrimonial Causes Act 1950 provides that "on a petition for divorce *it shall be the duty of the Court to inquire*, so far as it reasonably can, into the facts alleged, and whether there has been any connivance or condonation on the part of the petitioner and whether any collusion exists between the parties, and also to inquire into any countercharge which is made against the petitioner", and proceeds—"if the Court *is satisfied* on the evidence that the case for the petitioner has been proved . . . it shall pronounce a decree". *Cf. in New Zealand*, section 28 of the Matrimonial Proceedings Act 1963.

which must itself assume the duty of investigating the facts;[1] and the same principle applies to a *negative* finding in earlier matrimonial litigation as regards countercharges raised in the later proceedings by way of defence, for the court is positively required by the statute to "inquire" into such matters.

This duty of the court to inquire into countercharges raised by way of defence will avail to prevent the establishment of an estoppel *per rem judicatam* even where the bar to relief raised by way of defence is a discretionary bar, for whether a defence is established positively precluding relief, or whether it may in the discretion of the court avail to bar a decree, it is equally the duty of the court to make inquiry as to whether the countercharge is established.

In *Laws* v. *Laws*[2] a wife obtained a decree for restitution of conjugal rights against her husband in undefended proceedings on the ground of desertion; and on his failure to comply with the decree petitioned for judicial separation on the ground of non-compliance. The husband sought to allege cruelty by the wife, prior to the separation, as a defence to the petition for judicial separation. It was contended for the wife that he was estopped from doing so by reason of his failure to allege cruelty in the earlier proceedings. It was held that no estoppel would arise to preclude the husband's allegations, since the court on a petition for judicial separation had by virtue of section 4 (1) of the Matrimonial causes Act 1950 a duty to inquire into any countercharge made by the respondent; and it was pointed out that in terms of the proviso to section 4 (2) of the Act the court had a discretion to dismiss the petition if it found that during the marriage the petitioner had been guilty of cruelty.

"Estoppels do not bind the Divorce Court"

355 It has sometimes been said that in the Divorce jurisdiction the parties are estopped *inter se*, in accordance with the ordinary principle, by previous decisions of a court of competent jurisdiction, as to issues actually decided between them and fundamental to the previous decision; but that "the court is not to be estopped".[3] This is perhaps an over-abbreviated way of expressing the matter. The topic is developed in the judgment of DENNING L.J. in *Thompson* v. *Thompson*[4] as follows:

[1] *Harriman* v. *Harriman*, [1909] P. 123, C.A. per FLETCHER MOULTON L.J. at p. 142; per FARWELL L.J. at p. 144; *Hudson* v. *Hudson*, [1948] 1 All E.R. 773; [1948] P. 292 (Lord MERRIMAN P.); *Thompson* v. *Thompson*, [1957] P. 19 C.A. per DENNING L.J. at p. 29, per HODSON L.J. at p. 36, per MORRIS L.J. at p. 42. *In New Zealand* see *Keast* v. *Keast*, [1934] N.Z.L.R. 316, C.A.

[2] [1963] 3 All E.R. 398.

[3] "It cannot estop the Court"—per COZENS-HARDY M.R. in *Harriman* v. *Harriman*, [1909] P. 123, at pp. 131–132.

[4] [1957] P. 19, C.A.

"The question in this case is, however, whether those ordinary principles (of issue estoppel) do apply to the Divorce Division. The answer is, I think, that they do apply, but subject to the important qualification that it is the statutory duty of the Divorce Court to inquire into the truth of a petition—and of any counter-charge—which is properly before it, and no doctrine of estoppel by *res judicata* can abrogate that duty of the court. The situation has been neatly summarised by saying that in the Divorce Court 'estoppels bind the parties but do not bind the court': but this is perhaps a little too abbreviated. The full proposition is that, once an issue of a matrimonial offence has been litigated between the parties and decided by a competent court, neither party can claim as of right to re-open the issue and litigate it all over again if the other party objects (that is what is meant by saying that estoppels bind the parties): but the Divorce Court has the right, and indeed the duty in a proper case, to re-open the issue, or to allow either party to re-open it, despite the objection of the other party (that is what is meant by saying that estoppels do not bind the court). Whether the Divorce Court should re-open the issue depends on the circumstances. If the court is satisfied that there has already been a full and proper inquiry in the previous litigation, it will often hold that it is not necessary to hold another inquiry all over again. But if the court is not so satisfied, it has a right and a duty to inquire into it afresh. If the court does decide to re-open the matter, then there is no longer any estoppel on either party. Each can go into the matter afresh."[1]

DENNING L.J. expressly followed the earlier decision of Lord MERRIMAN P. in *Hudson* v. *Hudson*.[2] There it had been argued that the effect of *Harriman* v. *Harriman*[3] was simply that, while the parties were estopped by the previous finding of the court, the court was obliged to satisfy itself ("no estoppel will bind the court"); this it was said must be done without the assistance of the respondent or his counsel, since they would be estopped from active participation. Such an artificial and unreasonable procedural framework was rejected by Lord MERRIMAN, who said:

"It is suggested that, even if the respondent is entitled to file an answer, as he clearly must be until the question of estoppel is pleaded, he cannot be allowed to contest the effect of the earlier judgment. That means that although the party is there with his counsel and his witnesses the court is obliged to treat the case as an undefended one, and make such inquiries as it can by reason of the duty imposed on it without the assistance of cross-examination or the calling of witnesses for the respondent. I must say that it seems to me that that would be an extraordinary result of this legislation. Having asked the petitioner a few questions, the judge could not be prevented from calling the witnesses if he knew that they were there. I cannot believe that Parliament meant to reduce this procedure to such a farce as is suggested

---

1 At p. 29.
2 [1948] 1 All E.R. 773; [1948] P. 292 (Lord MERRIMAN P.).
3 [1909] P. 123 C.A.

by preventing the court assisting itself in the best way possible, that is by having the assistance of the person best qualified to assist it, namely the counsel who has to conduct the case on behalf of the other party. Having decided that the court is not bound to accept the earlier judgment as being conclusive of the commission of the offence charged, the only possible way to conduct the investigation is in my opinion in the usual way of a contest *inter partes*".[1]

Where no inquisitorial function involved in second proceeding

356 Where the invocation of an issue estoppel in the second proceeding will not have the effect of restricting or inhibiting any inquisitorial function of the court, such as is inherent in proceedings provided for in section 19 or section 28 of the Matrimonial Causes Act 1950, the ordinary rules as to issue estoppel will apply even in the Divorce jurisdiction.[2] It is sometimes said in this regard that where the earlier proceedings were in the High Court (for the rule has no application if the earlier proceedings were of a summary nature)[3] and the determination in such proceedings was a *negative* one, then the result, differently from that which follows from an affirmative examination, may be to found an estoppel; for to estop, in the second proceedings, the party who *unsuccessfully* put forward an allegation in the first is not always to offend against the statutory direction that the court must be "satisfied" of guilt before granting relief. It may be merely to apply the orthodox principle that a party, under a duty to his adversary in the first proceedings to put forward the whole of his case, who has failed to prove his allegation and has been refused relief accordingly, may not in a separate proceeding seek to relitigate the same matter.

So in *Finney* v. *Finney*[4] a wife petitioned the High Court for a judicial separation on the ground of cruelty; the petition was dismissed on the merits. She subsequently petitioned the High Court for divorce on the ground of adultery coupled with cruelty. It was held that since the issue of cruelty was the same as that which had been the subject of the earlier examination the petition must fail on the ground of estoppel.

In *Hopkins* v. *Hopkins and Castle*[5] the husband had been granted a decree of divorce against his wife on the ground of adultery with a named co-respondent. In subsequent proceedings he sued the co-respondent separately for damages; the latter raised defences of connivance and of conduct

---

[1] [1948] P. 292, at p. 301.

[2] *Conradi* v. *Conradi* (1868), L.R. 1 P. & D. 514. It is to be emphasised that where the second proceedings are not in the High Court in its divorce jurisdiction, the ordinary rules as to issue estoppel will apply, and the special considerations canvassed in this chapter will have no application. For the inquisitorial function from which these special considerations spring is an attribute solely of the High Court in its Divorce jurisdiction.

[3] See para. 359, *post*.

[4] (1868), L.R. 1 P. & D. 483.

[5] (1933), 50 T.L.R. 99.

inducing. It was held that the decree in the first proceedings necessarily rested on the court finding that no connivance existed; the co-respondent was therefore estopped in the second proceedings from raising this defence. The plea of estoppel was held, however, not to cover the defence of conduct inducing, which had not been raised in the first proceedings, and, not being more than a discretionary bar, could not be held necessarily to have been the subject of implicit adjudication.

And in *James* v. *James*[1] a husband had petitioned for divorce from his wife on the ground of adultery with a named co-respondent. Both the wife and the co-respondent denied adultery, and the petition was dismissed on the merits. Later the wife brought proceedings before justices for maintenance; the husband, in answer, repeated the same charges of adultery. It was held that he was precluded by the first decision from doing so, the matter being *res judicata* between the parties.

In *Field* v. *Field*[2] a husband in a suit for divorce had charged the wife with adultery. She counter-petitioned on the grounds of his adultery. At the hearing, the wife went into the witness box and denied adultery. The husband did not prosecute his petition further, and consented to the co-respondent being dismissed from the suit; the wife thereupon obtained a decree upon her counter-petition, the husband's petition being formally dismissed. On the husband's application, six years later, to vary the order made at the time of the divorce as to maintenance, he sought to re-allege his wife's adultery. It was held that he was estopped *per rem judicatam* from doing so; his petition for divorce, based on adultery, had been rejected, and the court must be taken to have found that the wife had not committed adultery, so as to estop the husband by the doctrine of *res judicata* from alleging it. It was particularly pointed out by WRANGHAM J. that in such proceedings as came before the court on the second proceeding (*viz.* an application for a variation of a maintenance order) the court had no inquisitorial duty such as arises under section 19 or section 28 of the Matrimonial Causes Act 1950.

357 But though the principle finds its application most often in circumstances in which the earlier determination has been a negative one, it is not strictly confined to these alone; for there may be affirmative determinations in the High Court which may satisfactorily serve as the foundation of estoppels without conflicting with any subsequent inquisitorial duty which lies upon the court in the second proceedings. So the parties in the second proceedings, for instance, will be estopped by a finding in the first,

---

[1] [1948] 1 All E.R. 214.

[2] [1964] P. 336. See also *Warren* v. *Warren*, [1962] 3 All E.R. 1031 (SCARMAN J.).

express or implied, that their marriage is valid and subsisting. In *Wilkins* v. *Wilkins*[1] a husband had unsuccessfully pleaded in the first proceeding that the marriage was bigamous; in the second, though the wife's first husband had turned up alive and well in the meantime, he was estopped nevertheless from averring his existence until he had first applied for and obtained an order for a new trial of the first proceedings! In *Woodland* v. *Woodland (otherwise Belin or Barton)*[2] too, a decree for restitution of conjugal rights was made by default against a husband who at the time of the suit had no ground for thinking that his marriage was bigamous. When he ascertained that it was so he was held estopped, as against the wife, so long as the first decree stood, from denying the validity of the first marriage.

An interesting case, in that the earlier finding was in form affirmative, though in substance negative, was *Hull* v. *Hull*.[3] Here a husband whose wife had in an undefended suit been granted a decree of divorce on the ground of desertion sought in later custody proceedings to allege that, contrary to the finding of the Judge in the first proceedings, so far from his having deserted his wife she had deserted him. It was held that, as the court which heard the suit had made an express finding that the husband had deserted the wife, and had based its decree on that finding, the doctrine of *res judicata* applied to estop the husband, in custody proceedings, from denying that he had deserted his wife. It is to be noted that in this case it was also sought by the husband, in the second proceedings, to allege that the wife had committed adultery other than that disclosed in the discretion statement which she had made in the first proceedings. SACHS J. held that no estoppel extended to the evidence of adultery, for no allegation of that offence had been pronounced upon at the earlier trial.[4]

Omissions may found an issue estoppel

358 The principles ordinarily governing issue estoppel require that each party to litigation should bring forward his whole case. In later litigation between the same parties a party who has been unsuccessful in the earlier suit will not be permitted to reopen a subject in respect of matter which might have been brought forward as part of the earlier contest, but which was not then brought forward; and this result applies in cases

---

1 [1896] P. 108, C.A.

2 [1928] P. 169 (HILL J.).

3 [1960] P. 118; [1960] 1 All E.R. 378.

4 Again in *Warren* v. *Warren*, [1962] 3 All E.R. 1031, SCARMAN J. held a wife estopped from setting up, to support a charge of desertion, the same facts which she had set up to support a charge of cruelty on an earlier petition which had been dismissed. But in the same case she was held not estopped from proceeding on the ground of desertion on different evidence. See, too, *Hill* v. *Hill*, [1954] 1 All E.R. 491; [1954] P. 291; *Holland* v. *Holland*, [1961] 1 All E.R. 226, C.A.

where the matter omitted from earlier consideration was omitted through the negligence or inadvertence of the party or his advisers, or even by accident.

> "The plea of *res judicata* applies, except in special cases, not only to points upon which the court was actually required by the parties to form an opinion and pronounce a judgment, but to every point which properly belonged to the subject of litigation and which the parties, exercising reasonable diligence, might have brought forward at the time."[1]

Only one requisite is essential—the point must be one the determination of which in the *successful* party's favour must have been fundamental to the judgment given.[2]

This rule applies fully in matrimonial cases,[3] as in others, subject, however to the limit which arises from the provisions of the statutes to which we have already referred—*viz.* that which follows from the duty of the court to assume an inquisitorial function as to certain matters within the Divorce jurisdiction.[4] It also follows, for a different reason, from what is said in the next paragraph, that no estoppel may be founded in the High Court in its Divorce jurisdiction from any omission to raise the same point in previous summary proceedings.[5]

Where the first proceedings are before Justices

359 Where the first proceedings have not been before the High Court, but before Magistrates, and have failed, the ordinary rules of issue estoppel, if applicable, would require the unsuccessful party to be estopped from repeating the same charges in later proceedings in the High Court; for it cannot be said, at least in the ordinary run of such cases, that there is

[1] *Henderson* v. *Henderson* (1843), 3 Hare 100, at p. 115 (Sir JAMES WIGRAM V.C.). This dictum was approved and applied by the Judicial Committee in *Hoystead* v. *Taxation Commissioner*, [1926] A.C. 155.

[2] In *Lake* v. *Lake*, [1955] 2 All E.R. 538; [1955] P. 336 the husband had petitioned for divorce on the ground of the wife's adultery. She denied adultery, and in the alternative pleaded condonation. The Commissioner dismissed the petition, finding on the facts that the wife's adultery had been proved, but that the defence of condonation succeeded. The wife attempted to appeal against the finding of adultery. It was held by the Court of Appeal that no appeal would lie, since she had succeeded on the petition; but the implications as to *res judicata* were discussed by members of the Court, and it is submitted that the judgment of Sir RAYMOND EVERSHED M.R. impliedly gives authority for the text as printed above. The reader may be referred, however, to the course taken by the Privy Council in *Australian Consolidated Press, Ltd.* v. *Uren*, [1967] 3 All E.R. 523, a decision which is examined, and made the subject of some criticism, in paragraph 216 *ante*.

[3] It is submitted that this result follows from what was said by Sir BOYD MERRIMAN P. in *Lindsay* v. *Lindsay*, [1934] P. 162, at p. 167.

[4] In *Winnan* v. *Winnan*, [1948] 2 All E.R. 862; [1949] P. 174, C.A. BUCKLEY L.J. disallowed the estoppel on the ground that the earlier proceedings had been before Justices and not in the High Court; but it is apparent from p. 185 that the estoppel would have been upheld if the earlier decision had been in the High Court. In *Bright* v. *Bright*, [1953] 2 All E.R. 939; [1954] P. 270 WILLMER J. applied *Hoystead* v. *Taxation Commissioner*, [1926] A.C. 155.

[5] *Winnan* v. *Winnan* was such a case, and the estoppel failed accordingly.

anything in the inquisitorial duty of the High court in its Divorce jurisdiction which must lead to a different result. But in practice the Divorce Court almost invariably investigates the charges afresh.[1] DENNING L.J. in his judgment in *Thompson* v. *Thompson*[2] explains the matter:

> "The reason is because it is known that magistrates are inclined to concentrate more on the question: ought this husband to pay maintenance to the wife, and less on the other issues, however relevant they may be. At any rate, the Divorce Court does not consider it satisfactory to allow the matter to be conclusively determined by the magistrates. The Divorce Court regards their finding as evidence, but not as conclusive, on the issue".[3]

Estoppel in summary matrimonial proceedings

360 When the second proceeding is one before justices the parties will be estopped by a finding on the same issue in earlier proceedings fundamental to the substantive judgment delivered,[4] and this whether the earlier proceedings have been in the High Court[5] or whether they have themselves been of a summary nature.[6] And moreover, provided the issue is identical, the estoppel will arise whether the previous determination has been of an affirmative or of a negative nature. For the inquisitorial duty which is laid upon the court by certain sections in the Divorce Acts is cast only upon the High Court in its Divorce jurisdiction, and has no place in summary proceedings, in which different considerations apply. So in *Whittaker* v. *Whittaker* (*supra*) the parties had separated under an agreement

---

[1] See, for example, *Winnan* v. *Winnan*, [1948] 2 All E.R. 862; [1949] P. 174, C.A. where a wife had obtained an order for maintenance before justices against her husband, he having failed to allege constructive desertion against her by way of defence. He later petitioned the High Court for a divorce, alleging the constructive desertion which he had previously omitted to raise. The wife set up estoppel. BUCKLEY L.J., delivering the judgment of the Court of Appeal, observed that if the principles enunciated in *Henderson* v. *Henderson* (1843), 3 Hare 100, at pp. 114–115 and *Hoystead* v. *Taxation Commissioner*, [1926] A.C. 155, at p. 170 were fully applicable, the plea of estoppel must succeed. But the Court disallowed the estoppel, for the reason that the earlier proceedings had been before justices. "If the principle applied in *Finney* v. *Finney* (1868), L.R. 1 P. & D. 483 is to be strictly applied to *proceedings before a Court of summary jurisdiction* followed by proceedings in the Divorce court, a previous finding of fact should act as an estoppel and prevent the guilty spouse from denying his guilt in answer to a divorce" said BUCKLEY L.J. at page 183. It is submitted, however, that he was speaking without fully taking into account the considerations which we have canvassed in an earlier paragraph when noting the inquisitorial function of the divorce court. BUCKLEY L.J. was perhaps nearer the mark when he said at page 187 "The point is bare of authority, and I do not find it easy to give any clear-cut reason why the rule of *res judicata* should not apply here . . ." It was to be left for DENNING L.J. in *Thompson* v. *Thompson*, [1957] 1 All E.R. 161; [1957] P. 19, C.A. to rationalise the decision. For his rationalisation, see printed text above. A later case is *Hayward* v. *Hayward*, [1961] 1 All E.R. 236; [1961] P. 152; PHILLIMORE J. said at p. 161 "In so far as there is any question of estoppel *per rem judicatam*, it can only arise from the decision of the Justices, which is not binding upon this Court".

[2] [1957] P. 19 C.A.

[3] At pp. 31–32.

[4] *Stokes* v. *Stokes*, [1911] P. 195 Div. Ct.

[5] As in *Sternberg* v. *Sternberg*, [1963] 3 All E.R. 319.

[6] *Whittaker* v. *Whittaker*, [1939] 3 All E.R. 833, D.C.

whereby the husband covenanted to pay his wife maintenance at a certain rate *dum casta*. Payments falling into arrears, the wife took proceedings in a County Court for their recovery. The husband pleaded her adultery as a defence; the County Court Judge found the adultery proved and gave judgment in the husband's favour. Subsequently the wife brought proceedings before justices alleging wilful failure to maintain. As a defence the husband relied on the earlier judgment of the County Court Judge. The justices thought that there was no estoppel, but on appeal a Divisional Court held that the wife was precluded from denying her adultery by the issue estoppel created against her by the judgment of the County Court Judge.

Decree refused:

361 If a decree is refused in the High Court, in a *defended* suit after the merits have been fully gone into, the result of the suit is no doubt *res judicata* between the parties in accordance with the general rule discussed in paragraph 356 above.[1] But if in an *undefended* suit a petition is dismissed—*e.g.* for insufficient proof—will such a dismissal be *res judicata* sufficient to preclude any re-litigation of the same allegation upon better proof becoming available? Here it is to be noticed that the respondent is often as anxious as the petitioner to have a decree granted; and the question of estoppel may not be specifically raised *inter partes* in the second suit. It is submitted that if the respondent does not raise the point in the second proceeding, no one else may do so;[2] the dismissal of the petition is not a judgment *in rem*.[3] But if the respondent in the second proceedings should defend, and raise the defence of estoppel, is the estoppel to be allowed? The point is obscure.

In pecuniary disputes between parties, considerations of convenience have been found on balance to require *ut sit finis litium*. But the consequences of a judgment dismissing a petition for divorce, if any re-litigation of the matter is thereby precluded *per rem judicatam*, are so much part of the stuff of life of the disputants that policy may well hesitate before deciding that the same result should follow on a dismissal in divorce, as follows on the dismissal of a civil claim. So in some jurisdictions it has been thought better to regard the dismissal of an undefended petition in divorce for lack of sufficient proof, as "in the nature of a non-suit"[4] and thus to allow the

[1] *Finney* v. *Finney* (1868), L.R. 1 P. & D. 483, at p. 484; *Bright* v. *Bright*, [1953] 2 All E.R. 939; [1954] P. 270 (WILLMER J.).

[2] See Chapter XIV, *post*.

[3] Counsel in the observance of his duty to the Court would certainly feel obliged to make disclosure of the position.

[4] *In New Zealand*, HUTCHISON J. held in *Hung* v. *Hung*, [1956] N.Z.L.R. 203 that this was the effect of a dismissal of an undefended petition; in a later decision of the Court of Appeal of that

presentation of a second petition on the same allegations with more thorough evidentiary support. There appears, however, to be no decision in this country expressly countenancing such a procedure.

The issues must be identical

362 In the divorce jurisdiction, as in other cases of issue estoppel, it is essential, if the doctrine is to be applied, to show that the issue is the same. It must be emphasised, moreover, that an issue estoppel (as has been pointed out in an earlier chapter) must relate to an *issue*, and not merely to evidence submitted in support of one. It is one thing to say that an issue of cruelty has been determined against a complainant, and that he or she is thereby estopped from re-litigating that issue; quite another to contend that the evidence which was submitted in support of the issue which failed cannot be resubmitted in a later proceeding where the issue is one of desertion.[1] So in *Cooper* v. *Cooper* (*No.* 2),[2] where in a court of summary jurisdiction a wife's charge of persistent cruelty against her husband had been dismissed and a subsequent charge of desertion and wilful failure to maintain was put forward in later proceedings, also of a summary nature, it was held that no estoppel arose with regard to the presentation of the same evidence as had earlier been given, for the issue was a different one. In *Bohnel* v. *Bohnel* (*No.* 2),[3] a wife petitioned for divorce on the ground of cruelty. The suit was undefended. The court held that the conduct complained of did not amount in law to cruelty, and accordingly dismissed the petition. The husband later petitioned for divorce on the ground of the wife's desertion. She filed an answer alleging that she had just cause for leaving her husband. On an application to strike out the answer on the ground that the wife was estopped from making the allegations contained therein it was held that she was not so estopped, since the issue of just cause had not been decided in the cruelty suit.

To exclude the estoppel it is sufficient to show that it is not perfectly

---

jurisdiction McGREGOR J. seems to have doubted the soundness of this decision—*Campbell* v. *Campbell*, [1957] N.Z.L.R. 1123 at p. 1127. *In Victoria* A'BECKETT J. considered such a dismissal as "in the nature of a non-suit" in *Gainsford* v. *Gainsford* (1899), 25 V.L.R. 176.

It has been said in both these jurisdictions, and there are similar dicta in this country, that the better course for the trial judge to adopt on an undefended petition which fails for insufficiency of proof, may be to stand it over for further consideration rather than to dismiss it out of hand; see, *in Victoria*, *Dean* v. *Dean* (1878), 5 V.L.R. (I.P. & M.) 116.

[1] *Foster* v. *Foster*, [1954] P. 67 D.C.

[2] *Cooper* v. *Cooper* (*No.* 2), [1955] P. 168 D.C. per Lord MERRIMAN P. at pp. 175–176; per KARMINSKI J. at p. 177, disapproving in this connection the observations of WILLMER J. in *Bright* v. *Bright* [1954], P. 270, at p. 287.

[3] [1963] 2 All E.R. 325 (CAIRNS J.). But in this case, even if the issue had been identical with that in the first proceeding, would not the Court still have been obliged to proceed with the inquiry whether the alleged desertion (by the wife) was desertion "without just cause"? See paras 354–355, *ante*.

clear from the previous record that the issues must be the same; and there has been a marked inclination shown in the decisions, particularly in the difficult areas of desertion, cruelty, and just cause for non-cohabitation, to refuse to allow an estoppel in a second proceeding where there is any real doubt as to whether the issue to be tried is absolutely identical with that held in the first.[1]

Issue estoppel in maintenance proceedings

363 Though in maintenance proceedings a duty is cast upon the Court, in assessing a wife's maintenance, to consider all relevant conduct of the parties both before and after marriage,[2] this rule does not allow the re-opening in the maintenance proceedings of an issue of fact upon which an issue estoppel may properly have been founded. In *Lindsay* v. *Lindsay*[3] a husband did not defend a wife's petition for divorce founded on an allegation of adultery, and the wife obtained a decree nisi, in which there was an order granting her the custody of the child of the marriage named in the petition. In a discretion statement the wife disclosed her own adultery on one specified occasion. Before the decree was made absolute, the wife filed a petition for maintenance for herself and the child. The husband by way of defence to this petition tendered affidavits to prove the wife's adultery during the marriage (on the same specified occasion only) and attempting to prove that the child named in the petition was not his, but the adulterer's. The wife pleaded estoppel *per rem judicatam* by virtue of the order for custody contained in the decree nisi. Sir BOYD MERRIMAN P., brushing aside in the manner noticed in the footnote[4] the difficulty as to the order being contained in the decree nisi, held that a decree which granted an order for custody, albeit by default, necessarily amounted to an adjudication as between petitioner and respondent of the legitimacy of the child, for it could not be made except as regards persons judicially held to be the children of the marriage; hence the issue of legitimacy was actually

[1] In *Cooper* v. *Cooper* (*No.* 2) (*supra*) Lord MERRIMAN P. at p. 172 in disallowing the submission of estoppel mentioned that there was "unquestionably an overlap" between the issues in the two proceedings. See also in the same regard, as to summary proceedings, *Molesworth* v. *Molesworth*, [1947] 2 All E.R. 842, D.C.; *Richards* v. *Richards*, [1952] 1 All E.R. 1384; [1952] P. 307 D.C.; in the High Court, *Thompson* v. *Thompson*, [1957] 1 All E.R. 161; [1957] P. 19, C.A.; *Fisher* v. *Fisher*, [1960] P. 36, C.A.

[2] *Restall* v. *Restall*, [1930] P. 189.

[3] [1934] P. 162 (Sir BOYD MERRIMAN P.).

[4] The case is complicated by the fact that at the time the wife's petition for maintenance was filed the decree nisi had not yet been made absolute. Sir BOYD MERRIMAN P., conceiving the Court to be bound by the decision in *The Delta* (1876), 1 P.D. 393, at p. 404, found some difficulty in holding that a plea of *res judicata* could be founded on a decree absolute not yet made at the date of the filing of the wife's petition, and this gave rise to a considerable excursus upon the theme that in this regard maintenance proceedings, following a divorce proceeding, constituted a special case. But the decision in *The Delta* has since been disapproved—see Chapter III, para. 100, *supra*.

determined, as between petitioner and respondent, by the decree, and the plea of *res judicata* was upheld.

Lindsay v. *Lindsay*[1] is direct authority for the proposition that in maintenance proceedings an issue which has necessarily been determined as fundamental to the decree of divorce cannot be relitigated between the parties; but in *Robinson* v. *Robinson*[2] the question arose as to whether it was permissible to raise in the maintenance proceedings conduct which would have amounted to a *discretionary* bar in the divorce proceedings, if it had been raised and proved there. HENN COLLINS J. held that though it could not be held barred by the doctrine of *res judicata*, since the finding on the issue could not be said to be fundamental and necessary to the decree, yet evidence of such conduct should be disallowed in the maintenance proceedings on the ground of "public policy". He said:[3]

> "The view to which I have come is that, although proceedings under section 190 sub-sec. (1) are separate proceedings from those for dissolution, a party ought not to be allowed to refrain from using at the hearing of a suit for divorce information which he had, or which, but for his carelessness he must have had, and then, when his pocket begins to be affected, propose to prove that information and put the petitioner to the expense of a separate issue".

364 This case was followed by the decision of PEARCE J. in *Duchesne* v. *Duchesne*.[4] In this case PEARCE J. was faced with the question which Sir BOYD MERRIMAN P. had put on one side in *Lindsay* v. *Lindsay*.[5] In the latter case it had been argued for the wife, setting up the plea of estoppel, that the husband was estopped in maintenance proceedings from disputing paternity of the child whose custody had been dealt with in the decree of divorce because (a) the question of paternity had necessarily been determined between the parties in the divorce court as a basis for the jurisdiction necessary to make a custody order, and (b) that alternatively the issue of paternity was crucial to a possible defence, as to the order for custody, on which the husband had chosen not to rely. The President had held in favour of the wife on the first point and deliberately left the second open.[6] It came up in *Duchesne* v. *Duchesne*.[7] A wife had obtained a decree in undefended divorce proceedings on the ground of desertion. On her application for maintenance the husband proposed to put forward evidence of the conduct of the parties during their married life. The submissions made by husband and

[1] [1934] P. 162 (Sir BOYD MERRIMAN P.).
[2] [1943] 1 All E.R. 251; [1943] P. 43 (HENN COLLINS J.).
[3] At p. 45.
[4] [1950] 2 All E.R. 784; [1951] P. 101 (PEARCE J.).
[5] [1934] P. 162.
[6] At p. 167.
[7] [1950] 2 All E.R. 784; [1951] P. 101.

wife respectively represented extreme points of view. For the husband it was contended, following *Mould* v. *Mould*,[1] that *all* conduct of the parties was admissible on a maintenance application; for the wife it was contended that, though the conduct of the parties was relevant to the issue of desertion, it was all to be excluded once that issue had been determined against the husband, except possibly some conduct such as might not have been known to the husband at the time of the hearing of the petition. PEARCE J. took an intermediate stand.[2] He "did not think that the authorities compelled him to either view in its extreme form". He proceeded:

> "The respondent is estopped in maintenance proceedings from asserting matters inconsistent with the decree. Further he is, for reasons of public policy, prohibited from asserting matters (of which he knew) which would reasonably have been expected, if proved either to provide an effective answer to the petition or to produce a different result at the trial (*e.g.* mutual decrees instead of a decree to the petitioner alone, or a discretionary decree instead of a decree as of right)."

Duchesne v. *Duchesne*[3] has been the subject of a good deal of criticism. What, it has been asked, is the basis upon which public policy may be said to preclude the tender of evidence, in respect of which the same public policy declines to apply the maxim *interest rei publicae . . .*? In *Brewer* v. *Brewer*[4] the High Court of Australia unanimously refused to follow *Duchesne* v. *Duchesne*.[3] In the judgment of WILLIAMS, WEBB, and TAYLOR JJ. it was said in criticism of PEARCE J.:[5]

> ". . . it adds nothing to his Lordship's statement to say, as he did, that it would also offend 'against public policy since it is a fraud on the Court', for the rules relating to estoppel are themselves based upon considerations of public policy and must, in general, be taken to express the full measure of what public policy requires in cases where they are called into play."

And FULLAGAR J., delivering the judgment of himself and DIXON J., said:[6]

> "The truth is that the rules of issue-estoppel have been carefully defined by the courts for the very purpose of determining as precisely as possible under what circumstances a party may put forward on a subsequent occasion material not put forward on a prior occasion. Such rules lose their value and their significance when attempts are made on vague grounds to give the effect of an estoppel to circumstances which admittedly create no estoppel".

---

1 *Mould* v. *Mould*, [1933] P. 76 (BATESON J.).
2 [1951] P. 101, at p. 113.
3 [1950] 2 All E.R. 784; [1951] P. 101.
4 *Brewer* v. *Brewer* (1953), 88 C.L.R. 1 (H. Ct. of Aus.).
5 At p. 9.
6 At p. 20.

It will be noticed that all the decisions cited above are of judges in courts of first instance, save the single exception of *Brewer* v. *Brewer*, which is a judgment, and a unanimous judgment, of the highest court in the Australian jurisdiction. In 1964 the point came up for further discussion before a court in this country; this was before WRANGHAM J. In *Field* v. *Field*[1] a husband had petitioned for divorce against his wife on the ground of adultery; there was a counter-petition by the wife against the husband, based on adultery and cruelty. At the hearing the husband abandoned his petition, which was dismissed by consent accordingly. The wife abandoned her allegation of cruelty, and proceeded as on an undefended petition with the charge of adultery only. She obtained a decree. There was an order for maintenance. Subsequently the husband made application for a variation of the maintenance order, on which he proposed to prove the adultery of the wife in respect of which he had previously suffered his petition to be dismissed. The wife contended that he was precluded from doing so by estoppel *per rem judicatam*.

It was clear that the plea of estoppel must succeed, since the adultery of the wife had been the subject of an actual adjudication (in the dismissal of the husband's petition). Anything, therefore, which WRANGHAM J. had to say on the decisions in *Lindsay* v. *Lindsay*,[2] *Robinson* v. *Robinson*[3] and *Duchesne* v. *Duchesne*[4] was *obiter*, and he so acknowledged.[5] Nevertheless the question of principle had been so fully canvassed before him, and by eminent Counsel, that he felt constrained to make some observations on the rule of "public policy" which had been noticed in, or created by, the decision of PEARCE J. WRANGHAM J. did not think that the statute invested the Court in maintenance proceedings with any inquisitorial function, such as it must assume on hearing a petition for divorce, and he came therefore to the conclusion that there was no rule of public policy such as had been laid down in *Robinson* v. *Robinson*[6] and *Duchesne* v. *Duchesne*.[7]

---

1 *Field* v. *Field*, [1964] 2 All E.R. 81; [1964] P. 336. It should be noticed that in the meantime a comparable question (the position in custody proceedings) had been discussed by SACHS J. in *Hull* v. *Hull*, [1960] 1 All E.R. 378; [1960] P. 118; he distinguished his own case from *Duchesne* v. *Duchesne* and showed little enthusiasm for any principle of public policy which transcended the ordinary rules of issue estoppel. See also *Baker* v. *Baker*, [1963] 3 All E.R. 901 (P.D.A.) where *Robinson* v. *Robinson* was "distinguished", and the Court allowed the evidence. As to whether, or how far, the doctrine of *res judicata* is applicable on a custody application, in which the interests of the child (not a party to the proceedings) are paramount, see *F.* v. *F.*, [1968] 2 All E.R. 946, C.A. where SALMON L.J. (with whom FENTON ATKINSON L.J. expressly agreed) queried at p. 950, notwithstanding the "careful judgment" of SACHS J. in *Hull* v. *Hull* (*supra*) whether the doctrine could be applicable in custody proceedings at all.

2 [1934] P. 162.

3 [1943] 1 All E.R. 251; [1943] P. 43.

4 [1950] 2 All E.R. 784; [1951] P. 101.

5 At p. 342.

6 [1943] 1 All E.R. 251; [1943] P. 43.

7 [1950] 2 All E.R. 784; [1951] P. 101.

With this conclusion the present writer, in agreement also with the High Court of Australia, is in respectful agreement. Public policy may support an issue estoppel when maintenance proceedings are before the court. If so, that estoppel succeeds because of the application of the ordinary rule *interest rei publicae sit finis litium*. But if the ordinary rules do not apply, it is because the maxim *interest rei publicae sit finis litium* does not apply; and if this maxim does not apply is there any room for contending that "public policy" will discountenance the production of the evidence? It is submitted that if no estoppel can be founded on what was determined on the divorce petition, no rule of public policy can be found to shut out evidence which is declared by the statute to be relevant.

Where decree nisi in former suit has been rescinded before being made absolute

365 It is of course clear that when a decree is rescinded it ceases, as a decree, to bind the parties; indeed it ceases as a decree to have any effect at all. In the case, then, of a decree nisi of divorce which is rescinded, should any issue estoppel, resulting from the findings of fact upon which the decree was granted, continue to bind the parties notwithstanding the rescission of the decree? Principle would appear, at least at first sight, to say "No"; once the judgment is extinguished, by virtue of which alone the issues become binding by way of estoppel on the parties, any estoppel should be extinguished likewise. This will indeed be the result where, if a decree nisi has been granted on the application of one party, it is rescinded, before being made absolute, on the application of the other, on some ground going to the making of the decree—on the ground, for instance, of fraud or misconduct in the proceedings. But there is a distinction to be made in this regard between decrees rescinded on the application of the unsuccessful party by reason of some factor which is deemed to invalidate the proceedings in which the finding is made, and decrees, good in all other respects, which the court has later seen fit to rescind on the intervention of the Queen's Proctor by reason of something extraneous to the proceedings—*e.g.* the conduct of the parties outside the court. The rescission being effected upon the application of a stranger, for reasons unconnected with the suit, it has been held that there is no reason why the parties should not be estopped by the findings leading to, and essential to, the grant of the decree nisi. This was decided by the Court of Appeal so long ago as 1894. In *Butler* v. *Butler*[1] a wife obtained a decree nisi of divorce against her husband on the ground of adultery; before it was made absolute it was rescinded on the application of the Queen's Proctor, who alleged against the petitioner-wife misconduct as regards which material facts had been

[1] [1894] P. 25, C.A.

suppressed in the suit. In subsequent proceedings A. L. SMITH J., delivering the judgment of the Court of Appeal, said:[1]

"But here arises the second point, for the decree nisi granted in the former suit has been rescinded, and it is said that as a verdict not followed by judgment is no evidence at all, as no judgment is now extant it is the same thing as if there had been no judgment at all. We think Mr Channell was well founded when he said, that in ordinary actions at law or issues directed by a court of Equity, a verdict given therein and not followed by a judgment, is no evidence at all. The Lord Chancellor (Lord COTTENHAM), in *O'Connor* v. *Malone* (1839), 6 Cl. & F. 572, at p. 596 said: 'It is a well-known rule of law that a verdict without judgment is no evidence at all, the reason being that there is nothing to shew that such verdict has not been set aside or may not have been acted upon by the Court'; and Sir JAMES WILDE, in *Bancroft* v. *Bancroft and Rumney* (1864), 3 Sw. & Tr. 597 above referred to, stated the same thing. It appears to us that in ordinary cases if a verdict be followed by a judgment, and such judgment is afterwards set aside, the verdict falls with the judgment, and, as was held in *O'Connor* v. *Malone* (1839), 6 Cl. & Fin. 572, neither party can give such verdict in evidence upon the second trial. But why is this? A judgment in such cases is set aside upon the ground that the verdict upon which it is founded was obtained either by fraud or by misdirection of the judge, or against evidence, or by surprise, or by some other means, which shewed that the verdict itself could not be supported, and consequently a judgment founded thereon was erroneous. In such cases the setting aside of the judgment vacates not only the judgment but the erroneous verdict, and places the parties in the same position as if no verdict had been given. But how does this apply to a case like the present? The verdict was followed by a judgment, and no fraud or error existed in the obtaining of that verdict, which stands unimpeached and upon which the decree nisi was founded. As regards the issues adjudicated upon between the parties, all was in order, and the judgment given thereon (*i.e.* the decree nisi) was perfectly valid and would have remained in force, and in due course would have become a decree absolute, had it not been that, dehors the verdict and wholly unconnected therewith, it was subsequently ascertained that the husband and wife had been guilty of conduct which disentitled them from reaping the benefit of the decree which both in this case so much desired. The material facts suppressed related to the conduct of the wife, not to the conduct of the husband. If any evidence favourable to him was suppressed he intentionally suppressed it, and he ought not to be allowed to reopen the case which was proved against him. If it could be shewn that the verdict in the first suit had been impeached, and that upon this ground the decree nisi had been set aside, we should have held that Mr Channell's argument was correct; but nothing of the sort can be shewn, for it is not the fact."

366 Notwithstanding that this judgment was one of the Court of Appeal, and notwithstanding that it has stood so long, and appears to be accepted without comment in many of the leading textbooks, it is sub-

[1] At p. 29.

mitted by the present writer that it was wrongly decided in principle. Doubtless its long standing will now constitute a considerable obstacle in the way of its reconsideration by a higher court; but it is submitted that a plea of *res judicata* ought not in principle to have been accepted on a judgment which had been set aside, and that a plea of issue estoppel can have no validity except as a special form of a plea of *res judicata*. Moreover a decree *nisi* is not a final judgment, and on this quite separate ground the decision in *Butler* v. *Butler* must be subject to serious criticism. This last point was glossed over by A. L. SMITH J. when he said:[1]

> "It cannot, we think, be doubted, if in the present suit the decree nisi had *remained unrescinded or had ripened into a decree absolute*, that then the verdict and decree in the former suit would have been conclusive evidence in the present suit of the husband's adultery and cruelty, and that it would not have been open to the husband in the present suit to controvert the fact of such adultery and cruelty having been committed by him."

It is here submitted that the consequence of the decree *nisi* "remaining unrescinded" and that of its "ripening into a decree absolute" are different consequences; in the latter case a decree becomes a final judgment, such as may found an issue estoppel, while in the former case there is no final judgment upon which an issue estoppel may be founded.

Cancellation and discharge of Decree Absolute

367 Once a decree has been finally made in a suit for divorce or nullity, if the status of the party was thereby changed or established the decree binds the world, being *in rem*. There may be cases in which, *e.g.* through mistake of fact or insufficient evidence being available, it transpires after the making of a final decree that the decision has been palpably wrong. In such a case the decree must continue to bind the world *in rem* until it is discharged by the court by some means; the proper procedure is to apply for a new trial, and for an enlargement of the time during which such an application may ordinarily be made. Then if justice requires it an order will be made accordingly, and on the new trial the true facts can be demonstrated. So in *Wilkins* v. *Wilkins*[2] a wife petitioned for judicial separation on the grounds of the husband's adultery. The husband pleaded that he was not validly married to the wife, and that she had a husband living at the time of his going through a ceremony of marriage with her. The jury found as a fact on the evidence that the first husband was dead at the time of the ceremony of marriage; and a decree of judicial separation was made.

---

[1] At p. 29.
[2] [1896] P. 108 C.A. See also *Woodland* v. *Woodland (otherwise Belin or Barton)*, [1928] P. 169.

Some months afterwards the first husband, who had not been heard of for more than thirty years, returned to England. The second husband commenced a suit for a decree of nullity of marriage. The wife pleaded estoppel, contending that notwithstanding the return of the first husband, the second husband was estopped (apparently) from alleging his existence. The court held that it could not make a decree of nullity while the decree in the first suit stood; but it allowed the husband to move in the first suit, notwithstanding that some three years had now gone by since the decree, for a new trial, and for an enlargement of the time within which such an application could be made.

Legitimacy

368 Questions of paternity frequently arise in divorce proceedings, and a decree in divorce, pronounced on a petition setting forth named children as the children of the marriage, in which an order for custody of those children is included, will estop either party in subsequent proceedings from averring that any child whose custody is so dealt with is not the legitimate child of the marriage.[1] But it is to be noticed that such a decree, though a judgment *in rem* as regards the matrimonial status of the parents, is not a judgment *in rem* as regards the children. And notwithstanding that they are the subjects of the order for custody, they are not parties to it; and they will not be bound thereby on questions of their own or each other's legitimacy, in respect of which any of them are free to take separate proceedings against their parents, and, if necessary, against each other.[2]

Withdrawal of summary application

368A The mere withdrawal of a matrimonial proceeding under the Summary Jurisdiction Acts does not give rise to an issue estoppel any more than the withdrawal of any other proceeding under those Acts; and this applies whether the withdrawal is made upon consideration of a preliminary point, or after the Court has begun to investigate the merits of the case, so

---

[1] *Lindsay* v. *Lindsay*, [1934] P. 162 (Sir BOYD MERRIMAN P.). For a more recent authority see *B.* v. *A.-G.*, [1965] 1 All E.R. 62; [1965] P. 278; there the estoppel is noted, but the case was one in which the children took action *inter se*, and they were held bound by no estoppel, not being parties to the earlier judgment.

[2] *B.* v. *A.-G.*, [1965] P. 278. "It seems to me", said WILLMER L.J., sitting as an additional judge in divorce, at p. 278, "that it would be absurd to suppose that, because a maintenance order may be embodied in the same document as that which determines the status of the parties, it is therefore to be regarded as an order binding *in rem*. I do not see that an order for custody should be regarded any differently, that is to say as anything other than an order binding upon the parties to the suit". *Cf. Nokes* v. *Nokes*, [1957] 2 All E.R. 535; [1957] P. 213. For the difficulties attending declarations of legitimacy as to persons not made parties to the suit, see *Aldrich* v. *A.-G.*, [1968] 1 All E.R. 345.

long as the summons has been withdrawn by the complainant before adjudication.[1]

---

[1] As in *Land* v. *Land*, [1949] 2 All E.R. 218; [1949] P. 405, where on the hearing of a summons under the provisions of the Summary Jurisdiction (Separation and Maintenance Acts) 1895–1925 on the ground of desertion the complainant withdrew her summons after she had been cross-examined. There was no adjudication by the court on the evidence which had been heard. In later proceedings it was held that no estoppel arose, such as to bar a reiteration of the allegations made in the first proceedings. See also *Molesworth* v. *Molesworth*, [1947] 2 All E.R. 842 (Lord MERRIMAN, P.).

CHAPTER XIII

Affirmative Answers to a Prima Facie Case of Estoppel Per Rem Judicatam

Introduction

369 If the party setting up the *res judicata* as an estoppel has alleged and established all the constituent elements of an estoppel of this nature, and if the opposite party is not in a position to meet by direct denial or disproof the case so made against him, it is still open to the latter to defeat the estoppel by setting up and establishing certain affirmative answers. Of these there are four main classes—fraud, cross-estoppel, contract, and public policy, each of which will be separately considered in this chapter. Following this discussion there will be some mention of certain spurious or ineffectual answers which from time to time have been suggested, but which have been found to lack validity.

Fraud: general considerations

370 "Acts of the highest judicial authority", though "not to be impeached from within", yet "are impeachable from without", for "although it is not permitted to shew that the Court was mistaken, it may be shewn that they were misled. Fraud is an extrinsic collateral act; which vitiates the most solemn proceedings of Courts of justice. Lord COKE says, it avoids all judicial acts, ecclesiastical or temporal".[1] The avoidance of a judicial act on the ground of fraud or collusion is effected not only by active proceedings for rescission[2] (which class of case does not

---

[1] *Duchess of Kingston's Case* (1776), 2 Smith L.C. (13th ed.) 644, per DE GREY C.J., delivering the opinion of the Judges summoned at p. 651.

[2] Though this is the most usual way of impeaching a judgment on this ground—*Jonesco* v. *Beard*, [1930] A.C. 298, H.L.

concern the present discussion, because an action or motion to set aside a judicial decision obviously presupposes that the decision is conclusive until set aside), but also by setting up the fraud as a defence to an action on the decision, or as an answer to any case which, whether by way of estoppel or otherwise, depends for its success on the decision being treated as incontrovertible. In the language of Lord BROUGHAM,[1] "you may at all times, . . . *either as actor or defender*, object to the validity" of the decision, "provided that it was pronounced through fraud, contrivance, or covin of any description, or not in a real suit", and such decision "shall avail nothing for, or against, the parties affected by it, to the prosecution of a claim or the defence of a right"; or, as Lord LANGDALE expressed it,[2] "if a sentence, decree, or judgment of any court can be shewn to have been obtained by fraud or collusion, *it is not to be used in any court as evidence against the right of the party who might be precluded by a sentence properly obtained*".

371 The fraud necessary to destroy a *prima facie* case of estoppel by *res judicata* includes every variety of *mala fides* and *mala praxis* whereby one of the parties misleads and deceives the judicial tribunal,[3] and also any form of judicial misconduct practised by the tribunal itself, with or without the concurrence and connivance of a party.[4] It may be constituted either by fraudulent misrepresentation, whether expressed in language or implied from acts and conduct, or, under certain conditions to be stated presently,

---

[1] *Earl Bandon* v. *Becher* (1835), 3 Cl. & Fin. 479 (at p. 510). This was a bill in the Irish Court of Chancery to redeem a mortgage, to which the defendant pleaded in bar a former decree in his favour for foreclosure and sale, and it was held a good answer to the estoppel that such decree had been obtained behind the plaintiff's back by the fraudulent collusion of the defendant and the other parties thereto.

[2] In *Perry* v. *Meddowcroft* (1846), 10 Beav. 122, at pp. 136, 137.

[3] In *Dsane* v. *Hagan*, [1962] Ch. 193 BUCKLEY J. rejected a plea of *res judicata* where in a second action it was sought to set aside a decree for specific performance made in default of appearance in earlier litigation, it being alleged on behalf of plaintiff, the executor of the defendant in the earlier suit (now deceased) that she (the defendant) had to the knowledge of the other party been incapable of contracting, and alternatively that the contract had been obtained by undue influence. BUCKLEY J., holding that the issues of fraud, lack of capacity, and undue influence were not raised by the earlier proceedings, declined to dismiss the second suit as incompetent because its subject-matter was *res judicata*, and went on to say, at p. 200–201 "In the circumstances such as these I think that it would be, at the least, unfortunate if the Court could not under its inherent jurisdiction recall its own judgment and allow the merits of the case to be litigated, if the circumstances are such as to suggest that the party who has obtained that judgment ought not fairly to be allowed to enforce it. In saying this I do not disregard the salutary maxim '*interest rei publicae ut sit finis litium*', but the court has never, I think, allowed that maxim to prevent the court from protecting itself from being deceived, and it seems to me to be at least arguable that, if the contract was obtained by fraud or was to the knowledge of the purchasers unenforceable for lack of capacity on the part of Mrs Hewson, the purchasers were guilty of deceiving the Court on the hearing of the summons under Order 14a. Such an argument would, I think, be open to the plaintiff on her present statement of claim."

[4] See paras. 380–1 *post*.

by silence and inaction. It defeats estoppels *in rem*, as well as estoppels *inter partes*;[1] and the rule applies, with one exception, to all English, and, without any exception, to all foreign, judicial decisions.

Fraud in relation to English judicial decisions other than awards

372 It has always been held, in the case of all English judicial decisions other than those of arbitral tribunals,[2] that, where it is definitely, and with sufficient precision and particularity, alleged, and substantially proved, that the decision was obtained by fraud or collusion, a good affirmative answer is thereby established to any *prima facie* case of estoppel founded on such decision as a *res judicata*, or to any action thereon,[3] or to any other proceeding dependent for its success upon the decision being held unimpeachable and conclusive, such as a petition in bankruptcy founded upon a judgment debt.[4]

It is the settled practice of the court that the proper method of impeaching a completed judgment on the ground of fraud is by action, in which the particulars of the fraud must be exactly given, and the allegations must be established by strict proof.[5]

373 Where the allegation, or the evidence, of the suggested fraud is inconclusive, or wanting in precision, or such as to give rise to no more than surmise, suspicion, or conjecture, the affirmative answer fails, and the

---

[1] See para. 382, *post*.

[2] See para. 374, *post*, as to this.

[3] As in *Loyd* v. *Mansell* (1722), 2 P. Wms. 73 (allegation that decree of foreclosure had been obtained by fraud upon the court held good by Lord MACCLESFIELD L.C., at p. 74); *Duchess of Kingston's Case*, *supra* (collusive sentence in a suit for jactitation of marriage); *Doe d. Davy* v. *Haddon* (1783), 3 Doug. K.B. 310 (sentence of dismissal by trustees of school against schoolmaster, alleged to have been fraudulently procured: *per* Lord MANSFIELD C.J., at p. 312); *Earl Bandon* v. *Becher*, *supra*, as to which see note 1, p. 323; *Harrison* v. *Southampton Corporation* (1853), 4 De G.M. & G. 137 (fraudulently and collusively obtaining decree of nullity of marriage: per KNIGHT-BRUCE L.J., at pp. 148–150, and TURNER L.J., at pp. 151–153); *Pearse* v. *Dobinson* (1865), 35 L.J. Ch. 110 (consent orders as to charges on estate alleged to have been procured by fraud and collusion (*per* KINDERSLEY V.C. at p. 112)). In the following cases, where the fraud or collusion was not established, it was recognized that, if and when established, either of these will defeat the estoppel: *Gregory* v. *Molesworth* (1747), 3 Atk. 626 (per Lord HARDWICKE L.C., at p. 627); *Brownsword* v. *Edwards* (1750), 2 Ves. Sen. 243 (per Lord HARDWICKE L.C., at p. 245); *Boaler* v. *Power*, [1910] 2 K.B. 229, C.A. (per FARWELL L.J., at p. 232), and the cases cited in the next note.

[4] For instance, by s. 7 of the Bankruptcy Act 1883, now s. 5 (3) of the Bankruptcy Act 1914, a duty is cast upon the bankruptcy court of inquiring into the consideration and circumstances of the debt upon which a petition is founded, before making a receiving order: for that purpose, in the case of a judgment debt, the court can "go behind" the judgment, and is not precluded by the statute from examining (as at common law also it would be bound to inquire) whether the judgment was collusive, or the debt fictitious: *Re Onslow, Ex parte Kibble*, (1875) 10 Ch.App. 373; *Re Blythe, Ex parte Banner* (1881), 17 Ch.D. 480, C.A.; *Re Lennox, Ex parte Lennox* (1885), 16 Q.B.D. 315, C.A.

[5] *Jonesco* v. *Beard*, [1930] A.C. 298, H.L.

estoppel is not displaced.[1] It should be noted here that grants of probate, though implied decisions that the will was validly executed, and, therefore, *inter alia*, without any fraud having been practised upon the testator,[2] do not necessarily involve a decision that no deceit was practised upon the court making the grant.

Fraud in relation to English awards

374 It has already been explained that, for the purposes of estoppel, the award of an English domestic tribunal stands generally on the same footing as other English judicial decisions, in all essentials.[3] It has nevertheless been held in a long line of authorities,[4] the result of which is now codified by statute,[5] that an award can be impeached for fraud or misconduct only by a motion to set it aside, and that such fraud or misconduct can never operate as a defence to an action on, or to summary proceedings for enforcing, the award, or support a plea of *nul tiel agard*,—in other words, an award procured by fraud upon, or by the judicial misconduct of, the arbitral tribunal is not a nullity, but a *res judicata*, unless and until set aside. Why there should be a distinction in this one respect only between the decisions of a domestic forum and those of the constituted judicial tribunals of the land, is not very clear.[6] Two different reasons have been assigned for the distinction by judges of high authority.[7] In neither case,

[1] As in *Burke* v. *Crosbie* (1811), 1 Ball & B. 489 (faint suggestion of fraud, not substantiated: per Lord MANNERS L.C. (Ir.) at p. 505); *Meddowcroft* v. *Huguenin* (1844), 4 Moore P.C. 386 ("responsive allegation" of fraud and collusion held bad on demurrer for want of precision and certainty: per Lord BROUGHAM, at pp. 398, 399); *Perry* v. *Meddowcroft* (1845), 10 Beav. 122 (where the fraud and collusion alleged was a mere "matter of surmise and inference from circumstances which do not of themselves necessarily lead to that conclusion": per Lord LANGDALE M.R., at p. 137); *Natal Land and Colonization Co.* v. *Good* (1868), L.R. 2 P.C. 121, 133; *Birch* v. *Birch*, [1902] P. 130, C.A., where the allegations of fraud were wanting in the necessary precision and particularity (per COZENS-HARDY L.J., at p. 138).

[2] *Allen* v. *M'Pherson* (1847), 1 H.L.C. 191 (per Lord LYNDHURST, at pp. 207–214, Lord BROUGHAM, at pp. 222–227, and Lord CAMPBELL, at pp. 232–238); *Melhuish* v. *Milton* (1876), 3 Ch.D. 27, C.A., per JAMES L.J., following the case last cited, at p. 33 ("a will obtained by fraud is not the will of the testator. A probate which is not recalled is conclusive proof in all other courts that the will is his will. Therefore no other court can listen to the allegation that the will was obtained by fraud"), MELLISH L.J., at p. 35, and BAGGALLAY L.J., at p. 36.

[3] See para. 26, *ante*.

[4] *Holland* v. *Brooks* (1795), 6 Term Rep. 161; *Braddick* v. *Thompson* (1807), 8 East 344; *Macarthur* v. *Campbell* (1834), 2 Ad. & El. 53; *Whitmore* v. *Smith* (1861), 7 H. & N. 509, Ex.Ch. *Woollen* v. *Bradford* (1864), 33 L.J. Q.B. 129; *Thorburn* v. *Barnes* (1867), L.R. 2 C.P. 384.

[5] The Arbitration Act 1889, now the Arbitration Act 1950. See *Bache* v. *Billingham*, [1894] 1 Q.B. 107, C.A., decided with reference to the former enactment.

[6] The passage is reprinted from Mr Spencer Bower's original text of 1924. But the difference is perhaps less than he supposed, when there are taken into account the procedural directions expressed and implied in *Jonesco* v. *Beard*, [1930] A.C. 298, H.L.

[7] In *Whitmore* v. *Smith*, *supra*; which was a case of alleged misconduct on the part of the arbitral tribunal, the Exchequer Chamber, whose judgment was delivered by WILLES J., suggested, at p. 519, as a reason of convenience for the distinction, that, on a plea of "no award", that is "no valid award", the court would have no other course open to them but to decide either that the

perhaps, is the explanation quite convincing; but, however this may be, the rule is now too firmly established to incur any danger of disturbance.

In the case of arbitrations under a statute which expressly or impliedly excludes the operation of the Arbitration Act 1950, the provisions of that statute must be carefully examined to see whether, as is sometimes the case, any exception is thereby created to the general rule above stated.[1]

Fraud in relation to foreign judicial decision

375 Fraud defeats a *prima facie* case of estoppel by a foreign, that is, a non-English,[2] *res judicata*, as effectually as it defeats an estoppel by an English *res judicata*;[3] indeed rather more so, for, in the case of a foreign decision, no question can ever arise as to any necessity of impeaching it by active proceedings in England, for the obvious reason, amongst others, that an English tribunal has no jurisdiction in that behalf.[4]

376 Accordingly, it has always been held that, whenever it is alleged and proved by the party against whom a foreign judgment is set up as a *res judicata* that such decision was obtained by the fraud or collusion of the opposite party, or by the judicial misconduct of the foreign tribunal, the answer is established, and the estoppel, or the action on the judgment,[5] as the case may be, is defeated,[6] but that where the fraud, collusion, or mis-

---

whole award is good, or that the whole award is bad, which might result in injustice on one side or the other, whereas, on a motion to set the award aside, the "peccant" portions of the award might, if severable, be set aside or remitted, leaving the residue to stand. Afterwards, in *Thorburn* v. *Barnes*, *supra*, where again, judicial misconduct of the arbitrators was made the subject of a replication amounting to "nul tiel agard", WILLES J., on this occasion speaking for himself alone, at p. 402, justified the distinction on a different ground, *viz.* that the arbitral tribunal is selected and appointed by the parties, whereas other English, and all foreign tribunals, are appointed by the State. Neither of these suggested reasons seems very sound, or even very plausible.

1 As to awards generally, see Chapter II; as to statutory arbitrations, see para. 90, *supra*.

2 As to "foreign" decisions, see Chapter II.

3 *Abouloff* v. *Oppenheimer* (1883), 10 Q.B.D. 295, C.A., per Lord COLERIDGE C.J., at p. 303: "it is a principle of law that no action can be maintained on a judgment of a court, *either in this country or in any other*, which has been obtained by the fraud of the person seeking to enforce it".

4 *Ibid.*, per BRETT L.J. at p. 305.

5 Which, as is explained in para. 11, *ante*, is possible only on the theory of estoppel.

6 As in *Blake* v. *Smith* (1810), unreported, but abstracted by SHADWELL V.C., at pp. 303, 304 of *Price* v. *Dewhurst*, *infra*, from the note in the registrar's book (a case in which the decree of a Portuguese court for dissolution of a partnership was treated as a nullity, having been procured by fraud); *Bowles* v. *Orr* (1836), 1 Y. & C. Ex. 464 (per Lord LYNDHURST C.B., at p. 473); *Price* v. *Dewhurst* (1837), 8 Sim. 279, per SHADWELL V.C., at p. 305, and on appeal (1838), 4 My. & Cr. 76, per Lord COTTENHAM L.C., at pp. 84, 85 (a case in which a Danish so-called "Executors' Court of Dealing" was shown to have consisted of the parties interested, who decided in their own favour); *Gossain* v. *Gossain* (1860), 8 W.R. 196, 199, P.C. (a decree of a British Indian Court embodying a compromise induced by *fraud*); *Abouloff* v. *Oppenheimer* (1882), 10 Q.B.D. 295, C.A. (defence to action on Russian judgment, alleging that the judgment had been obtained by misrepresentation to, and concealment from, the Russian tribunal, held good on demurrer: per Lord COLERIDGE C.J., at p. 303, and BRETT L.J., at p. 305); *Manger* v. *Cash* (1889), 5 T.L.R. 271, D.C. (the like); *Vadala* v. *Lawes* (1890), 25 Q.B.D. 310, C.A. (action on

conduct is not sufficiently alleged, or having been so alleged, is not sufficiently proved, the answer fails, and the estoppel remains unaffected.[1]

377 It is to be noted here that by the statute which facilitates and regulates the registration of Commonwealth judgments in this country[2] it is expressly provided that no such judgment shall be ordered to be registered if the judgment was obtained by fraud;[3] and that in the corresponding provision of the Foreign Judgments (Reciprocal Enforcement) Act 1933 it is provided that upon application in that behalf duly made by any party against whom a registered judgment may be enforced, the registration of the judgment shall be set aside if the registering Court is satisfied that the judgment was obtained by fraud.[4]

Collusion

378 On examining the authorities already cited, it will be found that fraud and collusion are so frequently associated, both in language and in fact, as to suggest that the latter is simply one of the many species or varieties of the former. This, however, is not strictly accurate. Collusion is essentially play-acting by two or more persons for one common purpose,—a concerted performance of a *fabula* disguised as a *judicium*,—an unreal and fictitious pretence of a contest by confederates whose game is the same.[5]

---

an Italian judgment against which the defendant successfully defended himself by proof that the judgment had been procured by fraudulent concealment of material facts from the Italian court: per LINDLEY L.J., at p. 316); *Bonaparte* v. *Bonaparte*, [1892] P. 402 (Scottish sentence of divorce obtained by fraud and collusion: per GORELL BARNES P., at pp. 409–411); *Codd* v. *Delap* (1905), 92 L.T. 510, H.L. (allegation in defendant's affidavit in answer to an application under O.XIV, in an action on a Canadian judgment, that the judgment had been obtained by fraud, held to entitle him to unconditional leave to defend (per Lord HALSBURY L.C., and Lord LINDLEY, at p. 511). For judicial statements of the rule, in cases where it was not necessary to decide whether the facts came within it or not, see *Godard* v. *Gray* (1870), L.R. 6 Q.B. 139 (per BLACKBURN J., at pp. 148, 149); *Ellis* v. *M'Henry* (1871), L.R. 6 C.P. 228 (*per Cur.*, at p. 239); *Messina* v. *Petrococchino* (1872), L.R. 4 P.C. 144, at p. 157; *Ochsenbein* v. *Papelier* (1873), 8 Ch.App. 695 (per Lord SELBORNE L.C., at pp. 698–700, and MELLISH L.J., at pp. 700, 701); *Macalpine* v. *Macalpine*, [1957] 3 All E.R. 134; [1958] P. 35 (a deliberate course of fraud by which a divorce was obtained in the State of Wisconsin without any notice to the respondent resulted in the decree being regarded as a nullity in this country); *Middleton* v. *Middleton*, [1966] 1 All E.R. 168; [1967] P. 62 (CAIRNS J.). Note: *In New Zealand* a different decision might have followed in these last two cases by virtue of the provisions of section 82 (1) (c) of the Matrimonial Proceedings Act 1963 whereby a decree is to be recognised if valid in a country where at least one of the parties is domiciled.

[1] As in *Shedden* v. *Patrick* (1854), 1 Macq., 535 H.L. (per Lord CRANWORTH L.C., at pp. 614–618, Lord BROUGHAM, at pp. 621–626, and Lord ST. LEONARDS, at pp. 641–648); *Cammell* v *Sewell* (1858), 3 H. & N. 617 (*per Cur.*, at p. 646); *Bater* v. *Bater*, [1906] P. 209, C.A. (*per* GORELL BARNES P., at pp. 218, 219, and COLLINS M.R., at pp. 228, 229). The onus of proof is heavy, and in *Blohn* v. *Desser*, [1962] 2 Q.B. 116, at p. 122, DIPLOCK L.J. held that "deep suspicion" was not enough.

[2] Administration of Justice Act 1920, as to which see para. 97 *ante*. [3] Section 9 (2) (d).

[4] Foreign judgments (Reciprocal Enforcement) Act 1933, s. 4. This statute is discussed in para. 98, *ante*.

[5] In the *Duchess of Kingston's Case* (1776), 20 State Tr. 355, the argument of WEDDERBURN S-G. (afterwards Lord LOUGHBOROUGH L.C.) contained the following passage, at coll. 478, 479,

The "play" it is true, is generally "foul play", but theoretically it need not be so, and there is a real distinction between the two concepts, and for some purposes, though not for those of estoppel, where the effect of fraud and collusion in defeating the estoppel is precisely the same,[1] it has been thought that there may be even a practical distinction as well.[2]

Concealment of material facts from the tribunal

379 The withholding of material facts from a party, or from the court, does not constitute either a cause of action, or a ground of defence, unless the party withholding those facts was under a duty of disclosure to the party from whom they were concealed, or to the court, as the case may be: and, similarly, non-disclosure, except under the conditions stated, is not deemed tantamount to a representation on which an estoppel can be founded.[3] On the same principle, when it is a question of shewing that the tribunal pronouncing the decision relied upon as a *res judicata* was imposed upon by the fraud of the successful party, no such fraud can be established by proof of the party's mere silence and inaction, as distinct from

---

which from frequent citation and adoption in subsequent judgments—*e.g.* that of Lord BROUGHAM, in *Earl Bandon* v. *Becher* (1835), 3 Cl. & Fin. 479, at pp. 510, 511, that of Lord CRANWORTH L.C., in *Shedden* v. *Patrick* (1854), 1 Macq. 535 H.L., at p. 608, and that of Lord SELBORNE L.C., in *Boswell* v. *Coaks* (1894), 6 Rep. 167, at pp. 168, 169,—has almost achieved judicial authority: "in order to make a sentence, there must be a real interest, a real argument, . . . a real defence, a real decision. Of all these requisites, not one takes place in case of a fraudulent and collusive suit: there is no judge; but a person, invested with the ensigns of a judicial office, is misemployed in listening to a fictitious cause proposed to him: there is no party litigating, . . . no real interest brought into question: and, to use the words of a very sensible civilian on this point, *fabula non judicium, hoc est; in scena, non in foro, res agitur*".

[1] Many of the cases mentioned in the preceding footnotes have been cases of collusion. In most of them the collusion was of a fraudulent character, or accompanied by fraud: but, in the following, collusion in itself, with or without fraud, was held, or stated, to be a good answer to the estoppel: *Brownsword* v. *Edwards* (1750), 2 Ves. Sr. 242 (per Lord HARDWICKE L.C., at p. 245: "if, indeed, there had been collusion, that might have been shewn . . .; because collusion affects everything"); *Earl Bandon* v. *Becher* (1835), 3 Cl. & Fin. 479 (per Lord BROUGHAM at p. 510: "you may . . . object to the validity of the decree, provided that it was pronounced through fraud, contrivance, or covin of any description, *or not in a real suit, or, if pronounced in a real substantial suit, between parties who were really not in contest with one another*"); *Re Onslow, Ex parte Kibble* (1875), 10 Ch.App. 373, a case of a collusive judgment given by an insolvent to his friends (per JAMES L.J., at p. 376, and MELLISH L.J. at p. 378); *Re Onslow's Trusts* (1875), L.R. 20 Eq. 677 (the like, per HALL V.C., at pp. 680, 681); *Re Blythe, Ex parte Banner* (1881), 17 Ch.D. 480, C.A. (the like: per JAMES L.J., at p. 488 BRETT L.J., at pp. 489–491, and COTTON L.J., at pp. 491–493); *Girdlestone* v. *Brighton Aquarium Co.* (1879), 4 Ex.D. 107, C.A.; a "former recovery" case—see note to para. 489, *post*—in which BRETT L.J. distinctly expressed the view (at pp. 108, 109) that the judgment there in question had *not* been procured by fraud, but (at pp. 109, 110) that, nevertheless, the judgment ought to be disregarded for the sole reason that the same parties were, in substance, both plaintiffs and defendants, and that the whole proceedings were fictitious and farcical. In *Re Leavesley* (1891), 64 L.T. 269, C.A., the principle was recognised, but the collusion was not made out.

[2] See the observations of Lord SELBORNE L.C., at pp. 168, 169, of *Boswell* v. *Coaks* (1894), 6 Rep. 167, H.L.

[3] See the authors' *Law of Estoppel by Representation* 2nd edn. paras. 62, 65, *et seq.*

positive statements or acts,—in other words, no *suppressio veri* can be considered equivalent to a *suggestio falsi*, unless the party owed a duty to the tribunal to speak, or act, in such a way as to reveal the undisclosed facts. In the absence of such a duty, no party litigant is bound to divulge to the court, any more than to his opponent, evidence against himself; he is entitled, for his own protection, and in the defence of his rights and interests, to use all that legitimate reticence and reserve which the Roman jurists denominated *dolus bonus*.[1] And it must further be shewn that the alleged undisclosed fact existed, that the party was cognisant, and the tribunal ignorant, thereof, and that it was material for the tribunal to know.[2]

But notwithstanding all that is said above, clearly cases will occur where it is the duty of the party obtaining judgment to draw the attention of the tribunal to facts within his knowledge, the existence of which must be fatal to his claim. Where, for instance, a plaintiff is aware that the defendant lacked capacity to contract, or, having capacity, was brought by undue influence to sign a contract, he is guilty of deceiving the court if he asks for and obtains a decree for specific performance in the absence of any appearance by the defendant; and if he does so, and the defendant or his representative in a subsequent action prays that the formal judgment be set aside, a plea of *res judicata* will not stand in the way of such a prayer.[3]

Upon whom, and by whom, the fraud must be shown to have been practised

380 The fraud must be proved to have misled the tribunal. If this be established, it is immaterial that the opposite party was not deceived: if not established, it is equally immaterial that he was. It is true that there is very seldom deception of the one without deception of the other, but the two facts are theoretically distinguishable facts. It is for this reason that, where, in support of a contention that the decision relied upon as *res judicata* was obtained by fraud practised upon the tribunal, the very same evidence was used which had been unsuccessfully adduced in the former proceedings for the purpose of shewing a fraud upon the party,[4] it was held that this course was unavoidable, and legitimate.[5]

---

1 See for instance *Bater* v. *Bater*, [1906] P. 209, C.A., per GORELL BARNES P., at pp. 218, 219, and, on appeal, per COLLINS M.R., at pp. 228, 229.

2 *Shedden* v. *Patrick* (1854), 1 Macq. 535 H.L. (per Lord BROUGHAM, at p. 622). In that case it was held that the undisclosed facts were not material, or that the facts alleged to have been concealed were not facts at all (per Lord CRANWORTH L.C., at pp. 614–618, Lord BROUGHAM, at pp. 621–6, and Lord ST. LEONARDS, at pp. 641–8). *Cp.* the case cited in the last note, for another illustration of non-materiality.

3 *Dsane* v. *Hagan*, [1961] 3 All E.R. 380; [1962] Ch. 193 (BUCKLEY J.).

4 As in *Abouloff* v. *Oppenheimer* (1883), 10 Q.B.D. 295, C.A.; *Vadala* v. *Lawes* (1890), 25 Q.B.D. 310, C.A.

5 *Vadala* v. *Lawes*, *supra* (per LINDLEY L.J., at pp. 316–320).

381 The fraud may have been practised by, not upon, the tribunal, using the term "fraud" in its largest sense, so as to include judicial misconduct, such as that of a *judex in sua causa*, or of one *qui statuit aliquid parte inaudita altera*. Of this there are one or two reported instances, where such judicial misconduct was held to defeat the estoppel as effectually as fraud practised by the party upon the court.[1] But the allegation and proof must be specific and precise: for instance, a mere vague suggestion of inveterate and notorious corruption in all the courts of a foreign State is quite futile and ineffective.[2]

382 When the decision was *inter partes*, the fraud to be established is the fraud of the party in whose favour the decision was given. But where the decision was *in rem*, the affirmative answer of fraud is as available for, or against, the world, as the decision itself is. On the one hand, it is enough in such a case, to establish that the fraud was practised upon the tribunal by anyone, whether a party or not:[3] on the other hand, anybody in the world can bring the fraud to the notice of the tribunal, and take the benefit of the answer to the estoppel,[4] even though he was himself implicated.[5]

---

[1] *Doe d. Davy* v. *Haddon* (1783), 3 Doug. K.B. 310 (per Lord MANSFIELD C.J., at p. 312: "whenever a judgment is obtained by fraud, it is open to go into it. *Here is a criminal charge against one of the judges*"); *Price* v. *Dewhurst* (1837), 8 Sim. 279, and, on appeal, (1838), 4 My. & Cr. 76, where gross judicial misconduct on the part of the tribunal was shown, as stated in note 6 on p. 326, *ante*, in which this case is cited; *Cammell* v. *Sewell* (1858), 3 H. & N. 617 (so stated by MARTIN B., delivering the judgment of the Court of Exchequer, at p. 646).

[2] In *Abouloff* v. *Oppenheimer* (1883), 10 Q.B.D. 295, C.A., there was, to the (original) author's knowledge, though the circumstance is not reported, a paragraph to this effect in the original defence, which was struck out in chambers.

[3] *Birch* v. *Birch*, [1902] P. 130, C.A., where the defendant objected that a judgment establishing a will, which he set up as a *res judicata*, could not be defeated by proof, adduced by the plaintiff, that the judgment was procured by the fraud of a third person, but the objection was overruled, on the ground that a will is either good against all the world, or bad against all the world (per COZENS-HARDY L.J., at pp. 137, 138): no fraud, however, was proved against anyone in this case.

[4] As in the *Duchess of Kingston's Case* (1776), 2 Smith L.C. (13th edn.) 644, where, in answer to the second of the two questions propounded to them, the judges summoned (per DE GREY C.J., at p. 652) expressed their opinion that, on the assumption that the sentence of a spiritual court in a suit for jactitation of marriage was binding upon the Crown, in other words, was a decision *in rem* (for the Crown was not a party to such suit), it was open to the Crown "to avoid the effect of such sentence by proving the same to have been obtained by fraud or collusion".

[5] As in *Re Lennox, Ex parte Lennox* (1885), 16 Q.B.D. 315, C.A., where a debtor had fraudulently consented to judgment for a debt gravely suspected to be fictitious, but nevertheless insisted that no receiving order ought to be made against him on the judgment, and the C.A., reversing the registrar, held that, having regard to the paramount interests of the whole body of creditors, the judgment ought not to be deemed conclusive, notwithstanding that the person bringing the fraud to the notice of the court was himself a party to it (per Lord ESHER M.R., at pp. 321, 322, COTTON L.J., at pp. 325, 326, and LINDLEY L.J., at pp. 328, 329); *Bonaparte* v. *Bonaparte*, [1892] P. 402, where it was held by GORELL BARNES J., at pp. 410, 411, that a divorce decree procured by fraud and collusion cannot operate as an estoppel even where the fraud is brought to the notice of the court, and relied upon, by one who had participated in it, the reason being that the decision was one affecting status and legitimacy.

Cross Estoppel

383 "Estoppel against estoppel setteth the matter at large", according to the oft-cited dictum of COKE. It is necessary, however, to examine this matter somewhat closely in order to determine within what limits a proposition of such sweeping generality can be accepted.

384 "Estoppel against estoppel" must mean that, when A. has established an estoppel against B., it is open to B. to set up, by way of affirmative answer, that A. is estopped from insisting upon such estoppel. Now, except possibly where the judicial decision was *in rem*, in which case it has been suggested that it may be open to the court to choose between two contradictory decisions as to status,[1] an estoppel *per rem judicatam* can never be defeated by another estoppel *per rem judicatam*, nor, indeed, can there, in strictness, be any question at all of any cross-estoppel, which presupposes two conflicting *res judicatae*, since the two decisions must either have related to the same subject-matter, in which case there is only one estoppel, namely that created by the earlier *res judicata*, or have related to different subject-matters, in which case there never could have been any estoppel at all.[2] In neither event is there any possibility of a pair of estoppels, one of which "crosses", or neutralizes, the other. There are, no doubt, cases in which an order or judgment of the tribunal, expressed to be "without prejudice to" other proceedings, has been held to be lacking in that finality which is an essential condition of any *res judicata* that is to operate as an estoppel: but this type of case, again, obviously raises no question of cross-estoppel.

385 On the other hand, where an estoppel *per rem judicatam* meets an estoppel by representation, there is a genuine cross-estoppel, in the strictest sense of the word. For here, A. having established a good estoppel by *res judicata* against B., B. confesses and avoids such estoppel by alleging and proving that A., by representation, has precluded himself from relying upon the *res judicata*. B. does not deny that he is estopped, but insists that A. is estopped from saying so. He destroys A's mine by a countermine, and so leaves the opposing forces in the same relative position and strength as before, or, in COKE's phrase, he "sets the matter at large".

---

[1] *R.* v. *Hutchings* (1881), 6 Q.B.D. 300, C.A. (per Lord SELBORNE L.C., at p. 303).

[2] As in *Poulton* v. *Adjustable Cover and Boiler Block Co.*, [1908] 2 Ch. 430, C.A., where it was held that an order for revocation of a patent did not create an estoppel upon the estoppel arising from a previous decision, in an action for infringement, that the patent was valid, since this decision and the subsequent order obviously did not determine the same question (per VAUGHAN WILLIAMS L.J., at p. 438, MOULTON L.J., at pp. 438, 439, and BUCKLEY L.J., at pp. 440, 441).

386 The representation giving rise to the cross-estoppel may be expressed in words, or (as is usually the case) implied from the representor's acts and conduct, or (when he is under a duty to speak or act) from his silence and inaction. The ordinary type of cross-estoppel by representation is that which arises upon the omission of the party in whose favour the decision was given to raise, at the earliest opportunity, the question of estoppel *per rem judicatam*, by pleading, objection to evidence, or otherwise, whereby he is deemed to have estopped himself from raising, or to have waived his right to raise, the question of *res judicata* once and for all.[1]

Contract

387 It is scarcely necessary to add that, if a party can by conduct or inaction estop himself from setting up estoppel *per rem judicatam*, an express contract to disregard any judicial decision which may be given on a specified point affords, *a fortiori*, a complete affirmative answer to an estoppel based upon such decision.[2]

Public policy: illegality

388 In the first edition of this work the opinion was expressed that "public policy, so potent a factor in defeating any estoppel by representation the allowance of which would result in the violation of some principle of statutory or common law affecting the community, and not the parties only, has . . . little or no importance in cases of estoppel by *res judicata*.[3] This view cannot be supported in the light of more recent authority, and it may now be asserted with confidence that considerations of illegality and public policy may avail to prevent an estoppel *per rem judicatam* from legalising that which a statute has declared illegal or which it is the policy of the law positively to prohibit. It is a commonplace of the law of estoppel by

---

[1] This is really a matter of Election. For illustrations see *Magrath* v. *Hardy* (1838), 4 Bing. N.C. 782, where, by not pleading estoppel *per rem judicatam*, as he might have done, the defendant was held to have "waived any benefit he might have derived from the estoppel" (per TINDAL C.J., at p. 798, after reviewing the previous authorities, at pp. 797, 798); *Litchfield* v. *Ready* (1850), 5 Exch. 939 (per PARKE B., at p. 945: "the record of a judgment . . . is conclusive evidence of the plaintiff's title, unless he *waives* his right of replying it by way of estoppel"); *Langdon* v. *Richards* (1917), 33 T.L.R. 325, D.C. where the Crown, by not raising orally (there was no question of pleading here) any objection to the jurisdiction of a statutory tribunal on the ground of a previous decision of a similar tribunal which operated as an estoppel, was held to have "waived" its right to rely on the estoppel (per Lord READING C.J., at pp. 326, 327, and RIDLEY and AVORY JJ., at p. 327). As to estoppel by conduct or inaction, amounting to a representation, on the part of litigants, see the authors' *Law of Estoppel by Representation*, 2nd edn. Chapter XIII, particularly para. 303.

[2] *Lothian* v. *Henderson* (1803), 3 Bos. & P. 499, H.L. (per Lord ELDON L.C., at pp. 546, 547, and Lord ALVANLEY, at pp. 547, 548). Conversely, a party can contract himself out of the right to set up an affirmative answer, such as fraud, to the estoppel, as in *Tullis* v. *Jacson*, [1892] 3 Ch. 441 (per CHITTY J., at pp. 443–446).

[3] 1st edn. para. 274.

representation that a party cannot set up such an estoppel in the face of a statute.[1] Thus it has been held that a corporation on which is imposed a statutory duty to carry out certain acts in the interests of the public cannot preclude itself by estoppel *in paiis* from performing its statutory duty and from asserting its legal rights accordingly.[2] And this principle is not confined to cases in which the policy of the law is made plain by statute; the common law itself may, for instance, prohibit the enforcement of certain contracts, such as those of an infant not for necessaries, and it cannot be supposed that it will the less refuse to base a judgment on an estoppel *in paiis* against an infant who has so contracted.[3]

389 It has seemed for some time to some Judges, that these principles should not be confined to estoppels by representation, and that there may be cases in which the same principles should apply to estoppels *per rem judicatam*.[4] This argument has in recent years begun to find its place in the decisions of the Courts; and it has begun to be clear that the most acceptable modern view is that the same principles which will destroy a plea of estoppel *in paiis* may now be applicable as regards a plea of estoppel *per rem judicatam*;[5] for in *Kok Hoong* v. *Leong Cheong Kweng Mines, Ltd.*[6] the Judicial Committee of the Privy Council, considering a plea of *res judicata*, and rejecting it on the primary ground that the plea was founded upon a judgment obtained by default, which in the circumstances was insufficient to found the estoppel, went on to consider a second ground of justification of the judgment appealed from—*viz.* that the prior judgment (on which the estoppel was founded) was one which resulted in the countenancing of the breach of a statute, and that on this account, too, no estoppel *per rem judicatam* could be successfully founded upon it. Their Lordships upheld the argument based upon illegality, and disallowed the plea of estoppel upon the same principles as have been above set out as applicable to estoppels *in paiis*. This decision must be regarded as clear authority recognising the affirmative answer of illegality and public policy to a plea of estoppel *per rem judicatam*.

In the course of the judgment of their Lordships, delivered by Viscount RADCLIFFE it was said:[7]

---

[1] See the authors' *Law of Estoppel by Representation*, 2nd edn. para. 139 *et seq.*

[2] *Maritime Electric Co., Ltd.* v. *General Dairies, Ltd.*, [1937] 1 All E.R. 748; [1937] A.C. 610, P.C.

[3] See the authors' *Law of Estoppel by Representation* 2nd edn. para. 144.

[4] For instance, to PHILLIMORE J. in *Hayward* v. *Hayward*, [1961] P. 152, at p. 159.

[5] See, for instance, *Griffiths* v. *Davies*, [1943] K.B. 618, C.A. *per* Lord GREENE M.R., at p. 619; *Langford Property Co., Ltd.* v. *Goldrich*, [1948] 2 All E.R. 439 (BIRKETT J.; affirmed on appeal in [1949] 1 All E.R. 402, C.A., at p. 408).

[6] [1964] A.C. 993, P.C.

[7] At p. 1016.

"It has been said that the question whether an estoppel is to be allowed or not depends on whether the enactment or rule of law relied on is imposed in the public interest or 'on grounds of general public policy' (see *Re a Bankruptcy Notice*, [1924] 2 Ch. at p. 97 per ATKIN L.J.). However a principle as widely stated as this might prove to be rather an elusive guide, since there is no statute, at least public general statute, for which this claim might not be made. In their Lordships' opinion a more direct test to apply in any case such as the present, where the laws of money lending or monetary security are involved, is to ask whether the law that confronts the estoppel can be seen to represent a social policy to which the court must give effect in the interests of the public generally or some section of the public, despite any rules of evidence as between themselves that the parties may have created by their conduct or otherwise. Thus the laws of gaming or usury (*Carter* v. *James* (1844), 2 Dow. & L. 236) override an estoppel: so do the provisions of the Rent Restriction Acts with regard to orders for possession of controlled tenancies (*Welch* v. *Nagy*, [1949] 2 All E.R. 868; [1950] 1 K.B. 455).

General social policy does from time to time require the denial of legal validity to certain transactions by certain persons. This may be for their own protection, as in the case of the infant or other category of person enjoying what is to some extent a protected status, or for the protection of others who may come to be engaged in dealings with them, as, for instance, the creditors of a bankrupt. In all such cases there is no room for the application of another general and familiar principle of the law that a man may, if he wishes, disclaim a statutory provision enacted for his benefit, for what is for a man's benefit and what is for his protection are not synonymous terms. Nor is it open to the court to give its sanction to departures from any law that reflects such a policy, even though the party concerned has himself behaved in such a way as would otherwise tie his hands. See *Re Stapleford Colliery Co., Barrow's Case* (1880), 14 Ch.D. 432 at p. 441 per BACON, V.-C. These principles, as their Lordships understand them, would point very directly to the conclusion that there can be no estoppel in face of the Moneylenders Ordinance, since the provisions on which the respondent seeks to rely render him a 'protected person' for this purpose, nor any estoppel in the face of the Bills of Sale Ordinance, the provisions of which, whatever other purposes they may serve, are at least intended for the protection of other creditors who may have dealings with the borrower. The analogy between the latter Ordinance and the Deeds of Arrangement Act 1914, which was the subject of decision in *Re a Bankruptcy Notice*, [1924] 2 Ch. 76, is very close."

390 And the judgment in *Kok Hoong* v. *Leong Cheong Kweng Mines, Ltd.*[1] goes even further; in an earlier passage it considers (though the passage is perhaps *obiter*) cases where illegality, and public policy, though derived from the common law and not from statute, may furnish an adequate answer to estoppel *per rem judicatam*. Their Lordships distinguished such

---

[1] [1964] A.C. 993, P.C.

cases from others such as *Humphries* v. *Humphries*,[1] in which it had been held no answer to such an estoppel to show that the judgment would make a contract enforceable which otherwise would be unenforceable by virtue of such a statute as the Statute of Frauds. Such a case, where the policy of the law is only to provide that the contract is to be unenforceable as a matter of evidence, is essentially different from the case, for instance, of an infant's contract, which is vitiated by much deeper considerations. The judgment in *Kok Hoong* v. *Leong Cheong Kweng Mines, Ltd.* deals with this distinction as follows:[2]

> "It does not appear to their Lordships that the principle invoked is confined to transactions that have been made the subject of legislation or that, where legislation is in question, the bare prescription that a transaction is to be void or unenforceable is sufficient by itself to justify the principle's application. Thus, on the one hand, the common law may itself prohibit the enforcement of certain contracts, such as those of an infant not for necessaries, and it cannot be supposed that it would any the less refuse to base a judgment on an estoppel against an infant who had so contracted. An infant who has obtained goods from a tradesman by representing himself to be of full age cannot be estopped from setting up his infancy, if sued for the price of the goods. On the other hand, there are statutes which, though declaring transactions to be unenforceable or void, are nevertheless not essentially prohibitory and so do not preclude estoppels. One example of these is the Statute of Frauds (see *Humphries* v. *Humphries*, [1910] 2 K.B. 531, C.A. in which it was no doubt considered that following *Leroux* v. *Brown* (1852), 12 C.B. 801, the statute ought to be treated as regulating procedure, not as striking at essential validity); another is the Stamp Act or Acts in their application to oral contracts of marine insurance, which, according to the decision in *Barrow Mutual Ship Insurance Co.* v. *Ashburner* (1885), 54 L.J.Q.B. 377, C.A. are not prohibited so much as penalised."

From this it would appear clear that it may indeed be an answer to a plea of estoppel *per rem judicatam* that the plea would, if allowed, result, *e.g.*, in the enforcement of a contract of which it is the policy of the common law to prevent the enforcement; but that the principle will not go so far as to disallow the estoppel when the result will be merely to authorise something which, though discountenanced by the law, yet cannot be elevated into this class.

Public policy: taxation cases

391 Another example of the impact of the doctrine of public policy on the operation of the doctrine of estoppel *per rem judicatam* is furnished by

---

[1] [1910] 2 K.B. 531, C.A. The first edition notes, as expressing a contrary view to that expressed in *Humphries* v. *Humphries*, the judgment of Lord Shaw in *Bradshaw* v. *M'Mullan*, [1920] 2 I.R. 412, H.L.

[2] [1964] A.C. 993, P.C. at p. 1015.

the taxation and rating cases. The extent to which issue estoppels would operate in assessment cases, so as to preclude dispute, on one year's assessment, of an issue which had been judicially decided in respect of a previous year's assessment, was for long in doubt. The uncertainty was finally resolved by the decision of the House of Lords in *Society of Medical Officers of Health* v. *Hope*,[1] and the later decision of the same House in *Caffoor* v. *Income Tax Commissioner*,[2] which made it plain that no issue estoppel could be set up in respect of an issue arising on one year's assessment, by virtue of a judicial determination of the same issue made in respect of an assessment in a different year. *Hope's* case left the principle upon which this point was decided somewhat obscure; it was said that the questions were different because the years were different. This rather general statement hardly satisfied the more exacting of the critics of the judgment; but in the judgment of Lord KEITH OF AVONHOLM, at least, the view was definitely set forth that the true *ratio* was to be found in public policy:

> "I emphasise these aspects of the functions of a valuation officer under the statute (he said) for they lead to what I regard the true foundation for the submission of the appellants, which is that a public officer in the position of the respondent cannot be estopped from carrying out his duties under the statute. The case is, I think, *a fortiori* of the judgment of the Board of the Privy Council in *Maritime Electric Co., Ltd.* v. *General Dairies, Ltd.* where it was held, in the circumstances of that case, that a public utility company could not be estopped from carrying out its duty under a statute. It has been said on other occasions that there is no estoppel against a statute".[3]

The following year in *Caffoor* v. *Income Tax Commissioner*[4] the Privy Council had to make a choice between their own conflicting decisions in *Broken Hill Pty. Co.* v. *Municipal Council of Broken Hill*[5] and *Hoystead* v. *Taxation Commissioner*[6] in 1926; and they followed *Society of Medical Officers of Health* v. *Hope*[7] in preferring the former decision. In giving the reason why they held for no estoppel their Lordships were content to say:[8]

> "It may be that the principles applied in these cases form a somewhat anomalous branch of the general law of estoppel *per rem judicatam* and are not easily derived from or transferred to the other branches of litigation in which such estoppels have to be considered; but in their Lordships' opinion they are well established in their own field, and it is not by any means to be assumed that the result is one that should be regretted in the public interest."

---

1 [1960] A.C. 551, H.L.
2 [1961] A.C. 584, P.C.
3 In *Society of Medical Officers of Health* v. *Hope*, [1960] A.C. 551, H.L. at p. 568.
4 [1961] A.C. 584, P.C.
5 [1926] A.C. 94, P.C.
6 [1926] A.C. 155, P.C.
7 [1960] A.C. 551, H.L.
8 [1961] A.C. 584, P.C. per Lord RADCLIFFE at pp. 599–600.

It may be thought that they, as much as Lord KEITH OF AVONHOLM, rested the exception by virtue of which taxation cases escaped the application of the rules of issue estoppel on public policy, which deems the interests of the state best served by making the doctrine inapplicable in this special case.

Public policy: divorce

392 We have already seen that the divorce cases furnish numerous illustrations of the public policy (in this case enshrined in the words of the statutory code) which concerns itself to forbid the operation of the ordinary principles of issue estoppel in such a way as to inhibit the inquisitorial functions with which the court is invested in certain aspects of its Divorce jurisdiction.[1]

Spurious answers: introductory

393 From time to time various matters have been vainly put forward, in the stress of desperate advocacy, as possible affirmative answers to a *prima facie* case of estoppel *per rem judicatam*. It appears convenient to conclude the present chapter with an examination of this group of heresies and fallacies, and to shew that none of them has won any permanent, and very few of them even any temporary, judicial acceptance.

Spurious answers: error in an English court

394 It is no answer to an estoppel to submit that the court pronouncing a prior judgment came to a wrong decision; it has already been noticed that a competent tribunal has jurisdiction to decide wrongly as well as rightly, and if it makes a mistake that mistake is conclusive between the parties, unless and until corrected by an appeal duly constituted.[2]

Spurious answers: error in a foreign court

395 It has never been doubted that estoppels founded on foreign, that is to say, non-English[3] judicial decisions, cannot be defeated, or affected in

---

[1] See Chapter XII *ante*.

[2] See Chapter I, para. 14 *ante*. The point was well put by ISAACS J. in the High Court of Australia in *Meyers* v. *Casey* (1913), 17 C.L.R. 90 (High Court of Australia) where he referred at p. 115 to "the well-known rule that a competent court or other tribunal has jurisdiction to give a wrong judgment, and if there is no appeal in the strict sense then its decision, right or wrong, must stand, and cannot be questioned in any subsequent proceedings elsewhere". The learned Judge proceeded to cite from *Malkarjun bin Shidramappa Pasare* v. *Narhari bin Shivappa* (1900), L.R. 27 I.A. 216, at p. 235 where their Lordships of the Judicial Committee said "In so doing the Court was exercising its jurisdiction. It made a sad mistake, it is true; but a Court has jurisdiction to decide wrong as well as right. If it decides wrong, the wronged party can only take the course prescribed by law for setting matters right; and if that course is not taken the decision, however wrong, cannot be disturbed".

[3] See Chapter II, para. 69, *ante*.

any way, by proof, as a fact,—for this, like all other questions of foreign *res judicatae*, is a question of fact,[1]—that the foreign tribunal misinterpreted, or misapplied, its own law,[2] or even, if professing to apply it, the law of England.[3] But it appears to have been at one time thought that, if error in the law of the foreign State, or mistake of fact, appears upon the face or the record of the foreign judgment, and can be thus established without resort to extrinsic evidence, a good answer to the estoppel is substantiated.[4] The dicta, however, to this effect,—they are nothing more, none of them being in the least necessary to the decision,—have been definitely rejected as unsound.[5] A modified and much more plausible proposition, to the effect that, at all events, a misinterpretation of English law, if disclosed upon the face of the record, is sufficient to negative the estoppel, was undoubtedly accepted in at least one of the earlier authorities,[6] but it eventually met with the same fate as the other exploded heresies, for the obvious reason that, if a foreign judgment is unimpeachable on the ground of a misapprehension of English law, it must be equally so whether the proof of the error is easy or difficult, simple or intricate.[7] It has, however, been held without any subsequent judicial disapprobation

---

[1] As explained in Chapter II, para. 75–6, *ante*, at p. 151 of *Godard* v. *Gray* (1870), L.R. 6 Q.B. 139 BLACKBURN J. observes that English law, as applied by a foreign tribunal, is as much a question of fact as the law of the foreign state.

[2] *Scott* v. *Pilkington* (1862), 2 B. & S. 11 (per COCKBURN C.J., at pp. 41, 42); *Vanquelin* v. *Bouard* (1863), 15 C.B. N.S. 341 (per ERLE C.J., at pp. 368, 369, and KEATING J., at p. 374); *Messina* v. *Petrococchino* (1872), L.R. 4 P.C. 144, at p. 159.

[3] *Dent* v. *Smith* (1869), L.R. 4 Q.B. 414 (per LUSH J., at pp. 450, 451, and HAYES J., at pp. 454, 455); *Castrique* v. *Imrie* (1870), L.R. 4 H.L. 414 (per BLACKBURN J., at pp. 432–7, Lord HATHERLEY L.C., at pp. 445–6, and Lord CHELMSFORD, at pp. 447–8); *Godard* v. *Gray* (1870), L.R. 6 Q.B. 139 (per BLACKBURN J., at pp. 149 *et seq.*); *Re Trufort, Trafford* v. *Blanc* (1887), 36 Ch.D. 600 (per STIRLING J., at pp. 613–6).

[4] In *Becquet* v. *MacCarthy* (1831), 2 B. & Ad. 951, Lord TENTERDEN C.J., at pp. 957, 958, said that the "apparent error" there relied upon was no answer to the estoppel, because it was not *clearly* disclosed on the face of the record, implying that if it had been so disclosed, the estoppel would have been defeated. In *Reimers* v. *Druce* (1857), 26 L.J. Ch. 196, ROMILLY M.R. stated, at pp. 199, 200, that he inclined to the above view that the estoppel is negatived by "apparent error", meaning "such error as shews upon the face of the judgment itself, without any extrinsic evidence, that the judge had come to an erroneous conclusion, *either of law or fact*", though he did not decide the case on this ground, and said that, before he could do so, he should require further argument. In *Messina* v. *Petrococchino* (1872), L.R. 4 P.C. 144, there is a dictum, not in the least necessary to the decision, at p. 157, that "a foreign judgment of a competent court may be impeached if it carries on the face of it manifest error".

[5] See *De Cosse Brissac* v. *Rathbone* (1861), 6 H. & N. 301, where amongst a collection of futile and "naughty" pleas to an action on a foreign judgment, all of which were curtly disposed of on demurrer (*per Cur.*, at p. 308), there was one which averred that error "on the merits" (whatever that expression may have been intended to cover,—presumably both law and facts) appeared upon the face of the judgment.

[6] This was held by the Court of King's Bench in *Novelli* v. *Rossi* (1831), 2 B. & Ad. 757 (per Lord TENTERDEN C.J., at pp. 764, 765), but in *Scott* v. *Pilkington* (1862), 2 B. & S. 11, COCKBURN C.J., delivering the judgment of the Court, at p. 42, mentions the point, but is careful to leave it open.

[7] See *Godard* v. *Gray* (1870), L.R. 6 Q.B. 139 (per BLACKBURN J. at pp. 151, 152).

that, where it is established that the foreign tribunal ought to have decided the case according to the law of England, the relevant rules of which are correctly set out in the record itself, but has nevertheless wilfully and deliberately ignored the English law applicable, for the supposed benefit of the subjects of the foreign State, there is not merely absence, but such a defiance, of international comity as to justify our courts in refusing to concede to the foreign decision the recognition to which, in accordance with that comity, it would otherwise have been entitled.[1]

Spurious answers: contrary to natural justice

396 In the first edition of this work, Mr Spencer Bower in a lengthy excursus expounded the proposition that the contention that "natural justice" has been denied by a foreign decision cannot amount to an answer to an estoppel founded upon it. In so far as the denial of natural justice which is relied upon is constituted by a failure to give due notice of the proceedings, the present writer is in some disagreement with him on this point. The topic has been fully discussed in an earlier chapter in this edition, and the reader is referred to Chapter IV for that discussion.[2]

---

[1] It was so held by WOOD V.C., at pp. 243–7 of *Simpson* v. *Fogo* (1863), 1 J. & H. 195, and mentioned as a possibly correct proposition by BLACKBURN J., at pp. 148–149 of *Godard* v. *Gray* (1870), L.R. 6 Q.B. 139.

[2] Chapter IV, paras. 157–162, *ante*.

CHAPTER XIV

Pleading and Procedure

Introduction

397 Any party litigant who is desirous of setting up estoppel *per rem judicatam* must do so by pleading it, or, if there is no possibility or opportunity of adopting this course, by objection *ore tenus* at the trial or hearing, and, in either case, as soon as facts and documents are first pleaded, or are first disclosed in evidence, as the case may be, on the other side, sufficient to constitute matter of estoppel, and to call for the question to be raised. These two modes of introducing a case of estoppel *per rem judicatam* require separate consideration.

Pleading

398 In all stages in the history of pleading before the passing of the Judicature Acts, the law rigidly required every estoppel *per rem judicatam* to be pleaded, if there was an opportunity of doing so, and, in that case, at the very earliest opportunity, under pain of losing the right to set up the estoppel at any later stage, or in any other form;[1] or, as the rule has been otherwise expressed, the party who omits to take this precaution, and to give timely notice to his opponent of his intention to rely upon a *res judicata*, is deemed to have impliedly represented to such opponent that he waives his right to insist on the estoppel, and so to have cross-estopped himself from doing so.[2]

399 The modern system of pleading introduced by the Judicature Acts, 1873 and 1875, and the Rules of Court framed thereunder, though per-

[1] *Vooght* v. *Winch* (1819), 2 B. & Ald. 662 (per ABBOTT C.J., at p. 668, BAGLEY J., at pp. 669, 670, and HOLROYD J., at pp. 671, 672); *Hannaford* v. *Hunn* (1825), 2 C. & P. 148 (per ABBOTT C.J., at p. 155); *Doe* v. *Huddart* (1835), 2 Cr.M. & R. 316 (*per Cur.*, at pp. 323, 324); *Magrath* v. *Hardy* (1838), 4 Bing. N.C. 782 (*per Cur.*, at p. 788); *Joly* v. *Swift* (1847), 11 I.Eq. R. 410, per BRADY L.C. (Ir.) at, p. 411; *Litchfield* v. *Ready* (1850), 5 Exch. 939 (per PARKE B., at p. 945); *Matthew* v. *Osborne* (1853), 13 C.B. 919 (per MAULE J., at p. 942, and CRESSWELL J., at pp. 942, 943).

[2] See para. 386, *ante*.

mitting, in point of form, much greater latitude (not to say laxity) than was formerly tolerated, is in point of substance quite as exacting. By the 1965 Rules of the Supreme Court it is provided that all matters must be pleaded which it is alleged "make any claim or defence of the opposite party not maintainable", or which "if not specifically pleaded might take the opposite party by surprise".[1] Clearly estoppel of any kind is covered by the language here used, and, therefore, the necessity of pleading it at the first available opportunity is still as vital as it ever was.[2]

400 If there is no opportunity of pleading the estoppel, of course there can be no penalty for omitting to do so, but, as will be seen hereafter, in that event it is the duty of the party to raise the question in some other form as soon as an occasion arises which calls for the disclosure.[3]

401 As long as there is no preceding pleading which necessarily involves a contradiction or impeachment of the *res judicata* on the merits, there is nothing to call for a plea of estoppel, and the party relying on the *res judicata* is under no duty to plead it: for instance, where in an action or indictment relating to land the defendant has pleaded simply "not guilty",[4] or that he "is in possession of the premises by himself or his tenants",[5] there is nothing on the record which of necessity involves an attack upon the plaintiff's title as declared or adjudged by the *res judicata*, or which therefore demands from him any special reply of estoppel. But it is otherwise where the defendant has pleaded that "the plaintiff is not possessed of the premises", for this plea is undoubtedly tantamount to an assertion that the title thereto is not in the plaintiff, and accordingly calls upon him to set up by way of estoppel any judicial decision to the contrary on which he intends to rely.[6] Two cases, which, however, are extremely difficult to understand, and unlikely to be followed, have gone so far as to decide that, in certain special circumstances, the duty of pleading the estoppel somewhere is so exigent and absolute that, even when there is no preceding plea which directly challenges the *res judicata*, or to which the plaintiff could be

---

[1] R.S.C. 1965: O. 18 r. 8.

[2] *Edevain* v. *Cohen* (1889), 43 Ch.D. 187, C.A. (per COTTON L.J., at p. 189).

[3] See paras. 416 *et seq.*, *post*.

[4] See *Armstrong* v. *Norton* (1839), 2 I.L.R. 96 (*per Cur.*, at pp. 100, 101: plea of "not guilty" to an action of trespass to land); *R.* v. *Blakemore* (1852), 21 L.J. M.C. 60 (plea of "not guilty" to an indictment for non-repair of a highway: per Lord CAMPBELL C.J., and PARKE B., at p. 64); *R.* v. *Haughton (Inhabitants)* (1853), 1 E. & B. 501 (a similar case: *per Cur.*, at p. 512).

[5] *Coppinger* v. *Norton*, *infra*, where it was held not only that the plaintiff need not, but also—a much more doubtful proposition—that he cannot properly, set up the estoppel in his reply: see note 1, p. 342.

[6] *Matthew* v. *Osborne*, *supra*, as cited in note (1), p. 340; *Wilkinson* v. *Kirby* (1854), 15 C.B. 430 (per JERVIS C.J., at p. 443, and MAULE J., at p. 446).

expected, or allowed, to reply the estoppel, it is incumbent upon him to raise it in his declaration, or statement of claim, by way of anticipation.[1]

402 The old system of pleading, for some not very intelligible reason, where the decision relied upon was *in rem*,[2] did not require the estoppel to be pleaded:[3] but it is quite clear that now a decision *in rem* would, if unpleaded, be held quite as "likely to take the opposite party by surprise", within the meaning of the more flexible canons of modern procedure already set out, as an unpleaded decision *inter partes*, and that an omission to plead the one would as effectually destroy the estoppel as an omission to plead the other.

403 In an action on a judgment, whether English or foreign, the very form of the action necessarily presupposes that the plaintiff is asserting that the decision is unimpeachable on the merits, and, therefore, he is not required to plead the estoppel expressly if the defendant limits his defence to a denial of the existence of the necessary conditions of a valid estoppel, or if, as he is at liberty to do, he merely raises as a point of law the question whether the plaintiff's pleading sufficiently discloses on the face of it, the existence of those conditions;[4] but, if the defendant pleads to the merits, the plaintiff then is in a position, and therefore under a duty, to raise the estoppel expressly in his reply,[5] or, if he thinks the plea bad on the face of it, by demurrer,[6] or its modern equivalents and substitutes.[7]

404 The ancient form of a plea of estoppel is of a very special character. It begins with a submission that the party said to be estopped "ought not to be admitted or received to plead", or "to say", the thing, or "to maintain the action", alleged to be the subject of the estoppel, by reason of the

---

[1] See *Doe* v. *Huddart* (1835), 2 Cr.M. & R. 316 (*per Cur.*, at pp. 323, 324); *Coppinger* v. *Norton*, [1902] 2 I. R. 232. Neither of these cases seems at all satisfactory. In the former, it is difficult to understand why the powerful argument for the plaintiff, at p. 319, as to the inconvenience of forcing a plaintiff to plead the estoppel by anticipation, and the injustice of penalizing him for not doing so, was not accepted, or even noticed, by the Court in its judgment. The latter decision is a still more astonishing one, for it cannot be excused or explained, as the earlier case can, by any suggestion that it belonged to a bygone period of extreme stringency and technicality in pleading. It is to be noted, however, that the decision was not unanimous, and that its harshness and unreasonableness is considerably mitigated by the circumstance that the Court offered to allow the plaintiff to amend his statement of claim by adding thereto a submission of the point of estoppel.

[2] Generally, as to decisions *in rem*, see Chapter VIII, *ante*.

[3] *Doe* v. *Huddart*, *supra* (per ALDERSON B., at p. 320, during the argument); *Cammell* v. *Sewell* (1858), 3 H. & N. 617 (*per Cur.*, at pp. 646, 647).

[4] Which was the course adopted in *Carpenter* v. *Thornton* (1819), 3 B. & Ald. 52 (action on a chancery decree); *Read* v. *Pope* (1834), 1 Cr.M. & R. 302 (action on county court judgment); *Austin* v. *Mills* (1853), 9 Exch. 288 (the like); *Hutchinson* v. *Gillespie* (1856), 11 Exch. 798 (action on order of Judicial Committee of Privy Council); *Vanquelin* v. *Bouard* (1863), 15 C.B. N.S. 341 (action on foreign judgment).

[5] See note 5, p. 345, *post*.

[6] See note 3, p. 307, *post*.

[7] See para. 414, *post*.

res judicata relied upon, the particulars of which are then set out, together with allegations of identity of subject-matter and parties, and of competent jurisdiction, all which allegations the pleader announces that he is "prepared to verify by the record", if there is any, and, if not, "to verify" simply: and the plea concludes with a prayer for the judgment of the court whether the party ought to be permitted, contrary to the *res judicata*, to plead, or say, or sue, etc., as the case may be.[1] Any deviation from this consecrated form, with its special exordium and conclusion, was originally held, in strictness, to vitiate the pleading altogether:[2] and, further, the formula was consecrated to estoppels in the sense that to use it in a case which was not strictly one of estoppel at all was deemed scarcely less profane than to omit its use where the case was one of estoppel.[3] In the course of time, however, more rational views began to prevail: in 1869, a Judge, considering a question of pleading in relation to estoppels, hazarded the observation that "pleas are not governed by their beginning and their ending, but by the substance of them",[4] and, in the following year, an instance is to be found of a plea which, without any regard to the ancient formalities, simply stated the facts raising the estoppel, and concluded with an averment that "all conditions had been fulfilled necessary to estop" the party, thus, for the first time introducing the word "estop", which (curiously) does not appear in the old type of plea.[5]

405 Before the Judicature Acts, in pleading *autrefois acquit*, which, as explained in an earlier chapter,[6] is neither more nor less than a plea of estoppel by a criminal judicial decision, the same form, with the necessary adaptations, was in common use.[7] As regards, however, certain classes of

[1] The skeleton form set out in the text was that used in civil proceedings, but, with the necessary modifications, it was also obligatory in criminal proceedings: see para. 405, above. It was of considerable antiquity. During the period when pleadings were required to be in Latin, there are Latin pleas of estoppel in the terms of the formula: see, for instance, *Groenvelt* v. *Burwell* (1699), 1 Ld. Raym. 454, where, at pp. 454–462, an elaborate plea is set out, which concludes as follows,—"et hoc parati sunt verificare; unde petunt judicium, si praedictus Johannes B. actionem suam praedictam inde versus eos habere seu manutenere debeat." In *Put and Hardy* v. *Rawsterne* (1682), T. Raym. 472, an abstract of the *res judicata* set up by the defendant is followed by the phrase "judgment *si actio*," which is evidently intended as a shorthand description of the prayer for judgment which concludes the formula.

[2] *General Steam Navigation Co.* v. *Guillou* (1843), 11 M. & W. 877 (per PARKE B., at p. 894).

[3] *Parkes* v. *Smith* (1850), 15 Q.B. 297 (per COLERIDGE J., at p. 312).

[4] *Commings* v. *Heard* (1869), L.R. 4 Q.B. 669 (per HAYES J., at p. 676; *cp.* the observations of LUSH J., at p. 674).

[5] *Newington* v. *Levy* (1870), L.R. 6 C.P. 180, Exch. Ch.

[6] See Chapter XI, para. 316, *ante*.

[7] See the very elaborate pleas of *autrefois acquit* set out in *R.* v. *Vandercomb and Abbott* (1796), 2 Leach 708, Ex. Ch. (at pp. 716–721); *R.* v. *Sheen* (1827), 2 C. & P. 634 (at p. 636); *R.* v. *Bird* (1851), 2 Den. 94 (at pp. 224–230); *R.* v. *Elrington* (1861), 1 B. & S. 688. In the second of these cases the plea was in the first instance pleaded *ore tenus*, but afterwards put into writing. The plea commenced with a statement that the accused "ought not to be put to answer the said indictment, he having been heretofore in due manner of law acquitted of the premises," and

offence punishable summarily, it was also open to the party to resort to the shorter and simpler form of plea sanctioned by the legislature in 1851.[1]

406 After the passing of the Judicature Acts, all these questions of form ceased to be of any importance whatever. Though the obligation to plead the estoppel remained, the courts became absolutely indifferent as to the phraseology of the pleading. It is now open to the pleader, if he chooses, to adhere to the old formula, wholly or in part,[2] or to set out the *res judicata* and claim an "estoppel" by reason thereof, *eo nomine*, without any other formality,[3] or, without using the word "estoppel" at all, to plead it as a "bar",[4] or simply to state his intention of "relying upon the doctrine of *res judicata*".[5]

Some latitude now allowed

407 Modern practice has been to relax the strictness of the rule requiring pleading as essential; and the tendency has been to inquire simply whether justice requires the disallowance of the estoppel by reason of failure to plead it. In *Winnan* v. *Winnan*[6] a wife had obtained a maintenance order before Justices on the ground of wilful failure to maintain. An allegation of constructive desertion, if put forward by her husband, would have been a defence in those proceedings. No such allegation was made. In later proceedings in the High Court the husband petitioned for divorce, alleging constructive desertion. The wife set up a plea of estoppel at the hearing of the petition, but there had been no mention of the point in the pleadings. A strong Court of Appeal[7] held that in the circumstances it was not too late to raise the point.[8]

---

concluded with a prayer for "the judgment of the Court here, if he ought to be put further to answer the said indictment, and whether our said Lord the King will or ought further to prosecute or impeach him on account of the premises in this present indictment contained".

[1] See s. 28 of the Criminal Procedure Act 1851. It is almost inconceivable that at the present day any consideration of mere form would be allowed to stand in the way of a plea of *autrefois acquit*, or its equivalent, having any real merit on the facts. For a full discussion of the plea, see Chapter XI, *ante*.

[2] As in *Bennett* v. *Gamgee* (1877), 46 L.J. Q.B. 204, C.A. (where the plea commenced as in the old form, but concluded differently); *Coppinger* v. *Norton*, [1902] 2 I.R. 232.

[3] As, for instance, in (amongst other cases) the following: *Mercantile Investment and General Trust Co.* v. *River Plate Trust Loan and Agency Co.*, [1894] 1 Ch. 578; *Beardsley* v. *Beardsley*, [1899] 1 Q.B. 746, D.C.; *Ritchie* v. *Malcolm*, [1902] 2 I.R. 403; *Hill* v. *Hill*, [1954] P. 291, at p. 292.

[4] As in *Hutton* v. *Ras S.S. Co.*, [1907] 1 K.B. 834, C.A.

[5] As in *Jones* v. *Lewis*, [1919] 1 K.B. 328, C.A. at p. 338; in *Bright* v. *Bright*, [1954] P. 270 the respondent had pleaded, in answer to certain allegations of constructive desertion in the pleadings, that the paragraphs setting these up were "identical in substance" with paragraphs in an earlier petition which had been dismissed, and that "petitioner ought not to be admitted to plead desertion and is estopped from pleading that . . . The merits of the said pleas are *res judicata*" (p. 275).

[6] *Winnan* v. *Winnan*, [1949] P. 174 C.A.

[7] Lord MORTON OF HENRYTON, BUCKNILL and ASQUITH L.JJ.

[8] At pp. 180–1. But the Court went on to hold that the plea failed for other reasons.

408 The practice which was occasionally resorted to, under the old system, of suing in equity to restrain a party from proceeding at law, on the ground of estoppel *per rem judicatam*,[1] has of course been rendered by the Judicature Acts unnecessary and improper.[2]

Leave to issue second writ required

409 In cases where the leave of the court is necessary before a writ is issued the plea of *res judicata* may be successfully put forward to prevent the issue of the writ instead of as an answer to the writ after issue. Thus in *In the Estate of Langton deceased*,[3] FAULKS J. refused leave to issue a writ claiming probate of a will in solemn form, which had been the subject of an earlier action in which the court had granted probate of a different will. The rules governing the issue of writs in probate actions required a Registrar's certificate before the writ issued: in the particular case the Registrar, being doubtful of the course which he should follow, withheld his certificate and referred the matter to FAULKS J. The learned judge, on considering the pleadings, refused the certificate, holding that the plaintiff was estopped *per rem judicatam* from raising the matters traversed in the statement of claim; and this decision was upheld by the Court of Appeal.

Plea must be raised promptly

410 The pleading in which the estoppel must be raised, if it is pleadable at all, is that which answers the first pleading on the opposite side manifesting an unmistakeable intention to canvass the merits of the *res judicata*, and containing allegations contradictory of any question of law or issue of fact thereby determined. If the statement of claim (or declaration, or bill, in former times) sets out matter of this character, then the defendant must plead the estoppel in his plea, answer, or defence;[4] if such matter first appears in a plea, or defence, then it is for the plaintiff to plead the estoppel in his replication or reply;[5] if the challenge is not made until the replication

---

1 As in *Waine* v. *Crocker* (1862), 3 De G.F. & J. 421.

2 *Ochsenbein* v. *Papelier* (1873), 8 Ch.App. 695 (per Lord SELBORNE L.C., at pp. 698–700, and MELLISH L.J., at pp. 700, 701). This was, it is true, an action in Chancery to restrain the defendant from suing on a foreign judgment in the Q.B., on the ground that it had been obtained by fraud, but the principle of the decision, *viz.* that complete relief can be obtained by way of defence to the common law action, in which, therefore, the matters sought to be raised should be pleaded, applies equally to the case of an action for an injunction to restrain a party from suing at common law in such a way as to controvert the *res judicata*.

3 [1964] P. 163.

4 See the cases cited in note (3) to para. 406, *supra*.

5 The estoppel was accordingly the subject of the replication before, and of the reply after, the Judicature Acts, in the following cases: *Outram* v. *Morewood* (1803), 3 East 346; *Doe* v. *Wright* (1839), 10 Ad. & El. 763; *Callow* v. *Jenkinson* (1851), 6 Exch. 666; *Wilkinson* v. *Kirby* (1854), 15 C.B. 430; *Sopwith* v. *Sopwith* (1861), 2 Sw. & Tr. 160; *Newall* v. *Elliott* (1863), 1 H. & C. 797; *Read* v. *Victoria Station and Pimlico Rail. Co.* (1863), 1 H. & C. 826; *Barber* v. *Nottingham*

or reply, the defendant must take it up in his rejoinder.[1] Where the claim itself necessarily involves the assertion of an estoppel, as in all cases of actions on judgments, there is no necessity for it to be expressly pleaded. It happens sometimes that a plaintiff, knowing that his claim may be subject to estoppel *per rem judicatam*, in the absence of any affirmative answer, and that, at all events, such estoppel is certain to be pleaded by the defendant, thinks it desirable to anticipate the impending attack by setting out the particulars of the *res judicata* in his own bill, declaration, or statement of claim, followed by a statement of facts constituting some affirmative answer, or special circumstances sufficient to justify the court in giving no effect to the estoppel which might otherwise be created, and in ignoring, or relieving him against, the *res judicata*:[2] in such cases, of course, the defendant is not required to plead over again the *res judicata* to which the plaintiff has already called attention, and in respect of which he has invoked the assistance of the court.

411 In certain very exceptional circumstances it has been held that a plaintiff is not at liberty to raise the estoppel by his replication or reply, in answer to a plea or defence which would ordinarily call for the adoption of such a course, but (since he is bound to raise the question in some pleading or other) must raise it by anticipation in his claim, if he is to save his rights.[3]

412 Until the abolition of demurrers,[4] it was considered quite proper, whenever a pleading on the other side disclosed sufficient facts and documents to invite such a course, to raise the estoppel by demurrer. For instance, a declaration, bill, or statement which set out the *res judicata* by way of anticipation, and claimed that, for certain reasons, it ought not to operate as an estoppel, obviously called for a demurrer, if those reasons appeared on the face of them to be insufficient in law. That course was not infrequently adopted under the old system,[5] and, in the time of the Year

and Grantham Rail. and Canal Co. (1864), 15 C.B. N.S. 726; *Scott* v. *Bennett* (1871), L.R. 5 H.L. 234; *Spencer and Spencer* v. *Williams* (1871), L.R. 2 P. & D. 230; *Flitters* v. *Allfrey* (1874), L.R. 10 C.P. 29; *Leggott* v. *Great Northern Rail. Co.* (1876), 1 Q.B.D. 599; *Ennis* v. *Rochford* (1884), 14 L.R. Ir. 285; *Webster* v. *Armstrong* (1885), 54 L.J. Q.B. 236; *Mercantile Investment and General Trust Co.* v. *River Plate Trust Loan and Agency Co.*, [1894] 1 Ch. 578; *Long* v. *Gowlett*, [1923] 2 Ch. 177.

[1] As in *Incledon (or Ingleton)* v. *Burges* (1688), Comb. 166; *Fisher* v. *Ogle* (1808), 1 Camp. 418; *Petrie* v. *Nuttall* (1856), 11 Exch. 569; *Hobbs* v. *Henning* (1864), 17 C.B. N.S. 791.

[2] As in *Loyd* v. *Mansell* (1722), 2 P. Wms. 73; *Pearse* v. *Dobinson* (1865), 35 L.J. Ch. 110; *Gossain* v. *Gossain* (1860), 18 W.R. 196, P.C.

[3] *Doe* v. *Huddart* (1835) 2 Cr.M. & R. 316; *Coppinger* v. *Norton*, [1902] 2 I.R. 232. As to these two cases, see note (1) on p. 342, *supra*.

[4] By O. 25, r. 1, of the R.S.C., 1883.

[5] As in *Bainbrigge* v. *Baddeley* (1847), 2 Ph. 705; *Simpson* v. *Fogo*, (1860) 1 John & H. 18; *Moss* v. *Anglo-Egyptian Navigation Co.* (1865), 1 Ch.App. 108.

Books when all pleadings were oral, and even as late as the Stuart period,[1] such demurrers were pleaded *ore tenus*, or "at the bar". If the defendant without formally demurring to a pleading of this anticipatory nature, contented himself with simply pleading as an estoppel the *res judicata* which had been already set out by the plaintiff, ignoring the facts on which the plaintiff claimed to be relieved of the estoppel, he was treated as having demurred, because, having impliedly admitted these facts, he clearly could not establish the estoppel, or displace the plaintiff's affirmative answer thereto, unless the facts stated disclosed no such answer in law.[2] So also, in the case of an action on a judgment, which necessarily involved an assertion of estoppel *per rem judicatam*, if the defendant pleaded solely to the merits, ignoring the effect of the judgment, and treating it as inconclusive, the obvious course for the plaintiff to take under the old practice was to demur.[3] Again, a defendant, having pleaded the estoppel in his plea or defence, was always permitted, if not expected, to demur to a replication which, in his view, was no answer in law to the case of estoppel set up by him,[4] and, similarly, it was considered quite legitimate for a plaintiff, who had first pleaded the estoppel in his replication or reply, to demur to an insufficient rejoinder.[5]

413 Under the old system, besides demurrers, there were other recognized means of raising the estoppel as a point of law on an admitted or given state of facts.[6]

414 When demurrers were abolished,[7] certain methods of raising points of law on agreed or admitted facts were substituted, to which parties

---

[1] See *Lord Say's Case* (1639), Cro. Car. 524, a case of "demurrer at the bar", whereby Charles I's Attorney-General set up the Ship Money judgment in the *Hampden* Case as an estoppel.

[2] *Loyd* v. *Mansell* (1722), 2 P. Wms. 73 (per Lord MACCLESFIELD L.C., at p. 74).

[3] See the following illustrations, in actions on English judgments: *Corrigal* v. *London and Blackwall Rail. Co.* (1843), 5 Man. & G. 219; *Read* v. *Victoria Station and Pimlico Rail. Co.* (1863), 1 H. & C. 826; *Barber* v. *Nottingham and Grantham Rail. Co. & Canal Co.* (1864), 15 C.B. N.S. 726. For instance of a demurrer by the plaintiff in an action on a foreign judgment to a plea canvassing the decision on the merits, see *Henderson* v. *Henderson* (1844), 6 Q.B. 288; *Bank of Australasia* v. *Nias* (1851), 16 Q.B. 717; *Frith* v. *Wollaston* (1852), 21 L.J. Ex. 108; *De Cosse Brissac* v. *Rathbone* (1861), 6 H. & N. 301; *Vanquelin* v. *Bouard* (1864), 15 C.B. N.S. 341.

[4] As in *Robinson* v. *Robinson* (1603), 5 Co. Rep. 32 b; *Mico* v. *Morris* (1685), 3 Lev. 234; *Dyson* v. *Wood* (1824), 3 B. & C. 449; *Eastmure* v. *Laws* (1839), 5 Bing. N.C. 444; *Hobbs* v. *Henning* (1864), 17 C.B. N.S. 791; *Thorburn* v. *Barnes* (1867), L.R. 2 C.P. 384.

[5] See *Doe* v. *Wright* (1839), 10 Ad. & El. 763; *Crawley* v. *Isaacs* (1867), 16 L.T. 529. For a case of an action on an award in which the plaintiff demurred to the rejoinder, see *Fisher* v. *Pimbley* (1809), 11 East 188.

[6] See *Moore* v. *Moore* (1840), 3 Moo. P.C.C. 84 (resisting application for leave to plead a "responsive allegation" in a matrimonial suit); *Shedden* v. *A.-G.* (1860), 30 L.J. (P. M. & A.) 217 (preliminary hearing of estoppel point); *Parker* v. *Simpson* (1869), 18 W.R. 204 (motion to stay proceedings).

[7] In 1883, by O. 25, r. 1, of the R.S.C. 1883.

have occasionally had recourse for the purposes of estoppel, such as applications to strike out a pleading "on the ground that it discloses no reasonable cause of action or defence", or motions for judgment where "the pleading is "scandalous, frivolous or vexatious, or otherwise an abuse of the process of the court"[1] or applications to have the point of estoppel set down and disposed of before trial.[2] It is a proper procedure, where estoppel *per rem judicatam* has been pleaded in the statement of defence for a plaintiff by way of reply to the defence thus raised in the pleadings to raise the availability of the estoppel as a preliminary question of law to be argued before trial.[3]

The question of estoppel may also be made the subject of the special

---

[1] R.S.C. (1883), O. 25, r. 4, now R.S.C. (1965), O. 18 r. 19. Such a course was adopted by the defendant in *Montgomery* v. *Russell* (1894), 11 T.L.R. 112, C.A., but unsuccessfully, because it did not appear on the face of the statement of claim that the plaintiff was estopped, nor was the action shewn by *the pleadings* to be "frivolous and vexatious". It was, however, shewn to be so by affidavit evidence of the *res judicata*, and it was dismissed, not under O. 25, r. 4, but under the inherent jurisdiction of the Court, as an abuse of its process. As to this procedure, which involves counter-evidence, and is, therefore, not an equivalent of, or analogous to, the old demurrer, see Appendix A, *post*. A more recent illustration of the use of this procedure is *Dixon* v. *Dixon*, [1953] 1 All E.R. 910; [1953] P. 103 where, after a petition and cross-petition for divorce containing counter-allegations of cruelty had both been dismissed it was sought to canvass some of the same evidence in new proceedings, in which the husband alleged desertion and the wife constructive desertion; each party then sought by summons an order striking out certain parts of the petition of the other, on the ground that they sought to set up a second time matters already determined in the former suit. The applications were dismissed by DAVIES J. "As we all know, there is abundant authority for the proposition that the summary course of striking out a pleading is only to be taken in plain and obvious cases. In my judgment it is impossible to say that the present case is a plain and obvious one" (p. 116). The procedure was invoked again (but again unsuccessfully on the merits) in *Re a Debtor* (*No. 472 of 1950*), [1958] 1 All E.R. 581. In *Marginson* v. *Blackburn Borough Council*, [1938] 2 All E.R. 539 the same procedure was invoked before LEWIS J., but was unsuccessful—on appeal to the Court of Appeal the estoppel was allowed: [1939] 2 K.B. 426. So, too, in *Greenhalgh* v. *Mallard*, [1947] 2 All E.R. 255 the procedure was successful in establishing an estoppel. See also *In the Estate of Langton Deceased*, [1964] P. 163, C.A.

[2] R.S.C. (1883) O. 25, r. 2. The application is now made under R.S.C. (1965), O. 18, r. 11 —see Supreme Court Practice, [1967] P. 245. For illustrations see *Houston* v. *Marquis of Sligo* (1885), 29 Ch.D. 448, C.A.; *Magnus* v. *National Bank of Scotland* (1888), 57 L.J. Ch. 902 (where, however, the point of estoppel was so futile that the Court refused the application to set it down for a preliminary hearing, or to treat it seriously in any way); *Nouvion* v. *Freeman* (1889), 15 App. Cas. 1, H.L. (as appears by the statement of Lord HERSCHELL, at p. 6); *Ritchie* v. *Malcolm* (1902), 2 I.R. 403; *R.* v. *Brixton Prison Governor, Ex parte Savarkar*, [1910] 2 K.B. 1056, C.A. (preliminary objection on the hearing of the appeal); *Robinson* v. *Fenner*, [1913] 3 K.B. 835, where the question of law as to the estoppel was set down for argument, and heard by CHANNELL J., as a preliminary point, under O. 24, r. 2, though, as we learn from p. 845 of the report, the C.A. considered that the case was not one for the application of the rule, and ordered the action to go down for trial in the ordinary way; *Bergerem* v. *Marsh* (1921), 125 L.T. 630.

[3] As was done in *Kok Hoong* v. *Leong Cheong Kweng Mines, Ltd.*, [1964] A.C. 993, P.C. "The issue is one of law. The relevant facts embrace nothing more than the circumstances of the earlier action, in which was given the judgment which is said to have created the estoppel, and the pleadings in the present action which is now pending"—per Lord RADCLIFFE at p. 995. *Cf.* the report in [1964] 1 All E.R. 300 at p. 302 where the procedure is especially mentioned.

In *Bright* v. *Bright*, [1954] P. 270 the question of estoppel was argued immediately before

case which in certain statutes is prescribed as the method of appeal from the tribunal created or invested with jurisdiction, thereby,[1] or it may be stated in a memorandum submitted for the information of the court by one of its officers.[2] Or it may arise incidentally upon an application to stay proceedings principally based upon some other ground. In a recent case occupying some space in the Reports the proceeding took the form of a summons for an order to stay proceedings and to dismiss the main action on the ground that the action was commenced without the plaintiff's authority; this latter question raised the question of *res judicata*, since it was contended that an earlier decision between the parties had determined the question of authority in favour of the defendant. The interlocutory application ultimately reached the House of Lords.[3]

415 Under the former practice, when it was necessary to obtain leave to plead estoppel with other pleas, such leave was not very readily granted,[4] and still less so when the application was for leave to amend a pleading for that purpose.[5] It would seem that, in respect of amendment for the purpose of introducing a case of estoppel not already set up, the modern system is not inclined to greater liberality or laxity than that which it has superseded.[6]

---

trial as a "preliminary point". WILLMER J. pointed out the disadvantages of so informal an approach at p. 278 and said "The proper way to deal with it would have been to apply in Chambers before trial for an order striking out the offending part or parts of the petition, so as to get these questions decided without waiting for the trial, and without incurring the expense of collecting the witnesses and making all the other preparations for trial". He pointed out that failure to follow the more economical procedure may be reflected in an award of costs. *In New Zealand* an order was made in *Baldwin* v. *Baldwin*, [1963] N.Z.L.R. 218 directing the formal argument before trial of the question of law "whether in the circumstances disclosed by the statement of claim the plaintiff is estopped from alleging (the matters set up in the proceedings)."

[1] As in *Lilley* v. *London County Council*, [1910] A.C. 1, H.L. (case stated under the London Building Act 1894).

[2] As in *Cox* v. *Dublin City Distillery Co.* (*No.* 3), [1917] 1 I.R. 203, where the question of estoppel was submitted by the chief clerk for the opinion of the Irish Court of Chancery in the form of a memorandum, stating the facts and documents.

[3] *Carl-Zeiss-Stiftung* v. *Rayner and Keeler, Ltd.*, [1966] 2 All E.R. 536, at pp. 542, 549.

[4] See *Collins* v. *Cave* (1858), 27 L.J. Ex. 146 (per MARTIN B., at p. 148); *Bancroft* v. *Bancroft* (1864), 3 Sw. & Tr. 597 (per Sir CRESSWELL CRESSWELL, at pp. 598, 599). In both these cases the application was refused. It was allowed, however, in *Hutt* v. *Morrell* (1849), 3 Exch. 240.

[5] In *Callandar* v. *Dittrich* (1842), 4 M. & G. 68, the Court declined to allow the amendment (per TINDAL C.J., at pp. 89, 90, COLTMAN J., at p. 90, ERSKINE J., at p. 92, and CRESSWELL J. at p. 94). On the other hand, an amendment for the purpose of properly raising the question of estoppel was offered to the plaintiff by the Court in *Coppinger* v. *Norton*, [1902] 2 I.R. 232.

[6] See *Edevain* v. *Cohen* (1889), 43 Ch.D. 187, C.A., a case of "former recovery", and as such cited in para. 499, note 3, *post*, in which NORTH J. having refused an application by the defendant, at the close of the plaintiff's evidence, for leave to amend his defence by adding a plea of *res judicata*, the C.A. held that the judge had exercised a sound discretion (per COTTON L.J. at p. 190.

Procedure for raising the estoppel, when not pleaded

416 In what is usually called the leading case on the subject, it was resolved by the judges summoned to advise the House of Lords that estoppel *per rem judicatam* "is, as a plea, a bar, or, as evidence, conclusive".[1] This statement, in the light of the subsequent authorities, must be taken to mean that the estoppel is conclusive in evidence if, but not unless, it has first been pleaded, or there never has been any opportunity of pleading it.

417 Where the party, being under a duty to plead the estoppel, has omitted to do so, he may thereafter not be allowed to rely upon the *res judicata* as conclusive, though it may be some evidence, at the trial or hearing, as has already been stated.[2]

418 Where on the other hand the party's omission to plead the estoppel was unavoidable or justifiable, his right to insist on the conclusiveness of the *res judicata* in evidence is not in the least prejudiced or impaired, provided that he takes the earliest available opportunity of raising the question in some other form, that is to say, as soon as the evidence of the party sought to be estopped discloses matter which is the proper subject of the estoppel.

419 Where the point is taken in a court of summary jurisdiction it may be impracticable to plead it at all—it is then proper to raise it at the hearing at the first convenient opportunity. In such a case if the matter goes to appeal the plea of estoppel will receive consideration as if it had been formally raised.[3]

420 The rules set out above apply, and the party desirous of raising the unpleaded estoppel has accordingly been held entitled to do so by objection to evidence *ore tenus* or otherwise at the earliest possible stage in the course of the proceedings, where, according to the practice of the tribunal adjudicating, pleadings are not permitted, as, for instance, in the case of a county court action,[4] proceedings before a court of summary jurisdiction,[5] a summons under the Vendor and Purchaser Act 1874,[6] a petition in

---

[1] *Duchess of Kingston's Case* (1776), 2 Smith L.C. (13th Ed.) 644 per DE GREY C.J. at p. 645.

[2] See para. 398, and the cases cited in note 1 thereto, *ante*.

[3] *Cooper* v. *Cooper* (*No.* 2), [1955] P. 168 at p. 172 per Lord MERRIMAN P.

[4] As in *Vaughton* v. *Bradshaw* (1860), 9 C.B. N.S. 103; *Hacking* v. *Lee* (1860), 9 W.R. 70; *Davis* v. *Hedges* (1871), L.R. 6 Q.B. 687; *Reed* v. *Nutt* (1890), 24 Q.B.D. 669; *River Ribble* (*Joint Committee*) v. *Croston Urban District Council*, [1897] 1 Q.B. 251, D.C.; *Anderson* v. *Collinson*, [1901] 2 K.B. 107, D.C.; *Humphries* v. *Humphries*, [1910] 2 K.B. 531, C.A.; *Cooke* v. *Rickman*, [1911] 2 K.B. 1125, D.C.

[5] In *R.* v. *Harrington* (1864), 12 W.R. 420, the objection not having been taken before the justices, the estoppel failed; the perhaps more liberal attitude of modern courts is illustrated by *Cooper* v. *Cooper* (*No.* 2), [1955] P. 168, per Lord MERRIMAN P. at p. 172.

[6] See *Re Allsop and Joy's Contract* (1889), 61 L.T. 213.

accordance with the practice prescribed by particular statutes[1], or proofs, claims, applications, and other proceedings in bankruptcy,[2] or in the winding up of companies,[3] or where, though pleadings are customary and requisite, the party said to be under a duty to plead the estoppel has been joined merely for conformity, and is therefore not the party from whom such a plea could properly be required;[4] or in the case of an interlocutory application for the distribution or disposition of a fund in court[5], or for a declaration in the course of the judicial administration of an estate,[6] before the pleading stage in the proceedings has been reached.

Plea first raised on appeal

421 Where the plea of *res judicata* is raised for the first time on appeal the submission of a previous decision of the matter in dispute not having been made to the court of first instance, the appellate court may be reluctant to allow the appeal out of hand, and may prefer to remit the matter to the court of first instance for a rehearing, where such a course is procedurally possible.[7]

Indeed it may be said that with some confidence that justice will seldom require an appellate court to allow the submission of issue estoppel to be made on appeal where it has not been put forward and the ground for it properly laid in the court below. A factual basis for the submission is necessary, just as in the case of estoppel by representation[8] and this can seldom, if ever, be properly laid in an appellate court. This point is referred to, though nothing was actually decided, in the advice of the Privy Council in *Broken Hill Proprietary Co., Ltd.* v. *Broken Hill Municipal Council.*[9] There the question before their Lordships was the construction of a

---

[1] As in *Waygood* v. *James* (1869), L.R. 4 C.P. 361 (election petition under the Parliamentary Elections Act 1868); *Stevens* v. *Tillett* (1870), L.R. 6 C.P. 147 (the like); *Re Selot's Trust*, [1902] 1 Ch. 488 (petition in an administration suit): *Re May* (1885), 28 Ch.D. 516 (petition under the National Debt Act 1870); *Re Deeley's Patent*, [1895] 1 Ch. 687 (petition for revocation of patent); *Thompson* v. *Thompson*, [1923] 2 Ch. 205 (petition in administration suit).

[2] As in *Re Bremner, Ex parte Harper* (1875), 10 Ch.App. 379; *Re Greaves, Ex parte Whitton* (1880), 43 L.T. 480; *Re Bond, Ex parte Bacon* (1881), 17 Ch.D. 447, C.A.; *Re Hilton, Ex parte March* (1892), 67 L.T. 594; *Re Graydon*, [1896] 1 Q.B. 417. See also the cases cited in note 4, p. 324, *ante*.

[3] As in *Re Bank of Hindustan, China, and Japan* (1873), 9 Ch.App. 1; *Re Orrell Colliery and Fire-brick Co.* (1879), 12 Ch.D. 681; *Re South American and Mexican Co., Ex parte Bank of England*, [1895] 1 Ch. 37, C.A.

[4] See *Whittaker* v. *Jackson* (1864), 2 H. & C. 926 (per POLLOCK C.B., at p. 931, and CHANNELL B., at pp. 932, 933).

[5] As in *Re Hazeldine's Trusts*, [1908] 1 Ch. 34 C.A.

[6] As in *Re Surfleet's Estate* (1911), 105 L.T. 582.

[7] *Sanders* v. *Sanders*, [1952] 2 All E.R. 767.

[8] *Muskham Finance, Ltd.* v. *Howard*, [1963] 1 All E.R. 81; [1963] 1 Q.B. 904; *Emmanuel Ayodeji Ajaji* v. *Briscoe*, [1964] 3 All E.R. 556, 559–560.

[9] *Broken Hill Proprietary, Ltd.* v. *Broken Hill Municipal Council*, [1926] A.C. 94, P.C.

revenue statute, the same provision having been previously construed in earlier litigation between the same parties. The question of construction was fully argued, both in the Full Court of New South Wales and in the High Court of Australia, without any submission of estoppel being raised; before the Privy Council the submission was made for the first time. Their Lordships were content to dismiss the argument for estoppel on its merits, deciding that the questions raised in the two proceedings were not *eadem quaestio*; but in doing so commented on the failure to raise the submission of estoppel earlier, in language which leaves a doubt whether the argument would have been considered at all at such a late stage, if it had appeared that the questions in the two proceedings were capable of being regarded as one and the same.[1]

---

[1] At p. 100—"It has been pointed out that no such question was raised or pleaded either before the District Court or before the Supreme Court in New South Wales, nor has there been any adjudication or finding upon it."

PART II

Res Judicata as a Bar to a Subsequent Recovery: The Doctrine of Merger in Judgment

CHAPTER XV

The Doctrine of Merger in Judgment: Preliminary

Introduction

422 *Res Judicata* has a twofold operation. Not only does it estop the parties from afterwards controverting any question or issue thereby decided, but it also bars the party who has obtained relief thereby from receiving again the same relief against the same party.

General Statement of the doctrine

423 The rule may be summarily stated as follows: any person in whose favour an English judicial tribunal of competent jurisdiction has pronounced a final judgment, whether civil or criminal, is precluded from afterwards recovering before any English tribunal a second judgment for the same civil relief on the same cause of action, or a second judgment of conviction for the same offence, against the same party. A bar or plea of this nature (known as "former recovery" in civil, and *autrefois convict* in criminal, cases) is essentially distinguishable from the estoppel *per rem judicatam* which has hitherto been the subject of inquiry, in two respects: in the first place, the latter prohibits contradiction, the former, repetition and reassertion; secondly, that which must not be controverted, in cases of estoppel, is the proposition of law, or finding of fact, expressly declared by, or necessarily involved in, the *res judicata*, the jussive or prohibitive part of which is of no importance whatever, except so far as it presupposes a determination of such question of law, or issue of fact;[1] whereas, in cases of former recovery, the situation is reversed, the thing which is not allowed to be sued for a second time being the relief and remedy granted by the jussive or prohibitive part of the *res judicata*, and the judicial

---

[1] *Cf.* Chapter VI, para 186, *ante*.

determination, express or implied, of any question of law, or issue of fact, being, as such, absolutely irrelevant.[1]

Terminology

424 The distinction between these two aspects and functions of *res judicata* is preserved in the terminology of the subject. Though, in both characters alike, the *res judicata* operates as an estoppel in the largest sense of the word, that is to say, as an obstacle to the reopening of matters once adjudicated upon, and though, indeed, in some few of the authorities "former recovery" has been pleaded, and even judicially described, as "estoppel",[2] yet, on the whole, the usual practice has been to reserve that term for use in cases of the class hitherto discussed, and to apply to "former recovery" other designations, such as "bar",[3] "exception",[4] "preclusion",[5] or "conclusiveness".[6]

Theory of the doctrine of former recovery or merger in judgment

425 The theoretical basis and justification of the doctrine of former

---

1 See *Outram* v. *Morewood* (1803), 3 East 346, per Lord ELLENBOROUGH C.J., at p. 354; "it is not the recovery, but the matter alleged by the party, and upon which the recovery proceeds, which creates the estoppel. The recovery itself in an action . . . is only a bar to the taking recovery of damages for the same injury, but the estoppel precludes parties and privies from contending to the contrary of that point, or matter of fact, which, having once been distinctly put in issue by them, . . . has been, on such issue jointed, solemnly decided against them." Further, as to the distinction between the bar of "former recovery" and estoppel *strictissimo sensu*, see the observations of PARKE B., at p. 502 of *King* v. *Hoare* (1844), 13 M. & W. 494, and of MAULE J., at p. 153 of *Buckland* v. *Johnson* (1854), 15 C.B. 145.

2 In *Bank of Australasia* v. *Harding* (1850), 9 C.B. 661, there was a plea of former recovery, set out at pp. 673–676, in the terms of the old plea of estoppel, as to which, see para. 404, *ante*, and there was a demurrer to this plea (see pp. 677, 678) on the ground (*inter alia*) that it was "improperly commenced and concluded as a plea of estoppel", but the Court did not find it necessary to deal with this question of the form of the pleading. On the other hand, a special demurrer to a plea of former recovery, on the ground that it did *not* commence or conclude in the manner prescribed by inveterate usage in the case of estoppels, *was* formally overruled in *King* v. *Hoare*, *supra*. In *Leggott* v. *Great Northern Rail. Co.* (1876), 1 Q.B.D. 599, the defendants pleaded a former recovery as an "estoppel" *eo nomine*, apparently without objection or comment from any quarter; whilst, in *Dewar & Sons, Ltd.* v. *Winder* (1895), 12 T.L.R. 54, and in *Sanders* v. *Hamilton* (1907), 96 L.T. 679, D.C., the bar was judicially described as an estoppel.

3 As in *Ferrer* v. *Arden* (1599), 6 Co.Rep. 7a; *Phillips* v. *Berryman* (1783), 3 Doug. K.B. 286 (per BULLER J., at pp. 288, 289); *Thorpe* v. *Cooper* (1828), 5 Bing. 116, Ex. Ch. *Dunn* v. *Murray* (1829), 9 B. & C. 780; *King* v. *Hoare* (1844), 13 M. & W. 494 (per PARKE B., at p. 504); *Buckland* v. *Johnson* (1854), 15 C.B. 145 (per JERVIS C.J., at p. 161); *Kendall* v. *Hamilton* (1879), 4 App. Cas. 504, H.L. (per Lord PENZANCE, at p. 526); *The Cella* (1888), 13 P.D. 82, C.A. (per HANNEN P., at p. 85); *R.* v. *Miles* (1890), 24 Q.B.D. 423, D.C. (per CHARLES J., at p. 438); *B. O. Morris, Ltd.* v. *Perrott and Bolton*, [1945] 1 All E.R. 567, C.A. per Lord GODDARD at p. 569.

4 As in *Nelson* v. *Couch* (1863), 15 C.B. N.S. 99 (per WILLES J., at p. 108).

5 As in *Bowden* v. *Horne* (1831), 7 Bing. 716 (per TINDAL C.J., at pp. 723, 724); *Russell & Sons* v. *Waterford and Limerick Rail. Co.* (1885), 16 L.R. Ir. 314; *Cambefort & Co.* v. *Champman* (1887), 19 Q.B.D. 229, D.C.; *The Cella*, *supra* (per HANNEN P., at p. 85).

6 As in *Hooper* v. *Hooper* (1825), 1 M'Cle. & Yo. 509 (*per Cur.*, at p. 513).

recovery has been put in three different ways. In the first place, from the point of view of public policy, it has always been insisted that the general interest of the community in the speedy and final termination of disputes between litigants demands the imposition and rigid observance of such a rule.[1] Coke and the lawyers of his school never ceased to enlarge upon the dishonour to the administration of justice which must necessarily result from the reagitation of causes finally adjudicated upon, from the multiplication of suits to the scandal of the common law, which "abhors infinity", and from the coexistence on the record of conflicting judgments of equal authority; and succeeding judges were no less outspoken and persistent supporters of the principle, *interest reipublicae ut sit finis litium*, and no less vigorous in their denunciation of, and warning against, the spirit of contentiousness which it was the object of the breed-bate and the speculative attorney to promote, and of the doctrine in question to repress.[2]

426 Secondly, the "former recovery" rule has been justified from the standpoint of private justice, and the interests of the individual litigant; *nemo debet bis vexari pro una et eadem causa*, or, adopting the formula to criminal cases, *nemo debet bis puniri pro uno et eodem delicto*[3]—and this notwithstanding that in particular cases the merits, apart from this principle, might have inclined the Court to consider a second claim.[4]

427 Thus far the theoretical groundwork of the rule is the same as that of the doctrine of estoppel *per rem judicatam*.[5] There is, however, a third theory on which the bar of "former recovery" has been rested, but which in no way supports the rules of estoppel. This theory, fully developed in Coke's time, though not perhaps meeting with universal or unqualified

---

[1] *Green* v. *Weatherill*, [1929] 2 Ch. 213 per MAUGHAM J. at p. 221.

[2] See *Ferrer* v. *Arden* (1599), 6 Co.Rep. 7a (*per Cur.*, at p. 9a); *Randal* v. *Higgens* (1605), 6 Co.Rep. 44b; *Stafford* v. *Clark* (1824), 2 Bing. 377 (per BEST C.J., at p. 382;) *Brinsmead* v. *Harrison* (1872), L.R. 7 C.P. 547, Ex. Ch. (per KELLY, C.B., at pp. 551, 552, and BLACKBURN J., at p. 553). *Cp.* the judicial observations, as to estoppel cases, which are cited in para. 10, notes 3 and 4, p. 10, *ante*.

[3] *Wemyss* v. *Hopkins* (1875), L.R. 10 Q.B. 378 (per BLACKBURN J., at pp. 381, 382, LUSH J., at p. 382, and FIELD J., at p. 382). *Cp.* the cases, with reference to estoppels, cited in note 4, p. 10, *ante*.

[4] See Lord ATKIN's speech in *Workington Harbour and Dock Board* v. *Trade Indemnity Co., Ltd.* (*No.* 2), [1938] 2 All E.R. 101, at p. 106: "The result is that the plaintiffs, who appear to have had a good cause of action for a considerable sum of money, failed to obtain it, and on what may appear to be technical grounds. Reluctant, however, as a judge may be to fail to give effect to substantial merits, he has to keep in mind principles established for the protection of litigants from oppressive proceedings. There are solid merits behind the maxim *nemo bis vexari debet pro eadem causa*. For a spirited statement of the opposite viewpoint in the same case, see the (dissenting) judgment of MACKINNON L.J. in the Court below reported in [1937] 3 All E.R. 139 at pp. 147–8.

[5] See para. 10, *ante*.

acceptance in the earliest periods of our jurisprudence,[1] is of the following nature. Any cause of action which results in a judgment of an English judicial tribunal, whereby relief is granted to the plaintiff, or other "actor" in the proceedings, is in contemplation of law merged in the judgment, as soon as pronounced, and thereby loses its individual vitality, and disappears as an independent entity, any English judgment even of the lowest degree being regarded as of a higher nature than any, even the most important, cause of action: *transit in rem judicatam*, whence it follows that after such "passing" and absorption, it cannot be the subject of a further action or proceeding for the recovery of similar relief.[2] Strongly though it savours of scholastic metaphysics, this view is perhaps, after all, the only one of the three which completely accounts for, and justifies, certain features in the doctrine of former recovery which differentiate it from the doctrine of estoppel; for instance, on this theory alone, and not on the

---

[1] As appears from p. 45b of *Randal* v. *Higgens* (1605), 6 Co. Rep. 44b, where there is a reference to a curious rule, which had prevailed during the reigns of E. 3, R. 2, and H. 4, though then extinct, requiring a defendant against whom judgment had been given on a deed to see that the deed was solemnly "damned" by the court, under pain of liability to be sued on the same deed again,—which means that, in that class of case at any rate, the cause of action was not in those days "drowned" in the judgment, but had to be excommunicated, or exorcised, by judicial bell, book, and candle, before it could be pronounced harmless.

[2] See, as regards civil proceedings, *Randal* v. *Higgens*, *supra* at pp. 44b, 45a; *Drake* v. *Mitchell* (1803), 3 East 251 (per Lord ELLENBOROUGH C.J., at p. 258: "I have always understood the principle of *transit in rem judicatam* to relate only to the particular cause of action in which the judgment is recovered operating as a change of remedy from its being of a higher nature than before"); *Bowden* v. *Horne* (1831), 7 Bing. 716 (*per Cur.*, at p. 723: "the nature of his original demand is changed, *quia transit in rem judicatam*"); *King* v. *Hoare* (1844), 13 M. & W. 494 (per PARKE B., at p. 504: "the cause of action is changed into matter of record, which is of a higher nature, and the inferior remedy is merged in the higher"); *Brinsmead* v. *Harrison* (1872), L.R. 7 C.P. 547, Exch. Ch. (per BLACKBURN J., at p. 553); *Kendall* v. *Hamilton* (1879), 4 App.Cas. 504, H.L. (per Lord PENZANCE, at p. 526, and Lord BLACKBURN, at p. 542). For a criminal case in which the same theory is put forward, see *Wemyss* v. *Hopkins* (1875), L.R. 10 Q.B. 378 (per BLACKBURN J., at pp. 381, 382, and LUSH and FIELD JJ., at p. 382). The language used in some of the above cases does not seem quite appropriate, in so far as an inferior remedy is said to be merged in one of a higher nature; for a cause of action is not a "remedy" at all: what is meant is that a mere assertion of the party becomes the declaration of the court, a claim passes into a decision, a pleading into a judgment. A clearer and more precise expression of the doctrine, in this respect, is to be found in the speech of Lord PENZANCE at p. 526 of *Kendall* v. *Hamilton*, *supra*: "when that which was originally only a right of action has been merged into a judgment, . . . the judgment is a bar to an action brought on the original cause of action." For a statement of the rule in Roman jurisprudence, see para. 511, Appendix B, *post*.

In *United Australia, Ltd.* v. *Barclays Bank, Ltd.*, [1941] A.C. 1 H.L., the House of Lords was dealing with the effect of proceedings taken against one person liable in respect of certain subject matter, upon the quite separate liability of another person in respect of the same subject matter. This was hardly a question of *res judicata*; yet their Lordships are to be found reflecting upon the topic, which indeed closely impinged upon the facts before them, though it could not be decisive upon them. On p. 28 Lord ATKIN considered the hypothetical case of a plaintiff to whom a given defendant is liable both in contract and in tort. Such a plaintiff obviously could not recover twice. "Hence he was restricted to one of the two remedies, and herein I think arose the doctrine of the 'waiver of the tort'. Having recovered in contract it is plain the plaintiff cannot go on to recover in tort. *Transit in rem judicatam*."

ground of either public convenience or private justice, can it be deemed right or reasonable to declare, as the law has declared, that a foreign judgment is no bar to a subsequent recovery,[1] and, on the other hand, that an unsatisfied English judgment, against one of two persons jointly liable in contract, is such a bar in favour of the other of them.[2]

The constituents of a good plea of former recovery

428 Any party who is desirous of setting up a former recovery as a bar to subsequent proceedings can succeed only if he alleges and establishes each and every of the following matters (except so far as expressly or impliedly admitted by the opposite party):

(i) That the former recovery relied upon was obtained by such a judgment as in law can be the subject of the plea.
(ii) That the former judgment was in fact pronounced in the terms alleged;
(iii) That the tribunal pronouncing the former judgment had competent jurisdiction in that behalf;
(iv) That the former judgment was final;
(v) That the plaintiff, or prosecutor, is proceeding on the very same cause of action, or for the same offence, as was adjudicated upon by the former judgment;
(vi) That the parties to the proceedings, or their privies, are the same as the parties to the former judgment, or their privies.

429 These several *alleganda et probanda* will be the subject of separate treatment in the above order.[3] There will then be a chapter in which the plea of *autrefois convict* is dealt with;[4] and the Part will conclude with chapters on the affirmative answers which may be raised to a *prima facie* case of former recovery,[5] and on the rules of procedure which prescribe and regulate the means by which the question may be raised.[6]

---

[1] As to this, see Chapter XVI, paras. 436–438, *post*.
[2] See Chapter XXI, paras. 464 *et seq.*, *post*. It is to be noticed that by virtue of the provisions of s. 6 of the Law Reform (Married Women and Tortfeasors) Act 1935 a different rule is applicable to persons jointly liable in tort.
[3] These six constituents are the subjects of Chapters XVI, XVII, XVIII, XIX, XX and XXI, *post*, respectively.
[4] See Chapter XXII, *post*.
[5] Dealt with in Chapter XXIII, *post*.
[6] Dealt with in Chapter XXIV, *post*.

CHAPTER XVI

The Doctrine of Merger in Judgment: What Constitutes Former Recovery

430 For the ascertainment of the necessary conditions of a good plea of former recovery, it is essential to examine closely the meaning, characteristics, effect, and operation of the three jural concepts,—"judgment", "merger", and "recovery". These will now be considered in their order.

"Judgment"

431 For the purposes of estoppel, the *res judicata* means, as has already been explained in the proper place,[1] a judicial determination of some controverted question of law or fact. But for present purposes, it means, and means only, a judgment granting relief and remedy to one of the parties.[2] Any judgment (or other judicial decision, such as a final order, or an award) which has this effect, or in so far as it has this effect, is a "judgment" within the meaning of the rule of former recovery, for it is something whereby the party may be said to have "recovered" money, or whatever other relief may have been awarded or granted. It is immaterial whether the cause of action sued upon was real or personal, breach of contract or tort,[3] common law or statutory;[4] nor does it matter whether the judgment operated *in rem* or *inter partes*,[5] or whether it was obtained after a trial, hearing, or other contest, or by default of appearance or pleading,[6]

[1] See para. 30, *ante*.

[2] See para. 423, *ante*.

[3] See, generally, the cases cited in the notes to this chapter for illustrations.

[4] *Wemyss* v. *Hopkins* (1875), L.R. 10 Q.B. 378 (per BLACKBURN J., at p. 381); *Girdlestone* v. *Brighton Aquarium Co.* (1879), 4 Ex. D. 107, C.A.

[5] See *Nelson* v. *Couch* (1863), 15 C.B. N.S. 99 (per WILLES J., at pp. 108–112).

[6] As in *Bowden* v. *Horne* (1831), 7 Bing. 716 (*per Cur.*, at p. 723); *Marston* v. *Phillips* (1863), 9 L.T. 289; *Girdlestone* v. *Brighton Aquarium Co.*, *supra*. For illustrations of default judgments in estoppel cases, see Part I, Ch. II, paras. 46 *et seq.*, *ante*.

or even whether, in point of strict form and accurate terminology, it was a "judgment" at all, provided that it was a judicial act of some kind operating as above stated.[1] It is immaterial that a judgment has been obtained by consent.[2]

It is sometimes said that a judgment is a "Contract of Record" in which is merged the antecedent right of action previously vested in the plaintiff. This concept of a judgment as a contract makes contractual capacity in the plaintiff a relevant factor, in rare cases, in deciding how far antecedent rights will effectually merge in the judgment. So in *Arabian* v. *Tuffnall and Taylor, Ltd.*[3] an infant and his next friend had joined in registering an agreement under the Workmen's Compensation Act which on registration had the effect of a County Court judgment. Upon the infant issuing proceedings for common law damages it was held that though the agreement barred further proceedings under the Workmen's Compensation Act, since the court in which it was registered had impliedly approved it to this end, yet it was not effective to bar proceedings at common law, provided that any payments of compensation were brought into account; for, the agreement not being shown to be for the infant's benefit if it extended so far, the court would limit the estoppel correspondingly to his capacity.

It is perhaps conceivable that a judgment taken or obtained *ultra vires* of a corporation may in special circumstances be subject to like considerations.[4]

432 The following do not satisfy the requirements mentioned, and, therefore, are not deemed "judgments" for the purposes of the plea of former recovery: a naked judicial declaration of rights and liabilities; a verdict not followed by judgment;[5] an unexercised right to sign judgment on default;[6] a compromise of an action on terms with which the defendant did not comply;[7] a balance order in the winding up of a company;[8] and,

---

[1] Such as, for instance, a decree, sentence, order, or award.

[2] See *Hammond* v. *Schofield*, [1891] 1 Q.B. 453, Div. Ct., which was a case of express consent. For an instance of implied consent, see *Wright* v. *London General Omnibus Co.* (1877), 2 Q.B. D. 271. As to consent judgments, in cases of estoppel, see Part I, Ch. II, paras. 41 *et seq.*, *ante*.

[3] [1944] K.B. 685 (WROTTESLEY J.).

[4] *Great North West Central Rail. Co.* v. *Charlebois*, [1899] A.C. 114; *cf. In Re Jon Beauforte (London), Ltd.*, [1953] 1 All E.R. 634; [1953] Ch. 131.

[5] *Morris* v. *Robinson* (1824), 3 B. & C. 196 (per BYLES J., at p. 205, and LITTLEDALE J., at p. 207).

[6] *Goldrei, Foucard & Son.* v. *Sinclair*, [1918] 1 K.B. 180, C.A. (per SARGANT J., at p. 191).

[7] *Thomas* v. *Exeter Flying Post Co.* (1887), 18 Q.B.D. 822.

[8] *Westmoreland Green and Blue Slate Co.* v. *Feilden*, [1891] 3 Ch. 15, C.A., where it was held that a balance order is not only not of a higher nature than the debt for calls, being less, rather than more, efficacious, but is not even a judgment at all, or (except as to the mode of enforcement by writ of *fieri facias*), in the least like a judgment (per LINDLEY L.J., at pp. 25, 26, and BOWEN L.J., at pp. 26, 27).

in criminal cases, a requisition upon the accused to enter into recognizances to keep the peace, made merely in the exercise of the general discretion of magistrates as conservators of the peace, and not intended, or taking effect, as a judgment of conviction.[1]

"*Merger*"

433 Any English cause of action, or prosecution, is deemed to be merged in, and effaced by, an English civil or criminal judgment pronounced thereon, and a civil judgment includes the decision of an arbitral tribunal, whether domestic or statutory;[2] but no foreign judgment has this, or any, effect upon the original cause of action.[3] It is desirable to discuss separately, in relation to the doctrine of merger, these three classes of judgment, English civil, English criminal and foreign.

434 In accordance with the principle stated, the bar or plea of former recovery is substantiated in any court by proof that the plaintiff has already recovered against the defendant, in respect of the same cause of action, the civil relief sued for in the second proceedings, and that such former recovery was effected by the judgment of an English civil tribunal,[4] whether a superior, or an inferior court, including an inferior criminal court exercising civil jurisdiction,[5] or an Admiralty

---

[1] *Hartley* v. *Hindmarsh* (1866), L.R. 1 C.P. 553 (per ERLE C.J., at p. 555, and WILLES, BYLES, and MONTAGUE SMITH JJ., at p. 556). Contrast the case cited in note 3 on p. 366, *post*, where there had been a judgment of conviction, which was none the less so because followed by a nominal sentence.

[2] See *Golightly* v. *Jellicoe* (1769), 4 Term Rep. 147 n. (domestic); *Ravee* v. *Farmer* (1791), 4 Term Rep. 146 (domestic); *Thorpe* v. *Cooper* (1828), 5 Bing. 116, Ex. Ch. (statutory), per BEST C.J., at pp. 129, 130; *Dunn* v. *Murray* (1829), 9 B. & C. 780 (domestic); *Harrison* v. *Creswick* (1853), 13 C.B. 399 (domestic); *Gueret* v. *Audouy* (1893), 62 L.J. Q.B. 633 (domestic), per LOPES L.J., at pp. 635–637, and A. L. SMITH L.J., at pp. 637–640; *Moakes* v. *Blackwell Colliery Co.*, [1917] 1 K.B. 565, C.A. (statutory); *Ayscough* v. *Sheed Thomson & Co., Ltd.* (1923), 129 L.T. 429, C.A. Generally, as to awards standing substantially in the same position for the purposes of the doctrine of *res judicata*, as other judicial decisions, see para. 26, *ante*. *In H. E. Daniels, Ltd.* v. *Carmel Exporters and Importers, Ltd.*, [1953] 2 Q.B. 242 PILCHER J. was inclined at p. 254 to doubt whether a commercial contract containing an agreement to submit disputes to arbitration necessarily implied that all disputes (*e.g.* as to merchantable quality, or as to misdescription of goods) should be submitted to the same arbitrator at the same time; at p. 255, however, he says: "I am inclined to think, however, that in spite of any technical difference which may exist in this connexion between judgments and awards, it might be difficult to argue successfully that, in so far as the point with which I am dealing is concerned, any valid distinction can properly be drawn between them."

[3] See paras. 439–441, *post*.

[4] That is to say, the party setting up the former recovery, in all the cases cited in the three following notes, either succeeded, or if not, failed solely because he had not established some one or more of the other conditions of a valid plea of former recovery.

[5] *Wright* v. *London General Omnibus Co.* (1877), 2 Q.B.D. 271, and *Sanders* v. *Hamilton* (1907), 96 L.T. 679, D.C., are instances of a former inferior court judgment barring a claim in an inferior court. For instances of inferior court judgments being set up in bar of actions in superior courts, see *Austin* v. *Mills* (1853), 9 Exch. 288; *Gibbs* v. *Cruikshank* (1873), L.R. 8 C.P. 454; *Clarke* v. *Yorke* (1882), 52 L.J. Ch. 32; *Brunsden* v. *Humphrey* (1884), 14 Q.B.D. 141, C.A. *Wright*

court,[1] or an arbitral tribunal invested with authority in that behalf either by the consent and submission of the parties, or by statute.[2]

435 The principle upon which a conviction of a person prosecuted in a criminal court may bar an attempt to proceed further against him criminally in respect of what was essentially the same transaction is discussed in a separate chapter devoted to the plea of *autrefois convict*.[3]

Foreign judgments

436 A foreign judgment[4] is not deemed of a higher nature than the original cause of action, as is an English judgment: therefore no such judgment operates as a merger, or as a bar to subsequent proceedings in an English court for the same relief, and on the same cause of action, as that which formed the subject of the foreign judgment.[5]

437 "Foreign" is here used in its strict technical sense of "non-English".[6] Accordingly a recovery in the courts of any British colony, or of any part of Her Majesty's Dominions, other than England, is no more a bar to a second recovery in an English court than is a foreign judgment in the popular sense of the word.[7]

---

v. *London General Omnibus Co.* (*supra*) has been severely criticised; see note 1 on p. 377, *post*. But an illustration not subject to the same criticism is furnished by *Birmingham Corporation* v. *Allsopp* (1919), 119 L.T. 775, in which a corporation, having been awarded in a criminal proceeding before justices, pursuant to s. 20 of the Gasworks Clauses Act 1847, a sum "by way of compensation" for damage done to a pillar box, was held precluded from suing civilly for the balance of the damage allegedly suffered. *In New Zealand*, where a Magistrate had dismissed on the merits a complaint made under ss. 9 and 10 of the Impounding Act 1908, asking for a summary award of damages for an alleged illegal impounding of cattle, the claimant was thereby held estopped from subsequently suing in a civil court for damages: *Banks* v. *Wilson* (1910), 29 N.Z.L.R. 832 (CHAPMAN J.). It is to be noted, however, that this decision must be regarded as based rather upon estoppel *per rem judicatam* than upon the doctrine of merger; but it is submitted that it would follow from it that had the decision been the other way, and had a sum been given by way of damages in the criminal proceedings, the claimant's rights would have been held to merge.

[1] See *Nelson* v. *Couch* (1863), 15 C.B. N.S. 99 (per WILLES J., at pp. 108–112).

[2] See the cases cited in note (2), p. 362 *supra*.

[3] Chapter XXII, *post*.

[4] As to foreign judgments generally, see Part I, Chapter II, paras. 69 *et seq*.

[5] *Hall* v. *Odber* (1809), 11 East 118 (per Lord ELLENBOROUGH C.J., at pp. 124, 125, GROSE J., at p. 125, and BAYLEY J., at pp. 126, 127); *Smith* v. *Nicolls* (1839), 5 Bing. N.C. 208 (per TINDAL C.J., at pp. 220–222, and BOSANQUET J., at p. 223); *Bank of Australasia* v. *Harding* (1850), 9 C.B. 661 (per WILDE C.J., at p. 686, CRESSWELL J., at p. 688, and TALFOURD J., at p. 689); *Barber* v. *Lamb* (1860), 8 C.B. N.S. 95 (per ERLE C.J., at p. 100); *Taylor* v. *Hollard*, [1902] 1 K.B. 676 (per JELF J., at p. 681, who, however, whilst recognizing the general rule that a foreign judgment is no bar, held that, in the circumstances of the case before him, the plaintiff had precluded himself by election from suing on the original cause of action).

[6] See Chapter II, paras. 69 *et seq*.

[7] See the cases cited in note 5, *supra*, in the first four of which the former judgments had been pronounced by colonial or consular tribunals.

438 But of course a colonial judgment, or a judgment of a court of any part of Her Majesty's Dominions, other than England, which accepts and administers the principles of our common law, operates as a merger, and a bar, in that colony or part:[1] and, *a fortiori*, an English judgment so operates in any such colony;[2] whether the same result would follow in any of the self-governing Dominions, however, is another matter, and it is submitted that in these jurisdictions an English judgment would be treated as a "foreign" one.

"*Recovery*"

439 A former recovery, the distinction between which and a former determination of some question of law or fact has already been explained,[3] is established by proof that the party against whom the plea or bar is set up has in previous litigation, whether as plaintiff, counterclaimant, or otherwise in the character of an *actor*,[4] obtained a judgment for the same relief as that which, in any of the above characters, he is claiming in the present litigation. A plea of payment under a former judgment is a totally different plea, for this can be alleged and proved without alleging or proving that the former judgment itself would have constituted a bar to the second proceedings.[5]

---

[1] See *Bank of Australasia* v. *Harding*, *supra*, where (per WILDE C.J., at p. 686) it was conceded that the judgment which had been recovered by the plaintiff in the Supreme Court of the colony of New South Wales operated as a merger, and a bar, in that colony; *Russell & Sons* v. *Waterford and Limerick Rail. Co.* (1885), 16 L.R. Ir. 314 (former Irish judgment a bar in Ireland); *Daly* v. *Dublin, Wicklow, & Wexford Rail. Co.* (1892), 30 L.R. Ir. 514 (the like, but no bar, because the causes of action were different); *Clarke* v. *Midland Great Western Rail. Co.*, [1895] 2 I.R. 294 (the like, but there again the plea failed because identity of causes of action was not established).

[2] See *Bayley* v. *Edwards* (1792), 3 Swan. 703, where it was recognized that a decree obtained by a plaintiff in the English Court of Chancery would be a bar to a suit for the same relief in a British colony, but here the plea of former recovery was held bad, because the recovery was not proved).

[3] See para 423, *ante*.

[4] See para. 463, *post*.

[5] See *Fisher* v. *Lane* (1772), 3 Wils K.B. 297; *Barber* v. *Lamb* (1860), 8 C.B. N.S. 95, per ERLE C.J., at p. 100 ("here the defence does not rest on merger, but on the principle that the plaintiff has obtained the judgment of a tribunal to which he has resorted for enforcing his debt, and that the judgment so obtained *has been satisfied by payment*"), and KEATING J., at p. 101 ("this is not a case of merger. It is not so pleaded. But the ground is that there has been a judgment of a court having jurisdiction over the subject-matter, and that *that judgment has been satisfied by payment*"); *Yeo* v. *Tatem* (1871), L.R. 3 P.C. 696, at p. 702. In neither of the two cases last cited could the defendant have succeeded on a mere plea of former recovery. The essential difference between a plea of former recovery and one of satisfaction by payment is interestingly illustrated in *Kohnke* v. *Karger*, [1951] 2 All E.R. 179; [1951] 2 K.B. 670. Here, A. was injured while driving in France in a collision between two vehicles driven by X. and Y. respectively. In penal proceedings brought in France against Y. only, Y. was held negligent and the proportions of responsibility for the accident, as between him and X. (who was not a party to the proceedings), was held to be two-thirds and one-third. £1,428 damages was awarded as against Y. The judgment was satisfied by payment. A. then brought proceedings in England against X., who resided within the jurisdiction, claiming damages. It was contended (and this was accepted by the Court) that on a claim brought in England £1,428 would have been an insufficient award. It was not contended

440 The question of whether there was a former recovery in the above sense is one of fact,[1] and, as such, must be established by evidence. If it be not shewn that in the former proceedings, the party recovered the precise relief alleged, whether by a judgment in an action,[2] by an award in an arbitration,[3] or by a conviction in a criminal case,[4] the plea fails.

441 "Recovery", however, means no more than recovery of the right, as judicially declared, to the relief granted: it does not mean physical or actual recovery of the money or other relief awarded by the judgment. The original cause of action is merged in the judgment as soon as it has been pronounced; it follows that everything which happens afterwards, in relation to its enforcement or fruition, is irrelevant. Accordingly, it has been held that a plea of former recovery, otherwise good, is none the less so merely because the former judgment was infructuous, the judgment creditor being either unwilling, or unable, to obtain satisfaction by payment, execution, or otherwise;[5] or merely because the party, *after* the judgment, elected to abandon his rights of execution, by *nolle prosequi*, or other formal act,[6] as distinct from an election to discontinue *before* judgment; or merely because, in county court proceedings, the party elected to "abandon the excess" over the pecuniary limit of the

---

that a plea of merger in judgment would lie as a defence to the claim against X, for no judgment against him had ever been obtained; but it was held that in any proceeding in England against X. A. must give credit for such moneys as had actually been received from Y. on account of the award.

[1] *Edevain* v. *Cohen* (1889), 43 Ch.D. 187, C.A. (per COTTON L.J., at pp. 189, 190).

[2] As in *Seddon* v. *Tutop* (1796), 6 Term Rep. 607, where the particular former recovery pleaded was not proved; *Edevain* v. *Cohen*, *supra*, where the former recovery set up at the trial had not been pleaded.

[3] As in *Golightly* v. *Jellicoe* (1769), 4 Term Rep. 147 n.; *Ravee* v. *Farmer* (1791), 4 Term Rep. 146; *Thorpe* v. *Cooper* (1828), 5 Bing. 116, Exch. Ch. (per BEST C.J., at pp. 129, 130). In all these cases the defendant failed to establish that the arbitral tribunal had in fact awarded to the plaintiff the precise compensation or relief which was then being sued for, or that the claim in the then action was either expressly or impliedly within the submission.

[4] As in *Hartley* v. *Hindmarsh* (1866), L.R. 1 C.P. 553, where no former conviction was proved, either in substance or in form (per ERLE C.J., at pp. 555, 556, and BYLES and MONTAGUE SMITH JJ., at p. 556). But see Chapter XXII for the further development of this topic.

[5] See *Randal* v. *Higgens* (1605), 6 Co. Rep. 44 b., where a plea of former recovery, without alleging execution of the judgment, was held good on demurrer; *King* v. *Hoare* (1844), 13 M. & W. 494 (immaterial that judgment unsatisfied); *Buckland* v. *Johnson* (1854), 15 C.B. 145 (per JERVIS C.J., at pp. 164, 165); *Kendall* v. *Hamilton* (1879), 4 App. Cas. 504, H.L.; *Re Hodgson* (1885), 31 Ch. D. 177, C.A.

[6] As in *Bowden* v. *Horne* (1831), 7 Bing. 716, where the plaintiff had in the former proceedings obtained judgment by default against the defendant for a certain sum on a bill of exchange, and a certain other sum as the price of goods sold, and work and labour, but, being at that time apprehensive that to insist on both claims might drive the defendant into bankruptcy, entered a *nolle prosequi* as to the second of the two sums recovered by the judgment, and it was held (per TINDAL C.J., at p. 723) that, "after the plaintiff has obtained a judgment in his favour, and has given up the damages upon the record in such terms as the present, he has precluded himself from suing

jurisdiction, pursuant to the provisions of the statute.[1] Nor is it any answer to a *prima facie* case of former recovery to show that, by suing in one of two possible forms of action on the former occasion, the plaintiff recovered a less measure of damages than he would have recovered if he had sued in the form which he proposes to adopt in the subsequent proceedings.[2] So also, the analogous plea of *autrefois convict* in criminal cases, if otherwise established, is not in the least invalidated by proof that, on such conviction, only a nominal sentence was passed.[3]

---

again on the original cause of action", though, as the Court intimated, at pp. 722, 723, the case would have been very different if there had been a *retraxit* (corresponding to the modern discontinuance before judgment).

1 As in *Clarke* v. *Yorke* (1882), 52 L.J. Ch. 32 (per PEARSON J., at p. 34).

2 See *Buckland* v. *Johnson* (1854), 15 C.B. 145 (per JERVIS C.J., at pp. 161–164, MAULE J. at p. 166, CRESSWELL J., at pp. 166, 167, and CROWDER J., at pp. 167, 168); *Wright* v. *London General Omnibus Co.* (1877), 2 Q.B.D. 271. *In New Zealand, Banks* v. *Wilson* (1910), 29 N.Z.L.R. 832, where CHAPMAN J. said: "*Prima facie*, where a plaintiff has his choice between two remedies and chooses to proceed for a statutory remedy rather than enforce his common law action, he is bound by the result, however disappointing".

3 See *R.* v. *Miles* (1890), 24 Q.B.D. 423, D.C., per CHARLES J., at p. 438: "It cannot be material that a magistrate has power by statute"—the Summary Jurisdiction Act 1879, s. 16 (2)—"to deal with a convicted person otherwise than by fine and imprisonment, for it is the conviction, and not the nature of the sentence, which constitutes the bar". Contrast the case cited in note 1 on p. 362, *ante*, where there had been no judgment at all, either of conviction, or acquittal.

CHAPTER XVII

The Doctrine of Merger in Judgment: Proof of the Former Judgment

442 The fact of the former judgment must, like any other fact, be proved by primary evidence, if producible, and, if not, by secondary evidence. That is to say, every such judgment must be "verified" by the official record, where there is one, and, where there is none, by the next best evidence available, as, for instance, the production of a minute or book from the custody of the officer of the court to whom the duty of recording the proceedings of such court is entrusted by custom or otherwise, and proof of compliance with such other or further rules of evidence as, in the particular case, may have been prescribed by statute.

443 These rules of evidence, in connection with the proper method of proving a judicial decision for the purposes of estoppel, to which of course they equally apply, have already been the subject of discussion and illustration,[1] followed by a classification of the records of different judgments, and of the statutory or other means whereby such records are respectively required to be proved.[2] It is sufficient, therefore, in this place, to refer to, without repeating, this previous discussion, and the references there given to the various relevant statutes, statutory rules, and authorities.

---

[1] In Part I, Chapter III, *ante*, wherein para. 101 deals with proof of record, and para. 104 with other modes of proof, when there is no record.

[2] See Part I, Chapter III, paras. 105 *et seq.*, *ante*. As to the proper mode of proving judgments of superior and inferior civil courts, see paras. 106–7, *ante*, respectively, and as to the mode of proving judgments of superior, and inferior, criminal courts, see paras. 108–109, *ante*, and the statutes, rules and cases referred to in these paragraphs. And see, further, as to proof of the judgment or process of an inferior civil court, *Fisher* v. *Lane* (1772), 3 Wils. 297, where a judgment of the Mayor's Court was proved by a minute in the books of the court, produced and read by the proper officer (*per Cur.*, at p. 304), and the existence of the custom of foreign attachment was established by oral evidence, it being intimated by the Court that this fact might also have been certified by the Recorder (*per Cur.*, at p. 303). And as to the proof of a summary conviction by a record, or an examined copy, see *Hartley* v. *Hindmarsh* (1866), L.R. 1 C.P. 553, where it was held that, even if the decision of the court of summary jurisdiction amounted to a conviction at all (which it did not), such conviction had not been proved in the proper form as above stated (per Erle C.J., and BYLES and MONTAGUE SMITH, JJ., at p. 556).

CHAPTER XVIII

The Doctrine of Merger in Judgment: Jurisdiction

444 As has already been explained,[1] it is essential to a case of estoppel *per rem judicatam* that the tribunal pronouncing the judicial decision should have had competent jurisdiction in that behalf. The justice and reasonableness of this rule, where a party to the decision is seeking to prevent his opponent from controverting it, seems obvious. It is not, however, quite so obvious, at the first blush, why jurisdiction should be equally essential in cases of former recovery, or why a party who has obtained a judgment from a court which had no jurisdiction to pronounce it should not suffer for his own mistake, or why it should lie in his mouth to bastardize a decision which he has sought, secured, and theretofore recognized as legitimate. Indeed, in one of the very early authorities, a hesitating opinion in the negative seems to have been expressed.[2] But a very little reflection must lead to an appreciation of the vital distinction between an unsatisfied or unexecuted judgment, which, nevertheless, if valid, operates as a bar, as has been pointed out at an earlier stage,[3] and a so-called judgment which never was a judgment at all, but always a nullity. It is precisely because the party afterwards discovers, or is advised, that he has obtained a mere piece of paper, which he cannot sue upon, or enforce by execution, that he is driven to sue on his original cause of action, which, there being in contemplation of law no judgment wherein it can be deemed to have been merged, still subsists. He suffers sufficiently for his own blunder by losing

---

[1] See Part I, Ch. IV, *ante*.

[2] In *Mico* v. *Morris* (1685), 3 Lev. 234, *per Cur.*, at p. 234; "if the judgment in London",—sc. in the Sheriff's Court of London, which judgment was held to have been void for want of jurisdiction,—"had been given for the plaintiff, it would have been a bar here, because he had recovered, and had a judgment for him." It would seem that either the Court, or the reporter, had some qualms as to this dictum, for the significant note is appended—"but *quaere* of that matter."

[3] See para. 441, *ante*.

the fruits of that which he intended to obtain, and thought he had obtained, by the judgment: there is no reason why he should further suffer by losing that which, *ex hypothesi*, has never ceased to be his. Accordingly, it has always been held that a judgment pronounced by a court having no jurisdiction in that behalf, whether a civil,[1] or criminal,[2] court, or a court of summary jurisdiction in the exercise of civil or quasi-civil functions conferred upon it by statute,[3] and whether the nullity of such judgment has been declared by an appellate tribunal or not, is no bar to further proceedings on the same cause of action, or for the same offence.

445 It seems doubtful whether the onus is on the party setting up the former recovery, as it is on the party setting up estoppel,[4] to allege and prove the jurisdiction, or for the other party to establish the absence of it.[5]

---

[1] See *Fisher* v. *Lane* (1772), 3 Wils. 297; *Smith* v. *Nicolls* (1839), 5 Bing. N.C. 208 (per TINDAL C.J., at p. 222, and VAUGHAN and BOSANQUET JJ., at p. 223).

[2] *R.* v. *Marsham*, [1912] 2 K.B. 362, D.C. (per Lord ALVERSTONE C.J., at p. 364, and AVORY J., at pp. 365, 366); *Conlin* v. *Patterson*, [1915] 2 I.R. 169 (where the conviction had been quashed for want of jurisdiction,—an *autrefois acquit* case, but the rule was stated by PALLES C.B., at pp. 174, 175, to apply equally to cases of *autrefois convict*); *Bannister* v. *Clarke*, [1920] 3 K.B. 598, D.C. (per Lord READING C.J., at pp. 605–607).

[3] *R.* v. *Brisby* (1849), 18 L.J. M.C. 157 (per Lord DENMAN C.J., at p. 159, PARKE B., at p. 159, PATTESON J., at pp. 159, 160, and COLTMAN and WILLIAMS JJ., at p. 160), a case of an affiliation order; *Midland Rail. Co.* v. *Martin & Co.*, [1893] 2 Q.B. 172, D.C., a case of an order by a magistrate under s. 40 of the Metropolitan Police Act 1839, for the delivery of goods illegally detained, where it was held not only that in fact the magistrate had not awarded any sum by way of special damage, but also that, if he had made any such order, it would have been a nullity for want of jurisdiction, and, therefore, could not have supported a plea of former recovery (per MATHEW J., at p. 174, and WRIGHT J., at pp. 174–5).

[4] See Part I, Chapter IV, para. 117 *et seq. ante*.

[5] In *Smith* v. *Nicolls* (1839), 5 Bing. N.C. 208, the court seems to have inclined to the view that it was for the party setting up the former recovery to allege that the judgment was "binding", in the sense that the tribunal had jurisdiction to pronounce it, but it was not necessary to decide the point, because, first, the judgment was a colonial one, which effects no merger, and secondly, the plaintiff had taken the precaution to plead the want of jurisdiction in his replication. As to the onus, in cases of alleged jurisdiction of the tribunal by custom, of proving the existence of the custom as a fact, and establishing its validity in law, see *Fisher* v. *Lane* (1772), 3 Wils. 297, and *cf.* the estoppel cases cited in the notes to para. 120, *ante*.

CHAPTER XIX

The Doctrine of Merger in Judgment: Finality

446 For the purposes of estoppel *per rem judicatam*, as has already been stated and illustrated in the proper place,[1] the judicial decision relied upon as creating the estoppel must be shown to have been final in both the senses there indicated:[2] that is to say, there is no estoppel if the judicial decision, as recorded, is imperfect, provisional, conditional, indefinite, or ambiguous,[3] or if, though *ex facie* appearing to be final, it is liable, whether at common law, or by statute, to be rescinded, varied, or re-opened by the tribunal which pronounced it.[4]

447 There is no reason why the same rule of finality should not be, and in fact it has always judicially been, applied to cases of "former recovery".[5] The party setting up this plea must allege and, if in controversy, must prove that the judgment relied upon as constituting the bar was complete and final in the sense that there was nothing in its terms which required anything further to be done judicially in order to render it effective and definite as a judgment. Thus, a judgment for damages to be assessed is clearly interlocutory, and is so described in the practice rules, and can never be final, or operate as a bar, unless and until the damages are so assessed by writ of inquiry, or by such other means as may be specified in the judgment.[6] And a judgment which may be rescinded or modified by the same court as that which pronounced it (as distinct from an appellate court) is

---

[1] In part I, Chapter V, *ante*.

[2] See para. 164, *ante*.

[3] This topic is dealt with, and illustrated, in Part I, Chapter V, paras. 165–171, *ante*.

[4] See Part I, Chapter V, paras. 172–174, *ante*.

[5] Accordingly, on the question of what constitutes finality, all the authorities cited in the notes to Part I Chapter V, *ante*, may serve as illustrations to the present chapter.

[6] As was held in *Marston* v. *Phillips* (1863), 9 L.T. 289, and in *Goldrei, Foucard & Son* v. *Sinclair*, [1918] 1 K.B. 180, C.A. (per SARGANT J., at p. 191). *Cf.* the analogous cases of estoppel referred to in para. 166, *ante*.

also wanting in finality: but not in a case where, though one section of a statute renders the judgment liable to such subsequent revision, it appears from other provisions thereof, and its general tenor, that the legislature intended to affix to the judgment the character of finality.[1]

---

[1] *Austin* v. *Mills* (1853), 9 Exch. 288 (*per Cur.*, at p. 293), a case which is cited and abstracted in note 1 on p. 139, *ante*.

CHAPTER XX

The Doctrine of Merger in Judgment: Identity of Causes of Action in the Two Proceedings

448 A former judgment cannot operate as a bar to any subsequent proceedings unless those proceedings are founded upon the same "cause" (in the largest sense of the word, and so including both ground of civil complaint, and criminal offence) as that upon which such former judgment proceeded.

The onus of allegation and proof

449 The burden of alleging,[1] and, having alleged it, of establishing this identity[2] lies upon the party who sets up the former judgment as a bar. Such onus is *prima facie* discharged by production of the record of the judgment, and of the pleadings, if any, in the former proceedings, and by reference to the pleadings (if any) in the second proceedings. If, on the mere comparison of these documents, it appears that the former judgment was in respect of a cause of action, or an offence, which could not, *ex facie*, have been the same as the cause of action, or the offence, on which the subsequent action or prosecution is founded,—which is a question of law,—the plea of former recovery, or (as the case may be) of *autrefois convict*, fails *in limine*.[3] If, however, it appears, on such comparison alone, that there is a possibility of the two causes of action, or the two offences, being

[1] See Chapter XXIV, *post*.

[2] See, generally, the cases cited in the notes to this chapter, for illustrations.

[3] *Wadsworth* v. *Bentley* (1853), 23 L.J. Q.B. 3 (per CROMPTON J., at p. 5: "the record, when produced, must be such as to shew on its face that the cause of action may be the same as that for which the judgment has been recovered in the former action"); *Guest* v. *Warren* (1854), 9 Exch. 379, where the plea set up a previous recovery of damages for assault and false imprisonment, whereas the action to which this plea was pleaded was one of malicious prosecution, and a demurrer to the plea was accordingly allowed (per PARKE, PLATT, and MARTIN B.B., at p. 383).

identical, there being nothing on the face of the documents to negative such possibility, then the plea is valid and adequate in point of law, and the party setting up the plea must proceed to establish the identity as a fact.[1]

450 The plea having averred the identity, it is for the opposite party to allege the absence of such identity, either by pleading *nul tiel record*, if he desires to set up that the effect of the former judgment has been incorrectly stated in the plea so as to show an identity which, on the production of the actual record, will not appear,[2] or by some other form of special replication or reply;[3] and, if any *prima facie* evidence is adduced in support of the identity, it is for him to displace it by counter-evidence, unless he is content to rely solely upon what is disclosed by the record of the two proceedings, when produced.[4]

451 For the purposes of the rule it makes no difference whether the former judgment was, or whether the proceedings in which the question is raised are, of a civil or of a criminal nature. It will be convenient, however, to deal with the subject of identity in connection with civil cases only, in this chapter, and to leave the topic of identity in criminal cases to be discussed in a later separate chapter wherein the plea of *autrefois convict* is examined.[5]

Identity of causes of action in civil proceedings

452 The following are illustrations of the failure to establish the plea of former recovery in civil proceedings by reason of substantial difference in the causes of action. Recovery on a negotiable instrument is no bar to a subsequent action on an instrument under seal whereby the judgment-debtor, jointly with others, has guaranteed payment of the debt for which the negotiable instrument was given:[6] a judgment in an action of defamation does not preclude the plaintiff from afterwards suing the defendant in

---

[1] *Stafford* v. *Clark* (1824), 2 Bing. 377 (per PARK J., at p. 381); *R.* v. *Tancock* (1876), 13 Cox C.C. 217, where a jury was empanelled to try certain issues of fact as to (*inter alia*) whether the person for whose murder the prisoner was being indicted was the person of whose manslaughter he had previously been convicted, and, on the jury finding in the affirmative, DENMAN J. proceeded to deal with the question of the identity of the offences as one of law.

[2] As in *Wadsworth* v. *Bentley*, *supra*; *Buckland* v. *Johnson* (1854), 15 C.B. 145.

[3] As in *Seddon* v. *Tutop* (1796), 6 Term Rep. 607 (replication); *Lord Bagot* v. *Williams* (1824), 3 B. & C. 235 (replication); *Holmes* v. *Wilson* (1839), 10 Ad. & El. 503 (new assignment); *Duke of Brunswick* v. *Pepper* (1848), 2 C. & K. 683 (new assignment).

[4] As in *Wadsworth* v. *Bentley*, *supra*.

[5] Chapter XXII, *post*.

[6] *Drake* v. *Mitchell* (1803), 3 East 251; *Wegg Prosser* v. *Evans*, [1895] 1 Q.B. 108, C.A. (per Lord ESHER M.R., at pp. 111–114, LOPES L.J., at pp. 114–116, and RIGBY L.J., at pp. 116–118), overruling *Cambefort & Co.* v. *Chapman* (1887), 19 Q.B.D. 229, D.C.

respect of another distinct publication of different, or even the same, defamatory matter:[1] judgment in trespass is no bar to a subsequent action for conversion;[2] judgment for damages in respect of acts of a defendant by which a river was polluted was held no bar to a further action for other acts of pollution of the same river;[3] the obtaining of an order by a court of summary jurisdiction for the delivery of illegally detained goods is no bar to a subsequent action for damages for their detention:[4] recovery of damages for assault and false imprisonment does not debar the plaintiff from afterwards suing the same defendant for malicious prosecution:[5] recovery of statutory compensation for loss to the survivors resulting from the death of a person caused by negligence of the defendant, under the Fatal Accidents Act, does not preclude any of the survivors so compensated from afterwards suing the same defendant at common law, in the character of personal representative of the deceased, for damage caused by the same negligence to the person or property of the deceased, for which he could have sued in his lifetime, and by which his estate has been diminished:[6] an Admiralty judgment *in rem* is no bar to a subsequent personal action in a common law court for the recovery of such sum (if any) as has not been realized on the enforcement of the maritime lien, or other security upon the ship, estab-

---

[1] *Duke of Brunswick* v. *Pepper* (1848), 2 C. & K. 683 (different dates and places of publication, and different newspapers); *Wadsworth* v. *Bentley* (1853), 23 L.J. Q.B. 3 (different defamatory matter).

[2] *Lacon* v. *Barnard* (1626), Cro. Car. 35, where the former judgment was for a nominal sum as damages for "taking and driving" (*ceperunt et abduxerunt*) 89 sheep, the property of the plaintiff, and the second action was for trover and conversion of these sheep by sale. The defendant pleaded that the two causes of action "be all one", and the plaintiff, in his replication, having alleged the above distinction, the defendant's demurrer thereto was overruled, on the ground that "both may stand together" (per HUTTON C.J., and HARVEY and COOKE JJ., diss. YELVERTON J., at p. 36).

[3] *Freshwater* v. *Bulmer Rayon Co., Ltd.*, [1933] Ch. 162.

[4] *Midland Rail. Co.* v. *Martin & Co.*, [1893] 2 Q.B. 172, D.C. (per MATHEW J., at p. 174, and WRIGHT J., at pp. 174, 175). Contrast the cases mentioned in note 1 on p. 381, *inf.*, in which both sets of proceedings were civil.

[5] *Guest* v. *Warren* (1854), 9 Exch. 379 (per PARKE, PLATT, and MARTIN BB., at p. 383).

[6] *Pym* v. *Great Northern Rail. Co.* (1863), 4 B. & S. 396 (per ERLE C.J., at p. 407: "the statute, as it appears to me, gives to the personal representative a cause of action beyond that which the deceased would have had if he survived, and based on a different principle"); *Barnett* v. *Lucas* (1872), 6I. C.L.R. 247, where it was held by the Irish Exchequer Chamber that a widow, suing as administratrix for damage for negligence whereby her deceased husband's estate had been diminished, was not debarred from doing so by a former recovery under the statute (*per Cur.*, at p. 255); *Leggott* v. *Great Northern Rail. Co.* (1876), 1 Q.B.D. 599, where, again, a former recovery under the statute was held no bar to an action by an administratrix for damages for personal injuries occasioned to her deceased husband by the defendant's negligence to the detriment of his personal estate: per MELLOR J., at pp. 604, 605, and QUAIN J., at pp. 606, 607; *Daly* v. *Dublin, Wicklow, and Wexford Rail. Co.* (1892), 30 L.R. Ir. 514, a similar case, per Lord ASHBOURNE L.C. (Ir.), at p. 518, and FITZGIBBON L.J. (Ir.), at p. 526. With these cases may be usefully contrasted that of *Read* v. *Great Eastern Rail. Co.* (1868), L.R. 3 Q.B. 555, where in both actions the widow sued for damages occasioned to the deceased during his lifetime, and the former recovery accordingly was held to be a bar to the subsequent proceedings.

lished by the *in rem* judgment, and *vice versa*:[1] a judgment by default against a company for rescission of a contract induced by misrepresentation, and for repayment of a sum of money paid thereunder, does not preclude the plaintiff from proceeding to trial on his other head of claim, in respect of which he has not signed judgment, against the promoter and the company, as joint tortfeasors, for damages for the same misrepresentation but, for the purposes of this head, alleged to be fraudulent:[2] recovery of damages for breach of a term in a contract is no bar to a subsequent action for the breach of another term of the same contract, which breach had not occurred at the time of the former proceedings.[3] And where an owner repossessed a chattel let out under a hire-purchase agreement, and sued the hirer for four instalments already due, the judgment on this claim was held no bar to a subsequent claim for damages for the final ascertained loss after the chattel had been resold.[4]

453 "Two actions may be brought in respect of the same facts, where these facts give rise to two distinct causes of action".[5] But if not only the

---

[1] The relief obtained by an admiralty judgment *in rem* is in the nature of a mortgage, charge, or lien upon the ship, to secure the debt or damages: if the security is insufficient, there is nothing incongruous in afterwards asserting a personal claim for the balance, in a court of common law, nor, after judgment in an action *in personam* is there anything improper in afterwards suing the ship *in rem* in the Admiralty Court, if the personal judgment is not fully satisfied, to establish and enforce a security upon the ship, by which means the unsatisfied balance may be realized: the two causes of action are distinct, and the remedies are cumulative, just as a security on land or chattels is distinct from a personal convenant or promise to pay. For illustrations of a judgment *in rem* in Admiralty, followed by a personal action in some other court, see *Nelson* v. *Couch* (1863), 15 C.B. N.S. 99, where it was held that a previous admiralty judgment against the ship and her freight in an action for collision at sea is no bar to an action in a common law court for the difference between the sum realized on the sale of the vessel and the full amount of the damages (per WILLES J. at pp. 108–111, and BYLES J., at p. 112). It is to be observed that, in accordance with a rule of the Admiralty Court, which may admittedly be productive of hardship, a judgment *in rem is* considered a bar to a subsequent action *in personam* in *that* court: see *The Hope* (1841), 1 W.Rob. 154 (per Dr LUSHINGTON, at pp. 158, 159), and the observations of WILLES J., at pp. 110, 111, of *Nelson* v. *Couch*, *supra*. For instances of the converse case of a common law personal judgment followed, without objection, by an action *in rem* in the Admiralty Court, see *The Bengal* (1859), Sw. 468 (per Dr LUSHINGTON, at p. 470); *The John and Mary* (1859), Swab. 472 (per Dr LUSHINGTON, at p. 473); *Yeo* v. *Tatem* (1871), L.R. 3 P.C. 696, at p. 702, where the principle was fully recognized, but, it being admitted that the plaintiff had been "fully satisfied" by the former personal judgment, he was held to be suing upon the same cause of action for the same remedy, which he was debarred from doing); *The Cella* (1888), 13 P.D. 82, C.A. (per HANNEN P., at p. 85: "an unsatisfied judgment *in personam* is no bar to proceedings *in rem*").

[2] *Goldrei, Foucard & Son* v. *Sinclair*, [1918] 1 K.B. 180, C.A. (per PICKFORD L.J., at pp. 185–188, and SARGANT J., at p. 192).

[3] *Bristowe* v. *Fairclough* (1840), 1 M. & G. 143 (per TINDAL C.J., at pp. 152, 153, and MAULE J., at p. 154). Cp. *Hadley* v. *Green*, *Few* v. *Backhouse*, and *Holmes* v. *Wilson*, cited in note 3 on pp. 379–380, *post*.

[4] *Overstone, Ltd.* v. *Shipway*, [1962] 1 All E.R. 52 C.A.

[5] *Brunsden* v. *Humphrey* (1884), 14 Q.B.D. 141, C.A. (per BRETT M.R., at p. 146). But questions of real difficulty may arise, as to whether the facts in a given case support one, or two, causes of action—*i.e.* whether two claims arise on one cause of action, or whether there are two separate causes of action on the same facts. *In New Zealand*, the Court of Appeal had recently to decide

facts are identical, but these identical facts give rise to substantially one and the same ground of complaint, the plea of former recovery prevails, notwithstanding that there may be technical and formal differences between the two causes of action, or that the two remedies may be called by different names.[1] The test is whether the second proceeding involves a new cause of action or whether it is merely an attempt to recover, on the original cause of action, under some heading of damage not previously invoked.[2] Thus, a judgment in replevin is a bar to a subsequent action under a statute for the taking of excessive distress, if the goods taken are the same, and the act of seizure is the same, in both cases.[3] So also, a recovery for conversion of goods by sale bars the plaintiff from afterwards issuing for the proceeds of that sale, as money had and received, there being no difference, in contemplation of law, between the goods, and the money which after their sale and receipt of the purchase money by the defendant, stood for the goods.[4] Where a plaintiff had obtained judgment for damages "for breach of contract to complete in a good and workmanlike manner" a bungalow, he was held precluded by the principle of *res judicata* from bringing a further action claiming damages for breach of an alleged term in the same contract to build "with proper materials". The particulars of damage were different from those alleged in the first claim; but "here there was but one promise, to complete the bungalow", and the cause of action in both claims was the same.[5] And it has even been held that acceptance by a person aggrieved, of statutory compensation in a court of summary jurisdiction, pursuant to an

whether one or two causes of action arose where, a patient having engaged a dental surgeon to extract certain teeth only, it was alleged that he had (a) extracted not only these but other unauthorised teeth and (b) failed to use due skill in what he did. All that the surgeon *did* was to extract certain teeth; and it was argued that all the damage which flowed from this one act must be contained in one cause of action. The New Zealand Court of Appeal held, however, that two causes of action were involved: *Rowley* v. *Wilkinson*, [1968] N.Z.L.R. 334 C.A. At the time of going to press the same question has agitated the Canadian Courts, and the Supreme Court of Canada in a 1968 decision has turned its back on *Brunsden* v. *Humphrey* (*supra*), holding that all causes of action (in the old sense) which arose out of a given "factual situation" must be litigated in one action, with the consequences as regards the doctrine of *res judicata* which must follow: *Cahoon* v. *Franks* (1967), 63 D.L.R. (2d) 274 (S.C. of Can.).

[1] "In my opinion it must be admitted that the cause of action in the two cases is strictly speaking not the same. On the other hand, the plea of *res judicata* is not a technical doctrine, but a fundamental doctrine based on the view that there must be an end to litigation"—MAUGHAM J. in *Green* v. *Weatherill*, [1929] 2 Ch. 213, at p. 221.

[2] Per FINLAY L.J., explaining the basis of *Brunsden* v. *Humphrey* (1884), 14 Q.B.D. 141 in *Derrick* v. *Williams*, [1939] 2 All E.R. 559, C.A. at p. 566. This was not strictly a case of *res judicata*, but one in which it was sought to initiate new proceedings notwithstanding the acceptance of moneys paid into Court in a previous action on the same facts; but the principle will be found the same.

[3] *Phillips* v. *Berryman* (1783), 3 Doug. K.B. 286 (per Lord MANSFIELD C.J., and WILLES and BULLER JJ., at p. 288).

[4] *Buckland* v. *Johnson* (1854), 15 C.B. 145 (per JERVIS C.J., at p. 161, and MAULE J., at p. 166).

[5] *Conquer* v. *Boot*, [1928] 2 K.B. 336. See also *Alfred Rowntree & Sons, Ltd.* v. *Allen* (1935), 41 Com. Cas. 90, in which GODDARD J. disallowed a second action on the same breach of

order which such a court is empowered by the statute to make, though only to a limited amount, is a bar to a subsequent action to recover damages *ultra*.[1]

454 Where an employer had made a claim for indemnity under the provisions in the Workmen's Compensation Acts which gave him an indemnity from a tort feasor who had injured the employee, it was held that the cause of action accrued due only upon actual payment to the employee; hence that a claim for monies paid to date did not preclude a further claim in respect of the same tortious acts for further compensation monies paid subsequently.[2] Where a plaintiff had sued his employer in the County Court under the Employers Liability Act 1880 (thereby avoiding a possible defence of Common Employment) claiming damages for personal injuries sustained in the course of his employment, and, the maximum amount recoverable under that act having been paid into Court, had uplifted the same in satisfaction, he was held precluded from pursuing a further claim in the High Court for damages at common law, since the causes of action at common law and under the Act were one and the same, the only difference between them being that under the Act the defence of common employment was not available, a "ceiling" being at the same time imposed on the damages recoverable by this procedure.[3]

But where exercising a statutory option pursuant to the provision of the Workmen's Compensation Acts an infant claimant and his next friend, electing to receive instalments of compensation rather than sue for damages at common law, had joined in an agreement with the employer to this end, the agreement being registered in the County Court and by this registration becoming "for all purposes enforceable as a County Court judgment", it was held that such judgment did no more than operate as an estoppel against

---

contract, based on new damage found to have been suffered. "He (plaintiff) can recover in one action for all damage actual or prospective, and if he does not ask for both he cannot afterwards bring a further action for damages for which he omitted to ask in the first action". See further *H. E. Daniels, Ltd.* v. *Carmel Exporters Ltd.*, [1953] 2 Q.B. 242, in which PILCHER J. had before him a second award by arbitrators awarding damages for misdescription of goods, where a previous arbitration had already made an award for defect of quality in respect of the supply of the same goods under the same contract; it would appear from the judgment that, had the plea of *res judicata* been properly before him, or a claim made in the Court (and not under arbitration) the learned judge would have followed and applied *Conquer* v. *Boot* (*supra*).

[1] *Birmingham Corporation* v. *Allsopp* (1919), 119 L.T. 775; the original text cited *Wright* v. *London General Omnibus Co.* (1877), 2 Q.B.D. 271, only to observe of this decision that it was "certainly a startling one". In the 1st edition of this work Mr Spencer Bower devoted a special appendix (Appendix G.) to a detailed criticism of it. This Appendix has been omitted in the present edition; but in the respectful view of the present editor the comment of the original author was justified, since the defendant company was not a party to the first proceeding.

[2] *A.-G.* v. *Arthur Ryan Automobiles, Ltd.*, [1938] 2 K.B. 16, C.A.

[3] *Hills* v. *Co-operative Wholesale Society, Ltd.*, [1940] 2 All E.R. 441 (MACNAGHTEN J.), affirmed by the Court of Appeal in [1940] 3 All E.R. 233.

any further proceedings under the Workmen's Compensation Act, and did not preclude an action for damages at common law, provided that in pursuing such an action the infant plaintiff brought back into account all payments of compensation which he had received. For the Court which registered this agreement, being bound to investigate its circumstances, must be taken to have certified that as regards Workmen's Compensation claims the agreement was for the benefit of the infant; but, having no corresponding duty to consider whether the infant might have a good common law claim, it could not be said to have adjudicated as to whether it was in the infant's interests to surrender or waive any such claim, and accordingly he was not estopped from pursuing it.[1]

455 Where the *same damage* is claimed against the same defendant upon *separate* causes of action, a judgment obtained, but not satisfied, in respect of one cause of action will not be a bar to a subsequent proceeding based on the other; but in so far as either judgment is satisfied credit must be given in respect of the other. If the same damage is claimed against separate defendants against whom a plaintiff has separate causes of action the same rule will apply.[2]

456 Questions of considerable nicety have from time to time arisen on the position of one who, having two causes of action against another, sues and recovers judgment upon one of them only. Is a plaintiff who had adopted such a course deemed to have recovered on both causes of action, or is he entitled to reserve for future proceedings the cause of action on which he has omitted to sue, without rendering himself liable to the bar of former recovery? And does it make any difference whether this omission was intentional and deliberate, or due to mere carelessness, accident, or mistake? The answer to these questions must be gathered from a number of authorities, some of which are, perhaps, not very easy to reconcile with one another. On the one hand, it is undoubtedly true that "there is no positive law (except so far as the County Court Acts have from a very early date dealt with the matter) against splitting demands which are essentially separable".[3] In other words, at common law, a man who has not in fact obtained judgment on a particular cause of action is not deemed in law to have done so, merely because he has recovered judgment on another cause of action as the result of proceedings in which he might have sued on the first cause of action also, provided that the two causes of action are "essentially separate" and distinct. And, if this is the only real test to apply for

---

[1] *Arabian* v. *Tuffnall and Taylor*, [1944] 2 All E.R. 317; [1944] K.B. 685 (WROTTESLEY J.).

[2] *Isaacs & Sons* v. *Salbstein*, [1916] 2 K.B. 139 C.A.; *in Australia*, *Bucknell* v. *O'Donnell* (1922), 31 C.L.R. 40 (H. Ct. of Aus.).

[3] Per BOWEN L.J., at p. 151 of *Brunsden* v. *Humphrey* (1884), 14 Q.B.D. 141, C.A.

the purpose of determining whether there is a bar to further proceedings on the omitted cause of action, it is not, technically or theoretically, material whether the conduct of the plaintiff was vexatious and oppressive, or excusably blundering or mistaken. But any concession to the party of his full legal right to "split his demands" which would result in multiplication of costs and aggravation of the burden of litigation is not accorded by the courts without the fullest and most sympathetic consideration being first bestowed upon those numerous "questions of great delicacy"[1] which nearly always arise in such cases; and, further, even when it cannot be judicially held that there is any bar, there is always an inherent jurisdiction in every court of the land to prevent, or (by special order as to costs) to penalize, an abuse of its process.[2]

457 Whenever, on the application of the above test to a case of "split demands", it has appeared that the demand not made the subject of the previous proceedings and judgment was essentially distinct from the demand which was made the subject thereof, it has always been held that the plaintiff was not debarred from asserting the former in a subsequent action.[3] And the same rule applied to awards as to judgments.[4]

[1] As was observed by Lord KENYON C.J., at p. 609 of *Seddon* v. *Tutop* (1796), 6 Term Rep. 607.

[2] As was pointed out by BOWEN L.J., at pp. 147, 148, and p. 151, of *Brunsden* v. *Humphrey*, *supra*. Generally, as to the inherent jurisdiction of the court in these matters, see Appendix A, *post*.

[3] As in *Seddon* v. *Tutop* (1796), 6 Term Rep. 607, where the plaintiff, having sued on a promissory note, and also for the price of goods sold and delivered, had judgment by default for both causes of action, but, on executing the writ of inquiry, not being prepared with proof on the second cause of action, took a verdict on the first only, and it was held that he was not thereby precluded from afterwards suing on the second (per Lord KENYON C.J., and GROSE J., at p. 609); *Hennell* v. *Fairlamb* (1800), 3 Esp. 104 (plaintiff held entitled to sue for balance of debt after deducting sum previously recovered by set off: per Lord KENYON C.J., at p. 105); *Hadley* v. *Green* (1832), 2 Cr. & J. 374 (per Lord LYNDHURST C.B., at pp. 375, 376, and BAYLEY B., at pp. 376, 377); *Few* v. *Backhouse* (1838), 8 Ad. & El. 789 (*per Cur.*, at p. 795); *Holmes* v. *Wilson* (1839), 10 Ad. & El. 503 (per Lord DENMAN C.J., at p. 511: "the former and the present action are for different trespasses. The former was for erecting the buttresses. This action was for continuing the buttresses so erected. The continued use of the buttresses for the support of the road, under such circumstances, was a fresh trespass"); *Florence* v. *Jenings* (1857), 2 C.B. N.S. 454, an action on a bill of exchange, in respect of which the defendant had agreed to pay a special rate of interest, if not honoured at maturity, but the plaintiff, having sued on the bill with ordinary commercial interest, without mentioning the special rate, took judgment therefor on the defendant's default, and was held to have precluded himself by such judgment from afterwards suing for the specially agreed rate of interest down to the date of the judgment, but not from recovering the amount payable at such special rate since the date (per COCKBURN C.J., at p. 466); *Gibbs* v. *Cruikshank* (1873), L.R. 8 C.P. 454, where the plaintiff having recovered damages in an action of replevin in the county court in respect of certain goods, though barred thereby from afterwards suing for damages for trespass thereto (per BRETT J., at p. 464: "he *could have* recovered the damage which he now claims: that he did not recover them is immaterial"), was held not precluded from recovering damages for trespass to the land on which the goods seized were at the date of seizure (per BOVILL C.J., at pp. 460, 461, KEATING J., at p. 462, and GROVE J., at p. 464); *Brunsden* v. *Humphrey* (1884), 14 Q.B.D. 141, C.A., where the plaintiff, having sued for damages for injury to his cab in a collision caused by the defendant's negligence, and

Footnote 4 on p. 380.

458 On the other hand, where there is substantially only one cause of action, and it is a case, not of "splitting separable demands", but of splitting one demand into two quantitative parts, the plea is sustained. In homely phrase, a party is entitled to swallow two separate cherries in successive gulps, but not to take two bites at the same cherry. He cannot limit his claim to a part of one homogeneous whole, and treat the inseparable residue as available for future use, like the good spots in the curate's egg. And it is immaterial how innocent, or even praiseworthy, his motives may have been in adopting this course, just as, conversely, in the cases where the demands are distinct, it does not signify how bad his motives may have been. Thus, where the omitted matter is a portion of the entire sum, or an item or parcel of the entire property, recoverable on a single cause of action, the judgment is a bar to any subsequent action in respect of such omitted matter.[1] So also, where there is only one right invaded, and one

---

taken a judgment for a small sum paid into court, was held entitled to sue for, and recover, damages in a second action for personal injuries to himself which had developed since the date of the former judgment (per BRETT M.R., at pp. 144–146, and BOWEN L.J., at pp. 146–152); *Clarke* v. *Midland and Great Western Rail. Co.*, [1895] 2 I.R. 294 (where a former judgment for damages for trespass was held no bar to a subsequent action for further acts of trespass after the date of the judgment). In *The Oropesa* [1943] P. 32 the Court of Appeal approved a decision of LANGTON J. at first instance reported in [1942] P. 140, holding that the parents of a seaman who had been drowned in a marine disaster were entitled to sue as his administrators under the Law Reform Act and as persons entitled under Lord Campbell's Act notwithstanding that as his personal representatives they had in a previous proceeding recovered property damage arising from the loss of his kit and equipment. But notice the recent Canadian case of *Cahoon* v. *Franks* (1967), 63 D.L.R. (2d) 274 (Supreme Court of Canada), reported as this volume goes to press, in which first the appellate division of the Supreme Court of Alberta, and then the Supreme Court of Canada declined to follow *Brunsden* v. *Humphrey* (*supra*) and held that property damage aud personal injury arising out of one tortious act gave only one cause of action.

[4] In the following cases a former award in favour of the plaintiff was held no bar to a subsequent action in respect of matters not submitted to, or in fact dealt with, by the arbitral tribunal:—*Golightly* v. *Jellicoe* (1769), 4 Term Rep. 147 n.; *Ravee* v. *Farmer* (1791), 4 Term Rep. 146 (per BULLER J., at p. 147); *Thorpe* v. *Cooper* (1828), 5 Bing. 116, Ex. Ch. (per BEST C.J., at pp 129, 130); *Gueret* v. *Audouy* (1893), 62 L.J. Q.B. 633 (per LOPES L.J., at pp. 635–637, and A.L. SMITH L.J., at pp. 637–640); *E. E. and Brian Smith* (1928) *Ltd.* v. *Wheatsheaf Mills, Ltd.*, [1939] 2 K.B. 302 (BRANSON J.).

[1] As in *Lord Bagot* v. *Williams* (1824), 3 B. & C. 235, where the plaintiff, having a claim against his agent for £7,000 money had and received, had sued for, and recovered, £4,000 only of that sum, in the belief that this was all that the defendant could then pay, and it was held that the former judgment barred him from afterwards recovering the balance of £3,000 (per ABBOTT C.J., at p. 240, and BAYLEY J., at pp. 240, 241, distinguishing *Seddon* v. *Tutop*, *supra*); *Russell & Sons* v. *Waterford and Limerick Rail. Co.* (1885), 16 L.R. Ir. 314, where the plaintiff, having a claim against the defendants for negligence in the carriage of 8½ sacks of flour, had sued, and taken a judgment, in respect of 6 sacks only, and was held precluded from afterwards suing in respect of the residue (per DOWSE B., at pp. 320, 321); *Sanders* v. *Hamilton* (1907), 96 L.T. 679, D.C., where a former judgment for £14 in detinue, though the real claim was for £35, was held a bar to the subsequent recovery of the residue (per DARLING J., at p. 679, and A. T. LAWRENCE J., at p. 680); *Furness, Withy & Co., Ltd.* v. *J. & E. Hall, Ltd.* (1909), 25 T.L.R. 233 (omission of an item of indemnity claimable in former proceedings: per CHANNELL J., at pp. 234, 235). *Cf.* the arbitration case of *Dunn* v. *Murray* (1829), 9 B. & C. 780, where the plaintiff, who had neglected to bring before the arbitrator one of the matters or items in dispute, and had obtained an award on the others, was held barred from afterwards recovering in respect of the omitted item

ground of complaint (*e.g.* detention of shares), a plaintiff who asks for and obtains one form of remedy, with which he is content (*e.g.* an injunction), is precluded from afterwards suing for further relief, such as damages for the detention.[1] Again, where there has been one act on the defendant's part giving rise to a claim for damages, which are assessed at the trial once for all and are given not only for past, but also all probable future, consequences of the injurious act, any recovery of such damages bars the plaintiff from a second recovery of further damages in respect of supervening and, it may be, entirely unforeseen, injuries resulting from the same act, as distinct from further damages for fresh acts of the same character, as in the case of a continuing trespass or nuisance. An extreme instance, but all the more striking because of its extremity (since a decision which will stand the strain of an attempted *reductio ad absurdum* will stand anything), is to be found in an ancient authority, never overruled, but on the contrary cited with approval in later judgments, the facts of which were that the plaintiff, having recovered damages "for an assault and battery in a drunken brawl", eight years afterwards sued the same defendant for further damages for that, since the judgment, "part of his skull by reason of the said battery had come out of his head". The defendant pleaded former recovery, to which the plaintiff demurred. It was strenuously argued for the defendant that the injury to the skull constituted a new cause of action.

> "*Quod Holt negavit.* And, *per totam curiam*, the jury in the former action considered the nature of the wound, and gave damages for all the damages that it had done to the plaintiff; and, therefore, a recovery in the said action is good here",

and, in the result, "the plaintiff could not obtain judgment, the Court inclining strongly against him",—which, we are to assume, was the reporter's polite way of indicating that the demurrer was overruled.[2] So also, in the case above referred to as to detention of shares, it was pointed

---

or matter (per Lord TENTERDEN C.J., at p. 788). See also *Derrick* v. *Williams*, [1939] 2 All E.R. 559—a case of payment into Court, and hence strictly not *res judicata*; but it is submitted that the principle will be the same—in which FINLAY L.J. said, explaining *Brunsden* v. *Humphrey* (1884), 14 Q.B.D. 141 C.A., at p. 566: "For a separate action or a reopening of the former action—it matters not which may be pursued— . . . the essential distinction, which is a perfectly obvious one, is between a distinct cause of action and some head of damages."

[1] *Serrao* v. *Noel* (1885), 15 Q.B.D. 549, C.A. (per Lord ESHER M.R., at pp. 557, 558, BAGGALAY L.J., at p. 559, and BOWEN L.J., at pp. 559, 560). *Cf. Gibbs* v. *Cruikshank* (1873), L.R. 8 C.P. 454, so far as it relates to the goods seized.

[2] *Fetter (or Ferrer)* v. *Beal (or Beale)* (1697), 1 Ld. Raym. 339, 692 (*per Cur.*, at pp. 339, 340, and again, at pp. 692, 693). This case was thus distinguished in *Holmes* v. *Wilson* (1839), 10 Ad. & El. 503, by Starkie (arguing for the plaintiff) with the approval of the Court: "the distinction is between an action for damages consequential upon an injury for which the plaintiff has already recovered a judgment, as in *Fetter* v. *Beale*, and an action for a continuing injury, repeated *de die in diem*". *Cf. Clarke* v. *Yorke* (1882), 52 L.J. Ch. 32 (per PEARSON J., at p. 34).

out that the plaintiff might, in the former proceedings, have recovered damages, not only for the original detention, but for any continued detention after the judgment, and until the shares should be redelivered.[1]

459 Questions as to the identity of a cause of action against one of two joint contractors with a cause of action against the other, are considered at a later stage, in the course of the discussion of the subject of parties.[2]

Identity of offences in criminal proceedings

460 The application of the requirement of identity to offences charged in successive criminal proceedings, the first of which has resulted in a conviction, is dealt with in a separate chapter[3] in which the plea of *autrefois convict* is discussed.

---

1 *Serrao* v. *Noel* (1885), 15 Q.B.D. 549, C.A., per BOWEN L.J., at p. 559.
2 See Chapter XXI, paras. 464 *et seq. post.*
3 Chapter XXII, *post.*

CHAPTER XXI

The Doctrine of Merger in Judgment: Identity of Parties in the Two Proceedings

Introductory

461 Just as there can be no estoppel *per rem judicatam*,[1] so also there can be no bar by former recovery, unless it be established that the parties to the former proceedings (or their privies) were identical, physically, or in contemplation of law, with the parties to the proceedings in which the question is raised.[2]

General Rules as to proof of identity of parties

462 It very rarely happens that the physical identity of a party is in issue: but, whenever such a matter is controverted, it must be established by the party setting up the plea of former recovery (or its criminal equivalent, *autrefois convict*) as a fact.[3]

463 One who, though in name a party to both proceedings, is shewn to have litigated in different characters or capacities is, in contemplation of law, not one person, but two. Though physically the same, he is jurally a different person in the second litigation from the person he was in the first, or, in the more accurate phraseology of the civilians, he wears separate and distinct *personae*, and plays separate and distinct parts, in the two proceedings; whence it follows that a judgment recovered by him in one character cannot be set up as a bar to a claim subsequently made by him for the same

[1] See Part I, Chapter VII, *ante*, the whole of the first part of which (together with the authorities cited in the notes thereto) may be resorted to in support and illustration of the present discussion.

[2] *Isaacs & Sons* v. *Salbstein*, [1916] 2 K.B. 139, C.A. (per SWINFEN EADY L.J., at pp. 149, 150, and BANKES L.J., at pp. 154, 155.

[3] *R.* v. *Tancock* (1876), 13 Cox C.C. 217, a case of *autrefois convict*, where a jury was empanelled, by direction of DENMAN J., to try two issues, one of which was whether the prisoner was the same man who had been convicted on the former occasion.

relief in another character,[1] any more than in estoppel cases, where a similar diversity of *personae* appears, a *res judicata* can be set up as an estoppel.[2] Conversely, whenever the former judgment has been recovered by one who, though physically distinct from the plaintiff in the subsequent proceedings, is yet united to him in interest, as in the case of two common informers, both representing the public in a sense,[3] there is, in contemplation of law, one *persona* only, and the identity of parties is accordingly established. There is, of course, no diversity of *personae* within the meaning of the above rule, merely because the party litigates as plaintiff in one of the proceedings, and in the other as counterclaimant,[4] or by way of set-off.[5]

Effect of a former judgment against one of two persons jointly liable

464 This class of case raises a variety of questions, formerly of considerable importance, but now not so important, to the solution of which much judicial attention has been devoted. It will accordingly receive some separate attention. First, as to persons jointly liable in contract. The general rule established by the authorities is that, where two or more persons are *jointly* liable in contract to another, a judgment recovered by that other against any one of the joint contractors, being in contemplation of law a judgment against all of them, debars the judgment creditor from instituting any subsequent proceedings against the other joint debtor, or debtors, for the debt or sum which is the subject of such joint contractual liability;[6] *secus*, where the liability was not purely joint, but joint and several.[7]

---

[1] See the cases cited in note 6 on p. 374, *ante*, in which it was held that a plaintiff obtaining compensation under the Fatal Accidents Act for the loss occasioned to the defendants by the death of the deceased is a different *persona*, because suing in a different character, from the same person, physically, suing as personal representative for damages which the deceased could have made the subject of an action in his lifetime. *Cf. Marginson* v. *Blackburn Borough Council*, [1939] 2 K.B. 426, C.A.

[2] See para. 232, Chapter VII, *ante*, and the cases cited in note 3 on p. 203, *ante*.

[3] As in *Girdlestone* v. *Brighton Aquarium Co.* (1879), 4 Ex.D. 107, C.A., where, though the plea of former recovery failed, the sole ground of the failure was that the former judgment had been obtained by collusion: no one disputed that the two informers constituted in law one *persona*, though physically distinct. *Cf.* the estoppel cases cited in note 3 on p. 204, *ante*.

[4] As in *Midland Rail. Co.* v. *Martin & Co.*, [1893] 2 Q.B. 172, D.C., where, however, the plea failed on the ground that identity of the causes of action was not established.

[5] See *Hennell* v. *Fairlamb* (1800), 3 Esp. 104 (per Lord KENYON C.J.), as to so much of the set-off as was required to countervail the claim in the former action.

[6] *Lechmere* v. *Fletcher* (1833), 1 Cr. & M. 623 (per BAYLEY J., at p. 635); *King* v. *Hoare* (1844), 13 M. & W. 494 (per PARKE B., at pp. 504–507); *Re Tyler, Ex parte Higgins* (1858), 3 De G. & J. 33 (per KNIGHT-BRUCE L.J., at pp. 37, 38, and TURNER L.J., at pp. 38, 39); *Kendall* v. *Hamilton* (1879), 4 App. Cas. 504, H.L. (per Lord O'HAGAN, at p. 533, Lord SELBORNE, at p. 540, and Lord BLACKBURN, at pp. 542–544); *Re Hodgson* (1885), 31 Ch.D. 177, C.A.; *Hammond* v. *Schofield*, [1891] 1 Q.B. 453, D.C. (per WILLS J., at p. 455, and VAUGHAN WILLIAMS J., at pp. 456, 457); *Hoare* v. *Niblett*, [1891] 1 Q.B. 781, D.C. (per A. L. SMITH J., at p. 782); *McLeod* v. *Power*, [1898] 2 Ch. 295 (per BYRNE J., at pp. 298, 299).

[7] *King* v. *Hoare*, *supra* (per PARKE B., at p. 505). Where the instrument does not expressly describe the liability as "joint", or as "several", or as "joint and several", the whole terms and

465 In tort, the same rule formerly applied, and a judgment against one of several *joint* tort-feasors precluded further proceedings against any other or others of them in respect of the same cause of action;[1] but this rule was abrogated by s. 17 of the Law Reform (Married Women and Tort-feasors) Act 1935, which now provides of judgments against one of several persons jointly liable in tort:

> "Where damage is suffered by any person as the result of a tort (whether a crime or not) . . . judgment recovered against any tort-feasor liable in respect of that damage shall not be a bar to an action against any other person who would, if sued, have been liable as a joint tort-feasor in respect of the same damage".[2]

466 As to liability in tort, then, the position of joint tort-feasors is assimilated to that of concurrent tort-feasors whose separate torts have caused or contributed to the same damage. In such cases, and in the case of persons severally liable in contract, the fact that judgment has been entered against one of them cannot preclude subsequent proceedings, to judgment, against the other or others.[3] When the stage of execution or satisfaction is reached, however, it is necessary that whatever is received on account of one of the judgments shall be properly taken into account on the other, so that the same damage or debt is not the subject of double payment;[4] but this is a subject matter of the law of appropriation, rather than one for consideration in a treatise on *res judicata*.

Theory and effect of the doctrine as regards persons jointly liable in contract

467 We now revert to the limited area in which the doctrine of *res judicata* will still serve to preclude proceedings against one of several

---

tenor of such instrument must be examined for the ascertainment of the parties' intention: *Parr* v. *Snell*, [1923] 1 K.B. 1, C.A. (per Lord STERNDALE M.R., at pp. 4, 5, and SCRUTTON L.J. at pp. 9, 10); *B. O. Morris, Ltd.* v. *Perrott and Bolton*, [1945] 1 All E.R. 567, C.A.

[1] In the first edition of this work (at p. 201) Mr Spencer Bower cites, in support of this proposition, at that time still good law: *Brown* v. *Wootton* (1695), Cro. Jac. 73; (joint conversion); *King* v. *Hoare*, *supra* (per PARKE B., at p. 506, as to joint torts generally); *Buckland* v. *Johnson* (1854), 15 C.B. 145 (joint conversion or trover: *per* JERVIS C.J., at p. 164); *Brinsmead* v. *Harrison* (1872), L.R. 7 C.P. 547, Ex. Ch. (joint detinue). In *Brown* v. *Wootton*, *supra*, at p. 68 of the report in Yelverton, a similar case, *Hickman* v. *Poyns* (joint battery) is referred to, as having been decided by the K.B. in "this very term", and joint trespass is also mentioned as another illustration of the rule.

[2] *In New Zealand*, s. 17 of the Law Reform Act 1936 contains a subsection in identical terms.

[3] *Isaacs & Sons* v. *Salbstein*, [1916] 2 K.B. 139, C.A. at p. 143; *United Australia, Ltd.* v. *Barclays Bank, Ltd.*, [1941] A.C. 1, H.L. *In Australia* see *Bucknell* v. *O'Donnell* (1922), 31 C.L.R. 40 (H. Ct. of Aus.). *A fortiori* where the torts committed are not concurrent, but successive, though contributing to the same aggregate damage—see *Freshwater* v. *Bulmer Rayon Co., Ltd.*, [1933] Ch. 162 (successive acts of pollution of the same river by different defendants).

[4] *United Australia, Ltd.* v. *Barclays Bank, Ltd.*, [1941] A.C. 1, H.L. per Lord ATKIN at p. 28: "He obviously could not compel the wrongdoer to recoup him for his losses twice over". The point is expressly covered in *B.O. Morris, Ltd.* v. *Perrott and Bolton*, [1945] 1 All E.R. 567.

persons jointly liable by reason of judgment having been entered against another of them. This consequence, as we have said, is now confined to the case of persons jointly liable *ex contractu*, and this and the following passages in the text must be read, since the passing of the Act of 1935, as exclusively applicable to such cases.[1]

468 The rule is not to be accounted for, or justified, or at all events not completely so, by considerations either of public policy, or of private justice as between the parties and the desirability of protecting them from oppressive multiplication of suits, though, as has been already explained,[2] these considerations constitute one, and not the least important, of the theoretical foundations on which the doctrine of former recovery in general is based. There would obviously be nothing on the face of it very unfair or oppressive in allowing a creditor who has obtained a judgment against A., without any appreciation of the fact that B. was jointly liable with A., or even of B.'s existence, and whose judgment is entirely unexecuted and unsatisfied, to sue B. afterwards, as soon as his joint liability is discovered; and yet, as will be seen presently,[3] this is precisely what according to the authorities he is precluded from doing. Nor can the rule in question be satisfactorily explained as a case of estoppel by election between two alternatively liable persons, which is a well-known application of the doctrine of estoppel by representation,[4] because, if this were the underlying principle, the estoppel would be defeated in the case supposed by proof that the judgment creditor was unaware of the alternative liability, or of his right of choice between two persons,[5] which circumstance, however, as will be noted immediately,[6] does not in the slightest degree affect the applicability or stringency of the special rule.

469 The only theory, therefore, on which the rule can be scientifically explained, if not ethically justified, is the other of the two main suggested bases of the doctrine of former recovery in general,[7] *viz.* the metaphysical theory of *transit in rem judicatam*, or the merger of the original cause of

---

[1] *In New Zealand*, this consequence does not obtain—the rule was abrogated in 1904 by the provisions now appearing in s. 94 of the Judicature Act 1908, in which it is provided that a judgment against one or more of several persons jointly liable shall not operate as a bar or defence to an action on another proceeding against any such persons against whom judgment has not been recovered, except to the extent to which the judgment has been satisfied.

[2] In paras. 425, 426, *ante*.

[3] See paras. 470, 471, *infra*.

[4] This topic is discussed in the authors' *Law of Estoppel by Representation* 2 Ed. Ch. XIII.

[5] *Kendall* v. *Hamilton* (1879), 4 App. Cas. 504, H.L. (per Lord CAIRNS L.C., at p. 515, and Lord BLACKBURN, at p. 542).

[6] See para. 470, *infra*.

[7] See para. 427, *ante*.

action in something which is of a higher nature.[1] Or, putting it in another way, where judgment has been obtained against A. alone, B. being jointly liable with him, and an action is afterwards brought against B., B. has a right in such second action to have A. joined with him as a defendant, of which right he is deprived where the plaintiff has disabled himself by the former judgment, and the merger which it has effected, from suing A. again.[2]

470 It follows from the adoption of the theory of merger, as the only true groundwork and explanation of the rule, that it is quite immaterial whether the plaintiff, when recovering against one of the two jointly liable persons, did or did not believe that the defendant was the only person liable to him.[3]

471 It is also a consequence of the rule, interpreted in the light of the above theory, that, as indeed in all other cases of former recovery,[4] the fact that the former judgment, at the time of the second action, remains wholly, or partly, unexecuted, unsatisfied, and infructuous, in no way defeats or impairs its operation as a bar.[5]

472 Where X. and Y. are jointly liable in contract to A., and A., after recovering judgment against X. only, enters into a collusive arrangement with him, without the consent or privity of Y., that an order of the court shall be, and it is accordingly, made, setting aside the judgment, and granting leave to amend the writ by adding Y. as a co-defendant, the right of Y. to set up the plea of former recovery to the action founded on the amended writ remains of course entirely unaffected.[6]

473 It makes no difference at common law,[7] whether the former judgment against one of two joint contractors, was recovered in a separate and independent action against that one, or was taken or signed in the

---

1 *King* v. *Hoare* (1844), 13 M. & W. 494 (per PARKE B., at p. 504: "there is only one cause of action, whether it be against a single person or many", and this one "cause of action is changed into matter of record which is of a higher nature, and the inferior remedy is merged in the higher"); *Kendall* v. *Hamilton*, *supra*, as cited in note 6 on p. 384, *supra*.

2 *Kendall* v. *Hamilton* (1879), 4 App.Cas. 504, H.L. (per Lord CAIRNS L.C., at pp. 515, 516).

3 *Ibid.* (per Lord CAIRNS L.C., at p. 523, and Lord BLACKBURN, at p. 544, who there observes that the hardship upon a plaintiff who was unaware of the joint liability is not really so great as, at first sight, it may appear to be, because the right which he loses through no fault of his own, but "by pure bad luck", is a right which he acquired without any merits of his own, by operation of law, and so "by pure good luck").

4 See note 5 on p. 365, *ante*.

5 *King* v. *Hoare* (1844), 13 M. & W. 494 (per PARKE B., at p. 504); *Buckland* v. *Johnson* (1854), 15 C.B. 145 (per JERVIS C.J., at pp. 164, 165).

6 *Hammond* v. *Schofield*, [1891] 1 Q.B. 453, D.C. (per WILLS J., at p. 456, and VAUGHAN WILLIAMS J., at pp. 458, 459).

7 For the statutory exceptions to the common law rule, see para. 476, *post*.

course of an action brought against both, whether by consent, or default, or otherwise.[1]

474 Where one is personally liable to another in contract on a particular instrument or cause of action, and also liable, jointly with others, on another instrument or cause of action, a judgment on the former instrument or cause of action is no bar to a subsequent action on the latter against the other party or parties to the joint obligation;[2] just as one of two persons jointly liable is not estopped from disputing the correctness of a judgment previously obtained against the other on any ground which, if he had then been joined as a defendant, would have afforded him a defence of a purely personal nature.[3]

475 Attempts have been made from time to time to induce the courts to extend the principle and benefit of this rule to relations which, whatever else they import, do not import joint liability. All such attempts have failed. Thus, it has been held that two persons related to one another as principal and surety, the liability of the one being primary, and of the other secondary, cannot possibly be described as jointly responsible to the creditor;[4] and that the relation of husband and wife does not, as such, involve any joint liability, being, at most, a *prima facie* relation of principal and agent, between whom the creditor may elect,[5] though of course the two spouses, like any other two persons, may be shewn by evidence to

---

[1] As in *Hoare* v. *Niblett*, [1891] 1 Q.B. 781, D.C.; *Weall* v. *James* (1893), 68 L.T. 515, C.A. (where the view expressed by LOPES L.J., to the contrary, at p. 516, was personal to himself, not in the least necessary to the decision, and not concurred in by either Lord ESHER M.R., or LINDLEY L.J.); and the husband and wife cases cited in note 5, *infra*.

[2] *Drake* v. *Mitchell* (1803), 3 East 251, where a judgment signed against one of three joint covenantors, not on the joint covenant, but on a bill of exchange accepted by him individually, was held no bar to an action afterwards brought against the three covenantors on the deed; *Wegg Prosser* v. *Evans*, [1895] 1 Q.B. 108, C.A. (judgment on cheque of one of two joint guarantors, held no bar to subsequent action against both guarantors on the instrument of joint suretyship (per Lord ESHER M.R., at pp. 111–114, LOPES L.J., at pp. 114, 115, and RIGBY L.J., at pp. 116–118), following, and applying, *Drake* v. *Mitchell*, *supra* and overruling *Cambefort & Co.* v. *Chapman* (1887), 19 Q.B.D. 229, D.C., in which, for no sufficient reason, FIELD and MANISTY JJ., had departed from the principle of the earlier case.

[3] See note 1 on p. 203, Chapter VII, *ante*.

[4] *Bermondsey Vestry* v. *Ramsey* (1871), L.R. 6 C.P. 247 (judgment obtained by local authority against owner of land for his assessed proportion of paving expenses, recoverable against "any present or future owner or occupier", by ss. 77, 96, of the Metropolis Management (Amendment) Act 1862, held no bar to a subsequent action against the occupier, the two statutory remedies being cumulative and independent, and the occupier and the owner being related to one another as principal and surety, rather than as persons under a joint liability: *per Cur.*, at pp. 251, 252).

[5] *Beck* v. *Pierce* (1889), 23 Q.B.D. 316, C.A. (per LINDLEY L.J., delivering the judgment of the Court, at p. 321); *Morel Brothers* v. *Earl and Countess of Westmorland*, [1904] A.C. 11, H.L. (per Lord HALSBURY L.C., at p. 14, and Lord DAVEY, at p. 15); *French* v. *Howie*, [1906] 2 K.B. 674, C.A.; *Moore* v. *Flanagan*, [1920] 1 K.B. 919, C.A.

have in fact made themselves by contract, or by conduct, jointly liable to the plaintiff in the particular case.[1]

Where in respect of the misapplication of the same sum of £5,000 one person was liable to the plaintiff as a stakeholder of that sum and another separately as the drawer of a cheque in the same amount, it was held that judgment against one did not bar the plaintiff from taking judgment against the other, and proceeding to execution upon it, so long as there was not double recovery of the sum claimed.[2]

476 It must be noticed, however, that statutory exemptions from the operation of the rule stated above are accorded to plaintiffs by three Practice regulations, in the circumstances therein respectively stated. The first of these provides that where a writ is indorsed with a claim against a defendant for a liquidated demand only, then, if that defendant fails to enter an appearance, the plaintiff may, after the time limited for appearing, enter final judgment against that defendant for a sum not exceeding that claimed in the writ and for costs, and may proceed with the action against any other defendants sued, notwithstanding the fact of his having taken such judgment.[3] By successive rules of the same Order a similar provision is made in the cases of claims in detinue or for possession of land; and in the case of a claim for unliquidated damages, provision is made for the entry of interlocutory judgment. In all these cases it is provided that the entry of such judgment as is taken shall not preclude the plaintiff from proceeding against the other defendant or defendants.[4]

The second of the regulations to which we have referred provides that in a case where more than one defendant is sued, and it appears to the court that any defendant has no defence, the plaintiff may apply to the court for a judgment against that defendant, and may, that judgment notwithstanding, proceed with the action against any other defendant or defendants.[5] The third extends the application of the first of these provisions to cases where default has been made by a defendant in serving a defence on the plaintiff

[1] See *Hoare* v. *Niblett*, [1891] 1 Q.B. 781, D.C., where the joint liability was established, and *Morel Brothers* v. *Earl and Countess of Westmorland*, *supra*, where the attempt to establish it failed.

[2] *B. O. Morris, Ltd.* v. *Perrott and Bolton*, [1945] 1 All E.R. 567, C.A.

[3] R.S.C. (1965) O. 13 r. 1. *McLeod* v. *Power*, [1898] 2 Ch. 295 is a case under the corresponding Rule formerly in force; but in that case BYRNE J. at p. 300 pointed out that the facts did not bring the case within the Rule, or that referred to in the next note.

[4] The supplementary provisions may be found in R.S.C. (1965) O. 13, rr. 3, 4, 22, respectively.

[5] R.S.C. (1965), O. 14, r. 1, r. 8. The corresponding rules formerly in force were O. 14, rr. 1 & 5 of the 1883 Code. Under these rules, in *Weall* v. *James* (1893), 68 L.T. 515, C.A., the plaintiff was held to have brought himself within the protection of the rule (per Lord ESHER, M.R., at pp. 515, 516, LINDLEY L.J., at p. 516, and LOPES L.J., at p. 516). In *McLeod* v. *Power*, *supra*, the case was not within the rule. In *Morel Brothers* v. *Earl and Countess of Westmorland*, *supra*, it was recognised that, if the joint liability of husband and wife had been established, which it had not been, the rule would have operated.

within the time fixed by the rules, in cases where the claim is for a liquidated demand only.[1]

Persons alternatively liable: election

477 Where one, and one only, of two persons is liable at the option of a plaintiff, and he elects to take judgment against one of them, his doing so will extinguish his cause of action against the other. *Transit in rem judicatam.*[2] Thus where an agent had contracted on behalf of an undisclosed principal, but the other party to the contract, having subsequently discovered the fact of agency and the identity of the principal, sued the latter and obtained judgment, it was held that he could not subsequently sue the agent, for the liability of the agent had been extinguished by the taking of judgment against the principal.[3] So, too, where proceedings were taken against both principal and agent, and, the agent not defending, judgment was taken by default against him, it was held that the action could not proceed against the principal, for the cause of action against him had disappeared.[4] Again where forwarding agents, in disregard of the owner's instructions, delivered goods to a customer, and the owner thereupon sued the customer for the price, and obtained judgment, he was thereby held precluded from subsequently suing the forwarding agents for conversion of the goods.[5]

But the principle above referred to has no application unless the plaintiff is put to his election by the circumstances of the case; cases frequently arise where it may be competent for a plaintiff to sue several persons independently for what may be the same damage. In such a case the plaintiff is not necessarily called upon to elect, the only limitation placed upon him being that he may not recover his damage more than once—*i.e.* if and in so far as he is *paid* by one or other of those liable to him, he must give to the others credit for what he has received.[6]

---

1 R.S.C. (1965) O. 19, r. 2. Rr. 3, 4, and 5, of this Order deal with unliquidated demands and claims in detinue and for possession of land. The corresponding Rules formerly in force were O. 27, Rr. 3 *et seq.* Mr Spencer Bower's note on the old rules refers to *Parr* v. *Snell*, [1923] 1 K.B. 1 C.A.

2 *Morel Brothers & Co., Ltd.* v. *Earl of Westmorland*, [1904] A.C. 11 H.L.; *R.M.K.R.M.* v. *M.R.M.V.L.*, [1926] A.C. 761, H.L. See, *in New Zealand*, *Banks* v. *Wilson* (1910), 29 N.Z.L.R. 832 (CHAPMAN J.).

3 *London General Omnibus Co.* v. *Pope* (1922), 38 T.L.R. 270 (ROCHE J.).

4 *Cross & Co.* v. *Matthews and Wallace* (1904), 91 L.T. 500.

5 *Verschures Creameries, Ltd.* v. *Hull and Netherlands S.S. Co.*, [1921] 2 K.B. 608, C.A.

6 "It is said that, if this is the rule of law, a person may recover a number of different judgments against different persons for the same sum of money. I see no great objection to this, having regard to the fact that a plaintiff cannot receive the amount claimed more than once"—per BANKES L.J. at p. 155 of *Isaacs & Sons* v. *Salbstein*, [1916] 2 K.B. 139, C.A. *Cf.* SWINFEN EADY L.J. at p. 141—"Where, however, the obligation binds two or more persons *severally*, a judgment against one is no bar to an action against another." *Cf. United Australia, Ltd.* v. *Barclays Bank, Ltd.*, [1941] A.C. 1, H.L.

CHAPTER XXII

The Doctrine of Merger in Judgment: The Plea of Autrefois Convict

Introduction

478 It is now convenient to deal with one special application of the principles of merger in judgment—the application of these principles to criminal proceedings which is commonly referred to as the plea of *autrefois convict*.

Nemo debet bis puniri pro uno delicto

479 As has been pointed out in a previous chapter,[1] the plea of *autrefois convict* is the process by which the doctrine of merger in judgment becomes effective in criminal jurisdiction. Once the accused has been tried for an offence, and convicted of it, that is an end to his criminal liability, and his conduct cannot serve as the basis of a second accusation of the same crime. As in civil, so in criminal law—*transit in rem judicatam*: the criminal liability of the prisoner for the offence which he has committed is merged in his conviction for that offence, once it has been obtained, and his liability to be punished is discharged by the punishment (if any) which has been inflicted in respect thereof.[2]

It is particularly to be noticed, however, that while the maxim *nemo debet bis puniri pro uno delicto* forbids a second verdict of guilty for the same *crime*, it does not forbid a second prosecution for the same *conduct*, in cases

---

[1] See Chapter XI, para. 317, *ante*.

[2] *Wemyss* v. *Hopkins* (1875), L.R. 10 Q.B. 378 per BLACKBURN J. at p. 381, quoted with approval by Lord MORRIS in *Connelly* v. *Director of Public Prosecutions*, [1964] A.C. 1254, H.L. at p. 1320; *ibid.* per Lord PEARCE at p. 1362.

in which such conduct may amount to two separate crimes.[1] Whether it is just to prosecute an accused again after one conviction, may be debated on the facts of the particular case; but the maxim will not forbid it. Neither will an exemption from criminal liability on the second charge follow from the application of the maxim *transit in rem judicatam*. What has passed into *res judicata* is the *offence* of which he was convicted, together with those other offences of which he could have been convicted on the same facts on the same indictment.[2] But if an accused is prosecuted to conviction (for instance) for aggravated assault, and after his conviction his victim dies of the assault, he may be prosecuted again for murder, and convicted of murder or of manslaughter, notwithstanding his previous conviction for assault.[3] For on the first occasion neither was he convicted of murder, or even charged with it, nor was it even possible so to charge him, since his victim was at that date still alive.

Autrefois convict distinct from issue estoppel

480 Although the pleas of *autrefois acquit* and *autrefois convict* are frequently mentioned in the same breath, and are indeed found to be dis-

---

[1] "It is quite plain that the learned Judge did not intend to lay down, and did not lay down, as a general principle of law that a man cannot be placed twice in jeopardy upon the same facts if the offences are different"—Lord READING C.J. delivering the judgment of the Court of Criminal Appeal in *R.* v. *Barron*, [1914] 2 K.B. 570. *R.* v. *Barron*, was an *autrefois acquit* case; but the learned judge referred to was HAWKINS J. in *R.* v. *King*, [1897] 1 Q.B. 214, an *autrefois convict* case. See, too, *R.* v. *Tonks*, [1916] 1 K.B. 443, C.A.; *R.* v. *Thomas*, [1950] 1 K.B. 26, C.C.A.—at p. 31—"It is not the law that the person shall not be liable to be punished twice for the same act; it has never been so stated in any case, and the Interpretation Act itself does not say so. What section 33 says is 'No person shall be liable to be punished twice for the same offence'." See, further, the speech of Lord MORRIS in *Connelly* v. *Director of Public Prosecutions*, [1964] A.C. 1254, at pp. 1307–1308: "The principle seems clearly to have been recognised that if someone had been either convicted or acquitted of an offence, he could not later be charged with the same offence or with what was in effect the same offence. In determining whether or not he was being so charged the court was not confined to an examination of the record. The reality of the matter was to be ascertained. That, however, did not mean that if two separate offences were committed at the same time a conviction or an acquittal in respect of one would be any bar to a subsequent prosecution in respect of the other. It was the offence or offences that had to be considered. Was there in substance one offence—or had someone committed two or more offences?"

[2] It is submitted that the test is whether the prisoner, convicted of one offence on the indictment, could have been convicted, even if he was not, *on that indictment* of the offence later charged. Such seems to have been the opinion of DENMAN J. in *R.* v. *Tancock* (1876), 13 Cox C.C. 217, where, the prisoner having been convicted on the first indictment of manslaughter, it was sought later to indict him for murder. It is clear from the judgment of DENMAN J. that the crucial question appeared to him to be "whether the (original) indictment was for murder or manslaughter". His willingness to disallow a plea of *autrefois convict* in the case where the earlier indictment had charged only manslaughter was the subject of the criticism at the hands of Lord MORRIS in *Connelly* v. *Director of Public Prosecutions*, [1964] A.C. 1254, at p. 1311; but in the respectful submission of the present writer the test proposed by DENMAN J. was the proper one.

[3] *R.* v. *Thomas*, [1950] 1 K.B. 26, C.C.A. At p. 28 HUMPHREYS J. delivering tb ejudgment of the court, said that this was "in accordance with the usual practice". See also *R.* v. *Tonks*, [1916] 1 K.B. 443, C.C.A.

cussed together in many of the judgments and texts,[1] they rest on completely different bases. *Autrefois acquit* serves to preclude the Crown from asserting in the second proceedings issues already decided in *favour of the accused* in the first.[2] *Autrefois convict* does not preclude the Crown from asserting an issue previously decided in favour of the accused; it precludes the Crown from reasserting an issue previously determined in its own favour —because the issue has merged in the previous conviction of the accused, whose account must be marked "paid in full" by virtue of the conviction, and of such punishment as has been meted out to him in consequence.[3]

How far the offence charged must be identical with that previously charged

481 While the two pleas of *autrefois acquit* and *autrefois convict* rest on different principles, the tests which determine their availability are much the same. *Autrefois convict* is, of course, available—this goes without saying—to preclude the same accused being charged again for the same offence, in respect of the same conduct, as formed the basis of a previous conviction. This is the purest, the most elementary, case. But, as in the case of *autrefois acquit*, the availability of the plea does not end there. The plea of *autrefois convict* will be available in favour of a prisoner who has been convicted, not only in respect of the offence of which he has been convicted, but also in respect of any offence with which he could in the previous proceedings, on the indictment as presented, have been convicted; and the plea will be available not only in respect of crimes of which he was or could have been convicted, but to other charges "in effect the same or substantially the same as either the principal or a different crime in respect of which he could have been or has been convicted".[4] In this respect the plea of *autrefois convict* in criminal proceedings is broader than that of merger in civil proceedings.

---

[1] As, for instance, in the speech of Lord MORRIS in *Connelly* v. *Director of Public Prosecutions*, [1964] A.C. 1254, H.L.

[2] The plea of *autrefois acquit* is discussed in Chapter XI.

[3] *Wemyss* v. *Hopkins* (1875), L.R. 10 Q.B. 378 per BLACKBURN J. at p. 381; *Connelly* v. *Director of Public Prosecutions*, [1964] A.C. 1254, H.L. at p. 1365.

[4] "It is quite clear that to enable a person to rely on that plea, the offence with which he is charged on the second action must be the same offence, *or practically the same offence*, as that with which he was charged on the first occasion"—SWIFT J., delivering the judgment of the Court of Criminal Appeal in *R.* v. *Kendrick and Smith* (1931), 23 Cr. App. Rep. 1, at p. 3. "It is plain that on May 2nd the accused was not convicted of that offence, (murder), nor of anything which is substantially the same offence or crime as that charged in the (later) indictment, nor could he have been since his wife was then alive. It follows that the plea of *autrefois convict* in the strict sense of the term is bound to fail, and does fail"—per HUMPHREYS J. delivering the judgment of the Court of Criminal Appeal in *R.* v. *Thomas*, [1950] 1 K.B. 26 at p. 29. In *Welton* v. *Taneborne* (1908), 99 L.T. 668 a driver had already been convicted of driving in a manner dangerous to the public, and the Magistrate in convicting him had expressly said that he convicted him on account of his excessive speed. A Divisional Court held that this conviction was in the circumstances a bar to a further charge on the same facts of driving at a speed exceeding 30 m.p.h.

One of the tests as to whether the plea is available in any given case is whether the evidence which is necessary to support the second indictment, or whether the facts which constitute the second offence, would have been sufficient to procure a legal conviction on the first indictment, either as to the offence charged, or as to an offence of which, on the indictment, the accused could have been found guilty.[1] But this principle must be read subject to the proviso that the offence charged in the second indictment has in fact been committed at the time of the first charge.[2] What has to be considered is whether the crime or offence charged in the later indictment is the same or is in effect or is substantially the same as the crime charged (or in respect of which there could have been a conviction) in a former indictment; and it is not decisive that the facts under examination, or the witnesses to be called, in the later proceedings are the same as those in the earlier proceedings. Finally it is to be noticed that apart from cases where indictments are preferred, and where pleas in bar may therefore be entered, the same fundamental principle always applies: a man is not to be prosecuted twice for the same crime.[3]

The principle behind the plea

482 It is often said that the principle upon which the rule of *autrefois convict* rests is that no man ought to be "placed in jeopardy" or "harassed" twice for the same offence.[4] But this is not quite an adequate explanation: if it were, the plea would be good, even if the former conviction had been a nullity *ab initio*, for want of jurisdiction, or if it had been quashed before plea pleaded, which, as has earlier been shewn,[5] is most certainly not the law; for in both these cases the party would have been twice in peril, and twice subjected to annoyance and anxiety. It is the former conviction, and not the former peril of conviction, which constitutes the bar, and the true

---

[1] Where a prisoner is charged with murder, and convicted of manslaughter, there can be no doubt that but the result will preclude a further charge of murder on the same facts; but what shall be the result if on a charge of manslaughter only he is convicted, and facts are later brought to light proving that the killing in fact amounted to murder? In *R.* v. *Tancock* (1876), 13 Cox. C.C. 217 DENMAN J. expressed the view that the earlier conviction would be no bar; but see the report of *R.* v. *Holcroft* (1578), 4 Co.Rep. 46b, and the disapproving passage in the judgment of Lord MORRIS in *Connelly* v. *Director of Public Prosecutions*, [1964] A.C. 1254, H.L. at pp. 1310–1311. It is submitted, with the utmost respect to Lord MORRIS, that the test must be as proposed by DENMAN J.—*viz.*, did the first indictment include a charge of murder?

[2] *R.* v. *Tonks*, [1916] 1 K.B. 443, C.C.A. at p. 450.

[3] Much of the text of this paragraph is taken *verbatim* from the speech of Lord MORRIS in *Connelly* v. *Director of Public Prosecutions*, [1964] A.C. 1254 H.L. at pp. 1305–1306. That case was, of course, concerned with a plea of *autrefois acquit*; but the two pleas were considered generally, and together, by Lord MORRIS at this point in his speech.

[4] *R.* v. *Haughton (Inhabitants)* (1853), 1 E. & B. 501 (per CROMPTON J., at p. 506: "*autrefois acquit* and *autrefois convict* depend upon the principle that a man shall not be twice in jeopardy for the same thing"); *R.* v. *Ollis*, [1900] 2 Q.B. 758, D.C. (per WRIGHT J., at p. 771).

[5] See notes 2 and 3 on p. 369, *ante*.

theory upon which the conviction alone is a bar is the same as that which lies at the root of the doctrine of former recovery in civil cases, namely, the absorptive potency of the *res judicata*.[1]

483 Whatever may be its true theory and underlying principle, the rule itself is now established beyond question, that a former conviction, whether by a superior or an inferior court,[2] is a bar to any further prosecution of the convict for the same offence in that, or any other, criminal court, superior or inferior,[3] in the same way, to the same extent, and subject to the same conditions, as a former civil recovery is a bar to any further civil proceedings against the defendant for the same cause of action.

484 The court which is relied on as having convicted the prisoner on the earlier occasion must be one possessing competent jurisdiction enabling it validly so to convict. So a finding of guilt accompanied by the imposition of a penalty, will not be sufficient to found the plea if the proceedings were before (*e.g.*) a domestic tribunal having no criminal jurisdiction.[4]

485 It should be noted here that, in the case of a conviction (or of an acquittal) by any court-martial, it is expressly provided by statute that no such conviction (or acquittal) is pleadable in bar of any subsequent prosecution or proceedings in any of the common law courts.[5]

When the plea should be put forward

486 A plea of *autrefois convict* is technically a plea in bar,[6] and should be advanced at the time of arraignment; if as a matter of law the judge is of opinion that there is a case to go to the jury upon it the proper procedure is to allow the jury to return a verdict on the plea.[7]

---

[1] *Wemyss* v. *Hopkins* (1875), L.R. 10 Q.B. 378, D.C. (per BLACKBURN J., at pp. 381, 382). See further *Connelly* v. *Director of Public Prosecutions*, [1964] A.C. 1254, H.L. per Lord MORRIS at p. 1320; per Lord PEARCE at p. 1362.

[2] By "inferior criminal court" is meant a court of summary jurisdiction.

[3] The following are cases in which a former conviction by a superior, or an inferior, criminal court was held a bar to a second conviction in a superior criminal court, or would have been so held, if the offence had been the same:—*R.* v. *Miles* (1890), 24 Q.B.D. 423; *R.* v. *Grimwood* (1896), 60 J.P. 809; *R.* v. *King*, [1897] 1 Q.B. 214; *R.* v. *Tonks*, [1916] 1 K.B. 443. For instances of former convictions operating as a bar to further proceedings in courts of summary jurisdiction, see *R.* v. *Brisby* (1849), 18 L.J. M.C. 157 (though the plea failed here on the ground that the former conviction was without jurisdiction); *Welton* v. *Taneborne* (1908), 99 L.T. 668, D.C.; *R.* v. *Marsham*, [1912] 2 K.B. 362, D.C.; but held that in this case, inasmuch as the magistrate had no jurisdiction to convict, the plea failed.

[4] As in *Lewis* v. *Mogan*, [1943] K.B. 376.

[5] Army Act 1881 s. 161. See, as to this enactment, *R.* v. *Aughet* (1918), 13 Cr. App. Rep. 101.

[6] *R.* v. *Thomas*, [1950] 1 K.B. 26, C.C.A. at p. 28.

[7] *R.* v. *Tonks*, [1916] 1 K.B. 443, C.C.A. at p. 448. *In New Zealand* the plea is disposed of by the judge without a jury—Crimes Act 1961 s. 357 *et seq.*

But where this is not done, and it is sought subsequently to advance the plea, and it appears that there are merits to support this course, the Court of Criminal Appeal will be slow to disallow a meritorious plea on a point of procedure. If the plea can be supported, no technicality will be likely to stop the Court of Criminal Appeal from doing what is right on the point.[1]

The residuary discretion of the court

487 There will be occasions on which, notwithstanding that the plea of *autrefois convict* will not be available on a strict application of the rules as above enunciated, it nevertheless appears unfair or unjust that the second prosecution should proceed. It is submitted that in such cases the court must assert itself as master of its own procedure, and must take such steps as will ensure that considerations of fairness and justice shall prevail.[2]

---

[1] *R.* v. *Tonks*, [1916] 1 K.B. 443, C.C.A. at pp. 446, 448.

[2] Instances may be seen in *R.* v. *Grimwood* (1896), 60 J.P. 809; *R.* v. *Nicholson* (1947), 32 Cr. App. Rep. 98. *Cf.* the powerful speech of Lord DEVLIN in *Connelly* v. *Director of Public Prosecutions*, [1964] A.C. 1254, H.L. at pp. 1346 *et seq.* This case turned, of course, on the plea of *autrefois acquit*; but several of their Lordships dealt with both pleas as governed by similar principles, Lord MORRIS and Lord DEVLIN seeming particularly to do so.

CHAPTER XXIII

The Doctrine of Merger in Judgment: Affirmative Answers to a Prima Facie Case of Former Recovery

488 At an earlier stage of this treatise the affirmative answers to a good *prima facie* case of estoppel *per rem judicatam*, consisting mainly of fraud, cross-estoppel, and public policy and illegality are examined and illustrated.[1] It is only seldom, however, that fraud or cross-estoppel can be set up as an answer to a *prima facie* case of former recovery; and public policy and illegality find no place in this chapter.

Fraud

489 Fraud, indeed, is not easy to imagine as an answer. However intelligible it may be that a party litigant should insist that an estoppel created *against* him by a former judicial decision is defeated by proof that his antagonist obtained that decision by fraud, it would obviously be an act of grotesque self-stultification, if one who has formerly recovered a judgment against his opponent, and is therefore *prima facie* barred from claiming the same relief against him in a second action, were to set up, as a means of destroying that bar, the fact that the former judgment was procured by the fraud, not of his opponent, but of himself.[2] Where, however, the plaintiffs in the two actions are two different individuals, though litigating in the same character or *persona* such as two common informers,

[1] See Part I, Chapter XIII, *ante*.

[2] *Nemo allegans suam turpitudinem est audiendus*,—a familiar maxim of the common law, which has been described as founded upon a sort of "moral estoppel" by EYRE C.B., at p. 611 of *Gibson* v. *Minet* (1791), as reported in 1 Hy.Bl. 569, H.L.

there may possibly be nothing inconsistent in the second plaintiff seeking to defeat the bar by proof that the first plaintiff obtained his judgment by fraudulent collusion with the defendant.[1]

Moreover it is submitted that a plaintiff, proceeding against a defendant, could be misled by circumstances, of which fraud by that defendant may be one, to take judgment against him for an amount, or for relief less than that which he would have claimed and received had the true position been disclosed to him. If this position should arise by reason of fraud of the defendant, it is submitted that the plaintiff should not be precluded, by reason of the judgment which he has mistakenly entered, from reopening the matter.[2]

Mistake

490 *In New Zealand* the position arising from mistake common to both parties in a specific performance action led to a cognate situation being considered. There, in a claim for specific performance of an agreement for a lease of land, the plaintiff mistakenly mis-described the piece of land in the pleadings on the first proceedings, so as to ask for a lease of less than the area to which he was entitled by the contract of the parties. The defendant did not notice the error, and the action was tried, and a decree made in plaintiff's favour, on the merits, on the foundation of the erroneous pleading; and subsequently a lease was executed in pursuance of the decree so made. When later the error was discovered, a second action was commenced, in which the same plaintiff claimed against the same defendant, under the same contract, a second decree for specific performance as to the balance of the area covered by the original contract. It was held, in these circumstances, that the plaintiff was not precluded by the decree in the first proceedings from obtaining the supplementary relief which he sought in the second.[3]

Cross-estoppel

491 The only instances of estoppel as an affirmative answer to a case of former recovery are to be found in the reports of those cases, to be considered hereafter, in which the party entitled to set up the bar may be deemed to have waived, or, in other words, to have estopped himself from exercising, his right to do so by omission to plead it, which has undoubtedly

---

[1] *Girdlestone* v. *Brighton Aquarium Co.* (1879), 4 Ex.D. 107, C.A. (per COTTON L.J., at pp. 111–113, and THESIGER L.J., at pp. 113, 114).

[2] The reader interested in authority to support this submission is referred to the closely-analogous (hypothetical) set of facts dealt with in para. 490, on this page.

[3] *Blinkhorne* v. *Brenchley* (1898), 16 N.Z.L.R. 498.

been held to be the effect of a similar omission to plead estoppel *per rem judicatam*, as has already been noted in the proper place.[1]

Other answers

492 Other affirmative answers are established by proof that before the date of the second action the former judgment has been reversed, for this is confession and avoidance,[2] or by bringing the case within some statutory exception.[3]

---

[1] See para. 386, Chapter XIII, *ante*, and para. 495, *post*.

[2] *Partington* v. *Hawthorne* (1888), 52 J.P. 807, D.C.

[3] Such as those created by the Army Act 1881 s. 161 (as to which, see para. 485, *ante*, and by the statutory rules referred to in para. 476, *ante*.

CHAPTER XXIV

The Doctrine of Merger in Judgment: Pleading and Procedure

493 Substantially, the rules of pleading and procedure which prescribe and regulate the mode in which estoppels *per rem judicatam* must be raised, as already enunciated and discussed,[1] are, *mutatis mutandis*, the same as those governing cases of former recovery.

494 Accordingly it has always been held that a case of former recovery, no less than a case of estoppel by *res judicata*, must be raised, and brought to the notice of the Court, and of the opposite party, at the first available moment, on pain of losing the right to insist, at the trial or hearing of the cause or matter, that the former judgment constitutes a bar to a second recovery.

Pleading

495 In all stages in the development of our procedure code, whether before or after the passing of the Judicature Acts,[2] the party desirous of setting up a former recovery in law of an action has been required to plead it at the earliest opportunity, where there is any opportunity at all of so doing. In the first edition of this work Mr Spencer Bower expresses the view that "any default in this respect, even though the defaulting party has resorted to what he may claim to have been equivalent measures, such as a

[1] In Part I, Chapter XIV, *ante*. Most of that chapter, and the cases cited in the notes thereto, may be referred to as, in principle, relevant to the subject matter of the present chapter.

[2] See *Edevain* v. *Cohen* (1889), 43 Ch.D. 187, C.A. (per COTTON L.J., at p. 189). And, generally, on this topic, see para. 399, Chapter XIV, *ante*.

motion to set aside, or stay, proceedings, has always been held fatal".[1] But it is submitted by the present author that so stern a view carries formalism further than modern practice justifies; and that the plea will be given due consideration, however raised, if its consideration will not in the circumstances, be unjust to the party against whom it is sought to set it up.

If pleaded the defence may, in a proper case, be made the subject of an argument on a question of law before trial. This course has been said to be preferable to a motion to dismiss the action as frivolous and vexatious, for it is desirable that such a question should be argued in court and not merely by a judge sitting in chambers or by a master.[2]

496 The plea of *autrefois convict*, as has been explained in an earlier chapter,[3] is the analogue, in criminal jurispurdence, of the plea of former recovery in civil. One would expect, therefore, the same pleading requirements to be imposed in the one class of case as in the other. And, in technical strictness, this is so: that is to say, a case of *autrefois convict* ought, as a general rule, to be pleaded in every case where written pleadings are obligatory or permissible, but,[4] *in favorem libertatis*, the criminal courts will on occasion forbear from insisting on a literal compliance with the rule. Thus, Mr Spencer Bower in the first edition of this work notices that in one of the authorities an oral plea of *autrefois convict* was received by the court on the eve of trial, on condition that it should immediately be put in writing;[5] that in another, the judge, on being apprised of the former conviction, though expressing astonishment that it had not been pleaded, nevertheless took note of it, and gave indirect effect to it by passing a merely nominal sentence;[6] and that, in a still later case, the court gave full effect to a former conviction as a bar, without taking the slightest notice of the fact that *autrefois convict* had never been pleaded.[7] It is submitted that more modern practice has relaxed formalities even further, and that a modern criminal court will not allow the justice of a plea of *autrefois convict* ever to be obscured by mere formalism.

497 The accepted and customary form of the plea of former recovery is as follows: "the plaintiff heretofore, in the Court of ——, sued the

---

1 The following are cited in a footnote to the original text: *Martin* v. *Kennedy* (1800), 2 Bos. & P. 69 (per Lord ELDON C.J., and HEATH J., at p. 71, and ROOKE J. at p. 72); *Stafford* v. *Clark* (1824), 2 Bing. 377 (per BEST C.J. at pp. 382, 383); *Ostell* v. *Le Page* (1852), 2 De G.M. & G. 892 (per Lord CRANWORTH L.J., at p. 892); *Edevain* v. *Cohen*, *supra*. (per COTTON L.J., at p. 189).

2 Per Lord ATKIN in *Workington Harbour and Dock Board* v. *Trade Indemnity Co.*, [1938] 2 All E.R. 101, H.L. at p. 102.

3 Chapter II, *ante*. The plea is separately dealt with in Chapter XXII, *ante*.

4 *R.* v. *Stanton* (1851), 5 Cox C.C. 324 (per ERLE J., at p. 325).

5 *R.* v. *Walker* (1843), 2 Mood & R. 446 (per PARKE B., who also ordered an oral demurrer to this plea to be "put on parchment").

6 *R.* v. *Stanton*, *supra*.

7 As in *R.* v. *Tonks*, [1916] 1 K.B. 443.

defendant in an action for the same cause of action as in the declaration (statement of claim) alleged, and such proceedings were thereupon had in that action that the plaintiff afterwards by the judgment of the said Court recovered against the defendant £—— for the said cause of action, and the said judgment still remains in force".[1] With the necessary adaptations, this is also the form of a plea of *autrefois convict*.[2]

498 If the plaintiff desires to dispute only the accuracy of the averments in the defendant's plea as to the contents of the record of the previous judgment, where the plea offers "verification by the record", he should reply *nul tiel record*, or some equivalent form of words:[3] but if he desires to controvert the allegations of a plea which makes no reference to the record, but simply asserts the identity of the causes of action, or of the offences, in the two actions, or prosecutions, as the case may be, or the identity of the parties, he must reply the fact of such non-identity, with or without special averments of the particular points of distinction.[4] If the plaintiff is minded to challenge the sufficiency in law of the allegations of identity contained in the plea,[5] or if the defendant is desirous of challenging the sufficiency in law of the plaintiff's reply in so far as it alleges dis-

---

[1] For illustrations, see, generally, the cases cited in the notes to this chapter. In *King* v. *Hoare* (1844), 13 M. & W. 494, it is pointed out by PARKE B., at p. 502, that "the plea does not operate by way of estoppel", and, therefore, it is quite wrong, indeed, self-contradictory and absurd, to plead former recovery as an estoppel, or in the form (with its special commencement and conclusion) which is consecrated to a plea of estoppel *per rem judicatam*, as to which see para. 404, Chapter XIV, *ante*. For instances of pleas by which former recovery was intended to be raised, and which were held bad, because pleaded wholly, or in part, as if estoppel had been intended, the vital distinction between the two bars in substance, and the corresponding distinction between the two pleas in form, being wholly ignored, see *Stewart* v. *Todd* (1846), 9 Q.B. 767, Ex. Ch. (*per Cur.*, at pp. 777, 778); *Bank of Australasia* v. *Harding* (1850), 9 C.B. 661 (the amazing 10th plea here is set out at pp. 693–696, and the grounds of the demurrer thereto at pp. 677, 678).

[2] See form of plea of *autrefois convict* which is set out at p. 218 of *R.* v. *Tancock* (1876), 13 Cox C.C. 217. But see, further, Chapter XXII as to this plea.

[3] As in *Wadsworth* v. *Bentley* (1853), 23 L.J. Q.B. 3; *Buckland* v. *Johnson* (1854), 15 C.B. 145; *Florence* v. *Jenings* (1857), 2 C.B. N.S. 454.

[4] As in the following cases of civil former judgments: *Lacon* v. *Barnard* (1626), Cro. Car. 35; *Seddon* v. *Tutop* (1796), 6 Term Rep. 607; *Lord Bagot* v. *Williams* (1824), 3 B. & C. 235; *Few* v. *Backhouse* (1838), 3 Ad. & El. 789; *Holmes* v. *Wilson* (1839), 10 Ad. & El. 503 (new assignment); *Stewart* v. *Todd* (1846); 9 Q.B. 767, Ex. Ch.; *Duke of Brunswick* v. *Pepper* (1848), 2 C. & K. 683 (new assignment); *Nelson* v. *Couch* (1863), 15 C.B. N.S. 99; *Girdlestone* v. *Brighton Aquarium Co.* (1879), 4 Ex.D. 107, C.A. For similar replies to a plea of *autrefois convict*, see *Holden* v. *King* (1876), 46 L.J. Q.B. 75; *R.* v. *Miles* (1890), 24 Q.B.D. 423, D.C.

[5] This course was adopted in the following cases where a civil judgment was set up as a bar:—*Brown* v. *Wootton* (1605), Cro. Jac. 73; *Randal* v. *Higgens* (1605), 6 Co. Rep. 44 b; *Fetter* v. *Beal* (1697), 1 Ld. Raym. 339; *Phillips* v. *Berryman* (1783), 3 Doug. K.B. 286; *Austin* v. *Mills* (1853), 9 Exch. 288; *Guest* v. *Warren* (1854), 9 Exch. 379; *Gibbs* v. *Cruikshank* (1873), L.R. 8 C.P. 454. For examples of demurrers to pleas of former criminal judgments, see *R.* v. *Walker* (1843), 2 Mood & R. 446; *Hartley* v. *Hindmarsh* (1866), L.R. 1 C.P. 553; *Masper* v. *Brown* (1875), 1 C.P.D. 97.

tinctions and differences,[1] it was always open to the party under the old system to demur to his opponent's pleading, and, since the Judicature Acts, it is open to him to resort to the equivalents of, or substitutes for, demurrer, which are thereby provided.[2]

499 Amendments of pleadings, for the purpose of introducing a plea of former recovery not previously pleaded, should be the subject of an application as early as possible, and leave may be refused if sought at too late a stage in the proceedings, for instance, if it is left till the trial on the conclusion of the plaintiff's evidence.[3] On the other hand, an amendment for this purpose is not only permissible, but obligatory, when the fact of the former judgment, though not known to the defendant, at the time of his original defence, yet becomes known at some date thereafter which leaves him ample time before the trial to make the application.[4]

Mode of raising the question of former recovery otherwise than by pleading

500 Where the party, being under a duty to plead the former judgment, omits to do so, he cannot afterwards rely upon it in bar of the action or prosecution, as has already been stated,[5] at least without the leave of the court granted as on an application to amend; though an unpleaded former judgment, even where there is such a duty, may still be used as evidence, with other facts, to establish a plea, not, indeed, of former recovery, but of payment.[6]

501 Where, however, the party's omission to plead the former judgment was not in breach of any duty, the effectiveness of the bar is in no way impaired, provided that he raises the objections in some other form at the earliest opportunity.

502 Accordingly, a party desirous of raising an unpleaded bar of former recovery, or former conviction, has been held entitled to do so *ore tenus* at, or on the first available occasion before, the trial, by way of preliminary objection or otherwise, whenever, by the practice of the court in which the question arises, written pleadings are not permitted, or prescribed,[7]

---

1 As in *Lacon* v. *Barnard* (1626), Cro. Car. 35; *Florence* v. *Jenings* (1857), 2 C.B. N.S. 454; *Brinsmead* v. *Harrison* (1872), L.R. 7 C.P. 547, Exch. Ch.

2 R.S.C. (1965) O. 25 and the rules therein contained.

3 *Edevain* v. *Cohen* (1889), 43 Ch.D. 187, C.A. (per COTTON L.J., at p. 190).

4 *McLeod* v. *Power*, [1898] 2 Ch. 295, where BYRNE J., on this ground, deprived the successful defendant of his costs.

5 See para. 495, *ante*.

6 *Stafford* v. *Clark* (1824), 2 Bing. 377 (per PARK J., at pp. 381, 382, BURROUGH J., at p. 382, and BEST C.J., at pp. 382, 383).

7 As in the County Court under the Act of 1888; in this connection see, amongst other cases, *Wright* v. *London General Omnibus Co.* (1877), 2 Q.B.D. 271; *Hoare* v. *Niblett* (1891), 1 Q.B. 781, D.C.; *Midland Rail. Co.* v. *Martin & Co.* (1893), 2 Q.B. 172, D.C.; *Isaacs & Sons* v. *Salbstein*, [1916] 2 K.B. 139, C.A.

as for instance, before a court of summary jurisdiction,[1] or in arbitrations, whether domestic,[2] or statutory;[3] or where, though pleadings are required by the procedure of the court in which the question arises, the party could not have pleaded the former judgment, because, at the time of delivering his defence, it had not been obtained.[4]

---

[1] *Wemyss* v. *Hopkins* (1875), L.R. 10 Q.B. 378; *Welton* v. *Taneborne* (1908), 99 L.T. 668, D.C.

[2] *Dunn* v. *Murray* (1829), 9 B. & C. 780.

[3] *Tyne Tees Shipping Co.* v. *Whilock* (1913), 6 B.W.C.C. 559, C.A.; *Watts* v. *Logan* (1914), 7 B.W.C.C. 82, C.A.; *Moakes* v. *Blackwell Colliery Co.*, [1917] 1 K.B. 565, C.A.

[4] This was the case in *McLeod* v. *Power*, [1898] 2 Ch. 295, where the former judgment relied upon was not obtained until after defence pleaded, and BYRNE J. accordingly gave effect to the unpleaded objection of former recovery, when orally raised at the trial, though he deprived the defendant of his costs on the ground that he might, and therefore should, have amended his defence by pleading the former judgment as a "matter arising pending the action".

Appendices

Inherent Jurisdiction of the Court in Cases Where Res Judicata is not Strictly Established

503 Every English court of justice is, and from time immemorial has been, invested with inherent jurisdiction, apart from, and independently of, all specific practice rules, to dismiss, or stay, or otherwise nullify all actions or proceedings which are shewn to its satisfaction to be vexatious or oppressive, or to constitute an abuse of its process.[1] Though very sparingly exercised in earlier and more technical times, this jurisdiction has, in modern practice, been resorted to with ever increasing freedom, and with most salutary effect.

504 In the exercise of this inherent authority, the courts have not infrequently intervened to prevent the perversion to base uses of a bare right to reopen matters already litigated, in cases where no estoppel *per rem judicatam*, or, as the case may be, no bar of "former recovery", has been strictly established.

505 Thus, where estoppel *per rem judicatam* has not been sufficiently pleaded, or made out, but nevertheless the circumstances are such as to render any reagitation of the questions formerly adjudicated upon a scandal and an abuse, the court will not hesitate to dismiss the action, or stay proceedings therein, or strike out the defence thereto, as the case may require.[2]

---

[1] The modern procedure substituted for demurrer, as to which see note 1 on p. 348, *ante*, and note 2 on p. 403, *ante*, leaves the much wider inherent jurisdiction of the Courts over their own proceedings entirely undiminished and untouched.

[2] For instance in *Reichel* v. *Magrath* (1889), 14 App.Cas. 665, H.L., though the defendant was not, strictly speaking, estopped by *res judicata*, the parties not being the same, the defence was struck out, and judgment given for the plaintiff, not under O. 25, r. 4, but in the exercise of the

506 Further, there are certain rules of conduct framed by the courts for their own guidance, and for the protection of litigants from oppression, in accordance with which, when applications for certain prerogative writs, and the like, have once been refused, a hearing will be denied to a second application for the same purpose, though any such refusal, as has already been explained, is not technically a judicial decision at all.[1] These rules, resting solely upon the inherent authority of the court over its own proceedings, are, it has been said, "if not altogether universal and inflexible, as nearly so as possible",[2] and have accordingly always been acted upon, except where the circumstances were very special, in cases of renewed applications for such writs as a writ of mandamus,[3] certiorari,[4] quo warranto,[5] or prohibition.[6]

507 In *Greenhalgh* v. *Mallard*[7] SOMERVELL L.J., in dealing with a submission apparently based (in the alternative) on the plea of inherent jurisdiction, said:[8]

> "I think that on the authorities to which I will refer it would be accurate to say that *res judicata* for this purpose is not confined to the issues which the court is actually asked to decide, but that it covers issues or facts which are

---

inherent jurisdiction (per Lord HALSBURY L.C., and Lord WATSON, at p. 668, and Lord HERSCHELL, at p. 669). In *Montgomery* v. *Russell* (1894), 11 T.L.R. 112, C.A., the case, again, was not strictly one of estoppel (because the two libel actions were not in respect of the same defamatory matter), nor did it come within the purview of O. 25, r. 4, but nevertheless the second action was dismissed as an abuse of the process (per Lord ESHER M.R., at p. 112). In *Horrocks* v. *Stubbs* (1896), 74 L.T. 58, C.A., it was held by the C.A. that KEKEWICH J. had rightly dismissed the action, which was for infringement of a patent, though not on the ground of *res judicata*, about which, in the opinion of the majority of the Court, there were considerable difficulties, the real justification for so disposing of the case being the inherent jurisdiction (per LINDLEY L.J., at p. 60, and A. L. SMITH L.J., at pp. 61, 62). Similarly, in *Stephenson* v. *Garnett*, [1898] 1 Q.B 677, C.A., an action was dismissed under the inherent jurisdiction, though the former decision, being an interlocutory, and not a final, order,—see Part I, Ch. V, *ante*,—was not technically a *res judicata* upon which an estoppel could be founded (per A. L. SMITH L.J., at pp. 680, 681, CHITTY L.J., at pp. 681, 682, and COLLINS L.J., at p. 682). See further the judgment of SCRUTTON L.J. (BANKES L.J. and ATKIN L.J. did not find it necessary to deal with this aspect of the case) in *Mackenzie-Kennedy* v. *Air Council*, [1927] 2 K.B. 517, at pp. 528–529; see also *Jaeger Co., Ltd.* v. *Jaeger* (1929), 46 R.P.C. 336 in the judgment of Lord HANWORTH M.R. at p. 344.

[1] As explained in Chapter II.

[2] Per Lord DENMAN C.J., at p. 427 of *R.* v. *Manchester and Leeds Rail. Co.* (1838), 8 Ad. & El. 413.

[3] *R.* v. *Pickles* (1842), 12 L.J. Q.B. 40; *R.* v. *Great Western Rail. Co.* (1844), 5 Q.B. 597; *Ex parte Thompson* (1845), 6 Q.B. 721; *R.* v. *Bodmin Corporation*, [1892] 2 Q.B. 21 (per DAY J., at p. 23, and CHARLES J., at p. 24).

[4] *R.* v. *Manchester and Leeds Rail. Co.*, *supra.*

[5] *R.* v. *Orde* (1831), 8 Ad. & El. 420, n.

[6] See the observations of SCRUTTON L.J., at p. 519 of *R.* v. *Kensington Income Tax Commissioners*, [1917] 1 K.B. 486, C.A.

[7] [1947] 2 All E.R. 255.

[8] At pp. 257–9.

> so clearly part of the subjectmatter of the litigation and so clearly could have been raised that it would be an abuse of the process of the court to allow a new proceeding to be started in respect of them.''

EVERSHED L.J. agreed that in the circumstances of that case, even if a plea of *res judicata* could not strictly be sustained, yet it was an abuse of the process of the court, and contrary to the principle that in the public interest there should be an end to litigation, to rely in the second action on the same concerted acts as formed the basis of the first proceedings.[1]

508 Other particular applications of the discretion which we have mentioned have been the subject of discussion in the text earlier in this work, under the headings of Divorce,[2] and of *Autrefois Acquit*.[3]

509 The inherent jurisdiction is exercised for the same purpose, and under the same conditions, in cases of ''former recovery''[4] or *autrefois convict*.[5]

---

[1] See further *Wright* v. *Bennett*, [1948] 1 All E.R. 227, C.A.; *In Re a Debtor*, [1958] 1 All E.R. 581, C.A.; *Public Trustee* v. *Kenward*, [1967] 2 All E.R. 870 (BUCKLEY J.).

[2] See Chapter XII, para. 364, where the decision of PEARCE J. in *Duchesne* v. *Duchesne*, [1951] P. 101 receives some critical consideration.

[3] See Chapter XI, paras. 334 *et seq.*, where Lord DEVLIN's view is considered.

[4] It was recognized in *Brunsden* v. *Humphrey* (1884), 14 Q.B.D. 141, C.A. (per BRETT M.R., at p. 144, and BOWEN L.J., at p. 151), and, again, in *Westmoreland Green and Blue Slate Co.* v. *Feilden*, [1891] 3 Ch. 15, C.A. (per LINDLEY L.J., at p. 25), that, even in cases where the cause of action is not the same in the two proceedings, and, therefore, technically, there is no ground for a plea of former recovery, the court will nevertheless exercise its inherent jurisdiction if any element of vexation or oppression is shown, either by staying proceedings in the second action, or by some special order as to costs. See, for a more recent instance of the exercise of this jurisdiction in a former recovery case *Green* v. *Weatherill*, [1929] 2 Ch. 213.

[5] See *R.* v. *King*, [1897] 1 Q.B. 214, D.C., where a conviction for larceny was quashed on the ground that the accused had been previously convicted of obtaining the same goods by false pretences, it being held that the two offences, though in strictness different, were ''practically the same'', and that ''the course adopted'' in the court below of allowing the man to be put upon his trial again was ''altogether inconsistent with what is right and just'' (per HAWKINS J., at p. 218).

APPENDIX B

The Doctrine of Res Judicata in Roman Law

(This Appendix is reproduced almost *verbatim* from Mr Spencer Bower's original text.)

510 Having regard to the undoubted fact that, in some respects, the English doctrine of *res judicata* is, if not founded upon, at least fortified and illustrated by the principles of the civil law, whilst, in others, our jurisprudence,[1] as indeed that of every civilized state,[2] has independently reached conclusions which are, in the main, identical with those of the Roman jurists, it may be useful and instructive to institute a comparison between the two systems in relation to this doctrine.

Sect. 1. *General view of the Exceptio Rei Judicatae in Roman jurisprudence*

511 Amongst the fundamental principles of Roman jurisprudence which are collected in the last book of the Digest,[3] is the maxim, *res*

---

[1] See *Barrs* v. *Jackson* (1842), 1 Y. & C. Ch. Cas. 585 (per KNIGHT-BRUCE V.-C., at pp. 588, 589: "with the rules of the civil law, rightly understood, . . . the law of England generally agrees"); *Nelson* v. *Couch* (1863), 15 C.B. N.S. 99 (per WILLES J., who, at p. 108, describes the English authorities on *res judicata* as being "entirely consistent", not only with one another, but also "with the rules of the civil law").

[2] See "The Times" of 17th March, 1916, in which appears, under the heading of "The Rule of Res Judicata", a short statement of some observations made by the Judicial Committee of the Privy Council in a case on appeal from Bengal, the parties to which are not named, and the "details" of which are described as having "no public interest". Sir HERBERT JENKINS, who delivered the judgment, "is there reported to have said that their Lordships desired to emphasize that the rule of *res judicata*, while founded on ancient precedent, was dictated by a wisdom which was for all time . . . Though the rule of the code might be traced to an English source, it embodied a doctrine in no way opposed to the spirit of the law as expounded by the Hindu commentators. Vijnanesvara and Nilakantha included the plea of a former judgment among those allowed by law, each citing for that purpose the text of Katyayana, who described the plea thus:—'if a person though defeated at law, sue again, he should be answered,—You were defeated formerly. This is called the plea of former judgment'".

[3] The collection of extracts from the commentaries of the most authoritative of the Roman jurists, which is commonly called "the Digest", is entitled "*Domini Nostri Sacratissimi Principis Justiniani juris enucleati ex omni vetere jure collecti Digestorum seu Pandectarum Libri Quinquaginta*". It

judicata pro veritate accipitur,[1] frequently cited in English judgments,[2] and closely corresponding with the "uncontrollable verity" which COKE postulates for the acts and proceedings of all courts of record in this country.[3] This means that, as with us, every *res judicata* was treated by the civilians as incontrovertible on the merits, if and when, but not unless or until, the fact of the former adjudication was brought to the notice of the tribunal.[4]

512 The justification of the Roman doctrine of *res judicata* is expressed in the Digest to consist in, first, the practical good of the community, who have a right to demand from the law protection against oppressive multiplication of suits, and the scandal of conflicting decisions,[5] and, secondly, the theoretical conception of a judicial decision as absorbing, when pronounced, that which had till then been a mere cause of action.[6] Of these theories the former is the basis, as has already been explained, of the English doctrine of estoppel *per rem judicatam*,[7] whilst the latter is

---

ought, therefore, properly to be called "the Digests". It is curious that, whilst the Greek title "Pandects" is always correctly used in the plural, jurists should have conspired to use the singular number in the case of the equally plural Latin equivalent. The mode of citation in the following notes is that now usually adopted: "D." stands for "Digest"; the first figure after the "D." indicates the number of the Book; the second, that of the Title, or Chapter; the third, that of the Section; and the fourth (where there is a fourth), that of the clause, or paragraph, or "fragment". When the clause is an introductory one, without a number, the abbreviation "pr." (for "*principium*") is used.

[1] D. 50. 17 (*Regulae Diversae*, Reg. 207, cited from Ulpian).

[2] For instance, by KNIGHT-BRUCE, V.-C., at pp. 588, 589, of *Barrs* v. *Jackson* (1842), 1 Y. & C. Ch. Cas. 585.

[3] 2 Co. Littl. 260a.

[4] Just. Inst. iv. 13.5: "*si judicio tecum actum fuerit sive in rem sive in personam, nihilominus ob id actio durat, et ideo ipso jure postea de eadem re adversus te agi potest: sed debes per exceptionem rei judicatae adjurari*". This means that, if the defendant, either intentionally or negligently, omits to inform the Praetor that he desires to raise a question of *res judicata* by an *exceptio*, no such question will be submitted to the judex in the "formula" or issue which he is directed to try, whereas, if such a question is properly raised, the issue will be so framed as to require the judex to deal with, and decide, it (the words, "*si ea res non judicata sit*", being added to the ordinary type of "formula").

[5] D. 44. 2. 6 (from Paulus *ad Edictum*, lib. lxx): "*ne aliter modus litium multiplicatus summam atque inexplicabilem faciat difficultatem, maxime si diversa pronuncientur*". This view appears to have accorded with Greek law and custom: see Soph. Ajax, 1239–1249 (a passage which includes the lines prefixed as a motto to this work on the title-page), where Agamemnon upbraids Teucer for daring to question the merits of the decision of the majority of the judges, and enlarges on the upheavals and confusion of all law, order, finality, and decency which would inevitably result from permitting a defeated party to canvass the correctness of a *res judicata*.

[6] In our jurisprudence the original cause of action is deemed to have been merged, once for all, in the *res judicata*, as soon as pronounced: but, in the view of the civilians, there were two mergers, or two stages in the merger; first, the claim or demand was absorbed in the action immediately upon the *litis contestatio*, or the commencement of the proceedings ("*res in judicium deducta*"), and, afterwards, on the adjudication, the claim in the action became merged in the *res judicata*.

[7] See para. 10, Chapter I, *ante*.

principally resorted to for the justification of our rules relating to "former recovery" or "merger in judgment".[1]

513 The Roman rule as to the *exceptio rei judicatae* is stated in general terms which very closely approximate to those in which the English rule is expressed. "The *exceptio*", says Ulpian, "is an effective bar to any proceeding in which the same question as that which has already been decided is put in controversy again between the same parties".[2]

514 It is to be observed that the Roman rule recognizes no such distinction as is drawn in our law between the effect of a *res judicata* as a bar to any contradiction, and its effect as a bar to any repetition, of that which has formerly been adjudged, but contents itself with a general prohibition of any reopening or re-agitation of the *res judicata*, in whatever form, and for whatever purpose.

Sect. 2. Roman and English law compared, as to identity of subject-matter

515 It has been pointed out, in the proper places, that, for the purposes both of estoppel, and of the plea of former recovery or merger in judgment our jurisprudence requires proof that the subject-matter (physical and metaphysical) of the former decision was identical with that of the subsequent proceedings.[3] The same requirement was made by the civilians.

516 As regards physical identity of subject-matter,[4] Roman jurisprudence required,[5] in order to constitute a valid plea of *res judicata*, proof that the two proceedings related to *idem corpus*, and *eadem quantitas*;[6] and that the point, or period, of time with which the judicial decision dealt was

[1] See Chapter XV, paras. 425 *et seq.*; and in connection with the rule as to former recovery against one of several persons jointly liable, see Chapter XXI, *ante*.

[2] D.44, 2. 7. 4, citing from Ulpian *ad Edictum*, lib. xv, a passage which he had adopted from Julian's *Digest*, lib. iii: "*generaliter, ut Julianus definit, exceptio rei judicatae obstat, quotiens inter easdem personas eadem quaestio revocatur, vel alio genere judicii*". Cp. D. 44. 2. 3, where the same rule is stated in slightly different language.

[3] See Chapter VI, (estoppel); Chapter XX, (former recovery).

[4] Chapter VI.

[5] Mr Spencer Bower was of the opinion that the same duality in the requirements as to identity of cause of action persisted in the English doctrine. The present writer is not as confident that this is so, and the reader is referred to paras. 206 *et seq.*, *ante*, in this regard.

[6] D.44 2. 13, citing Paulus *ad Edictum*, lib lxx (*cum quaeritur, haec exceptio noceat, necne, inspiciendum est, an* idem corpus *sit*), and D. 44, 2. 13, from Ulpian *ad Edictum*, lib. lxxv ("*quantitas eadem*"). In D. 44, 2. 7, a number of illustrations are given. Thus, it is said that the *exceptio* clearly applies to any one of the properties, or to any part of the land, building, ship, or goods, or to any fraction of the sum, forming the subject of the previous decision, but that questions as to whether the subject (in a physical sense) of the former adjudication extends to the income, or produce, or *fructus* of that subject (*e.g.* the produce of a tree, or of a *praegnans ancilla*) do not admit of an unqualified answer, and must be determined, in each case, by reference to the particular facts.

identical with that to which the subsequent proceedings related, and not prior, or subsequent thereto,[1] provided that, the mere subsequent discovery of *nova instrumenta* whereof the party had means of knowledge at the time of the former proceedings does not negative this identity, or make the subject-matter *alia res*.[2]

517 As regards what may be called the metaphysical identity of subject-matter, it has already been explained that, in English law, no plea of *res judicata* can succeed unless the question of law, or issue of fact, put in controversy is the very same question, or issue, which was determined by the former judgment.[3] So, in Roman law, no *exceptio rei judicatae* was effective, unless the subject-matter of the *res judicata*, and of the subsequent action, was *eadem quaestio*,[4] or, as it is variously expressed, *idem jus*[5], or unless the foundations of both the former judgment and the subsequent proceedings was *eadem causa petendi*.[6] For this purpose, *causa petendi* must be understood as meaning "ground of complaint", not "form of action or remedy"; for, not less than the English authorities,[7] the civilians are careful to insist that, if both proceedings related to the same controverted question of right, or title, it makes no difference that the former proceeding was instituted *alio genere judicii*,[8] *or diverso genere actionis*.[9]

Sect. 3. *The two systems compared, as to identity of parties*

518 Here again there is a close accord between the two systems, each of which requires proof of the identity of the parties (or their privies) to both proceedings as a condition of the validity of the plea of *res judicata*.[10]

519 It is part of the Roman doctrine of *res judicata*, as it is of the English,[11] that this identity of parties must be not only physical, but jural, that

[1] See D.44, 2. 17: "*si rem meam a te petiero, tu autem ideo fueris absolutus quod probaveris sine dolo malo te desiisse possidere, deinde postea coeperis possidere, et ego a te petam, non nocebit mihi exceptio rei judicatae*". Cp. several other examples which are given in D.44. 2. 11. 1–6, and in D.44. 2. 18, 19.

[2] D.44, 2, 27 (citing Neratius, lib. vii, *Membranarum*): "*nec jam interest . . . si quis, postea quam contra eum judicatum esset, nova instrumental causae suae reperisset.*"

[3] Chapter VI: Chapter XX.

[4] See the two citations in note 2 on p. 412, above.

[5] D.44, 2. 13 (from Ulpian *ad Edictum*, lib. lxxv).

[6] D.44, 2. 14. pr. ("*eadem causa petendi*").

[7] See, in Part I, para. 192: in Part II, para. 453.

[8] D.44, 2. 7. 4, is cited in note 2 on p. 412, above.

[9] D.44, 2. 5 (from Ulpian *ad Edictum*, lib. lxxiv): "*cum quis* actione mutata *experitur, etsi* diverso genere *actionis quam instituit videtur de eadem re agere*". An instance is then given,—an *actio mandati*, followed by an *actio negotiorum gestorum*.

[10] D.44, 2. 3 ("*inter eosdem*"), and D.44, 2. 7. 4 ("*inter easdem personas*"). For illustrations of privies, see D.44. 2. 11. 7–10, and D. 44. 2. 28. The English rules as to parties and privies entitled, and liable, to the exception of *res judicata* are stated in Ch. VII of Part I, *ante*, and in Chapter XXI of Part II *ante*.

[11] See in Part I, para. 232: in Part II, para. 463.

is to say that two distinct persons physically may have one and the same character, or *persona*, whilst one and the same person in a physical sense may, if litigating in two different capacities, constitute two distinct *personae*. Of this rule an illustration is given by Paulus, as cited in the Digest, who states that, where the first action was brought, and judgment obtained, against a man, as heir, in respect of the *dolus* of the deceased, there is no objection, on the ground of *res judicata*, to the subsequent institution of another action of fraud against the same man in his individual capacity.[1]

520 Roman jurisprudence recognised the distinction between actions *in rem* and actions *in personam*, at all events for the purposes of formulary procedure,[2] though the distinction does not seem to have played anything like the important part in the rules as to parties which it has always played in the English law of *res judicata*.[3] Illustrations of proceedings *in rem*, where the "actor" represented the entire community, and not himself alone, are to be found in many places of the Digest, such as the *popularis actio*, corresponding to the Scottish action of declarator[4], though unknown to the common law of England,[5] and actions for certain forms of sacrilege (*actio sepulchri violati*), for obstructing the administration of justice, for forgery or falsification of public records (*actio de albo corrupto*), and for certain public nuisances.[6] It does not appear, however, to what, if any, extent the Roman doctrine of *res judicata*, so far as regards the rule requiring proof of identity of parties, was affected by consideration of the special nature of these forms of action.

Sect. 4. References in English authorities to the Roman law of res judicata

521 The references in the English authorities to the Roman law of *res judicata*, though not numerous, are by no means unimportant. In one of these,[7] the judgment delivered by KNIGHT-BRUCE V.-C., a great master of the civil law, is prefaced by a citation of Ulpian's *res judicata pro veritate*

[1] D. 44. 2. 22 (from Paulus *ad Edictum*, lib. xxxi): "*etsi actio sit cum haerede de dolo defuncti, deinde de dolo haeredis agatur, exceptio rei judicatae non nocebit, quia de alia re agitur*".

[2] See the passage cited from Just. Inst. iv. 13. 5, in note 4, p. 411, *ante* ("*sive in rem sive in personam*"). In the case of an ordinary action *in personam*, the praetor's direction to the judex was:—"*si paret Numerium Negidium Aulo Agerio dare, facere, praestare . . . opportere, condemna*; *si non paret, absolvito*". In the case of an action *in rem*, on the other hand, such, for an example, as an action to determine the title to a slave, the formula ran,—"*si paret hominem ex jure Quiritium Auli Agerii esse, condemna*; *si non paret, absolvito*".

[3] As to English decisions *in rem*, and their conclusiveness on the community at large, see Part I, Ch. VIII.

[4] See para. 261, *ante*.

[5] See para. 261, *ante*.

[6] D. 9. 3 ("*De his quae effuderint vel dejecerint*"). These public offences entailed heavy penalties, specified in D. 9. 3. 1. pr. For a description of the perils and nuisances of the Roman streets which gave rise to this legislation, see *Juvenal*, Sat. iii, 266–277.

[7] *Barrs* v. *Jackson* (1842), 1 Y. & C. Ch. Cas. 585.

accipitur,[1] and a statement that "with the rules of the civil law, rightly understood, the law of England generally agrees",[2] which statement he proceeds to illustrate by a profusion of excerpts from the great Roman jurists, as transcribed in the Digest.[3] It must have been by reason of this careful and exhaustive exposition of the Roman doctrine of *res judicata* that the Vice-Chancellor's judgment is so frequently referred to in terms of laudation which might otherwise appear extravagant:[4] for the judgment itself is certainly not conspicuous for any other merit,—indeed it involved a rather gross misapplication of correctly stated principle to the facts of the case, and was on this ground reversed by Lord LYNDHURST L.C.[5]

522 The general statement of the rule of *res judicata*, adopted by Ulpian from Julian,[6] which has already been set forth,[7] was cited and relied upon not only by KNIGHT-BRUCE V.-C., in the judgment above referred to, but also, subsequently, by Lord MACNAGHTEN, delivering the opinion of the Judicial Committee of the Privy Council,[8] and by Lord SHAW in the House of Lords.[9]

523 Arnoldus Vinnius, a Dutch commentator, in his annotated edition of Justinian's Institutes, gathers up the various constituents of the Roman *exceptio rei judicatae*, in one comprehensive formula, as follows: "*exceptio rei judicatae non aliter petenti obstat quam si eadem quaestio inter eosdem revocetur; itaque ita demum nocet si omnia sint eadem, idem corpus, eadem quantitas, idem jus, eadem causa petendi, eadem conditio personarum*".[10] This formula, which is compounded of verbatim transcripts of passages in the Digest,[11] is properly and usefully quoted by KNIGHT-BRUCE V.-C., after a series of citations from the Digest itself, whence it derives its authority. It is also

---

[1] Transcribed in D. 50. 17 (*Diversae Regulae*), Reg. 207.

[2] At pp. 588, 589 of *Barrs* v. *Jackson* (1842), 1 Y. & C. Ch. Cas. 585.

[3] At p. 589 of *Barrs* v. *Jackson*, *supra*, where he collects all the passages from D. 44. 2. 6, 7, 12, 13, 14, 27, which are cited in the foregoing notes, and concludes with a reference to the summarised statement of Vinnius, set out in para. 523, above.

[4] *E.g.*, by WILLES J., at p. 119 of *Nelson* v. *Couch* (1863), 15 C.B. N.S. 99. There are many other laudatory references to this judgment in later authorities.

[5] See *Barrs* v. *Jackson* (1845), 1 Ph. 582.

[6] D. 44. 2. 7. 4.

[7] In note 2 on p. 412, *ante*.

[8] At p. 623 of *Badar Bee* v. *Habib Merican Noordin*, [1909] A.C. 615 P.C.

[9] At p. 423 of *Bradshaw* v. *M'Mullan* (1920) 2 Ir.R. 412, H.L. The passage is miscited in the reporter's note as D. 44. 7. 4, instead of D. 44. 2. 7. 4.

[10] In a note to the words "*per exceptionem rei judicatae*" in the passage from Just. Inst. IV. 13. 5, cited in note 4 on p. 411, *ante*.

[11] "*Eadem quaestio inter easdem personas*" is taken from D. 44. 2. 7. 4; "*idem corpus*", from D. 44. 2. 12; "*eadem quantitas, idem jus*", from D. 44. 2. 13; and "*eadem causa petendi, et eadem conditio personarum*", from D. 44. 2. 14.

quoted by Lord CAMPBELL L.C.,[1] and by KAY J.,[2] but, in both these instances, without any reference to the Digest at all, as if it were an original emanation from the unassisted intellect of Vinnius,—a mode of treatment which strikes one as hardly less odd than would be a judicial ascription of the authorship of an English enactment to the writer of a treatise on the statute containing it, instead of to the Legislature.

---

[1] At p. 176 of *Hunter* v. *Stewart* (1861), 4 De G. F. & J. 168.
[2] At p. 28 of *Caird* v. *Moss* (1886), 33 Ch.D. 22.

Civil Evidence Act 1968—Sections 11–13

Convictions, etc. as evidence in civil proceedings

11 *Convictions as evidence in civil proceedings.*—(1) In any civil proceedings the fact that a person has been convicted of an offence by or before any court in the United Kingdom or by a court-martial there or elsewhere shall (subject to subsection (3) below) be admissible in evidence for the purpose of proving, where to do so is relevant to any issue in those proceedings, that he committed that offence, whether he was so convicted upon a plea of guilty or otherwise and whether or not he is a party to the civil proceedings: but no conviction other than a subsisting one shall be admissible in evidence by virtue of this section.

(2) In any civil proceedings in which by virtue of this section a person is proved to have been convicted of an offence by or before any court in the United Kingdom or by a court-martial there or elsewhere—

(*a*) he shall be taken to have committed that offence unless the contrary is proved; and

(*b*) without prejudice to the reception of any other admissible evidence for the purpose of identifying the facts on which the conviction was based, the contents of any document which is admissible as evidence of the conviction, and the contents of the information, complaint, indictment or charge-sheet on which the person in question was convicted, shall be admissible in evidence for that purpose.

(3) Nothing in this section shall prejudice the operation of section 13 of this Act or any other enactment whereby a conviction or a finding of fact in any criminal proceedings is for the purposes of any other proceedings made conclusive evidence of any fact.

(4) Where in any civil proceedings the contents of any document are admissible in evidence by virtue of subsection (2) above, a copy of that document, or of the material part thereof, purporting to be certified or otherwise authenticated by or on behalf of the court or authority having custody of that document shall be admissible in evidence and shall be taken to be a true copy of that document or part unless the contrary is shown.

(5) Nothing in any of the following enactments, that is to say—

(*a*) section 12 of the Criminal Justice Act 1948 (under which a conviction leading to probation or discharge is to be disregarded except as therein mentioned);

(*b*) section 9 of the Criminal Justice (Scotland) Act 1949 (which makes similar provision in respect of convictions on indictment in Scotland); and

(*c*) section 8 of the Probation Act (Northern Ireland) 1950 (which corresponds to the said section 12) of any corresponding enactment of the Parliament of Northern Ireland for the time being in force,

shall affect the operation of this section; and for the purposes of this section any order made by a court of summary jurisdiction in Scotland under section 1 or section 2 of the said Act of 1949 shall be treated as a conviction.

(6) In this section "court-martial" means a court-martial constituted under the Army Act 1955, the Air Force Act 1955 or the Naval Discipline Act 1957 or a disciplinary court constituted under section 50 of the said Act of 1957, and in relation to a court-martial "conviction", as regards a court-martial constituted under either of the said Acts of 1955, means a finding of guilty which is, or falls to be treated as, a finding of the court duly confirmed and, as regards a court-martial or disciplinary court constituted under the said Act of 1957, means a finding of guilty which is, or falls to be treated as, the finding of the court, and "convicted" shall be construed accordingly.

12 *Findings of adultery and paternity as evidence in civil proceedings.*—(1) In any civil proceedings—

(*a*) the fact that a person has been found guilty of adultery in any matrimonial proceedings; and

(*b*) the fact that a person has been adjudged to be the father of a child in affiliation proceedings before any court in the United Kingdom,

shall (subject to subsection (3) below) be admissible in evidence for the purpose of proving, where to do so is relevant to any issue in those civil proceedings, that he committed the adultery to which the finding relates or, as the case may be, is (or was) the father of that child, whether or not he offered any defence to the allegation of adultery or paternity and whether or not he is a party to the civil proceedings; but no finding or adjudication other than a subsisting one shall be admissible in evidence by virtue of this section.

(2) In any civil proceedings in which by virtue of this section a person is proved to have been found guilty of adultery as mentioned in subsection (1)(*a*) above or to have been adjudged to be the father of a child as mentioned in subsection (1)(*b*) above—

(*a*) he shall be taken to have committed the adultery to which the finding relates or, as the case may be, to be (or have been) the father of that child, unless the contrary is proved; and

(*b*) without prejudice to the reception of any other admissible evidence for the purpose of identifying the facts on which the finding or adjudication was based, the contents of any document which was before the court, or which contains any pronouncement of the court, in the matrimonial or affiliation proceedings in question shall be admissible in evidence for that purpose.

(3) Nothing in this section shall prejudice the operation of any enactment whereby a finding of fact in any matrimonial or affiliation proceedings is for the purposes of any other proceedings made conclusive evidence of any fact.

(4) Subsection (4) of section 11 of this Act shall apply for the purposes of this section as if the reference to subsection (2) were a reference to subsection (2) of this section.

(5) In this section—

"matrimonial proceedings" means any matrimonial cause in the High Court or a county court in England and Wales or in the High Court in Northern Ireland, any consistorial action in Scotland, or any appeal arising out of any such cause or action;

"affiliation proceedings" means, in relation to Scotland, any action of affiliation and aliment;

and in this subsection "consistorial action" does not include an action of aliment only between husband and wife raised in the Court of Session or an action of interim aliment raised in the sheriff court.

13 *Conclusiveness of convictions for purposes of defamation actions.*—(1) In an action for libel or slander in which the question whether a person did or did not commit a criminal offence is relevant to an issue arising in the action, proof that, at the time when that issue falls to be determined, that person stands convicted of that offence shall be conclusive evidence that he committed that offence; and his conviction thereof shall be admissible in evidence accordingly.

(2) In any such action as aforesaid in which by virtue of this section a person is proved to have been convicted of an offence, the contents of any document which is admissible as evidence of the conviction, and the contents of the information, complaint, indictment or charge sheet on which that person was convicted, shall, without prejudice to the reception of any other admissible evidence for the purpose of identifying the facts on which the conviction was based, be admissible in evidence for the purpose of identifying those facts.

(3) For the purposes of this section a person shall be taken to stand convicted of an offence if but only if there subsists against him a conviction of that offence by or before a court in the United Kingdom or by a court-martial there or elsewhere.

(4) Subsections (4) to (6) of section 11 of this Act shall apply for the purposes of this section as they apply for the purposes of that section, but as if in the said subsection (4) the reference to subsection (2) were a reference to subsection (2) of this section.

(5) The foregoing provisions of this section shall apply for the purposes of any action begun after the passing of this Act, whenever the cause of action arose, but shall not apply for the purposes of any action begun before the passing of this Act or any appeal or other proceedings arising out of any such action.

APPENDIX D

Fifteenth Report of the Law Reform Committee (under the Chairmanship of Lord Pearson)

(Presented to Parliament by
the Lord High Chancellor
September 1967)*

Introduction

1. *Hollington* v. *F. Hewthorn & Co., Ltd. and Another*, [1943] K.B. 587, is the full title of the case in which the Court of Appeal laid down the rule of evidence which is the subject of our present Report, which forms part of our general review of the law of evidence in civil cases. In some recent judgments of the Court of Appeal, upon whom the rule in *Hollington* v. *Hewthorn* is still binding, it has been suggested that it requires reconsideration. We think so too.

2. The actual case in which the rule was laid down arose out of a collision between two cars upon the highway in which the plaintiff's car was damaged. The drivers of the two cars were the only eye-witnesses of the accident. It gave rise to both criminal and civil proceedings. The driver

---

* H.M.S.O., London, Cmnd. 3391.

of the defendant's car was prosecuted and convicted in the magistrates' court for the summary offence of careless driving under s. 12 of the Road Traffic Act 1930. That summary offence also constitutes the tort of negligence actionable at the suit of another user of the highway who sustains damage as a result of the careless driving. The plaintiff brought a civil action for this tort against the convicted driver and his employer. But, before the civil action came on for hearing, the driver of the plaintiff's car died. The plaintiff, deprived of his only witness, sought to put in evidence the conviction of the defendant driver to establish a *prima facie* case of negligence against him. The Court of Appeal held the conviction to be inadmissible in the civil action and, the defendant calling no evidence, the plaintiff's action failed for want of any admissible evidence of the defendant driver's negligence.

3. Rationalise it how one will, the decision in this case offends one's sense of justice. The defendant driver had been found guilty of careless driving by a court of competent jurisdiction. The onus of proof of culpability in criminal cases is higher than in civil; the degree of carelessness required to sustain a conviction for careless driving is, if anything, greater than that required to sustain a civil cause of action in negligence. Yet the fact that the defendant driver had been convicted of careless driving at the time and place of the accident was held not to amount even to *prima facie* evidence of his negligent driving at that time and place. It is not easy to escape the implication in the rule in *Hollington* v. *Hewthorn* that, in the estimation of lawyers, a conviction by a criminal court is as likely to be wrong as right. It is not, of course, spelt out in those terms in the judgment of the Court of Appeal, although, insofar as their decision was based mainly upon the ground that the opinion of the criminal court as to the defendant driver's guilt was as irrelevant as that of a bystander who witnessed the accident, the gap between the implicit and the explicit was a narrow one.

4. It is in a sense true that a finding by any court that a person was culpable or not culpable of a particular criminal offence or civil wrong is an expression of opinion by the court. But it is of a different character from an expression of opinion by a private individual. In the first place, it is made by persons, whether judges, magistrates or juries, acting under a legal duty to form and express an opinion on that issue. In the second place, in forming their opinion they are aided by a procedure, of which the law of evidence forms part, which has been evolved with a view to ensuring that the material needed to enable them to form a correct opinion is available to them. In the third place, their opinion, expressed in the form of a finding or verdict of guilty or not guilty in criminal proceedings or a judgment in civil pro-

ceedings, has consequences which are enforced by the executive power of the state.

5. Although the actual decision in *Hollington* v. *Hewthorn* related to the admissibility in civil proceedings of evidence of a previous criminal conviction of a party to those civil proceedings, the *ratio decidendi* extends to previous findings of culpability in civil proceedings not brought between the same parties. Where the previous civil proceedings were between the same parties, a different rule, that of estoppel *per rem judicatam*, applies. Estoppel lies outside the scope of our present Report, but with this exception we propose to consider the general problem of the admissibility and effect to be given to previous findings of culpability or lack of culpability on the part of any person by both criminal and civil courts.

6. A finding of culpability or lack of culpability by a court under our system of procedure may be the result of a number of component opinions reached in the course of the decision-making process: opinions as to the credibility of the accounts of individual witnesses of what they claim to have seen or heard, opinions as to the proper inferences to be drawn from primary facts established by credible testimony, opinions of law as to whether the facts proved and inferred constitute the criminal offence or civil wrong with which a person is charged. Basically the decision-making process is the same in both criminal and civil proceedings, but there are two significant differences which are relevant to the probative value of findings of culpability or lack of culpability by criminal courts and civil courts. A finding of culpability by a criminal court must not be made unless the court is satisfied beyond reasonable doubt that the accused is guilty of the offence with which he is charged. If not so satisfied, the criminal court must make a finding of lack of culpability, even though it may be of opinion that it is more likely than not that the accused was guilty. In civil proceedings a finding of culpability must be made upon the balance of probabilities, *i.e.* if the court is of opinion that it is more likely than not that a party was culpable of the civil wrong in respect of which he is sued. Secondly, although in both criminal and civil proceedings the court must form its opinion upon the evidence adduced before it, in civil proceedings in general the parties have complete liberty of choice as to how to conduct their respective cases and what material to place before the court, and, except in some matrimonial causes, the court has no duty to inquire whether all material relevant to its decision has been brought to its notice. In criminal cases, on the other hand, it is the practice and the duty of the prosecution, as well as adducing evidence which tends to show the culpability of the accused, either itself to adduce or to make available to the defence any material of which it has knowledge which tends to show his

non-culpability. There is no corresponding duty on the defence as respects evidence of culpability. It is also the duty of the presiding judge in trials on indictment to exclude evidence against the accused if he considers that its prejudicial effect would outweigh its true probative value. For these reasons, a finding of culpability against a person upon a contested trial in criminal proceedings is of higher probative value than a finding of culpability against him in civil proceedings, and a finding of lack of culpability against a person in criminal proceedings is of lower probative value than such a finding in civil proceedings.

7. Matrimonial causes in the High Court for dissolution of marriage differ from other civil proceedings in that the judge has a statutory duty to satisfy himself of the existence of valid grounds for dissolution and in so doing he is not confined to the evidence which the parties themselves choose to submit to him.

8. We approach the rule in *Hollington* v. *Hewthorn* from the premise stated in our Report on Hearsay Evidence (Thirteenth Report of the Law Reform Committee: Cmnd. 2964), that any material which has probative value upon any question in issue in a civil action should be admissible in evidence unless there are good reasons for excluding it. Our further premise is that any decision of an English court upon an issue which it has a duty to determine is more likely than not to to have been reached according to law and to be right rather than wrong. It may therefore constitute material of some probative value if the self-same issue arises in subsequent legal proceedings.

Criminal Proceedings

9. The issue in criminal proceedings is whether the conduct of the accused has been shown beyond reasonable doubt to constitute the criminal offence with which he has been charged. The same issue, save that culpability need only be shown upon the balance of probabilities, may arise in a civil suit in a number of different ways. It is most likely to arise in a civil suit against the person who was defendant in the criminal proceedings, for many criminal offences, at any rate if they cause damage to another person, are civil wrongs actionable at his suit. Exceptionally the defendant in the criminal proceedings may be the plaintiff in civil proceedings, as in an action for damages for a defamatory statement that he committed the offence of which he was acquitted or convicted. It may also arise in civil proceedings to which the defendant in the criminal proceedings is not a party, as in an action brought against his employer as vicariously liable for his tortious act or in an action brought against an insurer, as for example under a burglary policy. Provided that the issue decided in the criminal proceed-

ings is the same as an issue in the subsequent civil suit, we do not think that either the admissibility or the effect of the conviction or acquittal should depend upon who are the parties to the civil suit. We are concerned not with estoppel but with the probative value of the opinion of the criminal court expressed in its decision.

10. We deal later with the practical problem of identifying the conduct of the accused which constituted the criminal offence of which he was convicted or acquitted with his conduct which is relevant to an issue in the subsequent civil suit. At this stage we assume that the identification can be made. A criminal trial may have three results: a conviction upon a contested trial, a conviction upon plea of guilty, or an acquittal. The probative values of these three results upon the question in issue in the civil action, as to whether upon the balance of probabilities the conduct of the accused constituted the criminal offence with which he was charged, are not the same.

Conviction upon a contested trial

11. A conviction upon a contested trial is consistent only with the opinion of the criminal court's being that it has been established, not merely on the balance of probabilities, but beyond reasonable doubt, that the conduct of the accused did constitute the criminal offence with which he was charged and that it has been so established upon all the material known to the prosecution or the defence and considered by either to be relevant to the issue of guilt. Any layman would, we think, regard the fact of such conviction as a firm foundation for the belief that the accused had conducted himself in such a manner as to constitute the criminal offence of which he was convicted and, if such criminal offence would also constitute a civil wrong, that the accused had committed a civil wrong also. We, too, share this common-sense view. We consider that such a conviction has high probative value in establishing the cause of action in a subsequent civil action founded upon the same conduct, in which the onus of proof is lower. We have no doubt in principle that evidence of the conviction should be admissible.

Conviction upon Plea of Guilty

12. Under the existing law the fact that a person pleaded guilty to a criminal offence is admissible in a civil suit to which that person is a party as an admission by him—although technically the conviction resulting from the plea is not. A plea of guilty is not admissible in evidence-in-chief in a civil action to which the person who pleaded guilty is not a party, though it may be put to him in cross-examination if he is called as a witness.

Where a plea of guilty can be proved under the existing law, considerable weight attaches to it, for people, if they are innocent, do not usually plead guilty to criminal offences which render them subject to punishment. We see no reason in logic or in common sense why the conviction resulting from a plea of guilty should not have probative value in establishing that the accused, whether or not he is a party to the civil action, was guilty of the conduct of which he was convicted. We think it should be admissible in subsequent civil proceedings in the same way as a conviction upon a contested trial.

The Weight to be given to Convictions

13. We have considered whether in subsequent actions a conviction should be conclusive as to the culpability of the convicted person; but we do not think that, apart from certain actions for defamation, it would be right to go so far. Our premise is that the decision of an English criminal court upon an issue which it has a duty to determine is more likely to be right than wrong—not that it is infallible. Error may arise for a number of reasons. The evidence upon which the criminal court's decision was based may have been incomplete—particularly in summary proceedings for minor offences in which professional lawyers are not engaged. Further evidence may have come to light before the subsequent civil proceedings. The defence may have been inadequately presented at the criminal trial. Unreasonable inferences of fact may have been drawn by the court, or it may have fallen into error in law, but the smallness of the penalty imposed may have made it not worth while to appeal to a higher court. The accused may have pleaded guilty, particularly to a minor offence, not because he had no defence but for reasons of personal convenience—to save time and expense or to avoid disclosing some embarrassing though non-criminous fact which would come to light if the case were defended. We do not suggest that erroneous convictions for these or any other reasons are common, but they may occasionally occur and we do not think that a party to a civil action, who may not be the convicted person himself, should be debarred from proving if he can that a conviction was erroneous. But we have no doubt that the onus should be upon him to prove it. We accordingly recommend that, where any person has been charged with any conduct alleged to constitute a criminal offence and upon such charge has been convicted of such offence by any court of competent jurisdiction in the United Kingdom, the fact of such conviction shall be admissible in any civil proceedings and such person shall be taken to be guilty of such conduct and of such offence unless it is proved that such conviction was erroneous.

14. We have avoided using the expression *prima facie* evidence. It is,

we think, too vague a phrase in which to express our recommendation. To say that something is *prima facie* evidence of a material fact may mean no more than that it is evidence of that fact if there is no other evidence to displace it. It says no more about the weight of the *prima facie* evidence than that. Any legislation to give effect to our recommendation should make it clear that the onus lies upon the person seeking to displace the evidence constituted by the conviction to show that the conviction was erroneous.

Acquittal

15. Because of the higher onus of proof in criminal cases, an acquittal proves no more than that the criminal court was of opinion that it had not been proved beyond reasonable doubt that the conduct of the accused did constitute the criminal offence with which he was charged. That court may have been satisfied that the accused was innocent of the conduct alleged against him, but of itself a verdict of not guilty is equally consistent with that court's opinion being that on the balance of probabilities the accused's conduct did constitute the criminal offence—and this would be sufficient to establish his culpability in a civil action. Of itself, the mere fact that the accused was acquitted of a criminal offence is thus without probative value in a civil action based upon the same conduct. It is at first blush tempting to suggest that, while recognising that an acquittal may not have the same probative value as a conviction, evidence of an acquittal should nevertheless be admissible in subsequent civil proceedings "for what it is worth", and that it should be left to the civil court to determine what weight, if any, should be attached to it in the particular case. But, on reflection, we think this can be shown to be specious. In civil proceedings the onus of proving that the defendant's conduct constituted an actionable wrong lies upon the plaintiff. A previous conviction of the defendant based upon the same conduct would, if our recommendations were accepted, satisfy this onus and substitute an onus upon the defendant to show that the conviction was erroneous. But an acquittal is incapable of shifting the onus and the plaintiff would be obliged to adduce evidence of the conduct of the defendant which he alleges to be actionable. The civil court would have to form its own opinion whether the evidence adduced at the hearing established, not beyond reasonable doubt but only upon the balance of probabilities, that the defendant's conduct was such as to constitute a civil wrong. Even if that evidence were identical with the evidence adduced in the previous criminal proceedings, the civil court's conclusion, whether in favour of the plaintiff or the defendant, would be consistent with the defendant's acquittal in the criminal proceedings. So the acquittal, if admitted for "what it is worth", would be worth nothing: not only would

it have no effect upon the onus of proof but it would be without any probative value in the issue in the civil proceedings—which is another way of saying it is irrelevant.

Convictions under Appeal

16. Convictions may be reversed upon appeal and, if reversed, have the same effect as acquittals. They are no longer convictions and would be inadmissible under our recommendations. It is unlikely, in practice, that a civil action based upon the conduct of a defendant which was the subject of a criminal conviction would come on for trial while an appeal against the conviction was still pending. If this were to happen in an action in which a party was seeking to rely upon the conviction of another person, whether party to the action or not, the hearing of the civil action should be adjourned until after the final determination of the criminal appeal. We doubt if any specific rule of court would be necessary to ensure this; it could be safely left to the practice of the court.

Foreign Convictions

17. We have restricted our recommendation to convictions by courts of competent jurisdiction in the United Kingdom. We do not include convictions by foreign courts. This is for practical reasons. The substantive criminal law varies widely in different countries. So does criminal procedure and the law of evidence. The relevance of the foreign conviction to the issues in the English civil action could not be ascertained without expert evidence of the substantive criminal law of the foreign country. Its weight could not be judged without expert evidence of the procedural law of the foreign country and reliable information as to the standards of its courts. There are, of course, many countries whose standard of administration of criminal justice is as high as our own, but there are others in which one cannot be assured of this. It would be invidious to draw distinctions between one foreign country and another in the legislation needed to give effect to our recommendations. It would be impracticable to leave the admissibility and weight of a foreign conviction to the discretion of an English judge unfamiliar with the legal system and standards of criminal justice of the foreign country concerned. Furthermore, the burden of showing that a foreign conviction was erroneous would be difficult, perhaps impossible, to sustain, since there would be no way of compelling the witnesses in the foreign criminal proceedings to attend to give evidence in the English courts. The practical effect of making foreign convictions admissible might well be to make them conclusive, and the remoter the

country in which the conviction took place the more difficult it would be to dispute its correctness.

Convictions before courts-martial

18. We have considered whether our recommendations should also apply to findings of guilt by courts-martial, but on balance we have reached the conclusion that they should not. This does not imply any reflection upon the reliability of decisions of courts-martial, but is based upon practical considerations. When held in the United Kingdom, courts-martial are mainly confined to offences against military law. This is different from ordinary criminal law and the issues involved in a finding of guilt under military law would only very rarely be identical with any issues involved in civil proceedings. Acts done in the United Kingdom by service personnel which are offences against the ordinary criminal law and cause injury to the person or property of civilians are tried by criminal courts—not by courts-martial. The practical consequences of extending our recommendations to findings of guilt by courts-martial held in the United Kingdom would, we think, be minimal. Outside the United Kingdom courts-martial do more frequently try offences by service personnel against the ordinary criminal law of the United Kingdom and, if the act constituting the offence would constitute a tort if committed in the United Kingdom and is not lawful in the country where it was in fact committed, it could give rise to a civil action in England in which the issues were the same (subject to the lighter burden of proof) as those in the proceedings before the court-martial. But the difficulty of obtaining witnesses from outside the jurisdiction to establish that the conviction was erroneous, to which we have drawn attention in connection with convictions by foreign courts, would apply with equal force to findings of guilt by courts-martial held outside the United Kingdom. If the recommendations in our Report on Hearsay Evidence were adopted, the statements made by the witnesses at the court-martial would be admissible in the subsequent civil proceedings in England if the witnesses were abroad and not available for cross-examination. We do not think that we should further weight the scales against a party desirous of securing their attendance but unable to do so, by imposing upon him the additional express onus of proving that the finding of guilt by the court-martial was erroneous.

Coroners' Inquests

19. We should also make it clear that our recommendations do not extend to findings by coroners' courts. These are not criminal proceedings—though they may lead to them. There are no parties to an inquest; a person

against whom a verdict of murder or manslaughter may be brought has no right to cross-examine or to call evidence on his own behalf.

Identification of issues in Criminal Proceedings with those in Civil Proceedings

20. A conviction is of probative value in a subsequent civil action only if the convicted person's conduct which was the subject of the criminal charge against him is the same conduct as is in issue in the civil porceedings. In the judgment in *Hollington* v. *Hewthorn* considerable stress was laid upon the practical difficulties of identifying the conduct which is the subject-matter of a conviction. It was pointed out that the certificate of conviction, in that case of a motoring offence, did not itself contain any detailed particulars of the facts upon which it was based. It merely stated that the defendant was convicted of driving without due care and attention on a certain date in a certain parish or place. This, of itself, would not identify the careless driving of which he was convicted with the careless driving which caused damage to the plaintiff's car. We think that this judgment over-estimates the difficulty of identifying the subject-matter of a conviction even in the existing state of the law. It is not a novel problem, for in actions for tort which also constitute a felony the plaintiff must prove that the defendant has already been prosecuted for the felony[1]—proof of which involves the same problem of identification of conduct. The indictment, or the information in cases tried summarily, will contain more detailed particulars of the conduct which is the subject-matter of the conviction, and our recommendation in paragraph 13 is intended to cover the admissibility of the indictment or information on which the accused was convicted as well as the certificate of conviction itself. Unless it is admitted, oral evidence may be required to link the indictment or information with the conviction.

21. In most cases, however, of which *Hollington* v. *Hewthorn* was an example, the convicted person will be a party to the civil proceedings. The identification of the defendant's conduct which was the subject-matter of the criminal proceedings could readily be obtained by an interrogatory addressed to him. If the law is changed, as we recommend, it would normally be admitted without need to resort to interrogatories. But there may be some cases in which the convicted person is not a party to the civil proceedings, as for instance in a claim against an insurer under a burglary policy, and it is possible in such a case that the particulars in the indictment or information may be insufficient to identify the conduct which was the subject-matter of the criminal charge with the conduct relevant to the issue in the civil proceedings. In such a case, which would in practice,

1 This rule will no longer be effective when the Criminal Law Act 1967 comes into force on the 1st January 1968.

we think, be very rare, it would be necessary in the civil proceedings to investigate the evidence in the criminal proceedings and this, under the existing law, might involve re-calling on the issue of identification of conduct the witnesses called on the issue of guilt in the criminal proceedings. If, however, the recommendations made in our Report on Hearsay Evidence are given statutory force, this can be avoided and the transcript or notes of evidence in the criminal proceedings can be used on the issue of identification of conduct.

Procedural Matters

22. Where a party to civil proceedings wishes to rely upon the conviction of any person as evidence that he was guilty of the conduct constituting the criminal offence of which he was convicted, he should so state in his pleading, identifying the conduct and conviction upon which he will rely. The adverse party may wish (i) to deny the conviction, or (ii) to deny that the subject-matter of the conviction was the conduct alleged, or (iii) to allege that the conviction was erroneous, or to combine any two or more of these pleas. He should be required to specify in his defence or reply which of these pleas he intends to rely upon. The issues raised by pleas (i) and (ii), if not disposed of by interrogatories, could in most cases be dealt with at the trial by production of the indictment or information and the certificate of conviction and by oral evidence to identify the person named in the certificate. But in the exceptional case it might be necessary, in order to decide the issue raised by plea (ii), to show what was the evidence in the criminal proceedings on which the person was convicted. A note or transcript of such evidence would be admissible in the civil proceedings under the recommendations contained in our Report on Hearsay Evidence and would be the subject of a notice under the procedure recommended in that Report. Under plea (ii), however, the truth of the evidence upon which the conviction was based is not in issue and the other party should not be entitled to serve a counter-notice requiring the witnesses in the criminal proceedings to be called by the party relying on the conviction. Nor do we think he should be entitled to serve a counter-notice if plea (iii) is combined with plea (ii). The onus of proving that a conviction is erroneous lies upon the party who alleges that it is. It is for him to call his own witnesses to prove this. He should not be enabled by a procedural manoeuvre to insist upon the party relying on the conviction producing for fresh cross-examination on the issue of guilt the witnesses upon whose evidence he was convicted. To allow this would re-introduce in those cases where this manoeuvre was possible some of the practical consequences

of the rule in *Hollington* v. *Hewthorn* which our recommendation is intended to avoid.

Practical Consequences

23. We appreciate that quantitatively the abolition of the rule in *Hollington* v. *Hewthorn* may not have any decisive effect in a large number of cases. The commonest type of case in which there is a criminal conviction for conduct which also constitutes a civil wrong is the running-down action. In the majority of defended running-down actions contributory negligence is pleaded and the degree of fault (if any) of all parties is in issue. This is not in issue in criminal proceedings and, even though the onus of proof of one party's negligence is shifted, it will generally be necessary on the issue of contributory negligence to call in the civil proceedings the same witnesses who gave evidence in the criminal proceedings. In cases of this kind the abolition of the rule in *Hollington* v. *Hewthorn* is unlikely to result in much saving of time or expense. On the other hand, it will avoid such injustice as occurred in *Hollington* v. *Hewthorn* itself, where an essential witness has died before the hearing, and may discourage denials of liability where no contributory negligence can be alleged.

24. But the rule in *Hollington* v. *Hewthorn* not infrequently affects matrimonial causes where a respondent has been convicted of rape or some other sexual offence and dissolution of his marriage is sought on the grounds of adultery or cruelty. Such petitions are frequently undefended, but the evidence of the offence, often involving the testimony of a young victim, has to be given again in the High Court. The recommendation in our Report on Heresay Evidence would alleviate this in undefended cases, but not in defended cases in which a counter-notice was served. Only the abolition of the rule in *Hollington* v. *Hewthorn* would provide relief in such cases. In cases of homicide the abolition of the rule will also save costs in probate and administration actions.

25. We make no attempt to forecast the kind of material which would be sufficient to satisfy the onus of proof that a conviction was erroneous. This must necessarily depend on the particular circumstances of the case and be left to the common sense of the judge or the jury in the civil proceedings. But we do not regard the onus as a light one and, in the case of a conviction upon a contested trial, we should not normally expect it to be discharged by the testimony of the convicted person alone, unless supported by cogent corroborative evidence, or, in the case of a conviction upon plea, unless a convicing explanation were given by the convicted person of why he pleaded guilty.

Defamation

26. As will have been apparent, our general recommendations as to the admissibility in evidence in civil proceedings of convictions in previous criminal proceedings and the weight to be given to such convictions, and as to the non-admissibility of acquittals, have been based solely upon consideration of their respective probative values. But, as some recent cases have shown, the rule in *Hollington* v. *Hewthorn* can have practical consequences which raise a wider question of public policy to which our general recommendations may not provide a sufficient answer. The rule makes it possible in some circumstances to obtain what is in effect a re-trial of criminal proceedings in the guise of a civil action for defamation brought by the person who has been convicted or acquitted in the criminal proceedings. A fair and accurate report of criminal proceedings is, of course, absolutely privileged. But for a statement, not contained in such a report, which imputes that a person has committed a criminal offence, the only available defence is justification (whether standing by itself or joined with a defence of fair comment), unless the statement is made upon an occasion which is privileged for some other reason. If all that is said is that the plaintiff was convicted of the offence, proof of the conviction establishes the defence of justification; but if, as is likely to be the case, the statement imputes that he was guilty of the offence of which he was convicted, the defendant must prove the plaintiff's guilt *de novo* in the civil action for defamation. The conviction is not admissible evidence of guilt. Conversely, a defendant may justify a statement that the plaintiff was guilty of a criminal offence of which he was acquitted by proving his guilt *de novo* in the civil action.

Two recent cases will serve as illustrations. In one the plaintiff had been convicted of robbery and his conviction had been upheld by the Court of Criminal Appeal. Several years later he brought an action for libel against a defendant who had published a statement that the plaintiff was guilty of the robbery of which he had been convicted. The defendant upon whom, under the existing law, the onus lay of proving that the plaintiff had been guilty failed to discharge it and the plaintiff's action succeeded.[1] In the other, the plaintiff had been acquitted of murder, his defence being an alibi. Twenty years later he brought an action for libel against defendants who had published a statement which imputed that the plaintiff was guilty of the murder of which he had been acquitted. The defendants succeeded in sustaining the onus which lay upon them of proving on the balance of

[1] *Hinds* v. *Sparks*, [1964] Crim. L.R. 717.

probabilities that the plaintiff had been guilty of the murder of which he had been acquitted and the plaintiff's action failed.[1]

27. Our general recommendations about the admissibility in evidence of a conviction and the onus of proving that it was erroneous would have affected the conduct of the first case, but it would not have prevented the issue of guilt being retried in the civil proceedings and might not have altered the result of the action, for that issue was retried when the relevant evidence was inevitably very stale. The second case, since it arose out of an acquittal, would not have been affected by our general recommendations. In actions, other than those for defamation, to which our general recommendations apply, the materiality of the conviction is not to prove that the convicted person was guilty of the criminal offence of which he was convicted, but to prove that his conduct was such as to give rise to a civil liability on the part either of the convicted person himself or of another person such as his employer or an insurer. Because this liability is additional to the penal consequences of the conviction and may fall upon someone other than the convicted person, we have come to the conclusion, on balance, that the person upon whom the civil liability will fall should not be precluded from resisting it by proving, if he can, that the convicted person's conduct was not such as the criminal court found it to be. But in actions for defamation such as those which we have instanced, the only issue, other than that of damages, is whether a person who has been tried for a criminal offence was guilty of that criminal offence. The real purpose of the action in the case of a conviction, or the defence of justification in the case of an acquittal, is to obtain a re-trial of the criminal proceedings upon different evidence by a court which lacks jurisdiction to try crime and applies a procedure and standard of proof which the law regards as inappropriate in criminal proceedings.

28. This raises two related questions of public policy which do not depend upon the probative value of convictions and acquittals. The first is whether or not a civil court, in an action to which the Crown is not a party, ought to re-try upon a different standard of proof the precise issue of guilt of a criminal offence which has already been tried and determined by a criminal court of competent jurisdiction. The second is whether any person ought to be at risk of incurring civil liability for stating that another person was guilty of an offence of which he was convicted, so long as such conviction has not been set aside upon appeal, or ought ever to be entitled without incurring civil liability to state that another person was guilty of an offence for which he had been duly tried and acquitted.

29. We think that the answer to both these questions is "No". The

[1] *Loughans* v. *Odhams Press* (1963), Times, Feb. 14.

state, nominally the Crown, has a direct interest in all prosecutions for criminal offences. It has established a special system of trial and appellate courts for dealing with them. These courts apply a procedure different from that in civil actions and adopt a different standard or proof, the purpose of which is to safeguard the interests of the accused and to ensure that the innocent are not convicted. The penal sanctions which the criminal courts impose upon those whom they find guilty are enforced by the executive power of the state. No civil court has jurisdiction to alter or affect them. Those whom they acquit cannot be put on trial again. Their acquittal is final. It can only undermine public confidence in the administration of criminal justice if civil courts in actions between private individuals can be forced to re-try the issue of guilt which has already been determined by a criminal court and reach a different conclusion. To a trained lawyer it is no doubt intelligible that a civil court should reach a different conclusion from that of the criminal court without there having been any error in the finding of the criminal court. The re-trial in the civil action may take place many years later, when the witnesses, upon whose evidence the finding of guilty or not guilty at the criminal trial was based, have died or disappeared or forgotten what happened. Legal aid is not available in actions for defamation and one or other of the parties may lack the resources to trace witnesses and documents and marshall all the relevant evidence. In any event, the onus of proof will be different from that which the law regards as essential in a criminal trial. But this is much too technical for the layman. His reaction cannot fail to be: here are two English courts, one says that A was guilty, the other says that he was not; one of them must be wrong. And the law is made for laymen. It is on their behalf as citizens of the state that criminal prosecutions are brought. When such a prosecution brought in a court of competent jurisdiction results in a conviction which is not set aside upon appeal, any citizen should, we think, be entitled to say without risk of incurring any civil liability that the convicted person did commit the offence of which he was convicted. And, by parity of reasoning, when a prosecution results in an acquittal, we do not think that he is entitled to say that the acquitted person did commit the offence of which he was acquitted. In reaching this conclusion we have not overlooked the argument that there may be exceptional cases in which the public interest could be served by the Press, or a private citizen, being free to challenge the correctness of an acquittal, and that our recommendation could be criticised as tending to restrict freedom of discussion. But we think that, on balance, the greater public interest lies in inhibiting attempts to use defamation actions as a means of challenging the findings of criminal courts.

30. We recognise that this question of public policy may be classified as appertaining more to the substantive law of defamation than to the procedural law of evidence, and, as such, outside our terms of reference. But the change in the law which we think desirable would be a qualification of our general recommendation about the admissibility and effect of previous convictions in subsequent civil proceedings, by providing that in any civil action for defamation, brought in respect of a statement imputing that a person was guilty of any criminal offence, proof that such person stands convicted of such offence by a court of competent jurisdiction in the United Kingdom should be conclusive evidence that he was guilty of such offence, and proof that such person stands acquitted of such offence by a court of competent jurisdiction in the United Kingdom (or has been pardoned by the Crown) should be conclusive evidence that he was not guilty of such offence.

31. This proviso to our general recommendations would not affect any defences to actions for defamation other than that of justification, or fair comment insofar as the comment in question is based upon an allegation of criminal conduct. It would still be open to the defendant to rely upon privilege, whether absolute, or qualified, or leave and licence. It would not deprive a convicted plaintiff of a remedy for any defamatory imputation wider than that he was guilty of the actual offence of which he had been convicted, nor would it debar a defendant from proving that a plaintiff was guilty of any criminal offence other than the actual offence of which he had been acquitted. Its only object is to prevent the machinery of a civil action being used for the sole purpose of obtaining the re-trial of criminal proceedings which have already been heard and determined according to law by a court of criminal jurisdiction.

32. We also considered whether, notwithstanding the exclusion of convictions by courts-martial from our general recommendations as respects the probative effect of convictions in civil proceedings, our special recommendations as respects actions for defamation ought nevertheless to apply to convictions and acquittals before courts-martial. Our conclusion was that they should not be so extended: since our recommendations as respects actions for defamation are not based exclusively on the probative value of convictions and acquittals by criminal courts, the considerations set out in paragraph 18 are not conclusive so far as actions for defamation are concerned. Nevertheless, there appeared to us to be a number of special features affecting courts-martial which distinguish their findings from those of ordinary criminal courts. In particular, in respect of both the content and nature of the law applied and of the rights of appeal available to a convicted person, a court-martial is very different from the ordinary

criminal court. Nor, as we have already mentioned, is a court-martial in every sense necessarily a United Kingdom court, since it may, and often does, sit abroad. Thirdly, courts-martial form only a part of the criminal judicial system applicable to the Armed Forces and we should certainly not wish our recommendations to extend to those less formal adjudications which are made by commanding officers dealing summarily with military offences.

33. We have also considered to what extent our recommendations about defamation should apply to actions pending when the change in the law takes place. To make proof of conviction or acquittal *conclusive* evidence of guilt or innocence, as the case may be, operates to some extent as a change in the substantive law as well as in the law of evidence and we do not think that in this case it would be right to apply the normal rule whereby a change in the rules of evidence affects pending proceedings. On the other hand, we do think our recommendations ought to apply to all actions instituted after the change in the law, irrespective of the date on which the cause of action accrued, and we recommend accordingly.

Findings of Adultery in Matrimonial Cases

34. We have already drawn attention to the fact that in petitions for dissolution of marriage the judge is under a statutory duty to make inquiry to satisfy himself that the grounds for dissolution are made out. The only one of these grounds which is relevant for our present purposes is adultery, for this involves a stranger to the marriage sought to be dissolved. The alleged adulterer, whether co-respondent or woman named, is served with the proceedings and has the opportunity of defending himself or herself against the charge. But a finding of adultery against the co-respondent or woman named is not admissible as evidence of the adultery in a subsequent petition for dissolution of marriage by the spouse of the co-respondent or woman named. Having regard to the statutory duty of inquiry imposed upon the judge in suits for dissolution of marriage, and to the right of the alleged adulterer to defend the charge, we think that such a finding should be dealt with in the same way as a criminal conviction. In any subsequent civil proceedings the fact of such finding of adultery should be admissible and the person against whom the finding was made should be taken to have committed the adultery found against him, unless it is proved that such finding was erroneous. We draw attention to the fact that a similar recommendation was made in the Denning Report on Matrimonial Causes (1947 Cmd. 7024) and the Report of the Royal Commission on Marriage and Divorce (1956 Cmd. 9678).

35. Most findings of adultery are in undefended suits and there may be

good reasons, particularly when no claim for damages or costs is made against the alleged adulterer, for his not appearing and defending the suit, even though he might be able to do so successfully. Under our recommendation it would, of course, be open to him in the subsequent suit to put forward his explanation for not appearing to defend the charge in the former suit and to prove, if he could, that the finding was erroneous.

36. Findings of adultery are also made in proceedings in magistrates' courts as part of the grounds for making or discharging orders for maintenance. In these proceedings, although in practice the alleged adulterer is often informed of the proceedings and, if he attends, often gives evidence, he has no statutory right to be served with the proceedings, he is not a party to them and he has no enforceable right to take part in them or to be professionally represented. Since dissolution of the marriage is not involved, the magistrates' court is not under the same duty of inquiry as the High Court.[1] For these reasons, our recommendation as to findings of adultery in matrimonial suits in the High Court does not extend to such findings in proceedings in magistrates' courts. We think the matter should continue to be governed by section 3(1) and (2) of the Matrimonial Causes Act 1965 which provides:

> "(1) A person shall not be prevented from presenting a petition for divorce, or the court from granting a decree of divorce, by reason only that the petitioner has at any time, on the same facts or substantially the same facts as those proved in support of the petition, been granted a decree of judicial separation or an order under, or having effect as if made under, the Matrimonial Proceedings (Magistrates' Courts) Act 1960 or any corresponding enactments in force in Northern Ireland, the Isle of Man or any of the Channel Islands.
>
> (2) On a petition for divorce in such a case as is mentioned in the foregoing subsection, the court may treat the decree of judicial separation or the said order as sufficient proof of the adultery, desertion or other ground on which it was granted, but shall not grant a decree of divorce without receiving evidence from the petitioner."

Affiliation Orders

37. Affiliation orders are classified as orders made in civil proceedings, but a high standard of proof, including corroboration of the mother's evidence, is required and the putative father is a party to the proceedings and

---

[1] This duty will also be imposed on a county court judge under the Matrimonial Causes Act 1967, which gives the county court jurisdiction.

has full opportunity to defend them. His conduct in siring the child may be relevant to an issue of adultery in a subsequent matrimonial suit, or to the claims of the child in other civil proceedings. We think that a finding of paternity made in affiliation proceedings should be given the same evidential effect in subsequent civil proceedings as a conviction by a criminal court or a finding of adultery by the High Court.

Other Civil Proceedings

38. With the exceptions with which we have already dealt, an issue of fact in one civil action is seldom the same as an issue of act in another civil action between different parties. In practice it is only likely to arise where a number of different persons are injured in the same accident by the same acts of negligence. Such cases are most conveniently dealt with by all the injured parties joining in the same action, by consolidation, or by agreeing to treat one action as a test action. It is, however, theoretically possible (and has occasionally happened) that separate actions brought by different passengers in the same vehicle have been tried at different times by different courts with different results. This is undesirable and should be avoided by one or other of the means referred to above. But we do not think that, where there are two civil actions between different plaintiffs against the same defendant or by the same plaintiff against different defendants which do raise the same issue of fact, the finding of the court should be admissible in the second action. As we have already pointed out, in civil proceedings the parties have complete liberty of choice as to how to conduct their respective cases and what material to place before the court. The thoroughness with which their case is prepared may depend upon the amount at stake in the action. We do not think it just that a party to the second action who was not a party to the first should be prejudiced by the way the party to the first action conducted his own case, or that a party to both actions, whose case was inadequately prepared or presented in the first action, should not be allowed to avail himself of the opportunity to improve upon it in the second. The difference between ordinary civil actions and suits for dissolution of marriage in which there are findings of adultery is that in the latter, unlike the former, the parties are not at liberty to present their respective cases as they please and the judge himself is under a statutory duty of inquiry.

39. Finally, we should observe that this Report deals only with evidence in civil proceedings in English courts of law. Our recommendations are not intended to apply to proceedings before other tribunals, whether statutory or professional. Some of these have special rules as to the effect to be given to criminal convictions or particular findings by civil courts. We do not

suggest that any of these should be altered to conform with our recommendations for the ordinary civil courts. Nor do we recommend any change in the existing law as to the admissibility as evidence, in civil proceedings in courts of law, of findings of such tribunals.

* * *

Summary of Recommendations

41. Our recommendations may be summarised thus:—

(1) A conviction of a criminal offence before a court of competent jurisdiction in the United Kingdom should be admissible in subsequent civil proceedings (whether or not between the same parties) to show that the person concerned was guilty of the conduct constituting the offence (paragraph 11);

(2) no distinction should be made between a conviction on a plea of guilty and a conviction after a contested trial (paragraph 12);

(3) a person convicted of a criminal offence should, in subsequent civil proceedings in which the conviction is admitted, be taken to have been guilty of that offence unless the contrary is proved, the onus of proof being on the party seeking to show that the conviction was erroneous (paragraph 13);

(4) subject to recommendation (9) below, an acquittal should not be evidence in subsequent civil proceedings of the non-culpability of the person acquitted (paragraph 15);

(5) a conviction by a court outside the United Kingdom, or by a court-martial, should not be admissible in civil proceedings as evidence of the guilt of the person concerned (paragraphs 17 and 18);

(6) a finding by a coroner's court should not be admissible in subsequent civil proceedings (paragraph 19);

(7) for the purpose of identifying the criminal conduct of which the person concerned was convicted by a criminal court, the indictment or information, as well as the certificate of conviction, should be admissible (paragraph 20);

(8) a party to civil proceedings wishing to rely on a previous conviction of any person should so state in his pleadings and give particulars of the criminal conduct and the conviction in question, but the adverse party should not be entitled, whether he disputes either (i) the identification of the criminal conduct or (ii) the correctness of the conviction, to require the first party to call as his own witnesses those who gave evidence in the criminal proceedings (paragraph 22);

(9) in defamation actions, where the statement complained of alleges that the plaintiff has been guilty of a criminal offence, proof that he has been convicted of that offence and that the conviction has not been set aside should be conclusive evidence of his guilt, and proof that he was acquitted of that offence should be conclusive evidence of his innocence (paragraphs 26 to 33);

(10) findings of adultery by the High Court or by a county court under the Matrimonial Causes Act 1967 (but not by magistrates' courts) in matrimonial causes, and findings of paternity in affiliation proceedings, should be treated in subsequent civil proceedings in the same way as convictions by competent courts of criminal jurisdiction (paragraphs 34 to 37);

(11) previous judgments in other civil proceedings should not be admissible in subsequent civil proceedings between different parties as evidence of the facts on which they were founded (paragraph 38).

Index

B

C

J

S